W9-BNV-535

POCKET
REF

Compiled by
Thomas J. Glover
Third Edition

Sequoia Publishing, Inc.
Littleton, Colorado, U.S.A.

This POCKET REF belongs to:

NAME:

HOME ADDRESS:

HOME PHONE:

WORK PHONE:

BUSINESS ADDRESS:

In case of accident or serious illness, please notify:
Name:
Phone Number:

Copyright © 1989-2008 by Thomas J. Glover
   3rd Edition, 24th Printing - June 2008

All rights reserved.
No part of this book may be reproduced in any form, by
mimeograph, photocopying, information storage, re-
cording and retrieval systems, or any other means,
without permission in writing from the publisher.

Library of Congress Control Number: 2002091021
Printed in the United States of America

Sequoia Publishing, Inc.
   P.O. Box 620820, Dept. 101
   Littleton, CO 80162-0820
   (303) 932-1400
   Web Site: http://www.sequoiapublishing.com

ISBN 978-1-885071-33-0

Preface

Sequoia Publishing, Inc. has made a serious effort to provide accurate information in this book. However, the probability exists that there are errors and misprints and that variations in data values may also occur depending on field conditions. Information included in this book should only be considered as a general guide and Sequoia Publishing, Inc. does not represent the information as being exact.

The publishers would appreciate being notified of any errors, omissions, or misprints which may occur in this book. Your suggestions for future editions would also be greatly appreciated.

The information in this manual was collected from numerous sources and if not properly acknowledged, Sequoia Publishing, Inc. would like to express its appreciation for those contributions. See page 6 for specific trade name, trade mark, and credit information.

My deepest thanks to the following people for their tremendous effort in helping make the 3rd edition a reality:

> Richard Young - Research and writer
> Mary Glover - Research, photography, and writer
> Trish Glover - Research and graphics artist
> E. Craig Simmons - Geology chapter update
> Mary Miller - Research and writer
> Millie Young - 2nd Edition page layouts

A very special I love you and thanks goes to my wife Mary. Her patience, love, and understanding, not to mention her spoiling me to death, allow me to survive the rigors of the publishing world.

Thomas

Additional Products by Sequoia

AutoRef, 1st Edition ISBN 978-1-885071-48-4

Be A Cop, 1st Edition ISBN 978-1-885071-49-1

BoatRef, 1st Edition ISBN 978-1-885071-52-1 *>Coming soon <*

DeskRef, 3rd Edition ISBN 978-1-885071-44-6

Handyman In~Your~Pocket, 1st Edition, ISBN 978-1-885071-29-3

Measure for Measure 1st Edition ISBN 978-1-889796-00-0

Pocket Partner, 4th Edition ISBN 978-1-885071-55-2

Pocket PCRef, 13th Edition ISBN 978-1-885071-40-8

Seldovia, Alaska: An Historical Portrait
of Herring Bay 1st Edition ISBN 978-1-889796-03-1

TechRef, 13th Edition ISBN 978-1-885071-46-0

WinRef 98-95 In~Your~Pocket ISBN 1-885071-22-1

Personal Information

Name →				
Birthday				
Anniversary				
Favorite color				
Chest				
Gloves				
Hat				
Hips				
Inseam				
Neck				
Ring Size				
Shirt / Blouse				
Shoe				
Shoulder to Waist				
Sleeve Length				
Sock / Hose				
Suit/Dress				
Sweater				
Waist /belt				

Table Of Contents

References, Trade Names and Trade Marks

The following are Trade Names and Trade Marks included in Pocket Ref. If we missed your Trade Name or Trade Mark, we apologize, please let us know and we will insert it in the next printing.

AWS – American Welding Society
ANSI – American National Standards Institute
ASCII – American Standard Code for Information Interchange
Brown & Sharp
Cedarapids – Iowa Manufacturing Co.
ISO – International Organization for Standardization
Metropolitan Life Insurance Company
NCHS – National Center for Health Statistics
NEMA – National Electrical Manufacturers Association
Pioneer – Portec Pioneer Division
ROMEX –
SAE – Society of Automotive Engineers

Some of the references used in writing Pocket Ref include the following (They are all excellent references and should be added to any good reference library):

American Society of Heating, Refrigerating and Air Conditioning
Arco's New Complete Woodworking Handbook – J. T. Adams, Arco
Builders Vest Pocket Reference – W.J. Hornumg, Prentice–Hall,Inc
Cedarapids Reference Book – Iowa Manufacturing Company
Dana's Manual of Minerology – E.S. Dana, John Wiley & Sons
Electronic Engineers Master Catalog – Hearst Business Communications Inc.
Field Geologists Manual – Australian Institute of Mining and Met.
Grainger Catalog– W. W. Grainger, Inc
Handbook of Chemistry & Physics – The Chemical Rubber Co.
Handbook of Physical Calculations – Jan J. Tuma, McGraw–Hill
Information Please 1995 Almanac - Houghton Mifflin Co, New York
Machinery's Handbook – E.O. & F.D. Jones, Industrial Press Inc
Machinists' & Draftsmen's Handbook – A.M. Wagener & H.R. Arthur
Mechanical Engineers' Handbook – McGraw–Hill Book Co., Inc.
National Electrical Code – National Fire Protection Association
Pioneer Facts and Figures – Portec, Pioneer Division
Scientific Tables – Ciba–Geigy Ltd, New York
Standard Math Tables – The Chemical Rubber Co.
Technical Reference Handbook – E. P. Rasis, American Tech. Pub.
The Universal Almanac, 1995 - J.W.Wright, Andrews & McMeel
The World Almanac – Pharos Books
Water Well Handbook – K.E. Anderson, Missouri Water Well Assn.

NOTE: There are many more references, most of which are referenced on specific pages in Pocket Ref. If we have omitted a reference, we apologize, please let us know and we will include it in the next printing of Pocket Ref.

Air and Gases

O_2 He

(See WATER for Cyl. Fillage & Pollution, p. 634)

Composition Of Air

Component of Air	Symbol	Content – %Volume
Nitrogen	N_2	78.084 percent ⎤
Oxygen	O_2	20.947 percent ⎟
Argon	Ar	0.934 percent ⎟ 99.998%
Carbon dioxide	CO_2	0.033 percent ⎦
Neon	Ne	18.2 parts/million
Helium	He	5.2 parts/million
Krypton	Kr	1.1 parts/million
Sulfur dioxide	SO_2	1.0 parts/million
Methane	CH_4	2.0 parts/million
Hydrogen	H_2	0.5 parts/million
Nitrous oxide	N_2O	0.5 parts/million
Xenon	Xe	0.09 parts/million
Ozone – Summer	O_3	0.0 to 0.07 parts/million
Ozone – Winter	O_3	0.0 to 0.02 parts/million
Nitrogen dioxide	NO_2	0.02 parts/million
Iodine	I_2	0.01 parts/million
Carbon monoxide	CO	0.0 to trace
Ammonia	NH_3	0.0 to trace

The above table is an average for clean, dry air at sea level.
1 part/million = 0.0001 percent.

Physical Properties of Air

Density of dry air at Standard Temperature and Pressure
1.29274 kilograms/cu meter = 0.080703 pounds/cu foot

Universal Gas Constant (R): 0.08206 liter atmosphere/mole kelvin

8.31451 joule/mole kelvin

Standard Reference Conditions
(also known as Standard Temperature and Pressure - STP)

Standard Temperature = 0°C = 32°F = 273.15 K

Standard Pressure = 760 mm Hg =

14.696 pounds-force/sq inch = 2116.22 pounds-force/sq foot =

29.92 inch Hg = 1.01325×10^5 N/m² = 1.01325×10^5 Pa =

101.325 kPa

Speed of sound in dry air at STP
331.45 meters/sec = 1087.4 ft/sec = 741.4 miles/hr

ICAO Sea Level Air Standard Values
Atmospheric pressure = 760 mm Hg = 14.7 lbs-force/sq inch

Temperature = 15°C = 288.15 K = 59°F

Densities of Gases

Gas	Density (grams/liter)	Density (lb/cu ft)
Air @ STP	1.2928	0.08071
Air @ 59°F	1.2256	0.07651
Argon	1.7837	0.111353
Carbon Dioxide	1.9770	0.123420
Carbon Monoxide	1.2500	0.078035
Helium	0.1785	0.011143
Hydrogen	0.0899	0.005612
Neon	0.8999	0.056179
Nitrogen	1.2506	0.078072
Oxygen	1.4290	0.089210

All densities listed above assume a dry gas at standard temperature (0°C) and pressure (760 mm Hg) and under those conditions, one mole of any gas will occupy a volume of 22.41 liters = 0.02241 cubic meters = 0.7914 cubic feet.

Standard Atmosphere

The unit "1 Standard Atmosphere" is defined as the pressure equivalent to that exerted by a 760 mm column of mercury at 0°C (32°F), at sea level, and at standard gravity (32.174 ft/sec²). Atmospheric pressure is the weight of a column of air per area unit as measured from the top of the atmosphere to the reference point being measured. Atmospheric pressure decreases as altitude increases.

Equivalents to 1 atmosphere are as follows:

> 76 centimeters (760 mm) of mercury
> 29.921 inches of mercury
> 10.3322 meters of water
> 406.782 inches of water
> 33.899 feet of water
> 14.696 pounds-force per square inch
> 2,116.2 pounds-force per square foot
> 1.033 kilograms-force per square centimeter
> 101.325 kilopascal

General Gas Laws & Formulas

Perfect Gas Law

$$PV = nRT$$

P=Pressure in atmospheres
V=Volume in liters   n=Number of moles
R=Gas constant (0.0821 liter-atmospheres) / K / mole)
T=Temperature in K

If constant pressure $V1/V2 = T1/T2$
If constant temperature $P1/P2 = V2/V1$
If constant volume $P1/P2 = T1/T2$

Boyle's Law

If temperature is kept constant, the volume of a given mass of gas is inversely proportional to the pressure which is exerted upon it.

$$\frac{\text{Initial Pressure}}{\text{Final Pressure}} = \frac{\text{Final Volume}}{\text{Initial Volume}}$$

Charles' Law

If the pressure is constant, the volume of a given mass of gas is directly proportional to the absolute temperature.

$$\frac{\text{Initial Volume}}{\text{Initial Temperature K}} = \frac{\text{Final Volume}}{\text{Final Temperature K}}$$

Dalton's Law of Partial Pressures

The pressure which is exerted on the walls of a vessel is the sum of the pressures which each gas would exert if it were present alone.

$$PV = V (p_1 + p_2 + \dots p_n)$$

Graham's Law of Diffusion

Relative rates of diffusion of two gases are inversely proportional to the square roots of their densities.

Avogadro's Law

Equal volumes of gases, measured under the same conditions of temperature and pressure, contain equal numbers of molecules.

General Gas Laws & Formulas

Air Velocity in a Pipe

$$V = \sqrt{\frac{25,000 \, DP}{L}}$$

V = Air velocity in feet per second
D = Pipe inside diameter in inches
L = Length of pipe in feet
P = Pressure loss due to air friction in ounces-force/square inch
Using this equation and typical values of V, D, and L;
approximate values of P are computed as follows:

Velocity Ft/Sec	Pipe Diameter in inches, 10 feet long				
	1	2	4	6	10
1	0.0004	0.0002	0.0001	0.00007	0.00004
2	0.0016	0.0008	0.0004	0.0003	0.00016
5	0.0100	0.005	0.0025	0.0017	0.001
10	0.04	0.02	0.01	0.0067	0.004
15	0.09	0.045	0.0225	0.015	0.009
20	0.16	0.08	0.04	0.027	0.016
25	0.25	0.125	0.0625	0.0417	0.025
30	0.36	0.18	0.09	0.06	0.036

(Formula from B.F. Sturtevant Co)

Air Volume Discharged from Pipe

CFM = 60VA

CFM = Air volume in cubic feet per minute
V = Air velocity in feet per second as determined in the
equation at the top of this page.
A = Cross section area of pipe in square feet.

Theoretical Horsepower to Compress Air

$$HP = 0.2267 \, Q \left[\left[\frac{PSI}{14.7} + 1 \right]^{0.283} - 1 \right]$$

HP = Theoretical horsepower
Q = System air flow rate in cubic feet per minute
PSI = Outlet gage pressure in pounds-force per square inch
Conditions: (1) dry air at sea level, atmospheric pressure =
14.7 psi   (2) single stage adiabatic compression

Density of Moist Air

| mm | Air Temperature (Dew Point =10°C) | | | | |
Hg	0°C	10°C	20°C	40°C	60°C
1000	1.695	1.635	1.579	1.479	1.390
975	1.653	1.594	1.540	1.441	1.355
950	1.610	1.553	1.500	1.404	1.320
925	1.568	1.512	1.461	1.367	1.285
900	1.525	1.471	1.421	1.330	1.250
875	1.482	1.430	1.381	1.293	1.215
850	1.440	1.389	1.342	1.256	1.181
825	1.397	1.348	1.302	1.219	1.146
800	1.355	1.307	1.262	1.182	1.111
775	1.312	1.266	1.223	1.145	1.076
760	1.287	1.241	1.199	1.122	1.055
750	1.270	1.225	1.183	1.108	1.041
725	1.227	1.184	1.144	1.071	1.006
700	1.185	1.143	1.104	1.033	0.971
675	1.142	1.102	1.064	0.996	0.937
650	1.100	1.061	1.025	0.959	0.902
625	1.057	1.020	0.985	0.922	0.867
600	1.015	0.979	0.945	0.885	0.832
575	0.972	0.938	0.906	0.848	0.797
550	0.930	0.897	0.866	0.811	0.762
525	0.887	0.856	0.827	0.774	0.727
500	0.845	0.815	0.787	0.737	0.692
475	0.802	0.774	0.747	0.700	0.658
450	0.760	0.733	0.708	0.663	0.623
425	0.717	0.692	0.668	0.625	0.588
400	0.674	0.651	0.628	0.588	0.553
375	0.632	0.610	0.589	0.551	0.518
350	0.589	0.569	0.549	0.514	0.483
325	0.547	0.528	0.510	0.477	0.448
300	0.504	0.487	0.470	0.440	0.414
275	0.462	0.446	0.430	0.403	0.379
250	0.419	0.405	0.391	0.366	0.344
225	0.377	0.363	0.351	0.329	0.309
200	0.334	0.322	0.311	0.292	0.274
175	0.292	0.281	0.272	0.254	0.239
150	0.249	0.240	0.232	0.217	0.204
125	0.207	0.199	0.193	0.180	0.169
100	0.164	0.158	0.153	0.143	0.135
75	0.122	0.117	0.113	0.106	0.100

Moist air density (gms/liter) = 1.2929 x (273.13/T) x ((P−Vp)/760)

T=Absolute air temperature (Kelvin)

P=Barometric pressure (mm of mercury)

Vp=Vapor pressure of water (see table in WATER Chapter)

Elevation vs. Air & Water

| Elevation | | US Std Atmosphere | | Boiling | Speed |
Meters	Feet	Temp °F	Pressure lbf/sq in	Point H₂0(°F)	Sound m/sec
−1000	−3281	70.7	16.52	218.5	344.1
−500	−1640	64.9	15.59	215.2	342.2
0	0	59.0	14.70	212.0	340.3
250	820	56.1	14.26	210.4	339.3
500	1640	53.2	13.85	208.8	338.4
750	2461	50.2	13.44	207.2	337.4
1000	3281	47.3	13.03	205.7	336.4
1250	4101	44.4	12.64	204.1	335.5
1500	4921	41.5	12.26	202.6	334.5
1750	5741	38.5	11.89	201.0	333.5
2000	6562	35.6	11.53	199.5	332.5
2500	8202	29.8	10.83	196.5	330.6
3000	9843	23.9	10.17	193.5	328.6
3500	11483	18.1	9.54	190.6	326.6
4000	13123	12.2	8.94	187.7	324.6
4500	14764	6.4	8.38	184.8	322.6
5000	16404	0.5	7.84	182.0	320.5
5500	18045	−5.3	7.33	179.2	318.5
6000	19685	−11.1	6.85	176.4	316.5
6500	21325	−17.0	6.39	173.7	314.4
7000	22966	−22.8	5.96	171.0	312.3
7500	24606	−28.6	5.56	168.4	310.2
8000	26247	−34.5	5.17	165.8	308.1
8500	27887	−40.3	4.81	163.2	305.9
9000	29528	−46.2	4.47	160.7	303.8
9500	31168	−52.0	4.15	154.4	301.7
10000	32808	−57.8	3.84	151.3	299.5
11000	36089	−69.5	3.29	145.0	295.2
12000	39370	−69.5	2.81	138.9	295.1
13000	42651	−69.5	2.41	133.0	295.1
14000	45932	−69.5	2.06	127.0	295.1
15000	49213	−69.5	1.74	121.3	295.1
16000	52493	−69.5	1.50	115.7	295.1
17000	55774	−69.5	1.28	110.3	295.1
18000	59055	−69.5	1.10	104.7	295.1
19000	62336	−69.5	.94	99.7	295.1
20000	65617	−69.5	.80	94.5	295.1
25000	82021	−60.9	.37	70.5	298.4
30000	98425	−52.0	.17	49.3	301.7
32000	104987	−48.5	.13	41.5	303.0

Data in table based on ICAO Standard Atmosphere

Air and Gases   13

Dry Air Specific Heat & Sound Velocity at 1 Atmosphere, Various Temperatures

Specific Heat (also known as Specific Heat Capacity) is defined at either constant pressure (c_p) or constant volume (c_v). The Specific Heat Ratio (c_p / c_v) is dimensionless.

| Temperature | | Specific Heat (c_p) | | Ratio | Sound Velocity | |
°C	°F	Btu$_{IT}$ / lb °F*	kJ / kg K	c_v / c_v	ft / s	m / s
-173	-280	0.2456	1.028	-	651	198.4
-163	-262	0.2440	1.022	1.4202	685	208.8
-153	-244	0.2430	1.017	1.4166	717	218.5
-143	-226	0.2423	1.014	1.4139	747	227.7
-133	-208	0.2418	1.012	1.4119	776	236.5
-123	-190	0.2414	1.011	1.4102	804	245.1
-113	-172	0.2411	1.009	1.4089	831	253.3
-103	-154	0.2408	1.008	1.4079	856	260.9
-93	-136	0.2406	1.007	1.4071	882	268.8
-83	-118	0.2405	1.007	1.4064	906	276.1
-73	-100	0.2404	1.007	1.4057	930	283.5
-68	-91	0.2403	1.006	1.4055	941	286.8
-63	-82	0.2403	1.006	1.4053	953	290.5
-58	-73	0.2403	1.006	1.4050	964	293.8
-53	-64	0.2402	1.006	1.4048	976	297.5
-48	-55	0.2402	1.006	1.4046	987	300.8
-43	-46	0.2402	1.006	1.4044	998	304.2
-38	-37	0.2402	1.006	1.4042	1008	307.2
-33	-28	0.2401	1.005	1.4040	1019	310.6
-28	-19	0.2401	1.005	1.4038	1030	313.9
-23	-10	0.2401	1.005	1.4036	1040	317.0
-18	0	0.2401	1.005	1.4034	1051	320.3
-13	8	0.2401	1.005	1.4032	1061	323.4
-8	17	0.2402	1.006	1.4030	1071	326.4
-3	26	0.2402	1.006	1.4029	1081	329.5
2	35	0.2402	1.006	1.4026	1091	332.5
7	44	0.2402	1.006	1.4024	1101	335.6
12	53	0.2402	1.006	1.4022	1111	338.6
17	62	0.2403	1.006	1.4020	1120	341.4
20	68	0.2403	1.006	1.4019	1126	343.3
22	71	0.2403	1.006	1.4018	1130	344.4
27	80	0.2404	1.007	1.4017	1140	347.5
32	89	0.2404	1.007	1.4015	1149	350.2
37	98	0.2405	1.007	1.4013	1158	353.0
42	107	0.2405	1.007	1.4010	1167	355.7
47	116	0.2406	1.007	1.4008	1177	358.7
52	125	0.2407	1.008	1.4006	1186	361.5
57	134	0.2407	1.008	1.4004	1195	364.2
62	143	0.2408	1.008	1.4001	1204	367.0
67	152	0.2409	1.009	1.3999	1213	369.7

Dry Air Specific Heat & Sound Velocity at 1 Atmosphere, Various Temp (cont.)

Temperature		Specific Heat (c_p)		Ratio	Sound Velocity	
°C	°F	Btu$_{IT}$ / lb °F*	kJ / kg K	c_p / c_v	ft / s	m / s
72	161	0.2410	1.009	1.3996	1221	372.2
77	170	0.2411	1.009	1.3993	1230	374.9
82	179	0.2411	1.009	1.3990	1239	377.6
87	188	0.2412	1.010	1.3987	1247	380.1
92	197	0.2413	1.010	1.3984	1256	382.8
97	206	0.2415	1.011	1.3981	1264	385.3
102	215	0.2416	1.012	1.3978	1273	388.0
107	224	0.2417	1.012	1.3975	1281	390.4
112	233	0.2418	1.012	1.3971	1289	392.9
117	242	0.2420	1.013	1.3968	1298	395.6
122	251	0.2421	1.014	1.3964	1306	398.1
127	260	0.2422	1.014	1.3961	1314	400.5
137	278	0.2425	1.015	1.3953	1330	405.4
147	296	0.2428	1.017	1.3946	1346	410.3
157	314	0.2432	1.018	1.3938	1361	414.8
167	332	0.2435	1.019	1.3929	1377	419.7
177	350	0.2439	1.021	1.3920	1392	424.3
187	368	0.2443	1.023	1.3911	1407	428.9
197	386	0.2447	1.025	1.3901	1421	433.1
207	404	0.2451	1.026	1.3892	1436	437.7
217	422	0.2456	1.028	1.3881	1450	442.0
227	440	0.2460	1.030	1.3871	1464	446.2
237	458	0.2465	1.032	1.3861	1478	450.5
247	476	0.2469	1.034	1.3851	1492	454.8
257	494	0.2474	1.036	1.3840	1506	459.0
267	512	0.2479	1.038	1.3829	1520	463.3
277	530	0.2484	1.040	1.3818	1533	467.3
287	548	0.2490	1.043	1.3806	1546	471.2
297	566	0.2495	1.045	1.3795	1559	475.2
307	584	0.2500	1.047	1.3783	1572	479.1
317	602	0.2506	1.049	1.3772	1585	483.1
327	620	0.2511	1.051	1.3760	1597	486.8
347	656	0.2522	1.056	1.3737	1622	494.4
367	692	0.2533	1.061	1.3714	1647	502.0
387	728	0.2545	1.066	1.3691	1671	509.3
407	764	0.2556	1.070	1.3668	1695	516.6
427	800	0.2568	1.075	1.3646	1718	523.6
447	836	0.2579	1.080	1.3623	1742	531.0
467	872	0.2591	1.085	1.3601	1764	537.7
487	908	0.2602	1.089	1.3580	1787	544.7
507	944	0.2613	1.094	1.3559	1808	551.1
527	980	0.2624	1.099	1.354	1830	557.8
577	1070	0.2653	1.111	1.349	1883	573.9
627	1160	0.2678	1.121	1.345	1934	589.5

Dry Air Specific Heat & Sound Velocity at 1 Atmosphere, Various Temp (cont.)

| Temperature | | Specific Heat (c_p) | | Ratio | Sound Velocity | |
°C	°F	Btu_{IT} / lb °F*	kJ / kg K	c_p / c_v	ft / s	m / s
677	1250	0.2704	1.132	1.340	198	605.0
727	1340	0.2728	1.142	1.336	2032	619.4
827	1520	0.2774	1.161	1.329	2126	648.0
927	1700	0.2817	1.179	1.322	2215	675.1
1027	1880	0.2860	1.197	1.316	2300	701.0
1127	2060	0.2900	1.214	1.310	2381	725.7
1227	2240	0.2940	1.231	1.304	2459	749.5
1327	2420	0.2984	1.249	1.299	2535	772.7
1527	2780	0.3076	1.288	1.288	2676	815.6
1727	3140	0.3196	1.338	1.274	2807	855.6
2127	3860	0.3760	1.574	1.238	3033	924.5
2527	4580	0.5396	2.259	1.196	3225	983.0

* Btu_{IT} / lb °F is also equal to Btu_{IT} / lb °R = cal_{IT} / g °C = cal_{IT} / g K
  Btu_{IT} / lb °F = 4186.8 J / kg K

1 atmosphere (atm) is equal to the following:

   14.7 psia
   0.101325 MN/m^2
   0.101325 MPa
   1.01325 x 10^5 Pa

For ideal gases, the specific heat capacities differ by R, the molar gas constant, as shown in the following equation:
   c_p - c_v = R = 8.31 J / mole / K

Source: Tables of the Thermal Properties of Gases, National Bureau of Standards Circular 564, November 1955

Dry Air Specific Heat at 20°C Constant Temperature and Various Pressures

Specific Heat (also known as Specific Heat Capacity) is defined at either constant pressure (c_p) or constant volume (c_v). The Specific Heat Ratio (c_p / c_v) is dimensionless.

Specific Heat values in this table are based on a constant Temperature of 20°C = 68°F = 293 K

Pressure	c_p	c_p/c_v
0.01 atm 0.147 psia 0.00101325 MN/m²	0.2399	1.4002
0.1 atm 1.47 psia 0.0101325 MN/m²	0.2400	1.4003
0.4 atm 5.88 psia 0.04053 MN/m²	0.2401	1.4008
1 atm 14.7 psia 0.101325 MN/m²	0.2403	1.4019
7 atm 102.9 psia 0.70928 MN/m²	0.2427	1.4131
10 atm 147 psia 1.01325 MN/m²	0.2440	1.4188
40 atm 588 psia 4.053 MN/m²	0.2569	1.4763
70 atm 1029 psia 7.0928 MN/m²	0.2700	1.5323
100 atm 1470 psia 10.1325 MN/m²	0.2824	1.5828

Source: Tables of the Thermal Properties of Gases, National Bureau of Standards Circular 564, November 1955

Air Tool Requirements

Tool Category	Tool cfm	Tool Category	Tool cfm
Air Filter Cleaner	3	Hydr Lift 8000 lb	6*
Air Hammer	4	Hydr Floor Jack	6*
Air Hoist 1000#	5	Impact Wrenches:	
Air Motor 1 hp	6–10	1/4 inch drive	3
Air Motor 2 hp	12–15	3/8 inch drive	2–5
Air Motor 3 hp	18–20	1/2 inch drive	4–8
Bead Breaker	12*	3/4 inch drive	7–9
Bench Rammer	5	1 inch drive	10
Body Polisher	2	1 1/4 inch drive	14
Body Orbital Sander	5	Nutsetter – 3/8 inch	3–6
Brake Tester	4	Nutsetter – 3/4 inch	5–8
Burr Tool – small	4	Pneu. Garage Door	3*
Burr Tool – large	5–6	Radiator Tester	1
Carbon Remover	3	Rammers – small	3
Chain Saw	7–22	Rammers – medium	9
Circle Saw – 8 inch	12	Rammers – large	10
Circle Saw – 12 inch	17	Sander – 5 in Pad	8–10
Compression Riviter	1	Sander – 7 in Pad	15
Die Grinder	4–6	Sander – 9 in Pad	17–20
Drill 1/16–3/8 inch	4–6	Screwdriver #2–#6	1–3
Drill 3/8–5/8 inch	7–8	Screwdriver #6–up	3–6
Dust blow gun	3	Spray Cleaner	5
File/Saw Machine	3–5	Spray Paint Guns:	
Floor Rammer	7	Standard	5
Grease Gun	3*	Production	9
Grinder – 2 in Horz	5–10	Touch-up	4
Grinder – 4 in Horz	15	Undercoat	19
Grinder – 6 in Horz	15–17	Tamper Backfill	6–15
Grinder – 8 in Horz	20	Tapper – 3/8 inch	3–5
Grinder – 5 in Vert	8–10	Tire Changer	1*
Grinder – 7 in Vert	14–15	Tire inflation	2*
Grinder – 9 in Vert	17–20	Tire Rim Stripper	6*
Hammer – Chip	8	Tire Spreader	1*
Hammer – Fender	9	Transmission Flusher	3
Hammer – Rivet	8–15		
Hammer – Scale	3–4		
Hammer – Tire	12		
Hoist – Cyl type	2		

NOTE: Most tools listed above are rated at 90 to 100 pounds-force/sq inch, however, those items with a "*" next to the cfm rating require 125 to 160 pounds-force/sq inch.

<u>Always</u> check the manufacturers recommendations for both air pressure (psi – pounds-force per sq inch) and air flow (cfm – cubic feet per minute) requirements. The ratings listed above are only averages based on a 25% load factor (running 25% of the time).

CFM vs. PSI for Nozzles

Gauge PSI	CFM Free Air Flow @ Nozzle Diameter (inch)			
	1/64	1/32	3/64	1/16
1	0.03	0.11	0.2	0.4
5	0.06	0.24	0.5	1.0
10	0.08	0.34	0.8	1.4
15	0.11	0.42	0.9	1.7
20	0.12	0.49	1.1	2.0
25	0.14	0.56	1.3	2.2
30	0.16	0.63	1.4	2.5
40	0.19	0.77	1.7	3.1
50	0.23	1.06	2.1	3.7
60	0.26	1.06	2.4	4.2
70	0.30	1.20	2.7	4.8
80	0.33	1.34	3.0	5.4
90	0.37	1.48	3.3	5.9
100	0.41	1.62	3.7	6.5
110	0.44	1.76	4.0	7.1
120	0.48	1.91	4.3	7.6
130	0.51	2.05	4.6	8.2
140	0.55	2.19	4.9	8.8
150	0.58	2.33	5.2	9.3
175	0.67	2.68	6.0	10.7
200	0.76	3.04	6.8	12.1
PSI	3/32	1/8	3/16	1/4
1	1.0	1.7	3.9	6.8
5	2.2	3.9	8.7	15.4
10	3.1	5.4	12.3	21.8
15	3.8	6.7	15.1	26.9
20	4.4	7.9	17.7	31.4
25	5.1	9.0	20.2	35.9
30	5.7	10.1	22.8	40.5
40	7.0	12.4	27.9	49.5
50	8.2	14.6	32.9	58.6
60	9.5	16.9	38.0	67.6
70	10.8	19.2	43.1	76.7
80	12.1	21.4	48.2	85.7
90	13.3	23.7	53.3	94.8
100	14.6	26.0	58.4	104.0
110	15.9	28.2	63.5	113.0
120	17.1	30.5	68.6	122.0
130	18.4	32.7	73.7	131.0
140	19.7	35.0	78.8	140.0
150	21.0	37.3	83.9	149.0
175	24.2	42.9	96.6	172.0
200	27.3	48.6	109.0	194.0

PSI = pounds-force/square inch; CFM = cubic feet/minute
Values in table for Flow Coefficient = 1.0. For well rounded nozzles,
multiply by 0.97. For sharp edged nozzles, multiply by 0.65.

Air Hose Friction

Hose Size (inch)	CFM thru 50 ft Hose	Gage Pressure – Pounds-force/sq inch			
		50	70	90	110
		PSI Loss Over 50 foot Hose Length			
1/2	20	1.8	1.0	0.8	0.6
	30	5.0	3.4	2.4	2.0
	40	10.1	7.0	5.4	4.3
	50	18.1	12.4	9.5	7.6
	60	+	20.0	14.8	12.0
	70	+	28.4	22.0	17.6
	80	+	+	30.5	24.6
	90	+	+	41.0	33.3
	100	+	+	+	44.5
	110	+	+	+	+
3/4	20	0.4	0.2	0.2	0.1
	30	0.8	0.5	0.4	0.3
	40	1.5	0.9	0.7	0.5
	50	2.4	1.5	1.1	0.9
	60	3.5	2.3	1.6	1.3
	70	4.4	3.2	2.3	1.8
	80	6.5	4.2	3.1	2.4
	90	8.5	5.5	4.0	3.1
	100	11.4	7.0	5.0	3.9
	110	14.2	8.8	6.2	4.9
	120	+	11.0	7.5	5.9
	130	+	+	9.0	7.1
1	20	0.1	0.0	0.0	0.0
	30	0.2	0.1	0.1	0.1
	40	0.3	0.2	0.2	0.2
	50	0.5	0.4	0.3	0.2
	60	0.8	0.5	0.4	0.3
	70	1.1	0.7	0.6	0.4
	80	1.5	1.0	0.7	0.6
	90	2.0	1.3	0.9	0.7
	100	2.6	1.6	1.2	0.9
	110	3.5	2.0	1.4	1.1
	120	4.8	2.5	1.7	1.3
	130	7.0	3.1	2.0	1.5

PSI = Pressure in pounds-force/square inch
CFM = Air flow in cubic feet/minute

"+" means pressure loss is too great and therefore, the combination of Hose Size, CFM, and Gage Pressure is not recommended. Gage Pressure is the indicated air pressure, in pounds-force/square inch, at the source (ie, the air compressor receiver tank).

Air Line Recommended Sizes

Air Flow CFM	Length of Air Line in Feet			
	50	100	200	300
	Recommended Air Line Size in Inches			
5	1/2	1/2	1/2	1/2
10	1/2	1/2	1/2	3/4
15	1/2	1/2	3/4	3/4
20	1/2	3/4	3/4	3/4
25	3/4	3/4	1	1
30	3/4	3/4	1	1
35	3/4	3/4	1	1
40	3/4	1	1	1–1/4
50	1	1	1–1/4	1–1/4
75	1	1–1/4	1–1/4	1–1/4
100	1–1/4	1–1/4	1–1/2	1–1/2

Air Receiver Capacities

Tank Size (inches)	Tank Size (gallons)	Gauge Pressure on Tank (PSI)			
		0	100	150	200
		Cubic Feet Tank Capacity			
12 x 24	10	1.3	11	15	19
14 x 36	20	2.7	21	30	39
16 x 36	30	4.0	31	45	59
20 x 48	60	8.0	62	90	117
20 x 63	80	10.7	83	120	156
24 x 68	120	16.0	125	180	234
30 x 84	240	32.0	250	360	467

If your tank is not listed in the above table, use the following formula to calculate the Tank Size (gallons) and then estimate the Cubic Feet Tank Capacity at a given pressure from the table above.

$$\text{Tank Gallons} = \frac{\text{Tank Height} \times (\text{Tank Radius})^2}{73.53}$$

Height and Radius are in inches.

Limits for Air Contaminants

Pollutant	PEL[A]
Asbestos [B]	0.1 fiber / cc
Benzene [B]	1 ppm
Bromine	0.1 ppm
Cadmium (all forms) [C]	5 $\mu g/m^3$
Carbon dioxide	5,000 ppm
Carbon disulfide	20 ppm
Carbon monoxide	50 ppm
Carbon tetrachloride [C]	10 ppm
Chlorine	1 ppm [D]
Chloroform	50 ppm [D]
Cresol	5 ppm
Ethyl alcohol (ethanol)	1,000 ppm
Fluorine	.1 ppm
Formaldehyde [C]	0.75 ppm
Gasoline	300 ppm
Hydrogen cyanide	10 ppm
Iodine	0.1 ppm [D]
Iron oxide (fume)	10 mg/m^3
Isopropyl alcohol	400 ppm
Lead (all forms)	50 $\mu g/m^3$
Manganese compounds (as Mn)	5 mg/m^3
Mercury	1 $mg/10\ m^3$ [D]
Methyl alcohol (methanol)	200 ppm
Nitric oxide	25 ppm
Nitrogen dioxide	5 ppm [D]
Propane [E]	1000 ppm
Selenium compounds (as Se)	0.2 mg/m^3
Sulfur dioxide	5 ppm
Sulfuric acid	1 mg/m^3
Tellurium compounds (as Te)	0.1 mg/m^3
Tetraethyl lead (as Pb)	0.075 mg/m^3
Toluene	200 ppm
Turpentine	100 ppm
Vinyl chloride [B]	1 ppm
Zinc oxide (fume)	5 mg/m^3
Zinc oxide (dust)	15 mg/m^3

Notes
A = PEL = Permissible Exposure Limit, 8-hour time weighted average
B = Confirmed human carcinogen
C = Suspected human carcinogen
D = Acceptable ceiling concentration
E = Simple asphyxiant

Abbreviations
cc = cubic centimeter $\mu g/m^3$ = microgram per cubic meter
mg/m³ = milligram per cubic meter   **ppm** = part per million

Source: *OSHA (Occupational Safety and Health Administration).*
  [29 CFR 1920.1000,1001,1017,1025,1027,1028,1048]

See also WATER Chapter for pollution, page 636

Miles per Gallon Fuel Chart

Miles Traveled	Gallons of Fuel Used													
	0.25	0.5	0.75	1	2	3	4	5	6	7	8	9	10	11
5	20.00	10.00	6.67	5.00	2.50	1.67	1.25	1.00	0.83	0.71	0.63	0.56	0.50	0.45
10	40.00	20.00	13.33	10.00	5.00	3.33	2.50	2.00	1.67	1.43	1.25	1.11	1.00	0.91
20	80.00	40.00	26.67	20.00	10.00	6.67	5.00	4.00	3.33	2.86	2.50	2.22	2.00	1.82
30	120.00	60.00	40.00	30.00	15.00	10.00	7.50	6.00	5.00	4.29	3.75	3.33	3.00	2.73
40	160.00	80.00	53.33	40.00	20.00	13.33	10.00	8.00	6.67	5.71	5.00	4.44	4.00	3.64
50	200.00	100.00	66.67	50.00	25.00	16.67	12.50	10.00	8.33	7.14	6.25	5.56	5.00	4.55
60	240.00	120.00	80.00	60.00	30.00	20.00	15.00	12.00	10.00	8.57	7.50	6.67	6.00	5.45
70	280.00	140.00	93.33	70.00	35.00	23.33	17.50	14.00	11.67	10.00	8.75	7.78	7.00	6.36
80	320.00	160.00	106.67	80.00	40.00	26.67	20.00	16.00	13.33	11.43	10.00	8.89	8.00	7.27
90	360.00	180.00	120.00	90.00	45.00	30.00	22.50	18.00	15.00	12.86	11.25	10.00	9.00	8.18
100	400.00	200.00	133.33	100.00	50.00	33.33	25.00	20.00	16.67	14.29	12.50	11.11	10.00	9.09
110	440.00	220.00	146.67	110.00	55.00	36.67	27.50	22.00	18.33	15.71	13.75	12.22	11.00	10.00
120	480.00	240.00	160.00	120.00	60.00	40.00	30.00	24.00	20.00	17.14	15.00	13.33	12.00	10.91
130	520.00	260.00	173.33	130.00	65.00	43.33	32.50	26.00	21.67	18.57	16.25	14.44	13.00	11.82
140	560.00	280.00	186.67	140.00	70.00	46.67	35.00	28.00	23.33	20.00	17.50	15.56	14.00	12.73
150	600.00	300.00	200.00	150.00	75.00	50.00	37.50	30.00	25.00	21.43	18.75	16.67	15.00	13.64
160	640.00	320.00	213.33	160.00	80.00	53.33	40.00	32.00	26.67	22.86	20.00	17.78	16.00	14.55
170	680.00	340.00	226.67	170.00	85.00	56.67	42.50	34.00	28.33	24.29	21.25	18.89	17.00	15.45
180	720.00	360.00	240.00	180.00	90.00	60.00	45.00	36.00	30.00	25.71	22.50	20.00	18.00	16.36
190	760.00	380.00	253.33	190.00	95.00	63.33	47.50	38.00	31.67	27.14	23.75	21.11	19.00	17.27
200	800.00	400.00	266.67	200.00	100.00	66.67	50.00	40.00	33.33	28.57	25.00	22.22	20.00	18.18
210	840.00	420.00	280.00	210.00	105.00	70.00	52.50	42.00	35.00	30.00	26.25	23.33	21.00	19.09
220	880.00	440.00	293.33	220.00	110.00	73.33	55.00	44.00	36.67	31.43	27.50	24.44	22.00	20.00
230	920.00	460.00	306.67	230.00	115.00	76.67	57.50	46.00	38.33	32.86	28.75	25.56	23.00	20.91
240	960.00	480.00	320.00	240.00	120.00	80.00	60.00	48.00	40.00	34.29	30.00	26.67	24.00	21.82
250	1000.00	500.00	333.33	250.00	125.00	83.33	62.50	50.00	41.67	35.71	31.25	27.78	25.00	22.73
260	1040.00	520.00	346.67	260.00	130.00	86.67	65.00	52.00	43.33	37.14	32.50	28.89	26.00	23.64
270	1080.00	540.00	360.00	270.00	135.00	90.00	67.50	54.00	45.00	38.57	33.75	30.00	27.00	24.55
280	1120.00	560.00	373.33	280.00	140.00	93.33	70.00	56.00	46.67	40.00	35.00	31.11	28.00	25.45
290	1160.00	580.00	386.67	290.00	145.00	96.67	72.50	58.00	48.33	41.43	36.25	32.22	29.00	26.36

Miles per Gallon Fuel Chart (cont.)

Miles Traveled	Gallons of Fuel Used													
	0.25	0.5	0.75	1	2	3	4	5	6	7	8	9	10	11
300	1200.00	600.00	400.00	300.00	150.00	100.00	75.00	60.00	50.00	42.86	37.50	33.33	30.00	27.27
310	1240.00	620.00	413.33	310.00	155.00	103.33	77.50	62.00	51.67	44.29	38.75	34.44	31.00	28.18
320	1280.00	640.00	426.67	320.00	160.00	106.67	80.00	64.00	53.33	45.71	40.00	35.56	32.00	29.09
330	1320.00	660.00	440.00	330.00	165.00	110.00	82.50	66.00	55.00	47.14	41.25	36.67	33.00	30.00
340	1360.00	680.00	453.33	340.00	170.00	113.33	85.00	68.00	56.67	48.57	42.50	37.78	34.00	30.91
350	1400.00	700.00	466.67	350.00	175.00	116.67	87.50	70.00	58.33	50.00	43.75	38.89	35.00	31.82
360	1440.00	720.00	480.00	360.00	180.00	120.00	90.00	72.00	60.00	51.43	45.00	40.00	36.00	32.73
370	1480.00	740.00	493.33	370.00	185.00	123.33	92.50	74.00	61.67	52.86	46.25	41.11	37.00	33.64
380	1520.00	760.00	506.67	380.00	190.00	126.67	95.00	76.00	63.33	54.29	47.50	42.22	38.00	34.55
390	1560.00	780.00	520.00	390.00	195.00	130.00	97.50	78.00	65.00	55.71	48.75	43.33	39.00	35.45
400	1600.00	800.00	533.33	400.00	200.00	133.33	100.00	80.00	66.67	57.14	50.00	44.44	40.00	36.36
410	1640.00	820.00	546.67	410.00	205.00	136.67	102.50	82.00	68.33	58.57	51.25	45.56	41.00	37.27
420	1680.00	840.00	560.00	420.00	210.00	140.00	105.00	84.00	70.00	60.00	52.50	46.67	42.00	38.18
430	1720.00	860.00	573.33	430.00	215.00	143.33	107.50	86.00	71.67	61.43	53.75	47.78	43.00	39.09
440	1760.00	880.00	586.67	440.00	220.00	146.67	110.00	88.00	73.33	62.86	55.00	48.89	44.00	40.00
450	1800.00	900.00	600.00	450.00	225.00	150.00	112.50	90.00	75.00	64.29	56.25	50.00	45.00	40.91
460	1840.00	920.00	613.33	460.00	230.00	153.33	115.00	92.00	76.67	65.71	57.50	51.11	46.00	41.82
470	1880.00	940.00	626.67	470.00	235.00	156.67	117.50	94.00	78.33	67.14	58.75	52.22	47.00	42.73
480	1920.00	960.00	640.00	480.00	240.00	160.00	120.00	96.00	80.00	68.57	60.00	53.33	48.00	43.64
490	1960.00	980.00	653.33	490.00	245.00	163.33	122.50	98.00	81.67	70.00	61.25	54.44	49.00	44.55
500	2000.00	1000.00	666.67	500.00	250.00	166.67	125.00	100.00	83.33	71.43	62.50	55.56	50.00	45.45
510	2040.00	1020.00	680.00	510.00	255.00	170.00	127.50	102.00	85.00	72.86	63.75	56.67	51.00	46.36
520	2080.00	1040.00	693.33	520.00	260.00	173.33	130.00	104.00	86.67	74.29	65.00	57.78	52.00	47.27
530	2120.00	1060.00	706.67	530.00	265.00	176.67	132.50	106.00	88.33	75.71	66.25	58.89	53.00	48.18
540	2160.00	1080.00	720.00	540.00	270.00	180.00	135.00	108.00	90.00	77.14	67.50	60.00	54.00	49.09
550	2200.00	1100.00	733.33	550.00	275.00	183.33	137.50	110.00	91.67	78.57	68.75	61.11	55.00	50.00
560	2240.00	1120.00	746.67	560.00	280.00	186.67	140.00	112.00	93.33	80.00	70.00	62.22	56.00	50.91
570	2280.00	1140.00	760.00	570.00	285.00	190.00	142.50	114.00	95.00	81.43	71.25	63.33	57.00	51.82
580	2320.00	1160.00	773.33	580.00	290.00	193.33	145.00	116.00	96.67	82.86	72.50	64.44	58.00	52.73
590	2360.00	1180.00	786.67	590.00	295.00	196.67	147.50	118.00	98.33	84.29	73.75	65.56	59.00	53.64
600	2400.00	1200.00	800.00	600.00	300.00	200.00	150.00	120.00	100.00	85.71	75.00	66.67	60.00	54.55

Miles per Gallon Fuel Chart (cont.)

Miles Traveled	Gallons of Fuel Used													
	12	13	14	15	16	17	18	19	20	21	22	23	24	25
5	0.42	0.38	0.36	0.33	0.31	0.29	0.28	0.26	0.25	0.24	0.23	0.22	0.21	0.20
10	0.83	0.77	0.71	0.67	0.63	0.59	0.56	0.53	0.50	0.48	0.45	0.43	0.42	0.40
20	1.67	1.54	1.43	1.33	1.25	1.18	1.11	1.05	1.00	0.95	0.91	0.87	0.83	0.80
30	2.50	2.31	2.14	2.00	1.88	1.76	1.67	1.58	1.50	1.43	1.36	1.30	1.25	1.20
40	3.33	3.08	2.86	2.67	2.50	2.35	2.22	2.11	2.00	1.90	1.82	1.74	1.67	1.60
50	4.17	3.85	3.57	3.33	3.13	2.94	2.78	2.63	2.50	2.38	2.27	2.17	2.08	2.00
60	5.00	4.62	4.29	4.00	3.75	3.53	3.33	3.16	3.00	2.86	2.73	2.61	2.50	2.40
70	5.83	5.38	5.00	4.67	4.38	4.12	3.89	3.68	3.50	3.33	3.18	3.04	2.92	2.80
80	6.67	6.15	5.71	5.33	5.00	4.71	4.44	4.21	4.00	3.81	3.64	3.48	3.33	3.20
90	7.50	6.92	6.43	6.00	5.63	5.29	5.00	4.74	4.50	4.29	4.09	3.91	3.75	3.60
100	8.33	7.69	7.14	6.67	6.25	5.88	5.56	5.26	5.00	4.76	4.55	4.35	4.17	4.00
110	9.17	8.46	7.86	7.33	6.88	6.47	6.11	5.79	5.50	5.24	5.00	4.78	4.58	4.40
120	10.00	9.23	8.57	8.00	7.50	7.06	6.67	6.32	6.00	5.71	5.45	5.22	5.00	4.80
130	10.83	10.00	9.29	8.67	8.13	7.65	7.22	6.84	6.50	6.19	5.91	5.65	5.42	5.20
140	11.67	10.77	10.00	9.33	8.75	8.24	7.78	7.37	7.00	6.67	6.36	6.09	5.83	5.60
150	12.50	11.54	10.71	10.00	9.38	8.82	8.33	7.89	7.50	7.14	6.82	6.52	6.25	6.00
160	13.33	12.31	11.43	10.67	10.00	9.41	8.89	8.42	8.00	7.62	7.27	6.96	6.67	6.40
170	14.17	13.08	12.14	11.33	10.63	10.00	9.44	8.95	8.50	8.10	7.73	7.39	7.08	6.80
180	15.00	13.85	12.86	12.00	11.25	10.59	10.00	9.47	9.00	8.57	8.18	7.83	7.50	7.20
190	15.83	14.62	13.57	12.67	11.88	11.18	10.56	10.00	9.50	9.05	8.64	8.26	7.92	7.60
200	16.67	15.38	14.29	13.33	12.50	11.76	11.11	10.53	10.00	9.52	9.09	8.70	8.33	8.00
210	17.50	16.15	15.00	14.00	13.13	12.35	11.67	11.05	10.50	10.00	9.55	9.13	8.75	8.40
220	18.33	16.92	15.71	14.67	13.75	12.94	12.22	11.58	11.00	10.48	10.00	9.57	9.17	8.80
230	19.17	17.69	16.43	15.33	14.38	13.53	12.78	12.11	11.50	10.95	10.45	10.00	9.58	9.20
240	20.00	18.46	17.14	16.00	15.00	14.12	13.33	12.63	12.00	11.43	10.91	10.43	10.00	9.60
250	20.83	19.23	17.86	16.67	15.63	14.71	13.89	13.16	12.50	11.90	11.36	10.87	10.42	10.00
260	21.67	20.00	18.57	17.33	16.25	15.29	14.44	13.68	13.00	12.38	11.82	11.30	10.83	10.40
270	22.50	20.77	19.29	18.00	16.88	15.88	15.00	14.21	13.50	12.86	12.27	11.74	11.25	10.80
280	23.33	21.54	20.00	18.67	17.50	16.47	15.56	14.74	14.00	13.33	12.73	12.17	11.67	11.20
290	24.17	22.31	20.71	19.33	18.13	17.06	16.11	15.26	14.50	13.81	13.18	12.61	12.08	11.60

Miles per Gallon Fuel Chart (cont.)

Miles Traveled	Gallons of Fuel Used													
	12	13	14	15	16	17	18	19	20	21	22	23	24	25
300	25.00	23.08	21.43	20.00	18.75	17.65	16.67	15.79	15.00	14.29	13.64	13.04	12.50	12.00
310	25.83	23.85	22.14	20.67	19.38	18.24	17.22	16.32	15.50	14.76	14.09	13.48	12.92	12.40
320	26.67	24.62	22.86	21.33	20.00	18.82	17.78	16.84	16.00	15.24	14.55	13.91	13.33	12.80
330	27.50	25.38	23.57	22.00	20.63	19.41	18.33	17.37	16.50	15.71	15.00	14.35	13.75	13.20
340	28.33	26.15	24.29	22.67	21.25	20.00	18.89	17.89	17.00	16.19	15.45	14.78	14.17	13.60
350	29.17	26.92	25.00	23.33	21.88	20.59	19.44	18.42	17.50	16.67	15.91	15.22	14.58	14.00
360	30.00	27.69	25.71	24.00	22.50	21.18	20.00	18.95	18.00	17.14	16.36	15.65	15.00	14.40
370	30.83	28.46	26.43	24.67	23.13	21.76	20.56	19.47	18.50	17.62	16.82	16.09	15.42	14.80
380	31.67	29.23	27.14	25.33	23.75	22.35	21.11	20.00	19.00	18.10	17.27	16.52	15.83	15.20
390	32.50	30.00	27.86	26.00	24.38	22.94	21.67	20.53	19.50	18.57	17.73	16.96	16.25	15.60
400	33.33	30.77	28.57	26.67	25.00	23.53	22.22	21.05	20.00	19.05	18.18	17.39	16.67	16.00
410	34.17	31.54	29.29	27.33	25.63	24.12	22.78	21.58	20.50	19.52	18.64	17.83	17.08	16.40
420	35.00	32.31	30.00	28.00	26.25	24.71	23.33	22.11	21.00	20.00	19.09	18.26	17.50	16.80
430	35.83	33.08	30.71	28.67	26.88	25.29	23.89	22.63	21.50	20.48	19.55	18.70	17.92	17.20
440	36.67	33.85	31.43	29.33	27.50	25.88	24.44	23.16	22.00	20.95	20.00	19.13	18.33	17.60
450	37.50	34.62	32.14	30.00	28.13	26.47	25.00	23.68	22.50	21.43	20.45	19.57	18.75	18.00
460	38.33	35.38	32.86	30.67	28.75	27.06	25.56	24.21	23.00	21.90	20.91	20.00	19.17	18.40
470	39.17	36.15	33.57	31.33	29.38	27.65	26.11	24.74	23.50	22.38	21.36	20.43	19.58	18.80
480	40.00	36.92	34.29	32.00	30.00	28.24	26.67	25.26	24.00	22.86	21.82	20.87	20.00	19.20
490	40.83	37.69	35.00	32.67	30.63	28.82	27.22	25.79	24.50	23.33	22.27	21.30	20.42	19.60
500	41.67	38.46	35.71	33.33	31.25	29.41	27.78	26.32	25.00	23.81	22.73	21.74	20.83	20.00
510	42.50	39.23	36.43	34.00	31.88	30.00	28.33	26.84	25.50	24.29	23.18	22.17	21.25	20.40
520	43.33	40.00	37.14	34.67	32.50	30.59	28.89	27.37	26.00	24.76	23.64	22.61	21.67	20.80
530	44.17	40.77	37.86	35.33	33.13	31.18	29.44	27.89	26.50	25.24	24.09	23.04	22.08	21.20
540	45.00	41.54	38.57	36.00	33.75	31.76	30.00	28.42	27.00	25.71	24.55	23.48	22.50	21.60
550	45.83	42.31	39.29	36.67	34.38	32.35	30.56	28.95	27.50	26.19	25.00	23.91	22.92	22.00
560	46.67	43.08	40.00	37.33	35.00	32.94	31.11	29.47	28.00	26.67	25.45	24.35	23.33	22.40
570	47.50	43.85	40.71	38.00	35.63	33.53	31.67	30.00	28.50	27.14	25.91	24.78	23.75	22.80
580	48.33	44.62	41.43	38.67	36.25	34.12	32.22	30.53	29.00	27.62	26.36	25.22	24.17	23.20
590	49.17	45.38	42.14	39.33	36.88	34.71	32.78	31.05	29.50	28.10	26.82	25.65	24.58	23.60
600	50.00	46.15	42.86	40.00	37.50	35.29	33.33	31.58	30.00	28.57	27.27	26.09	25.00	24.00

Vehicle Miles Traveled

Speed miles/hr	0.25	0.50	0.75	1	2	3	4	5	6	7	8	9	10	11
								Time Traveled in hours						
10	2.50	5.00	7.50	10	20	30	40	50	60	70	80	90	100	110
15	3.75	7.50	11.25	15	30	45	60	75	90	105	120	135	150	165
20	5.00	10.00	15.00	20	40	60	80	100	120	140	160	180	200	220
25	6.25	12.50	18.75	25	50	75	100	125	150	175	200	225	250	275
30	7.50	15.00	22.50	30	60	90	120	150	180	210	240	270	300	330
35	8.75	17.50	26.25	35	70	105	140	175	210	245	280	315	350	385
40	10.00	20.00	30.00	40	80	120	160	200	240	280	320	360	400	440
45	11.25	22.50	33.75	45	90	135	180	225	270	315	360	405	450	495
50	12.50	25.00	37.50	50	100	150	200	250	300	350	400	450	500	550
55	13.75	27.50	41.25	55	110	165	220	275	330	385	440	495	550	605
60	15.00	30.00	45.00	60	120	180	240	300	360	420	480	540	600	660
65	16.25	32.50	48.75	65	130	195	260	325	390	455	520	585	650	715
70	17.50	35.00	52.50	70	140	210	280	350	420	490	560	630	700	770
75	18.75	37.50	56.25	75	150	225	300	375	450	525	600	675	750	825
80	20.00	40.00	60.00	80	160	240	320	400	480	560	640	720	800	880
85	21.25	42.50	63.75	85	170	255	340	425	510	595	680	765	850	935
90	22.50	45.00	67.50	90	180	270	360	450	540	630	720	810	900	990
95	23.75	47.50	71.25	95	190	285	380	475	570	665	760	855	950	1045
100	25.00	50.00	75.00	100	200	300	400	500	600	700	800	900	1000	1100
105	26.25	52.50	78.75	105	210	315	420	525	630	735	840	945	1050	1155
110	27.50	55.00	82.50	110	220	330	440	550	660	770	880	990	1100	1210
115	28.75	57.50	86.25	115	230	345	460	575	690	805	920	1035	1150	1265
120	30.00	60.00	90.00	120	240	360	480	600	720	840	960	1080	1200	1320
125	31.25	62.50	93.75	125	250	375	500	625	750	875	1000	1125	1250	1375
130	32.50	65.00	97.50	130	260	390	520	650	780	910	1040	1170	1300	1430

Vehicle Miles Traveled (cont.)

Speed miles/hr	Time Traveled in hours													
	0.25	0.50	0.75	1	2	3	4	5	6	7	8	9	10	11
135	33.75	67.50	101.25	135	270	405	540	675	810	945	1080	1215	1350	1485
140	35.00	70.00	105.00	140	280	420	560	700	840	980	1120	1260	1400	1540
145	36.25	72.50	108.75	145	290	435	580	725	870	1015	1160	1305	1450	1595
150	37.50	75.00	112.50	150	300	450	600	750	900	1050	1200	1350	1500	1650
155	38.75	77.50	116.25	155	310	465	620	775	930	1085	1240	1395	1550	1705
160	40.00	80.00	120.00	160	320	480	640	800	960	1120	1280	1440	1600	1760
165	41.25	82.50	123.75	165	330	495	660	825	990	1155	1320	1485	1650	1815
170	42.50	85.00	127.50	170	340	510	680	850	1020	1190	1360	1530	1700	1870
175	43.75	87.50	131.25	175	350	525	700	875	1050	1225	1400	1575	1750	1925
180	45.00	90.00	135.00	180	360	540	720	900	1080	1260	1440	1620	1800	1980
185	46.25	92.50	138.75	185	370	555	740	925	1110	1295	1480	1665	1850	2035
190	47.50	95.00	142.50	190	380	570	760	950	1140	1330	1520	1710	1900	2090
195	48.75	97.50	146.25	195	390	585	780	975	1170	1365	1560	1755	1950	2145
200	50.00	100.00	150.00	200	400	600	800	1000	1200	1400	1600	1800	2000	2200
205	51.25	102.50	153.75	205	410	615	820	1025	1230	1435	1640	1845	2050	2255
210	52.50	105.00	157.50	210	420	630	840	1050	1260	1470	1680	1890	2100	2310
215	53.75	107.50	161.25	215	430	645	860	1075	1290	1505	1720	1935	2150	2365
220	55.00	110.00	165.00	220	440	660	880	1100	1320	1540	1760	1980	2200	2420
225	56.25	112.50	168.75	225	450	675	900	1125	1350	1575	1800	2025	2250	2475
230	57.50	115.00	172.50	230	460	690	920	1150	1380	1610	1840	2070	2300	2530
235	58.75	117.50	176.25	235	470	705	940	1175	1410	1645	1880	2115	2350	2585
240	60.00	120.00	180.00	240	480	720	960	1200	1440	1680	1920	2160	2400	2640
245	61.25	122.50	183.75	245	490	735	980	1225	1470	1715	1960	2205	2450	2695
250	62.50	125.00	187.50	250	500	750	1000	1250	1500	1750	2000	2250	2500	2750

Speed miles/hr	Time Traveled in hours												
	12	13	14	15	16	17	18	19	20	21	22	23	24
10	120	130	140	150	160	170	180	190	200	210	220	230	240
15	180	195	210	225	240	255	270	285	300	315	330	345	360
20	240	260	280	300	320	340	360	380	400	420	440	460	480
25	300	325	350	375	400	425	450	475	500	525	550	575	600
30	360	390	420	450	480	510	540	570	600	630	660	690	720
35	420	455	490	525	560	595	630	665	700	735	770	805	840
40	480	520	560	600	640	680	720	760	800	840	880	920	960
45	540	585	630	675	720	765	810	855	900	945	990	1035	1080
50	600	650	700	750	800	850	900	950	1000	1050	1100	1150	1200
55	660	715	770	825	880	935	990	1045	1100	1155	1210	1265	1320
60	720	780	840	900	960	1020	1080	1140	1200	1260	1320	1380	1440
65	780	845	910	975	1040	1105	1170	1235	1300	1365	1430	1495	1560
70	840	910	980	1050	1120	1190	1260	1330	1400	1470	1540	1610	1680
75	900	975	1050	1125	1200	1275	1350	1425	1500	1575	1650	1725	1800
80	960	1040	1120	1200	1280	1360	1440	1520	1600	1680	1760	1840	1920
85	1020	1105	1190	1275	1360	1445	1530	1615	1700	1785	1870	1955	2040
90	1080	1170	1260	1350	1440	1530	1620	1710	1800	1890	1980	2070	2160
95	1140	1235	1330	1425	1520	1615	1710	1805	1900	1995	2090	2185	2280
100	1200	1300	1400	1500	1600	1700	1800	1900	2000	2100	2200	2300	2400
105	1260	1365	1470	1575	1680	1785	1890	1995	2100	2205	2310	2415	2520
110	1320	1430	1540	1650	1760	1870	1980	2090	2200	2310	2420	2530	2640
115	1380	1495	1610	1725	1840	1955	2070	2185	2300	2415	2530	2645	2760
120	1440	1560	1680	1800	1920	2040	2160	2280	2400	2520	2640	2760	2880
125	1500	1625	1750	1875	2000	2125	2250	2375	2500	2625	2750	2875	3000
130	1560	1690	1820	1950	2080	2210	2340	2470	2600	2730	2860	2990	3120

Vehicle Miles Traveled (cont.)

Speed miles/hr	Time Traveled in hours												
	12	13	14	15	16	17	18	19	20	21	22	23	24
135	1620	1755	1890	2025	2160	2295	2430	2565	2700	2835	2970	3105	3240
140	1680	1820	1960	2100	2240	2380	2520	2660	2800	2940	3080	3220	3360
145	1740	1885	2030	2175	2320	2465	2610	2755	2900	3045	3190	3335	3480
150	1800	1950	2100	2250	2400	2550	2700	2850	3000	3150	3300	3450	3600
155	1860	2015	2170	2325	2480	2635	2790	2945	3100	3255	3410	3565	3720
160	1920	2080	2240	2400	2560	2720	2880	3040	3200	3360	3520	3680	3840
165	1980	2145	2310	2475	2640	2805	2970	3135	3300	3465	3630	3795	3960
170	2040	2210	2380	2550	2720	2890	3060	3230	3400	3570	3740	3910	4080
175	2100	2275	2450	2625	2800	2975	3150	3325	3500	3675	3850	4025	4200
180	2160	2340	2520	2700	2880	3060	3240	3420	3600	3780	3960	4140	4320
185	2220	2405	2590	2775	2960	3145	3330	3515	3700	3885	4070	4255	4440
190	2280	2470	2660	2850	3040	3230	3420	3610	3800	3990	4180	4370	4560
195	2340	2535	2730	2925	3120	3315	3510	3705	3900	4095	4290	4485	4680
200	2400	2600	2800	3000	3200	3400	3600	3800	4000	4200	4400	4600	4800
205	2460	2665	2870	3075	3280	3485	3690	3895	4100	4305	4510	4715	4920
210	2520	2730	2940	3150	3360	3570	3780	3990	4200	4410	4620	4830	5040
215	2580	2795	3010	3225	3440	3655	3870	4085	4300	4515	4730	4945	5160
220	2640	2860	3080	3300	3520	3740	3960	4180	4400	4620	4840	5060	5280
225	2700	2925	3150	3375	3600	3825	4050	4275	4500	4725	4950	5175	5400
230	2760	2990	3220	3450	3680	3910	4140	4370	4600	4830	5060	5290	5520
235	2820	3055	3290	3525	3760	3995	4230	4465	4700	4935	5170	5405	5640
240	2880	3120	3360	3600	3840	4080	4320	4560	4800	5040	5280	5520	5760
245	2940	3185	3430	3675	3920	4165	4410	4655	4900	5145	5390	5635	5880
250	3000	3250	3500	3750	4000	4250	4500	4750	5000	5250	5500	5750	6000

Vehicle Hours to Travel a Distance

Distance miles	10	15	20	25	30	35	40	45	50	55	60	65	70	75
10	1.00	0.67	0.50	0.40	0.33	0.29	0.25	0.22	0.20	0.18	0.17	0.15	0.14	0.13
15	1.50	1.00	0.75	0.60	0.50	0.43	0.38	0.33	0.30	0.27	0.25	0.23	0.21	0.20
20	2.00	1.33	1.00	0.80	0.67	0.57	0.50	0.44	0.40	0.36	0.33	0.31	0.29	0.27
25	2.50	1.67	1.25	1.00	0.83	0.71	0.63	0.56	0.50	0.45	0.42	0.38	0.36	0.33
30	3.00	2.00	1.50	1.20	1.00	0.86	0.75	0.67	0.60	0.55	0.50	0.46	0.43	0.40
35	3.50	2.33	1.75	1.40	1.17	1.00	0.88	0.78	0.70	0.64	0.58	0.54	0.50	0.47
40	4.00	2.67	2.00	1.60	1.33	1.14	1.00	0.89	0.80	0.73	0.67	0.62	0.57	0.53
45	4.50	3.00	2.25	1.80	1.50	1.29	1.13	1.00	0.90	0.82	0.75	0.69	0.64	0.60
50	5.00	3.33	2.50	2.00	1.67	1.43	1.25	1.11	1.00	0.91	0.83	0.77	0.71	0.67
55	5.50	3.67	2.75	2.20	1.83	1.57	1.38	1.22	1.10	1.00	0.92	0.85	0.79	0.73
60	6.00	4.00	3.00	2.40	2.00	1.71	1.50	1.33	1.20	1.09	1.00	0.92	0.86	0.80
65	6.50	4.33	3.25	2.60	2.17	1.86	1.63	1.44	1.30	1.18	1.08	1.00	0.93	0.87
70	7.00	4.67	3.50	2.80	2.33	2.00	1.75	1.56	1.40	1.27	1.17	1.08	1.00	0.93
75	7.50	5.00	3.75	3.00	2.50	2.14	1.88	1.67	1.50	1.36	1.25	1.15	1.07	1.00
80	8.00	5.33	4.00	3.20	2.67	2.29	2.00	1.78	1.60	1.45	1.33	1.23	1.14	1.07
85	8.50	5.67	4.25	3.40	2.83	2.43	2.13	1.89	1.70	1.55	1.42	1.31	1.21	1.13
90	9.00	6.00	4.50	3.60	3.00	2.57	2.25	2.00	1.80	1.64	1.50	1.38	1.29	1.20
95	9.50	6.33	4.75	3.80	3.17	2.71	2.38	2.11	1.90	1.73	1.58	1.46	1.36	1.27
100	10.00	6.67	5.00	4.00	3.33	2.86	2.50	2.22	2.00	1.82	1.67	1.54	1.43	1.33
200	20.00	13.33	10.00	8.00	6.67	5.71	5.00	4.44	4.00	3.64	3.33	3.08	2.86	2.67
300	30.00	20.00	15.00	12.00	10.00	8.57	7.50	6.67	6.00	5.45	5.00	4.62	4.29	4.00
400	40.00	26.67	20.00	16.00	13.33	11.43	10.00	8.89	8.00	7.27	6.67	6.15	5.71	5.33
500	50.00	33.33	25.00	20.00	16.67	14.29	12.50	11.11	10.00	9.09	8.33	7.69	7.14	6.67
600	60.00	40.00	30.00	24.00	20.00	17.14	15.00	13.33	12.00	10.91	10.00	9.23	8.57	8.00
700	70.00	46.67	35.00	28.00	23.33	20.00	17.50	15.56	14.00	12.73	11.67	10.77	10.00	9.33
800	80.00	53.33	40.00	32.00	26.67	22.86	20.00	17.78	16.00	14.55	13.33	12.31	11.43	10.67
900	90.00	60.00	45.00	36.00	30.00	25.71	22.50	20.00	18.00	16.36	15.00	13.85	12.86	12.00
1000	100.00	66.67	50.00	40.00	33.33	28.57	25.00	22.22	20.00	18.18	16.67	15.38	14.29	13.33
1100	110.00	73.33	55.00	44.00	36.67	31.43	27.50	24.44	22.00	20.00	18.33	16.92	15.71	14.67
1200	120.00	80.00	60.00	48.00	40.00	34.29	30.00	26.67	24.00	21.82	20.00	18.46	17.14	16.00

Vehicle Speed in miles/hour

Vehicle Hours to Travel a Distance

Distance miles	Vehicle Speed in miles/hour													
	10	15	20	25	30	35	40	45	50	55	60	65	70	75
1300	130.00	86.67	65.00	52.00	43.33	37.14	32.50	28.89	26.00	23.64	21.67	20.00	18.57	17.33
1400	140.00	93.33	70.00	56.00	46.67	40.00	35.00	31.11	28.00	25.45	23.33	21.54	20.00	18.67
1500	150.00	100.00	75.00	60.00	50.00	42.86	37.50	33.33	30.00	27.27	25.00	23.08	21.43	20.00
1600	160.00	106.67	80.00	64.00	53.33	45.71	40.00	35.56	32.00	29.09	26.67	24.62	22.86	21.33
1700	170.00	113.33	85.00	68.00	56.67	48.57	42.50	37.78	34.00	30.91	28.33	26.15	24.29	22.67
1800	180.00	120.00	90.00	72.00	60.00	51.43	45.00	40.00	36.00	32.73	30.00	27.69	25.71	24.00
1900	190.00	126.67	95.00	76.00	63.33	54.29	47.50	42.22	38.00	34.55	31.67	29.23	27.14	25.33
2000	200.00	133.33	100.00	80.00	66.67	57.14	50.00	44.44	40.00	36.36	33.33	30.77	28.57	26.67
2100	210.00	140.00	105.00	84.00	70.00	60.00	52.50	46.67	42.00	38.18	35.00	32.31	30.00	28.00
2200	220.00	146.67	110.00	88.00	73.33	62.86	55.00	48.89	44.00	40.00	36.67	33.85	31.43	29.33
2300	230.00	153.33	115.00	92.00	76.67	65.71	57.50	51.11	46.00	41.82	38.33	35.38	32.86	30.67
2400	240.00	160.00	120.00	96.00	80.00	68.57	60.00	53.33	48.00	43.64	40.00	36.92	34.29	32.00
2500	250.00	166.67	125.00	100.00	83.33	71.43	62.50	55.56	50.00	45.45	41.67	38.46	35.71	33.33
2600	260.00	173.33	130.00	104.00	86.67	74.29	65.00	57.78	52.00	47.27	43.33	40.00	37.14	34.67
2700	270.00	180.00	135.00	108.00	90.00	77.14	67.50	60.00	54.00	49.09	45.00	41.54	38.57	36.00
2800	280.00	186.67	140.00	112.00	93.33	80.00	70.00	62.22	56.00	50.91	46.67	43.08	40.00	37.33
2900	290.00	193.33	145.00	116.00	96.67	82.86	72.50	64.44	58.00	52.73	48.33	44.62	41.43	38.67
3000	300.00	200.00	150.00	120.00	100.00	85.71	75.00	66.67	60.00	54.55	50.00	46.15	42.86	40.00
3100	310.00	206.67	155.00	124.00	103.33	88.57	77.50	68.89	62.00	56.36	51.67	47.69	44.29	41.33
3200	320.00	213.33	160.00	128.00	106.67	91.43	80.00	71.11	64.00	58.18	53.33	49.23	45.71	42.67
3300	330.00	220.00	165.00	132.00	110.00	94.29	82.50	73.33	66.00	60.00	55.00	50.77	47.14	44.00
3400	340.00	226.67	170.00	136.00	113.33	97.14	85.00	75.56	68.00	61.82	56.67	52.31	48.57	45.33
3500	350.00	233.33	175.00	140.00	116.67	100.00	87.50	77.78	70.00	63.64	58.33	53.85	50.00	46.67
3600	360.00	240.00	180.00	144.00	120.00	102.86	90.00	80.00	72.00	65.45	60.00	55.38	51.43	48.00
3700	370.00	246.67	185.00	148.00	123.33	105.71	92.50	82.22	74.00	67.27	61.67	56.92	52.86	49.33
3800	380.00	253.33	190.00	152.00	126.67	108.57	95.00	84.44	76.00	69.09	63.33	58.46	54.29	50.67
3900	390.00	260.00	195.00	156.00	130.00	111.43	97.50	86.67	78.00	70.91	65.00	60.00	55.71	52.00
4000	400.00	266.67	200.00	160.00	133.33	114.29	100.00	88.89	80.00	72.73	66.67	61.54	57.14	53.33
4100	410.00	273.33	205.00	164.00	136.67	117.14	102.50	91.11	82.00	74.55	68.33	63.08	58.57	54.67
4200	420.00	280.00	210.00	168.00	140.00	120.00	105.00	93.33	84.00	76.36	70.00	64.62	60.00	56.00

Vehicle Hours to Travel a Distance

Distance miles	Vehicle Speed in miles/hour													
	10	15	20	25	30	35	40	45	50	55	60	65	70	75
4300	430.00	286.67	215.00	172.00	143.33	122.86	107.50	95.56	86.00	78.18	71.67	66.15	61.43	57.33
4400	440.00	293.33	220.00	176.00	146.67	125.71	110.00	97.78	88.00	80.00	73.33	67.69	62.86	58.67
4500	450.00	300.00	225.00	180.00	150.00	128.57	112.50	100.00	90.00	81.82	75.00	69.23	64.29	60.00
4600	460.00	306.67	230.00	184.00	153.33	131.43	115.00	102.22	92.00	83.64	76.67	70.77	65.71	61.33
4700	470.00	313.33	235.00	188.00	156.67	134.29	117.50	104.44	94.00	85.45	78.33	72.31	67.14	62.67
4800	480.00	320.00	240.00	192.00	160.00	137.14	120.00	106.67	96.00	87.27	80.00	73.85	68.57	64.00
4900	490.00	326.67	245.00	196.00	163.33	140.00	122.50	108.89	98.00	89.09	81.67	75.38	70.00	65.33
5000	500.00	333.33	250.00	200.00	166.67	142.86	125.00	111.11	100.00	90.91	83.33	76.92	71.43	66.67
5100	510.00	340.00	255.00	204.00	170.00	145.71	127.50	113.33	102.00	92.73	85.00	78.46	72.86	68.00
5200	520.00	346.67	260.00	208.00	173.33	148.57	130.00	115.56	104.00	94.55	86.67	80.00	74.29	69.33
5300	530.00	353.33	265.00	212.00	176.67	151.43	132.50	117.78	106.00	96.36	88.33	81.54	75.71	70.67
5400	540.00	360.00	270.00	216.00	180.00	154.29	135.00	120.00	108.00	98.18	90.00	83.08	77.14	72.00
5500	550.00	366.67	275.00	220.00	183.33	157.14	137.50	122.22	110.00	100.00	91.67	84.62	78.57	73.33
5600	560.00	373.33	280.00	224.00	186.67	160.00	140.00	124.44	112.00	101.82	93.33	86.15	80.00	74.67
5700	570.00	380.00	285.00	228.00	190.00	162.86	142.50	126.67	114.00	103.64	95.00	87.69	81.43	76.00
5800	580.00	386.67	290.00	232.00	193.33	165.71	145.00	128.89	116.00	105.45	96.67	89.23	82.86	77.33
5900	590.00	393.33	295.00	236.00	196.67	168.57	147.50	131.11	118.00	107.27	98.33	90.77	84.29	78.67
6000	600.00	400.00	300.00	240.00	200.00	171.43	150.00	133.33	120.00	109.09	100.00	92.31	85.71	80.00
6100	610.00	406.67	305.00	244.00	203.33	174.29	152.50	135.56	122.00	110.91	101.67	93.85	87.14	81.33
6200	620.00	413.33	310.00	248.00	206.67	177.14	155.00	137.78	124.00	112.73	103.33	95.38	88.57	82.67
6300	630.00	420.00	315.00	252.00	210.00	180.00	157.50	140.00	126.00	114.55	105.00	96.92	90.00	84.00
6400	640.00	426.67	320.00	256.00	213.33	182.86	160.00	142.22	128.00	116.36	106.67	98.46	91.43	85.33
6500	650.00	433.33	325.00	260.00	216.67	185.71	162.50	144.44	130.00	118.18	108.33	100.00	92.86	86.67
6600	660.00	440.00	330.00	264.00	220.00	188.57	165.00	146.67	132.00	120.00	110.00	101.54	94.29	88.00
6700	670.00	446.67	335.00	268.00	223.33	191.43	167.50	148.89	134.00	121.82	111.67	103.08	95.71	89.33
6800	680.00	453.33	340.00	272.00	226.67	194.29	170.00	151.11	136.00	123.64	113.33	104.62	97.14	90.67
6900	690.00	460.00	345.00	276.00	230.00	197.14	172.50	153.33	138.00	125.45	115.00	106.15	98.57	92.00
7000	700.00	466.67	350.00	280.00	233.33	200.00	175.00	155.56	140.00	127.27	116.67	107.69	100.00	93.33

Vehicle Hours to Travel a Distance

Distance miles	Vehicle Speed in miles/hour														
	80	85	90	95	100	105	110	115	120	125	130	135	140	145	150
10	0.13	0.12	0.11	0.11	0.10	0.10	0.09	0.09	0.08	0.08	0.08	0.07	0.07	0.07	0.07
15	0.19	0.18	0.17	0.16	0.15	0.14	0.14	0.13	0.13	0.12	0.12	0.11	0.11	0.10	0.10
20	0.25	0.24	0.22	0.21	0.20	0.19	0.18	0.17	0.17	0.16	0.15	0.15	0.14	0.14	0.13
25	0.31	0.29	0.28	0.26	0.25	0.24	0.23	0.22	0.21	0.20	0.19	0.19	0.18	0.17	0.17
30	0.38	0.35	0.33	0.32	0.30	0.29	0.27	0.26	0.25	0.24	0.23	0.22	0.21	0.21	0.20
35	0.44	0.41	0.39	0.37	0.35	0.33	0.32	0.30	0.29	0.28	0.27	0.26	0.25	0.24	0.23
40	0.50	0.47	0.44	0.42	0.40	0.38	0.36	0.35	0.33	0.32	0.31	0.30	0.29	0.28	0.27
45	0.56	0.53	0.50	0.47	0.45	0.43	0.41	0.39	0.38	0.36	0.35	0.33	0.32	0.31	0.30
50	0.63	0.59	0.56	0.53	0.50	0.48	0.45	0.43	0.42	0.40	0.38	0.37	0.36	0.34	0.33
55	0.69	0.65	0.61	0.58	0.55	0.52	0.50	0.48	0.46	0.44	0.42	0.41	0.39	0.38	0.37
60	0.75	0.71	0.67	0.63	0.60	0.57	0.55	0.52	0.50	0.48	0.46	0.44	0.43	0.41	0.40
65	0.81	0.76	0.72	0.68	0.65	0.62	0.59	0.57	0.54	0.52	0.50	0.48	0.46	0.45	0.43
70	0.88	0.82	0.78	0.74	0.70	0.67	0.64	0.61	0.58	0.56	0.54	0.52	0.50	0.48	0.47
75	0.94	0.88	0.83	0.79	0.75	0.71	0.68	0.65	0.63	0.60	0.58	0.56	0.54	0.52	0.50
80	1.00	0.94	0.89	0.84	0.80	0.76	0.73	0.70	0.67	0.64	0.62	0.59	0.57	0.55	0.53
85	1.06	1.00	0.94	0.89	0.85	0.81	0.77	0.74	0.71	0.68	0.65	0.63	0.61	0.59	0.57
90	1.13	1.06	1.00	0.95	0.90	0.86	0.82	0.78	0.75	0.72	0.69	0.67	0.64	0.62	0.60
95	1.19	1.12	1.06	1.00	0.95	0.90	0.86	0.83	0.79	0.76	0.73	0.70	0.68	0.66	0.63
100	1.25	1.18	1.11	1.05	1.00	0.95	0.91	0.87	0.83	0.80	0.77	0.74	0.71	0.69	0.67
200	2.50	2.35	2.22	2.11	2.00	1.90	1.82	1.74	1.67	1.60	1.54	1.48	1.43	1.38	1.33
300	3.75	3.53	3.33	3.16	3.00	2.86	2.73	2.61	2.50	2.40	2.31	2.22	2.14	2.07	2.00
400	5.00	4.71	4.44	4.21	4.00	3.81	3.64	3.48	3.33	3.20	3.08	2.96	2.86	2.76	2.67
500	6.25	5.88	5.56	5.26	5.00	4.76	4.55	4.35	4.17	4.00	3.85	3.70	3.57	3.45	3.33
600	7.50	7.06	6.67	6.32	6.00	5.71	5.45	5.22	5.00	4.80	4.62	4.44	4.29	4.14	4.00
700	8.75	8.24	7.78	7.37	7.00	6.67	6.36	6.09	5.83	5.60	5.38	5.19	5.00	4.83	4.67
800	10.00	9.41	8.89	8.42	8.00	7.62	7.27	6.96	6.67	6.40	6.15	5.93	5.71	5.52	5.33
900	11.25	10.59	10.00	9.47	9.00	8.57	8.18	7.83	7.50	7.20	6.92	6.67	6.43	6.21	6.00
1000	12.50	11.76	11.11	10.53	10.00	9.52	9.09	8.70	8.33	8.00	7.69	7.41	7.14	6.90	6.67
1100	13.75	12.94	12.22	11.58	11.00	10.48	10.00	9.57	9.17	8.80	8.46	8.15	7.86	7.59	7.33
1200	15.00	14.12	13.33	12.63	12.00	11.43	10.91	10.43	10.00	9.60	9.23	8.89	8.57	8.28	8.00

Vehicle Hours to Travel a Distance

Distance miles	Vehicle Speed in miles/hour														
	80	85	90	95	100	105	110	115	120	125	130	135	140	145	150
1300	16.25	15.29	14.44	13.68	13.00	12.38	11.82	11.30	10.83	10.40	10.00	9.63	9.29	8.97	8.67
1400	17.50	16.47	15.56	14.74	14.00	13.33	12.73	12.17	11.67	11.20	10.77	10.37	10.00	9.66	9.33
1500	18.75	17.65	16.67	15.79	15.00	14.29	13.64	13.04	12.50	12.00	11.54	11.11	10.71	10.34	10.00
1600	20.00	18.82	17.78	16.84	16.00	15.24	14.55	13.91	13.33	12.80	12.31	11.85	11.43	11.03	10.67
1700	21.25	20.00	18.89	17.89	17.00	16.19	15.45	14.78	14.17	13.60	13.08	12.59	12.14	11.72	11.33
1800	22.50	21.18	20.00	18.95	18.00	17.14	16.36	15.65	15.00	14.40	13.85	13.33	12.86	12.41	12.00
1900	23.75	22.35	21.11	20.00	19.00	18.10	17.27	16.52	15.83	15.20	14.62	14.07	13.57	13.10	12.67
2000	25.00	23.53	22.22	21.05	20.00	19.05	18.18	17.39	16.67	16.00	15.38	14.81	14.29	13.79	13.33
2100	26.25	24.71	23.33	22.11	21.00	20.00	19.09	18.26	17.50	16.80	16.15	15.56	15.00	14.48	14.00
2200	27.50	25.88	24.44	23.16	22.00	20.95	20.00	19.13	18.33	17.60	16.92	16.30	15.71	15.17	14.67
2300	28.75	27.06	25.56	24.21	23.00	21.90	20.91	20.00	19.17	18.40	17.69	17.04	16.43	15.86	15.33
2400	30.00	28.24	26.67	25.26	24.00	22.86	21.82	20.87	20.00	19.20	18.46	17.78	17.14	16.55	16.00
2500	31.25	29.41	27.78	26.32	25.00	23.81	22.73	21.74	20.83	20.00	19.23	18.52	17.86	17.24	16.67
2600	32.50	30.59	28.89	27.37	26.00	24.76	23.64	22.61	21.67	20.80	20.00	19.26	18.57	17.93	17.33
2700	33.75	31.76	30.00	28.42	27.00	25.71	24.55	23.48	22.50	21.60	20.77	20.00	19.29	18.62	18.00
2800	35.00	32.94	31.11	29.47	28.00	26.67	25.45	24.35	23.33	22.40	21.54	20.74	20.00	19.31	18.67
2900	36.25	34.12	32.22	30.53	29.00	27.62	26.36	25.22	24.17	23.20	22.31	21.48	20.71	20.00	19.33
3000	37.50	35.29	33.33	31.58	30.00	28.57	27.27	26.09	25.00	24.00	23.08	22.22	21.43	20.69	20.00
3100	38.75	36.47	34.44	32.63	31.00	29.52	28.18	26.96	25.83	24.80	23.85	22.96	22.14	21.38	20.67
3200	40.00	37.65	35.56	33.68	32.00	30.48	29.09	27.83	26.67	25.60	24.62	23.70	22.86	22.07	21.33
3300	41.25	38.82	36.67	34.74	33.00	31.43	30.00	28.70	27.50	26.40	25.38	24.44	23.57	22.76	22.00
3400	42.50	40.00	37.78	35.79	34.00	32.38	30.91	29.57	28.33	27.20	26.15	25.19	24.29	23.45	22.67
3500	43.75	41.18	38.89	36.84	35.00	33.33	31.82	30.43	29.17	28.00	26.92	25.93	25.00	24.14	23.33
3600	45.00	42.35	40.00	37.89	36.00	34.29	32.73	31.30	30.00	28.80	27.69	26.67	25.71	24.83	24.00
3700	46.25	43.53	41.11	38.95	37.00	35.24	33.64	32.17	30.83	29.60	28.46	27.41	26.43	25.52	24.67
3800	47.50	44.71	42.22	40.00	38.00	36.19	34.55	33.04	31.67	30.40	29.23	28.15	27.14	26.21	25.33
3900	48.75	45.88	43.33	41.05	39.00	37.14	35.45	33.91	32.50	31.20	30.00	28.89	27.86	26.90	26.00
4000	50.00	47.06	44.44	42.11	40.00	38.10	36.36	34.78	33.33	32.00	30.77	29.63	28.57	27.59	26.67
4100	51.25	48.24	45.56	43.16	41.00	39.05	37.27	35.65	34.17	32.80	31.54	30.37	29.29	28.28	27.33
4200	52.50	49.41	46.67	44.21	42.00	40.00	38.18	36.52	35.00	33.60	32.31	31.11	30.00	28.97	28.00

Vehicle Hours to Travel a Distance

Distance miles	Vehicle Speed in miles/hour														
	80	85	90	95	100	105	110	115	120	125	130	135	140	145	150
4300	53.75	50.59	47.78	45.26	43.00	40.95	39.09	37.39	35.83	34.40	33.08	31.85	30.71	29.66	28.67
4400	55.00	51.76	48.89	46.32	44.00	41.90	40.00	38.26	36.67	35.20	33.85	32.59	31.43	30.34	29.33
4500	56.25	52.94	50.00	47.37	45.00	42.86	40.91	39.13	37.50	36.00	34.62	33.33	32.14	31.03	30.00
4600	57.50	54.12	51.11	48.42	46.00	43.81	41.82	40.00	38.33	36.80	35.38	34.07	32.86	31.72	30.67
4700	58.75	55.29	52.22	49.47	47.00	44.76	42.73	40.87	39.17	37.60	36.15	34.81	33.57	32.41	31.33
4800	60.00	56.47	53.33	50.53	48.00	45.71	43.64	41.74	40.00	38.40	36.92	35.56	34.29	33.10	32.00
4900	61.25	57.65	54.44	51.58	49.00	46.67	44.55	42.61	40.83	39.20	37.69	36.30	35.00	33.79	32.67
5000	62.50	58.82	55.56	52.63	50.00	47.62	45.45	43.48	41.67	40.00	38.46	37.04	35.71	34.48	33.33
5100	63.75	60.00	56.67	53.68	51.00	48.57	46.36	44.35	42.50	40.80	39.23	37.78	36.43	35.17	34.00
5200	65.00	61.18	57.78	54.74	52.00	49.52	47.27	45.22	43.33	41.60	40.00	38.52	37.14	35.86	34.67
5300	66.25	62.35	58.89	55.79	53.00	50.48	48.18	46.09	44.17	42.40	40.77	39.26	37.86	36.55	35.33
5400	67.50	63.53	60.00	56.84	54.00	51.43	49.09	46.96	45.00	43.20	41.54	40.00	38.57	37.24	36.00
5500	68.75	64.71	61.11	57.89	55.00	52.38	50.00	47.83	45.83	44.00	42.31	40.74	39.29	37.93	36.67
5600	70.00	65.88	62.22	58.95	56.00	53.33	50.91	48.70	46.67	44.80	43.08	41.48	40.00	38.62	37.33
5700	71.25	67.06	63.33	60.00	57.00	54.29	51.82	49.57	47.50	45.60	43.85	42.22	40.71	39.31	38.00
5800	72.50	68.24	64.44	61.05	58.00	55.24	52.73	50.43	48.33	46.40	44.62	42.96	41.43	40.00	38.67
5900	73.75	69.41	65.56	62.11	59.00	56.19	53.64	51.30	49.17	47.20	45.38	43.70	42.14	40.69	39.33
6000	75.00	70.59	66.67	63.16	60.00	57.14	54.55	52.17	50.00	48.00	46.15	44.44	42.86	41.38	40.00
6100	76.25	71.76	67.78	64.21	61.00	58.10	55.45	53.04	50.83	48.80	46.92	45.19	43.57	42.07	40.67
6200	77.50	72.94	68.89	65.26	62.00	59.05	56.36	53.91	51.67	49.60	47.69	45.93	44.29	42.76	41.33
6300	78.75	74.12	70.00	66.32	63.00	60.00	57.27	54.78	52.50	50.40	48.46	46.67	45.00	43.45	42.00
6400	80.00	75.29	71.11	67.37	64.00	60.95	58.18	55.65	53.33	51.20	49.23	47.41	45.71	44.14	42.67
6500	81.25	76.47	72.22	68.42	65.00	61.90	59.09	56.52	54.17	52.00	50.00	48.15	46.43	44.83	43.33
6600	82.50	77.65	73.33	69.47	66.00	62.86	60.00	57.39	55.00	52.80	50.77	48.89	47.14	45.52	44.00
6700	83.75	78.82	74.44	70.53	67.00	63.81	60.91	58.26	55.83	53.60	51.54	49.63	47.86	46.21	44.67
6800	85.00	80.00	75.56	71.58	68.00	64.76	61.82	59.13	56.67	54.40	52.31	50.37	48.57	46.90	45.33
6900	86.25	81.18	76.67	72.63	69.00	65.71	62.73	60.00	57.50	55.20	53.08	51.11	49.29	47.59	46.00
7000	87.50	82.35	77.78	73.68	70.00	66.67	63.64	60.87	58.33	56.00	53.85	51.85	50.00	48.28	46.67

Antifreeze Table

Cooling System Capacity Quarts	Temperature Rating °F at Quarts of Antifreeze Required			
	3	4	5	6
8	−8	−34	−69	
9	0	−21	−50	−85
10	4	−12	−34	−62
11	8	−6	−23	−47
12	10	0	−15	−34
13	13	3	−9	−25
14	15	6	−5	−17
15	16	8	0	−12
16	17	10	2	−8
17	18	12	5	−4
18	19	14	7	0
19	20	15	9	2
20	21	16	10	4

Cooling System Capacity Quarts	Temperature Rating °F at Quarts of Antifreeze Required			
	7	8	9	10
8				
9				
10	−84			
11	−75			
12	−57	−85		
13	−45	−66	−86	
14	−34	−54	−78	
15	−26	−43	−62	−85
16	−19	−34	−52	−69
17	−14	−27	−42	−58
18	−10	−21	−34	−50
19	−7	−16	−28	−42
20	−3	−12	−22	−34

NOTE: Never use more that 70% antifreeze in a cooling system or the antifreeze and boiling properties of the mixture become unfavorable. Commercial automotive antifreeze is an ethylene glycol based solution that, when mixed with radiator water, lowers the temperature at which the radiator water will freeze and also increases the temperature at which the water will boil. At a radiator cap pressure of 15 psi a 50% solution of antifreeze and water will increase the boiling point to 265° F and a 70% solution will increase it to 276 °F. Ethylene glycol is actually the chemical "1,2 Ethanediol" and has a chemical formula of $HOCH_2CH_2OH$. Antifreeze is poisonous and if swallowed, give two glasses of water, induce vomiting and call a physician. Portions of the above information are based on Prestone Anti Freeze by Union Carbide Corp.

Spark Plug Torque

Spark Plug Thread Size	Aluminum Head Ft lbf	Nm	Iron Head Ft lbf	Nm
10mm (Gasket)	8-11	11-15	8-12	11-16
12 mm (Gasket)	10-18	14-24	10-18	14-24
14 mm (Gasket)	18-22	24-30	26-30	35-41
14 mm (Taper seat)	7-15	9-20	7-15	9-20
18 mm (Gasket)	28-34	38-46	32-38	43-52
18 mm (Taper seat)	15-20	20-27	15-20	20-27
7/8-18 inch (Gasket)	31-39	42-53	31-39	42-53

NOTE: Ft lbf = Foot pound-force and Nm = Newton meter = 0.10197 Kilogram-force meter. If the engine manufacturers' torque specification is available, it should always take precedence over the values in the above table. Even with the above torque ranges, exercise care when tightening the spark plugs, since condition of the head threads, length of the threads and temperature all have an effect on the maximum torque. If a torque wrench is not available, simply tighten spark plug down to finger tight and then wrench tighten an additional 1/4 turn with gasket type plugs or 1/16 turn with taper seat plugs. It is recommended that a small amount of antiseize compound be used on threads in aluminum heads and a small amount of light weight oil be used in cast iron heads.

For additional information on torque ratings of various bolt specifications, see the HARDWARE Chapter, page 399.

Lead–Acid Battery Specific Gravity & Charge

Acids Specific Gravity	Charge Level
1.30 to 1.32	Overcharged
1.26 to 1.28	100%
1.24 to 1.26	75%
1.20 to 1.22	50%
1.15 to 1.17	25%
1.13 to 1.15	Very low capacity
1.11 to 1.12	Discharged

Battery Efficiency Changes with Temperature	
80°F=100% Charge	10°F=50% Charge
50°F=82% Charge	0°F=40% Charge
30°F=64% Charge	–10°F=33% Charge
20°F=58% Charge	–20°F=18% Charge

Oil Viscosity vs. Temperature

Engine Oil SAE Viscosity	Outside Temperature °F						
	−20	0	20	40	60	80	100
20W-20	no	no	yes	yes	yes	yes	yes
20W-40	no	no	yes	yes	yes	yes	yes
20W-50	no	no	yes	yes	yes	yes	yes
10W-30	no	yes	yes	yes	yes	yes	yes
10W-40	no	yes	yes	yes	yes	yes	yes
10W	no	yes	yes	yes	yes	no	no
5W-30	yes	yes	yes	yes	yes	no	no
5W-20	yes	yes	no	no	no	no	no

Gear Oil SAE Viscosity	Outside Temperature °F						
	−20	0	20	40	60	80	100
75W	yes	yes	yes	yes	no	no	no
80W	yes	yes	yes	yes	yes	no	no
80W-90	yes	yes	yes	yes	yes	yes	yes
85W	no	no	yes	yes	yes	yes	no
90	no	no	no	no	yes	yes	yes
140	no	no	no	no	yes	yes	yes

Table shows which viscosities are appropriate for different outside temperatures. Values are for average conditions and may vary depending on the type of equipment being used. Manufacturers specs should always take precedence over the above tables.

Auto Headlight Warning

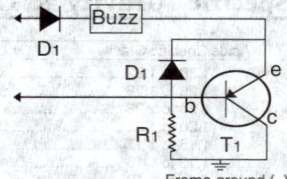

To taillight wire controlled by headlight switch.

To Ignition Switch "on" or coil-ignition terminal.

This simple circuit will buzz if you leave your headlights turned on when the ignition switch is turned off!
R1 = 150 ohm resistor, 10 watt
D1 = Silicon rectifier, almost any size such as 50 volt, 3 amp
Buzz = Small 12 volt buzzer
T1 = PNP 35 watt silicon switching transistor
"To taillight" is the wire that has 12 volts when the lights are ON
"To Ignition" is the wire that has 12 volts when the ignition is ON.

Automotive Trailer Wiring

There are 4 common configurations of connectors for trailers:

    4-Way: Utility trailers

    5-Way: Utility trailers for vehicles with Single Purpose Bulbs

    6-Way: Horse trailers, stock trailers and utility trailers

    7-Way: RV trailers and some horse and utility trailers

For each connector type, there are many different tow vehicle wiring color codes depending on the type of vehicle and application.

WARNINGS

1.   The following information should be used as a general guide only, **ALWAYS test before you connect your wiring.**

2. Some automotive manufacturers require a special wiring harness (included in their towing package) because the system has built-in sensor that prevents damage to the vehicles computer and lights. If your vehicle falls into this category, kits are available that allow you to connect directly to the vehicles battery instead of through the vehicles wire harness. Not using the correct wiring on these types of vehicles can cause severe (and very expensive) damage to the vehicles electrical system.

3. All foreign cars and some domestic vehicles use a lighting system where the turn-signal lights are in a different bulb than the brake lights (Single Purpose Bulb System). Most American systems use a bulb in which both the turn-signals and brake lights are in the same bulb (Dual Purpose Bulb System). In order for the trailer's lighting system to work properly, a "converter" must be used. See your local car or trailer parts dealer for details. (Note: if the vehicle has both amber and red tail lights, it is probably a Single Purpose Bulb System).

HELPFUL HINTS

1. For boat trailer users, it is recommended that you disconnect the trailers electrical connector BEFORE the trailer goes into the water. If you do not, there is a good chance that the trailers hot bulbs will crack when they encounter cold water.

2. Wipe a small amount of light waterproof grease or petroleum jelly on the contact surfaces to protect them from moisture and oxidation. Always protect both socket and plugs, when they are not connected, with a platic cap or plastic bag.

3. Solder all wire splices and wrap them with electrical tape or seal with heat shrink tubing (marine grade if possible).

4. Make sure that your tow vehicle is equipped with a heavy duty flasher. If a standard flasher is used, it will overload and cause both the vehicles and trailers turn signals to flash rapidly.

5. The two most common cause of trailer lights not working are a bad ground connection between vehicle and trailer or dirty connectors

6. If you plan on using electric brakes, you will need to install a brake controller in the vehicle first.

7. If the trailer does not use the same connector as the vehicle, you can purchase an adapter to make the connection instead of rewiring either the plug or socket.

Common US Vehicle Wire Colors and Functions

Function	Connector				GMC	Ford	Chrysler	Jeep
	4-Way	5-Way	6-Way	7-Way				
Ground					Black	Grey or black	Black	Black
Tail Lights & Clearance Lights					Brown	Brown	Black or black w/ yellow stripe	Blue
Right Turn & Brake Lights					Green	Orange w/ blue stripe	Brown	Brown
Left Turn & Brake Lights					Yellow	Lt green w/ orange stripe	Dark green	Grey w/ black stripe
Backup Lights					Lt Green	Black w/ pink stripe	Violet	Brown
Electric Trailer Brakes					Blue	Blue	Blue	Blue
Auxiliary Power/Battery Charge					Red or Orange	Red	Red	Red
Brake Lights with Single Purpose Bulbs					Pink or Lt Blue	Red w/ green stripe	White	Blue w/ black stripe

Common Import Vehicle Wire Colors and Functions

Function	Connector				Honda	Toyota	Mazda
	4-Way	5-Way	6-Way	7-Way			
Ground					Black	Black w/ white	Black
Tail Lights & Clearance Lights					Green w/ black stripe	Red w/ green stripe	Green w/ yellow stripe
Right Turn & Brake Lights					Green w/ yellow stripe	Green w/ yellow stripe	Green w/ yellow stripe
Left Turn & Brake Lights					Green w/ blue stripe	Green w/ black stripe	Dark Green
Backup Lights					--	--	--
Electric Trailer Brakes					Blue	Blue	Blue
Auxiliary Power/Battery Charge					Red	Red	Red
Brake Lights with Single Purpose Bulbs					Green w/ white stripe	Green w/ red or white stripe	Green or green w/ red stripe

Trailer Connector Wiring Guide

4-Way Connectors

4-Way connectors are designed primarily for Dual Purpose Bulb vehicles. If you have a Single Purpose Bulb vehicle (most imports and some American cars), you must use a converter for the trailer lights to work correctly. Factory installed wire harnesses frequently match the Flat 4 color layout.

Function	Color (gauge)	Car side layout
Ground	White (10)	Uncovered pin
Left turn & brake light	Yellow (14)	1st covered pin
Right turn & brake light	Green (14)	2nd covered pin
Tail and clearance lights	Brown (14)	3rd covered pin

Standard flat four pole plug (trailer side)   Round style four pole plug

5-Way Connectors

5-Way connectors are identical to 4-Way connectors except a fifth wire has been added to accommodate backup lights or trailer brake lock outs when you back up. The wire is usually Red.

5-Way connectors are also used in vehicles that use Single Purpose Bulbs and a converter

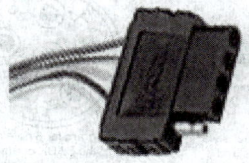

Standard flat five pole plug (vehicle side)

6-Way Trailer Connectors

6-Way connectors are designed to work with both Dual Purpose Bulb and Single Purpose Bulb systems. These connectors are most commonly used in horse trailers, stock trailers, and utility trailers. Note that there are two color layouts below, check carefully.

Function	Horse, Stock & Utility Trailer Color and (wire gauge)	Plug Mark
Ground	White (10)	GD
Left turn & brake light	Yellow (14)	LT
Right turn & brake light	Green (14)	RT
Tail and clearance lights	Brown (14)	TM
Battery, auxiliary power Connect to fuse block	Red or Black (14) but NOT both in the same connector	A
Electric Brakes	Blue (14)	S

Function	RV (Recreational Vehicle) Color Code	Plug Mark
Ground	White	GD
Left turn & brake light	Red	LT
Right turn & brake light	Brown	RT
Tail and clearance lights	Green	TM
Battery + auxillary power Connect to fues block	Black	A
Not used	Yellow	--
Electric Brakes	Blue	S

Rare Colors: black=stop light or electric brake; blue=stop light; brown=running & license plate lights; red=stop or electric brake.

1-1/4" diameter round knock-out style connector for 6 pole plug. Pins and sockets are round. This connector is on the trailer side.

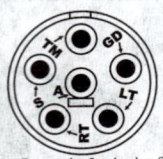

Wiring diagram for 6 pole plug (This view is of the BACK of the plug where the wires will be attached).

7-Way Trailer Connectors

7-Way connectors are designed to work with both Dual Purpose Bulb and Single Purpose Bulb systems. These connectors are most commonly used in RV's and heavier duty utility trailers. Note that Semi's and commercial trailers use a different 7-Way connector (round pins) and different color layouts.

Function	Horse, Stock & Utility Trailer Color and (wire gauge)	Plug Mark
Ground	White (10)	1
Electric brake	Blue (12)	2
Tail and clearance lights	Brown (14)	3
Battery + power	Black (10)	4
Left turn & brake light	Yellow (14)	5
Right turn & brake light	Green (14)	6
Auxiliary or backup	Orange or purple, not both (14)	7

Function	RV (Recreational Vehicle) Color and (wire gauge)	Plug Mark
Ground	White (10)	1
Electric brake	Blue (12)	2
Tail and clearance lights	Green (14)	3
Battery + power	Black (10)	4
Left turn & brake light	Red (14)	5
Right turn & brake light	Brown (14)	6
Auxiliary or backup	Yellow (14)	7

Rare Colors: blue=backup; brown=running & clearance; red=battery power & dome light; yellow=auxillary battery power.

2" diameter round connector for 7 pole, flat contact plug. Pins and sockets are flat instead of round.

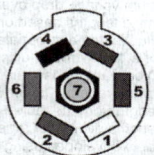

Wiring diagram for 7 pole plug (View is of the BACK of the plug where the wires will be attached).

Automotive Electric Wiring

Wire Gauge AWG	Maximum Wire Length (feet) for Car Wiring [1]					
	Current Load in Amps @ 12 Volts DC [2]					
	1	2	4	6	8	10
20	105	52	26	17	13	10
18	150	75	38	25	19	15
16	228	114	57	38	29	23
14	362	181	90	60	45	36
12	570	285	142	95	71	57
10	913	456	226	152	114	91
8	1447	723	362	241	181	145
6	--	1198	599	399	300	240
4	--	--	912	608	456	365
2	--	--	--	1017	763	610
1	--	--	--	1266	950	760
0	--	--	--	--	1209	967

Wire Gauge AWG	Maximum Wire Length (feet) for Car Wiring [1]					
	Current Load in Amps @ 12 Volts DC [2]					
	12	15	20	50	100	200
20	9	nr	nr	nr	nr	nr
18	13	nr	nr	nr	nr	nr
16	19	nr	nr	nr	nr	nr
14	30	24	nr	nr	nr	nr
12	47	38	28	nr	nr	nr
10	76	61	46	nr	nr	nr
8	121	96	72	nr	nr	nr
6	200	160	120	nr	nr	nr
4	304	243	182	73	nr	nr
2	508	407	305	122	nr	nr
1	633	507	380	152	76	nr
0	806	645	483	193	97	nr

(1) Maximum recommended wire lengths are based on a 1/2 volt maximum voltage drop over the length of the wire. If you want to determine lengths based on a different drop, simply multiply the table value by the appropriate factor (for example, if you want the values for a 1 volt drop, multiply the table value by 2).
(2) If you want the lengths for 6 volt or 24 volt systems, multiply the listed amperage by 0.5 for 6 volt or 2 for 24 volt and then select the wire length from the table.
(3) Lengths over 1,500 ft. are not shown.
(4) Table developed using SAE wire area.
"nr" means wire size is not recommended at selected current.
To be safe, always pick one wire size larger than you need for the specified wire length at the required current level.

Load Index vs. Load
P-metric & Euro Metric Tires

Load Index	Max. Load @ 35 psi		Load Index	Max. Load @ 35 psi	
	pounds	kilograms		pounds	kilograms
65	639	290	108	2,205	1,000
66	661	300	109	2,271	1,030
67	677	307	110	2,337	1,060
68	694	315	111	2,403	1,090
69	716	325	112	2,469	1,120
70	739	335	113	2,535	1,150
71	761	345	114	2,601	1,180
72	783	355	115	2,679	1,215
73	805	365	116	2,756	1,250
74	827	375	117	2,833	1,285
75	853	387	118	2,910	1,320
76	882	400	119	2,998	1,360
77	908	412	120	3,086	1,400
78	937	425	121	3,197	1,450
79	963	437	122	3,307	1,500
80	992	450	123	3,417	1,550
81	1,019	462	124	3,527	1,600
82	1,047	475	125	3,638	1,650
83	1,074	487	126	3,748	1,700
84	1,102	500	127	3,858	1,750
85	1,135	515	128	3,968	1,800
86	1,168	530	129	4,079	1,850
87	1,201	545	130	4,189	1,900
88	1,235	560	131	4,299	1,950
89	1,279	580	132	4,409	2,000
90	1,323	600	133	4,541	2,060
91	1,356	615	134	4,674	2,120
92	1,389	630	135	4,806	2,180
93	1,433	650	136	4,938	2,240
94	1,477	670	137	5,071	2,300
95	1,521	690	138	5,203	2,360
96	1,565	710	139	5,357	2,430
97	1,609	730	140	5,512	2,500
98	1,653	750	141	5,677	2,575
99	1,709	775	142	5,842	2,650
100	1,764	800	143	6,008	2,725
101	1,819	825	144	6,173	2,800
102	1,874	850	145	6,393	2,900
103	1,929	875	146	6,614	3,000
104	1,984	900	147	6,779	3,075
105	2,039	925	148	6,944	3,150
106	2,094	950	149	7,165	3,250
107	2,149	975	150	7,385	3,350

Tire Size vs. Load Rating

Tire Size (Bias, Bias-Belted, Radial)	Max Load lbs @ Cold Inflation 20 psi	32 psi
Passenger Car Tires:		
145R- 12 inch	600	780
6.00- 12 inch	605	845
155R- 12 inch	665	865
145/80R 12 inch	617	783
155/80R 12 inch	694	871
145R- 13 inch	660	825
145R- 13 inch	665	860
155R- 13 inch	730	950
155/80R- 13 inch	740	925
165/70R- 13 inch	750	880
6.00- 165R-, 165/75R- 13 inch	770	1010
175/70R- 13 inch	845	980
165/80R- 13 inch	816	1025
195/60R- 13 inch	825	1050
215/50R- 13 inch	840	1050
175/75R- 13 inch	850	1060
A78-, A70-, AR78-, AR70- 13 inch	810	1060
205/60R- 13 inch	835	1085
185/70R- 13 inch	870	1090
195/65R- 13 inch	880	1115
175/80R- 13 inch	905	1135
B13, 175R-, 205/60R- 13 inch	890	1150
6.50-, B78-, B70-, 175R-, BR78-, BR60-13	890	1150
185/75R- 13 inch	925	1170
195/70R- 13 inch	948	1210
195/70R- 13 inch	1045	1210
235/50R- 13 inch	970	1220
C-, C78-, C70-, CR78-, CR70-, 185/70R- 13 inch	950	1230
185/80R- 13 inch	990	1250
7.00-, 185R- 13 inch	980	1270
205/70R- 13 inch	1040	1300
D70-, DR78-, DR70- 13 inch	1010	1320
195R- 13 inch	1060	1370
E70-, ER78-, ER70-, ER60- 13 inch	1070	1400
155R- 14 inch	780	1010
A70-, AR70- 14 inch	810	1060
6.45-, 165R- 14 inch	860	1120
B78-, B70-, BR78-, BR70- 14 inch	890	1150
6.95- 14 inch	950	1230
C78-, C70-, CR78-, CR70- 14 inch	950	1230
D78-, D70-, DR78-, DR70-, 195/70- 14 inch	1010	1320
7.35- 185R- 14 inch	1040	1360
E78-, E70-, ER78-, ER70-, 205/70- 14 inch	1070	1400
7.75- 195R- 14 inch	1150	1500
F78-, F70-, F60-, FR78-, FR70-, 215/70-14	1160	1500
8.25- 205R- 14 inch	1250	1620
G78-, G70-, G60-, GR78-, GR70-, GR60- 14 inch	1250	1620
8.55- 215R- 14 inch	1360	1770
H78-, H70-, H60-, HR78-, HR70- 14 inch	1360	1770
8.85- 225R- 14 inch	1430	1860
6.85- C78-, C70-, 175R-, CR78-, CR70- 15 inch	950	1230
D78-, D70- 15 inch	1010	1320
7.35- 185R- 15 inch	1070	1390
E78-, E70-, E60-, ER78-, ER70-, ER60-, 205/70-15	1070	1400
7.75- 195R- 15 inch	1150	1490
F78-, F70-, F60-, FR78-, FR70-, FR60-, 215/70-15	1160	1500
205R- 15 inch	1240	1610
G78-, G70-, G60-, GR78-, GR70-, GR60- 225/70-15	1250	1620
8.25- 15 inch	1250	1620
215R- 15 inch	1340	1740

Tire Size vs. Load Rating

Tire Size (Bias, Bias-Belted, Radial)	Max Load lbs @ Cold Inflation	
	20 psi	32 psi
H78-,H70-,H60-,HR78-,HR70-,HR60- 15 inch	1360	1770
8.55- 15 inch	1360	1770
8.85-, 225R- 15 inch	1430	1860
J78-, J70-, J60-, JR78-, JR70- 15 inch	1430	1860
9.00- 15 inch	1460	1900
K70-, KR70- 15 inch	1460	1900
9.15-, 235R- 15 inch	1510	1970
L78-, L70-, L60-, LR78-, LR70-, LR60- 15 inch	1520	1970
205/55R- 16 inch	890	1150
225/50R- 16 inch	1000	1300
245/50R- 16 inch	1200	1510
255/50R- 16 inch	1280	1610

Light Truck Tires: (single tire) Tire Size (Bias, Bias-Belted, Radial)	Max Load lbs @ Cold Inflation	
	35 psi *Radial* 60 psi	
	30 psi *Bias* 75 psi	
E-, ER78-14LT	1140	1620
G-, GR78-14LT	1260	—
G-, GR78-15LT	1310	1870
H-, HR78-15LT	1440	2060
L-, LR78-15LT	1600	2290
F-, FR78-16LT	1270	1820
H-, HR78-16LT	1510	2150
L-, LR78-16LT	1670	2380
6.70-15LT	1210	2060
7.00-15LT	1350	2320
6.50-16LT	1270	2160
7.50-16LT	1620	2780
8.00-16.5LT	1360	2330
8.75-16.5LT	1570	2680
9.50-16.5LT	1860	3170
10.00-16.5LT	1840	3135
12.00-16.5LT	2370	4045
LT195/75-14	1115	1625
LT195/75-15	1165	—
LT215/75-15	1345	1960
LT235/75-15	1530	2230
LT255/75-16	1920	2800

Tire Size	30 psi *Radial* 50 psi	
	20 psi *Belted* 45 psi	
27 x 8.50-14LT	940	1515
30 x 9.50-15LT	1240	1990
31 x 10.50-15LT	1400	2250
31 x 11.50-15LT	1455	2340
32 x 11.50-15LT	1575	2530
33 x 12.50-15LT	1755	—

NOTE: Always check the current manufacturers specifications on a tire to verify the above approximations. If you want detailed information on tires, sizes, recommendations for different cars, etc, use a book entitled Tire Guide (get one for the current year), published by Tire Guides, Inc., 1101-6 S. Rogers Circle, Boca Raton, FL, 33487, (561) 997-9229, www.tireguides.com. The book is currently (2001) $14.95 and contains an abundance of information.

Tire Manufacturer Codes

Manufacturer	Codes
Alliance Tire & Rubber (Israel)	CD
Apollo Tyres (India)	8F, A6
Armstrong Rubber (USA)	CV
B.F. Goodrich Tire	BB, BC, BD, BK, BM, BN
Bandag (USA)	XX
Bridgestone Tire	1D, 1U, 1V, 2R, 7X, A7, A8, C8, EH to EP, H4, J2, L5, LH
Bridgestone/Firestone	0B, 0E, 1C, 2C, 3M, 3Y, 4D, 5D, 5T, 6T, 7B, 7G, 8B, 9B, D2, E2, HY, VA, VD, VE, VN, W1, W2, Y7
Carlisle Tire	4L, 8L, C4, UU
Ceat (India & Italy)	6K, 8H, HT, HU, WU
Cheng Shin Rubber (China & Taiwan)	7F, UY
CIA, Hulera Tornel (Mexico)	4F to 6F, T6
Continental	6Y, CL to CU, HW, LM, P1
Cooper Tire & Rubber (USA)	3D, U9, UP, UT
Cooper-Avon Tyres (England)	AT
Dayton Tire & Rubber (USA & Canada)	9X, HX, XV, XW, XY, Y2, Y4, YA to YK
Denman Tire (USA)	DY
Dunlop Tires	B2, D4, D5, D7, D8, DK, DL, F9, L8, W4, WM
Euzkadi Compania Hulera (Mexico)	WX, WY
Firestone Tire & Rubber	5C to 9C, 8T, 8X, E4 to E9, F2, F6, F7, V5, V6, VB, VC, VF to VM, VP, VT, VV, VX, VY, W5, W7, W9, WA, WC, WD, WF, WH
Gates Rubber (USA)	BW, BX, BY
General Tire	1H, 9V, A3, A9, AC, AD, AE, AH, H0, LV
Gentyre (Italy & S. Africa)	1L, HV
George Byers Sons (USA)	U4
Goodyear Dunlop Tires (USA)	DA, DB
Goodyear Tire & Rubber	1T, 1W, 4B, 7L, L1, M1, M6, M7, MB, MC, MD, MJ, MK, MT, MX, MY, NB, NC, ND, NH to NL, NP, NT, NU, NW, NY, PA to PD, T8, Y1
Hankook Tire (China & Korea)	1G, 5M, T1, T7
Hoosier Tire & Rubber (USA)	J7
Hung Ah Tire (Korea)	EF
Hurtublse Netread (USA)	N2
Inocce Rubber (Korea & Thailand)	J0
International Rubber (USA)	BV
Intreprinderea De Anvelope (Romania)	L7, N7
Ironsides Tire & Rubber (USA)	C7
J.K. Industries (India)	9F, X5
Kelly-Springfield Tire (USA)	P6, PJ, PK, PL
Kenda Rubber (SE Asia)	7Y, 8Y, K3
Kumho (Korea)	H2
Lee Tire & Rubber (Grem. & Luxem.)	KH, KM
Livingston's Tire Shop (USA)	V1
M & H Tire (USA)	V9
McCreary Tire & Rubber (USA)	C3
Metzier (Germany)	EA, EB, EC

Tire Manufacturer Codes

Manufacturer	Codes
Michelin	0C, 2X, 4M, 4V, 5E, 7V, A1, B1, B3, B6 to B9, C1, ED, F1, F3, FF to FN, FT to FY, H1, HA to HP, K0, L0, M3, M5
Mitsuboshi Belting (Japan)	LX, LY
Mohawk Rubber (USA)	CA, CB
MRF Limited (India)	0L, 9L, P9, T9, WT
Nankung Rubber Tire (Taiwan)	U8, WE
Ohtsu Tire & Rubber (Japan)	V4, VW
Panther Tyres (England)	L9
Phillips Petroleum (USA)	J1, K1
Phoenix Gummiwerke (Germany)	AX, AY
Pirelli	1B, 8U, XA to XT
Pirelli Armstrong Tire (USA)	CH, CK
Pneumant (Germany)	N5, N6, U6, U7
Pneumatiques Kleber (Germ. & France)	EW, EX, EY
Prelucrare Cauciuc (Romania)	L4, N4
Samson Tire & Rubber (Israel)	AW
Seiberling Tire & Rubber (USA & Can.)	AV, E3, PE, Y3, YM to YY
Semperit (Austria & Ireland)	BT, BU
South Pacific Tyres (Australia)	4C
SP Reifenwerke (Germany)	DM, DN
SP Tyres (England)	DD, DE
Specialty Tires (USA)	3U, CY
Sumitomo Rubber (Japan)	ET, EU, U2
Titan Tire (USA)	CF, F0, 3G
Tong Shin Chemical (Korea)	L3, X1
Toyo Tire (USA & Japan)	3C, CW, CX, N3
Trelleborg Ummifariks (Sweden)	LW
Uniroyal Goodrich Tire (USA & Mexico)	AN, AP, BA, BE, BF, BH, K4, LN
Uniroyal Tire	AJ, AK, AM, LJ, LL, LP, LT, LU, M9, T2, T3
United Tire & Rubber (Canada)	D3, D9
Universal Tire (USA)	VU
Vredestein (Netherlands)	DV, DW, DX, W3
Vsesojuznoe Ojedinenic (Russia)	V2, V7, X0, X3, X6 to X9
Yokohama (USA & Japan)	4U, 6B, CC, FA to FD
Zaklady Opon Samochodowych (Poland)	B5, C5

NOTE: The Alpha-Numeric tire code is located on the sidewall, near the rim and follows the letters "DOT". The code is "XXYY MMMM9999" where "XX" is the Manufacturer Plant Code in the above table, "YY" is the tire size (another letter type code), "MMMM" is an optional identification used by each manufacturer, and "9999" is the Date of Manufacture. The Date of Manufacture consists of four digits, the first two are the week of the year and the last two are the last two digits of the year. For example: "3197" means the 31st week of 1997. For tires sold in the United States, the Manufacturer Plant Codes will never contain the letters "G", "I", "O", "Q", "R", "S", or "Z". Data in the above table was compiled from *2001 Who Makes It And Where - Tire Directory*, Tire Guides, Inc., 1101-6 S. Rogers Circle, Boca Raton, FL 33487, (561) 997-9229 and the New Tire Manufacturer Database (newtire.mdb), National Highway Traffic Safety Administration.

Tire Size Codes - American Codes

P-Metric

P205/60R15 89H (New)

P = tire application: P = passenger tire, LT = light truck tire.
205 = tire width (millimeters) between sidewalls: "205" means 205 mm (8 in.) wide.
60 = aspect ratio, ratio of section heigth to tire width: "60" means section height is 60% of tire width or 123 mm (4.8 in.).
R = tire construction: R = radial, B = belted bias, D = diagonal or bias ply.
15 = rim diameter (inches): "15" means 15 in. (380 mm) diameter.
89 = load index A, maximum load (pounds or kilograms) at maximum pressure (psi or kPa).
H = speed ratingB, maximum service speed (mph or km/h).

P205/60HR15 (Old)

P = tire application: P = passenger tire, LT = light truck tire.
205 = tire width (millimeters) between sidewalls: "205" means 205 mm (8 in.) wide.
60 = aspect ratio, ratio of section heigth to tire width: "60" means section height is 60% of tire width or 123 mm (4.8 in.).
H = speed rating, maximum service speed (mph or km/h).
R = tire construction: R = radial, B = belted bias, D = diagonal or bias ply.
15 = rim diameter (inch): "15" means 15 in. (380 mm) diameter.

Numeric

6.00X13

6.00 = tire section width (inches) at widest point: "6.00" means 6 in. (150 mm) wide.
13 = rim diameter (inches): "13" means 13 in. (330 mm) diameter.
System no longer used on car or truck but still used on small tires such as camper trailer tires.

Alpha-Numeric

AR78HR13

A = size factor/load range, maximum load (pounds) at maximum pressure (psi): A = smallest tire/lowest load, L = largest tire/highest load.
R = tire construction: R = radial, blank = belted bias or diagonal/bias ply.
78 = aspect ratio, ratio of section heigth to tire width: "78" means section height is 78% of tire width. The term "series" was also used in place of aspect ratio.
HR = E & J speed rating (European & Japanese tires): HR = 112 mph (180 km/h),
SR = 130 mph (210 km/h), VR = 165 mph (265 km/h).
13 = rim diameter (inches): "13" means 13 in. (330 mm) diameter.

Light Truck Metric

LT235/85R15/D

LT = tire application: LT = light truck tire.
235 = tire width (millimeters) between sidewalls: "235" means 235 mm (9.25 in.) wide.
85 = aspect ratio, ratio of section heigth to tire width: "85" means section height is 85% oftire width or 200 mm (8 in.).
R = tire construction: R = radial, blank = belted bias or diagonal/bias ply.
15 = rim diameter (inches): "15" means 15 in. (380 mm) diameter.
D = load rangeC, maximum load (pounds) at maximum pressure (psi).

Light Truck High Flotation

31X10.5R15LT/C

31 = overall tire diameter (inches): "31" means overall diameter is 31 in. (780 mm).

10.5 = tire section width (inches): "10.5" means the tire is 10.5 in. (270 mm) wide.

R = tire construction: R = radial, blank = belted bias or diagonal/bias ply.
15 = rim diameter (inches): "15" means 15 in. (380 mm) diameter.
LT = tire application: LT = light truck tire.
C = load range, maximum load (pounds) at maximum pressure (psi).

Light Truck Numeric

8.75R16.5LT/D

8.75 = tire section width (inches): "8.75" means the tire is 8.75 in. (220 mm) wide.

R = tire construction: R = radial, blank = belted bias/diagonal/bias ply.
16.5 = rim diameter (inches): "16.5" means 16.5 in. (420 mm) diameter.
LT = tire application: LT = light truck tire.
D = load range, maximum load (pounds) at maximum pressure (psi).

European Sizing Codes

Euro Metric

205/60R15 89H (New)

205 = tire width (millimeters) between sidewalls: "205" means 205 mm (8 in.) wide.

60 = aspect ratio, ratio of section heigth to tire width: "60" means section height is 60% of tire width or 123 mm (4.8 in.).

R = tire construction: R = radial, B = belted bias, D = diagonal or bias ply.
15 = rim diameter (inches): "15" means 15 in. (380 mm) diameter.
89 = load index, maximum load (pounds or kilograms) at maximum pressure (psi or kPa).
H = speed rating, maximum service speed (mph or km/h).

205/60HR15 (Old)

205 = tire width (millimeters) between sidewalls: "205" means 205 mm (8 in.) wide.

60 = aspect ratio, ratio of section heigth to tire width: "60" means section height is 60% of tire width or 123 mm (4.8 in.).

H = speed rating, maximum service speed (mph or km/h).
R = tire conctruction: R = radial, B = belted bias, D = diagonal or bias ply.
15 = rim diameter (inches): "15" means 15 in. (380 mm) diameter.

155R13 78S (New)

155 = tire width (millimeters) between sidewalls: "155" means 155 mm (6.2 in.) wide.

R = tire construction: R = radial, blank = belted bias or diagonal/bias ply.
13 = rim diameter (inches): "13" means 13 in. (330 mm) diameter.
78 = load index, maximum load (pound or kilogram) at maximum pressure (psi or kPa).
S = speed rating, maximum service speed (mph or km/h).
Aspect ratio is assumed to be 82.

155SR13 (Old)

155 = tire width (millimeters) between sidewalls: "155" means 155 mm (6.2 in.) wide.

S = speed rating, maximum service speed (mph or km/h).
R = tire construction: R = radial, blank = belted bias or diagonal or bias ply.
13 = rim diameter (inch): "13" means 13 in. (330 mm) diameter.
Aspect ratio is assumed to be 82.

NOTES

(A) See Load Index vs. Load table.
(B) See Speed Rating Symbol table.
(C) Load Range is not the same as Load Index. Load Range varies with tire size while Load Index does not.

Tire Speed Rating Symbols

Symbols for P-metric and Euro Metric Tires					
Rating Symbol	Max. Service Speed		Rating Symbol	Max. Service Speed	
	mph	km/h		mph	km/h
B	31	50	P	93	150
C	37	60	Q	99	160
D	40	65	R	106	170
E	43	70	S	112	180
F	50	80	T	118	190
G	56	90	U	124	200
J	62	100	H	130	210
K	68	110	V	149	240
L	75	120	W	168	270
M	81	130	Y	186	300
N	87	140	ZR	>150	>240

Load Range vs. Ply Rating

Range-Rating	Range-Rating	Range-Rating	Range-Rating
A.......2	D.......8	G.......14	L.........20
B.......4	E.....10	H.......16	M.........22
C.......6	F.....12	J.......18	N.........24

Automotive Formulas

Engine Displacement = Stroke x Bore^2 x 0.7854 x Cylinders.
Engine Displacement is in cubic inches if Bore and Stroke are in inches or cubic centimeters (cc's) if Bore and Stroke are in centimeters. **To convert Displacement to Liters, multiply cubic inches by 0.01639 or cubic centimeters by 0.001.**
Cylinders is the number of engine cylinders (4, 6, 8, 12, etc)

CFM Engine Carburetor Air Flow:

4 Stroke Engine CFM = [CID x RPM x VE] / 3456

CFM is Cubic Feet per Minute air flow through the carburetor.
CID is the engine displacement in cubic inches.
RPM is the engine Revolutions Per Minute.
VE = engine Volumetric Efficiency, use 1 for 100% efficient.
(For a 2 Stroke Engine, divide by 1728, not 3456)

Fuel Consumption: Example 5 miles/gallon=47 liters/100 kilometers

X miles per US gallon = 235.214580 /X liters per 100 km

X miles per UK or Canadian gallon =
282.481060 / X liters per 100 km

Carpentry & Construction

(See also HARDWARE on page 399)
(See also PLUMBING on page 501)

Softwood Lumber Sizes

Nominal Size Inches	Actual Size Dry (Inches) (mm)	Actual Size Green (Inches) (mm)
THICKNESS:		
1	3/4 19	25/32 20
1–1/4	1 25	1–1/32 26
1–1/2	1–1/4 32	1–9/32 33
2	1–1/2 38	1–9/16 40
2–1/2	2 51	2–1/16 52
3	2–1/2 64	2–9/16 65
3–1/2	3 76	3–1/16 78
4	3–1/2 89	3–9/16 90
4–1/2	4 102	4–1/16 103
6	5–1/2	5–9/16
8	7–1/2	7–9/16
FACE WIDTH:		
2	1–1/2 38	1–9/16 40
3	2–1/2 64	2–9/16 65
4	3–1/2 89	3–9/16 90
5	4–1/2 114	4–5/8 117
6	5–1/2 140	5–5/8 143
7	6–1/2 165	6–5/8 168
8	7–1/4 184	7–1/2 190
9	8–1/4 210	8–1/2 216
10	9–1/4 235	9–1/2 241
11	10–1/4 260	10–1/2 267
12	11–1/4 286	11–1/2 292
14	13–1/4 337	13–1/2 343
16	15–1/4 387	15–1/2 394

Dry lumber is defined as lumber with less than 19 percent moisture and unseasoned or green is greater than 19 percent. All sizes listed above, both nominal and actual, conform to standards set by the *American Softwood Lumber Standards*.

Lumber is sold by a "feet board measure" or "board foot" rating. 1 board foot =144 cubic inches (for example 12 inch x 12 inch x 1 inch or 2 inch x 6 inch x 12 inch).
Board feet = thickness (in) x face width (in) x length (in)/144
   or = thickness (in) x face width (in) x length (ft)/12

The following are quick approximations for calculating board feet:
   for a 1 x 4, divide linear length (feet) by 3
   for a 1 x 6, divide linear length (feet) by 2
   for a 1 x 8, multiply linear length (feet) by 0.66
   for a 1 x 12, linear length (feet) = board feet
   for a 2 x 4, multiply linear length (feet) by 0.66
   for a 2 x 6, linear length (feet) = board feet
   for a 2 x 8, multiply linear length (feet) by 1.33
   for a 2 x 12, multiply linear length (feet) by 2

Softwood Lumber Grading

Softwood grading is based on the appearance, strength and stiffness of lumber. Grading systems are established by a variety of associations in different parts of the country but they all must follow the US Department of Commerce American Lumber Standards. The grading system is quite long and very detailed. *If you want more detailed information on softwood grading, obtain the book "Western Lumber Grading Rules 95" by the Western Wood Products Association, 522 S.W. Fifth, Portland, Oregon, 97204, (503)224-3930. The cost is only $4.00 and it is an excellent pocket reference.*

Softwood lumber comes from "conifer" trees, which means they have needle shaped leaves that stay green all year. Hardwoods come from "deciduous" trees, which means they have broad leaves and loose their leaves in the cold months. A list of tree types and their characteristics is given later in this chapter.

The first broad softwood classification is as follows:

> **Rough Lumber** – Sawn, trimmed, and edged, but the faces are rough and show saw marks.

> **Surfaced Lumber** (dressed) – Rough lumber that has been smoothed by a surfacing machine. Sub-categories are based on the number of sides and edges that have been smoothed:
> **S1S** – Surfaced 1 Side
> **S1E** – Surfaced 1 Edge
> **S2S** – Surfaced 2 Sides
> **S2E** – Surfaced 2 Edges
> **S1S1E** – Surfaced 1 Side and 1 Edge
> **S1S2E** – Surfaced 1 Side and 2 Edges
> **S2S1E** – Surfaced 2 Sides and 1 Edge
> **S4S** – Surfaced 4 Sides

> **Worked Lumber** – Surfaced lumber that has been matched, patterned, shiplapped or any combination thereof.

Another broad softwood classification (which is not a subcategory of the first classification above) is as follows:

> **Shop and Factory Lumber** – This is millwork lumber used for applications such as molding, door jambs, and window frames.
> **Yard Lumber** – Lumber used for house framing, concrete forms, and sheathing. It is also known as structural lumber.

Softwood Lumber Grading

Yard or structural softwood lumber is further subdivided into the following categories, based on size:

> **Boards** – Lumber must be no more than 1 inch thick and 4 to 12 inches wide.
>
> **Planks** – Lumber must be over 1 inch thick and more than 6 inches wide.
>
> **Timbers** – Lumber width and thickness must both be greater than 5 inches.

The most common softwood grading system places lumber into three main categories. Once again, bear in mind that some of these categories are very detailed and long; for example, the specific description of "#2 Common Board" is almost 2 pages long and covers details such as degree of cupping, twist, wane, knots, and raising of grain. The following descriptions cover the primary system only, see a grading manual for more detail:

1. **Select and Finish Materials** – These are "Appearance" grades and are used primarily for interior and exterior trim work, moldings, cabinets, and interior walls. Select grades are based on the best face and finish grades are based on the best face and 2 edges.

   > Select – B & BTR – 1 & 2 Clear
   > C Select
   > D Select
   > Superior Finish VG, FG or MG
   > Prime Finish VG, FG, MG
   > E Finish

2. **Boards** – Five grades referred to as "Commons" (1 Common through 5 Common) are used for general building, crafts, form lumber, flooring, sheathing, etc. "Alternate Board Grades" include the following (in order from best to worst):

   > Select Merchantable
   > Construction
   > Standard
   > Utility
   > Economy

   The final category of Boards is the "Stress Related Boards". These are special use products for light trusses, rafters, and box beams for factory built and mobile homes.

Softwood Lumber Grading

3. <u>**Dimension Lumber**</u> – This category is limited to surfaced softwood lumber that is 2 to 4 inches thick and is to be used as framing components. Category breakdowns are as follows:

   Light Framing – General framing and stud walls. Up to 4 inch wide. Grades are as follows:

   > Construction
   > Standard
   > Utility

   Structural Light Framing – This is suitable for higher stress applications such as roof trusses and concrete forms. Up to 4 inch wide. Grades are as follows:

Select Structural	No. 3
No. 1	Economy
No. 2	

   Studs – Load bearing and stud walls of 2 x 4 and 2 x 6 construction. Lengths are less than 10 feet. Up to 4 inch wide; and 5 inch and over.

   Structural Joists and Planks – Roof rafters, ceiling and floor joists. 5 inch and wider. Grades are as follows:

Select Structural	No. 3
No. 1	Economy
No. 2	

   Timbers – Heavy beam support and floor and ceiling supports.

Select Structural	No. 2
No. 1	No. 3

If you are confused by the softwood grading scheme, don't feel bad, you're not alone! Grading is not an exact science since it deals with both visual and strength analysis. A maximum of 5% variation below grade is allowable between grades. Note that the above grading is only a small portion of the actual code, there are literally hundreds of different grades.

Hardwood Lumber Size & Grade

Hardwood comes from "deciduous" trees, which have broad leaves and lose their leaves in the cold months. Oak and walnut constitute 50% of all hardwood production. Other common hardwoods include Basswood, Beech, Birch, Butternut, Chestnut, Cherry, Elm, Gum, Hickory, Maple, Mahogany, and Yellow Poplar. See the section later in this chapter that describes wood types and their general characteristics.

HARDWOOD SIZES

Nominal Size (Fraction In)	Rough Size (Inches)	Surface 2 Sides Actual Size Dry (Inches)
4/4	1	13/16
5/4	1-1/4	1-1/16
6/4	1-1/2	1-5/16
7/4	1-3/4	1-1/2
8/4	2	1-3/4
10/4	2-1/2	2-1/4
12/4	3	2-3/4
14/4	3-1/2	3-1/4
16/4	4	3-3/4

HARDWOOD GRADES

Grading is simpler than that used for Softwood and appearance is the prime consideration. Grades are based on the appearance of the poorest side, assuming that the board will be cut into pieces that are 2 to 7 feet long, each of which will have one clear face. There are numerous other requirements for grades of each of the various tree species, but the general grades of hardwood as determined by the National Hardwood Lumber Association are as follows (Listed in order from best to worst):

First and Second (FAS) – The best grade. Normally required for a natural or stained finish. A FAS board must be at least 6 inches wide, 8 to 16 feet long, and 83.3% clear on the worst face.

Select – No. 1 Common – Minimum 3 inches wide, 4 to 16 feet long, 66.66% clear wood.

Select – No. 2 Common

Select – No. 3 Common

If you want detailed information on the grading of hardwood, obtain a copy of the Hardwood Rule Book, National Hardwood Association, P.O. Box 34518, Memphis, Tennessee, 38184. Cost of the book is $6.00. It is an excellent source book.

Wood Moisture Content

Moisture content in wood affects both the size and strength of lumber. In general, the physical properties of wood can be improved by seasoning or drying. Although dependent on the tree species type, the strength of wood decreases as the moisture content goes up.

The following table is from Circular 108 of the U.S. Forest Service.

MOISTURE vs. COMPRESSIVE STRENGTH

% Moisture	Relative Maximum crushing strength compared to wood containing 2% moisture (compression parallel to the grain)		
	Red Spruce	Longleaf Pine	Douglas Fir
2	1.000	1.000	1.000
4	0.926	0.894	0.929
6	0.841 (c)	0.790	0.850
8	0.756	0.702	0.774
10	0.681	0.623	0.714
12	0.617	0.552	0.643
14	0.554 (b)	0.488	0.589
16	0.505	0.431	0.535
18	0.463	0.377	0.494
20	0.426	0.328(a)	0.458
22	0.394	0.278	0.428
24	0.362		0.398(a)
26	0.335		
28	0.314		
30	0.292		
32	0.271		
34	0.255		

(a) Green wood
(b) Air dried
(c) Kiln dried

The above table clearly indicates that high moisture content in wood significantly decreases the woods strength. As an example, Longleaf Pine has <u>half</u> the strength (0.552) with 12% moisture as is does with 2% moisture.

Additional information can be obtained from U.S. Department of Agriculture Bulletin 282 and Technical Bulletin 479.

Plywood & Panel Grading

Plywood is generally graded in terms of the quality of the veneer on both the front and back sides of the panel or by a "use type" name. Plywood is also grouped by the tree species type.

APA - The Engineered Wood Association Veneer Grades

N .....Smooth surface "natural finish" veneer. Select, all heartwood or all sapwood. Free of open defects. Allows not more than 6 repairs, wood only, per 4 x 8 panel, made parallel to grain and well matched for grain and color. Special Order.

A .....Smooth, paintable. Not more than 18 neatly made repairs, boat, sled, or router type, and parallel to grain, permitted. May be used for natural finish in less demanding applications.

B .....Solid surface. Shims, circular repair plugs and tight knots to 1 inch across grain permitted. Some minor splits permitted.

C .....Tight knots to 1–1/2 inch. Knotholes to 1 inch across grain and some to 1–1/2 inch if total width of knots and knotholes is within specified limits. Synthetic or wood repairs. Discoloration and sanding defects that do not impair strength permitted. Limited splits allowed. Stitching permitted.

C Plugged . . . Improved C veneer with splits limited to 1/8–inch width and knotholes and borer holes limited to 1/4 x 1/2 inch within specified limits. Admits some broken grain. Synthetic repairs permitted.

D .....Knots and knotholes to 2–1/2 inch width across grain and 1/2 inch larger within specified limits. Limited splits are permitted. Stitching permitted. Limited to Exposure 1 or Interior panels.

As an example, "C–D" grade panel would have one side conforming to the "C" grade and the other side conforming to the "D" grade. You must also specify the "Exposure Durability" (defined on the next page) to completely define the grade, e.g., EXTERIOR C–D.

NOTE: "CDX" is a very common grade of panel, but it does not have an "EXTERIOR" rating, it has an "EXPOSURE 1" rating.

A full description of the plywood and panel code can be obtained from the APA- The Engineered Wood Association P.O. Box 11700, Tacoma, Washington, 98411, (253) 565–6600.

Plywood & Panel Grading

EXPOSURE DURABILITY

EXTERIOR: Fully waterproof bond and designed for applications subject to permanent exposure to weather or moisture.

EXPOSURE 1: Fully waterproof bond but not for permanent exposure to weather or moisture.

EXPOSURE 2: Interior type with intermediate glue. Intended for protected construction applications where slight moisture exposure can be expected.

INTERIOR: Interior applications only.

GROUP CLASSIFICATION OF SPECIES

Group 1	Group 2	Group 3	Group 4	Group 5
Apitong	Cedar - Port	Alder–Red	Aspen	Basswd
Beech–Amer.	- Orford	Birch–Paper	Bigtooth	Poplar
Birch–Sweet	Cypress	Cedar-Alaska	Quaking	
Balsam				
–Yellow	Douglas Fir 2	Fir-Subalpine	Cativo	
Douglas Fir 1	Fir	Hemlock-East	Cedar	
Kapur	Balsam	Maple-Bigleaf	Incense	
Keruing	Calif. Red	Pine	West. Red	
Larch–West.	Grand	Jack	Cottonwood	
Maple-Sugar	Noble	Lodgepole	Eastern	
Pine	Pacific-Silver	Ponderosa	Black	
Caribbean	White	Spruce	West. Poplar	
Ocote	Hemlock-west	Redwood	Pine	
Pine South.	Lauan	Spruce	East. White	
Loblolly	Almon	Engelmann	Sugar	
Longleaf	Bagtikan	White		
Shortleaf	Mayapis			
Slash	Red			
Tanoak	Tangile			
	White			
	Maple–Black			
	Mengkulang			
	Meranti–Red			
	Mersawa			
	Pine–Pond, Red, Virginia, Western White			
	Spruce–Black, Red, and Sitka			
	Sweetgum			
	Tamarack			
	Yellow Poplar			

Group numbers are used to define the strength and stiffness of the panel, Group 1 being the strongest, Group 5 the weakest.

Wood Characteristics

Wood Name	Relative Cost/ Brd Ft (1)	Density Lbs per Cubic Ft	Hard	Split Resist	Grain
Alder	$$$	25–30	Med	Good	Low
Ash	$$	40–45	Hard	Good	Mod open
Aspen	$	25	Soft	Good	Mild fine
Balsa	$$$	8	V Soft	Good	Open
Basswood	$$	25–28	Soft	Good	Low, fine
Beech	$$	45	Hard	V Good	Mod, fine
Birch	$$$	40–45	Hard	V Good	Mod, fine
Butternut	$$$	27	Med	Good	Mod
Cedar, East	$$	29	M Hard	Poor	Fine, knots
Cedar, West	$$	25	Med	Poor	Fine
Cherry	$$$	35	M Hard	V Good	Mod, fine
Chestnut	$$	30	Hard	Good	Mod, coarse
Cottonwood		25	Med	Good	Low, fine
Cypress	$$	35	Hard	Poor	Wide, fine
Ebony	$$$$$	50–65	V Hard	V Good	V Low, fine
Elm, American	$$	35	M Hard	V Good	Mod, v fine
Elm, Rock		44	Hard	V Good	Mod, v fine
Fir, Douglas	$$	35	Med	Fair	Wide
Fir, White		25	Med	Fair	Wide
Gum, Black	$$	36	M Hard	V Good	Mod
Gum, Blue		50	Hard	V Good	Mod, open
Gum, Red	$$$	35	M Hard	V Good	Mod
Hackberry	$$	38	M Hard	Poor	Coarse
Hickory	$$	40–55	Hard	Good	Mod, pores
Holly	$$$$	40	M Hard	V Good	None, fine
Lignum Vitae	$$$$$	80	V Hard	V Good	Mod, v fine
Madrone	$$$$	45	Hard	Good	Mod, v fine
Magnolia		35	M Hard	Good	Fine
Mahogany					
African	$$$	30	M Hard	Good	Open, figure
Cuban		40	Hard	Good	Open, figure
Honduras	$$$$	35	M Hard	Good	Open, figure
Phillippine	$$$		Not a Mahogany, see Phillippine.		
Maple (hard)	$$$	35–44	M Hard	Good	Mod, fine
Myrtle	$$$$	40	Hard	Good	Mod, fine
Oak					
Amer. Red	$$	45	Hard	Good	Coarse,pores
Amer. White	$$	47	Hard	Good	Coarse,pores
English Brown	$$$$	45	Hard	Good	Coarse,pores
Pecan	$$	47	Hard	Good	Fine, pores
Persimmon	$$$	55	Hard	V Good	V fine
Philippine					
Red Luan	$$$	36	M Hard	Good	Mod,coarse
Tanguile		39	M Hard	V Good	Mod,coarse

Wood Characteristics

Wood Name	1995 Cost/ Brd Ft (1)	Density Lbs per Cubic Ft	Hard	Split Resist	Grain
Pine, White:					
Northern	$$	25	Soft	Poor	V coarse
Western	$$	27	Soft	Mod, fine	
Poplar, Yellow	$$	30	M Hard	Good	Mod, v fine
Redwood	$$$	28	Med	Poor	Fine
Rosewood:					
Bolivian	$$$$$	50	Hard	Good	Swirls,pores
East Indian	$$$$$	55	Hard	Good	Mod
Satinwood	$$$$$	67	V Hard	Good	Mod, fine
Spruce	$$$	28	Med	Poor	Mod, fine
Sycamore	$$$	35	M Hard	High	Mod, fine
Teak (Burma)	$$$$$	45	Hard	High	Mod to High
Walnut:					
Amer Black	$$$	38	Hard	Good	Mod, fine
Claro	$$$$	30	M Hard	Good	Mod, open
European	$$$$	35	M Hard	Good	Mod, open
Willow	$$	26	Soft	Good	Mod, fine
Zebrawood	$$$$	48	Hard	Good	High, fine

Hardness is a relative term between the different species. "V Soft" is an abbreviation for Very Soft, "V Hard" is Very Hard, and "M Hard" is moderately hard.

Split Resist refers to the susceptibility the lumber has to splitting. The scale ranges from "V Good" (Very Good) to "Good" to "Fair" to "Poor".

Grain defines the general appearance of the wood grain. "Mod" is moderate, "High" is very pronounced grain, "pores" is large open pores, "fine" is fine grained, "V fine" is very fine grained, and "coarse" is coarse grained.

(1) The relative cost per board foot column uses a cost scale from one dollar sign($) for the least expensive woods to five dollar signs ($$$$$) for the most expensive woods. Lumber costs are for the same grades and finishes. Thicker hardwood boards are usually more expensive, price increases of 10% to 40% are common for double the thickness.

An excellent book on woods is "Beautiful Woods", by the Frank Paxton Lumber Co, 4837 Jackson St, Denver, CO 80216, (303)399–6810, (complete with color photos!). Also, "Know Your Woods" by Albert Constantine, 1987, ISBN 0–684–14115–9.

Pressure Treated Lumber

Preservative Process

Pressure treated lumber refers to a class of wood products that are pressure treated with chemical preservatives. Under pressure, the preservatives are forced deep into the cellular structure of the wood and prevent decay due to fungi and resist attack from insects and microorganisms. Many pressure treated wood products have a usable life in excess of 40 years.

The pressure treatment process is basically the same for all preservatives. Wood products to be treated are stacked and loaded into a horizontal cylindrical treatment tank. The tank is sealed and evacuated to remove air and open the wood cells. A liquid preservative solution is pumped from a storage tank into the treatment tank. Pressure is applied to the liquid to force the preservative deep into the wood cells. Excess liquid is pumped back to the storage tank for reuse. The treatment tank is again evacuated to remove excess preservative. The wood products are removed from the treatment tank and allowed to dry.

Chemical Preservative Treatments

The following treatments are used in wood preservation.

Treatment	Chemicals
Oil-based Preservatives	
Copper Naphthenate	naphthenic acid, cupric salt
Creosote	creosote
Penta	pentachlorophenol
Water-based Preservatives	
Ammoniacal Copper Arsenate (ACA)	? ? ? ?
Ammoniacal Copper Quat (ACQ)	copper oxide, didecyldimethylammonium chloride
Ammoniacal Copper Zinc Arsenate (ACZA)	ammonia, copper oxide, zinc oxide, arsenic pentoxide
Chromated Copper Arsenate (CCA)	chromic acid, copper oxide, arsenic acid
Copper Azole	copper carbonate, boric acid, tebuconazole
Copper Citrate	ammonia, copper citrate
Disodium Octaborate Tetrahydrate (DOT)	disodium octaborate, tetrahydrate

Pressure Treated Lumber (cont.)

Many of the chemicals used for wood preservation are classified as pesticides and are regulated in the US by the Environmental Protection Agency (EPA). The EPA has ruled that, as of March 31, 2003, treated wood products for residential use can not contain arsenic or chromium compounds. This ruling applies to the ACA, ACZA, and CCA treatments listed on the previous page. ACQ, copper azole, copper citrate, and DOT are approved substitutes.

Copper naphthenate, creosote, and penta are typically used on utility poles, cross arms, railroad ties, posts, and timbers. Creosote and penta preserved woods should not be use for playground equipment. Creosote is a distillate of coal tar.

Preservative Retention Rates in
Pounds of Preservative per Cubic Foot of Wood Fiber

Lumber Use	Water-based preservative ↓	Creosote	Penta
No ground contact, no moisture	0.25	8.0	0.40
Ground contact, high moisture	0.40	10.0	0.50
Wood foundations, structural timbers	0.60	12.0	0.60

Safe Handling and Disposal of Preserved Wood Products

The following precautions should be used when handling and disposing of any preserved wood product.

- Read product labels and information before using these materials.
- Never burn treated or preserved wood products in open fires, stoves, fireplaces, or residential boilers. This includes dimensional lumber, timbers, railroad ties, plywood, particleboard, and old furniture. Burning can release toxic chemicals from the wood product. Some co-generation or incinerator facilities are permitted to burn these materials. Some preserved wood products can be buried.
- Dispose of treated or preserved wood products as you would household trash. Do not compost or mulch the sawdust or scraps.
- Use standard safety equipment and common sense when working preserved wood products.

Pressure Treated Lumber (cont.)

- Use eye protection and a dust mask when sawing, sanding, or machining preserved wood products. Work with these materials outdoors, if possible, or use a dust collection system indoors.
- Use gloves to protect against splinters.
- Practice good housekeeping – wash hands with soap and water after handling preserved wood products - clean up sawdust and scrape wood and dispose of as recommended - wash your work clothes separately from other household clothing.

Fastener Materials

Use corrosion-resistant fasteners. The following materials are recommended for fasteners in a wide range of preserved wood products: hot-dipped galvanized steel, stainless steel, polymer-coated steel, silicon bronze, or copper.

Do not use brass or aluminum fasteners with preserved wood products.

Painting or Staining Preserved Wood Products

Like any wood product, preserved wood needs to be maintained. Periodic cleaning and coating is recommended. Most preserved wood products can be stained or painted. High quality latex-based and oil-based paints and stains are recommended. Applying water repellent coatings can enhance weathering performance.

Moisture in the wood from the pressure treatment can affect the penetration and drying of stains and paints. Make sure the preserved wood is dry and free from surface deposits before any coating is applied.

Construction Tips for Decks and Fences

- When appearance is important, attach boards bark side up to reduce cupping.
- Fasten thin members to thicker members to improve structural integrity.
- To help prevent splitting, drill pilot holes when screwing or nailing near the end or edge of a board.

Pressure Treated Lumber (cont.)

- Use either nails or screws. Nails are more convenient but screws have better holding power. Screws are also easier to tighten or remove and screws eliminate hammer impressions on surfaces.
- Separate deck boards to allow for expansion. If the wood is heavy and wet allow no more than 1/16" separation. If the wood is light and dry allow no more than 1/8" separation.
- Use enough nails or screws. Use two fasteners across a 2x4 and three across a 2x6. Drive nails at slight angles toward each other. Use 12-penny (12d) nails on nominal 2-inch decking. Use 2-1/2" or 3" deck screws on nominal 2-inch decking.
- If a board is bowed, install it crown up. The weight of objects, people, etc. and gravity will help to flatten the board.
- A board with a slight bend can be straightened as it is nailed or screwed in place.

Insulation Value of Materials

Insulation Material	Thickness (inches)	k*	C*	R Value
Air space				
non-reflective	3/4		0.99	1.01
reflective	3/4		0.29	3.48
reflective foil,				
2 reflective surfaces	1	0.72		1.39
Aluminum siding over sheathing			1.61	0.61
Architectural glass			10.00	0.10
Asbestos–cement board		4.0		0.25
	1/8		33.00	0.03
	1/4		16.50	0.06
Asphalt roll roofing	0.048		6.50	0.15
Asphalt shingle	0.048		2.27	0.44
Balsam wood	1	0.27		3.70
Brick, common	1	5.00		0.20
Brick, face	1	9.00		0.11
Built-up roofing	3/8		3.00	0.33
Carpet and fibrous pad			0.48	2.08
Carpeting with foam rubber pad			0.81	1.23
Cedar shingle			1.11	0.90
Cellose, loose fill, blown in	1	0.31		3.25
Cellular board	1	0.35		2.86
Cellular glass	1	0.38		2.63
	2		0.17	5.90
Cellulosics	1	0.29		3.50
Celotex	1	0.33		3.03
Cement fiber slab	1	0.50		2.00
Cement mortar	1	5.00		0.20
Cinder block, hollow	8		0.58	1.72
	12		0.53	1.89
Cinder block, hollow,				
with 1/2-inch of plaster	8–1/2		0.35	2.85
with 1/2-inch of plaster	12–1/2		0.33	3.03
Clay tile				
hollow, 1 cell deep	3		1.25	0.80
hollow, 1 cell deep	4		0.90	1.11
hollow, 2 cells deep	6		0.66	1.52
hollow, 2 cells deep	8		0.54	1.85
hollow, 2 cells deep	10		0.45	2.22
hollow, 3 cells deep	12		0.40	2.50
Concrete block				
hollow	8		0.90	1.11
hollow	12		0.78	1.28
hollow with:				
lightweight aggregate	8		0.50	2.00

Insulation Value . . . (cont.)

Insulation Material	Thickness (inches)	k*	C*	R Value
with 1/2-inch of plaster	8–1/2		0.49	2.04
with 1/2-inch of plaster	12–1/2		0.45	2.22
Concrete, poured, sand and gravel aggregate	1	12.50		0.08
Concrete, slab	4	3.13		0.32
Concrete, wall	8	1.56		0.64
Cork board	1	0.30		3.33
Cork tile	1/8	3.60		0.28
Felt, vapor-permeable		16.70		0.06
Fiberboard sheathing	1/2	0.76		1.32
	25/32	0.49		2.06
	1	0.42		2.36
Fiberglass batt	1	0.30		3.30
	2		0.16	6.30
	3–1/2		0.091	11.00
	6		0.053	19.00
	8		0.04	25.30
Fiberglass, loose fill	1	0.91		1.10
Floor tile, vinyl, etc.		20.00		0.05
Glass fiber, organic bonded		0.25		4.00
Glass fiber board	1	0.25		4.00
Glass wool	1	0.27		3.76
Ground surface		2.00		0.50
Gypsum board	3/8	3.10		0.32
	1/2	2.22		0.45
	5/8	1.78		0.56
Gypsum plaster on gypsum lath	1/2	3.12		0.32
Hardboard	1/4	5.56		0.18
high density		0.82		1.22
high density, std tempered		1.00		1.00
medium density	1	0.73		1.37
Hardwood	1	1.10		0.91
Hardwood floor	3/4	1.47		0.68
	25/32	1.43		0.70
Linoleum or rubber tile		20.00		0.05
Mineral fiber, loose fill, blown in	1	0.31		3.25
rock or glass		0.38		2.60
rock or glass	3–3/4 to 5			11.00
rock or glass	6–1/2 to 8–3/4		0.05	19.00
rock or glass	10–1/4 to 13–3/4		0.03	30.00
resin binder	1	0.29		3.45
loosefill, blown in	7–1/2 to 10			22.00
with resin binder		0.29		3.45

Insulation Value . . . (cont.)

Insulation Material	Thickness (inches)	k*	C*	R Value
Mineral fiberboard	1	0.29		3.45
(wet-felted) acoustical tile	1	0.36		2.78
(wet-felted) roof insulation	1	0.34		2.94
(wet-molded) acoustical tile	1	0.42		2.38
Mineral wool, batt	1	0.31		3.25
	1	0.24		4.16
	3 to 4		0.091	11.00
	5-1/2 to 6-1/2		0.053	19.00
	6 to 7 1/2		0.045	22.00
	9 to 10		0.033	30.00
	12 to 13		0.026	38.0
Particleboard	5/8	1.22		0.82
high density		1.18		0.85
low density		0.54		1.85
medium density	1	0.94		1.06
underlayment	5/8	1.22		0.82
Perlite, expanded	1	0.33		3.03
expanded, organic bonded		0.36		2.78
loose fill	1	0.37		2.70
Plaster	1	8.33		0.12
Plaster and metal lath	3/4	7.69		0.13
Plaster, cement, sand	3/8	13.3		0.08
	3/4	6.66		0.15
	1	5.00		0.20
Plaster, gypsum				
lightwt agg.	1/2	3.12		0.32
lightwt agg.	5/8	2.67		0.39
lightwt agg.	3/4	2.13		0.47
perlite agg.		1.5		0.67
sand	1/2	11.10		0.09
sand	5/8	9.10		0.11
sand	1	5.50		0.18
on metal lath	3/4	7.70		0.13
Plasterboard	3/8	3.10		0.32
	1/2	2.22		0.45
Plywood	1/4	3.20		0.31
	3/8	2.13		0.47
	1/2	1.60		0.62
	5/8	1.29		0.77
	1	0.80		1.25
Plywood (Douglas Fir)		0.80		1.25
Plywood or wood panels	3/4	1.07		0.93
Polycarbonate sheet	1/8	1.06		0.94
	3/16	1.01		0.99

Insulation Material	Thickness (inches)	k*	C*	R Value
Polycarbonate sheet (cont.)	1/4		0.96	1.04
	3/8		0.88	1.14
	1/2		0.81	1.23
Polyisocyanurate, cellular	1/2		0.278	3.60
	1		0.139	7.20
	2		0.069	14.40
Polyisocyanurate, smooth skin	1	0.14		7.20
Polystyrene	1	0.28		3.57
cut cell	1	0.25		4.00
expanded, molded beads	1	0.26		3.85
foamed in place	1	0.27		3.75
smooth skin (Styrofoam)	1	0.20		5.00
Polyurethane				
expanded	1	0.14		7.00
expanded board	1	0.16		6.25
expanded, aged	1	0.16		6.30
Redwood	1	0.57		1.75
Rock cork	1	0.33		3.05
Rock wool batt	1	0.27		3.70
Roofing, 1-ply membrane	0.048		2.00	0.50
Rubber, expanded, board	1	0.22		4.55
Sawdust	1	0.41		2.44
Sawdust/shavings	1	0.45		2.20
Sheep's wool	1	0.34		2.96
Slate shingle	1/2		20.00	0.05
Softwood	1	0.80		1.25
Stone	1	12.50		0.08
Structural insulation board	1/2		0.76	1.32
Stucco	1	5.00		0.20
Terrazzo	1	12.50		0.08
Tile, hollow	4		1.00	1.00
Urea-formaldehyde	1	0.24		4.20
Urethane, foamed in place	1	0.16		6.30
Vapor-seal, 2-layers of mopped 15-lb felt			8.35	0.12
Vapor–seal, plastic film				Minimal
Vegetable Fiber Board				
Sheathing				
regular density	1/2		0.76	1.32
regular density	25/32		0.49	2.06
intermediate density	1/2		0.82	1.22
nail–base	1/2		0.88	1.14
Shingle backer	3/8		1.06	0.94

Insulation Material	Thickness (inches)	k*	C*	R Value
Vegetable Fiber Board (cont.) 5/16			1.28	0.78
sound deadening board	1/2		0.74	1.35
tile lay–in panels		0.40		2.50
	1/2		0.80	1.25
	3/4		0.53	1.89
laminated paperboard		0.50		2.00
homo. board from				
repulped paper		0.50		2.00
Vermiculite	1	0.47		2.13
Vermiculite, loose fill	1	0.45		2.20
Wall, vertical exterior, 15 mph wind			5.88	0.17
Wall, vertical interior, still air			1.47	0.68
Wood				
bevel lap siding	1/2		1.23	0.81
bevel lap siding	3/4		0.95	1.05
drop siding	3/4		1.27	0.79
drop siding	1	1.27		0.79
fiber, soft wood	1	0.30		3.33
fiberboard	1	0.59		1.69
fiberboard, acoustical tile	1/2		0.80	1.25
fiberboard, acoustical tile	3/4		0.53	1.89
shingle			1.06	0.94
shingle siding			1.15	0.87
shingle with insulating backer board			0.71	1.40
shingle, double			0.84	1.19
subfloor	3/4		1.06	0.94
vertical tongue & groove	3/4		1.00	1.00

* "k" (in units of Btu in / ft^2 hr °F) is heat conductivity over a thickness of 1 inch and "C" is heat conductance (in units of Btu/ft^2 hr °F) over the specified thickness. "R Value" is the most common number used to compare the insulating properties of various materials and is typically marked on the wrapper or container of the insulator. The "R Value" is effectively the materials resistance to heat–flow and is based on the "k" and "C" values. "R Values" are the reciprocals of "k" (which is 1/k) or "C" (which is 1/C) for a given material.

Insulation Value . . . (cont.)

Two excellent references for information on the insulation values of various materials are as follows:

Pocket Handbook for Air Conditioning, Heating, Ventilation and Refrigeration. 1987
American Society of Heating, Refrigerating and Air-Conditioning (ASHRAE).   1791 Tullie Circle, NE, Atlanta, Georgia, 30329

National Institute of Standards and Technology.
Quince Orchard and Clopper Roads
Gaithersburg, Maryland 20899
(301) 975-2758 Main public number
(301) 975-3058 Publications information

Maximum Floor Joist Spans

Douglas Fir - Larch: Includes Douglas fir and Western larch. (See "Notes" at end of tables.)

Nominal Lumber Size (inches)	Joist Spacing Center to Center (inches)	Select Structural	No. 1	No. 2
		Lumber Grade		
		Maximum Span (feet - inches)		

Max Live load=30 lbf/ft^2; Max Dead Load=10 lbf/ft^2

Nominal Lumber Size (inches)	Joist Spacing Center to Center (inches)	Select Structural	No. 1	No. 2
2 x 6	12	12 - 06	12 - 00	11 - 10
	16	11 - 04	10 - 11	10 - 09
	24	09 - 11	09 - 07	09 - 01
2 x 8	12	16 - 06	15 - 10	15 - 07
	16	15 - 00	14 - 05	14 - 01
	24	13 - 01	12 - 04	11 - 06
2 x 10	12	21 - 00	20 - 03	19 - 10
	16	19 - 01	18 - 05	17 - 02
	24	16 - 08	15 - 00	14 - 01
2 x 12	12	25 - 07	24 - 08	23 - 00
	16	23 - 03	21 - 04	19 - 11
	24	20 - 03	17 - 05	16 - 03

Max Live load=40 lbf/ft^2; Max Dead Load=10 lbf/ft^2

Nominal Lumber Size (inches)	Joist Spacing Center to Center (inches)	Select Structural	No. 1	No. 2
2 x 6	12	11 - 04	10 - 11	10 - 09
	16	10 - 04	09 - 11	09 - 09
	24	09 - 00	08 - 08	08 - 01
2 x 8	12	15 - 00	14 - 05	14 - 02
	16	13 - 07	13 - 01	12 - 07
	24	11 - 11	11 - 00	10 - 03
2 x 10	12	19 - 01	18 - 05	17 - 09
	16	17 - 04	16 - 05	15 - 05
	24	15 - 02	13 - 05	12 - 07
2 x 12	12	23 - 03	22 - 00	20 - 07
	16	21 - 01	19 - 11	17 - 10
	24	18 - 05	15 - 07	14 - 07

Dead Load = weight of structure + fixed loads
Live Load = movable loads such as furniture, wind, snow, etc.

Douglas Fir - Larch: (cont.)

Nominal Lumber Size (inches)	Joist Spacing Center to Center (inches)	Lumber Grade		
		Select Structural	No. 1	No. 2
		Maximum Span (feet - inches)		

Max Live load=50 lbf/ft², Max Dead Load=10 lbf/ft²

2 x 8	12	13 - 11	13 - 05	13 - 01
	16	12 - 07	12 - 02	11 - 06
	24	11 - 00	10 - 00	09 - 05
2 x 10	12	17 - 09	17 - 01	16 - 03
	16	16 - 01	15 - 00	14 - 01
	24	14 - 01	12 - 03	11 - 06
2 x 12	12	21 - 07	20 - 01	18 - 10
	16	19 - 07	17 - 05	16 - 03
	24	17 - 01	14 - 03	13 - 04
2 x 14	12	25 - 05	22 - 06	21 - 00
	16	23 - 01	19 - 05	18 - 02
	24	19 - 02	15 - 11	14 - 10

Max Live load=60 lbf/ft², Max Dead Load=10 lbf/ft²

2 x 8	12	13 - 01	12 - 07	12 - 04
	16	11 - 11	11 - 05	10 - 08
	24	10 - 05	09 - 04	08 - 08
2 x 10	12	16 - 08	16 - 01	15 - 00
	16	15 - 02	13 - 11	13 - 00
	24	13 - 03	11 - 04	10 - 07
2 x 12	12	20 - 03	18 - 07	17 - 05
	16	18 - 05	16 - 01	15 - 01
	24	15 - 10	13 - 02	12 - 04
2 x 14	12	23 - 11	20 - 10	19 - 05
	16	21 - 08	18 - 00	16 - 10
	24	17 - 09	14 - 08	13 - 09

Dead Load = weight of structure + fixed loads
Live Load = movable loads such as furniture,
wind, snow, etc.

Douglas Fir - Larch: (cont.)

Nominal Lumber Size (inches)	Joist Spacing Center to Center (inches)	Lumber Grade		
		Select Structural	No. 1	No. 2
		Maximum Span (feet - inches)		

Max Live load=30 lbf/ft^2 , Max Dead Load=27 lbf/ft^2

2 x 6	12	12 - 06	11 - 06	10 - 09
	16	11 - 04	10 - 00-	09 - 04
	24	09 - 09	08 - 02	07 - 07
2 x 8	12	16 - 06	14 - 07	13 - 07
	16	15 - 00	12 - 07	11 - 10
	24	12 - 05	10 - 04	09 - 08
2 x 10	12	21 - 00	17 - 09	16 - 08
	16	18 - 07	15 - 05	14 - 05
	24	15 - 02	12 - 07	11 - 09
2 x 12	12	24 - 10	20 - 08	19 - 04
	16	21 - 06	17 - 10	16 - 09
	24	17 - 07	14 - 07	13 - 08

Max Live load=40 lbf/ft^2 , Max Dead Load=27 lbf/ft^2

2 x 6	12	11 - 04	10 - 07	09 - 11
	16	10 - 04	09 - 02	08 - 07
	24	09 - 00	07 - 06	07 - 00
2 x 8	12	15 - 00	13 - 05	12 - 07
	16	13 - 07	11 - 08	10 - 11
	24	11 - 11	09 - 06	08 - 11
2 x 10	12	19 - 01	16 - 05	15 - 04
	16	17 - 04	14 - 03	13 - 04
	24	14 - 00	11 - 07	10 - 10
2 x 12	12	22 - 11	19 - 00	17 - 10
	16	19 - 10	16 - 06	15 - 05
	24	16 - 02	13 - 05	12 - 07

Dead Load = weight of structure + fixed loads
Live Load = movable loads such as furniture,
wind, snow, etc.

Douglas Fir - Larch: (cont.)

Nominal Lumber Size (inches)	Joist Spacing Center to Center (inches)	Lumber Grade		
		Select Structural	No. 1	No. 2
		Maximum Span (feet - inches)		

Max Live load=50 lbf/ft^2 , Max Dead Load=27 lbf/ft^2

Nominal Lumber Size (inches)	Joist Spacing Center to Center (inches)	Select Structural	No. 1	No. 2
2 x 8	12	13 - 11	12 - 06	11 - 09
	16	12 - 07	10 - 10	10 - 02
	24	10 - 08	08 - 10	08 - 03
2 x 10	12	17 - 09	15 - 04	14 - 04
	16	16 - 00	13 - 03	12 - 05
	24	13 - 00	10 - 10	10 - 01
2 x 12	12	21 - 04	17 - 09	16 - 07
	16	18 - 06	15 - 04	14 - 05
	24	15 - 01	12 - 07	11 - 09
2 x 14	12	23 - 11	19 - 10	18 - 07
	16	20 - 08	17 - 02	16 - 01
	24	16 - 11	14 - 00	13 - 01

Notes :
1. Tabulated values developed from: Span Tables for Joists and Rafters, American Softwood Lumber Standard Sizes, 1993, American Wood Council, P.O. Box 5364, Madison, WI 53705-5364.
2. The tabulated values assume:
   (a) installation of at least three joists that are spaced no more than 24" on center
   (b) fully supported members, properly sheathed with adequate flooring, nailed on top edge of the joist
   (c) dry service conditions with wood moisture content not exceeding 19%
   (d) minimum bearing width of 1.5" and minimum bearing length of 1.5"
   (e) deflection is limited to span in inches divided by 360.
3. Tabulated spans apply to surfaced (S4S) lumber and are distances from face to face of supports
4. Lumber lengths over 20' are not common.
5. Another good reference: Western Lumber Span Tables, Western Wood Products Association, 522 SW Fifth Ave., Suite 400, Portland, OR 97204-2122

Maximum Floor Joist Spans

Hemlock-Fir: Includes Western hemlock, California red fir, Grand fir, Noble fir, Pacific silver fir, and White fir. (See "Notes" at end of tables.)

Nominal Lumber Size (inches)	Joist Spacing Center to Center (inches)	Lumber Grade		
		Select Structural	No. 1	No. 2
		Maximum Span (feet - inches)		

Max Live load=30 lbf/ft², Max Dead Load=10 lbf/ft²

Nominal Lumber Size (inches)	Joist Spacing Center to Center (inches)	Select Structural	No. 1	No. 2
2 x 6	12	11 - 10	11 - 07	11 - 00
	16	10 - 09	10 - 06	10 - 00
	24	09 - 04	09 - 02	08 - 09
2 x 8	12	15 - 07	15 - 03	14 - 06
	16	14 - 02	13 - 10	13 - 02
	24	12 - 04	12 - 00	11 - 04
2 x 10	12	19 - 10	19 - 05	18 - 06
	16	18 - 00	17 - 08	16 - 10
	24	15 - 09	14 - 08	13 - 10
2 x 12	12	24 - 02	23 - 07	22 - 06
	16	21 - 11	20 - 09	19 - 08
	24	19 - 02	17 - 00	16 - 01

Max Live load=40 lbf/ft², Max Dead Load=10 lbf/ft²

Nominal Lumber Size (inches)	Joist Spacing Center to Center (inches)	Select Structural	No. 1	No. 2
2 x 6	12	10 - 09	10 - 06	10 - 00
	16	09 - 09	09 - 06	09 - 01
	24	08 - 06	08 - 04	07 - 11
2 x 8	12	14 - 02	13 - 10	13 - 02
	16	12 - 10	12 - 07	12 - 00
	24	11 - 03	10 - 09	10 - 02
2 x 10	12	18 - 00	17 - 08	16 - 10
	16	16 - 05	16 - 00	15 - 02
	24	14 - 04	13 - 01	12 - 05
2 x 12	12	21 - 11	21 - 06	20 - 04
	16	19 - 11	18 - 07	17 - 07
	24	17 - 05	15 - 02	14 - 04

Maximum Floor Joist (cont.)

Hemlock-Fir: (cont.)

Nominal Lumber Size (inches)	Joist Spacing Center to Center (inches)	Lumber Grade		
		Select Structural	No. 1	No. 2
		Maximum Span (feet - inches)		

Max Live load=50 lbf/ft², Max Dead Load=10 lbf/ft²

Nominal Lumber Size (inches)	Joist Spacing Center to Center (inches)	Select Structural	No. 1	No. 2
2 x 8	12	13 - 01	12 - 10	12 - 03
	16	11 - 11	11 - 08	11 - 01
	24	10 - 05	09 - 09	09 - 03
2 x 10	12	16 - 09	16 - 05	15 - 07
	16	15 - 02	14 - 08	13 - 10
	24	13 - 03	11 - 11	11 - 04
2 x 12	12	20 - 04	19 - 07	18 - 06
	16	18 - 06	17 - 00	16 - 01
	24	16 - 02	13 - 10	13 - 01
2 x 14	12	24 - 00	21 - 11	20 - 09
	16	21 - 09	19 - 00	11 - 11
	24	18 - 10	15 - 06	14 - 08

Max Live load=60 lbf/ft², Max Dead Load=10 lbf/ft²

Nominal Lumber Size (inches)	Joist Spacing Center to Center (inches)	Select Structural	No. 1	No. 2
2 x 8	12	12 - 04	12 - 01	11 - 06
	16	11 - 03	11 - 00	10 - 06
	24	09 - 10	09 - 01	08 - 07
2 x 10	12	15 - 09	15 - 05	14 - 08
	16	14 - 04	13 - 07	12 - 10
	24	12 - 06	11 - 01	10 - 06
2 x 12	12	19 - 02	18 - 02	17 - 02
	16	17 - 05	15 - 09	14 - 10
	24	15 - 02	12 - 10	12 - 02
2 x 14	12	22 - 07	20 - 03	19 - 02
	16	20 - 06	17 - 07	16 - 07
	24	-	14 - 04	13 - 07

Dead Load = weight of structure + fixed loads
Live Load = movable loads such as furniture, wind, snow, etc.

Maximum Floor Joist (cont.)

Hemlock-Fir: (cont.)

Nominal Lumber Size (inches)	Joist Spacing Center to Center (inches)	Lumber Grade		
		Select Structural	No. 1	No. 2
		Maximum Span (feet - inches)		

Max Live load=30 lbf/ft^2, Max Dead Load=27 lbf/ft^2

Nominal Lumber Size (inches)	Joist Spacing Center to Center (inches)	Select Structural	No. 1	No. 2
2 x 6	12	11 - 10	11 - 02	10 - 07
	16	10 - 09	09 - 08	09 - 02
	24	09 - 04	07 - 11	07 - 06
2 x 8	12	15 - 07	14 - 02	13 - 05
	16	14 - 02	12 - 04	11 - 08
	24	12 - 00	10 - 00	09 - 06
2 x 10	12	19 - 10	17 - 04	16 - 05
	16	18 - 00	15 - 00	14 - 02
	24	14 - 11	12 - 03	11 - 07
2 x 12	12	24 - 02	20 - 01	19 - 00
	16	21 - 02	17 - 05	16 - 06
	24	17 - 03	14 - 03	13 - 05

Max Live load=40 lbf/ft^2, Max Dead Load=27 lbf/ft^2

Nominal Lumber Size (inches)	Joist Spacing Center to Center (inches)	Select Structural	No. 1	No. 2
2 x 6	12	10 - 09	10 - 04	09 - 09
	16	09 - 09	08 - 11	08 - 06
	24	08 - 06	07 - 04	06 - 11
2 x 8	12	14 - 02	13 - 01	12 - 05
	16	12 - 10	11 - 04	10 - 09
	24	11 - 03	09 - 03	08 - 09
2 x 10	12	18 - 00	16 - 00	15 - 02
	16	16 - 05	13 - 10	13 - 01
	24	13 - 09	11 - 04	10 - 08
2 x 12	12	21 - 11	18 - 07	17 - 07
	16	19 - 06	16 - 01	15 - 02
	24	15 - 11	13 - 01	12 - 05

Dead Load = weight of structure + fixed loads
Live Load = movable loads such as furniture, wind, snow, etc.

Maximum Floor Joist (cont.)

Hemlock-Fir: (cont.)

Nominal Lumber Size (inches)	Joist Spacing Center to Center (inches)	Lumber Grade		
		Select Structural	No. 1	No. 2
		Maximum Span (feet - inches)		

Max Live load=50 lbf/ft², Max Dead Load=27 lbf/ft²

Nominal Lumber Size (inches)	Joist Spacing Center to Center (inches)	Select Structural	No. 1	No. 2
2 x 8	12	13 - 01	12 - 03	11 - 07
	16	11 - 11	10 - 07	10 - 00
	24	10 - 05	08 - 08	08 - 02
2 x 10	12	16 - 09	14 - 11	14 - 01
	16	15 - 02	12 - 11	12 - 03
	24	12 - 10	10 - 07	10 - 00
2 x 12	12	20 - 04	17 - 04	16 - 04
	16	18 - 06	15 - 00	14 - 02
	24	14 - 10	12 - 03	11 - 07
2 x 14	12	23 - 06	19 - 04	18 - 03
	16	20 - 04	16 - 09	15 - 10
	24	-	13 - 08	12 - 11

Notes :
1. Tabulated values developed from: Span Tables for Joists and Rafters, American Softwood Lumber Standard Sizes, 1993, American Wood Council, P.O. Box 5364, Madison, WI 53705-5364.
2. The tabulated values assume:
   (a) installation of at least three joists that are spaced no more than 24" on center
   (b) fully supported members, properly sheathed with adequate flooring, nailed on top edge of the joist
   (c) dry service conditions with wood moisture content not exceeding 19%
   (d) minimum bearing width of 1.5" and minimum bearing length of 1.5"
   (e) deflection is limited to span in inches divided by 360.
3. Tabulated spans apply to surfaced (S4S) lumber and are distances from face to face of supports.
4. Lumber lengths over 20' are not common.
5. Another good reference: Western Lumber Span Tables, Western Wood Products Association, 522 SW Fifth Ave., Suite 400, Portland, OR 97204-2122.

Maximum Floor Joist Spans

Spruce-Pine-Fir (South): Includes Engelmann spruce, Sitka spruce, White spruce, and Lodgepole pine. (See "Notes" at end of tables.)

Nominal Lumber Size (inches)	Joist Spacing Center to Center (inches)	Lumber Grade		
		Select Structural	No. 1	No. 2
		Maximum Span (feet - inches)		

Max Live load=30 lbf/ft², Max Dead Load=10 lbf/ft²

2 x 6	12	11 - 00	10 - 09	10 - 05
	16	10 - 00	09 - 09	09 - 06
	24	08 - 09	08 - 06	08 - 03
2 x 8	12	14 - 06	14 - 02	13 - 09
	16	13 - 02	12 - 10	12 - 06
	24	11 - 06	11 - 03	10 - 08
2 x 10	12	18 - 06	18 - 00	17 - 06
	16	16 - 10	16 - 05	15 - 11
	24	14 - 08	13 - 10	13 - 00
2 x 12	12	22 - 06	21 - 11	21 - 04
	16	20 - 06	19 - 08	18 - 06
	24	17 - 11	16 - 01	15 - 01

Max Live load=40 lbf/ft², Max Dead Load=10 lbf/ft²

2 x 6	12	10 - 00	09 - 09	09 - 06
	16	09 - 01	08 - 10	08 - 07
	24	07 - 11	07 - 09	07 - 06
2 x 8	12	13 - 02	12 - 10	12 - 06
	16	12 - 00	11 - 08	11 - 04
	24	10 - 06	10 - 02	09 - 06
2 x 10	12	16 - 10	16 - 05	15 - 11
	16	15 - 03	14 - 11	14 - 03
	24	13 - 04	12 - 05	11 - 08
2 x 12	12	20 - 06	19 - 11	19 - 01
	16	18 - 07	17 - 07	16 - 06
	24	16 - 03	14 - 04	13 - 06

Spruce-Pine-Fir (South): (cont.)

Nominal Lumber Size (inches)	Joist Spacing Center to Center (inches)	Lumber Grade		
		Select Structural	No. 1	No. 2
		Maximum Span (feet - inches)		

Max Live load=50 lbf/ft², Max Dead Load=10 lbf/ft²

Nominal Lumber Size	Joist Spacing	Select Structural	No. 1	No. 2
2 x 8	12	12 - 03	11 - 11	11 - 07
	16	11 - 01	10 - 10	10 - 06
	24	09 - 09	09 - 03	08 - 08
2 x 10	12	15 - 07	15 - 02	14 - 09
	16	14 - 02	13 - 10	13 - 00
	24	12 - 05	11 - 04	10 - 07
2 x 12	12	19 - 00	18 - 06	17 - 05
	16	17 - 03	16 - 01	15 - 01
	24	15 - 01	13 - 01	12 - 04
2 x 14	12	22 - 04	20 - 09	19 - 05
	16	20 - 04	17 - 11	16 - 01
	24	-	14 - 08	13 - 09

Max Live load=60 lbf/ft², Max Dead Load=10 lbf/ft²

Nominal Lumber Size	Joist Spacing	Select Structural	No. 1	No. 2
2 x 8	12	11 - 06	11 - 03	10 - 11
	16	10 - 06	10 - 02	09 - 10
	24	09 - 02	08 - 07	08 - 01
2 x 10	12	14 - 08	14 - 04	13 - 11
	16	13 - 04	12 - 10	12 - 00
	24	11 - 08	10 - 06	09 - 10
2 x 12	12	17 - 11	17 - 02	16 - 01
	16	16 - 03	14 - 10	14 - 00
	24	14 - 02	12 - 02	11 - 05
2 x 14	12	21 - 01	19 - 02	18 - 00
	16	19 - 02	16 - 07	15 - 07
	24	-	13 - 07	12 - 09

Dead Load = weight of structure + fixed loads
Live Load = movable loads such as furniture, wind, snow, etc.

Spruce-Pine-Fir (South): (cont.)

Nominal Lumber Size (inches)	Joist Spacing Center to Center (inches)	Lumber Grade		
		Select Structural	No. 1	No. 2
		Maximum Span (feet - inches)		

Max Live load=30 lbf/ft^2, Max Dead Load=27 lbf/ft^2

2 x 6	12	11 - 00	10 - 07	10 - 00
	16	10 - 00	09 - 02	08 - 07
	24	08 - 09	07 - 06	07 - 01
2 x 8	12	14 - 06	13 - 05	12 - 07
	16	13 - 02	11 - 08	10 - 11
	24	11 - 06	09 - 06	08 - 11
2 x 10	12	18 - 06	16 - 05	15 - 05
	16	16 - 10	14 - 02	13 - 04
	24	14 - 04	11 - 07	10 - 11
2 x 12	12	22 - 06	19 - 00	17 - 10
	16	20 - 04	16 - 06	15 - 06
	24	16 - 08	13 - 05	12 - 08

Max Live load=40 lbf/ft^2, Max Dead Load=27 lbf/ft^2

2 x 6	12	10 - 00	09 - 09	09 - 02
	16	09 - 01	08 - 06	07 - 11
	24	07 - 11	06 - 11	06 -06
2 x 8	12	13 - 02	12 - 05	11 - 08
	16	12 - 00	10 - 09	10 - 01
	24	10 - 06	08 - 09	08 - 03
2 x 10	12	16 - 10	15 - 02	14 - 03
	16	15 - 03	13 - 01	12 - 04
	24	13 - 03	10 - 08	10 - 01
2 x 12	12	20 - 06	17 - 07	16 - 06
	16	18 - 07	15 - 02	14 - 03
	24	12 - 05		11 - 08

Dead Load = weight of structure + fixed loads
Live Load = movable loads such as furniture,
wind, snow, etc.

Maximum Floor Joist (cont.)

Spruce-Pine-Fir (South): (cont.)

Nominal Lumber Size (inches)	Joist Spacing Center to Center (inches)	Lumber Grade		
		Select Structural	No. 1	No. 2
		Maximum Span (feet - inches)		

Max Live load=50 lbf/ft², Max Dead Load=27 lbf/ft²

Nominal Lumber Size (inches)	Joist Spacing Center to Center (inches)	Select Structural	No. 1	No. 2
2 x 8	12	12 - 03	11 - 07	10 - 10
	16	11 - 01	10 - 00	09 - 05
	24	09 - 09	08 - 02	07 - 08
2 x 10	12	15 - 07	14 - 01	13 - 03
	16	14 - 02	12 - 03	11 - 06
	24	12 - 04	10 - 00	09 - 04
2 x 12	12	19 - 00	16 - 04	15 - 04
	16	17 - 03	14 - 02	13 - 04
	24	-	11 - 07	10 - 10
2 x 14	12	22 - 04	18 - 03	17 - 02
	16	19 - 07	15 - 10	14 - 10
	24	-	12 - 11	12 - 02

Notes :
1. Tabulated values developed from: Span Tables for Joists and Rafters, American Softwood Lumber Standard Sizes, 1993, American Wood Council, P.O. Box 5364, Madison, WI 53705-5364.
2. The tabulated values assume:
   (a) installation of at least three joists that are spaced no more than 24" on center
   (b) fully supported members, properly sheathed with adequate flooring, nailed on top edge of the joist
   (c) dry service conditions with wood moisture content not exceeding 19%
   (d) minimum bearing width of 1.5" and minimum bearing length of 1.5"
   (e) deflection is limited to span in inches divided by 360.
3. Tabulated spans apply to surfaced (S4S) lumber and are distances from face to face of supports.
4. Lumber lengths over 20' are not common.
5. Another good reference: Western Lumber Span Tables, Western Wood Products Association, 522 SW Fifth Ave., Suite 400, Portland, OR 97204-2122.

Maximum Floor Joist Spans

Southern Pine: Includes Loblolly pine, Longleaf pine, Shortleaf pine, and Slash pine. (See "Notes" at end of tables.)

Nominal Lumber Size (inches)	Joist Spacing Center to Center (inches)	Select Structural	No. 1	No. 2
		Maximum Span (feet - inches)		

Max Live load=30 lbf/ft^2, Max Dead Load=10 lbf/ft^2

Nominal Lumber Size (inches)	Joist Spacing Center to Center (inches)	Select Structural	No. 1	No. 2
2 x 6	12	12 - 03	12 - 00	11 - 10
	16	11 - 02	10 - 11	10 - 09
	24	09 - 09	09 - 07	09 - 04
2 x 8	12	16 - 02	15 - 10	15 - 07
	16	14 - 08	14 - 05	14 - 02
	24	12 - 10	12 - 07	12 - 04
2 x 10	12	20 - 08	20 - 03	19 - 10
	16	18 - 09	18 - 05	18 - 00
	24	16 - 05	16 - 01	14 - 02
2 x 12	12	25 - 01	24 - 08	24 - 02
	16	22 - 10	22 - 05	21 - 01
	24	19 - 11	19 - 06	17 - 02

Max Live load=40 lbf/ft^2, Max Dead Load=10 lbf/ft^2

Nominal Lumber Size (inches)	Joist Spacing Center to Center (inches)	Select Structural	No. 1	No. 2
2 x 6	12	11 - 02	10 - 11	10 - 09
	16	10 - 02	09 - 11	09 - 09
	24	08 - 10	08 - 08	08 - 06
2 x 8	12	14 - 08	14 - 05	14 - 02
	16	13 - 04	13 - 01	12 - 10
	24	11 - 08	11 - 05	11 - 00
2 x 10	12	18 - 09	18 - 05	18 - 00
	16	17 - 00	16 - 09	16 - 01
	24	14 - 11	14 - 07	13 - 01
2 x 12	12	22 - 10	22 - 05	21 - 09
	16	20 - 09	20 - 04	18 - 10
	24	18 - 01	17 - 05	15 - 05

Maximum Floor Joist (cont.)

Southern Pine: (cont.)

Nominal Lumber Size (inches)	Joist Spacing Center to Center (inches)	Lumber Grade		
		Select Structural	No. 1	No. 2
		Maximum Span (feet - inches)		

Max Live load=50 lbf/ft^2, Max Dead Load=10 lbf/ft^2

Nominal Lumber Size (inches)	Joist Spacing Center to Center (inches)	Select Structural	No. 1	No. 2
2 x 6	12	10 - 04	10 - 02	09 - 11
	16	09 - 05	09 - 03	09 - 01
	24	08 - 03	08 - 01	07 - 09
2 x 8	12	13 - 08	13 - 05	13 - 01
	16	12 - 05	12 - 02	11 - 11
	24	10 - 10	10 - 08	10 - 00
2 x 10	12	17 - 05	17 - 01	16 - 09
	16	15 - 10	15 - 06	14 - 08
	24	13 - 00	13 - 04	12 - 00
2 x 12	12	21 - 02	20 - 09	19 - 10
	16	19 - 03	18 - 10	17 - 02
	24	16 - 10	15 - 11	14 - 00

Max Live load=60 lbf/ft^2, Max Dead Load=10 lbf/ft^2

Nominal Lumber Size (inches)	Joist Spacing Center to Center (inches)	Select Structural	No. 1	No. 2
2 x 6	12	09 - 09	09 - 07	09 - 04
	16	08 - 10	08 - 08	08 - 06
	24	07 - 09	07 - 07	07 - 02
2 x 8	12	12 - 10	12 - 07	12 - 04
	16	11 - 08	11 - 05	11 - 03
	24	10 - 02	10 - 00	09 - 04
2 x 10	12	16 - 05	16 - 01	15 - 08
	16	14 - 11	14 - 07	13 - 07
	24	13 - 00	12 - 04	11 - 01
2 x 12	12	19 - 11	19 - 07	18 - 05
	16	18 - 01	17 - 09	15 - 11
	24	15 - 10	14 - 09	13 - 00

Dead Load = weight of structure + fixed loads
Live Load = movable loads such as furniture,
wind, snow, etc.

Maximum Floor Joist (cont.)

Southern Pine: (cont.)

Nominal Lumber Size (inches)	Joist Spacing Center to Center (inches)	Lumber Grade		
		Select Structural	No. 1	No. 2
		Maximum Span (feet - inches)		

Max Live load=40 lbf/ft^2, Max Dead Load=20 lbf/ft^2

2 x 6	12	11 - 02	10 - 11	10 - 09
	16	10 - 02	09 - 11	09 - 06
	24	08 - 10	08 - 08	07 - 09
2 x 8	12	14 - 08	14 - 05	14 - 02
	16	13 - 04	13 - 01	12 - 04
	24	11 - 08	11 - 03	10 - 00
2 x 10	12	18 - 09	18 - 05	16 - 11
	16	17 - 00	16 - 04	14 - 08
	24	14 - 11	13 - 04	12 - 00
2 x 12	12	22 - 10	22 - 05	19 - 10
	16	20 - 09	19 - 06	17 - 02
	24	18 - 01	15 - 11	14 - 00

Max Live load=50 lbf/ft^2, Max Dead Load=20 lbf/ft^2

2 x 6	12	10 - 04	10 - 02	09 - 11
	16	09 - 05	09 - 03	08 - 10
	24	08 - 03	08 - 01	07 - 02
2 x 8	12	13 - 08	13 - 05	13 - 01
	16	12 - 05	12 - 02	11 - 05
	24	10 - 10	10 - 05	09 - 04
2 x 10	12	17 - 05	17 - 01	15 - 08
	16	15 - 10	15 - 01	13 - 07
	24	13 - 10	12 - 04	11 - 01
2 x 12	12	21 - 02	20 - 09	18 - 05
	16	19 - 03	18 - 00	15 - 11
	24	16 - 10	14 - 09	13 - 00

Dead Load = weight of structure + fixed loads
Live Load = movable loads such as furniture, wind, snow, etc.

Maximum Floor Joist (cont.)

Southern Pine: (cont.)

Nominal Lumber Size (inches)	Joist Spacing Center to Center (inches)	Lumber Grade		
		Select Structural	No. 1	No. 2
		Maximum Span (feet - inches)		

Max Live load=60 lbf/ft², Max Dead Load=20 lbf/ft²

2 x 6	12	09 - 09	09 - 07	09 - 04
	16	08 - 10	08 - 08	08 - 03
	24	07 - 09	07 - 07	06 - 09
2 x 8	12	12 - 10	12 - 07	12 - 04
	16	11 - 08	11 - 05	10 - 08
	24	10 - 02	09 - 09	08 - 08
2 x 10	12	16 - 05	16 - 01	14 - 08
	16	14 - 11	14 - 02	12 - 08
	24	13 - 00	11 - 07	10 - 04
2 x 12	12	19 - 11	19 - 06	17 - 02
	16	18 - 01	16 - 10	14 - 11
	24	15 - 10	13 - 09	12 - 02

Notes :
1. Tabulated values developed from: Span Tables for Joists and Rafters, American Softwood Lumber Standard Sizes, 1993, American Wood Council, P.O. Box 5364, Madison, WI 53705-5364.
2. The tabulated values assume:
   (a) installation of at least three joists that are spaced no more than 24" on center
   (b) fully supported members, properly sheathed with adequate flooring, nailed on top edge of the joist
   (c) dry service conditions with wood moisture content not exceeding 19%
   (d) minimum bearing width of 1.5" and minimum bearing length of 1.5"
   (e) deflection is limited to span in inches divided by 360.
3. Tabulated spans apply to surfaced (S4S) lumber and are distances from face to face of supports.
4. Lumber lengths over 20' are not common.
5. Another good reference: Maximum Spans, Southern Pine Joints & Rafters, Southern Forest Products Association, P.O. Box 641700, Kenner, LA 70064-1700.

Maximum Floor Joist Spans

Redwood: (See "Notes" at end of tables.)

Nominal Lumber Size (inches)	Joist Spacing Center to Center (inches)	Lumber Grade		
		Select Structural	No. 1	No. 2
		Maximum Span (feet - inches)		

Max Live load=30 lbf/ft², Max Dead Load=10 lbf/ft²

Nominal Lumber Size	Joist Spacing	Select Structural	No. 1	No. 2
2 x 6	12	11 - 03	11 - 00	10 - 09
	16	10 - 03	10 - 00	09 - 09
	24	08 - 11	08 - 09	08 - 06
2 x 8	12	14 - 11	14 - 06	14 - 02
	16	13 - 06	13 - 02	12 - 10
	24	11 - 10	11 - 06	11 - 03
2 x 10	12	19 - 00	18 - 06	18 - 00
	16	17 - 03	16 - 10	16 - 05
	24	15 - 01	14 - 08	14 - 04
2 x 12	12	23 - 01	22 - 06	21 - 11
	16	21 - 00	20 - 06	19 - 11
	24	18 - 04	17 - 11	17 - 05

Max Live load=40 lbf/ft², Max Dead Load=10 lbf/ft²

Nominal Lumber Size	Joist Spacing	Select Structural	No. 1	No. 2
2 x 6	12	10 - 03	10 - 00	09 - 09
	16	09 - 04	09 - 01	08 - 10
	24	08 - 02	07 - 11	07 - 09
2 x 8	12	13 - 06	13 - 02	12 - 10
	16	12 - 03	12 - 00	11 - 08
	24	10 - 09	10 - 06	10 - 02
2 x 10	12	17 - 03	16 - 10	16 - 05
	16	15 - 08	15 - 03	14 - 11
	24	13 - 08	13 - 04	13 - 00
2 x 12	12	21 - 00	20 - 06	19 - 11
	16	19 - 01	18 - 07	18 - 01
	24	16 - 08	16 - 03	15 - 10

Dead Load = weight of structure + fixed loads
Live Load = movable loads such as furniture, wind, snow, etc.

Maximum Floor Joist (cont.)

Redwood: (cont.)

Nominal Lumber Size (inches)	Joist Spacing Center to Center (inches)	Select Structural	No. 1	No. 2
		Lumber Grade		
		Maximum Span (feet - inches)		

Max Live load=50 lbf/ft^2, Max Dead Load=10 lbf/ft^2

Nominal Lumber Size (inches)	Joist Spacing	Select Structural	No. 1	No. 2
2 x 6	12	09 - 06	09 - 03	09 - 01
	16	08 - 08	08 - 05	08 - 03
	24	07 - 07	07 - 04	07 - 02
2 x 8	12	12 - 07	12 - 03	11 - 11
	16	11 - 05	11 - 01	10 - 10
	24	10 - 00	09 - 09	09 - 06
2 x 10	12	16 - 00	15 - 07	15 - 02
	16	14 - 07	14 - 02	13 - 10
	24	12 - 08	12 - 05	12 - 01
2 x 12	12	19 - 06	19 - 00	18 - 06
	16	17 - 08	17 - 03	16 - 10
	24	15 - 05	15 - 01	14 - 08

Max Live load=60 lbf/ft^2, Max Dead Load=10 lbf/ft^2

Nominal Lumber Size (inches)	Joist Spacing	Select Structural	No. 1	No. 2
2 x 6	12	08 - 11	08 - 09	08 - 06
	16	08 - 02	07 - 11	07 - 09
	24	07 - 01	06 - 11	06 - 09
2 x 8	12	11 - 10	11 - 06	11 - 03
	16	10 - 09	10 - 06	10 - 02
	24	09 - 04	09 - 02	08 - 11
2 x 10	12	15 - 01	14 - 08	14 - 04
	16	13 - 08	13 - 04	13 - 00
	24	11 - 11	11 - 08	11 - 04
2 x 12	12	18 - 04	17 - 11	17 - 05
	16	16 - 08	16 - 03	15 - 11
	24	14 - 07	14 - 02	13 - 10

Dead Load = weight of structure + fixed loads
Live Load = movable loads such as furniture,
wind, snow, etc.

Maximum Floor Joist (cont.)

Redwood: (cont.)

Nominal Lumber Size (inches)	Joist Spacing Center to Center (inches)	Lumber Grade		
		Select Structural	No. 1	No. 2
		Maximum Span (feet - inches)		

Max Live load=40 lbf/ft², Max Dead Load=20 lbf/ft²

Nominal Lumber Size (inches)	Joist Spacing Center to Center (inches)	Select Structural	No. 1	No. 2
2 x 6	12	10 - 03	10 - 00	09 - 09
	16	09 - 04	09 - 01	08 - 10
	24	08 - 02	07 - 11	07 - 09
2 x 8	12	13 - 06	13 - 02	12 - 10
	16	12 - 03	12 - 00	11 - 08
	24	10 - 09	10 - 06	10 - 02
2 x 10	12	17 - 03	16 - 10	16 - 05
	16	15 - 08	15 - 03	14 - 11
	24	13 - 08	13 - 04	13 - 00
2 x 12	12	21 - 00	20 - 09	19 - 11
	16	19 - 01	18 - 07	18 - 01
	24	16 - 08	16 - 03	15 - 10

Max Live load=50 lbf/ft², Max Dead Load=20 lbf/ft²

Nominal Lumber Size (inches)	Joist Spacing Center to Center (inches)	Select Structural	No. 1	No. 2
2 x 6	12	09 - 06	09 - 03	09 - 01
	16	08 - 08	08 - 05	08 - 03
	24	07 - 07	07 - 04	07 - 02
2 x 8	12	12 - 07	12 - 03	11 - 11
	16	11 - 05	11 - 01	10 - 10
	24	10 - 00	09 - 09	09 - 06
2 x 10	12	16 - 00	15 - 07	15 - 02
	16	14 - 07	14 - 02	13 - 10
	24	12 - 08	12 - 05	12 - 01
2 x 12	12	19 - 06	19 - 00	18 - 06
	16	17 - 08	17 - 03	16 - 10
	24	15 - 05	15 - 01	14 - 08

Dead Load = weight of structure + fixed loads
Live Load = movable loads such as furniture,
wind, snow, etc.

Maximum Floor Joist (cont.)

Redwood: (cont.)

Nominal Lumber Size (inches)	Joist Spacing Center to Center (inches)	Lumber Grade		
		Select Structural	No. 1	No. 2
		Maximum Span (feet - inches)		

Max Live load=60 lbf/ft², Max Dead Load=20 lbf/ft²

Nominal Lumber Size (inches)	Joist Spacing Center to Center (inches)	Select Structural	No. 1	No. 2
2 x 6	12	08 - 11	08 - 09	08 - 06
	16	08 - 02	07 - 11	07 - 09
	24	07 - 01	06 - 11	06 - 09
2 x 8	12	11 - 10	11 - 06	11 - 03
	16	10 - 09	10 - 06	10 - 02
	24	09 - 04	09 - 02	08 - 11
2 x 10	12	15 - 01	14 - 08	14 - 04
	16	13 - 08	13 - 04	13 - 00
	24	11 - 11	11 - 08	11 - 04
2 x 12	12	18 - 04	17 - 11	17 - 05
	16	16 - 08	16 - 03	15 - 10
	24	14 - 07	14 - 02	13 - 10

Notes :
1. Tabulated values developed from: Span Tables for Joists and Rafters, American Softwood Lumber Standard Sizes, 1993, American Wood Council, P.O. Box 5364, Madison, WI 53705-5364.
2. The tabulated values assume:
   (a) installation of at least three joists that are spaced no more than 24" on center
   (b) fully supported members, properly sheathed with adequate flooring, nailed on top edge of the joist
   (c) dry service conditions with wood moisture content not exceeding 19%
   (d) minimum bearing width of 1.5" and minimum bearing length of 1.5".
   (e) deflection is limited to span in inches divided by 360.
3. Tabulated spans apply to surfaced (S4S) lumber and are distances from face to face of supports.
4. Lumber lengths over 20' are not common.
5. Another good reference: Redwood Deck Construction, California Redwood Association, 405 Enfrente Drive, Suite 200, Novato, CA 94949.

Strength of Wood Beams

Wood Species	Stress in Pounds per Square Inch (PSI)					
	Bending		Compression			
	Horizontal Shear F_b		Perpendicular to Grain $F_{c\perp}$		Parallel to Grain F_c	
	Wet	Dry	Wet	Dry	Wet	Dry
Aspen, Big Tooth	1006	1006	177	265	725	725
Aspen, Quaking	1006	1006	177	265	725	725
Beech, American	1417	1668	477	715	960	1200
Birch, Sweet	1417	1668	477	715	960	1200
Birch, Yellow	1417	1668	477	715	960	1200
Cedar, Alaska	1150	1150	283	425	800	1000
Cedar, Incense	1150	1150	283	425	800	1000
Cedar, N. White	891	891	247	370	750	750
Cedar, Port Orford	1150	1150	283	425	800	1000
Cedar, Western Red	1150	1150	283	425	800	1000
Cottonwood	1006	1006	213	320	620	775
Fir, Alpine	1222	1438	283	425	1120	1400
Fir, Amabilis	1271	1495	247	370	1320	1650
Fir, Balsam	1222	1438	283	425	1120	1400
Fir, California Red	1369	1610	270	405	1200	1500
Fir, Douglas	1417	1668	417	625	1360	1700
Fir, Grand	1369	1610	270	405	1200	1500
Fir, Noble	1369	1610	270	405	1200	1500
Fir, Pacific Silver	1369	1610	270	405	1200	1500
Fir, White	1369	1610	270	405	1200	1500
Hemlock, Eastern	1222	1438	370	555	960	1200
Hemlock, Mountain	1006	1006	223	335	840	1050
Hemlock, Western	1271	1495	247	370	1320	1650
Hickory, Bitternut	1417	1668	477	715	960	1200
Hickory, Mockernut	1417	1668	477	715	960	1200
Hickory, Nutmeg	1417	1668	477	715	960	1200
Hickory, Pecan	1417	1668	477	715	960	1200
Hickory, Pignut	1417	1668	477	715	960	1200
Hickory, Shagbark	1417	1668	477	715	960	1200
Hickory, Shellbark	1417	1668	477	715	960	1200
Hickory, Water	1417	1668	477	715	960	1200
Larch, Western	1417	1668	417	625	1360	1700
Maple, Black	1150	1150	413	620	700	875
Maple, Red	1271	1495	410	615	880	1100
Maple, Silver	1150	1150	413	620	700	875
Maple, Sugar	978	1150	413	620	700	875

Strength of Wood Beams

Wood Species	Stress in Pounds per Square Inch (PSI)					
	Bending		Compression			
	Horizontal Shear F_b		Perpendicular to Grain $F_{c\perp}$		Parallel to Grain F_c	
	Wet	Dry	Wet	Dry	Wet	Dry
Oak, Black	1369	1610	590	885	920	1150
Oak, Bur	1173	1380	533	800	880	1100
Oak, Cherrybark	1124	1323	547	820	800	1000
Oak, Chestnut	1173	1380	533	800	880	1100
Oak, Laurel	1124	1323	547	820	800	1000
Oak, Live	1173	1380	533	800	880	1100
Oak, Northern Red	1369	1610	590	885	920	1150
Oak, Overcup	1173	1380	533	800	880	1100
Oak, Pin	1369	1610	590	885	920	1150
Oak, Post	1173	1380	533	800	880	1100
Oak, Scarlet	1369	1610	590	885	920	1150
Oak, Southern Red	1124	1323	547	820	800	1000
Oak, Swamp Chestnut	1173	1380	533	800	880	1100
Oak, Swamp White	1173	1380	533	800	880	1100
Oak, Water	1124	1323	547	820	800	1000
Oak, White	1173	1380	533	800	880	1100
Oak, Willow	1124	1323	547	820	800	1000
Pine, Eastern White	1222	1438	223	335	960	1200
Pine, Idaho White	1006	1006	223	335	840	1050
Pine, Jack	1222	1438	283	425	1120	1400
Pine, Loblolly	1857	2185	377	565	1440	1800
Pine, Lodgepole	1222	1438	283	425	1120	1400
Pine, Longleaf	1857	2185	377	565	1440	1800
Pine, Norway	1271	1495	223	335	960	1200
Pine, Pitch	1222	1438	223	335	960	1200
Pine, Pond	1369	1610	377	565	1240	1550
Pine, Ponderosa	1006	1006	223	335	840	1050
Pine, Red	1271	1495	223	335	960	1200
Pine, Shortleaf	1857	2185	377	565	1440	1800
Pine, Slash	1857	2185	377	565	1440	1800
Pine, Sugar	1006	1006	223	335	840	1050
Pine, Virginia	1369	1610	377	565	1240	1550
Popular, Yellow	978	1150	280	420	720	900
Redwood	1320	1553	433	650	1200	1500

Strength of Wood Beams

Wood Species	Stress in Pounds per Square Inch (PSI)					
	Bending		Compression			
	Horizontal Shear F_b		Perpendicular to Grain $F_{c\perp}$		Parallel to Grain F_c	
	Wet	Dry	Wet	Dry	Wet	Dry
Spruce, Black	1222	1438	283	425	1120	1400
Spruce, Engelmann	1222	1438	283	425	1120	1400
Spruce, Red	1222	1438	283	425	1120	1400
Spruce, Sitka	1271	1495	223	335	960	1200
Spruce, White	1222	1438	283	425	1120	1400
Tamarack	1222	1438	370	555	960	1200

Notes:
Design conditions:
1. Visually graded dimension lumber
2. 2 to 4 inches thick
3. 12 inch nominal depth
4. Normal load duration
5. Members are used for joists, truss chords, rafters, studs, planks, or decking
6. Members in contact or spaced not more than 24 inches on centers, not less than 3 in number and joined by floor, roof or other load distributing elements to support the design load
7. Note from the above table, that all strength ratings of wood decrease dramatically when the wood is wet!

Source: Design values developed from Design Values for Wood Construction, National Design Specification, American Forest and Paper Association, Washington, D.C., 1993

Wood Gluing Characteristics

Wood gluing is a very common practice today, but there are a large number of glue types from which to choose and each of the different types of wood have different gluing properties. See the chapter on GLUE, page 377, for specific information on each of the common glue types.

The following 4 groups define the relative difficulty with which various woods can be glued:

Easy: Works with many different types of glues and under many gluing conditions.
Aspen, Western Red Cedar, Chestnut, Cottonwood, Cypress, White Fir, Larch, Redwood, Spruce, Willow, Yellow Poplar.

Moderate: More restricted gluing conditions than the Easy category. Different types of glue work fine.
Red Alder, Basswood, Butternut, Eastern Red Cedar, Douglas Fir, American and Rock Elm, Hackberry, Western Hemlock, Magnolia, Mahogany, Pine, Sweet Gum.

Difficult: Well controlled gluing conditions are required but still works with many different glue types.
White Ash, Alaskan Cedar, Cherry, Dogwood, Silver Maple (soft), Red and White Oak, Pecan, Sycamore, Black and Water Typelo, Black Walnut.

Very Difficult: Requires special glues and very close control of gluing conditions.
American Beech, Sweet and Yellow Birch, Hickory, Sugar Maple (hard), Osage—orange, Persimmon.

"Gluing conditions" is a function of proper sanding, letting surfaces to be glued become tacky before joining, using clamps to hold glue positions, and drying in a warm, dry area. Heat lamps will sometimes aid in the drying process

In addition to the above, the following generalities are also true:
Hardwoods are more difficult to glue than softwoods.
Heartwood is more difficult to glue than sapwood.
Heavy woods are more difficult to glue than lightweight woods.

Concrete

Concrete is a mixture of aggregate (typically sand and gravel), Portland cement, and water. Characteristics of each of these components are as follows:

Aggregate: A mixture of sand and gravel ranging in size from dust to 2–1/2 inches. Rounded fragments are generally better and do not use fragments larger than 1/4 the thickness of the concrete unit you are pouring (e.g. for a 4 inch slab, don't use greater than 1 inch gravel). The larger the gravel the more cost effective the concrete and there will be less problems from shrinkage.

Portland Cement: Cement comes in 1 cubic foot bags that weigh 94 lbs. It can also be purchased in bulk trailer loads. There are 5 basic types of cement:
   - Type I: The most common type sold by building suppliers.
   - Type II: A "sulfate resistant" variety used in bridges & pilings.
   - Type III: Quick hardening, used for rush jobs and winter use.
   - Type IV: Slow hardening, low heat for large structures.
   - Type V: Very high "sulfate resistance". (near water)

Water: Use clean, impurity free water, not muddy water.

Air: A fourth component of some concrete is millions of tiny air bubbles entrained in the mixture. This component helps the concrete withstand the effects of freezing and thawing and also makes the concrete lighter. Machine mixing is a must.

The strength of concrete increases when:
   1. The amount of cement in the mixture increases.
   2. The amount of water relative to cement decreases.
   3. The density of the concrete is higher.
   4. The aggregate is coarser.

The most common problems encountered in making concrete are adding too much water or sand, and poor mixing.

Other factors affecting the quality of the finished product include mixing and curing. Thorough mixing of the concrete is absolutely necessary in order to produce the strongest, most durable pour. Curing of concrete is necessary in order for the material to harden properly. The concrete must be kept moist for a period of 7 days and the temperature must not drop below 50°F. Although after 28 days, there is normally very little increase in the strength of concrete, most concrete does not completely cure for years.

Concrete

Typical Concrete Mixtures by Volume

Cement:Sand:Gravel

Ratio	Application
1:3:6	Normal static loads, no rebar; not exposed
1:2.5:5	Normal foundations & walls; exposed
1:2.5:4	Basement walls
1:2.5:3.5	Waterproof basement walls
1:2.5:3	Floors (light duty), driveways
1:2.25:3	Steps, driveways, sidewalks
1:2:4	Lintels
1:2:4	Reinforced roads, buildings, walls; exposed
1:2:3.5	Retaining walls, drive ways
1:2:3	Swimming pools, fence posts
1:1.75:4	Floors (light duty)
1:1.5:3	Watertight, reinforced tanks & columns
1:1:2	High strength columns, girders, floors
1:1:1.5	Fence posts

When mixing concrete, mix the sand and cement first until a uniform color is obtained then mix in the aggregate. Adding the correct amount of water is a difficult task. In the above table, the portion for water is about 1/2 but this will vary depending on whether the sand is dry, damp, or wet (the 1/2 ratio component is equal to about 6 gallons of water per sack of cement). Simply remember that you only want to add enough water to make the concrete mixture workable and that the less water in relation to cement, the stronger the final concrete will be.

The strength of concrete can also be increased by compacting or working the mixture into place. This is accomplished by walking in the wet mixture or tamping or vibrating. If vibrators are used be careful that you do not cause segregation of the aggregate.

Recommended Thickness of Slabs

Thickness (inches)	Application
4	Home basement floors, farm building floors
4 to 5	Home garage floors, porches
5 to 6	Sidewalks, barn and granary floors, small shed floors
6 to 8	Driveways

Concrete and Mortar

Calculating Cubic Volumes

Concrete and mortar are normally sold and used on a cubic volume basis (either cubic feet or cubic yards). Use the following to calculate the amount of concrete you need for a slab:

Cubic feet of Concrete = Slab thickness in feet x Slab width in feet x Slab length in feet

1 cubic yard = 27 cubic feet
1 cubic foot = 1,728 cubic inches

In using the above equations, note that the volume of the final concrete mixture is approximately 2/3's the volume of the original cement–aggregate mixture. This occurs because the sand and cement fill in the void spaces between the gravel fragments.

Standard Steel Reinforcing Bar (re–bar)

Bar Number	Diameter Fraction Inch	Diameter Inches	Diameter mm	Pounds per foot
2b	1/4	0.250	6.4	0.17
3	3/8	0.375	9.5	0.38
4	1/2	0.500	12.7	0.67
5	5/8	0.625	15.9	1.04
6	3/4	0.750	19.1	1.50
7	7/8	0.875	22.2	2.04
8	1	1.000	25.4	2.67
9	1–1/8	1.128	28.7	3.40
10	1–1/4	1.270	32.3	4.30
11	1–3/8	1.410	35.8	5.31
14	1–3/4	1.693	43.0	7.65
18	2–1/4	2.257	57.3	13.60

Coloring Concrete and Mortar

Color	Color material	lbs / sack Cement
Black	Black oxide or mineral Black	1 to 12
Blue	Ultramarine Blue	5 to 9
Brown–Red	Red iron oxide	5 to 9
Bright Red	Mineral Turkey Red	5 to 9
Purple–Red	Indian red	5 to 9
Brown	Metallic Brown Oxide	5 to 9
Buff to yellow	Yellow ocher or yellow oxide	2 to 9
Green	Chromium oxide or ultramarine	5 to 9

Mortar

Mortar is composed of basically the same material as concrete, except that its composition has been altered to increase the ease of workability and decrease the setting time of the mixture. As with concrete, the strength of mortar is a function of the proportions of its ingredients.

Mortar is a mixture of Portland cement, hydrated lime, sand (well graded and in a size range of 1/8 inch to 100 mesh) and water. Masonry cement, which already contains the hydrated lime, can be used instead of Portland cement.

The strength of mortar increases when:
1. The amount of cement in the mixture increases.
2. The amount of water relative to cement decreases. Unfortunately, there is no rule for the amount of water since it is a function of workability. Just use as little as possible.
3. The amount of hydrated lime decreases.
4. The amount of Portland cement relative to masonry cement increases.
5. Brick with low water absorption is used. If brick absorbs water readily, the bricks must be wetted before mortaring.
6. Clean sand is used. Organic matter and salts in the sand will drastically decrease the mortar strength. A higher percentage of coarse to fine sand increases strength.
7. Special epoxies are available that can be mixed with the mortar. These increase both the strength and bonding power of the mortar and in many cases will create mortar that is stronger than the brick. Note that this adds to the cost of the mortar.

The workability of mortar increases when:
1. The amount of hydrated lime in the mixture increases.
2. The amount of water increases.

As with concrete, thorough mixing of the mortar is imperative. A power mixer is best, but small quantities can be mixed by hand. Once the mortar has been mixed, it will begin to cure and stiffen. If the mortar begins to stiffen within 2 to 2.5 hours of mixing (above 80°F outside air temperature) you can add a small amount of water to increase workability. After the 2.5 hour time limit, the mortar should be thrown away and a new batch mixed. If the outside air temperatures are below 80°F, the 2.5 hour time limit can be increased to approximately 3.5 hours.

Mortar

Type numbers are used to define the various mortar mixes. The following are the four common types with their <u>volume</u> proportions of Portland cement (see also concrete section for different types of Portland), masonry cement (Type II unless otherwise stated), lime, and sand:

Type M: General use for foundations, walls, sidewalks and other situations in contact with the ground or below grade. 28 day compression strength 4900–5400 psi, depending on amount of water used.
Portland Mix: 1 Portland; 1/4 hydrated lime; 3 sand
Masonry Mix: 1 Portland; 1 masonry, 6 sand

Type S: General use for high resistance to sideways or lateral stress. 28 day compression strength 2100–2800 psi, depending on amount of water used.
Portland Mix: 1 Portland; 1/2 hydrated lime; 4.5 sand.
Masonry Mix: 1/2 Portland; 1 masonry; 4.5 sand

Type N: General use above grade for severe exposure walls. 28 day compression strength 800–1200 psi, depending on amount of water used.
Portland Mix: 1 Portland; 1 hydrated lime; 6 sand
Masonry Mix: 1 masonry; 3 sand

Type O: Low strength load bearing walls where excessive moisture and freezing are not present. Compression strength must be below 100 psi.
Portland Mix: 1 Portland; 2 hydrated lime; 9 sand
Masonry Mix: 1 masonry (Types I or II); 3 sand

If you need a small amount of general use mortar, the following will make about 1 cubic foot: 16 lbs Portland cement, 8.5 lbs hydrated lime, 100 lbs dry sand, and 2 to 3 gallons of water.

The amount of mortar required for a job varies tremendously, but the following average quantities may be helpful. With practice, you can lay 90–120 common bricks/hour.

Mortar required for Common Brick (8 in x 3-3/4 in x 2-1/4 in) assuming 20 bricks per cubic foot		
Joint Thickness inches	Cu ft Mortar/ 1000 brick	Cu ft Mortar/ Cu ft brick
1/4	9	0.2
3/8	14	0.3
1/2	20	0.4

Hand Signals for Crane & Hoist

Stop
Extend arm with palm down and rapidly move hand left and right.

Emergency Stop
Extend both arms with palms down and rapidly move both hands left and right.

Stop
Extend arm and hold forearm vertically with palm of hand vertical.

Hold Everything
Clasp hands in front of body.

Lower Load
Move hand in circular motion with forearm vertical downward and forefinger pointing down.

Raise Load or Hoist
Move hand in circular motion with forearm vertical and forefinger pointing up.

Hand Signals for Crane & Hoist

Raise Boom
Extend arm, close fingers, point thumb upward.

Lower Boom
Extend arm, close fingers, point thumb downward.

Extend Boom (telescoping)
Position both fists in front of body with thumbs pointing outward.

Retract Boom (telescoping)
Position both fists in front of body with thumbs pointing toward each other.

Raise Boom Lower Load
One arm extended, fingers closed, thumb pointing upward. Other hand pointing downward and rotating in a small horizontal circle.

Lower Boom Raise Load
One arm extended, fingers closed, thumb pointing downward. Other hand pointing upward and rotating in a small horizontal circle.

Hand Signals for Crane & Hoist

Use Main Hoist
Tap fist on head to indicate Main Hoist, then use other hand signals.

Use Whip Line (auxiliary hoist)
Tap palm of hand on elbow to indicate the Whip Line, then use other hand signals.

Swing
Extend arm and point a finger in the direction of desired boom swing.

Magnet Disconnected
Crane operator extends both arms away from body with both palms up.

Finished with Crane
Place arms above head and cross hands.

Multiple Trolleys
Hold up number of fingers to indicate which trolley signals are to follow. 2 fingers=trolley#2

Hand Signals for Crane & Hoist

Travel (Bridge Travel)
Extend arm forward with hand open and slightly raised. Make a pushing motion in the direction of travel.

Move Slowly
Place signal hand in front of your other motionless hand. Example shown is "Hoist Slowly".

Travel Both Tracks of Crane
Bend arms at elbow, clich fists, and rotate both forearms around each other. Forward or backward by direction of revolving fists.

Travel One Track of Crane
Lock track on side indicated by clinched, raised fist. Bend other arm at elbow, clinch fist, rotate forearm in circular motion. Move track in direction of revolving fist.

Chemistry & Physics

(See Oxide Conversions in GEOLOGY, page 352)

(See also WEIGHTS OF MATERIALS, page 655)

Element Tables

Element Name	Symbol	Atomic Number	Atomic Weight	Valence	Redox Potential
Actinium	Ac	89	(227.0278)	3	
Aluminum	Al	13	26.981538	3	$Al^{3+}=+1.66$
Americium	Am	95	(243.0614)	3,4,5,6	$Am^{3+}=+2.32$
Antimony	Sb	51	121.760	3,5	
Argon	Ar	18	39.948	0	
Arsenic	As	33	74.92160	3,5	
Astatine	At	85	(209.9871)	1,3,5,7	
Barium	Ba	56	137.327	2	$Ba^{2+}=+2.90$
Berkelium	Bk	97	(247.0703)	3,4	
Beryllium	Be	4	9.012182	2	$Be^{2+}=+1.85$
Bismuth	Bi	83	208.98038	3,5	
Bohrium	Bh	107	(262.1229)		(Approved name)
Boron	B	5	10.811	3	
Bromine	Br	35	79.904	1,5	$2Br-,Br_2=-1.066$
Cadmium	Cd	48	112.411	2	$Cd^{2+}=+0.40$
Calcium	Ca	20	40.078	2	$Ca^{2+}=+2.87$
Californium	Cf	98	(251.0796)	3	
Carbon	C	6	12.0107	2,4	
Cassiopeium	Cp	see Lutetium			
Cerium	Ce	58	140.116	3,4	$Ce^{3+}=+2.48$
Cesium	Cs	55	132.90545	1	$Cs=+2.92$
Chlorine	Cl	17	35.4527	1,3,5,7	$2Cl-,Cl_2=-1.36$
Chromium	Cr	24	51.9961	2,3,6	$Cr^{3+}=+0.74$
Cobalt	Co	27	58.93320	2,3	$Co^{2+}=+0.28$
Columbium	Cb	see Niobium			
Copper	Cu	29	63.546	1,2	$Cu^{2+}=-0.34$
Curium	Cm	96	(247.0703)	3	
Dubnium	Db	105	(262.1138)		(Approved name)
Dysprosium	Dy	66	162.50	3	
Einsteinium	Es	99	(252.0827)	3	
Emanation	Em	see Radon			
Erbium	Er	68	167.26	3	
Europium	Eu	63	151.964	2,3	
Fermium	Fm	100	(257.0951)	3	
Fluorine	F	9	18.9984032	1	$2F-,F_2=-2.85$
Francium	Fr	87	(223.0197)	1	
Gadolinium	Gd	64	157.25	3	$Gd^{3+}=+2.4$
Gallium	Ga	31	69.723	3	$Ga^{3+}=+0.53$
Germanium	Ge	32	72.61	4	
Glucinium	Gl	see Berylium			
Gold	Au	79	196.96655	1,3	$Au^{3+}=-1.50$
Hafnium	Hf	72	178.49	4	$Hf^{4+}=+1.70$
Hassium	Hs	108	(265)		(Approved name)

Element Tables

Element Name	Symbol	Atomic Number	Atomic Weight	Valence	Redox Potential
Helium	He	2	4.002602	0	
Holmium	Ho	67	164.93032	3	
Hydrogen	H	1	1.00794	1	$H^+=+2.10$
Illinium	Il	see Promethium			
Indium	In	49	114.818	3	$In^{3+}=+0.34$
Iodine	I	53	126.90447	1,5,7	$2I^-, I_2=-0.54$
Iridium	Ir	77	192.217	2,3,4,6	
Iron	Fe	26	55.845	2,3	$Fe^{2+}=+0.44$
Krypton	Kr	36	83.80	0	
Lanthanum	La	57	138.9055	3	$La^{3+}=+2.52$
Lawrencium	Lr	103	(262.1053)	3	
Lead	Pb	82	207.19	2,4	$Pb^{2+}=+0.13$
Lithium	Li	3	6.941	1	$Li^+=+3.04$
Lutetium	Lu	71	174.967	3	$Lu^{3+}=+2.25$
Magnesium	Mg	12	24.3050	2	$Mg^{2+}=+2.37$
Manganese	Mn	25	54.938049	2,3,4,6,7	$Mn^{2+}=+1.18$
Meitnerium	Mt	109	(266)	(Approved name)	
Mendelevium	Md	101	(256.094)	2,3	
Mercury	Hg	80	200.59	1,2	$2Hg^{2+}=-0.79$
Molybdenum	Mo	42	95.94	2,3,4,5,6	$Mo^{3+}=+0.20$
Neodymium	Nd	60	144.24	3	$Nd^{3+}=+2.44$
Neon	Ne	10	20.1797	0	
Neptunium	Np	93	(237.0482)	3,4,5,6	$Np^{3+}=+1.86$
Nickel	Ni	28	58.6934	2,3	$Ni^{2+}=+0.25$
Niobium	Nb	41	92.90638	3,5	$Nb^{3+}=+1.1$
Niton	Nt	see Radon			
Nitrogen	N	7	14.00674	1,2,3,4,5	
Nobelium	No	102	(259.1009)	2,3	
Osmium	Os	76	190.23	2,3,4,6,8	
Oxygen	O	8	15.9994	2	
Palladium	Pd	46	106.42	2,4,	$Pd^{2+}=-0.99$
Phosphorus	P	15	30.973762	3,4,5	
Platinum	Pt	78	195.078	2,4	$Pt^{2+}=-1.2$
Plutonium	Pu	94	(244.0642)	3,4,5,6	$Pu^{3+}=+2.07$
Polonium	Po	84	(209.9828)	2,4	
Potassium	K	19	39.0983	1	$K^+=+2.925$
Praseodymium	Pr	59	140.90765	3,4	
Promethium	Pm	61	(144.9127)	3	
Protactinium	Pa	91	231.03588	4,5	
Radium	Ra	88	(226.0254)	2	$Ra^{2+}=+2.92$
Radon	Rn	86	(222.0114)	0	
Rhenium	Re	75	186.207	1,2,4,6,7	
Rhodium	Rh	45	102.90550	2,3,4	$Rh^{3+}=-0.8$

Element Tables

Element Name	Symbol	Atomic Number	Atomic Weight	Valence	Redox Potential
Rubidium	Rb	37	85.4678	1	$Rb^+ = +2.92$
Ruthenium	Ru	44	101.07	2,3,4,6,8	
Rutherfordium	Rf	104	(261.1087)	*(Approved name)*	
Samarium	Sm	62	150.36	2,3	$Sm^{3+} = +2.41$
Scandium	Sc	21	44.955910	3	$Sc^{3+} = +2.08$
Seaborgium	Sg	106	(263.1182)	*(Approved name)*	
Selenium	Se	34	78.96	2,4,6	$Se^{2-}Se = +0.78$
Silicon	Si	14	28.0855	4	
Silver	Ag	47	107.8682	1	$Ag^+ = +0.799$
Sodium	Na	11	22.989770	1	$Na^+ = +2.71$
Strontium	Sr	38	87.62	2	$Sr^{2+} = +2.89$
Sulphur	S	16	32.066	2,4,6	$S^{2-}, S = +0.92$
Tantalum	Ta	73	180.9479	5	
Technetium	Tc	43	(97.9072)	4,6,7	
Tellurium	Te	52	127.60	2,4,6	$Te^{2+} = +0.51$
Terbium	Tb	65	158.92534	3,4	
Thallium	Tl	81	204.3833	1,3	$Tl^+ = +0.34$
Thorium	Th	90	232.0381	4	$Th^{4+} = +1.9$
Thulium	Tm	69	168.93421	2,3	
Tin	Sn	50	118.710	2,4	$Sn^{2+} = +0.14$
Titanium	Ti	22	47.867	2,3,4	$Ti^{2+} = +1.63$
Tungsten	W	74	183.84	2,3,4,5,6	
Uranium	U	92	238.0289	3,4,5,6	$U^{3+} = +1.80$
Vanadium	V	23	50.9415	2,3,4,5	$V^{2+} = +1.18$
Wolfram	W		see Tungsten		
Xenon	Xe	54	131.29	0	
Ytterbium	Yb	70	173.04	2,3	
Yttrium	Y	39	88.90585	3	
Zinc	Zn	30	65.398	2	$Zn = +0.76$
Zirconium	Zr	40	91.224	4	$Zr^{4+} = +1.53$

Table of atomic weights based on carbon isotope C^{12}. Numbers in parenthesis represent the mass (Atomic Weight) of the most stable isotope. "Redox Potential" lists the end product (or beginning and end product if two are given) and electrode potential.

"*Approved Name*" is the name approved by vote of the International Union of Pure and Applied Chemistry (IUPAC), August, 1997

Element Properties

Element Name	State	Atomic Number	Density g/cc	Melting Point °C	Boiling Point °C
Actinium		89	10.07	1050	3200
Aluminum		13	2.6989	660.37	2467
Americium		95	13.67	994	2607
Antimony		51	6.618	630.5	1750
Argon	gas	18	1.784	−189.2	−185.7
Argon	liquid	18	1.402(−186°)	−189.2	−185.7
Argon	solid	18	1.65(−223°)	−189.2	−185.7
Arsenic	gray	33	5.73	817@28 atm	613
Arsenic	yellow	33	1.97	358	
Astatine		85		302	337
Barium		56	3.51	725	1640
Berkelium		97	14	1050	
Beryllium		4	1.848	1278	2970
Bismuth		83	9.747	271.3	1560
Boron	amorph.	5	2.37		
Boron	black	5	2.34	2300	2550
Bromine	gas	35	7.59	−7.2	58.78
Bromine	liquid	35	3.12	−7.2	58.78
Cadmium		48	8.65	320.9	765
Calcium		20	1.55	842	1484
Californium		98		900	
Carbon	amorph.	6	1.8-2.1	3550	4827
Carbon	graphite	6	1.9-2.3	3550	4827
Carbon	diamond	6	3.15-3.53	3550	4827
Cerium		58	6.67(25°)	798	3443
Cesium		55	1.873	28.4	671
Chlorine	gas	17	3.214	−100.98	−34.6
Chlorine	liquid	17	1.56(−34°)	−100.98	−34.6
Chromium		24	7.19	1857	2672
Cobalt		27	8.9	1495	2927
Copper		29	8.96	1083	2567
Curium		96	13.51	1345	
Dysprosium		66	8.540(25°)	1412	2561
Einsteinium		99		860	
Erbium		68	9.066(25°)	1529	2863
Europium		63	5.244(25°)	822	1596
Fermium		100		1527	
Fluorine	gas	9	1.696	−219.6	−188.1
Fluorine	liquid	9	1.108(−188°)	−219.6	−188.1
Francium		87		677	27
Gadolinium		64	7.90(25°)	1313	3264
Gallium	liquid	31	6.095(30°)	29.8	2403
Gallium	solid	31	5.9(5°)	29.8	2403
Germanium		32	5.32(25°)	937	2830
Gold		79	19.32	1064	2808
Hafnium		72	13.31	2233	4602

Element Properties

Element Name	State	Atomic Number	Density g/cc	Melting Point °C	Boiling Point °C
Helium	gas	2	0.1785	−272.2 @26atm	−268.9
Helium	liquid	2	0.147(−270.3)	−272.2 @26atm	−268.9
Holmium		67	8.795(25°)	1474	2694
Hydrogen	gas	1	0.08988	−259.34	−252.87
Hydrogen	liquid	1	0.074(−253°)	−259.34	−252.87
Hydrogen	solid	1	70.6(−262)	−259.34	−252.87
Indium		49	7.31	156.6	2080
Iodine	gas	53	11.27	113.5	184.4
Iodine		53	4.93	113.5	184.4
Iridium		77	22.42(17°)	2410	4129
Iron		26	7.87	1535	3000
Krypton	gas	36	3.733	−156.6	−152.3
Krypton	liquid	36	2.155(−152.9)		
Lanthanum		57	6.15(25°)	920	3455
Lawrencium		103		1627	
Lead		82	11.35	327.5	1740
Lithium		3	0.534	180.5	1342
Lithium	liquid	3	0.507(200°)	180.5	1342
Lutetium		71	9.84(25°)	1663	3393
Magnesium		12	1.738	650	1090
Manganese		25	7.43	1246	1962
Mendelevium		101		827	
Mercury	liquid	80	13.546	−38.87	356.58
Molybdenum		42	10.22	2623	4639
Neodymium		60	7.008	1021	3068
Neon	gas	10	0.8999	−248.7	−246.0
Neon	liquid	10	1.207(−246°)	−248.7	−246.0
Neptunium		93	20.25	640	3902
Nickel		28	8.9(25°)	1455	2732
Niobium		41	8.57	2468	4744
Nitrogen	gas	7	1.2506	−209.86	−195.79
Nitrogen	liquid	7	0.808(−196°)	−209.86	−195.79
Nitrogen	solid	7	1.026(−252°)	−209.86	−195.79
Nobelium		102		827	
Osmium		76	22.57	3033	5012
Oxygen	gas	8	1.429	−218.8	−182.95
Oxygen	liquid	8	1.14(−183°)	−218.8	−182.95
Oxygen	solid	8	1.426(−252.5)	−218.8	−182.95
Palladium		46	12.02	1555	2963
Phosphorus	white	15	1.82	44.1	280
Phosphorus	red	15	2.20	590 @43 atm	
Phosphorus	black	15	2.25-2.69		
Phosphorus	violet	15	2.36	590	
Platinum		78	21.45	1772	3827
Plutonium		94	19.84(25°)	641	3232
Polonium		84	9.32	254	962

Element Properties

Element Name	State	Atomic Number	Density g/cc	Melting Point °C	Boiling Point °C
Potassium		19	0.862	63.7	760
Praseodymium		59	6.773	931	3510
Promethium		61	7.264(25°)	1042	3000
Protactinium		91	15.37	1572	
Radium		88	5.0	700	1140
Radon	gas	86	9.73	−71	−61.8
Radon	liquid	86	4.4(−62°)	−71	−61.8
Radon	solid	86	4	−71	−61.8
Rhenium		75	21.02	3180	5596
Rhodium		45	12.41	1964	3695
Rubidium	liquid	37	1.475(39°)	38.89	688
Rubidium	solid	37	1.532	38.89	688
Ruthenium		44	12.41	2334	1450
Samarium		62	7.54(25°)	1072	1791
Scandium		21	2.989	1541	2830
Selenium	amorph.	34	4.28	50	685
Selenium	gray	34	4.79(25°)	217	685
Silicon		14	2.33(25°)	1410	2355
Silver		47	10.5	962	2163
Sodium		11	0.971	97.8	883
Strontium		38	2.54	769	1384
Sulphur	monoclinic	16	1.96	119.0	444.6
Sulphur	rhombic	16	2.07	115.2	444.6
Tantalum		73	16.6	3020	5458
Technetium		43	11.5	2204	4265
Tellurium		52	6.24	449	989
Terbium		65	8.27	1356	3223
Thallium		81	11.85	303	1457
Thorium		90	11.70	1750	4788
Thulium		69	9.321(25°)	1545	1947
Tin	gray	50	5.75	231.9	2270
Tin	white	50	7.31	231.9	2603
Titanium		22	4.54	1660	3287
Tungsten		74	19.3	3410	5660
Uranium		92	18.95	1132	3818
Vanadium		23	6.11(19°)	1890	3380
Xenon	gas	54	5.88	−112	−108
Xenon	liquid	54	3.52(−109°)	−112	−108
Xenon	solid	54	2.7(−140)		
Ytterbium		70	6.977	819	1194
Yttrium		39	4.47(25°)	1523	3337
Zinc		30	7.13(25°)	419.5	907
Zirconium		40	6.056	1852	4409

The elements above are in a "solid" state and density of gases are given in grams/liter measured at 760mm Hg and 0°C and other elements are measured at 20°C (all unless otherwise indicated).

Periodic Table of Elements

IA	IIA		IIIB	IVB	VB	VIB	VIIB	VIII			IB	IIB	IIIA	IVA	VA	VIA	VIIA	VIIIA
1 H																		2 He
3 Li	4 Be												5 B	6 C	7 N	8 O	9 F	10 Ne
11 Na	12 Mg												13 Al	14 Si	15 P	16 S	17 Cl	18 Ar
19 K	20 Ca		21 Sc	22 Ti	23 V	24 Cr	25 Mn	26 Fe	27 Co	28 Ni	29 Cu	30 Zn	31 Ga	32 Ge	33 As	34 Se	35 Br	36 Kr
37 Rb	38 Sr		39 Y	40 Zr	41 Nb	42 Mo	43 Tc	44 Ru	45 Rh	46 Pd	47 Ag	48 Cd	49 In	50 Sn	51 Sb	52 Te	53 I	54 Xe
55 Cs	56 Ba		57 La	72 Hf	73 Ta	74 W	75 Re	76 Os	77 Ir	78 Pt	79 Au	80 Hg	81 Tl	82 Pb	83 Bi	84 Po	85 At	86 Rn
87 Fr	88 Ra		89 Ac	104* Rf	105* Db	106* Sg	107* Bh	108* Hs	109* Mt									

58 Ce	59 Pr	60 Nd	61 Pm	62 Sm	63 Eu	64 Gd	65 Tb	66 Dy	67 Ho	68 Er	69 Tm	70 Yb	71 Lu
90 Th	91 Pa	92 U	93 Np	94 Pu	95 Am	96 Cm	97 Bk	98 Cf	99 Es	100* Fm	101* Md	102* No	103* Lr

*International Union of Pure & Applied Chemistry (IUPAC)
approved element names. August 1997*

pH of Common Acids

Acids (pH < 7)	Normality	pH
Acetic	1 N	2.4
Acetic	0.1N	2.9
Acetic	0.01N	3.4
Alum	0.1N	3.2
Arsenious	Saturated	5.0
Benzoic	0.1N	3.0
Boric	0.1N	5.3
Carbonic	Saturated	3.8
Citric	0.1N	2.1
Formic	0.1N	2.3
Hydrochloric	1 N	0.1
Hydrochloric	0.1N	1.0
Hydrochloric	0.01N	2.0
Hydrocyanic	0.1N	5.1
Hydrogen Sulfide	0.1N	4.1
Lactic	0.1N	2.4
Malic	0.1N	2.2
Nitric	0.1N	1.0
Orthophosphoric	0.1N	1.5
Oxalic	0.1N	1.3
Succinic	0.1N	2.7
Salicylic	Saturated	2.4
Sulfuric	1 N	0.3
Sulfuric	0.1N	1.2
Sulfuric	0.01N	2.1
Sulfurous	0.1N	1.5
Tartaric	0.1N	2.0
Trichloracetic	0.1N	1.2

pH of Common Bases

Bases (pH > 7)	Normality	pH
Ammonia	1 N	11.6
Ammonia	0.1N	11.1
Ammonia	0.01N	10.6
Barbital Sodium	0.1N	9.4
Borax	0.01N	9.2
Calcium Carbonate	Saturated	9.4
Calcium Hydroxide	Saturated	12.4
Ferrous Hydroxide	Saturated	9.5
Lime	Saturated	12.4
Magnesia	Saturated	10.5
Potassium Acetate	0.1N	9.7
Potassium Bicarbonate	0.1N	8.2
Potassium Carbonate	0.1	11.5

pH of Common Bases (cont.)

Bases (pH > 7)	Normality	pH
Potassium Cyanide	0.1N	11.0
Potassium Hydroxide	1 N	14.0
Potassium Hydroxide	0.1N	13.0
Potassium Hydroxide	0.01N	12.0
Sodium Acetate	0.1N	8.9
Sodium Benzoate	0.1N	8.0
Sodium Bicarbonate	0.1N	8.4
Sodium Carbonate	0.1N	11.6
Sodium Hydroxide	1 N	14.0
Sodium Hydroxide	0.1N	13.0
Sodium Hydroxide	0.01N	12.0
Sodium Metasilicate	0.1N	12.6
Sodium Sesquicarbonate	0.1N	10.1
Trisodium Phosphate	0.1N	12.0

pH Indicators

Indicator	Acid Color	Low pH	High pH	Base Color
Methyl violet	yellow	0.0	1.6	blue
Cresol red (1st range)	red	0.0	1.8	yellow
Crystal violet	yellow	0.0	1.8	blue
Malachite green	yellow	0.2	1.8	blue-green
Methyl green	yellow	0.2	1.8	blue
Metanil yellow	red	1.2	2.4	yellow
m-Cresol purple (1st range)	red	1.2	2.8	yellow
Metacresol purple (1st range)	red	1.2	2.8	yellow
Thymol blue (1st range)	red	1.2	2.8	yellow
Orange IV (Tropeolin 00)	red	1.3	3.2	yellow
4-o-Tolylazo-o-toluidine	orange	1.4	2.8	yellow
2,6-Dinitrophenol	colorless	1.7	4.4	yellow
Benzyl orange	red	1.9	3.3	yellow
2,4-Dinitrophenol	colorless	2.0	4.7	yellow
Erythrosin, disodium salt	orange	2.2	3.6	red
Benzopurpurine 48	violet	2.2	4.2	red
p-Dimethylaminoazobenzene	red	2.9	4.0	yellow
Methyl yellow	red	2.9	4.0	yellow
Bromochlorophenol blue	yellow	3.0	4.6	purple
Bromophenol blue	yellow	3.0	4.6	blue
Congo red	blue	3.0	5.0	red
Methyl orange	red	3.1	4.4	orange
Ethyl orange	red	3.4	4.8	yellow
Bromocresol green	yellow	3.8	5.6	blue
Resazurin	orange	3.8	6.4	violet
2,5-Dinitrophenol	colorless	4.0	5.8	yellow

pH Indicators (cont.)

Indicator	Acid Color	Low pH	High pH	Base Color
Methyl red	red	4.2	6.3	yellow
Azolitmin (litmus)	red	4.4	6.6	blue
Alizarin red S	yellow	4.6	6.0	red
Propyl red	red	4.6	6.6	yellow
Chlorophenol red	yellow	4.6	7.0	red
p-Nitrophenol	colorless	4.7	7.9	yellow
Bromophenol red	yellow	4.8	6.8	purple
Bromocresol purple	yellow	5.2	6.8	purple
p-Nitrophenol	colorless	5.4	6.6	yellow
Bromothymol blue	yellow	6.0	7.6	blue
Phenol red	yellow	6.4	8.4	red
m-Nitrophenol	colorless	6.4	8.8	yellow
Brilliant yellow	yellow	6.6	7.8	red
Neutral red	red	6.8	8.0	yellow
Rosolic acid	brown	6.9	8.0	red
Cresol red (2nd range)	yellow	7.0	8.8	red
α-Naphtholphthalein (Geigy)	brown	7.3	8.7	green
Metacresol purple (2nd range)	yellow	7.4	9.0	purple
m-Cresol purple (2nd range)	yellow	7.4	9.2	purple
Orange I (Tropeolin 000 No. 1)	yellow	7.6	8.9	rose
Thymol blue (2nd range)	yellow	8.0	9.6	blue
Phenolphthalein	colorless	8.0	10.0	red
o-Cresolphthalein	colorless	8.2	9.8	red
α-Naphtholphthalein (Lange)	yellow	9.0	11.0	blue
Thymolphthalein	colorless	9.4	10.6	blue
Alizarin yellow GG	yellow	10.0	12.0	orange
β-Naphthol violet	yellow	10.0	12.0	violet
Alizarin yellow R	yellow	10.1	12.2	red
Nitramine	colorless	10.8	13.0	brown
Poirrier blue	blue	11.0	13.0	red
Resorcin yellow (Tropeolin 0)	yellow	11.0	13.0	orange
Benzene sulfonic acid	yellow	11.4	12.6	orange
Indigosulfonic acid	blue	11.4	13.0	yellow
Clayton yellow	yellow	12.2	13.2	amber

pH values are approximate. pH values stated above may vary substantially from one user to another. pH values are affected by illumination, ion strength, and temperature. Values assume a temperature of 25°C (77°F).

Elementary Particles

Particle Name	Lifespan Seconds	Mass MeV	Charge	Spin
Baryons				
Proton	Stable	938.2720	+1	1/2
Antiproton	Stable	938.2720	−1	1/2
Neutron	886.7	939.5653	0	1/2
Antineutron	886.7	939.5653	0	1/2
Lambda hyperon	2.632×10^{-10}	1115.683	0	1/2
Lambda antihyperon	2.632×10^{-10}	1115.683	0	1/2
Positive Sigma	8.018×10^{-9}	1189.37	+1	1/2
Neutral Sigma	7.4×10^{-20}	1192.642	0	1/2
Negative Sigma	1.479×10^{-10}	1197.49	−1	1/2
Neutral Xi	2.9×10^{-10}	1314.83	0	1/2
Negative Xi	1.639×10^{-10}	1321.31	−1	1/2
Negative Omega	8.21×10^{-11}	1672.45	−1	1/2
Gluons				
Red to blue	Stable	0	0	1
Red to green	Stable	0	0	1
Green to red	Stable	0	0	1
Green to blue	Stable	0	0	1
Blue to red	Stable	0	0	1
Blue to green	Stable	0	0	1
Neutral (1)	Stable	0	0	1
Neutral (2)	Stable	0	0	1
Leptons				
Electron Neutrino	Stable	3×10^{-3}	0	1/2
Electron Antineutrino	Stable	3×10^{-3}	0	1/2
Muon Neutrino	Stable	<0.19	0	1/2
Muon Antineutrino	Stable	<0.19	0	1/2
Tau Neutrino	Stable	<18.2	0	1/2
Tau Antineutrino	Stable	<18.2	0	1/2
Electron	Stable	0.51099	−1	1/2
Positron	Stable	0.51099	+1	1/2
Muon	2.197×10^{-6}	105.658	−1	1/2
Antimuon	2.197×10^{-6}	105.658	+1	1/2
Tau	2.906×10^{-13}	1777.03	−1	1/2
Antitau	2.906×10^{-13}	1777.03	+1	1/2

Elementary Particles

Particle Name	Lifespan Seconds	Mass MeV	Charge	Spin
Mesons				
Positive Pion	2.6×10^{-8}	139.570	+1	0
Negative Pion	2.6×10^{-8}	139.570	−1	0
Neutral Pion	8.4×10^{-17}	134.977	0	0
Positive Kaon	1.239×10^{-8}	493.677	+1	0
Neutral Kaon–short	8.935×10^{-11}	497.672	0	0
Neutral Kaon–long	5.17×10^{-8}	497.672	0	0
Negative Kaon	1.239×10^{-8}	493.677	−1	0
Eta		547.30	0	0
Positive B	16.53×10^{-13}	5279.0	+1	0
Negative B	16.53×10^{-13}	5279.0	−1	0
Neutral B	15.48×10^{-13}	5279.4	0	0
Positive D	10.51×10^{-13}	1869.3	+1	0
Negative D	10.51×10^{-13}	1869.3	−1	0
Neutral D	4.126×10^{-13}	1864.5	0	0
Neutral Kaon		497.672	0	0
J/psi	10^{-20}	3096.87	0	1
Quarks				
Up	Stable	1 to 5	+2/3	1/2
Down	Stable	3 to 9	−1/3	1/2
Strange	Stable	75 to 170	−1/3	1/2
Charm		1150 to 1350	+2/3	1/2
Top		174300	+2/3	1/2
Bottom	$<5 \times 10^{-12}$	4000 to 4400	−1/3	1/2
Gauge & Higgs Bosons				
Photon	Stable	0	0	1
Positive W	10^{-20}	80419	+1	1
Negative W	10^{-20}	80419	−1	1
Neutral Z	10^{-20}	91188	0	1
Gluon		0	0	1

Note that there are many more subatomic particles than those listed in this table, but the above list contains most of the "common" particles. For detailed information see references such as the *Handbook of Chemistry and Physics* by The Chemical Rubber Company.

Radioisotope Half Lives

Isotope	Half Life	Isotope	Half Life
^{110}Ag	24.6 seconds	^{99}Mo	2.7476 days
^{241}Am	432.2 years	^{22}Na	2.605 years
^{243}Am	7370 years	^{24}Na	14.96 hours
^{198}Au	6.18 days	^{63}Ni	100 years
^{133}Ba	10.53 years	^{237}Np	2.14 million yrs
^{140}Ba	12.75 days	^{32}P	14.28 days
^{7}Be	53.28 days	^{210}Pb	22.6 years
^{210}Bi	5.01 days	^{103}Pd	16.99 days
^{82}Br	35.304 hours	^{109}Pd	13.43 hours
^{14}C	5715 years	^{147}Pm	2.6234 years
^{45}Ca	162.7 days	^{210}Po	138.38 days
^{109}Cd	462.0 days	^{144}Pr	17.28 minute
^{144}Ce	284.6 days	^{232}Pu	34.0 minutes
^{36}Cl	301,000 years	^{233}Pu	20.9 minutes
^{242}Cm	162.8 days	^{234}Pu	8.8 hours
^{244}Cm	18.11 years	^{235}Pu	25.3 minutes
^{60}Co	5.271 years	^{236}Pu	2.87 years
^{51}Cr	27.70 days	^{237}Pu	45.2 days
^{134}Cs	2.065 years	^{238}Pu	87.74 years
^{137}Cs	30.3 years	^{239}Pu	24,110 years
^{64}Cu	12.701 hours	^{240}Pu	6,537 years
^{55}Fe	2.73 years	^{241}Pu	14.4 years
^{59}Fe	44.51 days	^{242}Pu	375,000 years
^{72}Ga	14.10 hours	^{243}Pu	4.956 hours
^{68}Ge	270.8 days	^{244}Pu	82 million years
^{3}H	12.32 years	^{245}Pu	10.5 hours
^{203}Hg	46.61 days	^{246}Pu	10.85 days
^{131}I	8.04 days	^{86}Rb	18.65 days
^{115}In	440 trillion years	^{87}Rb	48.8 billion yrs
^{192}Ir	73.83 days	^{102}Rh	2.9 years
^{40}K	1.26 billion years	^{106}Rh	29.9 seconds
^{42}K	12.36 hrs	^{106}Ru	1.020 years
^{85}Kr	10.73 years	^{35}S	87.2 days
^{140}La	40.272 hours	^{125}Sb	2.758 years
^{54}Mn	312.2 days	^{46}Sc	83.81 days

Radioisotope Half Lives (cont.)

Isotope	Half Life	Isotope	Half Life
^{75}Se	119.78 days	^{232}U	68.9 years
^{32}Si	160 years	^{233}U	159,000 years
^{113}Sn	115.1 days	^{234}U	245,000 years
^{89}Sr	50.52 days	^{235}U	704 million years
^{90}Sr	29.1 years	^{236}U	23.4 million years
^{182}Ta	114.43 days	^{237}U	6.75 days
^{99}Tc	213,000 years	^{238}U	4.46 billion years
^{123}Te	13 trillion yrs	^{239}U	23.5 minutes
^{201}Tl	72.912 hours	^{240}U	14.1 hours
^{170}Tm	128.6 days	^{242}U	16.8 minutes
^{222}U	1 microsecond		
^{225}U	0.08 seconds	(See more U below)	
^{226}U	0.5 seconds		
^{227}U	1.1 minutes	^{50}V	140,000 trillion yrs
^{228}U	9.1 minutes	^{90}Y	2.67 days
^{229}U	58 minutes	^{65}Zn	243.8 days
^{230}U	20.8 days	^{95}Zr	64.02 days
^{231}U	4.2 days		

URANIUM 238 DECAY SERIES

Rnuclide	Element	Half–Life	Energy (MeV)
^{238}U	Uranium	4.46 billion yrs	4.1-4.2 Alpha
^{234}Th	Thorium	24 days	0.3 Beta
^{234}Pa	Protactinium	6.69 hours	2.2 Beta
^{234}U	Uranium	245,000 years	4.7-4.8 Alpha
^{230}Th	Thorium	80,000 years	4.6-4.7 Alpha
^{226}Ra	Radium	1,600 years	4.6-4.8 Alpha
^{222}Rn	Radon	3.82 days	5.5 Alpha
^{218}Po	Polonium	3.05 minutes	6.0 Alpha
^{214}Pb	Lead	26.8 minutes	0.7-1.0 Beta
^{214}Bi	Bismuth	19.7 minutes	3.3 Beta
^{214}Po	Polonium	0.16 milliseconds	7.7 Alpha
^{210}Pb	Lead	22.6 years	0.1 Beta
^{210}Bi	Bismuth	5 days	1.2 Beta
^{210}Po	Polonium	138 days	5.3 Alpha
^{206}Pb	Lead	Stable	

Galvanic Series of Metals in Seawater

Cathode end, Noble metals	Platinum
	Gold
	Graphite
	Titanium
	Silver
	Chlorimet 3 (62 Ni + 18 Cr + 18 Mo) Hastelloy C (62 Ni + 17 Cr + 15 Mo)
	18-8 Mo stainless steel - passive 18-8 Stainless steel - passive Chromium stainless steel 11 to 30% Cr - passive
	Inconel (80 Ni + 13 Cr + 7 Fe) - passive Nickel - passive
	Silver solder
	Monel (70 Ni + 30 Cu) Cupronickels (60 to 90 Cu + 40 to 10 Ni) Bronzes (Cu + Sn) Copper Brasses (Cu + Zn)
	Chlorimet 2 (66 Ni + 32 Mo + 1 Fe) Hastelloy B (60 Ni + 30 Mo + 6 Fe + 1 Mn)
	Inconel - active Nickel - active
	Tin
	Lead
	Lead-Tin solders
	Hastelloy A
	18-8 Mo stainless steel - active 18-8 stainless steel - active
	Ni-resist - high Ni cast iron
	Chromium stainless steel, 13% Cr - active
	Cast iron Steel or iron
	2024 aluminum (4.5 Cu + 1.5 Mg + 0.6 Mn)
	Alclad 35
	Cadmium
	Aluminum, commercially pure - 1100
Anode end, Active metals	Zinc
	Magnesium and magnesium alloys

Computers

Megabytes and Kilobytes

1 kilobyte = 2^{10} bytes = exactly 1,024 bytes
1 megabyte = 2^{20} bytes = exactly 1,048,576 bytes
1 gigabyte = 2^{30} bytes = exactly 1,073,741,824 bytes
1 terabyte = 2^{40} bytes = exactly 1,099,511,627,776 bytes
1 petabyte = 2^{50} bytes = exactly 1,125,899,906,842,620 bytes
1 byte = 8 bits (bit is short for binary digit)
8 bit computers move data in 1 byte chunks
16 bit computers move data in 2 byte chunks
32 bit computers move data in 4 byte chunks
64 bit computers move data in 8 byte chunks

Computer ASCII Codes

The following ASCII (**A**merican **S**tandard **C**ode for **I**nformation **I**nterchange) tables are used by most of the microcomputer industry. The codes occur in two sets: the "low–bit" set, from Dec 0 to Dec 127, and the "high–bit" set, from Dec 128 to Dec 255. The "low–bit" set is standard for almost all microcomputers but the "high–bit" set varies between the different computer brands. For instance, in the case of Apple computers and Epson printers, the "high–bit" set repeats the "low–bit" set except that the alphanumeric characters are italic. In the case of IBM and many other MSDOS systems, the "high–bit" set is composed of foreign language and box drawing characters and mathematic symbols.

Hex	Dec	Description	Abbr	Character	Control
00	0	Null	Null		Control @
01	1	Start Heading	SOH	☺	Control A
02	2	Start of Text	STX	♥ ☻	Control B
03	3	End of Text	ETX	♥ ♦	Control C
04	4	End Transmit	EOT		Control D
05	5	Enquiry	ENQ	♣ ♠	Control E
06	6	Acknowledge	ACK		Control F
07	7	Beep	BEL	•	Control G
08	8	Back space	BS	■	Control H
09	9	Horizontal Tab	HT	○	Control I
0A	10	Line Feed	LF	◙	Control J
0B	11	Vertical Tab	VT	♂	Control K
0C	12	Form Feed	FF	♀	Control L
0D	13	Carriage Ret.	CR	♪	Control M
0E	14	Shift Out	SO	♫	Control N
0F	15	Shift In	SI	☼	Control O
10	16	Device Link Esc	DLE	►	Control P
11	17	Dev Cont 1 X-ON	DC1	◄	Control Q
12	18	Dev Control 2	DC2	↕	Control R
13	19	Dev Cont 3 X-OFF	DC3	‼	Control S
14	20	Dev Control 4	DC4	¶	Control T
15	21	Negative Ack	NAK	§	Control U
16	22	Synchronous Idle	SYN		Control V
17	23	End Trans Block	ETB	↨	Control W
18	24	Cancel	CAN	↑	Control X
19	25	End Medium	EM	↓	Control Y
1A	26	Substitute	SUB	→	Control Z
1B	27	Escape	ESC	←	Control [

Computer ASCII Codes

Hex	Dec	Description	Abbr	Character	Control
1C	28	Cursor Right	FS	└	Control /
1D	29	Cursor Left	GS	↔	Control]
1E	30	Cursor Up	RS	▲	Control ^
1F	31	Cursor Down	US	▼	Control –

Hex	Dec	Character	Description
20	32		Space (SP)
21	33	!	Exclamation Point
22	34	"	Double Quote
23	35	#	Number sign
24	36	$	Dollar sign
25	37	%	Percent
26	38	&	Ampersand
27	39	'	Apostrophe
28	40	(	Left parenthesis
29	41	)	Right parenthesis
2A	42	*	Asterisk
2B	43	+	Plus sign
2C	44	,	Comma
2D	45	–	Minus sign
2E	46	.	Period
2F	47	/	Right or Front slash
30	48	0	Zero
31	49	1	One
32	50	2	Two
33	51	3	Three
34	52	4	Four
35	53	5	Five
36	54	6	Six
37	55	7	Seven
38	56	8	Eight
39	57	9	Nine
3A	58	:	Colon
3B	59	;	Semicolon
3C	60	<	Less than
3D	61	=	Equal sign
3E	62	>	Greater than
3F	63	?	Question mark
40	64	@	"at" symbol

Computer ASCII Codes

Hex	Dec	Character	Description
41	65	A	
42	66	B	
43	67	C	
44	68	D	
45	69	E	
46	70	F	
47	71	G	
48	72	H	
49	73	I	
4A	74	J	
4B	75	K	
4C	76	L	
4D	77	M	
4E	78	N	
4F	79	O	
50	80	P	
51	81	Q	
52	82	R	
53	83	S	
54	84	T	
55	85	U	
56	86	V	
57	87	W	
58	88	X	
59	89	Y	
5A	90	Z	
5B	91	[	Right bracket
5C	92	\	Left or Back Slash
5D	93	]	Left bracket
5E	94	^	Caret
5F	95	_	Underline
60	96	`	Accent
61	97	a	
62	98	b	
63	99	c	
64	100	d	
65	101	e	
66	102	f	
67	103	g	

Computer ASCII Codes

Hex	Dec	Standard Character	Description
68	104	h	
69	105	i	
6A	106	j	
6B	107	k	
6C	108	l	
6D	109	m	
6E	110	n	
6F	111	o	
70	112	p	
71	113	q	
72	114	r	
73	115	s	
74	116	t	
75	117	u	
76	118	v	
77	119	w	
78	120	x	
79	121	y	
7A	122	z	
7B	123	{	Left brace
7C	124	l	Vertical line
7D	125	}	Right brace
7E	126	~	Tilde
7F	127	DEL	Delete

Hex	Dec	Standard Character	IBM Set	Standard Description
80	128	Null	Ç	Null
81	129	SOH	ü	Start Heading
82	130	STX	é	Start of Text
83	131	ETX	â	End of Text
84	132	EOT	ä	End Transmit
85	133	ENQ	à	Enquiry
86	134	ACK	å	Acknowledge
87	135	BEL	ç	Beep
88	136	BS	ê	Back Space
89	137	HT	ë	Horiz Tab
8A	138	LF	è	Line Feed

Computer ASCII Codes

Hex	Dec	Standard Character	IBM Set	Standard Description
8B	139	VT	ï	Vertical Tab
8C	140	FF	î	Form Feed
8D	141	CR	ì	Carriage Return
8E	142	SO	Ä	Shift Out
8F	143	SI	Å	Shift In
90	144	DLE	É	Device Link Esc
91	145	DC1	æ	Device Cont 1 X–ON
92	146	DC2	Æ	Device Control 2
93	147	DC3	ô	Device Cont 3 X–OFF
94	148	DC4	ö	Device Control 4
95	149	NAK	ò	Negative Ack
96	150	SYN	û	Synchronous Idle
97	151	ETB	ù	End Transmit Block
98	152	CAN	ÿ	Cancel
99	153	EM	Ö	End Medium
9A	154	SUB	Ü	Substitute
9B	155	ESC	¢	Escape
9C	156	FS	£	Cursor Right
9D	157	GS	¥	Cursor Left
9E	158	RS	Pt	Cursor Up
9F	159	US	ƒ	Cursor Down
A0	160	Space	á	Space
A1	161	!	í	Italic Exclamation point
A2	162	"	ó	Italic Double quote
A3	163	#	ú	Italic Number sign
A4	164	$	ñ	Italic Dollar sign
A5	165	%	Ñ	Italic Percent
A6	166	&	ª	Italic Ampersand
A7	167	'	º	Italic Apostrophe
A8	168	(	¿	Italic Left parenthesis
A9	169	)	⌐	Italic Right parenthesis
AA	170	*	¬	Italic asterisk
AB	171	+	½	Italic plus sign
AC	172	,	¼	Italic comma
AD	173	–	¡	Italic minus sign
AE	174	.	«	Italic period
AF	175	/	»	Italic right slash
B0	176	0		Italic Zero
B1	177	1		Italic One

Computer ASCII Codes

Hex	Dec	Standard Character	IBM Set	Standard Description
B2	178	*2*		Italic Two
B3	179	*3*		Italic Three
B4	180	*4*		Italic Four
B5	181	*5*		Italic Five
B6	182	*6*		Italic Six
B7	183	*7*		Italic Seven
B8	184	*8*		Italic Eight
B9	185	*9*		Italic Nine
BA	186	*:*		Italic colon
BB	187	*;*		Italic semicolon
BC	188	*<*		Italic less than
BD	189	*=*		Italic equal
BE	190	*>*		Italic greater than
BF	191	*?*		Italic question mark
C0	192	*@*		Italic "at" symbol
C1	193	*A*		Italic A
C2	194	*B*		Italic B
C3	195	*C*		Italic C
C4	196	*D*		Italic D
C5	197	*E*		Italic E
C6	198	*F*		Italic F
C7	199	*G*		Italic G
C8	200	*H*		Italic H
C9	201	*I*		Italic I
CA	202	*J*		Italic J
CB	203	*K*		Italic K
CC	204	*L*		Italic L
CD	205	*M*		Italic M
CE	206	*N*		Italic N
CF	207	*O*		Italic O
D0	208	*P*		Italic P
D1	209	*Q*		Italic Q
D2	210	*R*		Italic R
D3	211	*S*		Italic S
D4	212	*T*		Italic T
D5	213	*U*		Italic U
D6	214	*V*		Italic V
D7	215	*W*		Italic W
D8	216	*X*		Italic X

Computers

Computer ASCII Codes

Hex	Dec	Standard Character	IBM Set	Description
D9	217	Y	⌐	Italic Y
DA	218	Z	⌐	Italic Z
DB	219	[	■	Italic left bracket
DC	220	\	■	Italic left or back slash
DD	221	]	▌	Italic right bracket
DE	222	^	▐	Italic caret
DF	223	_	▀	Italic underline
E0	224	`	α	Italic accent / alpha
E1	225	a	β	Italic a / beta
E2	226	b	Γ	Italic b / gamma
E3	227	c	π	Italic c / pi
E4	228	d	Σ	Italic d / sigma
E5	229	e	σ	Italic e / sigma
E6	230	f	μ	Italic f / mu
E7	231	g	γ	Italic g / gamma
E8	232	h	Φ	Italic h / phi
E9	233	i	θ	Italic i / theta
EA	234	j	Ω	Italic j / omega
EB	235	k	δ	Italic k / delta
EC	236	l	∞	Italic l / infinity
ED	237	m	Ø	Italic m / slashed zero
EE	238	n	∈	Italic n
EF	239	o	∩	Italic o
F0	240	p	≡	Italic p
F1	241	q	±	Italic q
F2	242	r	≥	Italic r
F3	243	s	≤	Italic s
F4	244	t	⌠	Italic t
F5	245	u	⌡	Italic u
F6	246	v	÷	Italic v
F7	247	w	≈	Italic w
F8	248	x	°	Italic x
F9	249	y	•	Italic y
FA	250	z	•	Italic z
FB	251	{	√	Italic left bracket
FC	252	|	^{n}	Italic vertical line
FD	253	}	2	Italic right bracket
FE	254	~		Italic tilde
FF	255	Blank	Blank	Blank

Constants

Constant Symbol Value

Constant	Symbol	Value
Acceleration due to gravity	g	32.174049 ft/sec²
		9.80665 m/sec²
		980.665 cm/sec²
		386.08858 in/sec²
		21.936831 miles/hr sec
Air, density @ 0°C, 760mm Hg		1.29274 kg/m³
Atomic Mass Unit, unified	u	1.66053873 × 10⁻²⁷ kg
Astronomical unit	AU	149.59787 × 10⁶ km
Atomic mass constant, unified	m_u	1.66053873 × 10⁻²⁷ kg
Atomic specific heat constant	h/k	4.799215664 × 10⁻¹¹ sec K⁻¹
Avogadro constant	N_A	6.02214199 × 10²³ mol⁻¹
Barn Cross Section		10⁻²⁸ cm²
Bohr Magneton	μ_B	9.27400899 × 10⁻²⁴ J T⁻¹
Bohr radius	a_o	5.291772083 × 10⁻⁹ cm
Equation for above		$\alpha / 4 \pi R_\infty$
Boltzmann constant	k	1.3806503 × 10⁻²³ J K⁻¹
Classical electron radius	r_e	2.817940285 × 10⁻¹⁵ m
Compton wavelength	λ_c	2.426310215 × 10⁻¹² m
Earth, equatorial radius		6378.137 km, 3963.16 mi
Earth, polar radius		6356.752km, 3949.90 mi
Earth, mass	M	5.9736 × 10²⁴ kg
		6.585 × 10²¹ tons
Earth, mean density		344.3 lb / ft³ (5515 kg/m³)
Electric field constant	ε_o	8.854187817 × 10⁻¹²F m⁻¹
(also known as Permittivity of free space)		
Equation for above		$1 / \mu_o c^2$
Electron, Atomic mass	Nm	5.485794249 × 10⁻⁴ u
Electron charge to mass ratio	$-e/m_e$	-1.758820174 × 10¹¹C kg⁻¹
(also known as Electron specific charge)		
Electron, magnetic moment	μ_e	-9.28476362 ×10⁻²⁴ J T⁻¹
Electron mass	m_e	9.10938188 × 10⁻³¹ kg
Electron volt	eV	1.60217215 × 10⁻¹⁹J

Constant Symbol Value

Constant	Symbol	Value
Elementary charge	e	$1.602176462 \times 10^{-19}$ C
Euler's constant	γ	0.577215664901532860606
Faraday constant	F	9.64853415×10^{4} C mol^{-1}
Gas constant, Universal	R	8.314510 J K^{-1}mol^{-1}
	R	8.20578×10^{-2} l atm/K mole
	R	1545.33 lbf ft / lb mole °R
Golden Ratio	ϕ	1.61803398874989484820458683465
Gravitational constant	G	6.67259×10^{-11} m^{3} kg^{-1}s^{-2}
Hydrogen, Atomic mass	H	1.007825035 u
Hydrogen atom, mass		1.673534×10^{-24} g
Ice–point temperature	T_{ice}	2.731500×10^{2} K
Impedance of free space	Z_o	376.731 ohms
Light, speed of in a vacuum	C_o	2.99792458×10^{8} m/sec
	C_o	186,282.397 miles/sec
Logarithmic constant	e	2.71828182845904523536028747 1352
Loschmidt's constant	n_o	2.6867775×10^{25} m^{-3}
Magnetic field constant	μ_o	$1.2566370614 \times 10^{-6}$ H/m
(also known as Permeability of a vacuum)		
Equation for above		$4\pi 10^{-7}$ N A^{-2}
Mercury, density @ 0°C		1.359508×10^{4} kg/m^{3}
Neutron mass	m_n	$1.67492716 \times 10^{-27}$ kg
Parsec	pc	2.062648×10^{5} AU
Permeability of free space	μ_o	$12.566370614 \times 10^{-7}$ N A^{-2}
Permittivity of free space	ε_o	$8.854187817 \times 10^{-12}$ F/m
Pi (ratio circle circum/diameter)	π	3.14159265358979323846264338327950288419716939937511
	2π	6.283185306
	π^2	9.86960440108935861883

Physical & Math Constants 135

Constant Symbol Value

Pi (ratio circle circum/diameter) .... $\sqrt{\pi}$	1.772453851
$\pi / 4$	0.785398163
Planck constant .... h	$6.62606876 \times 10^{-34}$ J s
	$6.62606876 \times 10^{-27}$ erg sec
1st radiation constant..................... c_1	$3.74177107 \times 10^{-16}$ W m^{-2}
2nd radiation constant .... c_2	1.4387752×10^{-2} m K
Proton, Atomic mass .... Nm$_p$ ...	1.007276470 u
Proton mass .... m_p	$1.67262158 \times 10^{-27}$ kg
Proton, Compton wavelength ...... $\lambda_{c,p}$ ...	$1.321409847 \times 10^{-15}$ m
Quantum charge ratio .... h/e	$4.135667273 \times 10^{15}$ J s/C
Rydberg constant, infinite mass..... R∞	$1.0973731568549 \times 10^{7}$ m^{-1}
Sound, velocity in dry air @ 0°C	331.45 m/sec
	1087.4 ft/sec
	741.4 miles/hour
Sound, velocity in distilled water @ 20°C...	1482.36 m/sec
	4863.3858 ft/sec
Stefan-Boltzmann Constant.......... σ	5.670400×10^{-8} W m^{-2}K^{-4}
Vacuum permeability .... μ_o......	$4\pi \times 10^{-7}$ N A^{-2}
Water, density @ 3.98°C...........................	999.9750 kg m^{-3}
	0.03613 lb/in^3
	62.43 lb/ft^3
Water, heat of fusion @ 0°C	79.72 cal/g
Water, heat of vaporization @ 100°C........	539.056 cal/g
Water, viscosity @ 20°C	1.002 centipoise
	0.01002 dyne sec/cm^2
Wavelength, krypton 86 orange-red line ..0.605780211 μm
Wien displacement constant........ b	2.8977686×10^{-3} m K
Zeeman displacement .... μ_1/hc....	
	4.668583×10^{-5} cm^{-1}gauss^{-1}

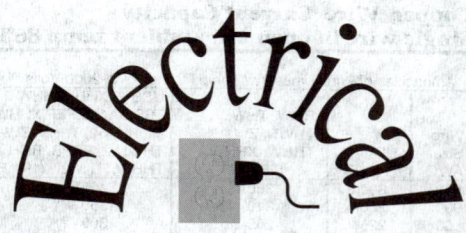

Electrical

Copper Wire Current Capacity
Single wire in open air, ambient temp 86°F

Ampacities of Wire Types (w/ Temp Rating) @ 0–2000 Volts

Wire Size AWG	TW UF (140°F)	RHW, THW, THWN, ZW THHW, XHHW (167°F)	USE-2, XHH, XHHW-2 TBS,SA,SIS,FEP,XHHW MI, RHW-2, THHN, ZW-2 THWN-2, FEPB, RHH THHW,THW-2 (194°F)
0000	300	360	405
000	260	310	350
00	225	265	300
0	195	230	260
1	165	195	220
2	140	170	190
3	120	145	165
4	105	125	140
6	80	95	105
8	60	70	80
10	40	50	55
12	30	35	40
14	25	30	35
16	–	–	24
18	–	–	18

Note: Type **TW** is the most common for house wiring. **TW** is for dry or wet conditions and is covered with a single layer of plastic.

If the ambient temperature[1] is over 86°F (30°C), then the following corrections should be applied by multiplying the above ampacities by the correction factor below.

Ambient[1] Temp °F	Ampacity Correction for above Wire types		
	140°F	167°F	194°F
96-104	0.82	0.88	0.91
105-113	0.71	0.82	0.87
114-122	0.58	0.75	0.82
123-131	0.41	0.67	0.76
132-140	...	0.58	0.71
141-158	...	0.33	0.58
159-176	...	...	0.41

NOTE: The information on pages 138 and 139 has been extracted from the National Electrical Code ®, National Fire Protection Association, Quincy, Massachusetts 02269, Copyright 2005 and does not represent the complete code.

Copper Wire Current Capacity
Three wires in cable, ambient temp 86°F

Ampacities of Wire Types (w/ Temp Rating) @ 0–2000 Volts

Wire Size AWG	TW UF (140°F)	RHW, THHW, ZW, THWN XHHW, THW, USE (167°F)	USE-2, XHH, XHHW-2 TBS,SA,SIS,FEP,XHHW MI, RHW-2, THHN, ZW-2 THWN-2, FEPB, RHH THHW,THW-2 (194°F)
0000	195	230	260
000	165	200	225
00	145	175	195
0	125	150	170
1	110	130	150
2	95	115	130
3	85	100	110
4	70	85	95
6	55	65	75
8	40	50	55
10	30	35	40
12	25	25	30
14	20	20	25
16	–	–	18
18	–	–	14

Note: All notes on ambient temperature and TW types on the previous page also apply to this Three Wire section.

Flexible Cords and Cables
Current Capacities

Wire Size AWG	Current Capacity in Amps for Wire Types: C,E,EO,ET,ETLB,ETP,ETT,PD,S,SE,SEO,SEOOW,SEOW,SEW,SJ, SJE,SJEO,SJEOOW,SJEOW,SJEW,SJO,SJOO,SJOOW,SJOW, SJT,SJTO,SJTOO,SJTOOW,SJTOW,SJTW,SO,SOO,SOOW,SOW, SP-1,SP-2,SP-3,SPE-1,SPE-2,SPE-3,SPT-1,SPT-1W,SPT-2, SPT-2W,SPT-3,SRD,SRDE,SRDT,ST,STO,STOO,STOOW,STOW, SV,SVE,SVEO,SVO,SVOO,SVT,SVTO,SVTOO	
	2 Conductor	3 Conductor
10	30	25
12	25	20
14	18	15
16	13	10
18	10	7

Note: In all Copper Wire Types listed on pages 138 and 139 overcurrent protection should not exceed 15 amps for 14 AWG, 20 amps for 12 AWG, and 30 amps for 10 AWG. This is not true if specifically permitted elsewhere in the Code.

Aluminum Wire Amp Capacity
Single wire in open air, ambient temp 86°F

Ampacities of Wire Types (w/ Temp Rating) @ 0–2000 Volts

Wire Size AWG	UF TW (140°F)	RHW THW, THWN XHHW, THHW (167°F)	THWN-2, XHH, USE-2 TBS, SA, THHW, SIS, RHH, THW-2, THHN, XHHW, RHW-2 XHHW-2, ZW-2 (194°F)
500kcmil	405	485	545
400kcmil	355	425	480
300kcmil	290	350	395
0000	235	280	315
000	200	240	275
00	175	210	235
0	150	180	205
1	130	155	175
2	110	135	150
3	95	115	130
4	80	100	110
6	60	75	80
8	45	55	60
10	35	40	40
12	25	30	35

Note: Type **TW** is the most common for house wiring. **TW** is for dry or wet conditions and is covered with a single layer of plastic.
This table also applies to copper-clad aluminum
If the ambient[1] temperature is over 86°F (30°C), then the following corrections should be applied by multiplying the above ampacities by the correction factor below. kcmil=1000 circular mil

Ambient[1] Temp °F	Ampacity Correction for above Wire Types 140°F	167°F	194°F
96-104	0.82	0.88	0.91
105-113	0.71	0.82	0.87
114-122	0.58	0.75	0.82
123-131	0.41	0.67	0.76
132-140	...	0.58	0.71
141-158	...	0.33	0.58
159-176	...	...	0.41

NOTE: The information on pages 140 and 141 has been extracted from the National Electrical Code ®, National Fire Protection Association, Quincy, Massachusetts 02269, Copyright 2005 and does not represent the complete code.

[1] Ambient temperature is the temperature of the material (air, earth, etc) surrounding the wire.

Aluminum Wire Amp Capacity
Three wires in cable, ambient temp 86°F

Ampacities of Wire Types (w/ Temp Rating) @ 0–2000 Volts

Wire Size AWG	UF TW (140°F)	RHW, USE THW, THWN XHHW, THHW (167°F)	THWN-2, XHH, USE-2 TBS, SA, THHW, SIS, RHH, THW-2, THHN, XHHW, RHW-2 XHHW-2, ZW-2 (194°F)
500kcmil	260	310	350
400kcmil	225	270	305
300kcmil	190	230	255
0000	150	180	205
000	130	155	175
00	115	135	150
0	100	120	135
1	85	100	115
2	75	90	100
3	65	75	85
4	55	65	75
6	40	50	60
8	30	40	45
10	25	30	35
12	20	20	25

Note: All notes on ambient temperature and TW types on the previous page also apply to this Three Wire section. kcmil=1000 circular mil

This table also applies to copper-clad aluminum

Current Adjustment for More Than 3 Wires in a Cable

Number of Conductors	Percentage of amperage value listed in amperage tables on the previous 4 pages.
4 to 6	80%
7 to 9	70%
10 to 20	50%
21 to 30	45%
31 to 40	40%
over 41	35%

Basically, the above table reflects the rule that the higher the temperature (more wires=higher temperature) the lower the current carrying capacity of the wire.

NOTE: In all Aluminum and Copper Clad Aluminum Wire Types listed on pages 140 and 141 overcurrent protection should not exceed 15 amps for 12 AWG and 25 amps for 10 AWG. This is not true if specifically permitted elsewhere in the Code.

Copper Wire Resistance

Gauge A.W.G.*	Feet per Ohm @ 77°F	Ohms per 1000 ft @ 77°F	Feet per Ohm @ 149°F	Ohms per 1000 ft @ 149°F
0000	20000	0.050	17544	0.057
000	15873	0.063	13699	0.073
00	12658	0.079	10870	0.092
0	10000	0.100	8621	0.116
1	7936	0.126	6849	0.146
2	6289	0.159	5435	0.184
3	4975	0.201	4310	0.232
4	3953	0.253	3425	0.292
5	3135	0.319	2710	0.369
6	2481	0.403	2151	0.465
7	1968	0.508	1706	0.586
8	1560	0.641	1353	0.739
9	1238	0.808	1073	0.932
10	980.4	1.02	847.5	1.18
11	781.3	1.28	675.7	1.48
12	617.3	1.62	534.8	1.87
13	490.2	2.04	423.7	2.36
14	387.6	2.58	336.7	2.97
15	307.7	3.25	266.7	3.75
16	244.5	4.09	211.4	4.73
17	193.8	5.16	167.8	5.96
18	153.6	6.51	133.2	7.51
19	121.9	8.21	105.5	9.48
20	96.2	10.4	84.0	11.9
21	76.3	13.1	66.2	15.1
22	60.6	16.5	52.6	19.0
23	48.1	20.8	41.7	24.0
24	38.2	26.2	33.1	30.2
25	30.3	33.0	26.2	38.1
26	24.0	41.6	20.8	48.0
27	19.0	52.5	16.5	60.6
28	15.1	66.2	13.1	76.4
29	12.0	83.4	10.4	96.3
30	9.5	105	8.3	121
31	7.5	133	6.5	153
32	6.0	167	5.2	193
33	4.7	211	4.1	243
34	3.8	266	3.3	307
35	3.0	335	2.6	387
36	2.4	423	2.0	488
37	1.9	533	1.6	616
38	1.5	673	1.3	776
39	1.2	848	1.0	979
40	0.93	1070	0.81	1230

* American Wire Gauge (formerly Brown & Sharp)

Standard Copper Wire Specs

Gauge A.W.G	Diameter in mils (1000th in)	Diameter Millimeters	Area in Circular Mils	Weight Lbs per 1000 feet	Turns / inch Enamel
0000	460.0	11.684	212000	641.0	2.2
000	410.0	10.414	168000	508.0	2.4
00	365.0	9.271	133000	403.0	2.7
0	325.0	8.255	106000	319.0	3.0
1	289.0	7.348	83700	253.0	3.3
2	258.0	6.544	66400	201.0	3.8
3	229.0	5.827	52600	159.0	4.2
4	204.0	5.189	41700	126.0	4.7
5	182.0	4.621	33100	100.0	5.2
6	162.0	4.115	26300	79.5	5.9
7	144.0	3.665	20800	63.0	6.5
8	128.0	3.264	16500	50.0	7.6
9	114.0	2.906	13100	39.6	8.6
10	102.0	2.588	10400	31.4	9.6
11	91.0	2.305	8230	24.9	10.7
12	81.0	2.053	6530	19.8	12.0
13	72.0	1.828	5180	15.7	13.5
14	64.0	1.628	4110	12.4	15.0
15	57.0	1.450	3260	9.86	16.8
16	51.0	1.291	2580	7.82	18.9
17	45.0	1.150	2050	6.2	21.2
18	40.0	1.024	1620	4.92	23.6
19	36.0	0.912	1290	3.90	26.4
20	32.0	0.812	1020	3.09	29.4
21	28.5	0.723	810	2.45	33.1
22	25.3	0.644	642	1.94	37.0
23	22.6	0.573	509	1.54	41.3
24	20.1	0.511	404	1.22	46.3
25	17.9	0.455	320	0.970	51.7
26	15.9	0.405	254	0.769	58.0
27	14.2	0.361	202	0.610	64.9
28	12.6	0.321	160	0.484	72.7
29	11.3	0.286	127	0.384	81.6
30	10.0	0.255	101	0.304	90.5
31	8.9	0.227	79.7	0.241	101
32	8.0	0.202	63.2	0.191	113
33	7.1	0.180	50.1	0.152	127
34	6.3	0.160	39.8	0.120	143
35	5.6	0.143	31.5	0.095	158
36	5.0	0.127	25.0	0.0757	175
37	4.5	0.113	19.8	0.0600	198
38	4.0	0.101	15.7	0.0476	224
39	3.5	0.090	12.5	0.0377	248
40	3.1	0.080	9.9	0.0200	282

* American Wire Gauge (formerly Brown & Sharp)

Wire Classes & Insulation

Standard cable, as used in home and general construction, is classified by the wire size, number of wires, insulation type and dampness condition of the wire environment. Example: a cable with the code "12/2 with Ground – Type UF – 600V – (UL)" has the following specifications:

> Wire sizes are 14 gauge for copper, 12 gauge for aluminum (minimum size for 0 to 2000 volts), See National Electric Code.
>
> The " / 2 " indicates there are two wires in the cable.
>
> "Ground" indicates there is a third wire in the cable to be used as a grounding wire.
>
> "Type UF" indicates the insulation type and acceptable dampness rating.
>
> "600V" means the wire is rated at 600 volts maximum.
>
> "UL" indicates the wire has been certified by Underwriters Laboratory to be safe.

Cables are dampness rated as follows:

> DRY: No dampness normally encountered. Indoor location above ground level.
>
> DAMP: Partially protected locations. Moderate amount of moisture. Indoor location below ground level.
>
> WET: Water saturation probable, such as underground or in concrete slabs or outside locations exposed to weather.

There are literally hundreds of different types of insulation used in wire and cable. To make things simple, the following descriptions are for wires commonly used in home wiring:

"BX" Type "AC". Armor covered with flexible, galvanized steel. Normally used in dry locations. Not legal to use in some states such as California.

"ROMEX" Although actually a trade name, it is used to describe a general class of plastic coated cable. Each wire is plastic wrapped except possibly the ground wire, which is sometimes bare or paper covered. Very flexible. There are three general types:
"NM" – Dry only, 2 or 3 wire, ground wire plastic wrapped.
"NMC" – Dry/moist, 2 or 3 wire, all wires in solid plastic.
"UF" – Wet, 2 or 3 wire, all wires in solid, water resistant plastic. Use also instead of conduit. Underground feeder.

Types "NM" & "NMC" can be placed in conduit where protection from physical damage is needed.

Wire Classes & Insulation

Wire types are typically coded by the type of insulation, temperature range, dampness rating, and type and composition of the
jacket. The following are some of the "Type Codes":

"T..."	Very common, dry only, full current load temperature must be less than 60°C (140°F).
"F"	Fixture wire. CF has cotton insulation (90°C), AF has asbestos insulation (150°C), SF has silicone insulation (200°C).
"R..."	Rubber (natural, neoprene, etc) covered.
"S..."	Appliance cord, stranded conductors, cotton layer between wire and insulation, jute fillers, rubber outer jacket. S is extra hard service, SJ lighter service, SV light service.
"SP..."	Lamp cord, rubber insulation.
"SPT..."	Lamp cord, plastic insulation.
"X..."	Insulation is a cross linked synthetic polymer. Very tough and heat and moisture resistant.
"FEP..."	Fluorinated ethylene propylene insulation. Rated over 90°C (194°F). Dry only.
"...B"	Suffix indicating an outer braid is used, such as glass.
"...H"	Suffix indicating Higher loaded current temperatures may be used, up to 75°C (167°F).
"...HH"	Suffix indicating much higher loaded current temperatures may be used, up to 90°C (194°F).
"...L"	Suffix indicating a seamless lead jacket.
"...N"	Suffix indicating the jacket is extruded nylon or thermoplastic polyester and is very resistant to gas and oil and is very tough.
"...O"	Suffix indicating neoprene jacket.
"...W"	Suffix indicating WET use type.

Examples of some of the more common wire types are "T", "TW",
"THWN", "THHN", "XHHW", "RHH", and "RHW".

Standard Wiring Color Codes

Standard wire color codes are very different between electronic circuitry and household 110 Volt AC wiring.

Household wiring (or other AC applications in the 100+ volt range) uses the following color codes:

Wire Color	Circuit type
Black	"Hot" wire. In an outlet, it is always wired to the narrow spade or brass colored terminal.
Green	"Ground" wire, always wired to the green terminal. Also called chassis ground. This wire is sometimes green w/ yellow stripe.
Red	"Second hot" wire used in connecting 3–way switches. Connects power between the 3–way switches. Sometimes call a "traveler".
White/Gray	"Neutral" wire. In an outlet, it is always wired to the wide spade or silver colored terminal.

Typically, the following color codes are used for **electronic applications** (as established by the Electronic Industries Association – EIA):

Wire Color (solid)	Circuit type
Black	Chassis grounds, returns, primary leads
Blue	Plate leads, transistor collectors, FET drain
Brown	Filaments, plate start lead
Gray	AC main power leads
Green	Transistor base, finish grid, diodes, FET gate
Orange	Transistor base 2, screen grid
Red	B plus dc power supply
Violet	Power supply minus
White	B–C minus of bias supply, AVC–AGC return
Yellow	Emitters-cathode and transistor, FET source

Stereo Audio Channels are color coded as follows:

Wire Color (solid)	Circuit type
White	Left channel high side
Blue	Left channel low side
Red	Right channel high side
Green	Right channel low side

Standard Wiring Color Codes

Power Transformers are color coded as follows:

Wire Color (solid)	Circuit type
Black	If a transformer does not have a tapped primary, both leads are black.
Black	If a transformer does have a tapped primary, the black is the common lead.
Black & Yellow	Tap for a tapped primary.
Black & Red	End for a tapped primary.

AF Transformers (audio) are color coded as follows:

Wire Color (solid)	Circuit type
Black	Ground line.
Blue	Plate, collector, or drain lead. End of primary winding.
Brown	Start primary loop, opposite to blue lead.
Green	High side, end secondary loop.
Red	B plus, center tap push–pull loop.
Yellow	Secondary center tap.

IF Transformers (Intermediate Frequency) are color coded as follows:

Wire Color (solid)	Circuit type
Blue	Primary high side of plate, collector, or drain lead.
Green	Secondary high side for output.
Red	Low side of primary returning B plus.
Violet	Secondary outputs.
White	Secondary low side.

Voltage Drop vs. Wire Size

Voltage drop is the amount of voltage lost over the length of a circuit. Voltge drop changes as a function of the resistance in the wire and should be less than 2% if possible. If the drop is greater than 2%, efficiency of the equipment in the circuit is severely decreased and life of the equipment will be decreased. As an example, if the voltage drop on an incandescent light bulb is 10%, the light output of the bulb decreases over 30%!

Voltage drop can be calculated using Ohm's Law, which is
Voltage Drop = Current in amperes x Resistance in ohms.
For example, the voltage drop over a 200 ft. long, #14 copper, 2 wire cable supplying a 1000 watt floodlight is calculated as follows:

Current = 1000 watts / 120 volts = 8.33 amperes
Resistance of solid #14 copper wire = 2.58 ohms / 1000 feet @ 77°F
Resistance of power line = 2 x 200 feet x 0.00258 ohms/foot
= 1.032 ohms
Voltage drop = 8.33 amperes x 1.032 ohms = 8.60 volts
Percent voltage drop = 8.60 volts / 120 volts = 7.2 %

The 7.2% drop is over the maximum 2% so the diameter of the wire must be increased(a decrease in wire gauge number). If #8 solid copper wire were used in the above example, the voltage drop would have been 1.8%. Resistance values for various size wire are contained in the Copper Wire Resistance table on page 142.

A more commonly used method of calculating voltage drop is as follows:

$$\text{Voltage drop} = \frac{K \times P \times \text{Wire length in ft.} \times \text{Current in amperes}}{\text{Wire area in circular mils}}$$

K = Approximate specific resistivity in ohm - circular mils / foot.

Wire	Temp	K	Temp	K
Solid Copper	77°- 121°F	11	122°-167°F	12
Solid Aluminum	77°- 121°F	18	122°-167°F	20
Stranded Copper	77°- 121°F	11	122°-167°F	12
Sttranded Aluminum	77°- 121°F	19	122°-167°F	20

P = Phase constant = 2 for single phase, 1.732 for three phase

Using values from the Ohm's Law example at the top of this page: #14 solid copper wire has an area of 4110 circular mils, K=11 @ 77°F, then voltage drop in a single phase circuit is (11 x 2 x 200 x 8.33) / 4110 = 8.92 volts or in percent, 8.92 volts / 120 volts = 7.4%. Wire area in circular mils is given in the Standard Copper Wire Specs table on page 143.

It is interesting to note that if the line voltage doubles (120 volts to 240 volts), the amperage is cut in half (8.33 to 4.17) and the voltage drop in percent decreases by a factor of 4. That means that a line can carry the same power 4 times further! Higher voltage lines are more efficient.

Wire Size vs. Voltage Drop

Copper Wire, solid, 2-conductor, K=11 (77°-121°F)
Max Footage @ <u>120</u> Volts, 1 Phase, 2% Max Voltage Drop

Amps	Volt-Amps	#14	#12	#10	#8	#6
1	120	450	700	1100	1800	2800
5	600	90	140	225	360	575
10	1200	45	70	115	180	285
15	1800	30	47	75	120	190
20	2400	...	36	57	90	140
25	3000	...	...	45	72	115
30	3600	...	...	38	60	95
40	4800	...	...	...	45	72
50	6000	...	...	...	...	57

Amps	Volt-Amps	#4	#2	1/0	2/0	3/0
1	120	4500	7000	...	...	...
5	600	910	1400	2250	2800	...
10	1200	455	705	1100	1400	1800
15	1800	305	485	770	965	1200
20	2400	230	365	575	725	900
25	3000	180	290	460	580	720
30	3600	150	240	385	490	600
40	4800	115	175	290	360	440
50	6000	90	145	230	290	360
60	7200	76	120	190	240	305
70	8400	65	105	155	205	260
80	9600	...	90	144	180	230

Max Footage @ <u>240</u> Volts, 1 Phase, 2% Max Voltage Drop

Amps	Volt-Amps	#14	#12	#10	#8	#6
1	240	900	1400	2200	3600	5600
5	1200	180	285	455	720	1020
10	2400	90	140	225	360	525
15	3600	60	95	150	240	350
20	4800	...	70	110	180	265
25	6000	...	...	90	144	210
30	7200	...	...	75	120	175
40	9600	...	...	...	90	130
50	12000	...	...	...	...	105

Amps	Volt-Amps	#4	#2	1/0	2/0	3/0
1	240	9000	...	...	...	...
5	1200	1750	2800	4500	5600	7000
10	2400	910	1400	2200	2800	3600
15	3600	605	965	1500	1900	2400
20	4800	455	725	1100	1400	1800
25	6000	365	580	920	1100	1440
30	7200	300	485	770	970	1200
40	9600	230	360	575	725	880
50	12000	180	290	460	580	720
60	14400	150	240	385	485	600
70	16800	130	205	330	415	520
80	19200	...	180	290	365	440
100	24000	...	...	230	280	360
150	36000	...	...	185	190	240
200	48000	...	...	...	...	180

Note: For K=12 (122°-167°F) multiply values in table by 0.92.

Conduit Size vs. Wire Size

Wire Size AWG	Minimum Conduit Size (inches) per Number of Type TW Wires. Number of Wires Inside Conduit				
	2	3	4	5	6
14	1/2	1/2	1/2	1/2	1/2
12	1/2	1/2	1/2	1/2	1/2
10	1/2	1/2	1/2	1/2	3/4
8	1/2	3/4	3/4	1	1
6	3/4	1	1	1-1/4	1-1/4
4	1	1	1-1/4	1-1/4	1-1/2
2	1	1-1/4	1-1/4	1-1/2	2
1/0	1-1/4	1-1/2	2	2	2-1/2
2/0	1-1/4	1-1/2	2	2	2-1/2
3/0	1-1/2	2	2	2-1/2	2-1/2

See the National Electric Code for conduit sizes when using wire types other than Type TW.

Box Size vs. Number of Wires

Box Size in inches	Maximum Number of Wires in a Junction Box Wire Size AWG			
	#14	#12	#10	#8
Outlet Boxes				
4-11/16 x 1-1/4 square	12	11	10	8
4-11/16 x 1-1/2 square	14	13	11	9
4-11/16 x 2-1/8 square	21	18	16	14
4 x 1-1/4 octagon or rou	6	5	5	5
4 x 1-1/2 octagon or rou	7	6	6	5
4 x 2-1/8 octagon or rou	10	9	8	7
4 x 1-1/4 square	9	8	7	6
4 x 1-1/2 square	10	9	8	7
4 x 2-1/8 square	15	13	12	10
Switch Boxes				
3 x 2 x 1-1/2	3	3	3	2
3 x 2 x 2	5	4	4	3
3 x 2 x 2-1/4	5	4	4	3
3 x 2 x 2-1/2	6	5	5	4
3 x 2 x 2-3/4	7	6	5	4
3 x 2 x 3-1/2	9	8	7	6
4 x 2-1/8 x 1-1/2	5	4	4	3
4 x 2-1/8 x 1-7/8	6	5	5	4
4 x 2-1/8 x 2-1/8	7	6	5	4

The above numbers are maximums and you should deduct 1 wire for each outlet, switch, cable clamp, fixture stud, or similar part that is also installed in the box.

Average Electric Motor Specs

NOTE: Use the following table as a general guide only! These numbers are for normal fan, furnace, appliance, pump, and normal duty applications. The exact specifications for any given motor can vary greatly from those listed below. For 230V motors simply divide the indicated amps by 2.

Specs for 115 volt, 60 Hz, 1 Phase, AC Electric Motors

Motor Horsepower	RPM	Full Load Amps	Motor Horsepower	RPM	Full Load Amps
1/20	3000	1.5–2.9	1/5	10,000	2.9–3.1
	1550	1.6–3.5		1050	6.0–8.0
	1050	2.0–3.1	1/4	3450	3.5–4.1
1/15	5000	1.2		1725	3.0–6.3
	3000	1.8–2.4		1140	5.6–6.2
	1550	1.3–3.2		1075	3.3–4.0
	1500	1.7		1050	8.5–9.4
	1050	1.6–4.0		850	6.9
	1000	2.7	1/3	3450	4.9–8.6
	950	3.7		1725	4.0–7.8
1/12	1725	2.1–2.9		1650	5.6
	1550	1.6		1140	6.2–8.6
	1450	3.1		1075	4.2–5.1
	1140	2.4		850	9.2
	1050	1.9–3.6		825	4.5
	1000	4.0	1/2	10,000	6.3–7.3
	850	3.2		3450	6.3–9.6
1/10	10,000	1.5		1140	8.6–10.4
	5000	1.5		1110	8.8
	1550	3.1–4.6		1075	7.0
	1100	4.2		825	6.0
	1050	3.4–4.7	3/4	3450	9.2–14.8
	1000	4.5		2850	9.8
1/9	3000	0.7		1725	9.8–13.3
1/8	3450	2.4		1140	10.6–12.6
	3000	1.8		1075	9.2
	1725	1.6–4.0	1	10,000	12.1
	1550	4.5		3450	11.4–19.2
	1140	3.8		1740	13.8–14.4
	1075	2.3		1725	12.6–15.0
	1050	4.3–5.5		1140	12.6
	850	4.6		1075	13.0
	700	2.0	1–1/2	3500	16.4
1/7	10,000	2.0		3450	15.4–22.0
	3450	2.0–2.4		1740	18.4–22.0
1/6	1725	3.0–4.2		1725	14.0–20.4
	1550	5.0	2	3500	18.8–20.8
	1140	3.7–4.6		3450	15.0–23.0
	1075	2.2–2.6		1740	19.0–25.6
	1050	5.6–7.1		1730	22.8
	850	5.6–6.1		1725	19.0–24.6

The above general specifications are based on motor data from the *1988 Graingers Catalog, Chicago, Illinois.*

Electrical Motor Frame Dimensions (NEMA - 1984)

Frame Designation	NEMA Frame Dimensions in inches						
	D	E	2F	(BA)	(N - W)	V	U
42	2-5/8	1-3/4	11/16	2-1/16	1-1/8	- - -	3/8
42C	2-5/8	1-3/4	11/16	2-1/16	1- /8	- - -	3/8
48	3	2-1/8	2-3/4	2-1/2	1-1/2	- - -	1/2
48C	3	2-1/8	2-3/4	2-1/2	1-1/2	- - -	1/2
48H	3	2-1/8	4-3/4	2-1/2	1-1/2	- - -	1/2
56	3-1/2	2-7/16	3	2-3/4	1-7/8	- - -	5/8
56C	3-1/2	2-7/16	- - -	2-3/4	1-7/8	- - -	5/8
56H	3-1/2	2-7/16	5	2-3/4	1-7/8	- - -	5/8
56HZ	3-1/2	2-7/16	5	2-3/4	2-1/4	2	7/8
56J	3-1/2	2-7/16	- - -	2-3/4	2-7/16	- - -	5/8
66	4-1/8	2-15/16	5	3-1/8	2-1/4	- - -	3/4
140T	3-1/2	2-3/4	4	2-3/4	2-1/4	- - -	7/8
142AT	3-1/2	2-3/4	3-1/4	2-3/4	1-3/4	1-1/2	7/8
143AT	3-1/2	2-3/4	4	2-1/4	1-3/4	1-1/2	7/8
143JM	3-1/2	2-3/4	4	2-1/4	- - -	- - -	7/8
143JP	3-1/2	2-3/4	4	2-1/4	- - -	- - -	7/8
143T	3-1/2	2 - 3/4	4	2 - 1/4	2 - 1/4	2	7/8
143TC	3-1/2	2 - 3/4	4	2 - 3/4	2 - 1/4	- - -	7/8
143TR	3-1/2	2-3/4	4	2-1/4	2-5/8	1-3/4	7/8
144AT	3-1/2	2-3/4	4-1/2	2-3/4	1-3/4	1-1/2	7/8
145AT	3-1/2	2-3/4	5	2-3/4	1-3/4	1-1/2	7/8
145JM	3-1/2	2-3/4	5	2-1/4	- - -	- - -	7/8
145JP	3-1/2	2-3/4	5	2-1/4	- - -	- - -	7/8
145T	3-1/2	2-3/4	5	2-1/4	2-1/4	2	7/8
145TC	3-1/2	2-3/4	5	2-3/4	2-1/4	- - -	7/8
145TR	3-1/2	2-3/4	5	2-1/4	2-5/8	1-3/4	7/8
146AT	3-1/2	2-3/4	5-1/2	2-3/4	1-3/4	1-1/2	7/8
146ATC	3-1/2	2-3/4	5-1/2	2-3/4	2-1/4	- - -	7/8
147AT	3-1/2	2-3/4	6-1/4	2-3/4	1-3/4	1-1/2	7/8
148AT	3-1/2	2-3/4	7	2-3/4	1-3/4	1-1/2	7/8
149AT	3-1/2	2-3/4	8	2-3/4	1-3/4	1-1/2	7/8
1410AT	3-1/2	2-3/4	9	2-3/4	1-3/4	1-1/2	7/8
1411AT	3-1/2	2-3/4	10	2-3/4	1-3/4	1-1/2	7/8
1412AT	3-1/2	2-3/4	11	2-3/4	1-3/4	1-1/2	7/8
1412ATC	3-1/2	2-3/4	11	2-3/4	2-1/4	- - -	7/8
162AT	4	3-1/8	4	2-1/2	1-3/4	1-1/2	7/8
163AT	4	3-1/8	4-1/2	2-1/2	1-3/4	1-1/2	7/8
164AT	4	3-1/8	5	2-1/2	1-3/4	1-1/2	7/8
165AT	4	3-1/8	5-1/2	2-1/2	1-3/4	1-1/2	7/8
166AT	4	3-1/8	6-1/4	2-1/2	1-3/4	1-1/2	7/8
167AT	4	3-1/8	7	2-1/2	1-3/4	1-1/2	7/8

Electric Motor Frame Dimensions (cont.)

Frame Designation	NEMA Frame Dimensions in inches						
	D	E	2F	(BA)	(N - W)	V	U
168AT	4	3-1/8	8	2-1/2	1-3/4	1-1/2	7/8
169AT	4	3-1/8	9	2-1/2	1-3/4	1-1/2	7/8
1610AT	4	3-1/8	10	2-1/2	1-3/4	1-1/2	7/8
182	4-1/2	3-3/4	4-1/2	2-3/4	2-1/4	2	7/8
L182ACY	4-1/2	3-3/4	4-1/2	2-3/4	2-1/4	2	7/8
182AT	4-1/2	3-3/4	4-1/2	2-3/4	2-1/4	2	1-1/8
L182AT	4-1/2	3-3/4	4-1/2	2-3/4	2-1/4	2	1-1/8
182JM	4-1/2	3-3/4	4-1/2	2-3/4	- - -	- - -	7/8
182JP	4-1/2	3-3/4	4-1/2	2-3/4	- - -	- - -	7/8
182T	4-1/2	3-3/4	4-1/2	2-3/4	2-3/4	2-1/2	1-1/8
182TC	4-1/2	3-3/4	4-1/2	2-3/4	2-3/4	- - -	1-1/8
182TR	4-1/2	3-3/4	4-1/2	2-3/4	3-3/8	2-1/4	1-1/8
183AT	4-1/2	3-3/4	5	2-3/4	2-1/4	2	1-1/8
184	4-1/2	3-3/4	5-1/2	2-3/4	2-1/4	2	7/8
184AT	4-1/2	3-3/4	5-1/2	2-3/4	2-1/4	2	1-1/8
184JM	4-1/2	3-3/4	5-1/2	2-3/4	- - -	- - -	7/8
184JP	4-1/2	3-3/4	5-1/2	2-3/4	- - -	- - -	7/8
184TC	4-1/2	3-3/4	5-1/2	2-3/4	2-3/4	- - -	1-1/8
184T	4-1/2	3-3/4	5-1/2	2-3/4	2-3/4	2-1/2	1-1/8
184TR	4-1/2	3-3/4	5-1/2	2-3/4	3-3/8	2-1/4	1-1/8
185AT	4-1/2	3-3/4	6-1/4	2-3/4	2-1/4	2	1-1/8
186ACY	4-1/2	3-3/4	7	2-3/4	2-1/4	2	7/8
186AT	4-1/2	3-3/4	7	2-3/4	2-1/4	2	1-1/8
L186AT	4-1/2	3-3/4	7	2-3/4	2-1/4	2	1-1/8
186ATC	4-1/2	3-3/4	7	2-3/4	2-1/4	- - -	1-1/8
187AT	4-1/2	3-3/4	8	2-3/4	2-1/4	2	1-1/8
188AT	4-1/2	3-3/4	9	2-3/4	2-1/4	2	1-1/8
189AT	4-1/2	3-3/4	10	2-3/4	2-1/4	2	1-1/8
189ATC	4-1/2	3-3/4	10	2-3/4	2-1/4	- - -	1-1/8
1810AT	4-1/2	3-3/4	11	2-3/4	2-1/4	2	1-1/8
203	5	4	5-1/2	3-1/8	2-1/4	2	3/4
204	5	4	6-1/4	3-1/8	2-1/4	2	3/4
213	5-1/4	4-1/4	5-1/2	3-1/2	3	2-3/4	1-1/8
213AT	5-1/4	4-1/4	5-1/2	3-1/2	2-3/4	2-1/2	1-3/8
213JM	5-1/4	4-1/4	5-1/2	3-1/2	- - -	- - -	7/8
213JP	5-1/4	4-1/4	5-1/2	3-1/2	- - -	- - -	1-1/4
213T	5-1/4	4-1/4	5-1/2	3-1/2	3-3/8	3-1/8	1-3/8
213TC	5-1/4	4-1/4	5-1/2	3-1/2	3-3/8	- - -	1-3/8
213TR	5-1/4	4-1/4	5-1/2	3-1/2	4-1/8	2-5/8	1-3/8
214AT	5-1/4	4-1/4	6-1/4	3-1/2	2-3/4	2-1/2	1-3/8
215	5-1/4	4-1/4	7	3-1/2	3	2-3/4	1-1/8

Electric Motor Frame Dimensions (cont.)							
Frame Designation	NEMA Frame Dimensions in inches						
	D	E	2F	(BA)	(N - W)	V	U
215AT	5-1/4	4-1/4	7	3-1/2	2-3/4	2-1/2	1-3/8
215JM	5-1/4	4-1/4	7	3-1/2	---	---	7/8
215JP	5-1/4	4-1/4	7	3-1/2	---	---	1-1/4
215T	5-1/4	4-1/4	7	3-1/2	3-3/8	3-1/8	1-3/8
215TC	5-1/4	4-1/4	7	3-1/2	3-3/8	---	1-3/8
215TR	5-1/4	4-1/4	7	3-1/2	4-1/8	2-5/8	1-3/8
216AT	5-1/4	4-1/4	8	3-1/2	2-3/4	2-1/2	1-3/8
217AT	5-1/4	4-1/4	9	3-1/2	2-3/4	2-1/2	1-3/8
218AT	5-1/4	4-1/4	10	3-1/2	2-3/4	2-1/2	1-3/8
219AT	5-1/4	4-1/4	11	3-1/2	2-3/4	2-1/2	1-3/8
219ATC	5-1/4	4-1/4	11	3-1/2	2-3/4	---	1-3/8
2110AT	5-1/4	4-1/4	12-1/2	3-1/2	2-3/4	2-1/2	1-3/8
2110ATC	5-1/4	4-1/4	12-1/2	3-1/2	2-3/4	---	1-3/8
224	5-1/2	4-1/2	6-3/4	3-1/2	3	2-3/4	1
225	5-1/2	4-1/2	7-1/2	3-1/2	3	2-3/4	1
253AT	6-1/4	5	7	4-1/4	3-1/4	3	1-5/8
254	6-1/4	5	8-1/4	4-1/4	3-3/8	3-1/8	1-1/8
254AT	6-1/4	5	8-1/4	4-1/4	3-1/4	3	1-5/8
254T	6-1/4	5	8-1/4	4-1/4	4	3-3/4	1-5/8
254TC	6-1/4	5	8-1/4	4-1/4	4	---	1-5/8
254TR	6-1/4	5	8-1/4	4-1/4	4-1/2	2-7/8	1-5/8
254U	6-1/4	5	8-1/4	4-1/4	3-3/4	3-1/2	1-3/8
255AT	6-1/4	5	9	4-1/4	3-1/4	3	1-5/8
256AT	6-1/4	5	10	4-1/4	3-1/4	3	1-5/8
256T	6-1/4	5	10	4-1/4	4	3-3/4	1-5/8
256TC	6-1/4	5	10	4-1/4	4	---	1-5/8
256TR	6-1/4	5	10	4-1/4	4-1/2	2-7/8	1-5/8
256U	6-1/4	5	10	4-1/4	3-3/4	3-1/2	1-3/8
257AT	6-1/4	5	11	4-1/4	3-1/4	3	1-5/8
258AT	6-1/4	5	12-1/2	4-1/4	3-1/4	3	1-5/8
259AT	6-1/4	5	14	4-1/4	3-1/4	3	1-5/8
283AT	7	5-1/2	8	4-3/4	3-3/4	3-1/2	1-7/8
284	7	5-1/2	9-1/2	4-3/4	3-3/4	3-1/2	1-1/4
284AT	7	5-1/2	9-1/2	4-3/4	3-3/4	3-1/2	1-7/8
284T	7	5-1/2	9-1/2	4-3/4	4-5/8	4-3/8	1-7/8
284TC	7	5-1/2	9-1/2	4-3/4	4-5/8	---	1-7/8
284TR	7	5-1/2	9-1/2	4-3/4	3-1/4	3-1/8	1-7/8
284TS	7	5-1/2	9-1/2	4-3/4	3-1/4	3	1-5/8
284U	7	5-1/2	9-1/2	4-3/4	4-7/8	4-5/8	1-5/8
285AT	7	5-1/2	10	4-3/4	3-3/4	3-1/2	1-7/8
286AT	7	5-1/2	11	4-3/4	3-3/4	3-1/2	1-7/8

Electric Motor Frame Dimensions (cont.)

Frame Designation	NEMA Frame Dimensions in inches						
	D	E	2F	(BA)	(N - W)	V	U
286T	7	5-1/2	11	4-3/4	4-5/8	4-3/8	1-7/8
286TC	7	5-1/2	11	4-3/4	4-3/4	---	1-7/8
286TR	7	5-1/2	11	4-3/4	4-3/4	3-1/8	1-7/8
286TS	7	5-1/2	11	4-3/4	3-1/4	3	1-5/8
286U	7	5-1/2	11	4-3/4	4-7/8	4-5/8	1-5/8
287AT	7	5-1/2	12-1/2	4-3/4	3-3/4	3-1/2	1-7/8
288AT	7	5-1/2	14	4-3/4	3-3/4	3-1/2	1-7/8
289AT	7	5-1/2	16	4-3/4	3-3/4	3-1/2	1-7/8
323AT	8	6-1/4	9	5-1/4	4-1/4	4	2-1/8
324	8	6-1/4	10-1/2	5-1/4	4-7/8	4-5/8	1-5/8
324AT	8	6-1/4	10-1/2	5-1/4	4-1/4	4	2-1/8
324TR	8	6-1/4	10-1/2	5-1/4	5-1/4	3-1/2	2-1/8
324TS	8	6-1/4	10-1/2	5-1/4	3-3/4	3-1/2	1-7/8
324U	8	6-1/4	10-1/2	5-1/4	5-5/8	5-3/8	1-7/8
325AT	8	6-1/4	11	5-1/4	4-1/4	4	2-1/8
326	8	6-1/4	12	5-1/4	4-7/8	4-5/8	1-5/8
326AT	8	6-1/4	12	5-1/4	4-1/4	4	2-1/8
326T	8	6-1/4	12	5-1/4	5-1/4	5	2-1/8
326TR	8	6-1/4	12	5-1/4	5-1/4	3-1/2	2-1/8
326TS	8	6-1/4	12	5-1/4	3-3/4	3-1/2	1-7/8
326U	8	6-1/4	12	5-1/4	5-5/8	5-3/8	1-7/8
327AT	8	6-1/4	14	5-1/4	4-1/4	4	2-1/8
328AT	8	6-1/4	16	5-1/4	4-1/4	4	2-1/8
329AT	8	6-1/4	18	5-1/4	4-1/4	4	2-1/8
363AT	9	7	10	5-7/8	4-3/4	4-1/2	2-3/8
364	9	7	11-1/4	5-7/8	5-5/8	5-3/8	1-7/8
364AT	9	7	11-1/4	5-7/8	4-3/4	4-1/2	2-3/8
364S	9	7	11-1/4	5-7/8	3-1/4	3	1-5/8
364T	9	7	11-1/4	5-7/8	5-7/8	5-7/8	2-3/8
364TR	9	7	11-1/4	5-7/8	5-3/4	3-3/4	2-3/8
364TS	9	7	11-1/4	5-7/8	3-3/4	3-1/2	1-7/8
364U	9	7	11-1/4	5-7/8	6-3/8	6-1/8	2-1/8
365	9	7	12-1/4	5-7/8	5-5/8	5-3/8	1-7/8
365AT	9	7	12-1/4	5-7/8	4-3/4	4-1/2	2-3/8
365T	9	7	12-1/4	5-7/8	5-7/8	5-7/8	2-3/8
324T	8	6-1/4	10-1/2	5-1/4	5-1/4	5	2-1/8
365TR	9	7	12-1/4	5-7/8	5-3/4	3-3/4	2-3/8
365TS	9	7	12-1/4	5-7/8	3-3/4	3-1/2	1-7/8
365U	9	7	12-1/4	5-7/8	6-3/8	6-1/8	2-1/8
366AT	9	7	14	5-7/8	4-3/4	4-1/2	2-3/8
364AT	9	7	11-1/4	5-7/8	4-3/4	4-1/2	2-3/8

Electric Motor Frame Dimensions (cont.)

Frame Designation	NEMA Frame Dimensions in inches						
	D	E	2F	(BA)	(N - W)	V	U
367AT	9	7	16	5-7/8	4-3/4	4-1/2	2-3/8
368AT	9	7	18	5-7/8	4-3/4	4-1/2	2-3/8
369AT	9	7	20	5-7/8	4-3/4	4-1/2	2-3/8
403AT	10	8	11	6-5/8	5-1/4	5	2-5/8
404AT	10	8	12-1/4	6-5/8	5-1/4	5	2-5/8
404T	10	8	12-1/4	6-5/8	7-1/4	7	2-7/8
404TR	10	8	12-1/4	6-5/8	6-5/8	4-3/8	2-7/8
404TS	10	8	12-1/4	6-5/8	4-1/4	4	2-1/8
404U	10	8	12-1/4	6-5/8	7-1/8	6-7/8	2-3/8
405AT	10	8	13-3/4	6-5/8	5-1/4	5	2-5/8
405T	10	8	13-3/4	6-5/8	7-1/4	7	2-7/8
405TR	10	8	13-3/4	6-5/8	6-5/8	4-3/8	2-7/8
405TS	10	8	13-3/4	6-5/8	4-1/4	4	2-1/8
405U	10	8	13-3/4	6-5/8	7-1/8	6-7/8	2-3/8
406AT	10	8	16	6-5/8	5-1/4	5	2-5/8
407AT	10	8	18	6-5/8	5-1/4	5	2-5/8
408AT	10	8	20	6-5/8	5-1/4	5	2-5/8
409AT	10	8	22	6-5/8	5-1/4	5	2-5/8
440	11	9	10	7-1/2	---	---	---
443AT	11	9	12-1/2	7-1/2	5-3/4	5-1/2	2-7/8
444AT	11	9	14-1/2	7-1/2	5-3/4	5-1/2	2-7/8
444T	11	9	14-1/2	7-1/2	8-1/2	8-1/4	3-3/8
444TR	11	9	14-1/2	7-1/2	7-1/2	5	3-3/8
444TS	11	9	14-1/2	7-1/2	4-3/4	4-1/2	2-3/8
444U	11	9	14-1/2	7-1/2	8-5/8	8-3/8	2-7/8
445AT	11	9	16-1/2	7-1/2	5-3/4	5-1/2	2-7/8
445T	11	9	16-1/2	7-1/2	8-1/2	8-1/4	3-3/8
445TR	11	9	16-1/2	7-1/2	7-1/2	5	3-3/8
445TS	11	9	16-1/2	7-1/2	4-3/4	4-1/2	2-3/8
445U	11	9	16-1/2	7-1/2	8-5/8	8-3/8	2-7/8
446AT	11	9	18	7-1/2	5-3/4	5-1/2	2-7/8
447AT	11	9	20	7-1/2	5-3/4	5-1/2	2-7/8
447T	11	9	20	7-1/2	8-1/2	8-1/8	3-3/8
447TS	11	9	20	7-1/2	4-3/4	4-1/2	2-3/8
448AT	11	9	22	7-1/2	5-3/4	5-1/2	2-7/8
449AT	11	9	25	7-1/2	5-3/4	5-1/2	2-7/8
449T	11	9	25	7-1/2	8-1/2	8-1/4	3-3/8
449TS	11	9	25	7-1/2	4-3/4	4-1/2	2-3/8
500	12-1/2	10	11	8-1/2	---	---	---
502AT	12-1/2	10	12-1/2	8-1/2	6-1/2	6-1/4	3-1/4
503AT	12-1/2	10	14	8-1/2	6-1/2	6-1/4	3-1/4

Electric Motor Frame Dimensions (cont.)

Frame Designation	NEMA Frame Dimensions in inches						
	D	E	2F	(BA)	(N - W)	V	U
504AT	12-1/2	10	16	8-1/2	6-1/2	6-1/4	3-1/4
505AT	12-1/2	10	18	8-1/2	6-1/2	6-1/4	3-1/4
506AT	12-1/2	10	20	8-1/2	6-1/2	6-1/4	3-1/4
507AT	12-1/2	10	22	8-1/2	6-1/2	6-1/4	3-1/4
508AT	12-1/2	10	25	8-1/2	6-1/2	6-1/4	3-1/4
509AT	12-1/2	10	28	8-1/2	6-1/2	6-1/4	3-1/4
583A	14-1/2	11-1/2	16	10	9-3/4	9-1/2	3-1/4
584A	14-1/2	11-1/2	18	10	9-3/4	9-1/2	3-1/4
585A	14-1/2	11-1/2	20	10	9-3/4	9-1/2	3-1/4
586A	14-1/2	11-1/2	22	10	9-3/4	9-1/2	3-1/4
587A	14-1/2	11-1/2	25	10	9-3/4	9-1/2	3-1/4
588A	14-1/2	11-1/2	28	10	9-3/4	9-1/2	3-1/4
683A	17	13-1/2	20	11-1/2	10-7/8	10-5/8	3-5/8
684A	17	13-1/2	22	11-1/2	10-7/8	10-5/8	3-5/8
685A	17	13-1/2	25	11-1/2	10-7/8	10-5/8	3-5/8
686A	17	13-1/2	28	11-1/2	10-7/8	10-5/8	3-5/8
687A	17	13-1/2	32	11-1/2	10-7/8	10-5/8	3-5/8
688A	17	13-1/2	36	11-1/2	10-7/8	10-5/8	3-5/8

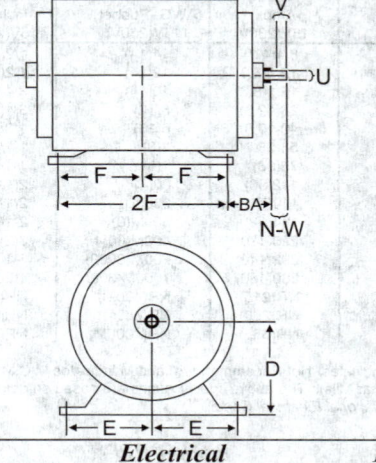

NEMA Electric Enclosures

Enclosure Type	Class	Description
NEMA Type 1	General Purpose	Indoor use where no oil, water or dust is present.
NEMA Type 2	Drip Tight	Indoor use where minimal dripping moisture occurs.
NEMA Type 3	Rain Tight	Outside use for protection against snow, rain & sleet.
NEMA Type 4	Water Tight	Outside use for protection against massive amounts of water, such as hosing.
NEMA Type 5	Dust Tight	Protection against dust.
NEMA Type 9	Dust Tight	Protection against dusts that are combustible.
NEMA Type 12	Industrial	Protection against oil, coolants, lints, and a variety of dusts.

DC Motor Wiring Specs

HP	Full Load Amps 115V(230V)	Wire Size Minimum (AWG–Rubber) 115V(230V)	Conduit Size Inches 115V(230V)
1	8.4(4.2)	14(14)	1/2(1/2)
1.5	12.5(6.3)	12(14)	1/2(1/2)
2	16.1(8.3)	10(14)	3/4(1/2)
3	23(12.3)	8(12)	3/4(1/2)
5	40(19.8)	6(10)	1(3/4)
7.5	58(28.7)	3(6)	1-1/4(1)
10	75(38)	1(6)	1-1/2(1)
15	112(56)	00(4)	2(1-1/4)
20	140(74)	000(1)	2(1-1/2)
25	184(92)	300M(0)	2-1/2(2)
30	220(110)	400M(00)	3(2)
40	292(146)	700M(0000)	3-1/2(2-1/2)
50	360(180)	1000M(300M)	4(2-1/2)
60	NR(215)	NR(400M)	NR(3)
75	NR(268)	NR(600M)	NR(3-1/2)
100	NR(355)	NR(1000M)	NR(4)

NR indicates "Not Recommended" and M indicates M.C.M (1000 Circular Mils). The above specifications are based on data from the *National Electrical Code*.

3 Phase Electric Motor Specs

HP	Full Load Amps 230V(460V)	Wire Size Minimum (AWG–Rubber) 230V(460V)	Conduit Size Inches 230V(460V)
1	3.3(1.7)	14(14)	1/2(1/2)
1.5	4.7(2.4)	14(14)	1/2(1/2)
2	6(3.0)	14(14)	1/2(1/2)
3	9(4.5)	14(14)	1/2(1/2)
5	15(7.5)	12(14)	1/2(1/2)
7.5	22(11)	8(14)	3/4(1/2)
10	27(14)	8(12)	3/4(1/2)
15	38(19)	6(10)	1-1/4(3/4)
20	52(26)	4(8)	1-1/4(3/4)
25	64(32)	3(6)	1-1/4(1-1/4)
30	77(39)	1(6)	1-1/2(1-1/4)
40	101(51)	00(4)	2(1-1/4)
50	125(63)	000(3)	2(1-1/4)
60	149(75)	200M(1)	2-1/2(1-1/2)
75	180(90)	0000(0)	2-1/2(2)
100	245(123)	500M(000)	3(2)
125	310(155)	750M(0000)	3-1/2(2-1/2)
150	360(180)	1000M(300M)	4(2-1/2)
200	480(240)	NR(500M)	NR(3)
250	580(290)	NR(NR)	NR(NR)
300	696(348)	NR(NR)	NR(NR)

NR indicates "Not Recommended" and "M" indicates M.C.M (1000 Circular Mils).

Note that starting currents for the above motors can be many times the Full Load Amps and fuses must be adjusted accordingly. If the powerline becomes too long, voltage drop will exceed safe limits and the wire size should be adjusted to the next larger (smaller AWG number) gauge wire. See the Copper Wire Specifications table in this chapter for more specific information on wire.

The above specifications are from the *National Electrical Code*.

HP vs. Torque vs. RPM – Motors

HP	Torque in Inch Pounds-force @ Motor R.P.M.					
	3450	2000	1725	1550	1140	1050
1	18	32	37	41	55	60
1.5	27	47	55	61	83	90
2	37	63	73	81	111	120
3	55	95	110	122	166	180
5	91	158	183	203	276	300
7.5	137	236	274	305	415	450
10	183	315	365	407	553	600
15	274	473	548	610	829	900
20	365	630	731	813	1106	1200
25	457	788	913	1017	1382	1501
30	548	945	1096	1220	1659	1801
40	731	1261	1461	1626	2211	2401
50	913	1576	1827	2033	2764	3001
60	1096	1891	2192	2440	3317	3601
70	1279	2206	2558	2846	3870	4202
80	1461	2521	2923	3253	4423	4802
90	1644	2836	3288	3660	4976	5402
100	1827	3151	3654	4066	5529	6002
125	2284	3939	4567	5083	6911	7503
150	2740	4727	5480	6099	8293	9004
175	3197	5515	6394	7116	9675	10504
200	3654	6303	7307	8132	11057	12005
225	4110	7090	8221	9149	12439	13505
250	4567	7878	9134	10165	13821	15006
275	5024	8666	10047	11182	15203	16507
300	5480	9454	10961	12198	16586	18007
350	6394	11029	12788	14231	19350	21008
400	7307	12605	14614	16265	22114	24010
450	8221	14181	16441	18298	24878	27011
500	9134	15756	18268	20331	27643	30012
550	10047	17332	20095	22364	30407	33013
600	10961	18908	21922	24397	33171	36014

Torque in Inch Pounds-force = $\dfrac{\text{Horsepower} \times 63025}{\text{Motor RPM}}$

To convert to Foot Pounds-force, divide the torque by 12.

HP vs. Torque vs. RPM – Motors

HP	Torque in Inch Pounds-force @ Motor R.P.M.					
	1000	850	750	600	500	230
1	63	74	84	105	126	274
1.5	95	111	126	158	189	411
2	126	148	168	210	252	548
3	189	222	252	315	378	822
5	315	371	420	525	630	1370
7.5	473	556	630	788	945	2055
10	630	741	840	1050	1261	2740
15	945	1112	1261	1576	1891	4110
20	1261	1483	1681	2101	2521	5480
25	1576	1854	2101	2626	3151	6851
30	1891	2224	2521	3151	3782	8221
40	2521	2966	3361	4202	5042	10961
50	3151	3707	4202	5252	6303	13701
60	3782	4449	5042	6303	7563	16441
70	4412	5190	5882	7353	8824	19182
80	5042	5932	6723	8403	10084	21922
90	5672	6673	7563	9454	11345	24662
100	6303	7415	8403	10504	12605	27402
125	7878	9268	10504	13130	15756	34253
150	9454	11122	12605	15756	18908	41103
175	11029	12976	14706	18382	22059	47954
200	12605	14829	16807	21008	25210	54804
225	14181	16683	18908	23634	28361	61655
250	15756	18537	21008	26260	31513	68505
275	17332	20390	23109	28886	34664	75356
300	18908	22244	25210	31513	37815	82207
350	22059	25951	29412	36765	44118	95908
400	25210	29659	33613	42017	50420	109609
450	28361	33366	37815	47269	56723	123310
500	31513	37074	42017	52521	63025	137011
550	34664	40781	46218	57773	69328	150712
600	37815	44488	50420	63025	75630	164413

Torque in Inch Pounds-force = $\dfrac{\text{Horsepower} \times 63025}{\text{Motor RPM}}$

NOTE: Ratings below 500 RPM are for gear motors.
To convert to Foot Pounds-force, divide the torque by 12.

HP vs. Torque vs. RPM – Motors

| HP | Torque in Inch Pounds-force @ Motor R.P.M. | | | | | |
	190	155	125	100	84	68
1	332	407	504	630	750	927
1.5	498	610	756	945	1125	1390
2	663	813	1008	1261	1501	1854
3	995	1220	1513	1891	2251	2781
5	1659	2033	2521	3151	3751	4634
7.5	2488	3050	3782	4727	5627	6951
10	3317	4066	5042	6303	7503	9268
15	4976	6099	7563	9454	11254	13903
20	6634	8132	10084	12605	15006	18537
25	8293	10165	12605	15756	18757	23171
30	9951	12198	15126	18908	22509	27805
40	13268	16265	20168	25210	30012	37074
50	16586	20331	25210	31513	37515	46342
60	19903	24397	30252	37815	45018	55610
70	23220	28463	35294	44118	52521	64879
80	26537	32529	40336	50420	60024	74147
90	29854	36595	45378	56723	67527	83415
100	33171	40661	50420	63025	75030	92684
125	41464	50827	63025	78781	93787	115855
150	49757	60992	75630	94538	112545	139026
175	58049	71157	88235	110294	131302	162197
200	66342	81323	100840	126050	150060	185368
225	74635	91488	113445	141806	168817	208539
250	82928	101653	126050	157563	187574	231710
275	91220	111819	138655	173319	206332	254881
300	99513	121984	151260	189075	225089	278051
350	116099	142315	176470	220588	262604	324393
400	132684	162645	201680	252100	300119	370735
450	149270	182976	226890	283613	337634	417077
500	165855	203306	252100	315125	375149	463419
550	182441	223637	277310	346638	412664	509761
600	199026	243968	302520	378150	450179	556103

$$\text{Torque in Inch Pounds-force} = \frac{\text{Horsepower} \times 63025}{\text{Motor RPM}}$$

NOTE: Ratings below 500 RPM are for gear motors.
To convert to Foot Pounds-force, divide the torque by 12.

World Electric and TV

Most countries of the world provide some type of electric, TV and telephone service to their populations. The following are notes about the general differences between the standards:

Of the 204 countries listed in the following tables, virtually all use AC power. DC power sources are rare and will NOT operate AC devices.

Most countries in the Western Hemisphere, above the equator, provide 110 volt AC power. The rest of the world normally operates at voltages of 220 to 250 volts AC. Voltage converters are available to adapt devices to either power standard.

AC power operates at one of two frequency standards - 50 hertz or 60 hertz. A 60 hertz frequency is standard in those countries that provide 110 volt power and 50 hertz is standard in those countries operating at 220 to 250 volts. Although most appliances will operate at either frequency, clocks and other timing devices may not work correctly. No converter devices are available to convert between either of the frequencies.

Many European countries have switched over to the 230 volt from the 220 volt standard.

There are five different television standards used in the world today: NTSC, SECAM, PAL, N-PAL, and M-PAL. All of these standards operate at different frequencies and with a different number of scanning lines and are therefore not compatible with each other. i.e. a PAL TV can not receive NTSC transmissions.

Telephones are fairly standardized in the world today and most use the North American "RJ-11" socket. There are only about 25 countries that require special adapter plugs. See page 178.

World Electric and TV

Drawings of the various electric plugs are included on page 172.

Country	Single Phase	Three Phase	Frequency	Plug #	TV Standard
Afghanistan	220	380	50Hz	C,D	PAL
Albania	110/220	380	50Hz	C	PAL
Algeria	127/220	220/380	50Hz	C,D,F	PAL
American Samoa	120/240	240/480	60Hz	A	NTSC
Andorra	220		50Hz	C	PAL
Angola[1,2,3]	220	380	50Hz	C	PAL
Anguilla	110		60Hz	A	
Antigua & Barbuda	110/220		50Hz	B,G	NTSC
	230/400	400	60Hz		
Argentina	220	380/440	50Hz	C,J	PAL
Armenia	220		50Hz	C	SECAM
Aruba	115/127	230	60Hz	A	NTSC
Australia[1,2]	240/415	415	50Hz	H,J	PAL
Austria[1,2]	220	380	50Hz	C	PAL
Azerbaijan	220		50Hz	C	SECAM
Azores	110/220	380	50Hz	C	PAL
Bahamas	120/240	240	60Hz	A	NTSC
	120/208	208	60Hz		
Bahrain[1,2]	220	400	50Hz	C,D,G	PAL
	110/115		60Hz		
Bangladesh[1,2,3]	220/230	440	50Hz	A,C,D	PAL
	220/380	380	50Hz		
Barbados[1,2]	115/230	230	50Hz	A,B	NTSC
	115/200	200	50Hz		
Belarus	220	380	50Hz	C	SECAM
Belgium[1,2]	220	400	50Hz	A,C,E	PAL
	127/220	220	50Hz		
	220/380	380	50Hz		
	230		50Hz		
Belize[1,2]	110/220	220	60Hz	A,B,G	NTSC
	220/440	440	60Hz		
Benin	220	380	50Hz	D	SECAM
Bermuda[1,2,3]	120/240	240	60Hz	A,B	NTSC
	120/208	208	60Hz		
Bhutan	220		50Hz	C,G	PAL
Bolivia	110/220	220	50Hz	A,C	NTSC
	115/230	230	50Hz		
	220	380	50Hz		
	230/400	400	50Hz		
Bosnia	220		50Hz	C	PAL
Botswana	231	400	50Hz	C,D,G	PAL/SECAM
	220	380	50Hz		
Brazil[1]	110/220	220	60Hz	A,B,C	PAL
	115/220	220	60Hz		
	115/230	230	60Hz		
	125/216	216	60Hz		
	127/220	220	60Hz		
	220/380	380	60Hz		

Country	Single Phase	Three Phase	Freq- uency	Plug #	TV Standard
Brazil (cont.)	120	240	60Hz		
	220/440	440	50Hz		
	230/400	400	60Hz		
Brunei[1,2]	240	415	50Hz	C,G	PAL
	230		50Hz		
Bulgaria	220	380	50Hz	C,F	SECAM
Burkina Faso	220	380	50Hz	C,E	SECAM
Burma[1,2,3]	230/400	400	50Hz	C,D,F	NTSC
	220		50Hz		
Burundi[3]	220	380	50Hz	C,E	SECAM
Cambodia	220/380	380	50Hz	A,C	NTSC
	110/208	208	50Hz		
Cameroon	220/380	380	50Hz	C,E	PAL
	127	220	50Hz		
	230/400	400	50Hz		
Canada[1]	120/240	240	60Hz	A,B	NTSC
		575	60Hz		
Canary Islands	110/220		50Hz	C,E	PAL
	127/220	220	50Hz		
	220/380	380			
Cape Verde[2]	220/380	380	50Hz	C,F	PAL
Cayman Islands[1,3]	120/240	240	60Hz	A,B	NTSC
Central African Rep.[2,3]	220	380	50Hz	C,E	SECAM
Chad	220	380	50Hz	C,D,E	SECAM
Chile	220/380	380	50Hz	C,N	NTSC
China	220	380	50Hz	A,C,G	PAL
Colombia	110/220	220	60Hz	A,B	NTSC
	120/208	208	60Hz		
Comoros	110/220		50Hz	C	SECAM
Congo, Democratic Republic of the[1,2]	220	380	50Hz	C	SECAM
Congo, Rep. Of[1,2,3]	220	380	50Hz	C,E	SECAM
Cook Islands	220/240		50Hz	J,H	PAL
Costa Rica	120/240	240	60Hz	A,B	NTSC
Cote d'Ivoire	220	380	50Hz	C,E	SECAM
Croatia	230		50Hz	C	PAL
Cuba	110/220		60Hz	A,C	NTSC
Cyprus[1,2]	240	415	50Hz	C,G	SECAM/PAL
	220		50Hz		
Czech Republic	220/380	380	50Hz	A,C,E	SECAM/PAL
Denmark	220/380	380	50Hz	C,L	PAL
	230		50Hz		
Djibouti, Rep. Of	220	380	50Hz	C,E	SECAM
Dominica	230	400	50Hz	G	NTSC
Dominican Republic	110/220	220	60Hz	A	NTSC
Ecuador[1]	120/208	208	60Hz	A,B	NTSC
	127/220	220	60Hz		
	110/220		60Hz		
Egypt	220/380	380	50Hz	C	SECAM/PAL
	110/220		50Hz		
El Salvador[1]	115/230	230	60Hz	A,B,C,D,E,F,G,J,M,N	NTSC

World Electric and TV

Country	Single Phase	Three Phase	Freq-uency	Plug #	TV Standard
	110/220		60Hz		
Equatorial Guinea	220			C,E	SECAM
Eritrea	220	380	50Hz	C	PAL
Estonia	220/230		50Hz	C	SECAM/PAL
Ethiopia	220	380	50Hz	C	PAL
Faroe Islands	220/380	380	50Hz	C	PAL
Fiji[1]	240/415	415	50Hz	J	PAL
	220		50Hz		
Finland	230	400	50Hz	C,F	PAL
	220	380	50Hz		
France	220	380	50Hz	C,E	SECAM
	230		50Hz		
	110	190	50Hz		
	110	220	50Hz		
	127	220	50Hz		
French Guiana	220/380	380	50Hz	C	SECAM
Gabon[1,2]	220	380	50Hz	C	SECAM
Gambia, The[1,2]	220	380	50Hz	C,G	PAL
Germany[1,2,3]	230	400	50Hz	C,F	SECAM/PAL
	220	380	50Hz		
Ghana	240	415	50Hz	C,D,G	PAL
	230		50Hz		
	220	400	50Hz		
Gibralter	240	415	50Hz	C,G	PAL
	220		50Hz		
Greece	220	380	50Hz	C,F	SECAM/PAL
	230		50Hz		
Greenland	220/380	380	50Hz	C,L	NTSC/PAL
Grenada[1,2,3]	230	400	50Hz	G	NTSC
	220/240		50Hz		
Guadeloupe	220/380	380	50Hz	C	SECAM
Guam	110/220	220	60Hz	A	NTSC
	120/208	208	60Hz		
Guatemala	120/240	240	60Hz	A,B,G,J	NTSC
	110		60Hz		
Guinea	220/380	380	50Hz	C,F,L	SECAM/PAL
Guinea-Bissau	220/380	380	50Hz	C	PAL
Guyana[1,2]	110/220	220	60Hz	A,D,G	NTSC/SECAM
	110/220	220	60Hz		
Haiti	110/220	220	50Hz	A,B	NTSC
	110/220	220	60Hz		
	120/208	208	60Hz		
Honduras	110/220	220	60Hz	A	NTSC
Hong Kong	200	346	50Hz	G	PAL
	230		50Hz		
Hungary[3,3]	220/380	380	50Hz	C,F	SECAM/PAL
Iceland	220/380	380	50Hz	C	PAL
	230		50Hz		
India[3]	230	400	50Hz	C,D,G	PAL
	220	380	50Hz		

Country	Single Phase	Three Phase	Freq-uency	Plug #	TV Standard
	240		50Hz		
Indonesia[1]	110	220	50Hz	C,F	PAL
	220	380	50Hz		
Iran	220	380	50Hz	C	SECAM
Iraq	220	380	50Hz	C,D,G	SECAM
Ireland[1,2,3]	220	380	50Hz	C,G	PAL
	230		50Hz		
Israel[1,2,4]	220	380	50Hz	C,K	PAL
	230	400	50Hz		
Italy[1,2,4]	127	220	50Hz	C,N	PAL
	230		50Hz		
	220	380	50Hz		
Jamaica[1,3]	110/220	220	50Hz	A,B	NTSC
Japan[1]	100/200	200	50Hz	A,B	NTSC
	100/200	200	60Hz		
Jordan[1,2]	220/380	380	50Hz	C,F,G	PAL
Kazakstan	220	380	50Hz	C,G,K	SECAM
Kenya[2,3]	240	415	50Hz	C,D,G	PAL
	220		50Hz		
Kiribati	110		60Hz	A,J	PAL
	220		50Hz		
Korea, Dem People's Rep. (North Korea)	110/220		60Hz	C	SECAM/PAL
Korea Rep. Of (South)[1,2,3]	110/220	380	60Hz	A,C	NTSC
Kuwait[3]	240	415	50Hz	C,D,G	PAL
	220		50Hz		
Laos	220	380	50Hz	A,B,C,E,F	PAL
Latvia	220		50Hz	C	SECAM/PAL
Lebanon[1]	110	190	50Hz	B,C,D,G	SECAM/PAL
	220	380	50Hz		
Lesotho[1,2]	220	380	50Hz	D,P	PAL
Liberia[1]	120/240	240	60Hz	A,B	PAL
Libya	127/230	220	50Hz	C,D	SECAM
Lithuania	220		50Hz	C	SECAM/PAL
Luxembourg[1,2]	230/400		50Hz	C,F	SECAM/PAL
	110/220		50Hz		
	120/208	208	50Hz		
	220/380	380	50Hz		
Macao	220/380	380	50Hz	D	PAL
Macedonia	220	380	50Hz	C,F	PAL
Madagascar[1,2]	127/220	380	50Hz	C,D,E,M,L	SECAM
	220/380	380	50Hz		
Malawi[3]	230/400	400	50Hz	G	PAL
	220		50Hz		
Malaysia[1,2]	240	415	50Hz	C,G	PAL
	220		50Hz		
Maldives	220		50Hz	D	PAL
	230	400	50Hz		
Mali[1,2]	220	380	50Hz	C,E	SECAM
Malta[1,2]	240	415	50Hz	C,G	PAL
	220		50Hz		

World Electric and TV

Country	Single Phase	Three Phase	Freq-uency	Plug #	TV Standard
Martinique	220/380	380	50Hz	C,D	SECAM
Mauritania[1,2,3]	220	380	50Hz	C	SECAM
Mauritius[1,2]	230	400	50Hz	C,G	SECAM
	220		50Hz		
Mexico[1]	127/220	220	60Hz	A	NTSC
	110/220		60Hz		
Micronesia, Federated State of	120		60Hz	A	NTSC
Monaco	127	220	50Hz	C,D,E,F	PAL/SECAM
	220	380	50Hz		
Mongolia	220		50Hz	C	SECAM
Montserrat	110/230	400	60Hz	A	NTSC
Morocco[1,2]	127	220	50Hz	C,E	SECAM
	110/220		50Hz		
	220	380	50Hz		
Mozambique[2]	220/380	380	50Hz	C,F	PAL
Namibia[1,2]	220	380	50Hz	C,D	PAL
Nauru	220/240		50Hz	J,H	
Nepal[1]	220	380	50Hz	C,D	PAL
	220	440	50Hz		
Netherlands[1]	220	380	50Hz	C,F	PAL
	230		50Hz		
Netherlands Antilles	127/220	220	50Hz	A,C	NTSC
	220/380	380	50Hz		
	120/208	208	60Hz		
	110/220		50Hz		
New Caledonia	220/380	380	50Hz	C	SECAM
New Zealand[1,2]	230/400	400	50Hz	H,J	PAL
Nicaragua	120/240	240	60Hz	A	NTSC
Niger	220/380	380	50Hz	A,C,E	SECAM
Nigeria[1]	220	380	50Hz	C,D,G	PAL
	230	415	50Hz		
Norway	220	380	50Hz	C,F	PAL
	230		50Hz		
Oman[2]	240	415	50Hz	C,D,G	PAL
	220		50Hz		
Pakistan[1]	230/400	400	50Hz	C,D,G	PAL
	220/380	380	50Hz		
Palau	120	240	60Hz	A,B	NTSC
Panama	120	240	60Hz	A,B,J	NTSC
	110/220	220	60Hz		
Papua New Guinea	240	415	50Hz	J,H	PAL
Paraguay	220	380	50Hz	C	PAL
Peru	220	380	60Hz	A,C	NTSC
	110/220	220	60Hz		
	110/220	220	50Hz		
Philippines[1,2,3]	110/220	220	60Hz	A,B,C	NTSC
	115/230	230	60Hz		
Poland	220/380	380	50Hz	C,E	SECAM/PAL
	230		50Hz		

Country	Single Phase	Three Phase	Frequency	Plug #	TV Standard
Portugal[1]	220/380	380	50Hz	C,F	PAL
	230		50Hz		
Puerto Rico	120/240	240	60Hz	A	NTSC
Qatar	240	415	50Hz	C,D,G	PAL
	220		50Hz		
Reunion	220		50Hz	C	SECAM
Romania[3]	220	380	50Hz	C,F	SECAM/PAL
	230		50Hz		
Russia	220/380	380	50Hz	Q	SECAM
Rwanda	220	380	50Hz	C,M	SECAM
Saint Kitts & Nevis	230	400	60Hz	D,G	NTSC
	220		50Hz		
Saint Lucia	240	416	50Hz	C,G	NTSC
	220		50Hz		
Saint Vincent	230	400	50Hz	C,G	NTSC
	110/220		50Hz		
Saudi Arabia[3]	127	220	60Hz	A,B,C,G	SECAM/PAL
	220	380	50Hz		
Senegal[1,3]	127/220	220	50Hz	C,D,E,L	SECAM
Seychelles	240	450	50Hz	C,D,G	PAL
	240	240	50Hz		
	220		50Hz		
Sierra Leone	230	400	50Hz	D,G	PAL
	220		50Hz		
Singapore[1]	230	400	50Hz	C,D,G	PAL
	220		50Hz		
Slovakia	220	380	50Hz	E	SECAM/PAL
	230		50Hz		
Slovenia	220		50Hz	C	PAL
Somalia	220	380	50Hz	C	PAL
	110	220	50Hz		
	220	440	50Hz		
	230		50Hz		
South Africa[1,2,3]	220/380	380	50Hz	C,D,P	PAL
	230/400	400	50Hz		
	250/433	433	50Hz		
	250	430	50Hz		
Spain[1]	220/380	380	50Hz	C,F	PAL
	127/220	220	50Hz		
	230		50Hz		
Sri Lanka[1,3]	230	400	50Hz	C,D	PAL
Sudan[1]	240	415	50Hz	C,D	PAL
	220		50Hz		
Suriname	127/220	220	50Hz	C,F	NTSC
	127		60Hz		
	110		50Hz		
	110		60Hz		
	115/230	230	60Hz		
Swaziland	230	400	50Hz	C,P	PAL
	220		50Hz		
Sweden[1,2]	230	400	50Hz	C,F	PAL
	220/380	380	50Hz		
Switzerland[1,2]	220/380	380	50Hz	C,M	PAL

World Electric and TV

Country	Single Phase	Three Phase	Frequency	Plug #	TV Standard
	230		50Hz		
Syria	220/380	380	50Hz	C	SECAM
	115/200		50Hz		
Tahiti	127/220	220	60Hz	A	SECAM
	110/220		60Hz		
	110/220		50Hz		
Taiwan[1]	110/220	220	60Hz	A,B	NTSC
Tajikistan	220	380	50Hz	C,J	SECAM
Tanzania[1,2,3]	220	380	50Hz	C,D,G	PAL
	230/400	400	50Hz		
Thailand[9]	220/380	380	50Hz	A,C	PAL
Togo	127	220	50Hz	C	SECAM
	220	380	50Hz		
Tonga	240/415	415	50Hz	J	NTSC
	115		60Hz		
Trinidad and Tobago[9]	115/230	230	60Hz	A,B,C	NTSC
	110/220		60Hz		
	230/400	400	60Hz		
Tunisia[1,2,3]	127	220	50Hz	C,E	SECAM
	110/220		50Hz		
	220	380	50Hz		
Turkey[1]	220/380	380	50Hz	C,F	PAL
Turkmenistan	220	380	50Hz	B,F	SECAM
Uganda[1,2]	240/415	415	50Hz	D,G	PAL
	220		50Hz		
Ukraine[1]	220	380	50Hz	C	SECAM
United Arab Emirates	220/380	380	50Hz	C,D,G	PAL
	230/400	400	50Hz		
	240/415	415	50Hz		
United Kingdom[1,2,3]	230	415	50Hz	C,D,G	PAL
	240	415	50Hz		
	230	400	50Hz		
	220	380	50Hz		
	240/480		50Hz		
United States of America	120/208	208	60Hz	A,B	NTSC
	120/240	240	60Hz		
		460	60Hz		
	110		60Hz		
Uruguay[2,3,6]	220	380	50Hz	C,F,J,N	PAL
Uzbekistan	220	380	50Hz	C,J	SECAM
Venezuela	120/240	240	60Hz	A,B	NTSC
Vietnam	220	380	50Hz	A,C	NTSC/PAL/SECAM
	127	220	50Hz		
Vietnam (cont.)	120	208	50Hz		
	127/230		50Hz		
	110		60Hz		
Virgin Islands	110/220		60Hz	A	NTSC
	120/240	240	60Hz		

Country	Single Phase	Three Phase	Frequency	Plug #	TV Standard
Western Samoa	230/400	400	50Hz	H	NTSC/PAL
Yemen	220	380	50Hz	A,C,D,G	PAL
	230	400	50Hz		
Zambia[1,2,4]	220	380	50Hz	C,D,G	PAL
	230	400	50Hz		
Zimbabwe[4]	220/380	380	50Hz	C,D,G	PAL
	230/400	400	50Hz		

Footnotes

1. The neutral wire of the secondary distribution system is grounded.
2. A grounding conductor is required in the electrical cord attached to appliances.
3. Voltage tolerance is plus or minus 4 to 9%
4. Voltage tolerance is plus or minus 10%
5. Voltage tolerance is plus or minus 20 to 30%
6. Voltage tolerance is plus or minus 4.5 to 20.5%

World Electric Connectors

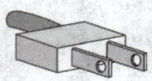

Plug A
Ungrounded: North America, South America, Japan, many of the Caribbean islands.

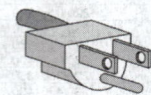

Plug B
Grounded: North America, South America, Japan, many of the Caribbean islands.

Plug C
Europlug: The most common plug pattern in the world. Also Africa, Middle East, Asia, Europe

Plug D
India and Africa and some in the Middle East

Plug E
France, Belgium, Czech Republic, Poland, some in Africa.

Plug F
Schuko plug: Germany, Greece, Hungary, Scandinavia, Portugal, Romania and Spain.

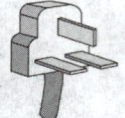

Plug G
United Kingdom, Ireland & present/former UK colonies. Also Africa, India, Asia, Mid East

Plug H
Ungrounded: Australia, New Zealand, China, Argentina, throughout South Pacific

World Electric Connectors

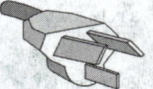

Plug J
Grounded: Australia, New Zealand, China, Argentina, throughout South Pacific

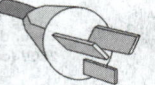

Plug K
Israel (unique to Israel)

Plug L
Denmark and limited use in Africa

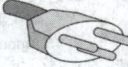

Plug M
Switzerland
(usually very tightly recessed)

Plug N
Italy, Ethiopia and most of Chile

Plug P
South Africa and India
(Old British style)

Plug Q
Russia
Similar to Plug C (Europe's plug) but pins are only 4 mm

NEMA Receptacle Configurations

Straight Blade Receptacles

2 Pole, 2 Wire PLUGS-next 3 only

125V

15 Ampere (#1-15)

250 V

20 Ampere (#2-20)

30 Ampere (#2-30)

2 Pole, 3 Wire, Grounding

125V

15 Ampere (#5-15)

20 Ampere (#5-20)

30 Ampere (#5-30)

50 Ampere (#5-50)

250V

15 Ampere (#6-15)

20 Ampere (#6-20)

2 Pole, 3 Wire, Grounding (cont.)

250V (cont.)

30 Ampere (#6-30)

50 Ampere (#6-50)

277V

15 Ampere (#7-15)

20 Ampere (#7-20)

30 Ampere (#7-30)

50 Ampere (#7-50)

347 V

15 Ampere (#24-15)

20 Ampere (#24-20)

30 Ampere (#24-30)

50 Ampere (#24-50)

3 Pole, 3 Wire

125/250V

20 Ampere (#10-20)

30 Ampere (#10-30)

50 Ampere (#10-50)

3 Phase 250 V

15 Ampere (#11-15)

20 Ampere (#11-20)

30 Ampere (#11-30)

50 Ampere (#11-50)

3 Pole, 4 Wire, Grounding

125/250V

15 Ampere (#14-15)

20 Ampere (#14-20)

30 Ampere (#14-30)

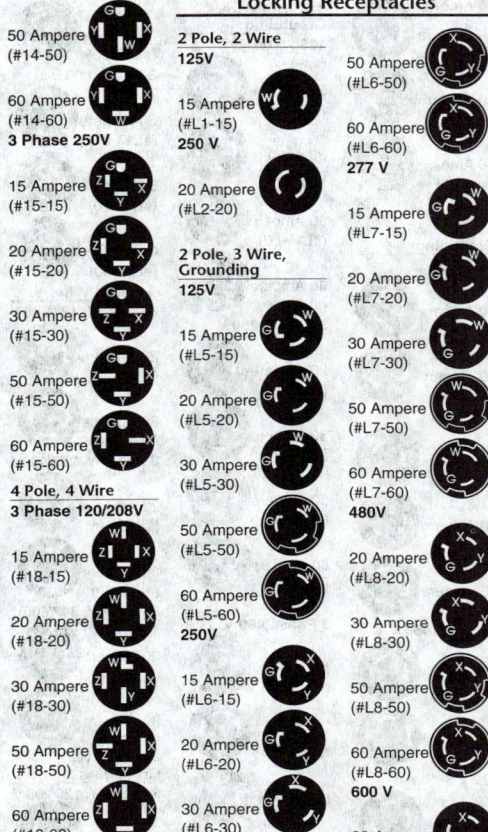

Locking Receptacles

50 Ampere (#14-50)

60 Ampere (#14-60)
3 Phase 250V

15 Ampere (#15-15)

20 Ampere (#15-20)

30 Ampere (#15-30)

50 Ampere (#15-50)

60 Ampere (#15-60)

4 Pole, 4 Wire
3 Phase 120/208V

15 Ampere (#18-15)

20 Ampere (#18-20)

30 Ampere (#18-30)

50 Ampere (#18-50)

60 Ampere (#18-60)

2 Pole, 2 Wire
125V

15 Ampere (#L1-15)
250 V

20 Ampere (#L2-20)

2 Pole, 3 Wire,
Grounding
125V

15 Ampere (#L5-15)

20 Ampere (#L5-20)

30 Ampere (#L5-30)

50 Ampere (#L5-50)

60 Ampere (#L5-60)
250V

15 Ampere (#L6-15)

20 Ampere (#L6-20)

30 Ampere (#L6-30)

50 Ampere (#L6-50)

60 Ampere (#L6-60)
277 V

15 Ampere (#L7-15)

20 Ampere (#L7-20)

30 Ampere (#L7-30)

50 Ampere (#L7-50)

60 Ampere (#L7-60)
480V

20 Ampere (#L8-20)

30 Ampere (#L8-30)

50 Ampere (#L8-50)

60 Ampere (#L8-60)
600 V

20 Ampere (#L9-20)

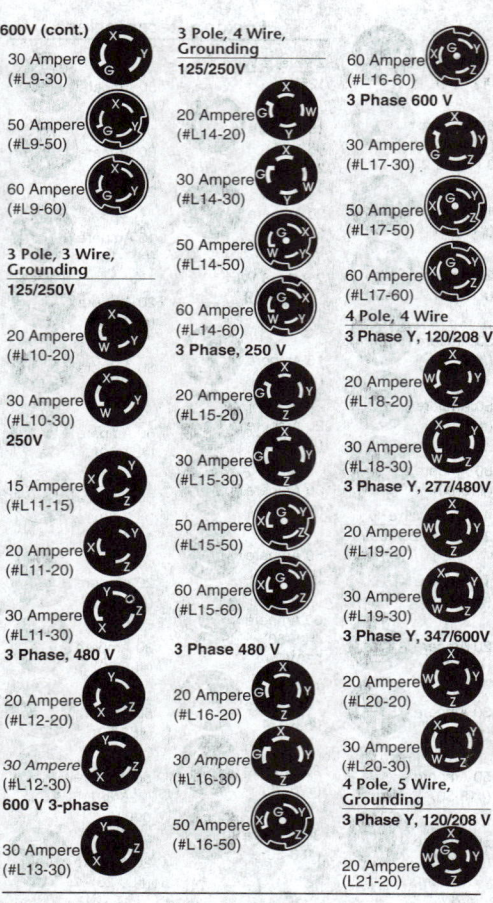

600V (cont.)

30 Ampere (#L9-30)

50 Ampere (#L9-50)

60 Ampere (#L9-60)

3 Pole, 3 Wire, Grounding
125/250V

20 Ampere (#L10-20)

30 Ampere (#L10-30)

250V

15 Ampere (#L11-15)

20 Ampere (#L11-20)

30 Ampere (#L11-30)

3 Phase, 480 V

20 Ampere (#L12-20)

30 Ampere (#L12-30)

600 V 3-phase

30 Ampere (#L13-30)

3 Pole, 4 Wire, Grounding
125/250V

20 Ampere (#L14-20)

30 Ampere (#L14-30)

50 Ampere (#L14-50)

60 Ampere (#L14-60)

3 Phase, 250 V

20 Ampere (#L15-20)

30 Ampere (#L15-30)

50 Ampere (#L15-50)

60 Ampere (#L15-60)

3 Phase 480 V

20 Ampere (#L16-20)

30 Ampere (#L16-30)

50 Ampere (#L16-50)

60 Ampere (#L16-60)

3 Phase 600 V

30 Ampere (#L17-30)

50 Ampere (#L17-50)

60 Ampere (#L17-60)

4 Pole, 4 Wire
3 Phase Y, 120/208 V

20 Ampere (#L18-20)

30 Ampere (#L18-30)

3 Phase Y, 277/480V

20 Ampere (#L19-20)

30 Ampere (#L19-30)

3 Phase Y, 347/600V

20 Ampere (#L20-20)

30 Ampere (#L20-30)

4 Pole, 5 Wire, Grounding
3 Phase Y, 120/208 V

20 Ampere (L21-20)

30 Ampere
(#L21-30)

50 Ampere
(#L21-50)

60 Ampere
(#L21-60)

3 Phase Y, 277/480V

20 Ampere
(#L22-20)

30 Ampere
(#L22-30)

50 Ampere
(#L22-50)

60 Ampere
(#L22-60)

3 Phase Y, 347/600V

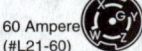

20 Ampere
(#L23-20)

30 Ampere
(#L23-30)

50 Ampere
(#L23-50)

60 Ampere
(#L23-60)

347V
20 Ampere
(#L24-20)

FSL Configurations

2 Pole 3 Wire Grounding
28V DC

30 Ampere
(#FSL-1)

120V/400hZ

30 Ampere
(#FSL-2)

120V/400hZ, 3-Phase

30 Ampere
(#FSL-3)

4 Pole 5 Wire Grounding
120/208V 3 phase Y 400 hZ

30 Ampere

Midget Locking

2 Pole 2 Wire
125 V

15 Ampere
(#ML-1)

2 Pole 3 Wire Grounding
125V

15 Ampere
(#ML-2)

125/250V

15 Ampere
(#ML-3)

Marine Ship to Shore

2 Pole 3 Wire Grounding
125 V

50 Ampere
(#SS1-50)

3 Pole 4 Wire Grounding
125/250V

50 Ampere
(#SS2-50)

Travel Trailer

2 pole, 3 Wire Grounding
120 V AC

30 Ampere
(#TT)

World Telephone Connectors

Telephones are fairly standardized in the world today and most use the North American "RJ-11" socket. There are approximately 33 countries that require special adapter plugs and these adapters are readily available through catalogs and stores that specialize in foreign travel.

Non Standard Countries
Afghanistan - Russian
Australia - mix of Australian and RJ-11
Austria - Austrian
Belgium - mix of Belgium and RJ-11
Brazil - mix of Brazil and RJ-11
Bulgaria - mix of Russian & RJ-11
Chad - French
Columbia - mix of Columbia and RJ-11
Cuba - mix of Russian & RJ-11
Denmark - Danish
Finland - Finnish/Norwegian
France - French
Germany - mix of German (5 types) and RJ-11 & RJ-45
Greenland - Danish
Hong Kong - - mix of British & RJ-45
Hungary - mix of Hungary, Austria and RJ-11
India - mix of old British & RJ-11
Israel - mix of Israel (2 types) and British
Italy - mix of Italy (2 types) and RJ-11
Japan - mix of Japan and RJ-11
Korea - mix of Korean and RJ-11
Macedonia - mix of Yugoslavian and RJ-11
Middle East - mix of Turkish, Jordan/Saudi, RJ-11
Netherlands - mix of Dutch, RJ-11 & RJ-45
Norway - mix of Finnish/Norwegian and RJ-45
Poland - mix of Russian and RJ-11
Portugal - mix of Portuguese, Danish, and RJ-11
Russia - Russian
Saudi Arabia - mix of British, French, Saudi & RJ-11
Scandinavia - Finish/Norwegian, RJ-45
Slovakia Republic - Czech
South Africa - mix of South African & RJ-11
Sweden - mix of Swedish & RJ-11
Switzerland - mix of Swiss (2 types) & RJ-45
Turkey - mix of Turkish & RJ-11
United Kingdom - British
Venezuela - mix of Venezuelan & RJ-11
Yugoslavia (former)

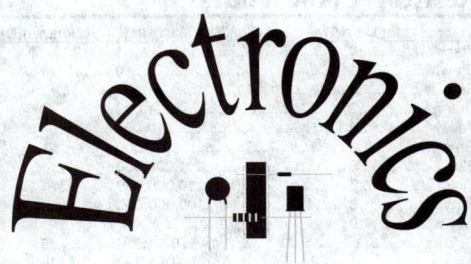

Electronics

(See also Frequency Spectrum on page 332)
(See also ELECTRIC Chapter on page 137)

Resistor Color Codes

Color	1st Digit(A)	2nd Digit(B)	Multiplier(C)	Tolerance(D)
Black	0	0	1	
Brown	1	1	10	1%
Red	2	2	100	2%
Orange	3	3	1,000	3%
Yellow	4	4	10,000	4%
Green	5	5	100,000	
Blue	6	6	1,000,000	
Violet	7	7	10,000,000	
Gray	8	8	100,000,000	
White	9	9	10^9	
Gold			0.1 (EIA)	5%
Silver			0.01 (EIA)	10%
No Color				20%

Example: Red–Red–Orange = 22,000 ohms, 20%

Additional information concerning the Axial Lead resistor can be obtained if Band A is a wide band. Case 1: If only Band A is wide, it indicates that the resistor is wirewound. Case 2: If Band A is wide and there is also a blue fifth band to the right of Band D on the Axial Lead Resistor, it indicates the resistor is wirewound and flame proof.

Axial Lead Resistor

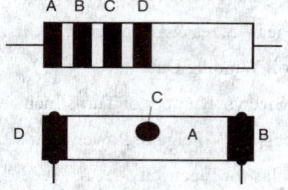

Radial Lead Resistor

Resistor Standard Values

Standard Resistor Values for 5% class
k = kilohms = 1,000 ohms   M = megohms = 1,000,000 ohms

1	10	100	1.0k	10k	100k	1.3M
1.1	11	110	1.1k	11k	110k	1.5M
1.2	12	120	1.2k	12k	120k	1.6M
1.3	13	130	1.3k	13k	130k	1.8M
1.5	15	150	1.5k	15k	150k	2.0M
1.6	16	160	1.6k	16k	160k	2.2M
1.8	18	180	1.8k	18k	180k	2.4M
2.0	20	200	2.0k	20k	200k	2.7M
2.2	22	220	2.2k	22k	220k	3.0M
2.4	24	240	2.4k	24k	330k	3.3M
2.7	27	270	2.7k	27k	360k	3.6M
3.0	30	300	3.0k	30k	390k	3.9M
3.3	33	330	3.3k	33k	430k	4.3M
3.6	36	360	3.6k	36k	470k	4.7M
3.9	39	390	3.9k	39k	510k	5.1M
4.3	43	430	4.3k	43k	560k	5.6M
4.7	47	470	4.7k	47k	620k	6.2M
5.1	51	510	5.1k	51k	680k	6.8M
5.6	56	560	5.6k	56k	750k	7.5M
6.2	62	620	6.2k	62k	820k	8.2M
6.8	68	680	6.8k	68k	910k	9.1M
7.5	75	750	7.5k	75k	1.0M	10.0M
8.2	82	820	8.2k	82k	1.1M	
9.1	91	910	9.1k	91k	1.2M	

Telephone Wire Color Codes

Wiring and Wire Pair Order
Wire Order·······white, red, black, yellow, violet
Trace Order·····blue, orange, green, brown, slate

Wire Pairs to Phone Solid Wire Colors
white/blue ·········green
blue/white ·········red
white/orange·····black
orange/white·····yellow
white/green·······white
green/white·······blue

Capacitor Color Codes

Color	1st Digit(A)	2nd Digit(B)	Multiplier(C)	Tolerance(D)
Black	0	0	1	20%
Brown	1	1	10	1%
Red	2	2	100	2%
Orange	3	3	1,000	3%
Yellow	4	4	10,000	4%
Green	5	5	100,000	5%
Blue	6	6	1,000,000	6%
Violet	7	7	10,000,000	7%
Gray	8	8	100,000,000	8%
White	9	9	10^9	9%
Gold			0.1 (EIA)	5%
Silver			0.01 (EIA)	10%
No Color				20%

Color Codes for Ceramic Capacitors

Color	Decimal Multiplier(C)	Tolerance (D) Above 10pf	Tolerance (D) Below 10pf	Temp Coef ppm/°C (E)
Black	1	20	2.0	0
Brown	10	1		−30
Red	100	2		−80
Orange	1000			−150
Yellow				−220
Green		5	0.5	−330
Blue				−470
Violet				−750
Gray	0.01		0.25	30
White	0.1	10	1.0	500

Ceramic disc capacitors are usually labeled. If the number is <1 then the value is picofarads, if >1 the value is microfarads. The letter R is sometimes used as a decimal, eg, 4R7 is 4.7.

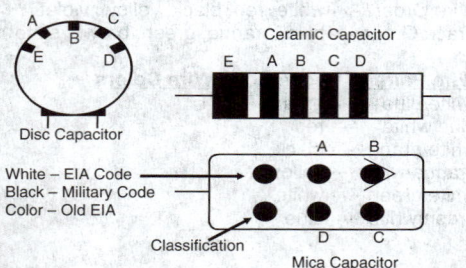

Disc Capacitor

Ceramic Capacitor

White – EIA Code
Black – Military Code
Color – Old EIA

Classification

Mica Capacitor

Capacitor Standard Values

pF	μF	μF	μF	μF
10	0.001	0.1	10	1000
12	0.0012			
13	0.0013			
15	0.0015	0.15	15	
18	0.0018			
20	0.002			
22	0.0022	0.22	22	2200
24				
27				
30				
33	0.0033	0.33	33	3300
36				
43				
47	0.0047	0.47	47	4700
51				
56				
62				
68	0.0068	0.68	68	6800
75				
82				
100	0.01	1.0	100	10,000
110				
120				
130				
150	0.015	1.5		
180				
200				
220	0.022	2.2	220	22,000
240				
270				
300				
330	0.033	3.3	330	
360				
390				
430				
470	0.047	4.7	470	47,000
510				
560				
620				
680	0.068	6.8		
750				
820				82,000
910				

pF = picofarads = 1×10^{-12} farads
μF = microfarads = 1×10^{-6} farads

Pilot Lamps

Lamp Number	Bead Color	Base Type	Bulb Volts	Amps	Type
12		2 Pin	6.3	0.15	G3-1/2
12PSB		Slide	12	0.17	T2
13	Green	Screw	3.7	0.30	G3-1/2
14	Blue	Screw	2.47	0.30	G3-1/2
19		2 Pin	14.4	0.10	G3-1/2
24PSB		Slide	24	0.073	T2
27		Screw	4.9	0.30	G4-1/2
28PSB		Slide	28	0.04	T2
31		Screw	6.15	0.30	G4-1/2
40	Brown	Screw	6.3	0.15	T3-1/4
40A	Brown	Bayonet	6.3	0.15	T3-1/4
41	White	Screw	2.5	0.5	T3-1/4
42	Green	Screw	3.2	0.35/0.5	T3-1/4
43	White	Bayonet	2.5	0.5	T3-1/4
44	Blue	Bayonet	6.3	0.25	T3-1/4
45	White/Grn	Bayonet	3.2	0.35/0.5	T3-1/4
46	Blue	Screw	6.3	0.25	T3-1/4
47	Brown	Bayonet	6.3	0.15	T3-1/4
48	Pink	Screw	2.0	0.06	T3-1/4
49	Pink	Bayonet	2.0	0.06	T3-1/4
49A	White	Bayonet	2.1	0.12	T3-1/4
50	White	Screw	7.5	0.22	G3-1/2
51	White	Bayonet	7.5	0.22	G3-1/2
53		Bayonet	14.4	0.12	G3-1/2
55	White	Bayonet	7.0	0.41	G4-1/2
57	White	Bayonet	14	0.24	G4-1/2
63		Bayonet	7.0	0.63	G6
67		Bayonet	13.5	0.59	G6
73		Wedge	14	0.08	T1-3/4
81		Bayonet	6.5	1.02	G5
82		Dbl Bayonet	6.5	1.02	G5
85		Wedge	28	0.04	T1-3/4
86		Wedge	6.3	0.20	T1-3/4
87		Bayonet	6.8	1.91	S8
88		Dbl Bayonet	6.8	1.91	S8
89		Bayonet	13.0	0.58	S8
93		Bayonet	12.8	1.04	S8
112		Screw	1.2	0.22	TL-3
120MB		Min. Bayonet	120.0	0.025	T2
123		Screw	1.25	0.30	G3-1/2
136		Bayonet	1.25	0.60	G4-1/2
158		Wedge	14.0	0.24	T3-1/4
161		Wedge	14.0	0.19	T3-1/4
168		Wedge	14.0	0.35	T3-1/4
194		Wedge	14.0	0.27	T3-1/4
222	White	Screw	2.25	0.25	TL-3
292	White	Screw	2.9	0.17	TL-3
292A	White	Bayonet	2.9	0.17	TL-3
301		Bayonet	28.0	0.17	G5
302		Dbl Bayonet	28.0	0.17	G5
303		Bayonet	28.0	0.30	G6
305		Bayonet	28.0	0.51	S8
307		Bayonet	28.0	0.67	S8
308		Dbl Bayonet	28.0	0.67	S8
309		Bayonet	28.0	0.90	S11
313		Min. Bayonet	28.0	0.17	T3-1/4

Pilot Lamps

Lamp Number	Bead Color	Base Type	Bulb Volts	Amps	Type
327		Mig. Flanged	28.0	0.04	T1-3/4
328		Mig. Flanged	6.0	0.20	T1-3/4
330		Mig. Flanged	14.0	0.08	T1-3/4
331		Mig. Flanged	1.35	0.06	T1-3/4
334		Mig. Grooved	28.0	0.04	T1-3/4
335		Mig. Screw	28.0	0.04	T1-3/4
344		Mig. Flanged	10.0	0.014	T1-3/4
381		Mig. Flanged	6.3	0.20	T1-3/4
382		Mig. Flanged	14.0	0.08	T1-3/4
385		Mig. Flanged	28.0	0.04	T1-3/4
387		Mig. Flanged	28.0	0.04	T1-3/4
388		Mig. Grooved	28.0	0.04	T1-3/4
656		Wedge	28.0	0.06	T3-1/4
680		Wires	5.0	0.06	T1
682		Mig. Flange	5.0	0.06	T1
683		Wires	5.0	0.06	T1
683AS15		Wires	5.0	0.06	T1
685		Mig. Flange	5.0	0.06	T1
713		Wires	5.0	0.075	T1
714		Wires	5.0	0.075	T1
715		Wires	5.0	0.115	T1
715AS15		Wires	5.0	0.115	T1
718		Mig. Flange	5.0	0.115	T1
755		Min. Bayonet	6.3	0.15	T3-1/4
756		Min. Bayonet	14.0	0.08	T3-1/4
757		Min. Bayonet	28.0	0.08	T3-1/4
1003		Bayonet	12.8	0.94	B6
1004		Dbl Bayonet	12.8	0.94	B6
1034		Bayonet	12.8	1.80	S8
1076		Dbl Bayonet	12.8	1.80	S8
1133		Bayonet	6.2	3.91	RP11
1156		Bayonet	12.8	2.10	S8
1157		DC Bayonet	12.8	2.10	S8
1176		Dbl Bayonet	12.8	1.34	S8
1195		Bayonet	12.5	3.0	RP11
1251		Bayonet	28.0	0.23	G6
1445		Bayonet	14.4	0.135	G3-1/2
1447		Screw	18	0.15	G3-1/2
1455	Brown	Screw	18.0	0.25	G5
1455A	Brown	Bayonet	18.0	0.25	G5
1458		Bayonet	20.0	0.25	G5
1487		Screw	14	0.2	T3-1/4
1488		Bayonet	14	0.15	T3-1/4
1490	White	Bayonet	3.2	0.16	T3-1/4
1495		Bayonet	28.0	0.30	T4-1/2
1705		Wires	14.0	0.08	T1-3/4
1764		Wires	28.0	0.04	T1-3/4
1784		Wires	6.0	0.20	T1-3/4
1813		Bayonet	14.4	0.10	T3-1/4
1815		Bayonet	14	0.20	T3-1/4
1816		Bayonet	13.0	0.33	T3-1/4
1819	White	Min. Bayonet	28.0	0.04	T3-1/4
1820		Min. Bayonet	28.0	0.10	T3-1/4
1822		Min. Bayonet	36.0	0.10	T3-1/4
1829		Min. Bayonet	28.0	0.07	T3-1/4
1847	White	Bayonet	6.3	0.15	T3-1/4

Pilot Lamps

Lamp Number	Bead Color	Base Type	Bulb Volts	Amps	Type
1864		Min. Bayonet	28.0	0.17	T3-1/4
1891	Pink	Bayonet	14	0.24	T3-1/4
1892	White	Min. Bayonet	14.4	0.12	T3-1/4
1895		Min. Bayonet	14.0	0.27	G4-1/2
2181		Wires	6.3	0.20	T1-3/4
2182		Wires	14.0	0.08	T1-3/4
2187		Wires	28.0	0.04	T1-3/4
3150		Mig. Flange	5.0	0.06	T1-3/4
6838		Wires	28.0	0.024	T1
6839		Mig. Flange	28.0	0.024	T1
7327		Bi Pin	28.0	0.04	T1-3/4
7333		Mig. Flange	5.0	0.06	T1-3/4
7361		Bi Pin	5.0	0.06	T1-3/4
7381		Bi Pin	6.3	0.20	T1-3/4
7382		Bi Pin	14.0	0.08	T1-3/4
7387		Bi Pin	28.0	0.04	T1-3/4
7632		Bi Pin	28.0	0.04	T1-1/4
7839		Bi Pin	28.0	0.024	T1
8623		Thr. Knurled	28.0	0.04	T1-1/4
8627		Wires	28.0	0.04	T1-1/4
PR-2	Blue	Flange	2.38	0.50	B3-1/2
PR-3	Green	Flange	3.57	0.50	B3-1/2
PR-4	Yellow	Flange	2.33	0.27	B3-1/2
PR-6	Brown	Flange	2.47	0.30	B3-1/2
PF-7		Flange	3.7	0.30	B3-1/2
PR-12	White	Flange	5.95	0.50	B3-1/2
PR-13		Flange	4.75	0.50	B3-1/2
PR-18		Flange	7.2	0.50	B3-1/2

Neon Number	Resistor Required	Base Type	Bulb Volts	Milli-amps	Type
NE-2 (A1A)	150k	Wire	110VAC	0.5	T2
NE-2A (A2A)	220k	Wire	110VAC	0.3	T2
A1B	220k	Wire	110VAC	0.3	T2
A1C	47k	Wire	110VAC	1.2	T2
NE-2D (C7A)	100k	Midg. Flange	110VAC	0.6	T2
NE-2E (A9A)	100k	Wire	110VAC	0.6	T2
NE-2H (C2A)	30k	Wire	110VAC	1.7	T2
NE-2J (C9A)	30k	Flange	110VAC	1.7	T2
NE-2M	150k	Wire	110VAC	0.5	T2
NE-2P	30k	Wire	110VAC	1.7	T2
NE-7 (B4A)	30k	Wire	110VAC	2.0	
NE-17 (B5A)	30k	DC Bayonet	110VAC	2.0	T4-1/2
NE-21 (B6A)	30k	Wire	110VAC	2.0	
NE-30	None	Screw	110VAC	12.0	S11
NE-34		Screw	110VAC	18.0	S14
NE-42			110VAC	30.0	
NE-45 (B7A)	30k	Candelabra S	110VAC	2.0	T4-1/2
NE-47 (B8A)	30k	SC Bayonet	110VAC	2.0	T4-1.2
NE-48	30k	DC Bayonet	110VAC	2.0	T4-1/2
NE-51 (B1A)	200k	Min. Bayonet	110VAC	0.3	T3-1/4
NE-51H (B2A)	45k	Min. Bayonet	110VAC	1.2	T3-1/4
NE-56	None	Screw	220VAC	5.0	S11
NE-57	None	Candelabra S	110VAC	2.0	T4-1/4
NE-58 (F4A)	100k	Candelabra S	220VAC	2.0	T4-1/4
NE-79	7.5k	DC Bayonet	110VAC	12.0	S7
6S6DC		Dbl Bayonet	120V	6 watt	S6
7C7		Candelabra S	115-0125	7 watt	S7

Fuses – Small Tube Type

TYPE	Description	Diameter Inches	Length Inches
3AB	Ceramic body, normal, 200% 15sec	1/4	1-1/4
1AG	Auto Glass, fast blow, 200% 5sec	1/4	5/8
2AG	Auto Glass, fast blow, 200% 10sec	0.177	0.57
3AG	Auto Glass, fast blow, 200% 5sec	1/4	1-1/4
4AG	Auto Glass, fast blow, 200% 5sec	9/32	1-1/4
5AG	Auto Glass, fast blow, 200% 5sec	13/32	1-1/2
7AG	Auto Glass, fast blow, 200% 5sec	1/4	7/8
8AG	Auto Glass, fast blow, 200% 5sec	1/4	1
9AG	Auto Glass, fast blow, 200% 5sec	1/4	1-7/16
216	Metric, fast blow, high int.,210% 30m	5mm	20mm
217	Glass, Metric, fast blow, 210% 30m	5mm	20mm
218	Glass, Metric, slow blow, 210% 2 min	5mm	20mm
ABC	No Delay, Ceramic, 110% rating, Will blow at 135% load in one hour	1/4	1-1/4
AGC	Fast Acting, glass tube, 110% rating, Will blow at 135% load in one hour	1/4	1-1/4
AGX	Fast Acting, glass tube	1/4	1
BLF	No delay, 200% 15sec	13/32	1-1/2
BLN	No delay, military, 200% 15sec	13/32	1-1/2
BLS	Fast clearing, 600V, 135% 1hr	13/32	1-3/8
FLA	Time delay, indicator pin, 135% 1hr	13/32	1-1/2
FLM	Dual element, delay, 200% 12 sec	13/32	1-1/2
FLQ	Dual element, delay,500V,200%12sec	3/32	1-1/2
FNM	Slow Blow Time Delay	13/32	1-1/4
FNA	Slow Blow, Indicator, silver pin pops out when blown, Dual Element	13/32	1-1/2
GBB	Rectifier Fuse, Fast, low let through	1/4	1-1/4
GLD	Indicator Fuse, silver pin pops out to show blown fuse. 110% rating	1/4	1-1/4
GGS	Metric, fast acting	5mm	20mm
KLK	Fast, current limiting, 600V, 135% 1hr	13/32	1-1/2
KLW	Fast, protect solid state, 250% 1sec	13/32	1-1/2
MDL	Dual Element, Time Delay, glass tube	1/4	1-1/4
MDX	Dual Element, glass tube	1/4	1-1/4
MDV	Dual Element, glass tube, Pigtail	1/4	1-1/4
SC	Slow Blow, Time Delay	13/3	1-5/16to
	Size rejection also		2-1/4
218000	Slow blow, glass body, 200% 5sec	0.197	0.787
251000	Pico II™ Subminiature, fast blow	Wire lead	
273000	Microfuse, fast blow, 200% 5sec	Wire lead	
313000	Slow blow, glass body, 200% 5sec	1/4	1-1/4
326000	Slow Blow, ceramic, 200% 5sec	1/4	1-1/4

Note: The 200% 10 sec figures above indicate that a 200% overload will blow the fuse in 10 seconds.

Battery Characteristics

Battery (1)	Anode	Cathode	Voltage(2)	Amp-hrs/kg
Ammonia	Mg	m–DNB	2.2 (1.7)	1,400
Cadmium–Air (C)	Cd	O_2	1.2 (0.8)	475
Cuprous chloride	Mg	CuCl	1.5 (1.4)	240
Edison (C)	Fe	NiO	1.5 (1.2)	195
H_2–O_2 (C)	H_2	O_2	1.23 (0.8)	3,000
Lead–Acid (C)	Pb	PbO_2	2.1 (2.0)	55
Leclance (NC)	Zn	MnO_2	1.6 (1.2)	230
Lithium–High Temp, 350°C, with fused salt				
	Li	S	2.1 (1.8)	685
Lithium Ion (C)	C	LiCoO	4.2 (3.7)	?
Lithium (NC)	Li	CFx	3.6 (3.0)	?
Lithium (NC)	L	MnO_2	3.6 (3.0)	?
Magnesium (NC)	Mg	MnO_2	2.0 (1.5)	270
Mercury (NC)	Zn	HgO	1.34 (1.2)	185
Mercad (NC)	Cd	HgO	0.9 (0.85)	165
MnO_2 alkaline (NC)	Zn	MnO_2	1.5 (1.15)	230
NiCad (C)	Cd	NiO	1.35 (1.2)	165
NiMH (C)	Ni	KOH	1.35 (1.2)	?
Organic Cath.(NC)	Mg	m–DNB	1.8 (1.15)	1,400
Silver Cadmium (C)	Cd	AgO	1.4 (1.05)	230
Silver Chloride	Mg	AgCl	1.6 (1.5)	170
Silver Oxide	Zn	AgO	1.85 (1.5)	285
Silver–Poly	Ag	Polyiodide	0.66 (0.6)	180?
Sodium – High Temp, 300°C, with β–alumina electrolyte				
	Na	S	2.2 (1.8)	1,150
Thermal	Ca	Fuel	2.8 (2.6)	240
Zinc-Air (NC)	Zn	O_2	1.6 (1.1)	815
Zinc–Nickel (C)	Zn	Ni oxides	1.75 (1.6)	185
Zinc-Silver Ox	Zn	AgO	1.85 (1.5)	285

Fuel Cells:

Hydrogen	H_2	O_2	1.23 (0.7)	26,000
Hydrazine	N_2H_4	O_2	1.5 (0.7)	2,100
Methanol	CH_2OH	O_2	1.3 (0.9)	1,400

(1) (NC) after the name indicates the cell is a Primary Cell and can-not be recharged. (C) indicates the cell is a Secondary Cell and can be recharged.
(2) The first voltage is the theoretical voltage developed by the cell and the value in parenthesis is the typical voltage generated by a working cell. Amp–hrs/kg is the theoretical capacity of the cell.

Battery data listed above was obtained from the *Electronic Engineers Master Catalog, Hearst Business Communications Inc., 1986–1987.*

Batteries - Sizes & Capacities

Primary Non-Rechargeable Systems

Size	ANSI/NEDA No.	IEC No.	Duracell	Energizer	Kodak	Panasonic	Rayovac	Voltage volts	Capacity mAh [A]
Carbon Zinc Cells (also called Zinc Chloride or Heavy Duty)									
AAA	24D	R03	---	1212	---	UM-4	3AAA	1.5	540
AA	15D	R6	---	1215	---	UM-3	5AA	1.5	950
C	14D	R14	---	1235	---	UM-2	4C	1.5	3,000
D	13D	R20	---	1250	---	UM-1	6D	1.5	5,900
Lantern	915	4R25	---	510S	---	---	---	6.0	11,000
Lantern	908D	4R25	---	1209	---	---	---	6.0	12,000
9V	1604D	6F22	---	1222	006P	---	D1604	9.0	400
Zinc/Manganese Dioxide (also known as Alkaline or Alkaline-Manganese Dioxide)									
---	1166A	LR44	---	---	KA76	---	---	1.5	125
---	---	LR9	---	---	KA625	---	---	1.5	200
AAAA	25A	---	---	E96	---	---	---	1.5	595
N	910A	LR1	MX2500	E90	KN	---	810	1.5	1,000
AAA	24A	LR03	MN2400	E92	K3A	AM-4PI	824	1.5	1,150
AA	15A	LR6	MN1500	E91	KAA	AM-3PI	815	1.5	2,850
C	14A	LR14	MN1400	E93	KC	AM-2PI	814	1.5	8,350
D	13A	LR20	MN1300	E95	KD	AM-1PI	813	1.5	18,000
---	1414A	4LR44	---	---	K28A	---	---	6.0	100
J	1412AP	4LR61	7K67	539	KJ	---	MEDJ-1	6.0	595
Lantern	908A	4LR25X	MN908	529	---	---	---	6.0	26,000
Lantern	915A	---	---	528	---	---	---	6.0	26,000
Lantern	918A	4LR25-2	MN918	521	---	---	---	6.0	52,000
9V	1604A	6LR61	MX1604	522	K9V	6AM-6PI	A1604	9.0	595
---	1811A	---	---	---	K23A	---	---	12.0	33

Batteries - Sizes & Capacities

Size	ANSI / NEDA No.	IEC No.	Duracell	Energizer	Kodak	Panasonic	Rayovac	Voltage volts	Capacity [A] mAh
Lithium/Manganese Dioxide: Cylindrical Batteries (also known as Lithium)									
AA	15LF	---	---	L91	---	---	---	1.5	2,900
1/3 N	5008LC	CR11108	DL1/3N	---	K58L	---	---	3.0	160
---	---	CR15H270	DLCR2	EL1CR2	---	CR2	RLCR2	3.0	750
CR2	5046LC	CR2	DLCR2	EL1CR2	KCR2	CR2	RLCR2	3.0	850
2/3 A	5018LC	CR17345	DL123A	EL123AP	K123LA	CR123A	RL123A	3.0	1,300
2/3 A	5017LC	CR17335	DL2/3A	---	---	---	---	3.0	1,400
2 x 1/3 N	1406LC	2CR11108	PX28L	---	K28L	---	---	6.0	160
2 x 2/3 A	5024LC	CR-P2	DL223A	EL223AP	K223LA	CR-P2	RL223A	6.0	1,300
2 x 2/3 A	5032LC	2CR5	DL245	EL2CR5	KL2CR5	2CR5	RL2CR5	6.0	1,300
---	1604LC	---	---	L522	---	---	---	9.0	1,200
Lithium/Manganese Dioxide: Button, Coin, or Miniature Batteries (also known as Lithium)									
---	5034LC	CR1216	DL1216	CR1216	---	CR1216	---	3.0	29
---	5033LC	CR1025	DL1025	CR1025	---	CR1025	CR1025	3.0	30
---	5012LC	CR1220	---	CR1220	---	CR1220	---	3.0	40
---	5020LC	CR1225	---	CR1225	---	---	---	3.0	50
---	5021LC	CR1616	DL1616	CR1616	---	CR1616	CR1616	3.0	55
---	---	CR2012	---	CR2012	---	CR2012	---	3.0	58
---	5009LC	CR1620	DL1620	CR1620	---	CR1620	CR1620	3.0	79
---	5000LC	CR2016	DL2016	CR2016	KCR2016	CR2016	CR2016	3.0	90
---	5020LC	CR2320	---	CR2320	---	CR2320	---	3.0	135
---	5003LC	CR2025	DL2025	CR2025	KCR2025	CR2025	CR2025	3.0	170
---	5004LC	CR2032	DL2032	CR2032	KCR2032	CR2032	CR2032	3.0	230
---	---	CR2330	---	---	---	CR2330	---	3.0	265
---	5011LC	CR2430	DL2430	CR2430	---	---	---	3.0	300

—	—	—	—	—	—	CR3032	CR3032	3.0	500
—	—	—	—	—	—	CR2354	CR2354	3.0	560
5029LC	—	—	—	CR2450	—	DL2450	CR2450	3.0	600
5045LC	—	—	—	—	—	—	—	9.0	1,400
Lithium/Carbon Monofluoride: Button, Coin, or Miniature Batteries (also known as Lithium)									
5020LB	—	—	—	—	—	BR1225	BR1225	3.0	50
5000LB	—	—	—	—	—	BR2016	—	3.0	70
—	—	—	—	—	—	BR2020	—	3.0	100
—	—	—	—	—	—	BR2320	—	3.0	110
5002LB	—	—	—	—	—	—	BR1632	3.0	130
5004LB	—	—	—	—	—	BR2325	—	3.0	180
—	—	—	—	—	—	BR2032	—	3.0	195
—	—	—	—	—	—	—	BR2330	3.0	255
—	—	—	—	—	—	BR2335	BR2335	3.0	300
—	—	—	—	—	—	BR3032	BR3032	3.0	500
—	—	—	—	—	—	—	BR2477	3.0	1,000
Silver Oxide: Button, Coin, or Miniature Batteries									
SR512SW	—	—	335	—	—	—	—	1.55	5
SR610SW	—	—	333	—	—	—	—	1.55	5
SR416SW	—	—	337	—	—	—	—	1.55	7.5
SR713SW	—	—	346	—	—	—	—	1.55	9
SR614SW	—	—	339	—	—	—	—	1.55	9.5
SR910SW	—	—	311	—	—	—	—	1.55	10.5
SR62	1185SO	—	317	317	—	—	—	1.55	11.5
SR714SW	1192SO	—	341	—	—	—	—	1.55	13.5
SR63	1191SO	D379	379	379	—	—	—	1.55	14
SR65	1174SO	—	321	321	—	—	—	1.55	14
SR716W	—	—	314	—	—	—	—	1.55	17
SR64	1186SO	—	319	319	—	—	—	1.55	18

Batteries - Sizes & Capacities

Size	ANSI / NEDA No.	IEC No.	Duracell	Energizer	Kodak	Panasonic	Rayovac	Voltage volts	Capacity [A] mAh
---	1175SO	SR60	D364	364	---	---	364	1.55	19
---	1187SO	SR67	---	315	---	---	315	1.55	21
---	1173SO	SR58	D361	361	---	---	361	1.55	23
---	1158SO	SR58	D362	362	---	---	362	1.55	23
---	---	SR66	---	376	---	---	---	1.55	25
---	1172SO	SR68	---	373	---	---	373	1.55	26
---	1176SO	SR66	D377	377	---	---	377	1.55	27
---	1177SO	SR1116SW	---	366	---	---	---	1.55	30
---	---	SR1116W	---	365	---	---	---	1.55	30
---	1163SO	SR59	D396	396	---	---	396	1.55	31.5
---	1164SO	SR59	D397	397	---	---	397	1.55	33
---	1171SO	SR69	D371	371	---	---	371	1.55	34
---	1188SO	SR69	D370	370	---	---	370	1.55	35
---	---	SR731SW	---	329	---	---	---	1.55	36
---	1179SO	SR41	---	S312E	---	---	312G	1.55	38
---	1134SO	SR41	D384	384	---	---	384	1.55	42
---	1135SO	SR41	D392	392	---	---	392	1.55	42
---	1170SO	SR55	D381	381	---	---	381	1.55	49
---	1160SO	SR55	D391	391	---	---	391	1.55	49
---	1162SO	SR57	D395	395	---	---	395	1.55	52
---	1165SO	SR57	D399	399	---	---	399	1.55	52
---	1161SO	SR45	---	394	---	---	394	1.55	60
---	1181SO	SR48	---	S13E	---	---	13G	1.55	68
---	1136SO	SR48	D309	309	---	---	---	1.55	70
---	1137SO	SR48	D393	393	---	---	393	1.55	70
---	1138SO	SR54	D389	389	---	---	389	1.55	85
---	1159SO	SR54	D390	390	---	---	390	1.55	85

1139SO	SR42	---	344	---	---	344	1.55	105
---	SR42	---	350	---	---	---	1.55	105
1132SO	SR43	D301	301	---	---	---	1.55	110
1133SO	SR43	D386	386	---	---	386	1.55	120
1183SO	SR44	D303	S41E	---	---	---	1.55	125
1130SO	SR44	D357	303	---	---	---	1.55	175
1131SO	SR44	MS76	357	---	---	357	1.55	175
1184SO	SR44	---	S76E	---	---	675G	1.55	195
1107SOP	SR44	---	EPX76	---	---	---	1.55	200
1406SOP	4SR44	---	544	---	---	KS76	6.2	200
Zinc Air								
7012ZD	PR63	DA10	AC5	---	PR521	10	1.4	33
7005ZD	PR70/PR536	---	AC10/230	---	PR536	---	1.4	70
7002ZD	PR41	DA312	AC312	---	PR41	312	1.4	130
7002ZD	PR48	DA13	AC13	---	PR48	113	1.4	255
7003ZD	PR44	DA675	AC675	---	PR44	675	1.4	600
7004Z	---	DA146	AC146X	---	---	---	8.4	1,100
9V	---	---	---	---	---	---	---	---
Rechargable Systems								
Alkaline								
AAA	---	---	---	---	---	724	---	---
AA	---	---	---	---	---	715	---	1,600
C	---	---	---	---	---	714	---	---
D	---	---	---	---	---	713	---	---
Nickel/Cadmium (also known as Ni-Cad)								
N	---	---	---	---	P-11AA/FT	---	1.2	120
H	---	---	---	---	P-11AAH/FT	---	1.2	120
N	---	---	---	---	P-18N/FT	---	1.2	190
N	---	---	---	---	P-22AAA	---	1.2	250

Batteries - Sizes & Capacities

Size	ANSI / NEDA No.	IEC No.	Duracell	Energizer	Kodak	Panasonic	Rayovac	Voltage volts	Capacity [A] mAh
R	---	---	---	---	---	P-22AAAR/FT	---	1.2	250
N	---	---	---	---	---	P-25AAA	---	1.2	280
R	---	---	---	---	---	P-25AAAR/FT	---	1.2	280
R	---	---	---	---	---	P-30AAR/FT	---	1.2	330
H	---	---	---	---	---	P-50AAH/FT	---	1.2	580
AA	---	KR15/51	---	ETM-600AA	---	---	---	1.2	600
N	---	---	---	---	---	P-60AA	---	1.2	640
R	---	---	---	---	---	P-60AAR/FT	---	1.2	640
AA	---	KR15/51	---	E-650AA	---	---	---	1.2	650
AA	10015	KR15/51	---	E-650AAC	---	---	---	1.2	650
S	---	---	---	---	---	P-60AS	---	1.2	660
AAA	1.2H4	HR03	---	---	K3AHR	---	---	1.2	700
N	---	---	---	---	---	P-70AA	---	1.2	740
R	---	---	---	---	---	P-70AARC/FT	---	1.2	740
AA	---	KR15/51	---	EC-800AA	---	---	---	1.2	800
S	---	---	---	---	---	P-80AAS/FT	---	1.2	880
S	---	---	---	---	---	P-100AASJ	---	1.2	1,080
S	---	---	---	---	---	P-100AAS/FT	---	1.2	1,080
S	---	---	---	---	---	P-110AS	---	1.2	1,180
S	---	---	---	---	---	P-110AAS/FT	---	1.2	1,180
H	---	---	---	---	---	P-120AH	---	1.2	1,250
S	---	---	---	---	---	P-120AS	---	1.2	1,280
S	---	---	---	---	---	P-120AAS/FT	---	1.2	1,280
C	---	KR23/43	---	EP-1300Cs	---	---	---	1.2	1,300
H	---	---	---	---	---	P-120SCH	---	1.2	1,350

Type					Part No.			Price
K					P-120SCK	---	1.2	1,350
P					P-120SCPJ	---	1.2	1,350
P					P-120SCPM	---	1.2	1,350
R					P-120SCRJ	---	1.2	1,350
S					P-130ASJ	---	1.2	1,420
R					P-130SCC	---	1.2	1,450
R					P-130SCR	---	1.2	1,450
C		KR23/43	EP-1500Cs			---	1.2	1,500
S					P-140AS	---	1.2	1,500
S					P-150AS	---	1.2	1,530
R					P-140SCC	---	1.2	1,530
R					P-140SCR	---	1.2	1,550
C			E-1600Cs			---	1.2	1,550
AA	1.2H3	HR6		KAAHR		---	1.2	1,600
S					P-160AS	---	1.2	1,600
C		KR23/43	EPP-1700Cs			---	1.2	1,690
C		KR23/43	ECF-1800Cs		P-170SCRP	---	1.2	1,700
P					P-180SCR	---	1.2	1,800
R					P-200SCP	---	1.2	1,800
P					P-200CK	---	1.2	1,950
K					P-230SCS	---	1.2	2,100
S					P-230CH	---	1.2	2,300
H					P-240C	---	1.2	2,490
N					P-280CR	---	1.2	2,500
R						---	1.2	2,600
D		KR35/62	E-4300D			---	1.2	3,000
H					P-400DH	---	1.2	4,300
K					P-400DK	---	1.2	4,400
N					P-440D	---	1.2	4,600

Batteries - Sizes & Capacities

Size	ANSI/NEDA No.	IEC No.	Duracell	Energizer	Kodak	Panasonic	Rayovac	Voltage volts	Capacity [A] mAh
D	---	KR35/62	---	EC-5000D	---	---	---	1.2	5,000
R	---	---	---	---	---	P-500DR	---	1.2	5,500
D	---	KR35/62	---	EC-5700D	---	---	---	1.2	5,700
Nickel/Metal Hydride (also known as Ni-MH)									
AAA	---	---	---	EMH-550AAA	---	---	---		550
AAA	---	---	---	---	---	HHR55AAA/FT	---	1.2	550
AAA	---	---	---	---	---	HHR60AAA/FT	---	1.2	600
AAA	---	---	---	---	---	HHR65AAAJ/FT	---	1.2	650
L-AAA	---	---	---	---	---	HHR65AAA	---	1.2	650
LL-AAAA	---	---	---	---	---	HHR7OQA	---	1.2	670
AAA	---	---	---	NH12	---	---	---	1.2	700
L-AAA	---	---	---	---	---	HHR70AAA	---	1.2	700
---	---	---	---	---	---	HHF75S	---	1.2	730
L-AAA	---	---	---	---	---	HHR75AAA	---	1.2	750
LL-AAA	---	---	---	---	---	HHR95AAA	---	1.2	950
AA	---	---	---	EMH-1100AA	---	---	---	1.2	1,100
AA	---	---	---	EMH-1100AAC	---	---	---	1.2	1,100
AA	---	---	---	---	---	HHR110AAO	---	1.2	1,100
4/5AA	---	---	---	---	---	HHR120AA	---	1.2	1,150
AA	---	---	---	NH15	---	---	---	1.2	1,200
AA	---	---	---	EMH-1200AA	---	---	---	1.2	1,200
---	---	---	---	---	---	HHF125T	---	1.2	1,250
AA	---	---	---	---	---	HHR130AA	---	1.2	1,300
AA	---	---	---	---	---	HHR150AA	---	1.2	1,500
4/5C	---	---	---	EMH-1550Cs	---	---	---	1.2	1,550

					V	mAh
4/5A	...	...	...	HHR160A	1.2	1,600
4/5SC	...	...	...	HHR200SCP	1.2	1,900
4/5A	...	...	...	HHR200A	1.2	2,000
A	...	NH35	...	HHR210A	1.2	2,100
C	...	EMP-2200Cs	...	...	1.2	2,200
C	...	NH50	...	...	1.2	2,200
D	...	...	...	...	1.2	2,200
C	...	EMX-2500Cs	...	...	1.2	2,500
SC	...	...	...	HHR300SCP	1.2	2,800
L-A	...	...	...	HHR380A	1.2	3,700
L-FAT A	...	...	...	HHR450A	1.2	4,200
D	...	...	...	HHR650D	1.2	6,500
D	...	EMX-7000D	...	...	1.2	7,000
9V	...	NH22	...	...	7.2	150
Lithium Ion (also known as Li-Ion)						
Cylindrical	...	...	...	CGR17500	3.7	830
Cylindrical	...	...	...	CGR17670HC	3.7	1,250
Cylindrical	...	...	...	CGR18650	3.7	1,400
Cylindrical	...	...	...	CGR18650H	3.7	1,500
Cylindrical	...	...	...	CGR18650HM	3.7	1,630
Cylindrical	...	...	...	CGR18650HG	3.7	1,800
Prismatic	...	...	...	CGP30486	3.7	630
Prismatic	...	...	...	CGP345006	3.7	875
Prismatic	...	...	...	CGP345010	3.7	1,400
Prismatic	...	...	...	CGP345010G	3.7	1,550
Sealed Lead-Acid						
...	...	...	...	LC-R061R3PU	6.0	1,300
...	...	...	...	LC-R063R4P	6.0	3,400
...	...	...	...	LC-RB064P	6.0	4,000

Batteries - Sizes & Capacities

Size	ANSI / NEDA No.	IEC No.	Duracell	Energizer	Kodak	Panasonic	Rayovac	Voltage volts	Capacity* mAh
---	---	---	---	---	---	LC-R065P	---	6.0	5,000
---	---	---	---	---	---	LC-R067R2P	---	6.0	7,200
---	---	---	---	---	---	LC-P067R2P	---	6.0	7,200
---	---	---	---	---	---	LC-P0612P	---	6.0	12,000
---	---	---	---	---	---	LC-R0612P	---	6.0	12,000
---	---	---	---	---	---	LC-R121R3PU	---	12.0	1,300
---	---	---	---	---	---	LC-T122PU	---	12.0	2,000
---	---	---	---	---	---	LC-TA122PU	---	12.0	2,000
---	---	---	---	---	---	LC-SD122EU	---	12.0	2,000
---	---	---	---	---	---	LC-R122R2P	---	12.0	2,200
---	---	---	---	---	---	LC-SA122R3EU	---	12.0	2,300
---	---	---	---	---	---	LC-R123R4P	---	12.0	3,400
---	---	---	---	---	---	LC-R125P	---	12.0	5,000
---	---	---	---	---	---	LC-R127R2P	---	12.0	7,200
---	---	---	---	---	---	LC-P127R2P	---	12.0	7,200
---	---	---	---	---	---	LC-RA1212P	---	12.0	12,000
---	---	---	---	---	---	LC-RD1217P	---	12.0	17,000
---	---	---	---	---	---	LC-X1220P	---	12.0	20,000
---	---	---	---	---	---	UP-RW1220P	---	12.0	20,000
---	---	---	---	---	---	LC-X1228P	---	12.0	28,000
---	---	---	---	---	---	LC-XC1228P	---	12.0	28,000
---	---	---	---	---	---	UP-RW1232P	---	12.0	32,000
---	---	---	---	---	---	LC-LA1233P	---	12.0	33,000
---	---	---	---	---	---	LC-X1242P	---	12.0	42,000
---	---	---	---	---	---	UP-RW1245P	---	12.0	45,000

...	...	...	...	...	...	...	LC-X1265P	...	12.0	65,000
...	...	...	...	...	...	...	LC-XA12100P	...	12.0	100,000
...	...	...	...	...	...	...	UP-RW2447P1	...	24.0	47,000

Notes:

A - Capacity: Average service capacity in milliampere hours (mAh).
Individual batteries may vary from these values.

Sources:
Duracell, Berkshire Corporate Park, Bethel, CT 06801
Energizer, 533 Maryville University, St. Louis, MO 63141
Eastman Kodak Company, 343 State St., Rochester, NY 14650
Panasonic, Matsushita Electric Corporation of America, One Panasonic Way, Secaucus, NJ 07094
Rayovac Corporation, P.O. Box 44960, Madison, WI 53744-4960

RF Coil Winding Data

The inductance (I), in microhenrys, of air–core coil can be calculated to within 1% or 2% with the following formulas:

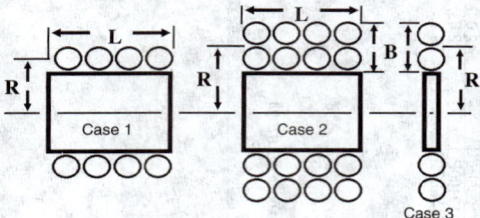

CASE 1: Single Layer Coil

$$I = \frac{R^2 N^2}{9R + 10L}$$

CASE 2: Multiple Layer Coil

$$I = \frac{0.8\,(R^2 N^2)}{6R + 9L + 10B}$$

CASE 3: Multiple Layer, Single Row Coil

$$I = \frac{R^2 N^2}{8R + 11B}$$

In all of the above equations, N = number of turns and I is the inductance in microhenrys. L, B and R are measured in inches.

Wire Size vs. Turns/Inch

Gauge AWG	Number of Turns Per Inch of Length		
	Enamel	S.S.C.	D.C.C
1	...	...	3.3
2	...	...	3.6
3	...	...	4.0
4	...	...	4.5
5	...	...	5.0
6	...	...	5.6
7	...	...	6.2
8	7.6	...	7.1
9	8.6	...	7.8
10	9.6	...	8.9
11	10.7	...	9.8
12	12.0	...	10.9
13	13.5	...	12.0
14	15.0	...	13.8
15	16.8	...	14.7
16	18.9	18.9	16.4
17	21.2	21.2	18.1
18	23.6	23.6	19.8
19	26.4	26.4	21.8
20	29.4	29.4	23.8
21	33.1	32.7	26.0
22	37.0	36.5	30.0
23	41.3	40.6	31.6
24	46.3	45.3	35.6
25	51.7	50.4	38.6
26	58.0	55.6	41.8
27	64.9	61.5	45.0
28	72.7	68.6	48.5
29	81.6	74.8	51.8
30	90.5	83.3	55.5
31	101.0	92.0	59.2
32	113.0	101.0	62.6
33	127.0	110.0	66.3
34	143.0	120.0	70.0
35	158.0	132.0	73.5
36	175.0	143.0	77.0
37	198.0	154.0	80.3
38	224.0	166.0	83.6
39	248.0	181.0	86.6
40	282.0	194.0	89.7

The above values will vary slightly depending the manufacturer of the wire and thickness of enamel.

Decibels vs. Volt & Power Ratios

Voltage	Power	+ DB −	Power	Voltage
1.000	1.000	0.0	1.000	1.000
1.059	1.122	0.5	0.891	0.944
1.122	1.259	1.0	0.794	0.891
1.189	1.413	1.5	0.708	0.841
1.259	1.585	2.0	0.631	0.794
1.334	1.778	2.5	0.562	0.750
1.413	1.995	3.0	0.501	0.708
1.496	2.239	3.5	0.447	0.668
1.585	2.512	4.0	0.398	0.631
1.679	2.818	4.5	0.355	0.596
1.778	3.162	5.0	0.316	0.562
1.884	3.548	5.5	0.282	0.531
1.995	3.981	6.0	0.251	0.501
2.113	4.467	6.5	0.224	0.473
2.239	5.012	7.0	0.200	0.447
2.371	5.623	7.5	0.178	0.422
2.512	6.310	8.0	0.158	0.398
2.661	7.079	8.5	0.141	0.376
2.818	7.943	9.0	0.126	0.355
2.985	8.913	9.5	0.112	0.335
3.162	10.000	10.0	0.100	0.316
3.350	11.220	10.5	0.089	0.299
3.548	12.589	11.0	0.079	0.282
3.758	14.125	11.5	0.071	0.266
3.981	15.849	12.0	0.063	0.251
4.217	17.783	12.5	0.056	0.237
4.467	19.953	13.0	0.050	0.224
4.732	22.387	13.5	0.045	0.211
5.012	25.119	14.0	0.040	0.200
5.309	28.184	14.5	0.035	0.188
5.623	31.623	15.0	0.032	0.178
5.957	35.481	15.5	0.028	0.168
6.310	39.811	16.0	0.025	0.158
6.683	44.668	16.5	0.022	0.150
7.079	50.119	17.0	0.020	0.141
7.499	56.234	17.5	0.018	0.133
7.943	63.096	18.0	0.016	0.126
8.414	70.795	18.5	0.014	0.119
8.913	79.433	19.0	0.013	0.112
9.441	89.125	19.5	0.011	0.106
10.0	100	20.0	0.010	0.100
31.6	1000	30.0	0.001	0.0316
100.0	10000	40.0	0.0001	0.01
316.2	10^5	50.0	0.00001	0.00316
1000	10^6	60.0	10^{-6}	0.001
3162	10^7	70.0	10^{-7}	0.000316
10000	10^8	80.0	10^{-8}	0.0001
31620	10^9	90.0	10^{-9}	0.0000316
10^5	10^{10}	100.0	10^{-10}	10^{-5}
316200	10^{11}	110.0	10^{-11}	0.0000032
10^6	10^{12}	120.0	10^{-12}	10^{-6}

Formulas for Electricity

(1) Ohm's Law (DC Current):

$$\text{Current in amps} = \frac{\text{Voltage in volts}}{\text{Resistance in ohms}} = \frac{\text{Power in watts}}{\text{Voltage in volts}}$$

$$\text{Current in amps} = \sqrt{\frac{\text{Power in watts}}{\text{Resistance in ohms}}}$$

Voltage in volts = Current in amps x Resistance in ohms

Voltage in volts = Power in watts / Current in amps

$$\text{Voltage in volts} = \sqrt{\text{Power in watts x Resistance in ohms}}$$

Power in watts = $(\text{Current in amps})^2$ x Resistance in ohms

Power in watts = Voltage in volts x Current in amps

Power in watts = $(\text{Voltage in volts})^2$ / Resistance in ohms

Resistance in ohms = Voltage in volts / Current in amps

Resistance in ohms = Power in watts / $(\text{Current in amps})^2$

(2) Resistors in Series (values in ohms):

Total Resistance = $\text{Resistance}_1 + \text{Resistance}_2 + \ldots \text{Resistance}_n$

(3) Two Resistors in Parallel (values in ohms):

$$\text{Total Resistance} = \frac{\text{Resistance}_1 \text{ x } \text{Resistance}_2}{\text{Resistance}_1 + \text{Resistance}_2}$$

(4) Multiple Resistors in Parallel (values in ohms):

$$\text{Total Resistance} = \frac{1}{1/\text{Resistance}_1 + 1/\text{Resistance}_2 + \ldots 1/\text{Resistance}_n}$$

Formulas for Electricity

(5) Ohm's Law (AC Current):

In the following AC Ohm's Law formulas, θ is the phase angle in degrees by which current lags voltage (in an inductive circuit) or by which current leads voltage (in a capacitive circuit). In a resonant circuit (such as normal household 120VAC) the phase angle is 0° and Impedance = Resistance.

$$\text{Current in amps} = \frac{\text{Voltage in volts}}{\text{Impedance in ohms}}$$

$$\text{Current in amps} = \sqrt{\frac{\text{Power in watts}}{\text{Impedance in ohms} \times \cos\theta}}$$

$$\text{Current in amps} = \frac{\text{Power in watts}}{\text{Voltage in volts} \times \cos\theta}$$

$$\text{Voltage in volts} = \text{Current in amps} \times \text{Impedance in ohms}$$

$$\text{Voltage in volts} = \frac{\text{Power in watts}}{\text{Current in amps} \times \cos\theta}$$

$$\text{Voltage in volts} = \sqrt{\frac{\text{Power in watts} \times \text{Impedance in ohms}}{\cos\theta}}$$

Impedance in ohms = Voltage in volts / Current in amps

Impedance in ohms = Power in watts / (Current amps^2 × cos θ)

Impedance in ohms = (Voltage in volts^2 × cos θ) / Power in watts

Power in watts = Current in amps^2 × Impedance in ohms × cos θ

Power in watts = Current in amps × Voltage in volts × cos θ

$$\text{Power in watts} = \frac{(\text{Voltage in volts})^2 \times \cos\theta}{\text{Impedance in ohms}}$$

Formulas for Electricity

(6) Resonance: – f

Resonant frequency in hertz (where $X_L = X_C$) =

$$\frac{1}{2\pi \sqrt{\text{Inductance in henrys} \times \text{Capacitance in farads}}}$$

(7) Reactance: – X

Reactance in ohms of an inductance is X_L
Reactance in ohms of a capacitance is X_C

$X_L = 2\pi(\text{frequency in hertz} \times \text{Inductance in henrys})$

$X_C = 1 / (2\pi(\text{frequency in hertz} \times \text{Capacitance in farads}))$

(8) Impedance: – Z

Impedance in ohms = $\sqrt{\text{Resistance in ohms}^2 + (X_L - X_C)^2}$
(series)

$$\text{Impedance in ohms (parallel)} = \frac{\text{Resistance in ohms} \times X_C}{\sqrt{\text{Resistance in ohms}^2 + X_C{}^2}}$$

(9) Susceptance: – B

Susceptance in mhos =

$$\frac{X_L}{\text{Resistance in ohms}^2 + X_L{}^2}$$

(10) Admittance: – Y

Admittance in mhos =

$$\frac{1}{\sqrt{\text{Resistance in ohms}^2 + (X_L - X_C)^2}}$$

Admittance in mhos = 1 / Impedance in ohms

Formulas for Electricity

(11) Power Factor: – pf

Power Factor = cos (Phase Angle)
Power Factor = True Power / Apparent Power
Power Factor = Power in watts / (volts x current in amps)
Power Factor = Resistance in ohms / Impedance in ohms

(12) Q or Figure of Merit: – Q

Q = Inductive Reactance in ohms / Series Resistance in ohms
Q = Capacitive Reactance in ohms / Series Resistance in ohms

(13) Efficiency of any Device:

Efficiency = Output / Input

(14) Sine Wave Voltage and Current:

Effective (RMS) value = 0.707 x Peak value
Effective (RMS) value = 1.11 x Average value
Average value = 0.637 x Peak value
Average value = 0.9 x Effective (RMS) value
Peak Value = 1.414 x Effective (RMS) value
Peak Value = 1.57 x Average value

(15) Decibels: – db

db = 10 Log_{10} (Power in Watts #1 / Power in Watts #2)
db = 10 Log_{10} (Power Ratio)
db = 20 Log_{10} (Volts or Amps #1 / Volts or Amps #2)
db = 20 Log_{10} (Voltage or Current Ratio)
Power Ratio = $10^{(db/10)}$
Voltage or Current Ratio = $10^{(db/20)}$

If impedances are not equal:

$$db = 20 \text{ Log}_{10} \left[(\text{Volt}_1 \sqrt{Z_2}) / (\text{Volt}_2 \sqrt{Z_1}) \right]$$

Formulas for Electricity

(16) Capacitors in Parallel (values in any farad):

Total Capacitance = Capacitance$_1$ + Capacitance$_2$ + ... Capacitance$_n$

(17) Two Capacitors in Series (values in any farad):

$$\text{Total Capacitance} = \frac{\text{Capacitance}_1 \times \text{Capacitance}_2}{\text{Capacitance}_1 + \text{Capacitance}_2}$$

(18) Multiple Capacitors in Series (values in farads):

$$\text{Total Capacitance} = \frac{1}{1/\text{Capacitance}_1 + 1/\text{Capacitance}_2 + \ldots 1/\text{Capacitance}_n}$$

(19) Quantity of Electricity in a Capacitor: – Q

Q in coulombs = Capacitance in farads × Volts

(20) Capacitance of a Capacitor: – C

Capacitance in picofarads =

$$0.0885 \times \frac{\text{Dielectric constant} \times \text{area in cm}^2 \times (\text{\# of plates} - 1)}{\text{thickness of dielectric in cm}}$$

(21) Self Inductance:

Use the same formulas as those for Resistance, substituting inductance for resistance. When including the effects of coupling, add 2 x mutual inductance if fields are adding and subtract 2 x mutual inductance if the fields are opposing. e.g.

Series: $L_t = L_1 + L_2 + 2M$ or $L_t = L_1 + L_2 - 2M$

Parallel: $L_t = 1 / \left[(1/L_1 + M) + (1/L_2 + M) \right]$

Formulas for Electricity

(22) Frequency and Wavelength: f and λ

Frequency in kilohertz = (300,000) / wavelength in meters
Frequency in megahertz = (300) / wavelength in meters
Frequency in megahertz = (984) / wavelength in feet
Wavelength in meters = (300,000) / frequency in kilohertz
Wavelength in meters = (300) / frequency in megahertz
Wavelength in feet = (984) / frequency in megahertz

(23) Length of an Antenna:

Quarter–wave antenna:
   Length in feet = 246 v / frequency in megahertz

Half–wave antenna:
   Length in feet = 492 v / frequency in megahertz

In the formulas above, v = velocity factor.

For homemade, 600-ohm, open wire antennas v = 0.95.

For twin-lead, 300-ohm, solid dielectric v = 0.80-0.85

For coaxial cable, RG-58/U, solid dielectric antennas v = 0.66.

(24) LCR Series Time Circuits:

Time in seconds =
   Inductance in henrys / Resistance in ohms

Time in seconds =
   Capacitance in farads x Resistance in ohms

(25) 70 Volt Loudspeaker Matching Transformer:

Transformer Primary Impedance =
   (Amplifier output volts)^2 / Speaker Power

(26) Time Duration of One Cycle:

10 megahertz = 100 nanoseconds cycle
4 megahertz = 250 nanoseconds cycle
1 megahertz = 1 microsecond cycle
250 kilohertz = 4 microsecond cycle
100 kilohertz = 10 microsecond cycle

CAUTION

This section is intended for use by personnel who have already been trained in first aid; it is not a substitute for such training, nor for the expert care and advice of a licensed physician. Sequoia Publishing, Inc. does not give medical advice and is not responsible for any use which may be made of this information. Recommended procedures change often as knowledge increases; this section may become outdated.

The most critical emergency procedures are listed in the front for ease of access. Be sure to follow any procedures required by your agency or the protocol listed on page 210.

Priorities

1. Make sure that it's safe to help the victim.
2. Check for life-threatening conditions:
   - Unconsciousness
   - No breathing
   - No pulse
   - Heavy bleeding

A. CHECK FOR UNCONSCIOUSNESS

- **Ask "Are you OK?"** Tap the victim on one shoulder if it is safe to do so.
- **If no response**, call an ambulance before doing anything else.
- **If the victim is conscious**, ask permission to give first aid before continuing.

B. CHECK FOR BREATHING AND PULSE

- If the victim is lying on their stomach, carefully roll them over by raising the arm closest to you above the victim's head, then, with one of your hands on the victim's hip and the other on his shoulder, roll him over smoothly and evenly to prevent further injury.
- **Look** to see if their chest is rising and falling, **listen** for breathing sounds, and **feel** for air coming from the victim's mouth and/or nose for about 5 seconds. **If you find no sign of breathing, immediately give the victim a couple of breaths** (see Mouth to Mouth breathing on page 214).

- Check for a pulse by placing your fingertips at the left side of the victim's neck on the carotid artery. If the victim is an infant, check at the inside of the arm between the shoulder and the elbow. If there is no pulse nor heartbeat, **begin CPR (page 212)**.

C. CHECK FOR BLEEDING

Bleeding may not be obvious, especially in the dark. If you suspect that someone is bleeding but cannot see, feel around (gently) for moist, sticky areas. Look for other signs of serious blood loss such as:

- Cool, damp skin
- Pallor (paleness)
- Profuse sweating
- Fast, weak pulse (faster than 60-80 bpm in an adult)
- Thirst
- Blurred vision
- Faintness or giddiness
- Shallow breathing with yawning or sighing
- Acts restless and talkative

Signs of Internal Bleeding:

- Bruises or wounds to the chest
- Signs of fractured ribs
- Tender, swollen, bruised or rigid abdomen
- Vomiting blood
- Excessive thirst
- Rectal or vaginal bleeding
- Impaired breathing or irregular pulse
- Skin feels damp and cool

If any of these signs are present, **call for an ambulance immediately,** monitor the victim carefully and be ready to give CPR (page 212). Make sure none of the victim's clothes are impeding his breathing or circulation. Roll the victim onto his side to drain fluids out of his mouth. Treat for shock (page 227).

CPR (1 Rescuer per Victum)

Before beginning, see Priorities on page 210.

- Place person on his back and open his mouth.

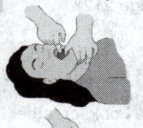

- Sweep your index finger through the person's mouth to dislodge any obstruction, being careful not to force anything farther down the throat. Never do finger sweeps on an infant or small child when you can't see into the throat.

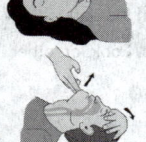

- If nothing is dislodged, put one hand on the victim's forehead and the other under his chin to tilt his head back and open the airway.

- Pinch his nose closed and blow two (2) full breaths into his mouth, pausing in between to take a breath yourself.

- If victim does not begin to breathe, straddle his thighs or kneel next to him.
- Put the **heel of one hand just above the notch at the bottom of the breast bone.** Cover that hand with your other hand, fingers interlaced.

- Keeping your elbows straight, shoulders directly above the hands, push sharply inward and upward about 1 ½ - 2 inches, 30 times in 18 seconds.
- After 30 compressions, retilt his head, and blow twice (2) into his mouth slowly, with the nose pinched closed, pausing in between to breathe for yourself. Minimize compression interruption to 10 seconds or less.
- **If the victim is a child (>1 year old)** Use the same technique as an adult, however, the initial 2 breaths are very important, make sure chest rises or clear airway and do 2 breaths again - use only enough air to make chest rise. The cycle is still 30 compressions and 2 breaths. Each compression should be about 1/3 to 1/2 the depth of the chest.
- **If the victim is an infant (less than 1 year old)**
- Remove clothing on chest, place small pad under shoulders; carefully clear airway (tongue is the most common obstruction.) Tilt head back with your palm on his forehead and lift chin with your fingers.

— If not breathing, place your mouth over the infant's mounth and nose (airtight seal) and give 2 slow, gentle breaths that make the chest rise. Only use enough air to make the chest rise. Remember adult lungs are larger.

— If no pulse, start chest compressions: Put 2 fingers on the infant's breast bone just below an imaginary line between the nipples. Press hard and fast at a rate of 30 compressions and 2 breaths. Each compression should be about 1/3 to 1/2 the depth of the chest. Minimize compression interruption to 10 seconds or less.

=> **Continue CPR for adult, child or infant as follows:**

- Repeat the cycle four times, then check for a pulse.
- When you feel a pulse in the neck, stop compressing, but continue mouth-to-mouth until the person starts breathing on his own.
- Continue the cycle of compressions and breaths until
  — the person begins to breathe on his own
  — another trained person takes over from you
  — you are exhausted and unable to continue
  — or the scene becomes unsafe

Heimlich Maneuver

If the victim is conscious:

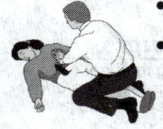

- Stand behind the victim.
- Put your arms around the victim's waist.
- Make a fist with one hand, and put the thumb against the victim's abdomen, below the breast bone and above the navel, even with his bottom rib.
- Grasp your fist with the other hand, and thrust it sharply upward into the victim's abdomen, keeping your elbows out.
- Repeat until the object is expelled. If the victim becomes unconscious, see below.

If the victim is unconscious, call an ambulance, then:

- Lay the victim on his back and open his mouth.
- Sweep your index finger in a hooking motion to remove the object, being careful not to push it farther down the throat. Never perform blind finger sweeps on an infant or small child.

- If that doesn't dislodge the object, put one hand on the victim's forehead and the other under his chin to tilt his head back, opening the airway.
- Pinch his nose closed and blow two full breaths into his mouth, pausing in between to breathe yourself.
- If the victim does not begin to breathe, straddle his thighs. Put the heel of one hand in the **center of his abdomen, between the breastbone and the navel.** Put your other hand on top of the first one, with fingers interlaced.
- Keep your elbows straight, press the abdomen sharply inward and upward, 6-10 times.
- Check the victim's mouth again to see if the obstruction has been forced out. If so, sweep it out with your finger.
- Repeat these steps until the object comes out or medical help arrives.

To clear a blocked airway in an infant, give back blows and chest thrusts:

- Hold the infant face down on your forearm, with its face in your hand.
- Strike the infant between the shoulder blades 5 times with your other hand.

- Turn the infant over and put 2 or 3 fingers in the center of its breast bone. Give 5 thrusts with your fingers, each about 1 inch deep.
- Repeat sequence of back blows and chest thrusts as needed.

Mouth to Mouth Breathing

- Open the victim's airway by putting the heel of your hand against his forehead and your fingertips under his jaw. Push the forehead down and lift the jaw until it is pointing straight up.

- Pinch his nose closed and blow two full breaths into his mouth, pausing in between to breathe yourself.
- If you feel a pulse, but the victim is not breathing, continue with mouth-to-mouth breathing; 1 breath every 5 seconds for an adult, every 3 seconds for an infant.

Bleeding

Bleeding wound:
- Apply pressure directly on the wound with a piece of cloth, or your hand if nothing else is available. Keep the pressure in place; if the victim bleeds through the dressing, just put a new one over it.
- If bleeding continues, elevate the wound above the level of the heart. Do not elevate a broken arm or leg.
- If the victim is still bleeding, apply pressure at a pressure point:

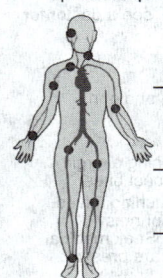

— Arms - inside of the wrist (radial artery) or inside of the upper arm (Brachial artery)

— Legs - at the crease in the groin (femoral artery).

— Check to sure you have not impaired the victim's circulation. Ease pressure if pulse rate slows, or fingertips or toes turn bluish.

- If bleeding continues, wrap a roll of gauze (or whatever is available) tightly around the dressing. Again, check to be sure the bandage isn't cutting off the victim's circulation.
- If a foreign object is embedded in the wound, don't try to remove it. Removal may increase the bleeding.
  — Hold the edges of the wound together around the object for up to ten minutes.
  — If holding the wound together is ineffective, put a thick "doughnut" of clean cloth, thicker than the

object if possible, over the wound. Hold the cloth in place with diagonal strips of bandage that do not go directly over the object.
— Get the victim to a hospital immediately.

Bleeding from nose, mouth or ear:
- Position the victim so that the bleeding organ points downward and blood can flow out. Put a dressing underneath to catch blood, but do not apply pressure. Call an ambulance. If the victim loses consciousness, roll him on his side and monitor for pulse and breathing.

Bites

Animal Bites:
- If the victim is not bleeding heavily, clean the wound thoroughly with soap and water, apply antibiotic, and cover. A severe wound should be cleaned only by trained medical personnel.
- Because of the danger of infection, see a doctor for all bites.

Snake Bites:
- Wash wound with soap and water.
- Keep the bite lower than the heart, and don't move it.
- Call for emergency medical help.

Insect Bites (and stings): Life-threatening allergic reactions are the major danger with insect bites.
Symptoms: Swelling of throat, pain, itching, hives, redness at the site of the bite, difficult or noisy breathing, decreased consciousness. Seek medical help immediately if any of these signs are present.
Treatment:
- Remove the stinger if there is one.
- Wash the wound with soap and water.
- Use a cold compress to relieve pain and swelling.
- Keep the stung area lower than the heart to slow circulation of the venom.

Spider or Scorpion Stings:
- Wash the wound with soap and water.
- Use a cold compress to relieve pain and swelling.
- Get medical care to receive antivenin.
- If reaction is severe, seek emergency medical help.

Broken Bones

Fractures, sprains, strains and dislocations are difficult to diagnose and should all be handled as if they were breaks. **All such injuries require professional medical attention.**

Symptoms: Pain, tenderness, swelling, bruising, inability to move the injured part. Victim may feel as though two bones are rubbing together.

Treatment:

- Control bleeding (page 215)
- Treat for shock (page 227)
- Apply cold packs to reduce pain and swelling
- Splint if necessary, and possible without causing the victim more pain
- **Do not try to move the victim** unless he is still in danger due to his location. If you MUST move a person, stabilize his head and neck first, and keep the spinal cord as still as possible in the process.

Burns

All serious burns - second or third degree; burns of the eye, mouth or nose; or burns that cover 15% or more of the body - **require professional medical attention.**

Burn depth is categorized into three levels of severity:

Symptoms:

- **First degree**: Redness, discoloration, mild swelling and some pain. Sunburn is a common example.
- **Second degree:** Deeper layers of skin are burned, skin is red or mottled and has blisters. Fluids may be lost through the damaged skin. Since nerve endings have not been destroyed, second degree burns are very painful.
- **Third degree**: Most serious. Skin may look either white or charred, and is damaged throughout all of its layers. If victim has no pain, it means nerve endings have been destroyed; severe pain indicates that nerve endings are intact.

Treatment:

- Cool the burn by flushing with water.
- Cover the burn with a dry, sterile dressing.
- Keep the victim comfortable and do not let him or her become chilled.
- Get professional medical attention for all second or third degree burns.

Do NOT use butter or other greasy substances to treat burns. Water is the most effective first aid.

Burns caused by chemicals: Remove contaminated clothing and flush the affected area with lots of water for 15 to 30 minutes. Do not try to use another chemical to neutralize the first one.

Choking

If a person is choking, but can speak or cough forcibly, encourage them to keep coughing and stand by.

If a choking person CANNOT speak or cough, the airway obstruction must be cleared via the **Heimlich Maneuver (page 213).**

Diabetic Emergencies

Insulin shock and diabetic coma are two opposite types of emergencies. Insulin shock results from too much insulin in the body; diabetic coma from too much sugar/too little insulin. If a person is unconscious, check for a bracelet identifying the victim as a diabetic. **Call an ambulance immediately.**

Symptoms:
  - **Insulin Shock:** Symptoms include rapid breathing and pulse, dizziness, weakness, change in level of consciousness, vision difficulties, sweating, headache, numbness in hands or feet, and hunger. May appear to be drunk without the smell of alcohol.
  - **Diabetic Coma:** Develops slowly; preceding symptoms include drowsiness, confusion, deep and fast breathing, thirst, dehydration, fever, sweet or fruity smelling breath, change in level of consciousness.
  - It can be hard to tell which reaction a person is having.

    ASK **"Have you eaten today?"** If "yes":

    ASK **"Did you take your medication today?"**

  - Has eaten/no medication = Diabetic Coma
  - Has NOT eaten, has taken medication = Insulin Shock

Treatment:
  - Feed the person something high in sugar immediately - candy, fruit juice, soft drink. <u>Insulin shock is life threatening</u>, and sugar can literally be a life saver and won't hurt someone in diabetic coma.

Electric Shock

Do not touch the victim until you have eliminated risk of shock to yourself.

- Unplug appliances or turn off power at the fuse box.
- If you cannot turn off the electricity, use a nonconductive material, like dry fabric or wood, to move the victim away from the power source.
- Always **get professional help** for someone who has been shocked, since injuries can be internal, and electrical burns can cause electrolyte imbalance, muscle breakdown and even kidney failure.

High-Voltage Electricity from power lines and industrial equipment, or from railway, subway or streetcar systems can produce shock up to 20 ft. away. Stay clear and call an ambulance or 911.

- If victim is unconscious and not breathing, perform CPR (page 212).
- If victim is unconscious and breathing, roll him on his side and wait for help.
- Treat burns appropriately (page 217)

Lightning injuries can range from a minor stun to death, and may cause heart attack, asphyxiation, severe burns, broken bones, and burn or melt clothing and jewelry.

- If the victim's clothes are on fire, extinguish the flames by rolling them on the ground, covering them with a heavy blanket, or dousing them with water.
- If the victim is unconscious and not breathing, administer CPR (page 212).
- If unconscious and breathing, roll them on their side and wait for help.
- Treat burns appropriately. (Page 217).

Eye Injuries

Eye injuries must be treated very, very gently. **Prompt medical help is important to save the person's eyesight.**

- If you can see something floating in the eye, try to flush it out with water. If that doesn't work, seek medical attention.

- If something is embedded in the eye, do not try to remove it. Bandage both eyes and go to an emergency room or clinic. Place a paper cup upside down on the injured eye and hold it in place with a bandage.
- **Chemical burns:** Flush the eye with lots of lukewarm water for 15-30 minutes, then bandage both eyes and get medical attention.

Frostbite

If a person has frostbite, be alert for signs of hypothermia as well. Call 911 or a doctor for advice on how to handle the frostbite.

Symptoms:
- *Superficial frostbite:* Skin has white or gray patches and feels firm, but not hard. Once frostbite sets in, it is not painful. No tissue loss will occur if it is treated properly.
- *Deep frostbite* may involve an entire finger or toe or other body part. The skin feels hard and cold; affected tissue looks white or gray. Skin does not rebound when pressed. No pulse can be felt in the affected area.

Treatment:
- It is best not to rewarm the tissue in the field, unless there is no alternative.
  - The risk of damage due to improper warming is greater than the risk of delaying treatment
  - Tissue that is thawed and then refreezes nearly always dies. Frostbitten tissue must be handled extremely gently.
- DO NOT:
  - rub the frozen tissue
  - apply ice or snow
  - use cold water or high temperatures to try to thaw the frozen part
  - give the victim alcohol or tobacco
  - break any blister which may form
- If possible, take the patient to a hospital while protecting the frozen area from further damage.
- If thawing in the field is necessary, use water warmed to 100-106°F in a container large enough for the whole frostbitten area to be submerged without touching the bottom or sides. Water must be maintained at this temperature, so an additional source of water is necessary. Gently circulate the water around the frozen area until the tip becomes flushed.

- Warmed tissue is extremely painful. Get advice from a physician for pain relief. Pain after rewarming usually indicates that treatment has been successful.
- Keep rewarmed extremities above heart level if possible.
- If feet have been frostbitten and rewarmed, do not allow the patient to walk on them unless their life (or yours) depends on it.

Head and Spine Injuries

Symptoms:
- Bleeding, bumps or depression on the head, neck or back; bruises around eyes or behind ears
- Changes in consciousness
- Inability to move any body part
- Pain in the head, neck or back
- Numbness or tingling in fingers, toes, hands or feet
- Seizures
- Persistent headache
- Nausea or vomiting, loss of balance
- Difficulty seeing or breathing after the injury

Treatment:
- Immobilize the head and neck as much as possible
- Keep airway open
- Monitor breathing, pulse, consciousness
- Control bleeding
- Maintain victim's normal body temperature
- Get professional medical attention

Heat Emergencies

Heat Cramps
- **Symptoms:** Heavy exertion results in muscle pain and spasms, usually in leg or abdominal muscles.
- **Treatment:** Get victim to a cool place and give him one-half glass of cool water every 15 minutes.

Heat Exhaustion
- **Symptoms:** Cool, pale, moist skin, heavy sweating, dilated pupils, headache, nausea, dizziness & vomiting. Body temperature appears to be near normal.
- **Treatment:** Move victim to a cool place. Have victim lie on back with feet elevated. Remove or loosen clothing. Apply cold packs, wet towels or sheets, or fan the victim if these are not available. Give water every 15 minutes, if the victim is conscious.

Heat Stroke is *Life threatening - begin to cool the victim and call for medical help immediately!*

- **Symptoms:** Sweat glands shut down - no perspiration. Hot, dry, red skin. Pupils contracted very small. Body temperature very high, even up to 105°. Victim may refuse water, vomit or lose consciousness.
- **Treatment:** ACT IMMEDIATELY! Cool the victim as soon as possible in any way you can. Place in a bathtub of cool water, wrap in wet sheets, or put in an air conditioned room. Do not wait for help to arrive! Treat for shock, and do not give anything by mouth.

Heart Attack

Symptoms:

- **Chest Pain** which the victim may describe as pressure, tightness, aching, crushing, fullness, constricting, heaviness. Many victims think they have heartburn!
  - The pain may be in the center of the chest, one or both shoulders or arms, the neck, jaw or back. Pain does not go away when the victim stops moving.
- **Sweating**
- **Nausea**
- **Shortness of breath**
- **Changes in pulse rate**
- **Pale or bluish skin color.**

Treatment: Recognize the symptoms of a heart attack, **call 911 immediately**. Do not wait to be sure!

- Calm the victim so that fear does not make the problem worse.
- Have the victim stop activity and sit or lie in a comfortable position.
- Loosen clothing as needed to ease circulation and breathing.
- Monitor victim's condition.

A victim who is unconscious and/or whose heart has stopped will need CPR (page 212).

Hypothermia

Mild:

- **Symptoms:** Shivering, loss of coordination, complains of being cold.

- **Treatment:**
  - Move victim to someplace warm and dry.
  - Add more clothing, or replace wet clothing with dry.
  - Cover the person's head and/or neck.
  - Put a barrier between the person and the ground.
  - Cover the person with a space blanket or other vapor barrier.
  - Offer warm nonalcoholic liquids or food.
  - Encourage the person to move around to generate more heat.
  - Apply heat packs to head, neck, underarms, sides of chest, or groin; insulate heavily to prevent further heat loss.
  - Warm shower or bath if available and victim is alert.
  - As a last resort, have someone who is NOT hypothermic get into a sleeping bag with the victim. This method may endanger the rescuer. Two people who are hypothermic should not do this.

Moderate:
- **Symptoms:** Listless, confused, does not recognize problem; shivers uncontrollably, uncoordinated, speech slurred.
- **First Aid:** Same treatment as above, but cover the person rather than moving him. Do not allow victim to exercise or move, treat very gently. Check for other injuries, including frostbite. (Page 220)

Severe:
- **Symptoms:** Internal temperature of 90°F (32.2°C) or less. Unconsciousness, slow pulse and respiration, no shivering, physical collapse, unresponsive to pain or words.
- **First Aid:** *Life-threatening - call for professional care.*
  If pulse and respiration are present, treat as above, but don't give oral fluids unless completely conscious. Do not put the person in a warm shower or bath, and be careful to handle the person very gently. Do not rub hands or feet.
- If pulse and respiration are not present, take the above measures to rewarm the person, start CPR (page 212), and get to a medical facility ASAP.

Nose Injuries

Most nosebleeds can be controlled by having the victim

- sit down, pinch the nose shut
- lean *forward* in order to prevent blood from running into the throat.
- Since walking, talking or blowing the nose can start the bleeding again, the person should rest quietly until certain that the bleeding has stopped. A severe nosebleed can lead to shock if enough blood is lost.
- If nose bleed occurs in someone who has had a head, neck or back injury, DO NOT attempt to control the bleeding, as it may increase pressure on the injured area. **Get medical help immediately**.

Poisoning

Poisons cause very different symptoms, and require very different treatments. Call a certified Poison Control Center or 911 immediately if you suspect poisoning.

INHALED POISONS: Get the victim to fresh air and avoid breathing the fumes yourself. Open doors and windows if it can be done safely. Start CPR (page 212) if the victim is not breathing.

POISON IN THE EYE: Rinse the eye with lukewarm water from a pitcher or glass for 15 minutes. Do not force the eyelid open, but have the victim blink as much as possible while rinsing.

POISON ON THE SKIN: Remove any clothing that has the poison on it. Rinse the skin with running water for 15 minutes

SWALLOWED POISONS: Remove any remaining substance from the mouth.

- **Chemical or household products:** Give one glass of milk or water to drink, if the victim is conscious and is not having convulsions or unable to swallow. Do not force them to drink.
- **Medicines:** Do nothing until instructed by the Poison Control Center.

POISON CONTROL CENTERS (PCCs)

Telephone numbers for certified poison control centers are listed below. When you call, tell them:

- Name, age and sex of the victim.
- Exact name of the substance involved. Have the container at hand if possible.

- Estimate the amount of poison involved.
- The time the poisoning occurred.
- Any symptoms the victim has, and any preexisting medical conditions.
- How the poisoning occurred.
- Anything else you think the staff member should know.

Poison Centers other than 800-764-7661 are IN STATE ONLY 800 numbers

Alabama		
Birmingham	800-292-6678	205-939-9201
Tuscaloosa	800-462-0800	205-345-0600
Alaska	800-478-3193	907-261-3193
Arizona		
Tucson	800-362-0101	520-626-6016
Phoenix		602-253-3334
Arkansas	800-376-4766	
California	800-876-4766	
Sacramento	800-342-9293	
San Francisco	800-356-3129	
Colorado	800-332-3073	
Denver metro		303-629-1123
Connecticut		
Delaware	302-655-3389	215-386-2100
Florida	800-282-3171	
Jacksonville		904-549-4480
Tampa		813-253-4444
Georgia	800-282-5846	404-616-9000
Hawaii	800-362-3586	808-941-4411
Idaho	800-632-8000	208-334-4570
Illinois		
Normal		309-454-6666
Chicago	800-942-5969	312-942-5969
Springfield	800-252-2022	217-753-3330
Indiana	800-382-9097	317-929-2323
Iowa	800-352-2222	712-277-2222
Kansas	800-332-6633	913-588-6633
Kentucky	800-722-5725	502-629-7275
Louisiana	800-256-9822	318-362-5393
Maine	800-442-6305	207-871-2950
Maryland	800-492-2414	410-528-7701
Massachusetts	800-682-9211	617-232-2120
Michigan	800-764-7661	
Detroit		313-745-5711
Marquette		906-225-3497
Minnesota	800-222-1222	612-347-3141
Mississippi		601-354-7660
Missouri	800-366-8888	314-772-5200
Montana	800-525-5042	303-629-1123
Nebraska	800-955-9119	402-390-5555
Nevada	800-446-6179 (LV only)	303-629-1123
New Hampshire	800-562-8236	603-650-8000
New Jersey	800-764-7661	

New Mexico	800-432-6866	505-843-2551
New York		
Syracuse	800-252-5655	315-476-4766
Hudson Valley	800-336-6997	914-366-3030
Long Island		516-542-2323
New York City		212-340-4494
Buffalo	800-888-7655	716-878-7654
North Carolina	800-848-6946	704-355-4000
North Dakota	800-732-2200	701-234-5575
Ohio		
Akron	800-362-9922	330-379-8562
Columbus	800-682-7625	614-228-1323
Cincinnati	800-872-5111	513-558-5111
Cleveland		216-231-4455
Toledo	800-589-3897	419-381-3897
Oklahoma	800-522-4611	405-271-5454
Oregon	800-452-7165	503-494-8968
Pennsylvania		
Hershey	800-521-6110	
Philadelphia		215-386-2100
Pittsburgh		412-681-6669
Erie	800-822-3232	
Rhode Island		401-444-5727
South Carolina	800-922-1117	803-777-1117
South Dakota	800-952-0123	
Tennessee	800-288-9999	
Texas	800-764-7661	
Utah	800-456-7707	801-581-2151
Vermont	877-658-3456	802-658-3456
Virginia	800-451-1428	804-924-5543
Eastern & Central	800-552-6337	804-828-9123
Washington	800-732-6985	206-526-2121
Spokane	800-572-5842	
Tacoma	800-542-6319	253-552-1414
West Virginia	800-642-3625	304-348-4211
Wisconsin	800-815-8855	414-266-2222
Wyoming	800-955-9119	402-390-5555

Puncture Wounds to the Torso

Stab or bullet wounds to the chest or abdomen may create unusual problems:

"Sucking" Chest Wound

- When a lung or the chest cavity is punctured, air can move in and out through the wound, causing a "sucking" sound and preventing the lungs from functioning properly.
- Cover the wound with a dressing that air cannot pass through, and tape it down, leaving one corner loose.

Abdominal Wounds

- A puncture wound to the abdomen may cause organs to protrude outside the body.
- The victim should be placed on his or her back.
- Do not apply pressure to the protruding organ or try to push it back in.
- Remove any clothing that is near the wound.
- Cover the wound with a sterile, moist dressing.

Seizures

Symptoms: Uncontrollable muscle spasms, rigidity, unconsciousness, loss of bladder and bowel control. Breathing may stop temporarily.

Treatment:

- Don't try to restrain the person, or put anything in their mouth.
- Move furniture and equipment out of the way and loosen the person's clothes.
- If vomiting occurs, turn the person on their side.
- Stay with the victim until they are fully conscious.

Shock

Shock is insufficient blood supply to the heart, lungs and brain. It can occur with any type of injury, usually within an hour afterward. **Always take steps to prevent shock when you encounter an injured person.** Shock can be fatal if it goes untreated!

Symptoms:

- Restlessness or irritability; confused behavior
- Weak, trembling arms or legs
- Skin looks pale or bluish, feels cool and moist
- Rapid pulse and/or breathing
- Pupils are enlarged.

Treatment:

- Victim should lie down, with legs elevated unless there is a broken leg, or injury to the head or neck.
- Help maintain the victim's normal body temperature, but do not overheat.
- Control external bleeding, if any.
- If the victim vomits, lay them on their side.
- If they have trouble breathing, They should assume a semi-reclining position .
- Do not give victim anything to eat or drink.
- Get professional medical care for victim.

Stroke

A stroke is an interruption of the brain's blood supply that lasts long enough to damage the brain. Recognize the symptoms, and **call for professional help**.

Symptoms:

- Weakness or numbness in the face, arm or leg, especially on only one side
- Difficulty speaking
- Dizziness
- Confusion
- Headache
- Ringing ears
- Mood change
- Unconsciousness
- Uneven-sized pupils
- Breathing and swallowing difficult
- Loss of bowel and bladder control.

Treatment:

- Have the person rest.
- Keep the person comfortable and calm, but don't let them eat or drink anything.
- If the person vomits, allow the vomit to drain away from the mouth by turning him on his side.
- Keep an eye on the victim's breathing and circulation; be prepared to give CPR (page 212) if needed.

Sources:
American Red Cross, *Community First Aid and Safety*, St. Louis, MO: Mosby-Yearbook, Inc., 1993.

Brown, Robert E., *Emergency/Survival Handbook*, 5th Edition. Bellevue, WA: American Outdoor Safety League, 1990.

Tilton, Buck, Wilderness Medicine Institute, *Backcountry First Aid and Extended Care*, 2nd Edition. Merrillville, IN: ICS Books, Inc., 1994

Forgey, William W., M.D., *The Basic Essentials of Hypothermia*, Merrillville, IN: ICS Books., Inc., 1991

American Heart Association, Heart and Stroke Guide, available http://wwwamhrt.org/Heart_and_Stroke_A_Z_Guide/, May 5, 1998.

Kaiser Permanente, Kaiser Permanente's Health Reference: Cardiopulmonary Resuscitation, available http://www.scl.ncal.kaiperm.org/healthinfo/cpr/

MedicineNet, First Aid, available, http://www.medicinenet.com/hp.asp?li+MNI, 01/20/98

State of Alaska Cold Injuries and Cold Water Near Drowning Guidelines, (Rev. 01/96), available, http://www.westcst.com

Dawson, Chad P., U. Of Minnesota Sea Grant Program, Survival in cold water: Hypothermia Prevention, available http://www.d.umn.edu/seagr/tourism/hypothermia.html

Adventure Sports Online, Hypothermia, available: http://www.adventuresports.com/asap/ski/skihypo.htm

General Information

General Information   229

Holidays

Holiday	Date (listed in chronological order)
New Years Day	January 1
Epiphany	Sunday on or before January 6
Martin Luther King Day	3rd Monday January or January 15
Robert E. Lee Day	January 18
National Freedom Day	February 1
Groundhog Day	February 2
Lincoln's Birthday	February 12
Presidents Day	3rd Monday February
Valentine's Day	February 14
Susan B. Anthony Day	February 15
Washington's Birthday	February 22
Ash Wednesday	47 days before Easter
St Patrick's Day	March 17
St. Joseph's Day	March 19
Juarez' Birthday	March 21 (Mexico)
Palm Sunday	Sunday before Easter
Maundy Thursday	Thursday before Easter
Good Friday	Friday before Easter
Easter	1st Sunday after 1st full moon after the Spring equinox.
Pan American Day	April 14
Secretaries Day	Wednesday of the last full week in April
Arbor Day	Last Friday in April
Loyalty Day	May 1
Cinco de Mayo	May 5 (Mexico)
Ascension	40 days after Easter
Pentecost	50 days after Easter
Mother's Day	2nd Sunday in May
Armed Forces Day	3rd Saturday in May
National Maritime Day	May 22
Victoria Day	1st Monday before May 25
Memorial Day	Last Monday in May
Flag Day	June 14
Father's Day	3rd Sunday in June
Independence Day(US)	July 4
Assumption Day	August 15
Labor Day	1st Monday in September
Grandparent's Day	1st Sunday after Labor Day
Citizenship Day	September 17
Child Health Day	1st Monday in October
Columbus Day	2nd Monday in October
World Poetry Day	October 15
Boss Day	October 16
United Nations Day	October 24
Mother-in-Law's Day	4th Sunday in October

Holidays (cont.)

Holiday	Date (listed in chronological order)
Halloween	October 31
Reformation Day	October 31 (Protestant)
All Saints' Day	November 1
Election Day	1st Tues. in Nov. following 1st Mon.
Veterans' Day	November 11
Sadie Hawkins Day	1st Saturday after November 11
Thanksgiving Day	4th Thursday in November
Immaculate Conception	December 8
Bill of Rights Day	December 15
Wright Brothers Day	December 17
Christmas Eve	December 24 (In some states)
Christmas Day	December 25
National Day of Prayer	Set by president, any day but Sunday

Most Jewish holidays are not included because they are difficult to calculate (not on the same date) and require the Jewish calendar.

STATE SPECIFIC HOLIDAYS

Three Kings Day, Puerto Rico	January 6
Confederate Heroes Day, in the South	January 19
Kentucky, F. D. Roosevelt's Bday	January 30
Texas Independence Day	March 2
Alabama, Thomas Jefferson Bday	March 12
Louisiana & Alabama, Mardi Gras	Tues. before Ash Wed.
Alaska, Seward's Day	March 28
Alabama, Confederate Memorial Day	April 1
San Jacinto Day, Texas	April 21
Arbor Day, Nebraska	April 22
Mississippi, Confederate Memorial Day	April 24
Maine & Massachusetts, Patriots Day	3rd Monday in April
Missouri, Harry S. Truman's Bday	May 8
Mississippi, Jefferson Davis' Bday	May 29
Alabama, Jefferson Davis' Bday	1st Monday in June
Kentucky, Jefferson Davis' Bday	June 3
Kentucky, Confederate Memorial Day	June 3
Hawaii, King Kamehameha I Day	June 11
Texas, Emancipation Day	June 19
West Virginia Day	June 20
Utah, Pioneer Day	July 24
Puerto Rico Constitution Day	July 25
Colorado, Colorado Day	August 1
Victory Day, Rhode Island	August 14
Vermont, Bennington Battle Day	August 16
Defender's Day, Maryland	September 12
Alaska, Alaska Day	October 18
Nevada, Nevada Day	Last Friday in October
New York, Verrazano Day	April 7

Season & Clock Dates

Season	Date
Northern Hemisphere	
Spring Equinox (Spring begins, sun crosses equator, hours of day and night approximately equal lengths all over the earth)	Mar. 20 or 21
Daylight Saving Time, Start, move 1 hour ahead (spring forward), 2 a.m. on the second Sunday in March (this new date started in 2007)	
Summer Solstice (Summer begins, sun is highest in sky)	June 20 or 21
Autumn Equinox (Fall begins, sun crosses equator, hours of day and night approximately equal lengths all over the earth)	Sept. 22 or 23
Daylight Saving Time, End, move 1 hour back (fall back), 2 a.m. on the first Sunday in November (this new date started in 2007)	
Winter Solstice (Winter begins, sun is lowest in sky)	Dec. 21 or 22

Signs of the Zodiac

Name	Symbol	Dates
Aries	Ram	March 21–April 19
Taurus	Bull	April 20–May 20
Gemini	Twins	May 21–June 20
Cancer	Crab	June 21–July 22
Leo	Lion	July 23–Aug 22
Virgo	Virgin	Aug 23–Sept 22
Libra	Balance	Sept 23–Oct 22
Scorpio	Scorpion	Oct 23–Nov 21
Sagittarius	Archer	Nov 22–Dec 21
Capricorn	Goat	Dec 22–Jan 19
Aquarius	Water Bearer	Jan 20–Feb 18
Pisces	Fishes	Feb 19–March 20

Flowers for Each Month

Month	Flower
January	Carnation
February	Violet
March	Jonquil
April	Sweet Pea
May	Lily of the Valley
June	Rose
July	Larkspur
August	Gladiola
September	Aster
October	Calendula
November	Chrysanthemum
December	Narcissus

Birthstones

Month	Stone	Significance
January	Garnet	Constancy
February	Amethyst	Sincerity
March	Jasper, bloodstone, aquamarine	Wisdom
April	Diamond	Innocence
May	Emerald, chrysoprase	Love
June	Pearl, moonstone, alexandrite	Wealth
July	Ruby, carnelian	Freedom
August	Sardonyx, peridot	Friendship
September	Sapphire, lapis lazuli	Truth
October	Opal, tourmaline	Hope
November	Topaz	Loyalty
December	Turquoise, zircon, lapis lazuli	Success

Anniversary Names

Anniversary Year	Traditional	Modern
1	paper	clocks
2	cotton, straw, calico	china
3	leather	crystal or glass
4	flowers, fruit, books	appliances
5	wood	silverware
6	iron or sugar (sweets)	wood
7	copper, wool, brass	desk sets
8	bronze, rubber	linens & laces
9	pottery,	leather
10	tin or aluminum	diamond jewelry
11	steel	fashion jewelry
12	silk or fine linen	pearls
13	lace	textiles or furs
14	ivory or agate	gold jewelry
15	crystal, glass	watches
20	china	platinum
25	silver	silver
30	pearl	diamond
35	coral	jade
40	ruby or garnet	ruby
45	sapphire	sapphire
50	gold	gold
55	emerald, turquoise	emerald
60	diamond	diamond
75	diamond	diamond

Proofreaders Marks

Symbol	Description	Example
=	Align horizontally	grapes and berries
‖	Align vertically	‖grapes and berries
⟧ or ctr	Center horizontally	⟧An American Tale⟦
bf	Change to **boldcase**	He must arrive today
cap/s or c	Change to Capitals (letter or entire word)	sally ran to the door He lives in the usa
ital	Change to *Italics*	He slept too late
lf	Change to lightface	He **slept** too late
lc	Change to lowercase	The Big dog
rom	Change to roman	He *slept* too late
sm cap or sc	Change to SMALL CAPITALS	It is 9:00pm
∧	Change to subscript (or inferior)	Water or H2O
∨	Change to superscript (or superior)	The 4th of July
◡	Close up	He liv es in the USA
Delete	Delete	He likes likes candy
Delete & Close up	Delete & Close up	He likes candy

Proofreaders Marks

Symbol	Description	Example
ℒℓ#	Delete line space	He drove the car. Then he went to work.
eq#	Equalize space	He lives ✓in✓the✓USA
1/M	Insert 1 em dash (long)	a rain–like smell
☐	Insert 1 em space	Figure A The graph
☐☐	Insert 2 em space	1. The Lecture a. History
1/N	Insert 1 en dash (short)	1999 2002
◩	Insert 1 en space	1 The Lecture
⸜	Insert an apostrophe	Marys car
:	Insert a colon	The list
⸜	Insert a comma	Mary the judge waited
= or ⸞	Insert a hyphen	multicolored
ℓ#	Insert line space	He drove the car. Then he went to work.
⊙	Insert a period	She bought a house
;	Insert a semicolon	vegetables fruit
#	Insert a space	A verylong trip
[/]	Insert brackets	Mary said
(/)	Insert parentheses	a very long trip

Proofreaders Marks

Symbol	Description	Example
“ ”	Insert quotation marks	“No Problem,” I said
^ or ˅	Insert something (a letter or word etc., or mark an error or note)	She bought a house
stet	Let stand-ignore marks	The ~~big~~ dog
ⓧ	Letters not clear	He ~~should~~ be there
[	Move to the left	[He drove the car
]	Move to the right	He] drove the car
⊔	Move word or letter down	The big dog
⊓	Move word or letter up	The big dog
¶	New paragraph	¶The big dog
no ¶ or *run in*	No paragraph, or run in	He drove the car.
Note	Question, comment or instruction to author	Christmas events *Which?*
/	Separates error marks	He drove car #/ the/#
sp	Spell out	12 Days of Christmas
break	Start new line	He drove the car. In other news
tr	Transpose	He the car drove
	Turn over an inverted letter	He drove the car
wf	Wrong font size or style	He **drove** the car

Plastic Recycling Symbols

SPI [A] Symbol	Plastic Type	Common Containers
1 PETE	PETE Polyethylene Terephthalate	Soda bottles, water bottles, juice bottles, detergent bottles, peanut butter jars
2 HDPE	HDPE Digh-density Polyethylene	Milk bottles, detergent bottles oil bottles, motor oil bottles, plastic bags, toys, bleach bottles, water jugs
3 V	V Vinyl or Polyvinyl Chloride (PVC)	Food wrap, vegetable oil bottles, blister packages window cleaner bottles
4 LDPE	LDPE Low-density	Plastic bags, shrink wrap, garment bags, flxible film packaging
5 PP	PP Polypropylene	Refrigerated containers, some bags, most bottle tops, some carpets, some food wrap, yogurt tubs, straws
6 PS	PS Polystyrene	Throwaway utensils, meat packaging, protective packaging, egg cartons, plates, carry-out containers
7 OTHER	Other	Usually layered or mixed plastics not mentioned above. Can not be recycled.

A = SPI, Society of the Plastics Industry

Paper Sizes

Paper Size	Standard	Millimeters	Inches
4A0	ISO	1,682 x 2,378	66.22 x 93.62
2A0	ISO	1,189 x 1,682	46.81 x 66.22
Eight Crown	UK	1,060 x 1,461	41.75 x 57.50
B0	ISO	1,000 x 1,414	39.37 x 55.67
Arch-E	Arch	914 x 1,219	36.00 x 48.00
SRA0	ISO	900 x 1,280	35.43 x 50.39
ANSI-E	ANSI	864 x 1,118	34.00 x 44.00
RA0	ISO	860 x 1,220	33.86 x 48.03
A0	ISO	841 x 1,189	33.11 x 46.81
Quad Demy	UK	826 x 1,118	32.50 x 44.00
Quad Crown	UK	762 x 1,016	30.00 x 40.00
Antiquarian	UK	737 x 1,321	29.00 x 52.00
Double Princess	UK	711 x 1,118	28.00 x 44.00
B1	ISO	707 x 1,000	27.83 x 39.37
Double Elephant	UK	686 x 1,016	27.00 x 40.00
SRA1	ISO	640 x 900	25.20 x 35.43
RA1	ISO	610 x 860	24.02 x 33.86
Arch-D	Arch	610 x 914	24.00 x 36.00
A1	ISO	594 x 841	23.39 x 33.11
Double Demy	UK	572 x 889	22.50 x 35.00
ANSI-D	ANSI	559 x 864	22.00 x 34.00
Imperial	UK	559 x 762	22.00 x 30.00
Princess	UK	546 x 711	21.50 x 28.00
B2	ISO	500 x 707	19.69 x 27.83
Demy	UK	470 x 584	18.50 x 23.00
Arch-C	Arch	457 x 610	18.00 x 24.00
SRA2	ISO	450 x 640	17.72 x 25.20
ANSI-C	ANSI	432 x 559	17.00 x 22.00
RA2	ISO	430 x 610	16.93 x 24.02
A2	ISO	420 x 594	16.54 x 23.39
B3	ISO	353 x 500	13.90 x 19.69
Brief	UK	333 x 470	13.13 x 18.50
Arch-B	Arch	305 x 457	12.00 x 18.00
A3	ISO	297 x 420	11.69 x 16.54
ANSI-B	ANSI	279 x 432	11.00 x 17.00
B4	ISO	250 x 353	9.84 x 13.90
Arch-A	Arch	229 x 305	9.00 x 12.00
Legal	US	216 x 356	8.50 x 14.00
ANSI-A	ANSI	216 x 279	8.50 x 11.00
Demy Quarto	UK	216 x 273	8.50 x 10.75
Foolscap Folio	UK	210 x 333	8.25 x 13.13
A4	ISO	210 x 297	8.27 x 11.69
Crown Quarto	UK	184 x 242	7.25 x 9.50
B5	ISO	176 x 250	6.93 x 9.84
Foolscap Quarto	UK	165 x 206	6.50 x 8.13
Royal Octavo	UK	152 x 241	6.00 x 9.50
A5	ISO	148 x 210	5.83 x 8.27
Demy Octavo	US	140 x 216	5.50 x 8.50
Demy Octavo	UK	137 x 213	5.38 x 8.38
-	US	127 x 178	5.00 x 7.00
B6	ISO	125 x 176	4.92 x 6.93
Crown Octavo	UK	121 x 181	4.75 x 7.13
A6	ISO	105 x 148	4.13 x 5.83
-	US	102 x 127	4.00 x 5.00
B7	ISO	88 x 125	3.46 x 4.92
-	US	76 x 127	3.00 x 5.00
A7	ISO	74 x 105	2.91 x 4.13

Paper Size	Standard	Millimeters	Inches
B8	ISO	62 x 88	2.44 x 3.46
A8	ISO	52 x 74	2.05 x 2.91
B9	ISO	44 x 62	1.73 x 2.44
A9	ISO	37 x 52	1.46 x 2.05
B10	ISO	31 x 44	1.22 x 1.73
A10	ISO	26 x 37	1.02 x 1.46

Abbreviations for the above table are:
ANSI	American National Standards Institute
Arch	Architects Standard, US
ISO	International Organization for Standardization
UK	United Kingdom
US	United States

English – Greek Alphabet

English	Greek	Greek Name
A, a	A, α	alpha
B, b	B, β	beta
G, g	Γ, γ	gamma
D, d	Δ, δ	delta
E, e	E, ε	epsilon
Z, z	Z, ζ	zeta
E, e	H, η	eta
Th, th	Θ, θ	theta
I, i	I, ι	iota
K, k	K, κ	kappa
L, l	Λ, λ	lambda
M, m	M, μ	mu
N, n	N, ν	nu
X, x	Ξ, ξ	xi
O, o	O, o	omicron
P, p	Π, π	pi
R, r	P, ρ	rho
S, s	Σ, σ	sigma
T, t	T, τ	tau
U, u	Y, υ	upsilon
Ph, ph	Φ, ϕ	phi
Ch, ch	X, χ	chi
Ps, ps	Ψ, ψ	psi
O, o	Ω, ω	omega

Phonetic Alphabet

LetterWord	Intl/Radio	Pronunciation	Law Enforcement
A	Alpha	Al Fah	Adam
B	Bravo	Bra Voh	Boy
C	Charlie	Char Lee	Charles
D	Delta	Del Tah	David
E	Echo	Ek Oh	Edward
F	Foxtrot	Foks Trot	Frank
G	Golf	Golf	George
H	Hotel	Ho Tell	Henry
I	India	In Dee Ah	Ida
J	Juliett	Jew Lee Ett	John
K	Kilo	Key Loh	King
L	Lima	Lee Mah	Lincoln
M	Mike	Mike	Mary
N	November	No Vem Ber	Nora
O	Oscar	Oss Cahr	Ocean
P	Papa	Pah Pah	Paul
Q	Quebec	Ke Beck	Queen
R	Romeo	Row Me Oh	Robert
S	Sierra	See Air Rah	Sam
T	Tango	Tang Go	Tom
U	Uniform	You Nee Form	Union
V	Victor	Vick Ter	Victor
W	Whiskey	Wiss Key	William
X	X-Ray	Ecks Ray	X-Ray
Y	Yankee	Yang Key	Young
Z	Zulu	Zoo Loo	Zebra

Morse Code

Letter	Code	Letter	Code	Letter	Code
A	•—	Q	——•—	1	•————
B	—•••	R	•—•	2	••———
C	—•—•	S	•••	3	•••——
D	—••	T	—	4	••••—
E	•	U	••—	5	•••••
F	••—•	V	•••—	6	—••••
G	——•	W	•——	7	——•••
H	••••	X	—••—	8	———••
I	••	Y	—•——	9	————•
J	•———	Z	——••	0	—————
K	—•—	Error	••••••••	.	•—•—•—
L	•—••	Wait	•—•••	,	——••——
M	——	End Msg	•—•—•	:	———•••
N	—•	End Work	•••—•—	=	—•••—
O	———	Inv Xmit	—•—	)	—•——•—
P	•——•	/	—••—•	(	—•——•
				?	••——••

Semaphore Alphabet

A&1		K&0		U	
B&2		L		V	
C&3		M		W	
D&4		N		X	
E&5		O		Y	
F&6		P		Z	
G&7		Q		Numeric follows	
H&8		R		Alphabetic follows	
I&9		S		Cancel	
J		T			
Error	Alternate ʻↃʼ then ⚐ (move up and down)				

Braille Alphabet

A	⠁	M	⠍	Y	⠽
B	⠃	N	⠝	Z	⠵
C	⠉	O	⠕	1	⠁
D	⠙	P	⠏	2	⠃
E	⠑	Q	⠟	3	⠉
F	⠋	R	⠗	4	⠙
G	⠛	S	⠎	5	⠑
H	⠓	T	⠞	6	⠋
I	⠊	U	⠥	7	⠛
J	⠚	V	⠧	8	⠓
K	⠅	W	⠺	9	⠊
L	⠇	X	⠭	0	⠚

"Ten" Radio Codes

10-1	Receiving poorly, bad signal
10-2	Receiving OK, signal strong
10-3	Stop transmitting
10-4	Message received
10-5	Relay message
10-6	Busy, please stand by
10-7	Out of service
10-8	In service
10-9	Repeat message
10-10	Finished, standing by
10-11	Talk slower
10-12	Visitors present
10-13	Need weather or road conditions
10-16	Pickup needed at
10-17	Urgent Business
10-18	Is there anything for us
10-19	Nothing for you, return to base
10-20	My location is
10-21	Use a telephone
10-22	Report in person to
10-23	Stand by
10-24	Finished last assignment
10-25	Can you contact ?
10-26	Disregard last information
10-27	I'm changing to channel
10-28	Identify your station
10-29	Your time is up for contact
10-30	Does not conform to FCC rules
10-32	I'll give you a radio check
10-33	Emergency traffic at this station
10-34	Help needed at this station
10-35	Confidential information
10-36	The correct time is
10-37	Wrecker needed at
10-38	Ambulance needed at
10-39	Your message has been delivered
10-41	Please change to channel
10-42	Traffic accident at
10-43	Traffic congestion at
10-44	I have a message for
10-45	All units within range please report in
10-50	Break channel
10-60	What is the next message number
10-62	Unable to copy, please call on the phone
10-63	Net directed to
10-64	Net clear
10-65	Standing by, awaiting your next message
10-67	All units comply
10-70	Fire at
10-71	Proceed with transmission in sequence
10-73	Speed trap at
10-75	Your transmission is causing interference
10-77	Negative contact
10-81	Reserve hotel room for
10-82	Reserve room for
10-84	My telephone number is
10-85	My address is
10-89	Radio repairman is needed at
10-90	I have TVI
10-91	Talk closer to the microphone
10-92	Your transmitter needs adjustment
10-93	Check my frequency on this channel
10-94	Please give me a long count
10-95	Transmit dead carrier for 5 seconds
10-99	Mission completed, all units secure
10-200	Police needed at

Military Rank - Air Force

Grade	Rank	Insignia

Enlisted (black trim, silver stripes)

E1	Airman Basic ·············· No insignia	
E2	Airman ·······································	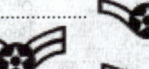
E3	Airman 1st Class ·········	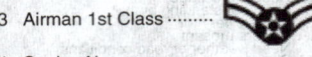
E4	Senior Airman ·····························	
E5	Staff Sergeant ··············	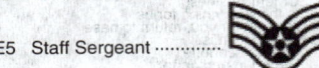
E6	Technical Sergeant ·····························	
E7	Master Sergeant ·········	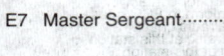
E7	First Sergeant ·····························	
E8	Senior Master Sergeant	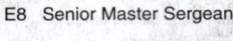
E8	First Sergeant ·····························	
E9	Chief Master Sergeant	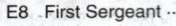
E9	First Sergeant ·····························	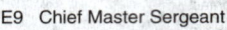 

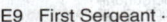

Grade	Rank	Insignia

Enlisted (cont.)

E9 Command Chief Master

E9 Chief Master Sergeant of Air Force ·····

Officer

W1,2,3,4 ·· No Warrant Officers

O1 2nd Lieutenant (brass) ·······················

O2 1st Lieutenant (silver) ·············

O3 Captain (silver) ································

O4 Major (gold) ·····················

O5 Lieutenant Colonel (silver) ·····················

O6 Colonel (silver) ····················

O7 Brigadier General (silver) ·····························

O8 Major General (silver) ·············

O9 Lieutenant General (silver) ·····················

O10 General (silver) ·····················

–   General of the Air Force (silver)·················
     (Reserved for war time only - 1 person)

Grade	Rank	Navy & Coast Guard

Enlisted

E1 Seaman Recruit·····················No insignia

E2 Seaman Apprentice·······························

E3 Seaman···············

E4 Petty Officer 3rd Class·······························

E5 Petty Officer 2nd Class············

E6 Petty Officer 1st Class·······························

E7 Chief Petty Officer

E8 Sr Chief Petty Officer·······································

E9 Mst Chief Petty Officer············

E9 Fleet/Command Master·······························
    Chief Petty Officer

    Mst Chief Petty Officer of·······
    Navy and Coast Guard

Military Rank - Navy & Coast Guard

Grade	Rank	Navy & Coast Guard
Officer		
W1	Warrant Officer	No longer in use
W2	Chief Warrant Officer 2	
W3	Chief Warrant Officer 3	
W4	Chief Warrant Officer 4	
W5	Chief Warrant Officer 5	None
O1	Ensign (brass)	
O2	Lieutenant Jr. Grade (silver)	
O3	Lieutenant (silver)	
O4	Lieutenant Commander (gold)	
O5	Commander (silver)	
O6	Captain (silver)	

Military Rank - Navy & Coast Guard

Grade   Rank   Insignia

Officer (cont.)

O7   Rear Admiral (lower half) (silver) ....

O8   Rear Admiral (upper half) ....

O9   Vice Admiral (silver) ....

O10 Admiral (silver) ....

–   Fleet Admiral (silver) ....
      (Reserved for wartime only)

Military Rank - Army

Grade   Rank   Insignia

Enlisted (black trim, orange stripes)

E1   Private ....No insignia

E2   Private ....

E3   Private 1st Class ....

E4   Corporal or Specialist ....

Grade	Rank	Insignia

Enlisted (black trim, yellow stripes)

E4 Specialist

E5 Sergeant

E6 Staff Sergeant

E7 Sergeant 1st Class

E8 Master Sergeant

E8 1st Sergeant

E9 Command Sergeant Major

E9 Sergeant Major

E9 Sergeant Major of the Army

Military Rank - Army

Grade	Rank	Insignia

Officer

W1 Warrant Officer

W2 Chief Warrant Officer

W3 Chief Warrant Officer

W4 Chief Warrant Officer

W5 Master Warrant Officer

O1 2nd Lieutenant (brass)

O2 1st Lieutenant (silver)

O3 Captain (silver)

O4 Major (gold)

O5 Lieutenant Colonel (silver)

O6 Colonel (silver)

O7 Brigadier General (silver)

O8 Major General (silver)

O9 Lieutenant General (silver)

O10 General-Chief of Staff (silver)

– Gen of Army (silver)
(Reserved for wartime only)

Military Rank - Marines

Grade	Rank	Insignia
Enlisted (red base, green stripes)		
E1	Private	No insignia
E2	Private 1st Class	
E3	Lance Corporal	
E4	Corporal	
E5	Sergeant	
E6	Staff Sergeant	
E7	Gunnery Sergeant	
E8	Master Sergeant	
E8	1st Sergeant	
E9	Sergeant Major	
E9	Master Gunnery Sergeant	
E9	Sergeant Major of the Marines	

Military Rank - Marines

Grade	Rank	Insignia

Officer

Grade	Rank	Insignia
W1	Warrant Officer	
W2	Chief Warrant Officer 2	
W3	Chief Warrant Officer 3	
W4	Chief Warrant Officer 4	
W5	Master Warrant Officer	
O1	2nd Lieutenant (brass)	
O2	1st Lieutenant (silver)	
O3	Captain (silver)	
O4	Major (gold)	
O5	Lieutenant Colonel (silver)	
O6	Colonel (silver)	
O7	Brigadier General (silver)	
O8	Major General (silver)	
O9	Lieutenant General (silver)	
O10	General (silver)	

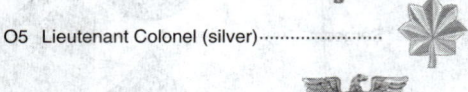

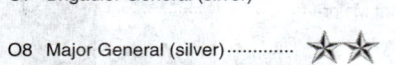

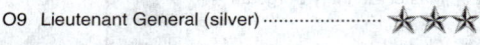

Chili Pepper Hotness Scale

Name	Scoville Units	Hotness
Pure capsicin	15,000,000-16,000,000	Maximum
Pepper spray (Std US)	2,000,000-5,500,000	Very Hot
Jolokia (Dorset Naga)	855,000-1,000,000	Very Hot
Habanero, Red Savina	225,000-550,000	Very Hot
Habanero, yellow and orange	100,000 - 325,000	Very Hot
Scotch Bonnet	100,000 – 350,000	Very Hot
Thai	75,000 – 150,000	Very Hot
Piquin	70,000 – 100,000	Very Hot
Tepin	40,000 – 70,000	Hot
Cayenne	30,000 - 55,000	Hot
Tabasco	30,000 – 50,000	Hot
De Arbol	15,000 – 30,000	Hot
Chipotle	15,000	Hot
Casabel	5,000-15,000	Medium
Louisiana Hot	4,000 - 10,000	Medium
Chilcostle	3,500 - 5,000	Medium
Jalapeno, green, red	2,500 - 5,000	Medium
Mirasol or Aji Mirasol	2,500 – 5,000	Medium
Serrano	2,000 – 4,500	Medium
Pasilla or Pasilla de Oaxaca or Poblano	1,000 – 1,500	Mild
Ancho or Ancho Poblano	1,000 – 1,500	Mild
New Mxico Big Jim	1,000 – 1,400	Mild
New Mexico #6	800 - 1,400	Mild
Anaheim	100 - 250	Mild
Pimento	0-100	Mild
Bell Pepper (green, yellow, orange, red)	0	No Heat

The Scoville Heat Scale was developed by Dr. Wilbur Scoville in 1912 and is simply a ratio of the amount of sugar water to chili before a person cannot detect any flavor or hotness. For example, the Anaheim chili takes 200 cups of sugar water to 1 cup of product before one cannot detect any hotness. There are 6 capsaicinoid compounds found in chili and the hottest of these is capsaicin which causes the burning sensation. The best product to break the painful stimuli is a glass of milk. Milk contains a protein called casein and casein breaks the bond between the pain receptors and the capsaicin. Today laboratories use a high-performance liquid chromatograph (HPCL) for measuring hotness. This procedure is more accurate and takes less time to produce a result; however, the Scoville Heat Scale is the one that is widely used. There are claims that a chili hotter than the Red Habanero chile was found in the Central Assamese town of Tezpur (boarder region between Indian and Burma). This chill is purported to have measured 855,000 on the Scoville Scale. If so, it would not be an edible chili but could be used in pepper spray weapons.

Bed & Sheet Sizes - USA

Bed Size	Width x Length (inches)	Width per Person	Fitted Sheet (inches)	Flat Sheet (inches)
Crib	27-28 x 48-52		28 x 52	42 x 72
Cot	31 x 74	31		
Single or Twin	39 x 75	39	39 x 75	66 x 96
Twin (narrow)	30 x 80	30		
Twin X-Long	39 x 80	39	39 x 80	39 x 80
Twin X-Long	30 x 84	30		
XX-Long Twin	39 x 84	39		
Three Quarter	48 x 75	48		
Rice & Antique Bed	48 x 75	48		
Full Sofa Bed	54 x 72	27		
Standard Double/Full	54 x 75	27	54 x 75	81 x 96
XL Full	54 x 80	27		
XX-Long Full	54 x 84	27		
Queen Sofa Bed	60 x 74	30		
Queen	60 x 80	30	60 x 80	90 x 102
Dual Queen	60 x 80	30	60 x 80	90 x 102
X-Long Queen	60 x 84	30		
Standard King aka Eastern	76 x 80 or 78 x 80	38	76-79 x 80	108 x 102
California King aka Western	72 x 84	36	72 x 84	102 x 110
Dual Super Extra Wide King	108 x 80	54		
7 Foot Round	84 diameter			
8 Foot Round	96 diameter			
Super Single Waterbed	48 x 84	48		
Queen Waterbed	60 x 84	30		
King Waterbed	72 x 84	36		

Note: Sheets listed above are all standard size sheets. If a sheet is not listed for a particular bed you will need to use a larger standard size sheet.

Clothing Sizes - USA vs. Europe

Men's Clothing: Suits, Overcoats & Sweaters

American	British	European	Japanese
34 or S	34	44	S
36 or M	36	46	
38 or M	38	48	M
40 or L	40	50	
42 or XL	42	52	L
44 or XL	44	54	
46 or XL	46	56	LL

General Rules
Using the American size as a base:
  American and British suit and coat sizes are the same.
  European sizes are 10 more than American
  Japanese sizes are in letters

Women's Clothing: Suits and Dresses

American	British	European	Japanese
10	32	38	9
12	34	40	11
14	36	42	13
16	38	44	15
18	40	46	17
20	42	48	19
22	44	50	21

General Rules
Using the American size as a base:
  British sizes are 22-24 more than American
  European size is 28 more than American
  Japanese size is 1 less than American

Note: Sock, belt and glove sizes are generally the same universal sizes.

Clothing Sizes - USA vs. Europe

Men's Shirts (Neck Sizes)			
American	**British**	**European**	**Japanese**
14	14	36	36
14 ½	14 ½	37	37
15	15	38	38
15 ½	15 ½	39	39
16	16	40-41	40
16 ½	16 ½	41-42	41-42
17	17	42-43	42-43

General Rules
American and British are the same size
European sizes are 22 more than American (round up)
Japanese sizes are the same as the European

Women's Blouses/Sweaters			
American	**British**	**European**	**Japanese**
6 or S	8	34-36	5
8 or M	10	36-38	7
10 or M	12	38-40	9
12 or L	14	40-42	11
14 or L	16	42-44	13
16 or XL	18	44-46	15
18	20	46-48	17
20	22	48	19

General Rules
British sizes are 2 more than American
European sizes are 28-30 more than American
Japanese are 1 less than American

Note: Sock, belt and glove sizes are generally the same universal sizes.

Clothing Sizes - USA vs. Europe

Men's Shoe Sizes

American	British	European	Japanese
6		39	24
6 ½	5-6	39-40	24 ½
7	5-6	39-40	24 ½ - 25
7 ½	6-7	40-41	25 ½ -26
8	7-8	41	25 ½ -26
8 ½	7-8	42	26 ½
9	8-9	42	27
9 ½	9	43	27 ½
10	9-10	43	28
10 ½	10	44	28-28 ½
11	10-11	45	29
11 ½	11-11 ½	46	29-29 ½
12	11 ½ - 12	47	30

General Rules
Using the American size as a base:
  British sizes are ½ to 1 less than American
  European sizes are 33 to 34 more than American
  Japanese sizes are 19 more than American

Women's Shoe Sizes

American	British	European	Japanese
4 ½	3	34-45	21 ½
5	3 ½	35-36	22
5 ½	4	36 ½	22 ½
6	4 ½	36-37	23-23 ½
6 ½	5	37 ½	23 ½-23 ¾
7	5 ½	38	24 - 24 ½
7 ½	6	38-38 ½	24 ½
8	6 ½	38-40	25
8 ½	7	39-40	25 ½
9	7 ½	40-42	26

General Rules
Using the American size as a base:
  British sizes are 1 ½ less than American
  European sizes are 30 more than American (round up)
  Japanese sizes are 17 more than American

Consanguinity Table

Common Ancestor (Relative #2)	Child	Grandchild	Great Grandchild	2nd Great Grandchild	3rd Great Grandchild	4th Great Grandchild	5th Great Grandchild	6th Great Grandchild
Child	Sibling	Niece or Nephew	Grand Niece / Nephew	Great Grand Niece / Nephew	2nd Great Grand Niece / Nephew	3rd G-Grand Niece / Nephew	4th G-Grand Niece / Nephew	5th G-Grand Niece / Nephew
Grandchild	Niece or Nephew	First Cousin	First Cousin 1X Removed	First Cousin 2X Removed	First Cousin 3X Removed	First Cousin 4X Removed	First Cousin 5X Removed	First Cousin 6X Removed
Great Grandchild	Grand Niece / Nephew	First Cousin 1X Removed	Second Cousin	2nd Cousin 1X Removed	2nd Cousin 2X Removed	2nd Cousin 3X Removed	2nd Cousin 4X Removed	2nd Cousin 5X Removed
2nd Great Grandchild	Great Grand Niece / Nephew	First Cousin 2X Removed	2nd Cousin 1X Removed	Third Cousin	3rd Cousin 1X Removed	3rd Cousin 2X Removed	3rd Cousin 3X Removed	3rd Cousin 4X Removed
3rd Great Grandchild	2nd Great Grand Niece / Nephew	First Cousin 3X Removed	2nd Cousin 2X Removed	3rd Cousin 1X Removed	Fourth Cousin	4th Cousin 1X Removed	4th Cousin 2X Removed	4th Cousin 3X Removed
4th Great Grandchild	3rd G-Grand Niece / Nephew	First Cousin 4X Removed	2nd Cousin 3X Removed	3rd Cousin 2X Removed	4th Cousin 1X Removed	Fifth Cousin	5th Cousin 1X Removed	5th Cousin 2X Removed
5th Great Grandchild	4th G-Grand Niece / Nephew	First Cousin 5X Removed	2nd Cousin 4X Removed	3rd Cousin 3X Removed	4th Cousin 2X Removed	5th Cousin 1X Removed	Sixth Cousin	6th Cousin 1X Removed
6th Great Grandchild	5th G-Grand Niece / Nephew	First Cousin 6X Removed	2nd Cousin 5X Removed	3rd Cousin 4X Removed	4th Cousin 3X Removed	5th Cousin 2X Removed	6th Cousin 1X Removed	Seventh Cousin

Relative #1

Consanguinity Table

Definition

Consanguinity is the relationship between persons descending from the same ancestor.

Directions

1) Determine relationship to Common Ancestor for Relative #1 - locating box in top row
2) Determine relationship to Common Ancestor for Relative #2 - locating box in 1st column
3) Take line down graph for #1 and line across for #2 - where they intersect is the relationship between the two relatives

Notes

"Removed" Cousin - Removed designates the cousins are not of the same generation. 1st Cousin 1X Removed would be the child of your 1st Cousin. 1st Cousin 2X Removed would be the grandchild of your 1st Cousin

Consanguinity relationships are either lineal or collateral. Lineal is a direct line descendant. In the chart above, a lineal descendant is either the first row from left to right or the first column from the top cell to the bottom cell. (Even though the cells have stopped with 6th Great grandchild, the chart could be extended infinitely). All other cells within the chart are collateral descendants.

"Half" - denotes that within the family tree, one of the parental units married and had children, thereby giving "half" of a blood line;

"Step" - denotes that within the family tree, a blood relative married and although there is a relative relationship, there is no blood line.

"Double" 1st Cousins - This can occur if the children of two marriages where two blood siblings of one family marry the two blood siblings of another family; any resulting issue would be a Double 1st Cousin. Sequentially, if triplets of one family marry triplets of another family, then the children of the marriages would be Triple 1st Cousins.

Social Security Numbers

1st 3 Num. ···· Location	1st 3 Num. ···· Location
000 ·········· Unused	525 ·········· New Mexico
001-003 ···· New Hampshire	526-527 ···· Arizona
004-007 ···· Maine	528-529 ···· Utah
008-009 ···· Vermont	530 ·········· Nevada
010-034 ···· Massachusetts	531-539 ···· Washington
035-039 ···· Rhode Island	540-544 ···· Oregon
040-049 ···· Connecticut	545-573 ···· California
050-134 ···· New York	574 ·········· Alaska
135-158 ···· New Jersey	575-576 ···· Hawaii
159-211 ···· Pennsylvania	577-579 ···· District of Columbia
212-220 ···· Maryland	580 ·········· Virgin Islands
221-222 ···· Delaware	581-584 ···· Puerto Rico
223-231 ···· Virginia	585 ·········· New Mexico
232-236 ···· West Virginia	586 ·········· Pacific Islands (PI)*
237-246 ···· North Carolina	587-588 ···· Mississippi*
247-251 ···· South Carolina	589-595 ···· Florida
252-260 ···· Georgia	596-599 ···· Puerto Rico
261-267 ···· Florida	600-601 ···· Arizona
268-302 ···· Ohio	602-626 ···· California
303-317 ···· Indiana	627-645 ···· Texas
318-361 ···· Illinois	646-647 ···· Utah
362-386 ···· Michigan	648-649 ···· New Mexico
387-399 ···· Wisconsin	650-653 ···· Colorado
400-407 ···· Kentucky	654-658 ···· South Carolina*
408-415 ···· Tennessee	659-665 ···· Louisiana*
416-424 ···· Alabama	667-675 ···· Georgia*
425-428 ···· Mississippi	676-679 ···· Arkansas*
429-432 ···· Arkansas	680 ·········· Nevada*
433-439 ···· Louisiana	691-699 ···· Virginia*
440-448 ···· Oklahoma	700-728 ···· Railroad workers
449-467 ···· Texas	Through 1963
468-477 ···· Minnesota	750-751 ···· Hawaii*
478-485 ···· Iowa	756-763 ···· Tennessee*
486-500 ···· Missouri	763-899 ···· Unassigned;
501-502 ···· North Dakota	for future use
503-504 ···· South Dakota	900-999 ···· Not valid -used for
505-508 ···· Nebraska	program purposes
509-515 ···· Kansas	
516-517 ···· Montana	* Numbers newly allocated to
518-519 ···· Idaho	this area.
520 ·········· Wyoming	
521-524 ···· Colorado	

State Population - Year 2000

State	Abbreviation	Population	+/-%	Capital
United States	USA	281,421,906	13.2	Washington, DC
Alabama	AL	4,447,100	10.1	Montgomery
Alaska	AK	626,932	14.0	Juneau
Arizona	AZ	5,130,632	40.0	Phoenix
Arkansas	AR	2,673,400	13.7	Little Rock
California	CA	33,871,648	13.8	Sacramento
Colorado	CO	4,301,261	30.6	Denver
Connecticut	CT	3,405,565	3.6	Hartford
Delaware	DE	783,600	17.6	Dover
Dist. of Columbia	DC	572,059	-5.7	Washington, DC
Florida	FL	15,982,378	23.5	Tallahassee
Georgia	GA	8,186,453	26.4	Atlanta
Hawaii	HI	1,211,537	9.3	Honolulu
Idaho	ID	1,293,953	28.5	Boise
Illinois	IL	12,419,293	8.6	Springfield
Indiana	IN	6,080,485	9.7	Indianapolis
Iowa	IA	2,926,324	5.4	Des Moines
Kansas	KS	2,688,418	8.5	Topeka
Kentucky	KY	4,041,769	9.7	Frankfort
Louisiana	LA	4,468,976	5.9	Baton Rouge
Maine	ME	1,274,923	3.8	Augusta
Maryland	MD	5,296,486	10.8	Annapolis
Massachusetts	MA	6,349,097	5.5	Boston
Michigan	MI	9,938,444	6.9	Lansing
Minnesota	MN	4,919,379	12.4	St. Paul
Mississippi	MS	2,844,658	10.5	Jackson
Missouri	MO	5,595,211	9.3	Jefferson City
Montana	MT	902,195	12.9	Helena
Nebraska	NE	1,711,263	8.4	Lincoln
Nevada	NV	1,998,257	66.3	Carson City
New Hampshire	NH	1,235,786	11.4	Concord
New Jersey	NJ	8,414,350	8.9	Trenton
New Mexico	NM	1,819,046	20.1	Santa Fe
New York	NY	18,976,457	5.5	Albany
North Carolina	NC	8,049,313	21.4	Raleigh
North Dakota	ND	642,200	0.5	Bismarck
Ohio	OH	11,353,140	4.7	Columbus
Oklahoma	OK	3,450,654	9.7	Oklahoma City
Oregon	OR	3,421,399	20.4	Salem
Pennsylvania	PA	12,281,054	3.4	Harrisburg
Rhode Island	RI	1,048,319	4.5	Providence
South Carolina	SC	4,012,012	15.1	Columbia
South Dakota	SD	754,844	8.5	Pierre
Tennessee	TN	5,689,283	16.7	Nashville
Texas	TX	20,851,820	22.8	Austin
Utah	UT	2,233,169	29.6	Salt Lake City
Vermont	VT	608,827	8.2	Montpelier
Virginia	VA	7,078,515	14.4	Richmond
Washington	WA	5,894,121	21.1	Olympia
West Virginia	WV	1,808,344	0.8	Charleston
Wisconsin	WI	5,363,675	9.6	Madison
Wyoming	WY	493,782	8.9	Cheyenne

State Information - Year 2000

State	State Bird	State Flower	Statehood(Admit #)
United States	bald eagle		7-4-1776
Alabama	yellowhammer	camelia	12-14-1819 (22)
Alaska	willow ptarmigan	forget-me-not	1-3-1959 (49)
Arizona	cactus wren	saguaro cactus	2-14-1912 (48)
Arkansas	mockingbird	apple blossom	6-15-1836 (25)
California	california valley quail	golden poppy	9-9-1850 (31)
Colorado	lark bunting	columbine	8-1-1876 (38)
Connecticut	robin	mountain laurel	1-9-1788 (5)
Delaware	blue hen chicken	peach blossom	12-7-1787 (1)
Florida	mockingbird	orange blossom	3-3-1845 (27)
Georgia	brown thrasher	cherokee rose	1-2-1788 (4)
Hawaii	nene or Hawaiin goose	yellow hibiscus	8-21-1959 (50)
Idaho	mountain bluebird	syringa	7-3-1890 (43)
Illinois	cardinal	violet	12-3-1818 (21)
Indiana	cardinal	peony	12-11-1816 (19)
Iowa	eastern goldfinch	wild rose	12-28-1846 (29)
Kansas	western meadowlark	sunflower	1-29-1861 (34)
Kentucky	cardinal	goldenrod	6-1-1792 (15)
Louisiana	eastern brown pelican	magnolia	4-30-1812 (18)
Maine	chickadee	pine cone	3-15-1820 (23)
Maryland	baltimore oriole	black-eyed susan	4-28-1788 (7)
Massachusetts	chickadee	mayflower	2-6-1788 (6)
Michigan	robin	apple blossom	1-26-1837 (26)
Minnesota	common loon	lady's slipper	5-11-1858 (32)
Mississippi	mockingbird	magnolia	12-10-1817 (20)
Missouri	bluebird	hawthorn	8-10-1821(24)
Montana	western meadowlark	bitterroot	11-8-1889 (41)
Nebraska	western meadowlark	goldenrod	3-1-1867 (37)
Nevada	mountain bluebird	sagebrush	10-31-1864 (36)
New Hampshire	purple finch	purple lilac	6-21-1788 (9)
New Jersey	eastern goldfinch	purple violet	12-18-1787 (3)
New Mexico	roadrunner	yucca	1-6-1912 (47)
New York	bluebird	rose	7-26-1788 (11)
North Carolina	cardinal	dogwood	11-21-1789 (12)
North Dakota*	western meadowlark	wild rose	11-2-1889 (39)
Ohio	cardinal	carnation	3-1-1803 (17)
Oklahoma	scissor-tailed flycatcher	mistletoe	11-16-1907 (46)
Oregon	western meadowlark	oregon grape	2-14-1859 (33)
Pennsylvania	ruffed grouse	mountain laurel	12-12-1787 (2)
Rhode Island	rhode island red	violet	5-29-1790 (13)
South Carolina	great carolina wren	yellow jessamine	5-23-1788 (8)
South Dakota*	ring-necked pheasant	pasque	11-2-1889 (40)
Tennessee	mockingbird	purple iris	6-1-1796 (16)
Texas	mockingbird	bluebonnet	12-29-1845 (28)
Utah	california seagull	sego lily	1-4-1896 (45)
Vermont	hermit thrush	red clover	3-4-1791 (14)
Virginia	cardinal	dogwood	6-25-1788 (10)
Washington	willow goldfinch	rhododendron	11-11-1889 (42)
West Virginia	cardinal	rhododendron	6-20-1863 (35)
Wisconsin	robin	wood violet	5-29-1848 (30)
Wyoming	western meadowlark	indian paintbrush	7-10-1890 (44)

* North and South Dakota became states on the same day.

Climate Data in U.S. Cities

State, City	Temperature (°F)		Avg Precipitation (in.)	
	Winter	Summer	Rain	Snow
AL, Mobile	52.5	81.5	64.6	0.1
AK, Juneau	25.5	54.3	53.1	102.3
AZ, Phoenix	53.9	89.6	7.1	trace
AR, Little Rock	42.4	80.5	49.2	5.6
CA, Los Angeles	52.1	68.3	12.1	trace
CO, Denver	31.9	70.6	15.3	59.9
CT, Hartford	27.3	71.1	44.4	49.4
DC, Washington	37.2	77.0	39.0	16.7
DE, Wilmington	33.3	74.0	41.4	20.9
FL, Miami	67.8	82.0	57.5	0
GA, Atlanta	43.8	77.5	48.6	2.0
HI, Honolulu	73.2	80.0	23.5	0
ID, Boise	32.7	70.8	11.7	21.8
IL, Chicago	25.0	71.2	33.3	40.1
IN, Indianapolis	29.1	73.4	39.1	23.3
IA, Des Moines	22.9	73.9	30.8	35.0
KS, Wichita	33.0	79.0	28.6	16.3
KY, Louisville	35.2	75.9	43.6	17.3
LA, New Orleans	53.9	81.3	59.7	0.2
ME, Portland	23.4	65.6	43.5	72.0
MD, Baltimore	34.6	74.8	41.8	21.6
MA, Boston	31.3	71.1	43.8	41.6
MI, Detroit	25.9	70.0	31.0	41.3
MN, Minneapolis-St.Paul	16.0	70.6	26.4	49.9
MS, Jackson	47.8	80.7	52.8	1.1
MO, St. Louis	32.3	76.9	33.9	19.7
MT, Great Falls	23.7	66.2	15.2	59.1
NE, Omaha	24.9	75.3	30.3	31.1
NV, Reno	34.0	66.2	7.5	25.3
NH, Concord	22.2	67.1	36.5	64.4
NJ, Atlantic City	33.6	72.2	41.9	16.4
NM, Albuquerque	36.6	76.4	8.1	10.6
NY, New York	33.8	74.5	44.1	28.8
NC, Raleigh	41.1	76.2	41.8	7.5
ND, Bismarck	12.2	67.8	15.4	40.7
OH, Cleveland	28.0	69.8	35.4	54.0
OK, Oklahoma City	38.9	80.0	30.9	9.0
OR, Portland	41.0	63.8	37.4	7.0
PA, Pittsburgh	29.0	70.2	36.3	44.7
RI, Providence	29.9	70.1	45.3	36.6
SC, Columbia	46.2	79.6	49.1	1.9
SD, Sioux Falls	17.1	71.4	24.1	40.3
TN, Nashville	39.5	77.8	48.5	11.3
TX, Houston	53.3	82.1	44.8	0.4
UT, Salt Lake City	31.0	73.5	15.3	59.4
VT, Burlington	19.1	67.3	33.7	78.3
VA, Richmond	38.5	76.0	44.1	14.5
WA, Seattle	41.0	63.0	38.6	12.9
WV, Charleston	35.1	73.0	42.4	32.2
WI, Milwaukee	22.3	68.2	30.9	47.3
WY, Cheyenne	28.2	65.9	13.3	54.4

Temperature is average daily temperature (°F) in Dec, Jan, & Feb (Winter) and June, July, & Aug (Summer).
Rain is average annual rain plus snow, etc water equivalent.
Snow is the average depth of unmelted snow.
Data from U.S. NOAA, Climatography of the United States

Time Zones: Canada, Alaska & Hawaii

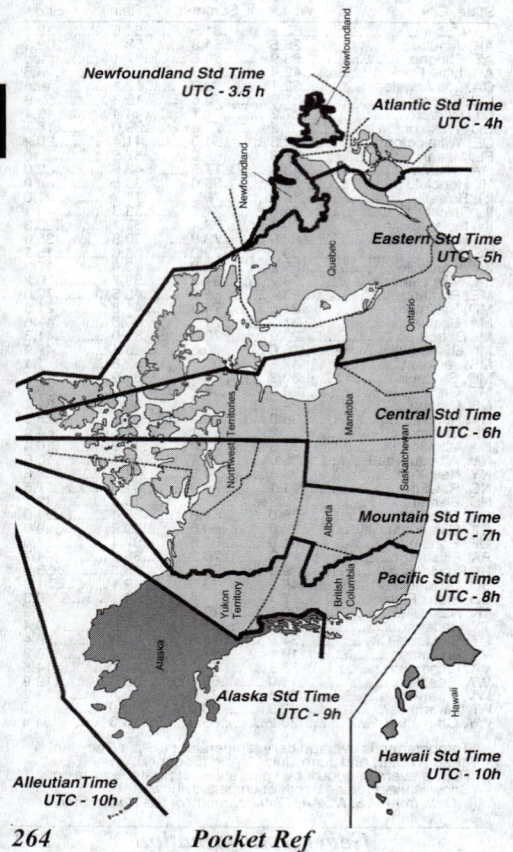

Newfoundland Std Time
UTC - 3.5 h

Atlantic Std Time
UTC - 4h

Eastern Std Time
UTC - 5h

Central Std Time
UTC - 6h

Mountain Std Time
UTC - 7h

Pacific Std Time
UTC - 8h

Alaska Std Time
UTC - 9h

Hawaii Std Time
UTC - 10h

Alleutian Time
UTC - 10h

Time Zones: U.S.A., Mexico & Carib-

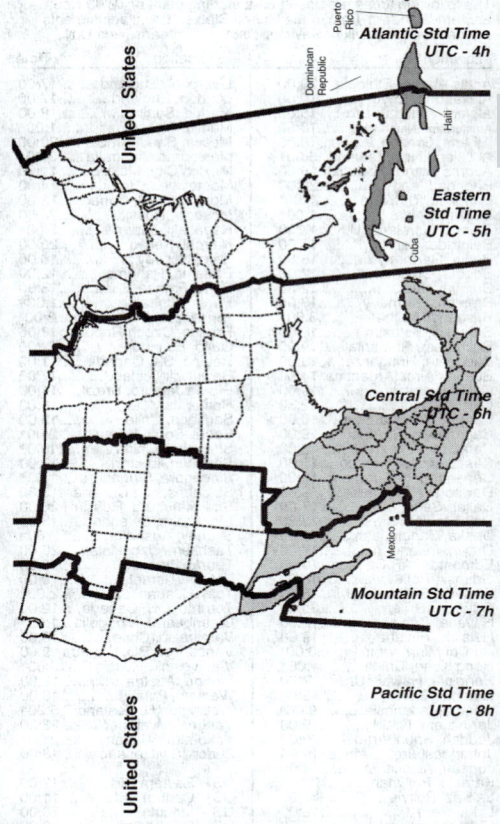

Time Zones In The World

The following times are based on a starting point of 12:00 Noon, Eastern Standard Time in the United States. Local adjustments are needed for Daylight Savings Time.   "*" means Next Day

Location	Time	Location	Time
Addis Ababa, Ethiopia	20:00	Liverpool, England	17:00
Alexandria, Egypt	19:00	London, England	17:00
Algiers, Algeria	18:00	Madrid, Spain	18:00
Amsterdam, Netherlands	18:00	Manila, Philippines	1:00*
Athens, Greece	19:00	Mecca, Saudi Arabia	20:00
Auckland,New Zealand	5:00*	Melbourne, Australia	3:00*
Azores Island, Portugal	16:00	Mexico City, Mexico	11:00
Baghdad, Iraq	20:00	Montevideo, Uruguay	14:00
Bangkok, Thailand	0:00*	Montreal, QC, Canada	12:00
Beijing, China	1:00*	Moscow, Russia	20:00
Belfast, N.Ireland, U.K.	17:00	Nagasaki, Japan	2:00*
Belgrade, Serbia	18:00	Nairobi, Kenya	20:00
Berlin, Germany	18:00	Oslo, Norway	18:00
Bogota, Colombia	12:00	Panama, Panama	12:00
Bombay, India	22:30	Paris, France	18:00
Bremen, Germany	18:00	Perth, Australia	1:00*
Brisbane, Australia	3:00*	Port Moresby, Papua NG	3:00*
Brussels, Belgium	18:00	Prague, Czech Republic	18:00
Bucharest, Romania	19:00	Quito, Ecuador	12:00
Budapest, Hungary	18:00	Regina, SK, Canada	11:00
Buenos Aires,Argentina	14:00	Reykjavik, Iceland	17:00
Cairo, Egypt	19:00	Rio de Janeiro, Brazil	14:00
Calcutta, India	22:30	Rome, Italy	18:00
Calgary, AB, Canada	10:00	Santiago, Chile	13:00
Cape Town, S. Africa	19:00	Seoul, South Korea	2:00*
Caracas, Venezuela	13:00	Shanghai, China	1:00*
Casablanca, Morocco	17:00	Shannon, Ireland	17:00
Copenhagen, Denmark	18:00	Singapore, Singapore	1:00*
Dawson, YT, Canada	9:00	St. Johns, NL, Canada	13:30
Dakar, Senegal	17:00	St. Petersburg, Russia	20:00
Delhi, India	22:30	Stockholm, Sweden	18:00
Dhaka, Bangladesh	23:00	Sydney, Australia	3:00*
Dublin, Ireland	17:00	Tashkent, Uzbekistan	23:00
Edmonton, AB,Canada	10:00	Tehran, Iran	20:30
Gdansk, Poland	18:00	Tel Aviv, Israel	19:00
Geneva, Switzerland	18:00	Tokyo, Japan	2:00*
Guam, U.S.Terr.	3:00*	Toronto, ON, Canada	12:00
Havana, Cuba	12:00	Ulaanbaatar, Mongolia	1:00*
Helsinki, Finland	19:00	Valparaiso, Chile	13:00
Ho Chi Minh, Vietnam	0:00*	Vancouver, BC, Canada	9:00
Hong Kong, China	1:00*	Vladivostok, Russia	3:00*
Honolulu, Hawaii, U.S.	7:00	Vienna, Austria	18:00
Istanbul, Turkey	19:00	Warsaw, Poland	18:00
Jakarta, Indonesia	0:00*	Wellington, N. Zealand	5:00*
Jerusalem, Israel	19:00	Yangon, Myanmar	23:30
Jeddah, Saudi Arabia	20:00	Yokohama, Japan	2:00*
Johannesburg, S.Africa	19:00	Zurich, Switzerland	18:00
Juneau, Alaska, U.S.	8:00		
Karachi, Pakistan	22:00	US – Eastern Std	12:00
La Paz, Bolivia	13:00	US – Central Std	11:00
Lima, Peru	12:00	US – Mountain Std	10:00
Lisbon, Portugal	17:00	US – Pacific Std	9:00

North American Area Codes by STATE

State / Country	City	Code
Alabama	Birmingham, Tuscaloosa	205
	Huntsville	256
	Mobile	251
	Montgomery	334
Alaska		907
American Samoa		684
Anguilla		264
Antigua, Barbuda		268
Arizona	Flagstaff, Yuma	928
	Tucson	520
	Phoenix (Central)	602
	Phoenix (E suburbs)	480
	Phoenix (W suburbs)	623
Arkansas	Fayetteville, Ft. Smith	479
	Little Rock, Hot Springs	501
	Jonesboro, Pine Bluff	870
Bahamas		242
Barbados		246
Bermuda		441
British Virgin Islands		284
California	Anaheim, Orange	714
	Bakersfield	661
	Burbank, Glendale	818
	Chico, Yreka	530
	Concord	925
	Del Mar, LaJolla	858
	Eureka, Santa Rosa	707
	Fresno	559
	Long Beach	562
	Los Angeles (Downtn)	213
	Los Angeles, Santa Monica	310
	Los Angeles (Metro)	323
	Modesto, Stockton	209
	Monterey, Santa Cruz	831
	Newport Beach	949
	Oakland, Berkeley	510
	Palm Springs, Barstow	760
	Palo Alto, San Mateo	650
	Pasadena	626
	Riverside	951
	Sacramento	916
	San Bernardino	909
	San Diego	619
	San Francisco	415
	San Jose, Gilroy	408
	Santa Barbara	805
Canada	Alberta, Calgary	403
	Alberta, Edmonton	780
	British Columbia	250
	BC, Vancouver	604, 778
	Manitoba	204
	New Brunswick	506
	Newfoundland	709

North American Area Codes by STATE

State / Country	City	Code
Canada (cont.)	Nova Scotia, P. Ed. Isl	902
	Ontario, Hamilton	905, 289
	Ontario, Windsor	519
	Ontario, Ottawa	613
	Ontario, Sault Ste Marie	705
	Ontario, Thunder Bay	807
	Ontario, Toronto(Metro)	416, 647
	Quebec, Montreal	514
	Quebec, Quebec City	418
	Quebec, Sherbrooke	819
	Quebec, Laval	450
	Saskatchewan	306
	Yukon, NW Territories	867
Cayman Islands		345
Colorado	Denver, Boulder	303, 720
	Colorado Springs, Pueblo	719
	Grand Junction, Ft.Collins	970
Connecticut	New Haven, Stamford	203
	Hartford	860
Delaware		302
District of Columbia	Washington DC	202
Dominica		767
Dominican Republic		809
Florida	Daytona Bh., Lake City	386
	Ft. Lauderdale	754, 954
	Gainesville	352
	Jacksonville	904
	Miami	786
	Miami, Key West	305
	Naples	239
	Okeechobee	863
	Orlando	407, 321, 689
	Pensacola, Tallahassee	850
	Sarasota, Ft. Myers	941
	St. Petersburg	727
	Tampa	813
	Vero Beach	772
	West Palm Beach	561
Georgia	Atlanta (Metro inside I285)	404, 770
	Atlanta (outside I285)	770, 678
	Columbus, Augusta	706
	Macon	478
	Savannah	912
	Valdosta	229
Grenada		473
Guam		671
Hawaii		808
Idaho		208
Illinois	Alton	618
	Champaign, Urbana	217
	Chicago	773
	Chicago (Central)	312
	Chicago (Central subs)	630

North American Area Codes by STATE

State / Country	City	Code
	Chicago (So.suburbs)	708
	Chicago (N,NW subs.)	847, 224
	Peoria	309
	Rockford	815
Indiana	Evansville	812
	Ft. Wayne	260
	Gary	219
	Indianapolis (Metro)	317
	Lafayette, Muncie	765
	South Bend	574
Iowa	Cedar Rapids	319
	Council Bluffs	712
	Davenport, Dubuque	563
	Des Moines	515
	Mason City, Ottumwa	641
Jamaica		876
Kansas	Dodge City, Emporia	620
	Kansas City	913
	Topeka, Colby	785
	Wichita	316
Kentucky	Ashland	606
	Bowling Green	270
	Frankfort, Louisville	502
	Lexington	859
Louisiana	Alexandria, Shreveport	318
	Baton Rouge	225
	Hammond, Houma	985
	Lafayette, Lake Charles	337
	New Orleans	504
Maine		207
Mariana Islands (CNMI)		670
Maryland	Baltimore	410, 443
	Silver Spring	301, 240
Massachusetts	Lowell, Salem	978, 351
	Cape Cod, Worcester	508, 774
	Springfield	413
	Boston (Metro)	617, 857
	Boston (Suburbs)	781, 339
Michigan	Ann Arbor	734
	Battle Creek	616
	Detroit	313
	Escanaba	906
	Flint	810
	Kalamazoo	269
	Lansing	517
	Muskegon	231
	Pontiac, Troy	248, 947
	Saginaw, Alpena	989
	Warren	586
Minnesota	Bloomington	952
	Brooklyn Park	763
	Duluth	218
	Minneapolis	612

North American Area Codes by STATE

State / Country	City	Code
	St. Paul	651
	St. Cloud	320
	Rochester	507
Mississippi	Biloxi & Gulf Coast	228
	Jackson, Natchez	601, 769
	Tupelo	662
Missouri	Jefferson City	573
	Kansas City, St. Joseph	816
	Sedalia	660
	Springfield	417
	St. Charles	636
	St. Louis	314
Montana		406
Montserrat		664
Nebraska	Lincoln, Omaha	402
	North Platte, Grand Isl.	308
Nevada	Las Vegas	702
	Reno, Ely, Elko	775
New Hampshire		603
New Jersey	Camden	856
	Elizabeth, Phillipsburg	908
	Hackensack	201, 551
	Newark	973, 862
	New Brunswick	732, 848
	Trenton, Atlantic City	609
New Mexico		505
New York	Albany	518
	Binghamton, Elmira	607
	Bronx, Brooklyn	718, 347, 917
	Buffalo	716
	Hempstead, Long Island	516
	Hudson Valley	845
	Long Island, Brentwood	631, 516
	Manhattan	212, 646, 917
	New York City	212, 347, 646
	New York City	718, 917
	Queens, Staten Island	718, 347, 917
	Rochester	585
	Syracuse	315
	White Plains, Yonkers	914
North Carolina	Asheville	828
	Charlotte	704, 980
	Fayetteville	910
	Greensboro	336
	Raleigh	919
	Rocky Mount, Greenville	252
North Dakota		701
Ohio	Akron, Canton	330, 234
	Cincinnati	513
	Cleveland (Metro)	216
	Cleveland (Suburbs)	440
	Columbus	614
	Dayton	937

North American Area Codes by STATE

State / Country	City	Code
	Marion, Zanesville	740
	Toledo	419, 567
Oklahoma	Oklahoma City	405
	Lawton	580
	Tulsa	918
Oregon	Portland, Salem	503, 971
	Eugene, Burns	541
	Tillamook, Astoria	503
Pennsylvania	Allentown	610, 484
	Altoona	814
	Harrisburg	717
	Philadelphia	215, 267
	Pittsburgh	412, 878
	Pittsburgh (Suburbs)	724, 878
	Scranton, Wilkes-Barre	570
Puerto Rico		787, 939
Rhode Island		401
South Carolina	Charleston	843
	Columbia	803
	Greenville	864
South Dakota		605
St. Kitts, Nevis		869
St. Lucia		758
St. Vincent, Grenadines		784
Tennessee	Celina, Clarksville	931
	Chattanooga, Bristol	423
	Jackson	731
	Knoxville	865
	Memphis	901
	Nashville	615
Texas	Abilene,	325
	Alpine, Midland	432
	Austin	512
	Brownsville	956
	Bryan, College Station	979
	Corpus Christi	361
	Dallas & Suburbs	214, 469
	Dallas & Suburbs	972, 469
	El Paso	915
	Fort Worth, Arlington	817, 682
	Galveston, Beaumont	409
	Houston	713, 281, 832
	Huntsville	936
	Kerrville	830
	Lubbock, Amarillo	806
	San Antonio	210
	Tyler	430, 903
	Waco	254
	Wichita Falls	940
Trinidad, Tabago		868
Turks and Caicos Islands		649
US Virgin Islands		340
Utah	Salt Lake City	801

State / Country	City	Code
Utah (cont.)	Logan, St, George	435
Vermont		802
Virginia	Arlington	703, 571
	Bristol	276
	Lynchburg	434
	Norfolk	757
	Richmond	804
	Roanoke	540
Washington	Bellevue, Edmonds	425
	Olympia, Vancouver	360
	Seattle	206
	Spokane	509
	Tacoma, Kent	253
West Virginia		304
Wisconsin	Eau Claire	715
	Green Bay	920
	Kenosha	262
	Madison	608
	Milwaukee	414
Wyoming		307

North American Area Codes by CODE

State / Country	City	Code
New Jersey	Hackensack	201
District of Columbia	Washington DC	202
Connecticut	New Haven, Stamford	203
Canada	Manitoba	204
Alabama	Birmingham, Tuscaloosa	205
Washington	Seattle	206
Maine		207
Idaho		208
California	Modesto, Stockton	209
Texas	San Antonio	210
New York	Manhattan, NY City	212
California	Los Angeles (Downtn)	213
Texas	Dallas & Suburbs	214
Pennsylvania	Philadelphia	215
Ohio	Cleveland (Metro)	216
Illinois	Champaign, Urbana	217
Minnesota	Duluth	218
Indiana	Gary	219
Illinois	Chicago (N NW suburbs)	224
Louisiana	Baton Rouge	225
Mississippi	Biloxi & Gulf Coast	228
Georgia	Valdosta	229
Michigan	Muskegon	231
Ohio	Akron, Canton	234
Florida	Naples	239
Maryland	Silver Spring	240
Bahamas		242
Barbados		246
Michigan	Pontiac, Troy	248
Canada	British Columbia	250
Alabama	Mobile	251
North Carolina	Rocky Mount, Greenville	252
Washington	Tacoma, Kent	253
Texas	Waco	254
Alabama	Huntsville	256
Indiana	Ft. Wayne	260
Wisconsin	Kenosha	262
Anguilla		264
Pennsylvania	Philadelphia	267
Antigua, Barbuda		268
Michigan	Kalamazoo	269
Kentucky	Bowling Green	270
Virginia	Bristol	276
Texas	Houston	281
British Virgin Islands		284
Canada	Ontario, Hamilton	289
Maryland	Silver Spring	301
Delaware		302
Colorado	Denver, Boulder	303
West Virginia		304
Florida	Miami, Key West	305
Canada	Saskatchewan	306
Wyoming		307

State / Country	City	Code
Nebraska	North Platte, Grand Island	308
Illinois	Peoria	309
California	Los Angeles, Santa Monica	310
Illinois	Chicago (Central)	312
Michigan	Detroit	313
Missouri	St. Louis	314
New York	Syracuse	315
Kansas	Wichita	316
Indiana	Indianapolis (Metro)	317
Louisiana	Alexandria, Shreveport	318
Iowa	Cedar Rapids	319
Minnesota	St. Cloud	320
Florida	Orlando	321
California	Los Angeles (Metro)	323
Texas	Abilene	325
Ohio	Akron, Canton	330
Alabama	Montgomery	334
North Carolina	Greensboro	336
Louisiana	Lafayette, Lake Charles	337
Massachusetts	Boston (Suburbs)	339
US Virgin Islands		340
Cayman Islands		345
New York	Bronx, Brooklyn, NY City	347
Massachusetts	Lowell, Salem	351
Florida	Gainesville	352
Washington	Olympia, Vancouver	360
Texas	Corpus Christi	361
Florida	Daytona Bh, Lake City	386
Rhode Island		401
Nebraska	Lincoln, Omaha	402
Canada	Alberta, Calgary	403
Georgia	Atlanta (Metro inside I285)	404
Oklahoma	Oklahoma City	405
Montana		406
Florida	Orlando	407
California	San Jose	408
Texas	Galveston, Beaumont	409
Maryland	Baltimore	410
Pennsylvania	Pittsburgh	412
Massachusetts	Springfield	413
Wisconsin	Milwaukee	414
California	San Francisco	415
Canada	Ontario, Toronto (Metro)	416
Missouri	Springfield	417
Canada	Quebec, Quebec City	418
Ohio	Toledo	419
Tennessee	Chattanooga, Bristol	423
Texas	Tyler	430
Texas	Alpine, Midland	432
Washington	Bellevue, Edmonds	425
Virgina	Lynchburg	434
Utah	Logan, St. George	435
Ohio	Cleveland (Suburbs)	440

North American Area Codes by CODE

State / Country	City	Code
Bermuda		441
Maryland	Baltimore	443
Canada	Quebec, Laval	450
Texas	Dallas	469
Grenada		473
Georgia	Macon	478
Arkansas	Fayetteville	479
Arizona	Phoenix (E suburbs)	480
Pennsylvania	Allentown	484
Arkansas	Little Rock, Hot Springs	501
Kentucky	Frankfort, Louisville	502
Oregon	Portland, Salem	503
Oregon	Astoria	503
Louisiana	New Orleans	504
New Mexico		505
Canada	New Brunswick	506
Minnesota	Rochester	507
Massachusetts	Cape Cod, Worcester	508
Washington	Spokane	509
California	Oakland, Berkeley	510
Texas	Austin	512
Ohio	Cincinnati	513
Canada	Quebec, Montreal	514
Iowa	Des Moines	515
New York	Hempstead, Long Island	516
Michigan	Lansing	517
New York	Albany	518
Canada	Ontario, Windsor	519
Arizona	Tucson, Flagstaff	520
California	Chico, Yreka	530
Virginia	Roanoke	540
Oregon	Eugene, Burns	541
New Jersey	Hackensack	551
California	Fresno	559
Florida	West Palm Beach	561
California	Long Beach	562
Iowa	Davenport, Dubuque	563
Ohio	Toledo	567
Pennsylvania	Scranton, Wilkes-Barre	570
Virginia	Arlington	571
Missouri	Jefferson City	573
Indiana	South Bend	574
Oklahoma	Lawton	580
New York	Rochester	585
Michigan	Warren	586
Mississippi	Jackson, Natchez	601
Arizona	Phoenix (Central)	602
New Hampshire		603
Canada	BC, Vancouver	604
South Dakota		605
Kentucky	Ashland	606
New York	Binghamton, Elmira	607
Wisconsin	Madison	608

North American Area Codes by CODE

State / Country	City	Code
New Jersey	Trenton, Atlantic City	609
Pennsylvania	Allentown	610
Minnesota	Minneapolis	612
Canada	Ontario, Ottawa	613
Ohio	Columbus	614
Tennessee	Nashville	615
Michigan	Battle Creek	616
Massachusetts	Boston (Metro)	617
Illinois	Alton	618
California	San Diego	619
Kansas	Dodge City, Emporia	620
Arizona	Phoenix (W suburbs)	623
California	Pasadena	626
Illinois	Chicago (Central sub.)	630
New York	Long Island, Brentwood	631
Missouri	St. Charles	636
Iowa	Ottumwa, Mason City	641
New York	Manhattan, N.Y. City	646
Canada	Ontario, Toronto	647
Turks and Caicos Islands		649
California	Palo Alto, San Mateo	650
Minnesota	St. Paul	651
Missouri	Sedalia	660
California	Bakersfield	661
Mississippi	Tupelo	662
Montserrat		664
Mariana Islands (CNMI)		670
Guam		671
Georgia	Atlanta (Inside&Outside I285)	678
Texas	Ft. Worth, Arlington	682
American Samoa		684
Florida	Orlando	689
North Dakota		701
Nevada	Las Vegas	702
Virginia	Arlington	703
North Carolina	Charlotte	704
Canada	Ontario, Sault Ste Marie	705
Georgia	Columbus, Augusta	706
California	Eureka, Santa Rosa	707
Illinois	Chicago (So.suburbs)	708
Canada	Newfoundland	709
Iowa	Council Bluffs	712
Texas	Houston	713
California	Anaheim, Orange	714
Wisconsin	Eau Claire	715
New York	Buffalo	716
Pennsylvania	Harrisburg	717
New York	Bronx, Brooklyn	718
New York	Queens, Staten Island	718
New York	New York City	718
Colorado	Colorado Springs, Pueblo	719
Colorado	Denver, Boulder	720
Pennsylvania	Pittsburgh (Suburbs)	724

North American Area Codes by CODE

State / Country	City	Code
Florida	St. Petersburg	727
Tennessee	Jackson	731
New Jersey	New Brunswick	732
Michigan	Ann Arbor	734
Ohio	Marion, Zanesville	740
Florida	Ft. Lauderdale	754
Virginia	Norfolk	757
St. Lucia		758
California	Barstow, Palm Springs	760
Minnesota	Brooklyn Park	763
Indiana	Lafayette, Muncie	765
Dominica		767
Mississippi	Jackson, Natchez	769
Georgia	Atlanta	770
Florida	Vero Beach	772
Illinois	Chicago	773
Massachusetts	Cape Cod, Worcester	774
Nevada	Reno, Ely, Elko	775
Canada	BC, Vancouver	778
Canada	Alberta, Edmonton	780
Massachusetts	Boston (Suburbs)	781
St. Vincent, The Grenadines		784
Kansas	Topeka, Colby	785
Florida	Miami	786
Puerto Rico		787
Utah	Salt Lake City	801
Vermont		802
South Carolina	Columbia	803
Virginia	Richmond	804
California	Santa Barbara	805
Texas	Amarillo, Lubbock	806
Canada	Ontario, Thunder Bay	807
Hawaii		808
Domin. Republic		809
Michigan	Flint	810
Indiana	Evansville	812
Florida	Tampa	813
Pennsylvania	Altoona	814
Illinois	Rockford	815
Missouri	Kansas City, St. Joseph	816
Texas	Fort Worth, Arlington	817
California	Burbank, Glendale	818
Canada	Quebec, Sherbrooke	819
North Carolina	Asheville	828
Texas	Kerrville	830
California	Monterey, Santa Cruz	831
Texas	Houston	832
South Carolina	Charleston	843
New York	Hudson Valley	845
Illinois	Chicago (N, NW subs)	847
New Jersey	New Brunswick	848
Florida	Pensacola, Tallahassee	850
New Jersey	Camden	856

North American Area Codes by CODE

State / Country	City	Code
Massachusetts	Boston (Metro)	857
California	Del Mar, LaJolla	858
Kentucky	Lexington	859
Connecticut	Hartford	860
New Jersey	Newark	862
Florida	Okeechobee	863
South Carolina	Greenville	864
Tennessee	Knoxville	865
Canada	Yukon, NW Territories	867
Trinidad, Tobago		868
St. Kitts, Nevis		869
Arkansas	Jonesboro, Pine Bluff	870
Jamaica		876
Pennsylvania	Pittsburgh	878
Tennessee	Memphis	901
Canada	Nova Scotia, P.Ed.Isl	902
Texas	Tyler	903
Florida	Jacksonville	904
Canada	Ontario, Hamilton	905
Michigan	Escanaba	906
Alaska		907
New Jersey	Elizabeth, Phillipsburg	908
California	San Bernardino	909
North Carolina	Fayetteville	910
Georgia	Savannah	912
Kansas	Kansas City	913
New York	White Plains, Yonkers	914
Texas	El Paso	915
California	Sacramento	916
New York	Manhattan, N. Y. City	917
Oklahoma	Tulsa	918
North Carolina	Raleigh	919
Wisconsin	Green Bay	920
California	Concord	925
Arizona	Flagstaff, Yuma	928
Tennessee	Celina, Clarksville	931
Texas	Huntsville	936
Ohio	Dayton	937
Puerto Rico		939
Texas	Wichita Falls	940
Florida	Sarasota, Ft. Myers	941
Michigan	Pontiac	947
California	Newport Beach	949
California	Riverside	951
Minnesota	Bloomington	952
Florida	Ft. Lauderdale	954
Texas	Brownsville	956
Colorado	Grand Junction, Ft. Collins	970
Oregon	Portland, Salem	971
Texas	Dallas (Suburbs)	972
New Jersey	Newark	973
Massachusetts	Lowell, Salem	978
Texas	Bryan, College Station	979

North American Area Codes by CODE

State / Country	City	Code
North Carolina	Charlotte	980
Louisiana	Hammond, Houma	985
Michigan	Alpena, Saginaw	989

World Wide Area Codes by LOCATION

Country	City/Area	Country /Area #	International Access Code

See page 289 for dialing instructions!

Country	City/Area	Country /Area #	International Access Code
Afghanistan		93	00
Albania		355	00
Algeria		213	00
American Samoa		684	00
Andorra		376	00
Angola		244	00
Antarctica		672	00
Argentina		54	00
	Buenos Aires	1	
	Cordoba	51	
Armenia		374	00
Aruba		297	00
	all points	8	
Ascension Is		247	01
Australia		61	0011
	Canberra	2	
	Melbourne	3	
	Sydney	2	
Austria		43	00
	Graz	316	
	Innsbruck	512	
	Vienna	1	
Azerbaijan		994	8~10
Bahrain		973	0
Bangladesh		880	00
	Dhaka	2	
Belarus		375	8~10
Belgium		32	00
	Antwerp	3	
	Brussels	2	
Belize		501	00
	Belize City	2	
Benin		229	00
Bhutan		975	00
Bolivia		591	00
	La Paz	2	
Bosnia-Herzegovina		387	00
	Sarajevo	33	
Botswana		267	00
Brazil		55	00
	Brasilia	61	
	Rio de Janeiro	21	
	Sao Paulo	11	
Brunei		673	00
Bulgaria		359	00
	Sofia	2	
Burkina Faso		226	00
Burundi		257	90
Cambodia		855	00
Cameroon		237	00
Canada (see North American tables, pages 267 and 271)			
Cape Verde Is		238	0
Central African Republic		236	19

World Wide Area Codes by LOCATION

Country	City/Area	Country Area #	International Access Code
See page 289 for dialing instructions!			
Chad		235	15
Chile		56	00
	Santiago	2	
China		86	00
	Beijing	10	
	Shanghai	21	
Christmas Is		61	00
Colombia		57	90
	Bogota	1	
	Cartagena	5	
Comoros		269	10
Congo		242	00
Congo, Dem Rep of		243	00
	Kinshasa	12	
Cook Is		682	00
Costa Rica		506	00
Croatia		385	00
	Zagreb	1	
Cuba		53	119
	Havana	7	
Curacao		599	00
Cyprus		357	00
	Nicosia	2	
Czech Republic		420	00
	Brno	5	
	Prague	2	
Denmark		45	00
Diego Garcia		246	00
Djibouti		253	00
East Timor		670	00
Easter Is		56	00
Ecuador		593	00
	Quito	2	
Egypt		20	00
	Alexandria	3	
	Cairo	2	
El Salvador		503	0
Equatorial Guinea		240	00
Eritrea		291	00
Estonia		372	8–00
Ethiopia		251	00
	Addis Ababa	1	
Faeroe Is		298	009
Falkland Is		500	0
Fiji Is		679	05
Finland		358	00
	Helsinki	9	
France		33	00
	Lyon	472	
	Marseille	491	
	Paris	1	
French Antilles		596	00
French Guiana		594	00

World Wide Area Codes by LOCATION

Country	City/Area	Country /Area #	International Access Code
See page 289 for dialing instructions!			
French Polynesia (Tahiti)		689	00
Gabon		241	00
Gambia		220	00
Georgia		995	8~10
Germany		49	00
	Berlin	30	
	Bonn	228	
	Dresden	351	
	Frankfurt	69	
	Hamburg	40	
	Leipzig	341	
	Munich	89	
Ghana		233	00
Gibraltar		350	00
Greece		30	00
	Athens	01	
	Thessoloniki	031	
Greenland		299	009
Guadeloupe		590	00
Guatemala		502	00
Guinea		224	00
Guinea-Bissau		245	00
Guyana		592	001
	Georgetown	2	
Haiti		509	00
Honduras		504	00
Hong Kong		852	001
Hungary		36	00
	Budapest	1	
Iceland		354	00
India		91	00
	Calcutta	33	
	Delhi	11	
Indonesia		62	001
	Jakarta	21	
Iran		98	00
	Tehran	21	
Iraq		964	00
	Baghdad	1	
Ireland		353	00
	Cork	21	
	Dublin	1	
Israel		972	00
	Haifa	4	
	Jerusalem	2	
	Tel Aviv	3	
Italy		39	00
	Milan	02	
	Naples	081	
	Rome	06	
	Venice	041	
Ivory Coast		225	00
Japan		81	001

World Wide Area Codes by LOCATION

Country	City/Area	Country /Area #	International Access Code

See page 289 for dialing instructions!

Country	City/Area	Country /Area #	International Access Code
	Hiroshima	82	
	Kobe	78	
	Osaka	66	
	Tokyo	3	
	Yokohama	45	
Jordan		962	00
	Amman	6	
Kazakhstan		7	8~10
Kenya		254	000
	Mombasa	11	
	Nairobi	2	
Kiribati		686	00
Korea (North)		850	00
Korea (South)		82	001
	Pusan	51	
	Seoul	2	
Kuwait		965	00
Kyrgyz Republic		996	8~10
Laos		856	14
Latvia		371	00
Lebanon		961	00
	Beirut	01	
Lesotho		266	00
Liberia		231	00
Libya		218	00
	Benghazi	61	
	Tripoli	21	
Liechtenstein		423	00
Lithuania		370	8~10
Luxembourg		352	00
Macau		853	00
Macedonia		389	00
Madagascar		261	00
Malawi		265	00
Malaysia		60	00
	Kuala Lumpur	3	
Maldives		960	00
Mali Republic		223	00
Malta		356	00
Marshall Is		692	01110
Martinique		596	00
Mauritania		222	00
Mauritius		230	00
Mayotte Is		269	10
Mexico		52	00
	Acapulco	744	
	Cancun	998	
	Mexico City	55	
	Puerto Vallarta	322	
Micronesia		691	011
Midway Is		808	00
Moldova		373	8-10
Monaco		377	00

World Wide Area Codes by LOCATION

Country	City/Area	Country /Area #	International Access Code

See page 289 for dialing instructions!

Country	City/Area	Country /Area #	International Access Code
Mongolia		976	00
Morocco		212	00
	Casablanca	22	
	Rabat	37	
Mozambique		258	00
Myanmar		95	0
Namibia		264	09
Nauru		674	00
Nepal		977	00
Netherlands		31	00
	Amsterdam	20	
	Rotterdam	10	
	The Hague	70	
Netherlands Antilles		599	00
	Bonaire	7	
	Curacao	9	
	Saint Maarten	5	
New Caledonia		687	00
New Zealand		64	00
	Auckland	9	
	Christchurch	3	
	Wellington	4	
Nicaragua		505	00
	Managua	2	
Niger		227	00
Nigeria		234	009
	Lagos	1	
Niue Is.		683	00
Norfolk Is		672	00
Norway		47	00
Oman		968	00
Pakistan		92	00
	Islamabad	51	
	Karachi	21	
Palau		680	011
Palestine		970	00
Panama		507	0
Papua New Guinea		675	05
Paraguay		595	00
	Asuncion	21	
Peru		51	00
	Lima	1	
Philippines		63	00
	Cebu City	32	
	Manila	2	
	Subic Bay	47	
Poland		48	0-0
	Krakow	12	
	Warsaw	22	
Portugal		351	00
	Lisbon	21	
Qatar		974	0
Reunion Is		262	00

World Wide Area Codes by LOCATION

Country	City/Area	Country Area #	International Access Code
See page 289 for dialing instructions!			
Romania		40	00
Russia		7	8-10
	Moscow	095	
Rwanda		250	00
Saint Helena		290	01
Saint Pierre & Miquelon		508	00
San Marino		378	00
Sao Tome & Principe		239	00
Saudi Arabia		966	00
	Dhahran	3	
	Jeddah	2	
	Makkah (Mecca)	2	
	Riyadh	1	
Senegal		221	00
Serbia		381	00
Seychelles Is		248	00
Sierra Leone		232	00
Singapore		65	001
Slovak Republic		421	00
Slovenia		386	00
Solomon Is		677	00
Somalia		252	19
South Africa		27	09
	Cape Town	21	
	Johannesburg	11	
	Pretoria	12	
Spain		34	00
	Barcelona	93	
	Palma de Mallorca	971	
	Madrid	91	
Sri Lanka		94	00
	Colombo	1	
Sudan		249	00
Suriname		597	00
Swaziland		268	00
Sweden		46	00
	Gothenburg	31	
	Stockholm	8	
Switzerland		41	00
	Berne	31	
	Geneva	22	
	Zurich	1	
Syria		963	00
	Damascus	11	
Taiwan		886	002
	Taipei	2	
Tajikistan		992	8-10
Tanzania		255	000
	Dar Es Salaam	22	
Thailand		66	001
	Bangkok	2	
Togo		228	00
Tokelau		690	00

World Wide Area Codes by LOCATION

Country	City/Area	Country /Area #	International Access Code

See page 289 for dialing instructions!

Country	City/Area	Country /Area #	International Access Code
Tonga Is		676	00
Tunisia		216	00
	Tunis	1	
Turkey		90	00
	Ankara	312	
	Istanbul Avrupa	212	
	Istanbul Asya	216	
	Izmir	232	
Turkmenistan		993	8~10
Tuvalu		688	00
Uganda		256	00
	Kampala	41	
Ukraine		380	8-10
United Arab Emirates		971	00
	Abu Dhabi	2	
	Dubai	4	
United Kingdom		44	00
	Belfast (North Ireland)	28	
	Cardiff (Wales)	29	
	Edinburgh (Scotland)	131	
	Glasgow (Scotland)	141	
	Liverpool (England)	151	
	London (England)	20	
United States of America		1	011
(USA see North America Area Codes in previous section)			
Uruguay		598	00
	Montevideo	2	
Vatican City		39	00
	all points	6	00
Venezuela		58	00
	Caracas	2	00
	Maracaibo	61	00
Yemen		967	00
	Sana'a	2	00
Yugoslavia		381	99
	Belgrade	11	99
	Zagreb	41	99
Zaire		243	NA
	Kinshasa	12	NA
Zambia		260	NA
	Lusaka	1	NA
Zimbabwe		263	NA
	Harare	4	NA

World Wide Area Codes by CODE

Country	Code	Country	Code
See page 289 for dialing instructions!			
Kazakhstan	7	Senegal	221
Russia	7	Mauritania	222
Egypt	20	Mali Republic	223
South Africa	27	Guinea	224
Greece	30	Ivory Coast	225
Netherlands	31	Burkina Faso	226
Belgium	32	Niger	227
France	33	Togo	228
Spain	34	Benin	229
Hungary	36	Mauritius	230
Italy	39	Liberia	231
Vatican City	39	Nigeria	234
Romania	40	Sierra Leone	232
Switzerland	41	Ghana	233
Austria	43	Nigeria	234
United Kingdom	44	Chad	235
Denmark	45	Central African Republic	236
Sweden	46	Cameroon	237
Norway	47	Cape Verde Is	238
Poland	48	Soa Tome & Principe	239
Germany, Fed Republic of	49	Equatorial Guinea	240
Peru	51	Gabon	241
Mexico	52	Congo	242
Cuba	53	Congo, Dem Rep of	243
Argentina	54	Angola	244
Brazil	55	Guinea-Bissau	245
Chile	56	Diego Garcia	246
Easter Is	56	Seychelles Is	248
Colombia	57	Sudan	249
Venezuela	58	Rwanda	250
Malaysia	60	Ethiopia	251
Australia	61	Somalia	252
Christmas Is	61	Djibouti	253
Indonesia	62	Kenya	254
Philippines	63	Tanzania	255
New Zealand	64	Uganda	256
Singapore	65	Burundi	257
Thailand	66	Mozambique	258
Japan	81	Zambia	260
Korea (South)	82	Madagascar	261
Vietnam	84	Reunion Is	262
China	86	Zimbabwe	263
Turkey	90	Namibia	264
India	91	Malawi	265
Pakistan	92	Lesotho	266
Afghanistan	93	Botswana	267
Sri Lanka	94	Swaziland	268
Myanmar	95	Mayotte Is	269
Iran	98	Saint Helena	290
Morocco	212	Eritrea	291
Algeria	213	Aruba	297
Tunisia	216	Faeroe Is	298
Libya	218	Greenland	299
Gambia	220	Gibralter	350

World Wide Area Codes by CODE

Country	Code	Country	Code

See page 289 for dialing instructions!

Country	Code	Country	Code
Portugal	351	Nauru	674
Luxembourg	352	Papua New Guinea	675
Ireland	353	Tonga Is	676
Iceland	354	Solomon Is	677
Albania	355	Vanuatu	678
Malta	356	Fiji Is	679
Cyprus	357	Palau	680
Finland	358	Wallis & Futuna Is	681
Bulgaria	359	Cook Is	682
Lithuania	370	Niue Is	683
Latvia	371	American Samoa	684
Estonia	372	Western Samoa	685
Moldova	373	Kiribati	686
Armenia	374	New Caledonia	687
Belarus	375	Tuvalu	688
Andorra	376	French Polynesia (Tahiti)	689
Monaco	377	Tokelau	690
San Marino	378	Micronesia	691
Ukraine	380	Marshall Is	692
Serbia	381	Midway Is	808
Yugoslavia	381	Wake Is	808
Croatia	385	Dominican Republic	809
Slovenia	386	Korea (North)	850
Bosnia-Herzegovina	387	Hong Kong	852
Macedonia	389	Macau	853
Czech Republic	420	Cambodia	855
Slovak Republic	421	Laos	856
Liechtenstein	423	Bangladesh	880
Falkland Is	500	Taiwan	886
Belize	501	Maldives	960
Guatemala	502	Lebanon	961
El Salvador	503	Jordan	962
Honduras	504	Syria	963
Nicaragua	505	Iraq	964
Costa Rica	506	Kuwait	965
Panama	507	Saudi Arabia	966
Saint Pierre & Miquelon	508	Yemen	967
Haiti	509	Oman	968
Guadeloupe	590	Palestine	970
Bolivia	591	United Arab Emirates	971
Guyana	592	Israel	972
Ecuador	593	Bahrain	973
French Guiana	594	Qatar	974
Paraguay	595	Bhutan	975
French Antilles	596	Mongolia	976
Martinique	596	Nepal	977
Suriname	597	Tajikistan	992
Uruguay	598	Turkmenistan	993
Curacao	599	Azerbaijan	994
Netherlands Antilles	599	Georgia	995
East Timor	670	Kyrgyz Republic	996
Antarctica	672	Uzbekistan	998
Norfolk Is	672		
Brunei	673		

Dialing Instructions for Countries

Dialing Instructions for countries listed in the tables World Wide Area Codes by Location and World Wide Area Codes by Code are as follows:

> First: Dial the International Access Code for the country you are calling FROM.

> Second: Dial the Country/Area# for the country you are calling TO.

> Third: Dial the City Code for the location you are calling TO. (Note: some countries do not require the City Code - in other words, the Country Code provides access to all locations in that country.)

> Fourth: Dial the Local Phone Number of the person you are calling. Allow up to 45 seconds for the ringing to start.

For example, from Denver, Colorado to Marseille, France, dial the following:

> 011 33 491 Local Number
> (011=USA, 33=France, and 491=Marseille)

To call from Marseille, France to Denver, Colorado, dial the following:

> 00 1 303 Local Number
> (00 = France, 1=USA, 303=Denver, Colorado)

State	City	Population	Airport Name	Code	Elev
AK	Anchorage	260283	Ted Stevens Anchorage Intl	ANC	152
AK	Barrow	4581	Wiley Post-Will Rogers	BRW	44
AK	Bethel	5471	Bethel	BET	123
AK	Coffmann Cove	99	Coffman Cove SB	KCC	0
AK	Cordova	2454	Merle K Mudhole Smith	CDV	42
AK	Craig	1397	Craig Seaplane Base	CGA	0
AK	Deadhorse	??	Deadhorse	SCC	61
AK	Dillingham	2466	Dillingham	DLG	86
AK	Dutch Harbor	??	Unalaska	DUT	22
AK	Fairbanks	30224	Fairbanks Intl	FAI	434
AK	Haines	1811	Haines	HNS	16
AK	Homer	3946	Homer	HOM	84
AK	Hoonah	860	Hoonah	HNH	20
AK	Hydaburg	382	Hydaburg SB	HYG	0
AK	Iliamna	102	Iliamna	ILI	186
AK	Juneau	30711	Juneau Intl	JNU	19
AK	Kenai	6942	Kenai Mun	ENA	99
AK	Ketchikan	7922	Ketchikan Intl	KTN	88
AK	King Salmon	442	King Salmon	AKN	57
AK	Kodiak	6334	Kodiak	ADQ	73
AK	Kotzebue	3082	Ralph Wien Mem	OTZ	11
AK	Metlakatla	1375	Metlakatla SB	MTM	0
AK	Nome	3505	Nome	OME	37
AK	Petersburg	3224	Petersburg James A Johnson	PSG	107
AK	Seldovia	286	Seldovia	SOV	29
AK	Sitka	8835	Sitka Rocky Gutierrez	SIT	21
AK	Skagway	862	Skagway	SGY	44
AK	Talkeetna	772	Talkeetna	TKA	358
AK	Thorne Bay	557	Thorne Bay SB	KTB	0
AK	Valdez	4036	Valdez Pioneer Fld	VDZ	120
AK	Wrangell	2308	Wrangell	WRG	44
AK	Yakutat	680	Yakutat	YAK	38
AL	Anniston	24276	Anniston Metro	ANB	612
AL	Birmingham	242820	Birmingham Intl	BHM	644
AL	Dothan	57737	Dothan Reg	DHN	401
AL	Gadsden	38978	Gadsden Mun	GAD	569
AL	Huntsville	158216	Huntsville Intl-Carl T Jones Fld	HSV	629
AL	Mobile	198915	Mobile Reg	MOB	219
AL	Montgomery	201568	Montgomery Reg-Dannelly Fld	MGM	221
AL	Muscle Shoals	11924	NW Alabama Reg	MSL	550
AL	*Tuscaloosa*	77906	Tuscaloosa Mun	TCL	170
AR	Fayetteville	58047	Drake Fld	FYV	1251
AR	Fort Smith	80268	Fort Smith Reg	FSM	469
AR	Little Rock	183133	Adams Fld	LIT	262
AR	Texarkana	26448	Texarkana Reg-Webb Fld	TXK	389
AZ	Bullhead City	33769	Laughlin-Bullhead City Intl	IFP	695
AZ	Flagstaff	52894	Flagstaff Pulliam	FLG	7014
AZ	Grand Canyon	1460	Grand Canyon Ntl Park	GCN	6606

State	City	Population	Airport Name	Code	Elev
AZ	Page	6809	Page Mun	PGA	4313
AZ	Phoenix	1321045	Phoenix Sky Harbor Intl	PHX	1135
AZ	Scottsdale	202705	Scottsdale	SDL	1510
AZ	Sierra Vista-		Libby AAF-		
AZ	Fort Huachuca		Sierra Vista Mun	FHU	4716
AZ	Tucson	486699	Tucson Intl	TUS	2641
AZ	Yuma	77515	Yuma Intl-Yuma MCAS	YUM	213
CA	Arcata-Eureka	42779	Arcata	ACV	218
CA	Bakersfield	247057	Meadows Fld	BFL	507
CA	Burbank	105555	Burbank-Glendale-Pasadena	BUR	775
CA	Chico	59954	Chico Mun	CIC	238
CA	Concord	121780	Buchanan Fld	CCR	23
CA	Crescent City	7461	Jack McNamara	CEC	57
CA	Death Valley Natl Mon	??	Furnace Creek	L06	-210
CA	Fresno	427662	Fresno Yosemite Intl	FAT	336
CA	Imperial	7560	Imperial Co	IPL	-55
CA	Inyokern	984	Inyokern	IYK	2455
CA	Long Beach	461522	Long Beach-Daugherty Fld	LGB	58
CA	Los Angeles	3694820	Los Angeles Intl	LAX	126
CA	Merced	63893	Merced Mun - Macready Fld	MCE	156
CA	Modesto	188856	Modesto City-Co / Harry Sham Fld	MOD	97
CA	Monterey	29674	Monterey Peninsula	MRY	254
CA	Oakland	399484	Metro Oakland Intl	OAK	6
CA	Ontario	158007	Ontario Intl	ONT	944
CA	Oxnard	170358	Oxnard	OXR	43
CA	Palm Springs	42807	Palm Springs Intl	PSP	474
CA	Palmdale	116670	Palmdale Prodn Flt-Test Instln AF Plant 42	PMD	2543
CA	Redding	80865	Redding Mun	RDD	502
CA	Sacramento	407018	Sacramento Intl	SMF	28
CA	San Diego	1223400	San Diego Intl - Lindbergh Fld	SAN	14
CA	San Francisco	776733	San Francisco Intl	SFO	11
CA	San Jose	894943	San Jose Intl	SJC	58
CA	San Luis Obispo	44174	San Luis Obispo Co-McChesney Fld	SBP	209
CA	Santa Ana	337977	John Wayne-Orange Co	SNA	56
CA	Santa Barbara	92325	Santa Barbara Mun	SBA	10
CA	Santa Maria	77423	Santa Maria Public - Cpt G A Hancock Fld	SMX	261
CA	Santa Rosa	147595	Sonoma Co	STS	125
CA	South Lake Tahoe	23609	Lake Tahoe	TVL	6264
CA	Stockton	243771	Stockton Metro	SCK	30
CA	Visalia	91565	Visalia Mun	VIS	295
CO	Aspen	5914	Aspen-Pitkin Co-Sardy Fld	ASE	7820
CO	Colorado Springs	360890	Colorado Springs Mun	COS	6184
CO	Denver	554636	Denver Intl	DEN	5431
CO	Durango	13922	Durango-La Plata Co	DRO	6685
CO	Eagle-Vail	7561	Eagle Co Reg	EGE	6535

State	City	Population	Airport Name	Code	Elev
CO	Grand Junction	41986	Walker Fld	GJT	4858
CO	Gunnison	5409	Gunnison Co	GUC	7678
CO	Hayden-Steamboat Sp	9815	Yampa Valley	HDN	6602
CO	Leadville	2821	Lake County	LXV	9927
CO	Montrose	12344	Montrose Reg	MTJ	5759
CO	Pueblo	102121	Pueblo Mem	PUB	4726
CO	Telluride	2221	Telluride Reg	TEX	9078
CT	Bridgeport	139529	Igor I Sikorsky Mem	BDR	10
CT	Groton-New London	39907	Groton-New London	GON	10
CT	New Haven	123626	Tweed-New Haven	HVN	14
CT	Windsor Locks	12043	Bradley Intl	BDL	173
DC	Washington	572059	Ronald Reagan Washington National	DCA	15
DC	Washington	572059	Washington Dulles Intl	IAD	313
FL	Boca Raton	74764	Boca Raton	BCT	13
FL	Daytona Beach	64112	Daytona Beach Intl	DAB	34
FL	Fort Lauderdale	152397	Fort Lauderdale-Hollywood Intl	FLL	9
FL	Fort Myers	48208	Page Fld	FMY	17
FL	Fort Myers	48208	SW Florida Intl	RSW	30
FL	Gainesville	85447	Gainesville Reg	GNV	152
FL	Jacksonville	735617	Jacksonville Intl	JAX	30
FL	Key West	25478	Key West Intl	EYW	3
FL	Marathon	10255	Florida Keys Marathon	MTH	7
FL	Melbourne	71382	Melbourne Intl	MLB	33
FL	Miami	362470	Miami Intl	MIA	8
FL	Naples	20976	Naples Mun	APF	8
FL	Orlando	185951	Orlando Intl	MCO	96
FL	Orlando	185951	Executive	ORL	113
FL	Panama City	36417	Panama City-Bay Co Intl	PFN	20
FL	Pensacola	56255	Pensacola Reg	PNS	121
FL	Sarasota-Bradenton	102219	Sarasota-Bradenton Intl	SRQ	27
FL	Tallahassee	150624	Tallahassee Reg	TLH	81
FL	Tampa	303447	Tampa Intl	TPA	26
FL	Valparaiso	6408	Eglin AFB	VPS	87
FL	Vero Beach	17705	Vero Beach Mun	VRB	24
FL	West Palm Beach	82103	Palm Beach Intl	PBI	18
GA	Albany	76939	SW Georgia Reg	ABY	197
GA	Athens	100266	Athens Ben Epps	AHN	808
GA	Atlanta	416474	William B Hartsfield-Atlanta Intl	ATL	1026
GA	Augusta	195182	Augusta Reg @ Bush Fld	AGS	144
GA	Brunswick	15600	Glynco Jetport	BQK	26
GA	Columbus	185781	Columbus Metro	CSG	397
GA	Macon	97255	Middle Georgia Reg	MCN	354
GA	Savannah	131510	Savannah Intl	SAV	50
GA	Valdosta	43724	Valdosta Reg	VLD	203
HI	Hilo	40759	Hilo Intl	ITO	38
HI	Honolulu	371657	Honolulu Intl	HNL	13
HI	Kahului	20146	Kahului	OGG	54

State	City	Population	Airport Name	Code	Elev
HI	Kailua-Kona	9878	Kona Intl @ Keahole	KOA	47
HI	Kaunakakai	2726	Molokai	MKK	454
HI	Lahaina	9118	Kapalua	JHM	256
HI	Lanai City	3164	Lanai	LNY	1308
HI	Lihue	5674	Lihue	LIH	153
IA	Burlington	26839	Burlington Reg	BRL	698
IA	Cedar Rapids	120758	Eastern Iowa	CID	864
IA	Des Moines	198682	Des Moines Intl	DSM	957
IA	Dubuque	57686	Dubuque Reg	DBQ	1076
IA	Fort Dodge	25136	Fort Dodge Reg	FOD	1157
IA	Mason City	29172	Mason City Mun	MCW	1213
IA	Sioux City	85013	Sioux Gateway	SUX	1098
IA	Waterloo	68747	Waterloo Mun	ALO	873
ID	Boise	185787	Boise Air Terminal-Gowen Fld	BOI	2868
ID	Hailey	6200	Friedman Mem	SUN	5317
ID	Idaho Falls	50730	Idaho Falls Reg	IDA	4740
ID	Lewiston	30904	Lewiston-Nez Perce Co	LWS	1438
ID	Pocatello	51466	Pocatello Reg	PIH	4452
ID	Twin Falls	34469	Joslin Fld-Magic Valley Reg	TWF	4151
IL	Bloomington	64808	Central IL Reg @ Bloomington-Normal	BMI	871
IL	Champaign-Urbana	103913	University of Illinois-Willard	CMI	754
IL	Chicago	2896016	Chicago Midway	MDW	620
IL	Chicago	2896016	Chicago O'Hare Intl	ORD	668
IL	Decatur	81860	Decatur	DEC	682
IL	Mattoon-Charleston	39330	Coles Co Mem	MTO	722
IL	Moline	43768	Quad City Intl	MLI	590
IL	Peoria	112936	Greater Peoria Reg	PIA	660
IL	Quincy	40366	Quincy Reg-Baldwin Fld	UIN	769
IL	Rockford	150115	Greater Rockford	RFD	742
IL	Springfield	111454	Capital	SPI	597
IN	Bloomington	69291	Monroe Co	BMG	846
IN	Elkhart	51874	Elkhart Mun	EKM	778
IN	Evansville	121582	Evansville Reg	EVV	418
IN	Fort Wayne	205727	Fort Wayne Intl	FWA	815
IN	Indianapolis	791926	Indianapolis Intl	IND	797
IN	Lafayette	56397	Purdue University	LAF	606
IN	South Bend	107789	South Bend Reg	SBN	799
IN	Terre Haute	59614	Terre Haute Intl-Hulman Fld	HUF	589
KS	Wichita	344284	Wichita Mid-Continent	ICT	1332
KY	Lexington	260512	Blue Grass	LEX	979
KY	Louisville	256231	Louisville Intl-Standiford Fld	SDF	501
KY	Owensboro	54067	Owensboro-Davies Co	OWB	406
KY	Paducah	26307	Barkley Reg	PAH	410
LA	Alexandria	46342	Alexandria Intl	AEX	89
LA	Baton Rouge	227818	Baton Rouge Metro-Ryan Fld	BTR	70

State	City	Population	Airport Name	Code	Elev
LA	Lafayette	110257	Lafayette Reg	LFT	42
LA	Lake Charles	71757	Chennault Intl	CWF	17
LA	Monroe	53107	Monroe Reg	MLU	79
LA	New Iberia	32623	Acadiana Reg	ARA	24
LA	New Orleans	484674	Louis Armstrong-New Orleans Intl	MSY	4
LA	Shreveport	200145	Shreveport Reg	SHV	258
MA	Boston	589141	General E Lawrence-Logan Intl	BOS	19
MA	Hyannis	11050	Barnstable Mun-Boardman-Polando Fld	HYA	55
MA	Nantucket	9520	Nantucket Mem	ACK	48
MA	Vineyard Haven	3120	Martha's Vineyard	MVY	68
MA	Worcester	172648	Worcester Reg	ORH	1009
MD	Baltimore	651154	Baltimore-Washington Intl BWI		146
MD	Hagerstown	36687	Hagerstown Reg-R A Henson Fld	HGR	703
MD	Salisbury	23743	Salisbury-Ocean City Wicomico Co	SBY	52
ME	Augusta	18560	Augusta State	AUG	352
ME	Bangor	31473	Bangor Intl	BGR	192
ME	Portland	64249	Portland Intl Jetport	PWM	74
ME	Presque Island	9511	N Maine Reg@ Presque Is	PQI	534
ME	Rockland	7609	Knox Co Reg	RKD	55
MI	Benton Harbor	11182	SW Michigan Reg	BEH	643
MI	Detroit	951270	Detroit City	DET	626
MI	Detroit	951270	Detroit Metro Wayne Co	DTW	640
MI	Escabana	13140	Delta Co	ESC	609
MI	Flint	124943	Bishop Intl	FNT	782
MI	Grand Rapids	197800	Gerald R Ford Intl	GRR	793
MI	Hancock	4323	Houghton Co Mem	CMX	1095
MI	Jackson	36316	Jackson Co-Reynolds Fld	JXN	1001
MI	Kalamazoo	77145	Kalamazoo-Battle Creek Intl	AZO	874
MI	Lansing	119128	Capital City	LAN	861
MI	Marquette	19661	Sawyer Intl	SAW	1221
MI	Muskegon	40105	Muskegon Co	MKG	628
MI	Pellston	771	Pellston Reg-Emmet Co	PLN	720
MI	Pontiac	66337	Oakland County Intl	PTK	980
MI	Saginaw	61799	MBS Intl	MBS	668
MI	Traverse City	14532	Cherry Capital	TVC	624
MN	Bemidji	11917	Bermidji-Beltrami Co	BJI	1390
MN	Brainerd	13178	Brainerd-Crow Wing Co Reg	BRD	1226
MN	Duluth	86918	Duluth Intl	DLH	1428
MN	Grand Rapids	7764	Grand Rapids/Itasca Co-Gordon Newstrom Fld	GPZ	1355
MN	Hibbing	17071	Chisholm-Hibbing	HIB	1353
MN	Intl Falls	8703	Falls Intl	INL	1185
MN	Minneapolis	382618	Minneapolis-St Paul Intl-		

State	City	Population	Airport Name	Code	Elev
			Wold-Chamberlain	MSP	841
MN	Rochester	85806	Rochester Intl	RST	1317
MN	Thief River Falls	8410	Thief River Falls Reg	TVF	1116
MO	Joplin	45504	Joplin Reg	JLN	981
MO	Kansas City	441545	Kansas City Intl	MCI	1026
MO	Saint Louis	348189	Lambert-Saint Louis Intl	STL	604
MO	Springfield	151580	Springfield-Branson Reg	SGF	1267
MS	Columbus-Starkville-West Point	59958	Golden Triangle Reg	GTR	264
MS	Greenville	41633	Mid Delta Reg	GLH	131
MS	Gulfport	71127	Gulfport-Biloxi Intl	GPT	28
MS	Hattiesburg-Laurel	63172	Hattiesburg-Laurel Reg.	PIB	298
MS	Jackson	184256	Jackson Intl	JAN	346
MS	Meridian	39968	Key Fld	MEI	297
MS	Tupelo	34211	Tupelo Reg	TUP	346
MT	Billings	89487	Billings Logan Intl	BIL	3649
MT	Bozeman	27509	Gallatin Fld	BZN	4474
MT	Butte	34606	Bert Mooney	BTM	5545
MT	Glasgow	3253	Wokal Fld-Glasgow Intl	GGW	2294
MT	Glendive	4729	Dawson Community	GDV	2456
MT	Great Falls	56690	Great Falls Intl	GTF	3677
MT	Havre	9621	Havre City-Co	HVR	2590
MT	Helena	25780	Helena Reg	HLN	3874
MT	Kalispell	14223	Glacier Park Intl	FCA	2977
MT	Lewistown	5813	Lewistown Mun	LWT	4167
MT	Miles City	8487	Frank Wiley Fld	MLS	2630
MT	Missoula	57053	Missoula Intl	MSO	3205
MT	Sidney	4774	Sidney-Richland Mun	SDY	1984
MT	West Yellowstone	1177	Yellowstone	WYS	6644
MT	Wolf Point	2663	LM Clayton	OLF	1986
NC	Asheville	68880	Asheville Reg	AVL	2165
NC	Charlotte	540828	Charlotte/Douglas Intl	CLT	748
NC	Fayetteville	121015	Fayetteville Reg-Grannis Fld	FAY	189
NC	Greensboro	223891	Piedmont Triad Intl	GSO	926
NC	Greenville	60476	Pitt-Greenville	PGV	27
NC	Hickory	37222	Hickory Reg	HKY	1189
NC	Jacksonville	66715	Albert J Ellis	OAJ	94
NC	Kinston	23688	Kinston Reg Jetport @ Stallings Fld	ISO	94
NC	New Bern	23128	Craven Co Reg	EWN	18
NC	Raleigh-Durham	463108	Raleigh-Durham Intl	RDU	435
NC	Rocky Mount	55893	Rocky Mount-Wilson Reg	RWI	159
NC	Wilmington	75838	Wilmington Intl	ILM	32
NC	Winston-Salem	185776	Smith Reynolds	INT	969
ND	Bismarck	55532	Bismarck Mun	BIS	1661
ND	Devils Lake	7222	Devils Lake Mun	DVL	1455
ND	Fargo	90599	Hector Intl	FAR	900
ND	Grand Forks	49321	Grand Forks Intl	GFK	844
ND	Jamestown	15527	Jamestown Mun	JMS	1498
ND	Minot	36567	Minot Intl	MOT	1716
ND	Williston	12512	Sloulin Fld Intl	ISN	1982
NE	Lincoln	225581	Lincoln Mun	LNK	1219

State	City	Population	Airport Name	Code	Elev
NE	Omaha	390007	Eppley	OMA	984
NH	Lebanon	12568	Lebanon Mun	LEB	603
NH	Manchester	107006	Manchester	MHT	242
NJ	Atlantic City	40517	Atlantic City Intl	ACY	75
NJ	Newark	273546	Newark Intl	EWR	18
NJ	Trenton	85403	Trenton Mercer	TTN	213
NM	Albuquerque	448607	Albuquerque Intl Sunport	ABQ	5355
NM	Farmington	37844	Four Corners Reg	FMN	5506
NV	Elko	16708	Elko Reg	EKO	5140
NV	Ely	4041	Ely Yelland Fld	ELY	6259
NV	Las Vegas	478434	McCarran Intl	LAS	2181
NV	Reno	180480	Reno-Tahoe Intl	RNO	4412
NY	Albany	95658	Albany Intl	ALB	285
NY	Binghamton	47380	Binghamton Reg-Edwin A Link Fld	BGM	1636
NY	Buffalo	292648	Buffalo Niagara Intl	BUF	724
NY	Elmira-Corning	41782	Elmira-Corning Reg	ELM	955
NY	Islip	20575	Long Island Mac Arthur	ISP	99
NY	Ithaca	29287	Ithaca Tompkins Reg	ITH	1099
NY	Jamestown	31730	Chautauqua Co/Jamestown	JHW	1723
NY	New York	8008278	John F Kennedy Intl	JFK	13
NY	New York	8008278	La Guardia	LGA	22
NY	Newburgh	28254	Stewart Intl	SWF	491
NY	Plattsburgh	18816	Plattsburgh Intl	PBG	235
NY	Poughkeepsie	29871	Dutchess Co	POU	165
NY	Rochester	219773	Greater Rochester Intl	ROC	560
NY	Syracuse	147306	Syracuse Hancock Intl	SYR	421
NY	Utica	60651	Oneida Co	UCA	742
NY	White Plains	53077	Westchester Co	HPN	439
OH	Akron	217074	Akron-Canton Reg	CAK	1228
OH	Cincinnati-Covington KY	374655	Cincinnati/N Kentucky Intl	CVG	897
OH	Cleveland	478403	Burke Lakefront	BKL	583
OH	Cleveland	478403	Cleveland Hopkins Intl	CLE	791
OH	Columbus	711470	Rickenbacker Intl	LCK	744
OH	Columbus	711470	Port Columbus Intl	CMH	815
OH	Dayton	166179	James M Cox Dayton Intl	DAY	1009
OH	Toledo	313619	Toledo Express	TOL	684
OH	Youngstown	82026	Youngstown-Warren Reg	YNG	1196
OK	Lawton	92757	Lawton-Fort Sill Reg	LAW	1110
OK	Oklahoma City	506132	Will Rogers World	OKC	1295
OK	Tulsa	393049	Tulsa Intl	TUL	677
OR	Eugene	137893	Mahlon Sweet Fld	EUG	369
OR	Klamath Fall	19462	Klamath Falls Intl	LMT	4095
OR	Medford	63154	Rogue Valley Intl-Medford	MFR	1335
OR	North Bend	9544	North Bend Mun	OTH	17
OR	Pendelton	16354	E Oregon Reg	PDT	1497
OR	Portland	529121	Portland Intl	PDX	30
OR	Redmond	13481	Roberts Fld	RDM	3077
OR	Salem	136924	McNary Fld	SLE	214
PA	Allentown	106632	Lehigh Valley Intl	ABE	394

State	City	Population	Airport Name	Code	Elev
PA	Altoona	49523	Altoona-Blair Co	AOO	1504
PA	Bradford	9175	Bradford Reg	BFD	2143
PA	Du Bois	8123	Du Bois-Jefferson Co	DUJ	1817
PA	Erie	103717	Erie Intl-Tom Ridge Fld	ERI	733
PA	Franklin	7212	Venango Reg	FKL	1540
PA	Harrisburg	48950	Harrisburg Intl	MDT	310
PA	Johnstown	23906	Johnstown-Cambria Co	JST	2284
PA	Lancaster	56348	Lancaster	LNS	403
PA	Latrobe	8994	Arnold Palmer Reg	LBE	1185
PA	Philadelphia	1517550	Philadelphia Intl	PHL	38
PA	Pittsburgh	334563	Pittsburgh Intl	PIT	1204
PA	Reading	81207	Reading Reg-Carl A Spaatz Fld	RDG	344
PA	Wilkes Barre-Scranton	119538	Wilkes-Barre-Scranton Intl	AVP	962
PA	Williamsport	30706	Williamsport Reg	IPT	529
RI	Providence	173618	Theodore Francis Green State	PVD	55
SC	Charleston	96650	Charleston AFB-Intl	CHS	46
SC	Columbia	116278	Columbia Metro	CAE	236
SC	Florence	30248	Florence Reg	FLO	148
SC	Greer	16843	Greenville-Spartanburg Intl	GSP	964
SC	Myrtle Beach	22759	Myrtle Beach Intl	MYR	25
SD	Aberdeen	24658	Aberdeen Reg	ABR	1302
SD	Brookings	18504	Brookings Mun	BKX	1648
SD	Huron	11895	Huron Reg	HON	1289
SD	Mitchell	14558	Mitchell Mun	MHE	1304
SD	Pierre	13876	Pierre Reg	PIR	1742
SD	Rapid City	59607	Rapid City Reg	RAP	3202
SD	Sioux Falls	123975	Joe Foss Fld	FSD	1429
SD	Watertown	20237	Watertown Mun	ATY	1748
TN	Bristol-Johnson City Kingsport	125195	Tri City Reg	TRI	1519
TN	Chattanooga	155554	Lovell Fld	CHA	682
TN	Jackson	59643	McKellar-Sipes Reg	MKL	434
TN	Knoxville	173890	McGhee Tyson	TYS	981
TN	Memphis	650100	Memphis Intl	MEM	341
TN	Nashville	569891	Nashville Intl	BNA	599
TX	Abilene	115930	Abilene Reg	ABI	1791
TX	Amarillo	173627	Amarillo Intl	AMA	3607
TX	Austin	656562	Austin-Bergstrom Intl	AUS	542
TX	Beaumont-Port Arthur	171621	SE Texas Reg	BPT	15
TX	College Station	67890	Easterwood Fld	CLL	321
TX	Corpus Christi	277454	Corpus Christi Intl	CRP	44
TX	Dallas	1188580	Dallas Love Fld	DAL	487
TX	Dallas-Fort Worth	1723274	Dallas-Ft Worth Intl	DFW	603
TX	El Paso	563662	El Paso Intl	ELP	3958
TX	Harlingen	57564	Valley Intl	HRL	36
TX	Houston	1953631	William P Hobby	HOU	46

State	City	Population	Airport Name	Code	Elev
TX	Houston	1953631	George Bush Inter-continental-Houston	IAH	97
TX	Killeen	86911	Killeen Mun	ILE	848
TX	Laredo	176578	Laredo Intl	LRD	508
TX	Longview	73344	Gregg Co	GGG	365
TX	Lubbock	199564	Lubbock Intl	LBB	3282
TX	McAllen	106414	McAllen Miller Intl	MFE	107
TX	Midland	94996	Midland Intl	MAF	2871
TX	San Angelo	88439	San Angelo Reg-Mathis Fld	SJT	1919
TX	San Antonio	1144646	San Antonio Intl	SAT	809
TX	Tyler	83650	Tyler Pounds Fld	TYR	544
TX	Waco	113726	Waco Reg	ACT	516
TX	Wichita Falls	104197	Wichita Falls Mun-Sheppard AFB	SPS	1019
UT	Cedar City	20527	Cedar City Reg	CDC	5622
UT	Saint George	49663	Saint George Mun	SGU	2941
UT	Salt Lake City	181743	Salt Lake City Intl	SLC	4227
UT	Vernal	7714	Vernal	VEL	5278
VA	Charlottesville	45049	Charlottesville-Albemarle	CHO	639
VA	Danville	48411	Danville Reg	DAN	571
VA	Lynchburg	65269	Lynchburg Reg-Preston Glenn Fld	LYH	938
VA	Newport News-Williamsburg	192148	Newport News-Williamsburg Intl	PHF	43
VA	Norfolk	234403	Norfolk Intl	ORF	26
VA	Richmond	197790	Richmond Intl	RIC	167
VA	Roanoke	94911	Roanoke Reg-Woodrum Fld	ROA	1176
VA	Staunton-Waynesboro-Harrisonburg	83841	Shenandoah Valley Reg	SHD	1201
VT	Burlington	38889	Burlington Intl	BTV	335
WA	Bellingham	67171	Bellingham Intl	BLI	170
WA	Moses Lake	14953	Grant Co	MWH	1185
WA	Pasco	32066	Tri-Cities	PSC	407
WA	Port Angeles	18397	William R Fairchild Intl	CLM	291
WA	Pullman	24675	Pullman-Moscow Reg	PUW	2555
WA	Seattle	563374	Seattle-Tacoma Intl	SEA	429
WA	Spokane	195629	Spokane Intl	GEG	2372
WA	Walla Walla	29686	Walla Walla Reg	ALW	1205
WA	Wenatchee	27856	Pangborn Mem	EAT	1249
WA	Yakima	71845	Yakima Air Terminal McAllister Fld	YKM	1095
WI	Appleton	70087	Outagamie Co	ATW	918
WI	Eau Claire	61704	Chippewa Valley Reg	EAU	907
WI	Green Bay	102313	Austin Straubel Intl	GRB	695
WI	La Crosse	51818	La Crosse Mun	LSE	654
WI	Madison	208054	Dane Co Reg-Truax Fld	MSN	887
WI	Milwaukee	596974	General Mitchell Intl	MKE	723
WI	Mosinee	6209	Central Wisconsin	CWA	1277
WI	Oshkosh	62916	Wittman Reg	OSH	808
WI	Rhinelander	7735	Rhinelander-Oneida Co	RHI	1623

State	City	Population	Airport Name	Code	Elev
WV	Beckley	17254	Raleigh Co Mem	BKW	2504
WV	Bluefield	11451	Mercer Co	BLF	2857
WV	Charleston	53421	Yeager	CRW	981
WV	Clarksburg	16743	Harrison-Marion Reg	CKB	1217
WV	Huntington	551475	Tri-State/ Milton J Ferguson Fld	HTS	828
WV	Lewisburg	3624	Greenbrier Valley	LWB	2302
WV	Morgantown	26809	Morgantown Mun- Walter L Bill Hart Fld	MGW	1248
WV	Parkersburg	33099	Wood Co- Gill Rob Wilson Fld	PKB	858
WY	Casper	49644	Natrona Co Intl	CPR	5348
WY	Cody	8835	Yellowstone Reg	COD	5098
WY	Gilette	19646	Gilette-Campbell Co	GCC	4363
WY	Jackson	8647	Jackson Hole	JAC	6447
WY	Laramie	27204	Laramie Reg	LAR	7278
WY	Rock Springs	18708	Rock Springs- Sweetwater Co	RKS	6760
WY	Sheridan	15804	Sheridan Co	SHR	4024
WY	Worland	5250	Worland Mun	WRL	4227

Airport City	Airport Name	Elevation Feet	AP Code
Algeria, Algiers	Houari Boumedienne	82	ALG
Argentina, Buenos Aires	Ministro Pistarini	66	EZE
Australia, Adelaide	Adelaide	20	ADL
Australia, Brisbane	Brisbane Intl	13	BNE
Australia, Darwin	Darwin Intl	103	DRW
Australia, Melbourne	Melbourne	434	MEL
Australia, Perth	Perth Intl	67	PER
Australia, Sydney	Sydney Intl	21	SYD
Austria, Vienna	Vienna Intl	600	VIE
Belarus, Minsk	Minsk	669	MSQ
Belgium, Brussels	Brussels	184	BRU
Bolivia, La Paz	El Alto Intl	13313	LPB
Bosnia-Herzegovina, Sarajevo	Sarajevo	1708	SJJ
Brazil, Recife	Guararapes	33	REC
Brazil, Rio de Janeiro	Rio de Janeiro-Galeão Intl	28	GIG
Brazil, Sao Paulo	Sao Paulo-Guarulhos Intl	2459	GRU
Bulgaria, Sofia	Sofia	1742	SOF
Canada, Calgary	Calgary Intl	3557	YYC
Canada, Edmonton	Edmonton Intl	2373	YEG
Canada, Halifax	Halifax Intl	477	YHZ
Canada, Montreal	Montréal-Trudeau Intl	117	YUL
Canada, Ottawa	Ottawa Intl	374	YOW
Canada, Toronto	Lester B Pearson Intl	569	YYZ
Canada, Vancouver	Vancouver Intl	14	YVR
Chile, Santiago	Arturo Merino Benitez intl	1554	SCL
China, Beijing	Capital Intl	116	PEK
China, Hong Kong	Hong Kong Intl	28	HKG
China, Shanghai	Hong Qiao Intl	10	SHA
Columbia, Bogota	El Dorado Intl	8361	BOG
Congo (Dem.Rep.of),Kinshasa	Kinshasa N'Djili Intl	1027	FIH
Costa Rica, San Jose	Juan Santamaria Intl	3021	SJO
Croatia, Zagreb	Zagreb	353	ZAG
Cuba, Havana	Jose Marti Intl	210	HAV
Czech Republic, Prague	Prague Ruzyne	1247	PRG
Denmark, Copenhagen	Copenhagen	17	CPH
Dominican Republic, Santo Domingo	Las Americas	59	SDQ
Ecuador, Quito	Mariscal Sucre Intl	9228	UIO
Egypt, Cairo	Cairo Intl	382	CAI
El Salvador, San Salvador	Comalapa Intl	101	SAL
Estonia, Tallinn	Tallinn Yulemiste	132	TLL
Ethiopia, Addis Ababa	Bole Intl	7621	ADD
Finland, Helsinki	Helsinki-Vantaa	167	HEL
France, Bordeaux	Bordeaux	161	BOD
France, Marseille	Marseille Provence	66	MRS
France, Nice	Nice Côte d'Azur	13	NCE
France, Paris	Paris Charles de Gaulle	387	CDG
France, Paris	Le Bourget	218	LBG
France, Paris	Paris Orly	291	ORY
Germany, Berlin	Tegel	121	TXL
Germany, Berlin	Tempelhof	164	THF
Germany, Cologne	Cologne-Bonn	300	CGN
Germany, Düsseldorf	Düsseldorf Intl	147	DUS

Major World Airports

Airport City	Airport Name	Elevation Feet	AP Code
Germany, Frankfurt	Frankfurt Main	364	FRA
Germany, Hamburg	Hamburg Intl	53	HAM
Germany, Munich	Munchen Intl	1486	MUC
Germany, Stuttgart	Stuttgart	1267	STR
Greece, Athens	Eleftherios Venizelos	68	ATH
Guatemala, Guatemala City	La Aurora	4952	GUA
Haiti, Port-au-Prince	Mais Gate	121	PAP
Honduras, Tegucigalpa	Toncontin	3294	TGU
Hungary, Budapest	Budapest Ferihegy	495	BUD
Iceland, Keflavik	Keflavik Intl	169	KEF
India, Calcutta	Calcutta Intl	17	CCU
India, Mumbai (Bombay)	Chhatrapati Shivaji Intl	26	BOM
India, New Delhi	Indira Gandhi Intl	776	DEL
Indonesia, Jakarta	Halim Perdana Kusuma Intl	85	HLP
Indonesia, Jakarta	Soekarno-Hatta Jakarta Intl	34	CGK
Iran, Tehran	Mehrabad Intl	3962	THR
Iraq, Baghdad	Baghdad Intl	113	BGW
Ireland, Dublin	Dublin	242	DUB
Ireland, Shannon	Shannon	46	SNN
Israel, Tel Aviv	Ben Gurion Intl	135	TLV
Italy, Bologna	Bologna G. Marconi Intl	125	BLQ
Italy, Milan	Milan Linate Intl	353	LIN
Italy, Milan	Milan Malpensa Intercontinent	768	MXP
Italy, Naples	Naples Intl	299	NAP
Italy, Pisa	Pisa Galileo Galilei	6	PSA
Italy, Rome	Rome Leonardo da Vinci-Fiumicino	14	FCO
Italy, Venice	Venice Marco Polo	5	VCE
Japan, Osaka	Kansai Intl	26	KIX
Japan, Tokyo	Tokyo Haneda Intl	35	HND
Japan, Tokyo	New Tokyo Intl	139	NRT
Jordan, Amman	Queen Alia Intl	2395	AMM
Kenya, Nairobi	Jomo Kenyatta Intl	5327	NBO
Kuwait, Kuwait City	Kuwait Intl	210	KWI
Lebanon, Beirut	Beirut Intl	87	BEY
Lithuania, Vilnius	Vilnius	646	VNO
Malaysia, Kuala Lampur	Kuala Lampur Intl	89	KUL
Mexico, Mexico City	Licenciado Benito Juarez Intl	7341	MEX
Morocco, Casablanca	Mohammad V.	656	CMN
Mynamar (Burma), Yangon	Yangon Intl	109	RGN
Nepal, Kathmandu	Tribhuvan Intl	4390	KTM
Netherlands, Amsterdam	Schiphol	11	AMS
New Zealand, Auckland	Auckland Intl	23	AKL
Nicaragua, Managua	Augusto Sandino	194	MGA
Nigeria, Managua	Augusto Sandino Intl	194	MGA
Norway, Oslo	Oslo	681	OSL
Pakistan, Islamabad	Islamabad Intl	1666	ISB
Panama, Panama City	Tocumen Intl	135	PTY
Papua New Guinea, Port Moresby	Port Moresby Jacksons Intl	146	POM
Paraguay, Asuncion	Silvio Pettirossi	292	ASU
Peru, Lima	Jorge Chávez Lima-Callao Intl	112	LIM
Philippines, Manila	Ninoy Aquino Intl	75	MNL
Poland, Warsaw	Warsaw Frederic Chopin	361	WAW

Major World Airports

Airport City	Airport Name	Elevation Feet	AP Code
Portugal, Lisbon	Lisboa	374	LIS
Romania, Bucharest	Otopeni	314	OTP
Russia, Moscow	Sheremetyevo Intl	630	SVO
Russia, Moscow	Vnukovo	686	VKO
Russia, St. Petersburg	Pulkovo	79	LED
Saudi Arabia, Jeddah	King Abdulaziz Intl	48	JED
Senegal, Dakar	Yoff	85	DKR
Singapore, Singapore	Singapore Changi	22	SIN
South Africa, Cape Town	Cape Town Intl	151	CPT
South Africa, Johannesburg	Johannesburg Intl	5559	JNB
South Korea, Seoul	Kimpo Intl	58	SEL
Spain, Balearic Islands	Palma de Mallorca	8	PMI
Spain, Madrid	Madrid Barajas	2000	MAD
Sri Lanka, Colombo	Katunayake	29	CMB
Sudan, Khartoum	Khartoum	1261	KRT
Sweden, Stockholm	Stockholm Arlanda	124	ARN
Switzerland, Geneva	Geneva Intl	1411	GVA
Switzerland, Zurich	Zurich	1416	ZRH
Syrian Arab Republic, Damascus	Damascus Intl	2020	DAM
Taiwan, Taipei	Chiang Kai Shek Intl	107	TPE
Thailand, Bangkok	Bangkok Intl	9	BKK
Tunisia, Tunis	Carthage	22	TUN
Turkey, Istanbul	Atatürk Intl	158	IST
Uganda, Kampala	Entebbe	3782	EBB
Ukraine, Kiev	Borispol	130	KBP
U.K. - England, Birmingham	Birmingham Intl	325	BHX
U.K. - England, London	Gatwick	196	LGW
U.K. - England, London	Heathrow	80	LHR
U.K. - England, London	London City	17	LCY
U.K. - England, London	London Stansted	348	STN
U.K. - England, London	London Luton	526	LTN
U.K. - England, Manchester	Manchester	257	MAN
U.K. - N. Ireland, Belfast	Belfast City	267	BHD
U.K. - Scotland, Edinburgh	Edinburgh	135	EDI
U.K. - Scotland, Glasgow	Glasgow	26	GLA
United Arab Emirates, Abu Dhabi	Abu Dhabi Intl	88	AUH
Uruguay, Montevideo	Carrasco	105	MVD
U.S. Territory, Guam Island	Guam Intl	298	GUM
Venezuela, Caracas	Simon Bolivar Intl	235	CCS
Vietnam, Ho Chi Minh City	Tan Son Nhut Intl	33	SGN
Yugoslavia, Belgrade	Belgrade	335	BEG

Airline Two Letter Codes

Code	Airline	Code	Airline
AA	American Airlines	CP	Canadian Airlines Intl
AB	Air Berlin	CQ	Sunshine Airlines
AC	Air Canada	CS	Continental Micronesia
AE	Mandarin Airlines	CU	Cubana Airlines
AF	Air France	CV	Cargolux
AG	Provincial Airlines	CW	Airline of the Marshall
AH	Air Algerie		Islands
AI	Air India	CX	Cathay Pacific Airways
AJ	Air Belgium	CY	Cyprus Airways
AK	Air Asia	CZ	China Southern Airlines
AM	Aeromexico	DB	Brit'Air
AN	Ansett Australia Airlines	DD	Bayu Air Indonesia
AP	Air One	DE	Condor Flugdienst
AQ	Aloha Airlines	DH	Alantic Coast
AR	Aerolineas Argentinas		Airlines-United Express
AS	Alaska Airlines	DI	Deutsche BA Luftfahrt
AT	Royal Air Maroc	DL	Delta Air Lines
AU	Austral Lineas Aereas	DM	Maersk Air (Denmark)
AV	Avianca	DO	Air Vallee
AW	Dirgantara Air Service	DP	Air 2000
AX	Binter Mediterraneo	DS	Air Senegal
AY	Finnair	DT	TAAG Angola Airlines
AZ	Alitalia	DU	Hemus Air
BA	British Airways	DV	Nantucket Airlines
BB	Balair	DX	Danish Air Transport
BC	Brymon Aviation	DY	Air Djibouti
BD	British Midland	EA	Eastern Air Lines
BG	Biman Bangladesh Airline	ED	CCAir-US Airways Express
BI	Royal Brunei Airlines	EF	Far Eastern Air Transport
BJ	Nouvelair Tunisie	EG	Japan Asia Airways
BL	Pacific Airlines	EH	SAETA Air Ecuador
BM	Air Sicilia	EI	Aer Lingus
BO	Bouraq Indonesia Airlines	EJ	New England Airlines
BP	Air Botswana	EK	Emirates Airlines
BQ	Virgin Express	EL	Air Nippon Airlines
BR	EVA Air	EM	Western Airlines Australia
BT	Air Baltic	EN	Air Dolomiti
BU	Braathens	EP	Pelita Air Service
BV	Sun Air	EQ	TAME
BW	BWIA West Indies Airway	ER	DHL Airways
BX	Coast Air	ET	Ethiopian Airlines
BY	Britannia Airways	EU	Ecuatoriana
CA	Air China	EV	Atlantic Southeast
CB	Scot Airways		Airlines-Delta Connection
CC	Air Atlanta Icelandic	EW	Eurowings Luftverkehrs
CD	Mindanao Express	EX	Air Santo Domingo
CE	Nationwide Air Charter	EZ	Sun-Air of Scandinavia
CG	Airline of Papua New Guinea	F9	Frontier Airlines
CI	China Airlines	FA	Safair
CJ	Colgan Air-US Airways	FB	Fine Air
CL	Lufthansa CityLine	FD	CityFlyer Express
CM	COPA Airlines	FG	Ariana Afghan Airlines
CO	Continental Airlines	FH	Futura International Airway

Airline Two Letter Codes

Code	Airline	Code	Airline
FI	Icelandair	IH	Falcon Air
FJ	Air Pacific	IL	Istanbul Airlines
FL	AirTran Airways	IN	Macedonian Airlines
FM	Shanghai Airlines	IQ	Augsburg Airways
FN	Regional Air Lines	IR	Iran Air
FO	Expedition Airways	IS	Island Airlines
FQ	Air Aruba	IV	Fujian Airlines
FR	Ryanair	IY	Yemenia
FS	STAF	IZ	Arkia Israeli Airlines
FU	Air Littoral	JA	Air Bosna
FX	FedEx	JB	Helijet Airways
GA	Garuda Indonesia Airway	JD	Japan Air System
GB	Airborne Express	JE	Manx Airlines
GC	Lina Congo	JG	Air Greece
GE	TransAsia Airways	JH	Amerijet International
GF	Gulf Air	JI	Midway Airlines
GG	Air Holland	JJ	TAM Linhas Aereas
GH	Ghana Airways	JK	Spainair
GI	Air Guinee	JL	JAL Japan Airlines
GJ	Eurofly	JM	Air Jamaica
GL	Greenland Air	JN	Japan Air Commuter
GM	Air Slovakia	JP	Adria Airways
GN	Air Gabon	JQ	Air Jamaica Express
GQ	Big Sky Airlines	JR	AeroCalifornia
GR	Aurigny Air Services	JS	Air Koryo
GT	Air Mandalay	JT	Jaro International
GU	Aviateca	JU	JAT Yugoslav Airlines
GV	Riga Airlines	JV	Bearskin Lake Air Services
GX	Air Ontario	JW	Arrow Air
GY	Guyana Airways	JY	Jersey European Airways
GZ	Air Rarotonga	JZ	Skyways AB
HA	Hawaiian Airlines	KA	DragonAir
HB	Malitas	KB	Druk Air
HF	Hapag-Lloyd Fluggesellschaft	KD	Kendell Airlines
HH	Islandsflug	KE	Korean Air
HI	Papillon Airways	KF	Air Botnia
HK	Yangon Airways	KH	Kyrnair
HM	Air Seychelles	KI	Air Atlantique
HN	KLM Cityhopper BV	KJ	British Mediterranean
HP	America West Airlines	KK	TAM Brasil
HQ	Business Express	KL	KLM Royal Dutch Airlines
HR	China United Airlines	KM	Air Malta
HT	Air Tchad	KQ	Kenya Airways
HV	Transavia Airlines	KR	Kitty Hawk Air Cargo
HY	Uzbekistan Airways	KS	Peninsula Airways
IA	Iraqi Airways	KT	Turtle Airways - Fiji
IB	Iberia	KU	Kuwait Airways
IC	Indian Airlines	KX	Cayman Airways
ID	Air Guyane	KZ	Nippon Cargo Airlines
IE	Solomon Islands Airlines	LA	LAN Chile
IF	Interflug	LB	LAB Lloyd Aereo Boliviano
IG	Meridiana	LC	Loganair
		LD	Air Hong Kong

Airline Two Letter Codes

Code	Airline	Code	Airline
LG	Luxair	NZ	Air New Zealand
LH	Lufthansa German Airlines	OA	Olympic Airways
LI	LIAT Airlines	OE	Westair Commuter Airlines-United Express
LJ	Sierra National Airlines		
LL	Allegro Air	OF	Sunstate Airlines
LM	Air ALM	OG	Austrian Air Transport
LN	Libyan Arab Airlines	OH	Comair-Delta Connection
LO	LOT Polish Airlines	OI	Asipring Air
LP	LAN Peru	OK	Air St. Barthelemy
LR	Lacsa	OK	CSA Czech Airlines
LT	LUT International Airways	OM	MIAT Mongolian Airlines
LV	Albanian Airlines	ON	Air Nauru
LW	Pacific Wings	OO	Sky West Airlines (USA)
LX	Crossair	OP	Chalk's Ocean Airways
LY	El Al Israel Airlines	OR	Crimea Air
LZ	Balkan Bulgarian Airlines	OS	Austrian Airlines
MA	Malev	OU	Croatia Airlines
MD	Air Madagascar	OV	Estonian Air
ME	MEA Middle East Air Lines	OX	Orient Thai Airlines
MF	Xiamen Airlines	OZ	Asiana Airlines
MG	Djibouti Airlines	PA	Pan Am
MH	Malaysia Airlines	PB	Air Burundi
MI	SilkAir	PC	Air Fiji
MJ	LAPA	PD	Pem-Air
MK	Air Mauritius	PE	Air Europe
MO	Calm Air International	PF	Palestinian Airlines
MP	Martinair Holland	PG	Bangkok Airways
MQ	Simmons Airlines-American Eagle	PH	Polynesian Airlines
		PI	Sunflower Airlines
MR	Air Mauritanie	PK	PIA Pakistan Intl Airlines
MS	EgyptAir	PL	AeroPeru
MU	China Eastern Airlines	PM	Tropic Air
MW	Maya Airways	PP	Jet Aviation
MX	Mexicana	PQ	Skippers Aviation
MY	Euroscot Express Airways	PR	Philippine Airlines
MZ	Merpati Nusantara Airlines	PS	Ukraine International Airline
NA	Executive Airlines American Eagle	PT	West Air Sweden
		PU	PLUNA
NC	National Jet Systems	PW	Precision Air
ND	Airlink	PX	Air Niugini
NF	Air Vanuatu	PY	Surinam Airways
NG	Lauda Air	PZ	LAPSA Air Paraguay
NH	All Nippon Airways	QA	Aerocaribe
NI	PGA Portugalia Airlines	QF	Qantas
NJ	Vanguard Airlines	QI	Cimber Air Denmark
NK	Spirit Airlines	QJ	Jet Airways
NL	Shaheen Air International	QK	Air Nova
NM	Mount Cook Airlines	QL	Air Lesotho
NT	Binter Canarias	QM	Air Malawi
NU	Japan Transocean Airlines	QO	Aeroexpress
NW	Northwest Airlines	QP	Airkenya
NX	Air Macau	QR	Qatar Airways
NY	Air Iceland		

Airline Two Letter Codes

Code	Airline	Code	Airline
QS	Tatra Air	TH	Transmile Air Services
QU	Uganda Airlines	TK	THY Turkish Airlines
QV	Lao Aviation	TL	Airnorth
QW	TCNA Turks and Caicos National Airline	TM	LAM Mozambique
		TN	Air Tahiti Nui
QX	Horizon Airlines	TP	TAP Air Portugal
QY	European Air Transport	TR	Transbrasil
RA	Royal Nepal Airlines	TS	Air Transat
RB	SyrianAir	TT	Air Lithuania
RC	Atlantic Airways	TU	Tunis Air
RE	Aer Arann	TX	Air Caraibes
RG	VARIG	TY	Air Caledonie
RI	Mandala Airlines	TZ	American Trans Air
RJ	Royal Jordanian Airlines	UA	United Airlines
RK	Air Afrique	UB	Myanmar Airways Intl
RL	Ultrair	UC	Ladeco Chilean Airlines
RM	Air Moldova International	UD	Hex'Air
RN	Euralair	UE	Transeuropean Airlines
RO	Tarom	UG	Tuninter
RQ	Air Engiadina	UK	KLM uk
RR	RAF Royal Air Force	UL	SriLankan Airlines
RS	Intercontinental Colombia	UM	Air Zimbabwe
RT	Airlines of South Australia	UN	Transaero Airlines
RU	Sky King	UP	Bahamasair
RV	Reeve Aleutian Airways	UR	British International Helicopters
RW	RAS Fluggesellschaft		
RZ	Sansa	US	US Airways
SA	South African Airways	UT	Linea Turistica Aereotuy
SB	Aircalin	UU	Air Austral
SC	Shandong Airlines	UW	Perimeter Airlines
SD	Sudan Airways	UX	Air Europa
SE	Wings of Alaska	UY	Cameroon Airlines
SK	SAS Scandinavian Airlines	VA	VIASA Venezuelan International Airways
SL	Rio-Sul Servicios Aereos Regionais	VB	Maersk Air (UK)
		VC	Servivensa
SM	Taino Airways	VD	Air Liberte
SN	Sabena Belgian World Airlines	VE	Avensa
		VF	British World Airways
SO	Swiss World Airways	VG	VLM Airlines
SP	SATA Air Azores	VH	Air Burkina
SQ	Singapore Airlines	VI	Volga-Dnepr Russian International Air
SR	Swissair		
SS	CorsAir International	VJ	Royal Air Cambodge
ST	Yanda Airlines	VL	North Vancouver Air
SU	Aeroflot	VM	Regional Airlines
SV	Saudi Arabian Airlines	VN	Vietnam Airlines
SW	Air Namibia	VO	Tyrolean Airways
SY	Sun County Airlines	VP	VASP
SZ	China Southwest Airlines	VQ	Impulse Airlines
TA	TACA International Airlines	VR	TACV Cabo Verde Airlines
TC	Air Tanzania	VS	Virgin Atlantic Airways
TE	Lithuanian Airlines	VT	Air Tahiti
TG	Thai Airways		

Airline Two Letter Codes

Code	Airline	Code	Airline
VU	Air Ivoire	YV	Mesa Airlines
VV	AeroSvit	YW	Air Nostrum
VW	Aeromar Airlines	YX	Midwest Express Airlines
VX	ACES Colombia	ZA	Access Air
VZ	Airtours Intl Airways	ZB	Monarch Airline
WA	Newair Airservice	ZC	Royal Swazi National
WB	SAN Ecuador		Airways
WC	Islena Airlines	ZD	Ross Aviation
WE	Rheintaflug Seewald	ZF	Airborne of Sweden
WF	Wideroes Flyveselska	ZG	Sabair Airlines
WG	Wasaya Airways	ZI	Aigle Azur
WH	China Northwest Airlines	ZK	Great Lakes Aviation-
WI	U-Land Airlines		United Express
WJ	Air Labrador	ZM	Scibe Airlift Cargo
WL	AeroPerlas	ZP	Air St. Thomas
WM	Winair-Windward Island	ZQ	Qantas New Zealand
	Airways International	ZR	Muk Air
WN	Southwest Airlines	ZS	AzzurraAir Airlines
WO	World Airways	ZT	Satena Colombia
WP	Island Air-Aloha Airlines	ZW	Air Wisconsin-United
WQ	Romavia		Express
WR	Royal Tongan Airlines	ZX	Air BC
WT	Nigeria Airways	ZY	ADA Air
WU	Wuhan Air Lines	ZZ	Buzz
WX	CityJet		
WY	Oman Air		
WZ	Acvilla Air		
XC	Air Caribbean		
XE	Southcentral Air		
XG	North American Airlines		
XJ	Mesaba Airlines		
XK	CCM Airlines		
XL	Affretair		
XM	Australian Air Express		
XO	Xinjiang Airlines		
XP	Casino Express		
XT	KLM Exel Netherlands		
XU	Freedom Air International		
XZ	Eastair		
YB	South African Express		
YC	Flight West Airlines		
YD	Gomelavia		
YG	Cocesna		
YH	Air Nunavut		
YI	Air Sunshine		
YJ	National Airlines		
YK	Cyprus Turkish Airlines		
YN	Air Creebec		
YO	Heli Air Monaco		
YP	Aero Lloyd Flugreisen		
YR	Scenic Airlines		
YT	Skywest Airlines (Australia)		
YU	Dominair		

Airline 1–800 Phone Numbers

Airline	Phone #	Airline	Phone #
ACES Colombia	846–2237	Lacsa	225–2272
Aeroflot	995–5555	Ladeco Chilean Airlines	432-2799
Aerolineas Argentinas	333-0276	LAN Chile	735–5526
Aeromexico	237-6639	LOT Polish Airlines	249-0739
AeroPeru	777–7717	Lufthansa German Airline	645–3880
Air Afrique	456-9192	Malaysia Airlines	421–8641
Air ALM	327–7197	Malev	223-6884
Air Canada	776–3000	Mesa Airlines	637–2247
Air France	237–2747	Mexicana	531–7921
Air India	223–7776	Midway Airlines	446–4392
Air Jamaica	523–5585	Midwest Express	452–2022
Air New Zealand	262–1234	Northwest Airlines	225–2525
Alaska Airlines	426–0333	Olympic Airways	223–1226
Alitalia	223–5730	Philippine Airlines	435-9725
All Nippon Airways	235–9262	Qantas	227–4500
Aloha Airlines	367–5250	Royal Air Maroc	344–6726
America West	235–9292	Royal Jordanian Airline	223–0470
American Air Cargo	227-4622	Sabena Belgian World Airlines	
American Airlines	433–7300		955–2000
American Eagle	433–7300	SAETA Air Ecuador	827–2382
American Trans Air	435-9282	SAS Scandinavian Airlines	
Austrian Airlines	843–0002		221–2350
Avianca	284–2622	Saudi Arabian Airlines	472–8342
Aviateca	327–9832	Singapore Airlines	742-3333
Big Sky Airlines	237–7788	South African Airways	722-9675
British Airways	247–9297	Southwest Airlines	435–9792
BWIA West Indies Airways		Sun Country Airlines	752-1218
	538-2942	Swissair	221–4750
Canadian Airlines Intl.	426–7000	TACA International Airlines	
Cathay Pacific Airways	233–2742		535–8780
Cayman Airways	422–9626	TAP Air Portugal	221–7370
China Airlines	227–5118	Thai Airways	426–5204
Continental Airlines	525–0280	THY Turkish Airline	874–8875
CSA Czech Airlines	223–2365	United Airlines	241–6522
Delta Air Lines	221–1212	United Cargo	822-2746
DHL Airways	225–5345	US Airways	428–4322
Egyptair	334-6787	Vanguard Airlines	826-4827
El Al Israel Airlines	223–6700	VARIG	468–2744
Emirates Airlines	777-3999	VIASA Venezuelan	468–4272
Finnair	950–5000		
Frontier Airlines	432-1359		
Guyana Airways	242-4210		
Hawaiian Airlines	367–5320		
Horizon Airlines	547–9308		
Iberia	772–4642		
Icelandair	223–5500		
Island Airlines	248-7779		
JAL Japan Airlines	525–3663		
KLM Royal Dutch Airline	374–7747		
Korean Air	438–5000		
LAB Lloyd Aereo Boliviano			
	327–7407		

Lost Credit Card Phone #'s

Carrier	USA Number	World Wide Number
84 Lumber	800-250-5411	---
American Express	800-528-4800	336-393-1111
Amoco/British Petroleum	800-850-6266	---
Beacon	800-333-3560	---
Chevron Oil Co	800-243-8766	---
Conoco/Phillips	800-242-1567	---
David's Bridal	Any Store	
Diners Club Int./Carte Bl.	800-234-6377	303-799-1504
Discover Card	800-347-2683	801-902-3100
Exxon/Mobil	800-288-6378	---
FamousBarr	Any Store	
Filene's	Any Store	
Foley's	Any Store	
Hecht's	Any Store	
Home Depot	800-677-0232	---
J.C. Penney	800-527-4403	---
Jones Store	Any Store	
Kohl's	866-887-8884	---
Kaufmann's	Any Store	
L S Ayres	Any Store	
Lord & Taylors	Any Store	
Lowes	800-445-6937	---
Marshall Field's	888-755-5856	---
Mastercard	800-622-7747	636-722-7111
May Department Stores	Any Store	
Meier & Frank	Any Store	
Mervyn's	888-755-5856	---
Robinsons May	Any Store	
Sears, Roebuck & Co.	800-819-9000	---
Shell Oil Co	800-331-3703	---
Sinclair Oil	800-325-3265	---
Strawbridge's	Any Store	
Target	888-755-5856	---
Texaco Oil Co	800-552-7827	---
Total	800-333-3560	---
Ultramar Diamond Shamrock	800-333-3560	---
Visa Worldwide	800-847-1130	410-581-9994

NOTES

MOST of the above carriers require that you have your credit card number in order to report it lost or stolen. You should carry a list of all your card numbers somewhere other than your wallet or purse (use the inside cover of this book if you want).

When calling the world wide number, try calling collect first. Many carriers, such as Visa, will accept a collect call to report a lost or stolen card. Some of the world wide numbers listed above are regional numbers, but they will be able to direct you to the correct number if they can't help.

Car Rental Phone Number

Car Rental Company	Toll Free Number (Local #/CORP #)	Countries where service is offered (see country code table, page 312)
Advantage Rent A Car	1-800-777-5500 (1-210-344-4712)	BE, CH, CR, DE, DO, ES, FR, GB, IE, IT, MX, NL, PT, US
Alamo Rent A Car	1-800-327-9633 (1-954-320-4000)	AG, AN, AW, BE, CA, CH, CL, CR, DE, DO, ES, FR, GB, GR, IE, IT, MX, NL, NI, PT, US
Avis	1-800-230-4898 (n/a)	AD, AE, AG, AR, AS, AT, AU, AW, AZ, BA, BE, BG, BH, BN, Bonaire, BR, BS, BW, BY, BZ, CA, CD, CF, CH, CI, CK, CL, CM, CR, CV, CY, CZ, DE, DK, DO, EC, EE, EG, ES, FI, FJ, FO, FR, GA, GB, GD, GE, GF, GH, GI, GP, GQ, GR, GT, GU, HK, HN, HR, HT, HU, ID, IE, IL, IN, IS, IT, JO, JP, KE, KM, KN, KR, KY, KZ, LB, LC, LK, LS, LT, LU, LV, MA, MD, MG, MK, MO, MQ, MT, MU, MW, MX, MY, NA, NC, NG, NL, NO, NZ, OM, PA, PE, PF, PG, PH, PK, PL, PR, PT, QA, RE, RO, SA, SC, SE, SG, SI, SK, SN, SR, St. Barthelemy, St. Martin, SV, SZ, TC, TD, TG, TH, TN, TO, TR, TT, UA, US, UY, VC, VE, VG, VI, VU, WS, ZA, ZM, ZW
Budget Rent A Car	1-800-527-0700 (1-972-404-7810)	AE, AG, AR, AS, AT, AU, AW, BA, BE, BG, BH, Bonaire, BR, BS, BW, BZ, CA, CH, CI, CK, CL, CN, CO, CR, Curacao, CY, CZ, DE, DK, DM, DO, EC, EE, EG, ES, FI, FJ, FR, GB, GI, GD, GF, GP, GR, GT, GU, GY, HN, HR, HT, HU, IE, IL, IN, IS, IT, JM, JO, JP, KE, KR, KW, KY, LB, LC, LK, LS, LT, LV, MA, MG, MH, MK, MP, MQ, MT, MU, MX, MY, NA, NC, NI, NL, NO, NZ, OM, PA, PE, PG, PH, PK, PL, PR, PT, PW, QA, RE, RO, RU, SA, SC, SE, SG, SI, SN, St. Barthelemy, St. Croix, St. Maarten, St. Martin, St. Thomas, SV, SY, TC, TH, TN, Tortola, TR, TT, US, UY, VE, VU, WS, ZA, ZW
Dollar Rent A Car/Sixt Rent A Car	1-800-800-4000 (n/a)	AG, AR, AU, AW, BO, BS, CA, CL, CO, CR, DO, FM, GD, GT, GU, HN, HT, JM, KY, MX, NI, PA, PE, PH, PR, St. Maarten, SV, US, UY, VG

Car Rental Company	Toll Free Number (Local #/CORP #)	Countries where service is offered (see country code table, page 312)
Enterprise Rent A Car	1-800-325-8007 (n/a)	CA, US
Hertz	1-800-654-3131 (1-516-747-4716)	AD, AE, AG, AI, AL, AM, AN, AO, AR, AT, AU, AW, AZ, BA, BD, BE, BG, BH, BN, BO, BR, BS, BZ, CA, CD, CH, CI, CL, CM, CO, CR, CV, CY, CZ, DK, DO, EC, EG, ES, FI, FJ, FR, GA, GB, GE, GF, GH, GI, GM, GP, GR, GT, GU, HK, HN, HR, HT, HU, ID, IE, IL, IN, IS, IT, JM, JO, JP, KE, KG, KR, KW, KY, LB, LC, LT, LU, LV, MA, MC, MD, MG, MK, MQ, MT, MU, MW, MX, MY, MZ, NA, NC, NG, NI, NL, NO, NZ, OM, PA, PE, PF, PG, PH, PK, PL, PR, PT, PY, QA, RE, RO, RU, SA, Saipan, SB, SC, SE, SG, SI, SK, SN, SR, SV, SY, TC, TN, TR, TT, TZ, UA, UG, US, UY, VE, VG, VI, VU, YE, ZA, ZW
National Car Rental	1-800-227-7368 (1-954-320-6600)	AN, AT, AU, BE, BF, CA, CH, CL, CO, CR, CY, CZ, DE, DK, DO, EE, ES, FR, GB, GF, GP, GR, GT, GU, HN, HR, HU, ID, IE, IL, IT, JP, KE, KR, LB, LV, MA, MP, MQ, MT, MU, MX, MY, NL, NO, NZ, PA, PE, PH, PL, PT, PY, RE, RO, SE, SG, SI, SK, SN, TH, TR, US, VG, ZA
Payless Car Rental	1-800-729-5377 (1-727-321-6352)	CR, CY, DO, EG, GR, GU, HU, JO, LB, MX, NI, PL, PR, US
Thrifty	1-800-847-4389 (1-918-665-3930)	AE, AI, AG, AR, AT, AU, AW, BH, BS, BZ, CA, CL, CR, CY, CZ, DE, DO, FJ, FR, GB, GP, GR, GU, HN, IE, IL, IT, JM, JO, KN, KW, KY, LB, MA, Marianna Islands, MT, MX, NC, NI, NZ, OM, PA, PG, PH, PR, QA, SA, SC, SE, SG, St. Maarten, SV, TR, TT, US, UY, VE, VI

Note: See Country Code table on page 312.

If local numbers are not shown, you will need to call directory assistance for a rental agency in that town.

Country Codes - 2 and 3 Letter

Country Name	Country Name Short Description	2 Letter Country Code	3 Letter Country Code
Afghanistan	Afghanista	AF	AFG
Albania	Albania	AL	ALB
Algeria	Algeria	DZ	DZA
American Somoa	Amer Somoa	AS	ASM
Andorra	Andorra	AD	AND
Angola	Angola	AO	AGO
Anguilla	Anguilla	AI	AIA
Antartica	Antartica	AQ	ATA
Antigua and Barbuda	Antigua/BA	AG	ATG
Argentina	Argentina	AR	ARG
Armenia	Armenia	AM	ARM
Aruba	Aruba	AW	ABW
Australia	Australia	AU	AUS
Austria	Austria	AT	AUT
Azerbaijan	Azerbaijan	AZ	AZE
Bahamas	Bahamas	BS	BHS
Bahrain	Bahrain	BH	BHR
Bangladesh	Bangladesh	BD	BGD
Barbados	Barbados	BB	BRB
Belarus	Belarus	BY	BLR
Belgium	Belgium	BE	BEL
Belize	Belize	BZ	BLZ
Benin	Benin	BJ	BEN
Bermuda	Bermuda	BM	BMU
Bhutan	Bhutan	BT	BTN
Bolivia	Bolivia	BO	BOL
Bosnia and Herzegovina	Bosnia	BA	BIH
Botswana	Botswana	BW	BWA
Bouvet Island	Bouvet ISL	BV	BVT
Brazil	Brazil	BR	BRA
British Indian Ocean Territory	British IO	IO	IOT
Brunei Darusslalam	Brunei	BN	BRN
Bulgaria	Bulgaria	BG	BGR
Berkina Faso	Burkina F	BF	BFA
Burundi	Burundi	BI	BDI
Central African Republic	C-African	CF	CAF
Cambodia	Cambodia	KH	KHM

Country Name	Country Name Short Description	2 Letter Country Code	3 Letter Country Code
Cameroon	Cameroon	CM	CMR
Canada	Canada	CA	CAN
Cape Verde	Cape Verde	CV	CPV
Cayman Islands	Cayman ISL	KY	CYM
Chad	Chad	TD	TCD
Chile	Chile	CL	CHL
China	China	CN	CHN
Christmas Island	Christmas	CX	CXR
Cocos Islands	Cocos ISL	CC	CCK
Colombia	Colombia	CO	COL
Comoros	Comoros	KM	COM
Congo	Congo	CG	COG
Cook Islands	Cook ISLDS	CK	COK
Costa Rica	Costa Rica	CR	CRI
Cote D'Ivoire	Cote DIvoi	CI	CIV
Croatia	Croatia	HR	HRV
Cuba	Cuba	CU	CUB
Cyprus	Cyprus	CY	CYP
Czech Republic	Czech Repl	CZ	CZE
Denmark	Denmark	DK	DNK
Djibouti	Djibouti	DJ	DJI
Dominica	Dominica	DM	DMA
Dominican Republic	Dominican	DO	DOM
East Timor	East Timor	TP	TMP
Ecuador	Ecuador	EC	ECU
Egypt	Egypt	EG	EGY
El Salvador	El Salvado	SV	SLV
Equatorial Guinea	Equat Guin	GQ	GNQ
Eritrea	Eritrea	ER	ERI
Estonia	Estonia	EE	EST
Ethiopia	Ethiopia	ET	ETH
Falkland Islands	Falkland	FK	FLK
Faroe Islands	Faroe ISL	FO	FRO
Fiji	Fiji	FJ	FJI
Finland	Finland	FI	FIN
France	France	FR	FRA
France Metropolitan	France MET	FX	FXX
French Guiana	French GUI	GF	GUF
French Polynesia	French POL	PF	PYF

Country Name	Country Name Short Description	2 Letter Country Code	3 Letter Country Code
French Southern Territories	French STH	TF	ATF
Gabon	Gabon	GA	GAB
Gambia	Gambia	GM	GMB
Georgia	Georgia	GE	GEO
Germany	Germany	DE	DEU
Ghana	Ghana	GH	GHA
Gibraltar	Gibraltar	GI	GIB
Greece	Greece	GR	GRC
Greenland	Greenland	GL	GRL
Grenada	Grenada	GD	GRD
Guadeloupe	Guadeloupe	GP	GLP
Guam	Guam	GU	GUM
Guatemala	Guatemala	GT	GTM
Guinea	Guinea	GN	GIN
Guinea-Bissau	Guinea-BIS	GW	GNB
Guyana	Guyana	GY	GUY
Haiti	Haiti	HT	HTI
Heard Island & McDonald Isl	Heard/MCDO	HM	HMD
Honduras	Honduras	HN	HND
Hong Kong	Hong Kong	HK	HKG
Hungary	Hungary	HU	HUN
Iceland	Iceland	IS	ISL
India	India	IN	IND
Indonesia	Indonesia	ID	IDN
Iran	Iran	IR	IRN
Iraq	Iraq	IQ	IRQ
Ireland	Ireland	IE	IRL
Israel	Israel	IL	ISR
Italy	Italy	IT	ITA
Jamaica	Jamaica	JM	JAM
Japan	Japan	JP	JPN
Jordan	Jordan	JO	JOR
Kazakhstan	Kazakhstan	KZ	KAZ
Kenya	Kenya	KE	KEN
Kiribati	Kiribati	KI	KIR
Korea, DEM People's Repl of	Korea	KP	PRK
Korea, Republic of	Korea-REPL	KR	KOR
Kuwait	Kuwait	KW	KWT
Kyrgyzstan	Kyrgystan	KG	KGZ

Country Name	Country Name Short Description	2 Letter Country Code	3 Letter Country Code
Lao, People's Democratic Repub	Lao	LA	LAO
Latvia	Latvia	LV	LVA
Lebanon	Lebanon	LB	LBN
Lesotho	Lesotho	LS	LSO
Liberia	Liberia	LR	LBR
Libyan Arab Jamahirya	Libyan A J	LY	LBY
Liechtenstein	Lichenstei	LI	LIE
Lithuania	Lithuania	LT	LTU
Luxembourg	Luxembourg	LU	LUX
Macau	Macau	MO	MAC
Madagascar	Madagascar	MG	MDG
Malawi	Malawi	MW	MWI
Malaysia	Malaysia	MY	MYS
Maldives	Maldives	MV	MDV
Mali	Mali	ML	MLI
Malta	Malta	MT	MLT
Marshall Islands	Marshall	MH	MHL
Martinique	Martinique	MQ	MTQ
Mauritania	Mauritania	MR	MRT
Mauritius	Mauritius	MU	MUS
Mayotte	Mayotte	YT	MYT
Mexico	Mexico	MX	MEX
Micronesia	Micronesia	FN	FSM
Moldova, Republic of	Moldova	MD	MDA
Monaco	Monaco	MC	MCO
Mongolia	Mongolia	MN	MNG
Monsterrat	Monsterrat	MS	MSR
Morocco	Morocco	MA	MAR
Mozambique	Mozambique	MZ	MOZ
Myanmar	Myanmar	MM	MMR
Northern Mariana Islands	N Mariana	MP	MNP
Namibia	Namibia	NA	NAM
Napal	Napal	NP	NPL
Nauru	Nauru	NR	NRU
Netherlands	Netherland	NL	NLD
Netherlands Antilles	Nethr Antl	AN	ANT
New Caledonia	New Caledo	NC	NCL
New Zealand	New Zealan	NZ	NZL

Country Name	Country Name Short Description	2 Letter Country Code	3 Letter Country Code
Nicaragua	Nicaragua	NI	NIC
Niger	Niger	NE	NER
Nigeria	Nigeria	NG	NGA
Niue	Niue	NU	NIU
Norfolk Island	Norfolk IS	NF	NFK
Norway	Norway	NO	NOR
Oman	Oman	OM	OMN
Pakistan	Pakistan	PK	PAK
Palau	Palau	PW	PLW
Panama	Panama	PA	PAN
Papua New Guinea	Papua Guin	PG	PNG
Paraguay	Paraguay	PY	PRY
Peru	Peru	PE	PER
Philippines	Philippine	PH	PHL
Pitcairn	Pitcairn	PN	PCN
Poland	Poland	PL	POL
Portugal	Portugal	PT	PRT
Puerto Rico	Puerto Ric	PR	PRI
Qatar	Qatar	QA	QAT
Reunion	Reunion	RE	REU
Romania	Romania	RO	ROM
Russian Federation	Russian Fe	RU	RUS
Rwanda	Rwanda	RW	RWA
South Africa	S Africa	ZA	ZAF
S Georgia and S Sandwich Isl	S Georgia	GS	SGS
San Marino	San Marino	SM	SMR
Sao Tome and Principe	San Tome	ST	STP
Saudi Arabia	Saudia Ara	SA	SAU
Senegal	Senegal	SN	SEN
Seychelles	Seychelles	SC	SYC
Sierra Leone	Sierra Leo	SL	SLE
Singapore	Singapore	SG	SGP
Slovakia	Slovakia	SK	SVK
Slovenia	Slovenia	SI	SVN
Solomon Islands	Solomon IS	SB	SLB
Somalia	Somalia	SO	SOM
Somoa	Somoa	WS	WSM
Spain	Spain	ES	ESP
Sri Lanka	Sri Lanka	LK	LKA

Country Name	Country Name Short Description	2 Letter Country Code	3 Letter Country Code
Saint Helena	St Helena	SH	SHN
Saint Kitts/Nevis	St Kitts	KN	KNA
Saint Lucia	St Lucia	LC	LCA
Saint Pierre/Miquelo	St Pierre	PM	SPM
Saint Vincent/Grena	St Vincent	VC	VCT
Sudan	Sudan	SD	SDN
Suriname	Suriname	SR	SUR
Svalbard and Jan Mayen	Svalbard	SJ	SJM
Swaziland	Swaziland	SZ	SWZ
Sweden	Sweden	SE	SWE
Switzerland	Switzerlan	CH	CHE
Syrian Arab Republic	Syrian	SY	SYR
Taiwan Province of China	Taiwan	TW	TWN
Tajikistan	Tajikistan	TJ	TJK
Tanzania, United Republic of	Tanzania	TZ	TZA
Thailand	Thailand	TH	THA
Togo	Togo	TG	TGO
Tokelau	Tokelau	TK	TKL
Tonga	Tonga	TO	TON
Trinidad and Tobago	Trinidad	TT	TTO
Tunisia	Tunisia	TN	TUN
Turkey	Turkey	TR	TUR
Turkmenistan	Turkmenist	TM	TKM
Turks and Caicos Islands	Turks/Caic	TC	TCA
Tuvalu	Tuvalu	TV	TUV
United Arab Emirates	U Arab EMI	AE	ARE
United Kingdom	U Kingdom	GB	GBR
United States	U S	US	USA
Uganda	Uganda	UG	UGA
Ukraine	Ukraine	UA	UKR
Uruguay	Uruguay	UY	URY
United States Minor Outlyng Is	US-Islands	UM	UMI
Uzbekistan	Uzbekistan	UZ	UZB
Vanuatu	Vanuatu	VU	VUT
Vatican City State	Vatican	VA	VAT
Venezuela	Venezuela	VE	VEN
Vietnam	Vietnam	VN	VNM
Virgin Islands British	Virgin BRT	VG	VGB
Virgin Islands U S	Virgin U S	VI	VIR

Country Name	Country Name Short Description	2 Letter Country Code	3 Letter Country Code
Western Sahara	W Sahara	EH	ESH
Wallis and Futuna Islands	Wallis	WF	WLF
Yemen	Yemen	YE	YEM
Yugoslavia	Yugoslavia	YU	YUG
Zaire	Zaire	ZR	ZAR
Zambia	Zambia	ZM	ZMB
Zimbabwe	Zimbabwe	ZW	ZWE

General Science

See also GEOLOGY for Richter Earthquake scales

See also WEATHER for natural disaster scales

Temperature Conversions

°C	°F	°C	°F	°C	°F
10000	18032	430	806	200	392.0
9500	17132	420	788	195	383.0
9000	16232	410	770	190	374.0
8500	15332	400	752	185	365.0
8000	14432	395	743	180	356.0
7500	13532	390	734	175	347.0
7000	12632	385	725	170	338.0
6500	11732	380	716	165	329.0
6000	10832	375	707	160	320.0
5500	9932	370	698	155	311.0
5000	9032	365	689	150	302.0
4500	8132	360	680	145	293.0
4000	7232	355	671	140	284.0
3500	6332	350	662	135	275.0
3000	5432	345	653	130	266.0
2500	4532	340	644	125	257.0
2000	3632	335	635	120	248.0
1500	2732	330	626	115	239.0
1000	1832	325	617	110	230.0
950	1742	320	608	105	221.0
900	1652	315	599	100	212.0
850	1562	310	590	99	210.2
800	1472	305	581	98	208.4
750	1382	300	572	97	206.6
700	1292	295	563	96	204.8
650	1202	290	554	95	203.0
600	1112	285	545	94	201.2
590	1094	280	536	93	199.4
580	1076	275	527	92	197.6
570	1058	270	518	91	195.8
560	1040	265	509	90	194.0
550	1022	260	500	89	192.2
540	1004	255	491	88	190.4
530	986	250	482	87	188.6
520	968	245	473	86	186.8
510	950	240	464	85	185.0
500	932	235	455	84	183.2
490	914	230	446	83	181.4
480	896	225	437	82	179.6
470	878	220	428	81	177.8
460	860	215	419	80	176.0
450	842	210	410	79	174.2
440	824	205	401	78	172.4

°C = *Degrees Celsius.* 1 unit is 1/100 of the difference between the temperature of melting ice and boiling water at standard temperature and pressure.

°F = *Degrees Fahrenheit.* 1 unit is 1/180 of the difference between the temperature of melting ice and boiling water at standard temperature and pressure.

Temperature Conversions

°C	°F	°C	°F	°C	°F
77	170.6	34	93.2	−9	15.8
76	168.8	33	91.4	−10	14.0
75	167.0	32	89.6	−11	12.2
74	165.2	31	87.8	−12	10.4
73	163.4	30	86.0	−13	8.6
72	161.6	29	84.2	−14	6.8
71	159.8	28	82.4	−15	5.0
70	158.0	27	80.6	−16	3.2
69	156.2	26	78.8	−17	1.4
68	154.4	25	77.0	−18	−0.4
67	152.6	24	75.2	−19	−2.2
66	150.8	23	73.4	−20	−4.0
65	149.0	22	71.6	−21	−5.8
64	147.2	21	69.8	−22	−7.6
63	145.4	20	68.0	−23	−9.4
62	143.6	19	66.2	−24	−11.2
61	141.8	18	64.4	−25	−13.0
60	140.0	17	62.6	−26	−14.8
59	138.2	16	60.8	−27	−16.6
58	136.4	15	59.0	−28	−18.4
57	134.6	14	57.2	−29	−20.2
56	132.8	13	55.4	−30	−22.0
55	131.0	12	53.6	−31	−23.8
54	129.2	11	51.8	−32	−25.6
53	127.4	10	50.0	−33	−27.4
52	125.6	9	48.2	−34	−29.2
51	123.8	8	46.4	−35	−31.0
50	122.0	7	44.6	−36	−32.8
49	120.2	6	42.8	−37	−34.6
48	118.4	5	41.0	−38	−36.4
47	116.6	4	39.2	−39	−38.2
46	114.8	3	37.4	−40	−40.0
45	113.0	2	35.6	−50	−58.0
44	111.2	1	33.8	−60	−76.0
43	109.4	0	32.0	−70	−94.0
42	107.6	−1	30.2	−80	−112.0
41	105.8	−2	28.4	−90	−130.0
40	104.0	−3	26.6	−100	−148.0
39	102.2	−4	24.8	−125	−193.0
38	100.4	−5	23.0	−150	−238.0
37	98.6	−6	21.2	−200	−328.0
36	96.8	−7	19.4	−250	−418.0
35	95.0	−8	17.6	−273	−459.4

$$°C = 5/9 \ (°F - 32) \qquad °F = 9/5 \ °C + 32$$
$$\text{Absolute Zero} = 0K = -273.16°C = -459.69°F$$

K = Kelvin (Absolute temperature). This scale is based on the average kinetic energy per molecule of a perfect gas and uses the same size unit as the Celsius scale, but the degree symbol (°) is not used. Zero (0K) on the scale is the temperature at which a perfect gas has lost all of its energy.

General Science 321

Sound Intensities

Decibels	Degree	Loudness or Feeling
225	Deafening	12" cannon @ 12 ft, in front & below
194		Saturn rocket, 50# of TNT @ 10'
140		Artillery fire, jet aircraft, ram jet
130		Threshold of pain
		>130 causes immediate ear damage
		Propeller aircraft at 5 meters
		Hydraulic press, pneumatic rock drill
120		Thunder, diesel engine room
		Nearby riviter
110		Close to a train, ball mill
100	Very Loud	Boiler factory, home lawn mower
		Car horn at 5 meters, wood saw
90		Symphony or a band
		>90 regularly can cause ear damage
		Noisy factory
		Truck without muffler
80	Loud	Inside a high speed auto
		Police whistle, electric shaver
		Noisy office, alarm clock
70		Average radio
		Normal street noise
60	Moderate	Normal conversation, close up
50		Normal office noise, quiet stream
45		To awaken a sleeping person
40	Faint	Normal private office noise
		Residential neighborhood, no cars
30		Quiet conversation, recording studio
20	Very Faint	Inside an empty theater
		Ticking of a watch
		Rustle of leaves
		Whisper
10		Sound proof room
		Threshold of hearing
0		Absolute silence

Sound intensities are typically measured in decibels (db). A decibel is defined as 10 times the logarithm of the power ratio (power ratio is the ratio of the intensity of the sound to the intensity of an arbitrary standard point.) Normally a change of 1 db is the smallest volume change detectable by the human ear.

Sound intensity is also defined in terms of energy (erg) transmitted per second over a 1 square centimeter surface. This energy is proportional to the velocity of propagation of the sound. The energy density in $erg/cm^3 = 2 \pi^2$ x density in g/cm^3 x frequency^2 in Hz x amplitude^2 in cm.

Sound Intensities

Permissible Noise Exposures

Hours Duration per Day	Sound Level in Decibels (Slow Response)
8	90
6	92
4	95
3	97
2	100
1.5	102
1	105
0.5	110
0.25	115

The above restrictions are based on the *Occupational Safety and Health Act of 1970*. That Code basically states that if the above exposures are exceeded, then hearing protection must be worn. Note that these are based on the "A scale" of a standard sound level meter at slow response and will change if some other standard is used. See the *OSHA Section 1910.95* for additional details on the differences.

Perception of Changes in Sound

Sound Level Change in Decibels	Perception
3	Barely perceptible
5	Clearly perceptible
10	Twice as loud

Note that the sound level scale in decibels is a logarithmic rather than linear scale. A sound level change of 3 decibels is double (or half) of the previous power level. The ear registers this as just noticeable. A change in power level of 10 decibels is a power change of 10 times, and the ear judges this as only twice (or half) as loud.

These relationships do not hold true at all power levels or at all frequencies, as the ear is a very non-linear device. See Fletcher-Munson hearing curves published in books on hearing.

Some human ears can hear sounds in the frequency range of 20Hz to 20,000Hz, however, the hearing for most people is limited to about 30Hz to 15,000Hz

Human Body Composition

Element	Percent	Pounds	Kilograms
Oxygen	65.	97.5	44.2
Carbon	18.	27.0	12.2
Hydrogen	10.	15.0	6.8
Nitrogen	3.	4.5	2.0
Calcium	1.5	2.25	1.0
Phosphorus	1.0	1.50	0.68
Sulfur	0.25	0.375	0.170
Potassium	0.20	0.300	0.136
Chlorine	0.15	0.225	0.102
Sodium	0.15	0.225	0.102
Magnesium	0.05	0.075	0.034
Iron	0.006	0.009	0.004
Fluorine	0.0037	0.00555	0.00252
Zinc	0.0032	0.00480	0.00218
Silicon	0.0020	0.00300	0.00136
Zirconium	0.0006	0.00090	0.00041
Rubidium	0.00046	0.00069	0.00031
Strontium	0.00046	0.00069	0.00031
Bromine	0.00029	0.000435	0.000197
Lead	0.00017	0.000255	0.000116
Niobium	0.00016	0.000240	0.000109
Copper	0.00010	0.000150	0.000068
Aluminum	0.000087	0.0001305	0.0000592
Cadmium	0.000072	0.0001080	0.0000490
Boron	0.000069	0.0001035	0.0000469
Barium	0.000031	0.0000465	0.0000211
Arsenic	0.000026	0.0000390	0.0000177
Vanadium	0.000026	0.0000390	0.0000177
Tin	0.000024	0.0000360	0.0000163
Mercury	0.000019	0.0000285	0.0000129
Selenium	0.000019	0.0000285	0.0000129
Manganese	0.000017	0.0000255	0.0000116
Iodine	0.000016	0.0000240	0.0000109
Gold	0.000014	0.0000210	0.0000095
Nickel	0.000014	0.0000210	0.0000095
Molybdenum	0.000013	0.0000195	0.0000088
Titanium	0.000013	0.0000195	0.0000088
Tellurium	0.000012	0.0000180	0.0000082
Antimony	0.000011	0.0000165	0.0000075
Lithium	0.0000031	0.00000465	0.00000211
Chromium	0.0000024	0.00000360	0.00000163
Cesium	0.0000021	0.00000315	0.00000143
Cobalt	0.0000021	0.00000315	0.00000143
Silver	0.0000010	0.00000150	0.00000068
Uranium	0.00000013	0.000000195	0.000000088
Beryllium	0.00000005	0.000000075	0.000000034
Radium	0.0000000000001	0.00000000000021	0.000000000001

Mass of the element assumes an average body mass of 150 pounds (68.04 kilograms). Source: Geigy Scientific Tables, Ciba-Geigy Limited, Basle, Switzerland, 1984

Ideal Body Weight vs. Height

Height in Feet–Inches	Small Frame (lbs)	Medium Frame (lbs)	Large Frame (lbs)
MEN			
5–2	128–134	131–141	138–150
5–3	130–136	133–143	140–153
5–4	132–138	135–145	142–156
5–5	134–140	137–148	144–160
5–6	136–142	139–151	146–164
5–7	138–145	142–154	149–168
5–8	140–148	145–157	152–172
5–9	142–151	148–160	155–176
5–10	144–154	151–163	158–180
5–11	146–157	154–166	161–184
6–0	149–160	157–170	164–188
6–1	152–164	160–174	168–192
6–2	155–168	164–178	172–197
6–3	158–172	167–182	176–202
6–4	162–176	171–187	181–207

Height in Feet–Inches	Small Frame (lbs)	Medium Frame (lbs)	Large Frame (lbs)
WOMEN			
4–10	102–111	109–121	118–131
4–11	103–113	111–123	120–134
5–0	104–115	113–126	122–137
5–1	106–118	115–129	125–140
5–2	108–121	118–132	128–143
5–3	111–124	121–135	131–147
5–4	114–127	124–138	134–151
5–5	117–130	127–141	137–155
5–6	120–133	130–144	140–159
5–7	123–136	133–147	143–163
5–8	126–139	136–150	146–167
5–9	129–142	139–153	149–170
5–10	132–145	142–156	152–173
5–11	135–148	145–159	155–176
6–0	138–151	148–162	158–179

Based on data from *Metropolitan Life Insurance Company*

Physical Growth % – BOYS

Select the age in years, read the weight/height on the same row and then read the top line for the Percentile category.

Age in Years	Boys Weight (Pounds) Percentile						
	5%	10%	25%	50%	75%	90%	95%
2	23	24	26	28	30	32	33
3	27	28	29	32	34	37	39
4	30	31	33	36	39	42	45
5	34	35	37	41	45	49	52
6	37	39	42	46	51	56	60
7	41	43	47	51	57	63	68
8	46	48	51	57	64	72	78
9	50	52	57	63	71	81	89
10	55	58	63	71	81	93	102
11	61	64	71	80	91	105	116
12	67	71	79	90	103	119	131
13	75	80	89	101	116	133	146
14	85	90	100	113	129	147	160
15	95	100	111	125	142	160	174
16	104	110	121	135	152	172	186
17	112	118	128	143	161	181	196
18	117	123	134	148	167	188	203

Age in Years	Boys Height (Inches) Percentile						
	5%	10%	25%	50%	75%	90%	95%
2	31.8	32.3	33.1	34.0	35.0	35.8	36.3
3	35.1	35.6	36.5	37.4	38.6	39.5	40.1
4	37.6	38.2	39.2	40.4	41.5	42.5	43.1
5	39.9	40.6	41.7	43.0	44.2	45.3	46.0
6	42.2	43.0	44.2	45.5	46.9	48.1	48.8
7	44.6	45.3	46.6	48.0	49.5	50.8	51.6
8	46.8	47.6	48.9	50.4	52.0	53.4	54.3
9	48.7	49.6	51.0	52.7	54.3	55.8	56.7
10	50.5	51.4	52.9	54.7	56.4	58.0	59.0
11	52.1	53.1	54.7	56.6	58.5	60.2	61.2
12	54.1	55.1	56.8	58.8	60.8	62.6	63.7
13	56.5	57.6	59.5	61.6	63.7	65.6	66.7
14	59.3	60.5	62.5	64.6	66.7	68.6	69.7
15	61.7	62.9	64.9	67.0	69.0	70.8	71.8
16	63.3	64.5	66.3	68.4	70.3	72.0	73.0
17	64.2	65.3	67.1	69.0	70.9	72.6	73.6
18	64.7	65.7	67.5	69.4	71.3	72.9	73.9

Data from the *National Center for Health Statistics (NCHS)*
Hyattsville, Maryland. Year 2000

Physical Growth % – GIRLS

Select the age in years, read the weight/height on the same row and then read the top line for the Percentile category.

Age in Years	Girls Weight (Pounds) Percentile						
	5%	10%	25%	50%	75%	90%	95%
2	23	23	25	27	29	31	32
3	26	27	28	31	33	36	38
4	29	30	32	36	38	42	45
5	32	34	36	40	44	49	52
6	36	38	41	45	50	56	60
7	40	42	46	50	57	64	69
8	44	47	51	57	64	73	80
9	49	52	57	64	73	84	92
10	55	58	64	73	84	97	106
11	61	65	72	82	95	110	121
12	69	73	81	92	107	123	136
13	76	81	89	101	117	135	149
14	84	88	97	109	125	145	160
15	90	94	103	115	131	151	167
16	96	99	107	119	135	155	172
17	98	102	110	122	137	158	175
18	100	104	112	124	140	161	178

Age in Years	Girls Height (Inches) Percentile						
	5%	10%	25%	50%	75%	90%	95%
2	31.2	31.7	32.5	33.5	34.4	35.2	35.7
3	34.6	35.1	36.0	37.1	38.1	39.1	39.7
4	37.0	37.6	38.6	39.8	41.0	42.0	42.7
5	39.5	40.2	41.3	42.5	43.8	45.0	45.7
6	42.1	42.8	43.9	45.3	46.7	48.0	48.8
7	44.5	45.2	46.5	47.9	49.4	50.8	51.7
8	46.7	47.5	48.8	50.3	51.9	53.4	54.3
9	48.5	49.3	50.8	52.4	54.1	55.7	56.6
10	50.2	51.1	52.6	54.4	56.2	57.9	58.9
11	52.1	53.1	54.9	56.8	58.7	60.5	61.6
12	54.8	55.9	57.7	59.6	61.6	63.3	64.4
13	57.4	58.4	60.1	61.9	63.8	65.4	66.4
14	58.9	59.9	61.4	63.2	64.9	66.5	67.4
15	59.6	60.5	62.0	63.7	65.5	67.0	68.0
16	59.8	60.7	62.3	64.0	65.7	67.3	68.2
17	60.0	60.9	62.4	64.1	65.9	67.4	68.3
18	60.0	61.0	62.5	64.2	65.9	67.5	68.4

Data from the *National Center for Health Statistics (NCHS)* Hyattsville, Maryland. Year 2000.

Life Expectancy Statistics

Persons Age Today	Men Life Expecancy	Women Life Expectancy	Persons Age Today	Men Life Expecancy	Women Life Expectancy
0	73.26	79.26	32	43.28	48.50
1	72.85	78.78	33	42.36	47.53
2	71.89	77.82	34	41.43	46.57
3	70.92	76.84	35	40.51	45.62
4	69.94	75.86	36	39.59	44.66
5	68.96	74.87	37	38.67	43.71
6	67.98	73.89	38	37.76	42.76
7	66.99	72.90	39	36.85	41.81
8	66.01	71.91	40	35.94	40.86
9	65.02	70.92	41	35.03	39.92
10	64.03	69.93	42	34.13	38.98
11	63.04	68.94	43	33.24	38.05
12	62.05	67.95	44	32.35	37.12
13	61.06	66.96	45	31.46	36.19
14	60.08	65.98	46	30.59	35.26
15	59.11	65.00	47	29.71	34.34
16	58.16	64.02	48	28.85	33.43
17	57.21	63.04	49	27.99	32.52
18	56.27	62.07	50	27.13	31.61
19	55.34	61.10	51	26.28	30.72
20	54.41	60.13	52	25.44	29.82
21	53.48	59.16	53	24.61	28.94
22	52.56	58.19	54	23.78	28.06
23	51.64	57.22	55	22.97	27.19
24	50.72	56.24	56	22.17	26.34
25	49.79	55.27	57	21.37	25.49
26	48.86	54.30	58	20.60	24.64
27	47.93	53.33	59	19.83	23.81
28	47.00	52.36	60	19.07	22.99
29	46.07	51.39	61	18.33	22.18
30	45.14	50.43	62	17.60	21.38
31	44.21	49.46	63	16.89	20.60

Life Expectancy Statistics (cont.)

Persons Age Today	Men Life Expectancy	Women Life Expectancy	Persons Age Today	Men Life Expectancy	Women Life Expectancy
64	16.19	19.82	88	4.26	5.34
65	15.52	19.06	89	3.98	4.97
66	14.86	18.31	90	3.73	4.63
67	14.23	17.58	91	3.49	4.31
68	13.61	16.85	92	3.27	4.01
69	13.00	16.14	93	3.06	3.73
70	12.41	15.44	94	2.88	3.48
71	11.82	14.75	95	2.71	3.26
72	11.24	14.06	96	2.55	3.05
73	10.67	13.40	97	2.41	2.87
74	10.12	12.74	98	2.29	2.70
75	9.58	12.09	99	2.17	2.54
76	9.06	11.46	100	2.05	2.39
77	8.56	10.85	101	1.94	2.25
78	8.07	10.25	102	1.84	2.11
79	7.61	9.67	103	1.74	1.98
80	7.16	9.11	104	1.64	1.86
81	6.72	8.57	105	1.55	1.74
82	6.31	8.04	106	1.46	1.63
83	5.92	7.54	107	1.37	1.52
84	5.55	7.05	108	1.29	1.41
85	5.20	6.59	109	1.21	1.32
86	4.86	6.15	110	1.14	1.22
87	4.55	5.74	111	1.06	1.13

Source: Social Security Administration Period Life Table, 1997 (published April 14, 2000)

Firewood / Fuel Comparisons

Fuel Type	Million Btu /Unit (1)	Available Units /million Btu (2)	Comment
Coals:			75% efficient
Anthracite	26.27/ton	0.0508	
Bituminous			
low/med volatile	28.72/ton	0.0464	
high volatile	24.74/ton	0.0539	
Subbituminous	19.19/ton	0.0695	
Lignite	13.95/ton	0.0956	
Charcoal	25.00/ton	0.0533	
Electricity: [3]	0.0034/kWh	308.5	95% efficient
Gases: [3]			
Butane	3.261/Mcf	0.3931	78% efficient
Methane	1.016/Mcf	1.230	80% efficient
Natural Gas	1.049/Mcf	1.192	80% efficient
Producer Gas	0.170/Mcf	7.347	80% efficient
Propane	2.531/Mcf	0.5065	78% efficient
Oils:			80% efficient
#1 Fuel Oil	0.1391/gallon	8.985	
#2 Fuel Oil	0.1426/gallon	8.766	
#4 Fuel Oil	0.1472/gallon	8.492	
#5 Fuel Oil	0.1508/gallon	8.289	
#6 Fuel Oil	0.1538/gallon	8.129	
Heating Oil	0.1342/gallon	9.313	
Kerosene	0.1308/gallon	9.556	
Woods:			55% efficient
Apple	28.72/cord	0.0633	L–smoke, L–spark
Ash	22.30/cord	0.0815	
Aspen	16.57/cord	0.1098	M–smoke, H–spark
Basswood	14.77/cord	0.1231	
Beech	23.33/cord	0.0779	
Birch	21.71/cord	0.0837	
Boxelder	18.10/cord	0.1005	
Buckeye	13.40/cord	0.1357	
Butternut	15.40/cord	0.1181	
Catalpa	16.40/cord	0.1109	
Cherry	21.30/cord	0.0854	
Chestnut	12.90/cord	0.1409	
Coffeetree	21.60/cord	0.0842	
Cottonwood	15.86/cord	0.1146	M–smoke, L–spark
Dogwood	27.00/cord	0.0673	
Douglas Fir	26.35/cord	0.0690	H–smoke, M–spark
Elm	19.77/cord	0.0920	M–smoke, M–spark
Hackberry	21.00/cord	0.0866	
Hemlock	16.91/cord	0.1076	
Hickory	29.21/cord	0.0622	L–smoke, L–spark
Ironwood	26.00/cord	0.0699	
Larch (Eastern)	18.65/cord	0.0975	
Locust	27.30/cord	0.0666	
Maple	21.59/cord	0.0842	L–smoke, L–spark
Mulberry	25.80/cord	0.0705	
Oak (Red & Wht)	26.39/cord	0.0689	L–smoke, L–spark

Fuel Type	Million Btu /Unit [1]	Available Units /million Btu [2]	Comment
Osage Orange	32.90/cord	0.0553	
Pine:			
Lodgepole	19.25/cord	0.0944	M–smoke, M–spark
Pinon	33.50/cord	0.0543	M–smoke, M–spark
Ponderosa	18.72/cord	0.0972	M–smoke, M–spark
Tamarack	21.15/cord	0.0860	
White	14.53/cord	0.1251	M–smoke, H–spark
Yellow	22.00/cord	0.0826	
Redcedar (East.)	19.80/cord	0.0918	
Spruce	15.98/cord	0.1138	M–smoke, H–spark
Sycamore	19.50/cord	0.0932	
Walnut (Black)	21.50/cord	0.0846	
Willow	13.15/cord	0.1383	

"L–" is Low, "M–" is Medium, and "H–" is High

To calculate the actual cost of heat for each fuel: Multiply the "Available Units/million Btu" by the current cost per unit. For example, if natural gas is currently $4.60 per Mcf, the cost of 1 million Btu is $4.60 x 1.192 = $5.48. For Pinon Pine, at $150/cord, the cost of 1 million Btu is $150 x 0.0543 = $8.15. Note that the wood efficiency can vary greatly, depending on moisture content and efficiency of the furnace, stove, or fireplace.

Notes:
(1) Million Btu/Unit defines the average amount of heat per unit that is available for that fuel, assuming 100% burning efficiency. For example, Aspen contains 16,570,000 Btu per dry cord.
(2) Available Units/million Btu defines the actual number of units required to produce 1,000,000 Btu. The efficiency of burning (shown in the Comment column) is considered, as well as the moisture content of wood (average 20% moisture for dry wood). For example, 0.1098 cords of Aspen burning at 55% efficiency will produce 1,000,000 Btu.
(3) kWh=Kilowatt Hours   Mcf=Thousand Cubic Feet

Sources:
1993 ASHRAE Handbook - Fundamentals, American Society of Heating, Refrigerating and Air-Conditioning Engineers, Inc., Atlanta, GA 30329
Blair & Ketchum's Country Journal, 1977, Country Journal Publishing Co., Brattleboro, VT 05301
Encyclopedia of Energy, 3rd Edition, 1976, McGraw-Hill, New York, NY
Energy Deskbook, Samuel Classtone, June 1982, DOE/IR/05114-1, US Dept. of Energy, Oak Ridge, TN 37830
Energy Reference Handbook, 2nd Edition, 1977, Government Institutes, Inc., Washington, DC 20014
Firewood Fact Sheet, Colorado State Forest Service
Firewood Facts, October 1987, The Family Handyman
Fuel Oil Facts, www.fueloil.com
Heat Values of Wood, www.hearth.com
HVAC Field Manual, R.O. Parmley, 1988, McGraw-Hill, New York, NY
Mark's Standard Handbook for Mechanical Engineers, 10th Edition, 1996, McGraw-Hill, New York, NY
Mechanical Engineers' Handbook, 1986, John Wiley & Sons, New York, NY
Natural Gas Facts, www.naturalgas.com
Nebraska Fuelwood Specifications
Wood Power, Its Promises & Problems, N. Engalichev & V.K. Mathur, February 1980, University of New Hampshire, Durham, NH 03824

Electromagnetic Frequency Spectrum

Frequency (Wavelength)	Name
0 Hertz................................	Steady direct current
15–20,000 Hz........................	Audio frequencies
30–15,000 Hz........................	Normal human hearing range
16–4186.01 Hz......................	Standard musical scales
Note: – Audio is mechanical not electromagnetic	
300-3000Hz (1,000-100km)	VF – Voice Frequency
10–16 kHz	ultrasonic
3–30 Hz (100Mm–10Mm)	ELF – Extremely Low Frequency
30–300 Hz (10Mm–1Mm)	SLF – Super Low Frequency
300-3000 Hz (1Mm–0.1Mm)	ULF – Ultra Low Frequency
3–30 kHz (100,000–10,000m)	VLF – Very Low Frequency
30 kHz to 30,000 MHz.............	Radio frequencies
30–300 kHz (10,000–1,000m)	LF – Low Frequency
30–535 kHz	Marine com & navigation, aero nav.
153-279 kHz	LW – Long Wave
531-1620 kHz	MW - Medium Wave
2310 - 25820 kHz	SW - Short Wave
300–3,000 kHz (1,000–100m) .	MF – Medium Frequency
535–1,705 kHz	AM broadcast bands
1,800–2,000 kHz	Amateur band, 160 meter
3–30 MHz (100–10m)	HF – High Frequency
3.5–3.75 MHz	Amateur band, 80 meter
3.75-4.0 Mhz	Amateur band, 75 meter
7–7.3 MHz	Amateur band, 40 meter
10.10–10.15MHz....................	Amateur band, 30 meter
14.0–14.35 MHz.....................	Amateur band, 20 meter
18.068–18.168MHz.................	Amateur band, 17 meter
21–21.45 MHz.......................	Amateur band, 15 meter
26.95–27.54 MHz...................	Industrial, scientific, & medical
24.89–24.99 MHz...................	Amateur band, 12 meter
28–29.7 MHz.........................	Amateur band, 10 meter
26.965–27.405 MHz................	Citizens band (Class D)
30–300 MHz (10–1m)	VHF – Very High Frequency
30–50 MHz............................	Police, fire, forest, highway, railroad
50–54 MHz............................	Amateur band, 6 meter
54–72 MHz............................	TV channels 2 to 4
72–76 MHz............................	Government, Aero. Marker 75MHz
76–88 MHz............................	TV channels 5 and 6
88–108 MHz..........................	FM broadcast band
108–117.95 MHz....................	Aeronautical navigation
118–135.95 MHz....................	Civil Aviation Communication Band

Electromagnetic Frequency Spectrum

Frequency (Wavelength)	Name
148–174 MHz	Government
144–148 MHz	Amateur band, 2 meter
174–216 MHz	TV channels 7 to 13
216–470 MHz	Amateur, government, CB Band, non–government, fixed or mobile aeronautical navigation
219–225 MHz	Amateur band, 1-1/4 meter
225–400 MHz	Military
420–450 MHz	Amateur band, 70 cm
462.55–563.20 MHz	Citizens band (Class A)
300–3,000 MHz(100–10cm)	UHF – Ultra High Frequency
470–890 MHz	TV channels 14 to 69
806–890 MHz	Cellular telephone
890–3,000 MHz	Aero navigation, amateur bands, government & non–government, fixed and mobile
1,300–1,600 MHz	Radar band
3,000–30,000 MHz(10–1cm)	SHF – Super High Frequency Government and non–government, amateur bands, radio navigation
30,000 MHz to 300 GHz (1–0.1cm)	EHF–Extremely High Frequency (weather, experimental, radar government)
30–0.76 μm	Infrared light and heat
0.76–0.39 μm	Visible light
6,470–7,000 ångstroms	Red light
5,850–6,740 ångstroms	Orange light
5,750–5,850 ångstroms	Yellow light
5,560–5,750 ångstroms	Maximum visibility
4,912–5,560 ångstroms	Green light
4,240–4,912 ångstroms	Blue light
4,000–4,240 ångstroms	Violet light
0.39–0.032 μm	Ultraviolet light
0.032–0.00001 μm	X-rays
0.00001–0.0000006 μm	Gamma rays
0.0005 ångstroms	Cosmic rays

μm = micrometer(10^{-6}m): m = meter: cm = centimeter

Hz= hertz: MHz= megahertz (10^6 Hz): kHz= kilohertz(10^3 Hz):

GHz= gigahertz(10^9 Hz): 1 ångstrom = 10^{-10} meters

Acceleration Due to Gravity

Degrees Latitude	Acceleration Due to Gravity at Sea Level Feet/second^2	Cm/second^2
0	32.08730	978.0327
5	32.08858	978.0719
10	32.09240	978.1884
15	32.09865	978.3786
20	32.10712	978.6370
25	32.11757	978.9556
30	32.12969	979.3249
31	32.13228	979.4039
32	32.13492	979.4843
33	32.13761	979.5662
34	32.14034	979.6494
35	32.14310	979.7337
36	32.14591	979.8192
37	32.14874	979.9056
38	32.15161	979.9930
39	32.15450	980.0811
40	32.15741	980.1698
41	32.16034	980.2592
42	32.16329	980.3489
43	32.16625	980.4391
44	32.16921	980.5294
45	32.17218	980.6199
46	32.17515	980.7104
47	32.17811	980.8008
48	32.18107	980.8910
49	32.18402	980.9809
50	32.18696	981.0704
51	32.18987	981.1593
52	32.19277	981.2476
53	32.19564	981.3351
54	32.19848	981.4217
55	32.20130	981.5074
56	32.20407	981.5921
57	32.20681	981.6755
58	32.20951	981.7577
59	32.21216	981.8385
60	32.21476	981.9178
65	32.22694	982.2890
70	32.23746	982.6096
75	32.24599	982.8698
80	32.25228	983.0616
85	32.25614	983.1791
90	32.25744	983.2186

Acceleration Due to Gravity (cm/s^2) at Altitude (h) =
Acceleration Due to Gravity (cm/s^2) at Sea Level − 0.3086h
where h is the altitude in kilometers.

Planetary Data

In the following tables, d=day, h=hour, m=minute, s or sec=second

SUN:

Mass	4.3852 x 10^{30} lb; 1.9891 x 10^{30} kg
Density	87.9 lb/ft^3; 1,408 kg/m^3
Mean Radius	432,474 mi; 696,000 km
Gravity relative to earth	28
Rotation period	25 d, 9 h, 7 m, 12 s
Escape velocity	383.8 mi/sec; 617.7 km/sec

MERCURY:

Mass	7.280 x 10^{23} lb; 3.302 x 10^{23} kg
Density	338.8 lb/ft^3; 5,427 kg/m^3
Mean Radius	1,516 mi; 2,440 km
Max distance from the sun	43,384,000 mi; 69,820,000 km
Min distance from the sun	28,583,000 mi; 46,000,000 km
Gravity relative to earth	0.378
Rotation period	58 d, 15 h, 36 m, 0 s
Revolution time around sun	87 d, 23 h, 15 m, 21 s
Orbital velocity	29.75 mi/sec; 47.87 km/sec
Number of moons	0
Escape velocity	2.7 mi/sec; 4.3 km/sec

VENUS:

Mass	1.073 x 10^{25} lb; 4.869 x 10^{24} kg
Density	327.3 lb/ft^3; 5,243 kg/m^3
Mean Radius	3760 mi; 6,052 km
Max distance from the sun	67,692,000 mi; 108,940,000 km
Min distance from the sun	66,785,000 mi; 107,480,000 km
Gravity relative to earth	0.907
Rotation period	243 d, 0 h, 30 m, 0 s
Revolution time around sun	224 d, 16 h, 49 m, 26 s
Orbital velocity	21.76 mi/sec; 35.02 km/sec
Number of moons	0
Escape velocity	6.44 mi/sec; 10.4 km/sec

EARTH:

Mass	1.317 x 10^{25} lb, 5.9736 x 10^{24} kg
Density	344.3 lb/ft^3; 5,515 kg/m^3
Mean Radius	3959 mi; 6,371 km
Max distance from the sun	94,511,000 mi; 152,100,000 km
Min distance from the sun	91,397,000 mi; 147,090,000 km
Gravity	32.1 ft/sec^2; 9.78 m/sec^2
Rotation period	23 h, 56 m, 4 s
Revolution time around sun	365 d, 6 h, 8 m, 38 s
Orbital velocity	18.5 mi/sec; 29.8 km/sec
Number of moons	1 (no official name other than "The Moon". Luna is latin for moon, selene is greek for moon.)
Escape velocity	6.95 mi/sec; 11.2 km/sec

Planetary Data

EARTH'S MOON:
Mass.....................................1.620×10^{23} lb, 7.349×10^{22} kg
Density.................................209.1 lb/ft^3; 3,350 kg/m^3
Mean Radius.........................1,079 mi; 1,737 km
Max distance from earth........251,970 mi; 405,500 km
Min distance from earth.........225,740 mi; 363,300 km
Gravity relative to earth.........0.17
Rotation period.....................27 d, 7 h, 43 m, 40 s
Orbital velocity.....................0.64 mi/sec; 1.02 km/sec
Escape velocity.....................1.48 mi/sec; 2.38 km/sec

MARS:
Mass.....................................1.415×10^{24} lb, 6.419×10^{23} kg
Density.................................245.5 lb/ft^3; 3,933 kg/m^3
Mean Radius.........................2106 mi; 3,390 km
Max distance from the sun......154,860,000 mi; 249,230,000 km
Min distance from the sun.......128,388,000 mi; 206,620,000 km
Gravity relative to earth.........0.38
Rotation period.....................1 d, 0 h, 37 m, 22 s
Revolution time around sun.....686 d, 23 h, 31 m, 12 s
Orbital velocity.....................14.99 mi/sec; 24.13 km/sec
Number of moons...................2: Deimos, Phobos
Escape velocity.....................3.13 mi/sec; 5.03 km/sec

JUPITER:
Mass.....................................4.186×10^{27} lb, 1.8986×10^{27} kg
Density (mean)......................82.8 lb/ft^3; 1,326 kg/m^3
Mean Radius.........................43,441 mi; 69,911 km
Max distance from the sun......507,424,000 mi; 816,260,000 km
Min distance from the sun.......460,138,000 mi; 740,520,000 km
Gravity relative to earth.........2.364
Rotation period.....................9 h, 55 m, 30 s
Revolution time around sun.....12 years (4,332 d, 14 h, 8 m, 9 s)
Orbital velocity.....................8.12 mi/sec; 13.07 km/sec
Number of moons...................61: Adrastea, Metis, Amalthea, Io,
    Thebe, Europa, Ganymede, Callisto, Leda, Himalia, Lysithea,
    Elara, Ananke, Carme, Pasiphae, Sinope & 45 others
Escape velocity.....................37.0 mi/sec; 59.5 km/sec

SATURN:
Mass.....................................1.253×10^{27} lb, 5.685×10^{26} kg
Density (mean)......................42.9 lb/ft^3; 687 kg/m^3
Radius (mean volumetric).......36,184 mi; 58,232 km
Max distance from the sun......941,067,000 mi; 1,514,500,000 km
Min distance from the sun.......840,436,000 mi; 1,352,550,000 km
Gravity relative to earth.........0.916
Rotation period.....................10 h, 39 m, 21 s
Revolution time around sun.....29 years (10,759 d, 5 h, 16 m, 47 s)
Orbital velocity.....................6.02 mi/sec; 9.69 km/sec

Planetary Data

SATURN (cont.):

Number of moons ....31: Atlas, Prometheus, Pandora, Janus, Epimetheus, Mimas, Enceladus, Tethys, Telesto, Calypso, Dione, Helene, Rhea, Titan, Hyperion, Iapetus, Phoebe, Pan and 13 others.

Escape velocity ....22.1 mi/sec; 35.5 km/sec

URANUS:

Mass...1.914 x 10^{26} lb, 8.683 x 10^{25}kg
Density ....79.3 lb/ft^3; 1,270 kg/m^3
Mean Radius ....15,759 mi; 25,362 km
Max distance from the sun ....1,866,363,000 mi; 3,003,620,000 km
Min distance from the sun ....1,703,365,000mi; 2,741,300,000 km
Gravity relative to earth 0.889
Rotation period ....17 h, 14 m. 23 s
Revolution time around sun .....84 years (30,685 d, 9 h, 36 m)
Orbital velocity ....4.23 mi/sec; 6.81 km/sec
Number of moons ....26: Cordelia, Ophelia, Bianca, Cressida, Desdemona, Juliet, Portia, Rosalind, Belinda, Puck, Miranda, Ariel, Umbriel, Titania, Oberon, Caliban, Prospero, Setebos, Stephano, Sycorax, Trinculo, and 5 unnamed.

Escape velocity ....13.2 mi/sec; 21.3 km/sec

NEPTUNE:

Mass..2.26 x 10^{26} lb, 1.024 x 10^{26}kg
Density ....102.3 lb/ft^3; 1,638 kg/m^3
Mean Radius ....15,301 mi; 24,624 km
Max distance from sun ....2,824,548,000 mi; 4,545,670,000 km
Min distance from sun ....2,761,653,000 mi; 4,444,450,000 km
Gravity relative to earth 1.12
Rotation period ....16 h, 6 m, 35 s
Revolution time around sun .....165 years (60,189 d)
Orbital velocity ....3.37 mi/sec; 5.43 km/sec
Number of moons ....13: Triton, Nereid, Naiad, Despina, Thalassa, Galatea, Larissa, Proteus and 5 unnamed.

Escape velocity ....14.6 mi/sec; 23.5 km/sec

PLUTO:

Mass..2.76 x 10^{22} lb, 1.25 x 10^{22}kg
Density ....109.2 lb/ft^3; 1,750 kg/m^3
Mean Radius ....742.5 mi; 1,195 km
Max distance from sun ....4,538,700,000 mi; 7,304,330,000 km
Min distance from sun ....2,755,775,000 mi; 4,434,990,000 km
Gravity relative to earth 0.059
Rotation period ....6 d, 9 h, 17 m, 34 s
Revolution time around sun .....248 years (90,465 d)
Orbital velocity ....2.93 mi/sec; 4.72 km/sec
Number of moons ....1: Charon
Escape velocity ....0.75 mi/sec; 1.2 km/sec

Torino Asteroid-Comet Destruction Scale

Torino damage potential scale for asteroid and comet impacts.

- 0 ······ The likelihood of a collision is zero, or well below the chance that a random object of the same size will strike the earth within the next few decades. This designation also applies to any small object to reach the earth's surface intact.

- 1 ······ The chance of collision is extremely unlikely, about the same as a random object of the same size striking the earth within the next few decades.

- 2 ······ A somewhat close, but not unusual, encounter. Collision is very unlikely.

- 3 ······ A close encounter, with 1% or greater chance of a collision capable of causing localized destruction.

- 4 ······ A close encounter, with 1% or greater chance of a collision capable of causing regional destruction.

- 5 ······ A close encounter, with a significant threat of a collision capable of causing regional devastation.

- 6 ······ A close encounter, with a significant threat of a collision capable of causing global catastrophe.

- 7 ······ A close encounter, with an extremely significant threat of a collision capable of causing global catastrophe.

- 8 ······ A collision capable of causing localized destruction. Such events occur somewhere on earth between once per 50 years and once per 1,000 years.

- 9 ······ A collision capable of causing regional destruction. Such events occur between once per 1,000 years and once per 100,000 years.

- 10 ····· A collision capable of causing a global climatic catastrophe. Such events occur between once per 100,000 years or less often.

NOTES

Examples of earth/asteroid impacts: the object which impacted and formed Meteor Crater in Arizona would have rated an 8 on the scale; the object which exploded over Tunguska, Siberia in 1908 would have rated an 8 on the scale; and the object which struck the earth 65 million years ago near what is now the town of Chicxulub, Mexico and ended the reign of the dinosaurs would have rated a 10 on the scale.

Developed by Richard P. Binzel, accepted by the International Astronomical Union (IAU) June 1999.

Source: Assessing the Hazard: The Development of the Torino Scale, Richard P. Binzel, The Planetary Report, Volume XIX, Number 6, November/December 1999.
On the web see http://128.102.38.40/impact/torino.cfm.

Geology

Dana's Manual of Mineralogy, Field Geologists' Manual and A Field Guide to Rocks and Minerals, Encyclopedia of Geochemistry ISBN 0412755009, The Continental Crust ISBN 0632011483, An Introduction to the Rock Forming Minerals ISBN 0582300940, webmineral.com, and Athena Minerology were used as source material for the Geology chapter, see page 2 for the reference.

(See also GENERAL SCIENCE on page 319)
(See also WEIGHTS OF MATERIALS on page 655)

Mineral Table Abbreviations

Abbreviations used in the "**Name**" column are:

(A)	=	Amphibole group
(B)	=	Bauxite component
(C)	=	Clay group or clay like
(Cb)	=	Carbonate group
(D)	=	Diopside series
(E)	=	Enstatite group
(F)	=	Feldspar group
(Fp)	=	Feldspathoid group
(G)	=	Garnet group
(H)	=	Hornblende
(J)	=	Jamesonite group
(M)	=	Mica group
(O)	=	Orthoclase
(Ov)	=	Olivine group
(P)	=	Pyroxene group
(R)	=	Rare Earth Oxide group
(S)	=	Spinel group
(Sc)	=	Scapolite series
(W)	=	Wolframite series
(Z)	=	Zeolite group

The "**Density**" column lists the density of the mineral in grams / cubic centimeter.

The "**Hard**" column lists hardness as defined by Mohs scale of hardness (see Mohs table, page 373, also in this geology section).

"**Sys**" column lists the crystal system of each mineral:

Is	=	Isometric
Hx	=	Hexagonal–Hexagonal
Tg	=	Trigonal (Hexagonal–rhombohedral)
Te	=	Tetragonal
Or	=	Orthorhombic
Mo	=	Monoclinic
Tr	=	Triclinic

Mineral Tables

Name	Composition	System	Density	Hard
Acanthite	Ag_2S	Mo	7.2-7.3	2
Achroite	Colorless Tourmaline			
Acmite (P)	$NaFe^{3+}Si_2O_6$	Mo	3.52	6-6.5
Actinolite (A)	$Ca_2(Mg,Fe^{2+})_5(Si_8O_{22})(OH)_2$	Mo	3.04	5.5
Adularia (O)	Clear orthoclase			
Agate	Banded Chalcedony			
Alabandite	MnS	Is	4	3.4-4
Alabaster	Fine-grained gypsum			
Albite (F)	$NaAlSi_3O_8$	Tr	2.62	7
Alexandrite	Chrysoberyl - gemstone			
Allanite	$(Ca,La,Ce,Y)_2(Al,Fe^{3+})_3(SiO_4)_3(OH)$	Mo	3.3-4.2	5.5
Allemontite	SbAs	Hx	6.15	3-4
Allophane (C)	$Al_2O_3 \cdot nSiO_2 \cdot nH_2O$ (variable)	Am	1.9	3
Almandine (G)	$Fe^{2+}_3Al_2(SiO_4)_3$ - red	Is	4.09-4.31	7-8
Altaite	PbTe	Is	8.14	2.5
Alunite	$KAl_3(SO_4)_2(OH)_6$	Tg	2.59-2.9	3.5-4
Amazonstone	Green Microcline			
Amblygonite	$(Li,Na)Al(PO_4)(F,OH)$	Tr	2.98-3.11	5.5-6
Amethyst	Purple quartz			
Amphibole	A group of minerals			
Analcime	$Na(AlSi_2O_6) \cdot H_2O$	Tr	2.3	5
Anatase	TiO_2	Te	3.9	5.5-6
Anauxite	Silicon-rich Kaolinite			
Andalusite	Al_2SiO_5	Or	3.15	6.5-7
Andesine (P)	$Ab_{70}An_{30}$-$Ab_{50}An_{50}$	Tr	2.67	7
Andradite (G)	$Ca_3Fe^{3+}_2(SiO_4)_3$	Is	3.7-4.1	6.5-7
Anglesite	$PbSO_4$	Or	6.3	2.5-3
Anhydrite	$CaSO_4$	Or	2.97	3.5
Ankerite (Cb)	$Ca(Fe^{2+},Mg,Mn)(CO_3)_2$	Rh	3.05	3.5-4
Annebergite	$Ni_3(AsO_4)_2 \cdot 8H_2O$	Mo	3.05	2
Anorthite (P)	$CaAl_2Si_2O_8$	Tr	2.73	6
Anorthoclase (O)	$(Na,K)AlSi_3O_8$	Tr	2.58	6
Anthophyllite (A)	$(Mg,Fe)_7(Si_8O_{22})(OH)_2$	Or	2.85-3.57	5-6
Antigorite	Serpentine			
Antimony	Sb	Tg	6.66	3-3.5
Antlerite	$Cu_3(SO_4)(OH)_4$	Or	3.9	3
Apatite	$Ca_5(PO_4)_3(F,OH,Cl)$	Hx	3.19	5
Apophyllite	$(K,Na)Ca_4Si_8O_{20}(F,OH) \cdot 8H_2O$	Te	2.34	4-5
Aquamarine	Green-blue beryl - gemstone			
Aragonite	$CaCO_3$	Or	2.93	3.5-4
Arfvedsonite (A)	$Na_3(Fe^{2+},Mg,Al)_5Si_8O_{22}(OH)_2$	Mo	3.44	5.5-6
Argentite	Ag_2S	Is	7.3	2-2.5
Arsenic	As	Tg	5.7	3.5
Arsenopyrite	FeAsS	Mo	6.07	5
Asbestos	A group of minerals			
Atacamite	$Cu_2Cl(OH)_3$	Or	3.76	3-3.5
Augite	$(Ca,Na)(Mg,Fe,Al,Ti)(Si,Al)_2O_6$	Mo	3.4	5-6.5
Aurichalcite	$(Zn,Cu)_5(CO_3)_2(OH)_6$	Mo	3.64-3.9	2
Autunite	$Ca(UO_2)_2(PO_4)_2 \cdot 10H_2O$	Te	3.15	2-2.5
Awaruite	Ni_3Fe to Ni_2Fe	Is	8	5
Axinite	$Ca_2(Fe^{2+},Mg,Mn)(BO_3)Si_4O_{12}(OH)$	Tr	3.28	6.5-7

Mineral Tables

Name	Composition	System	Density	Hard
Azurite	$Cu_3(CO_3)_2(OH)_2$	Mo	3.83	3.5-4
Balas Ruby	Red Spinel - gemstone			
Barite	$BaSO_4$	Or	4.48	3-3.5
Bastnaesite (R)	$(Ce,La)(CO_3)(F,OH)$	Hx	4.95	4-5
Bauxite	Aluminum hydroxide mixture			
Beidellite (C)	$Na_{.5}Al_3(Si_{3.5}Al_{.5}O_{10})(OH)_2 \cdot nH_2O$	Or	2.15	1-2
Bentonite (C)	Montmorillonite clay			
Beryl	$Be_3Al_2(Si_6O_{18})$	Hx	2.63-2.9	7.5-8
Biotite (M)	$K(Mg,Fe^{2+})_3(Al,Fe^{3+})Si_3O_{10}(OH)_2$	Mo	2.8-3.5	2.5-3
Bismite	Bi_2O_3	Mo	8.5-9.5	4-5
Bismuth	Bi	Tg	9.75	2-2.5
Black Jack	Sphalerite			
Blende	Sphalerite			
Bloodstone	Heliotrope			
Blue Vitriol	Chalcanthite			
Boehmite (B)	$AlO(OH)$	Or	3.03	3
Boracite	$Mg_3B_7O_{13}Cl$	Or	2.9	7
Borax	$Na_2B_4O_5(OH)_4 \cdot 8H_2O$	Mo	1.71	2-2.5
Bornite	Cu_5FeS_4	Or	5.09	3
Boulangerite	$Pb_5Sb_4S_{11}$	Mo	5.7-6.3	2.5
Brannerite	$(U,Ca,Ce)(Ti,Fe)_2O_6$	Mo	4.5-6.5	4-5
Braunite	$(Mn^{2+},Mn^{3+})_7SiO_{12}$	Te	4.76	6-6.5
Bravoite	$(Ni,Fe)S_2$	Is	5.01	6.5
Brochantite	$Cu_4(OH)_6SO_4$	Mo	3.97	3.5-4
Bromargyrite	$AgBr$	Is	5.8-6	1.5-2
Bronzite (E)	$(Mg,Fe)SiO_3$	Or	3.2-3.9	5.5-6
Brookite	TiO_2	Or	4.11	5.5-6
Brucite	$Mg(OH)_2$	Tg	2.39	2.5-3
Bytownite (P)	$Ab_{30}An_{70}-Ab_{10}An_{90}$	Tr	2.71	7
Cairngorm	Quartz - black to smoky			
Calamine	Hemimorphite			
Calaverite	$AuTe_2$	Mo	9.04	2.5
Calcite	$CaCO_3$	Tg	2.71	3
Californite	Idocrase - gemstone			
Calomel	Hg_2Cl_2	Te	6.45	1.5-2
Cancrinite (Fp)	$Na_6Ca_2Al_6Si_6O_{24}(CO_3)_2$	Hx	2.45	2.5
Carnallite	$KMgCl_3 \cdot 6H_2O$	Or	1.6	2.5
Carnelian	Chalcedony -red			
Carnotite	$K_2(UO_2)_2(VO_4)_2 \cdot 3H_2O$	Or	3.7-4.7	2
Cassiterite	SnO_2	Te	6.9	6-7
Cat's Eye	Chrysoberyl or quartz - gemstone			
Celestite	$SrSO_4$	Or	3.95	3-3.5
Celsian (F)	$BaAl_2Si_2O_8$	Mo	3.25	6-6.5
Cerargyrite	$AgCl$ - Chloroargyrite	Is	5.55	1-1.5
Cerussite (Cb)	$PbCO_3$	Or	6.58	3-3.5
Cervantite	Sb_2O_4	Or	6.5	4-5
Chabazite (Z)	$(Ca,Na_2,K_2,Mg)(Al_2Si_4O_{12}) \cdot 6H_2O$	Tg	2.09	4
Chalcanthite	$CuSO_4 \cdot 5H_2O$	Tr	2.21	2.5
Chalcedony	Cryptocrystalline quartz			
Chalcocite	Cu_2S	Or	5.5-5.8	2.5-3
Chalcopyrite	$CuFeS_2$	Te	4.19	3.5

Mineral Tables

Name	Composition	System	Density	Hard
Chalcotrichite	Cuprite - fibrous			
Chalk	Calcite - fine grained			
Chalybite	Siderite			
Chert	SiO_2 - cryptocrystalline quartz			
Chessylite	Azurite			
Chiastolite	Andalusite			
Chloanthite	Skutterudite - nickel variety			
Chlorite	$(Mg,Al,Fe)_6(Si,Al)_4O_{10}(OH)_8$	Mo	2.42	1-2
Chloritoid (M)	$(Fe^{2+},Mg,Mn)_2Al_4Si_2O_{10}(OH)_4$	Mo,Tr	3.51-3.8	6.5
Chondrodite	$(Mg,Fe)_5(SiO_4)_2(F,OH)_2$	Mo	3.15	6-6.5
Chromite	$Fe^{2+}Cr_2O_4$	Is	4.5-5.09	5.5
Chrysoberyl	$BeAl_2O_4$	Or	3.5-3.84	8.5
Chrysocolla	$(Cu,Al)_2H_2Si_2O_5(OH)_4 \cdot nH_2O$	Or	2-2.4	2.5-3.5
Chrysolite	Olivine			
Chrysoprase	Chalcedony - green			
Chrysotile	Serpentine asbestos			
Cinnibar	HgS	Tg	8.1	2-2.5
Cinnamon Stone	Grossularite garnet			
Citrine	Quartz - pale yellow			
Clay	A group of minerals			
Cleavelandite	Albite - white			
Cliachite	Al-hydroxide in bauxite			
Clinochlore	$(Mg,Fe^{2+})_5(Al,Si_3O_{10})(OH)_8$	Mo	2.65	2-2.5
Clinoclase	$Cu_3(AsO_4)(OH)_3$	Mo	4.29	2.5-3
Clinoenstatite (E)	$MgSiO_3$	Mo	3.4	5-6
Clinoferrosilite (E)	$(Fe,Mg)SiO_3$	Mo	4.1	5-6
Clinohumite	$(Mg,Fe^{2+})_9(SiO_4)_4(F,OH)_2$	Mo	3.26	6
Clinozoite	$Ca_2Al_3(SiO_4)_3(OH)$	Mo	3.34	7
Cobaltite	CoAsS	Or	6.33	5.5
Colemanite	$Ca_2B_6O_{11} \cdot 5H_2O$	Mo	2.42	4.5
Collophane	Apatite			
Columbite	$Fe^{2+}(Nb,Ta)_2O_6$	Or	5.3-7.3	6
Copper	Cu	Is	8.94	2.5-3
Copper glance	Chalcocite			
Coppery pyrites	Chalcopyrite			
Cordierite	$(Mg,Fe^{2+})_2Al_4Si_5O_{18}$	Or	2.55-2.77	7
Corundum	Al_2O_3	Tg	4.05	9
Covellite	CuS	Hx	4.68	1.5-2
Cristobalite	SiO_2	Te	2.27	6.5
Crocidolite	Riebeckite			
Crocoite	$PbCrO_4$	Mo	6	2.5-3
Cryolite	Na_3AlF_6	Mo	2.97	2.5-3
Cubanite	$CuFe_2S_3$	Or	4.7	3.5
Cummingtonite (A)	$(Fe^{2+},Mg)_7(Si_8O_{22})(OH)_2$	Mo	3.35	5-6
Cuprite	Cu_2O	Is	6.1	3.5-4
Cyanite	Kyanite			
Cymophane	Chrysoberyl			
Danburite	$CaB_2(SiO_4)_2$	Or	2.99	7
Datolite	$CaB(SiO_4)(OH)$	Mo	2.9	5.5
Davidite	Brannerite variety			
Demantoid	Andradite garnet - green gemstone			

Mineral Tables

Name	Composition	System	Density	Hard
Diallage	Diopside			
Diamond	C	Is	3.51	10
Diaspore	AlO(OH)	Or	3.4	6.5-7
Diatomite	Diatoms - siliceous			
Dichroite	Cordierite			
Dickite (C)	$Al_2Si_2O_5(OH)_4$ - Kaoline	Mo	2.6	1.5-2
Digenite	Cu_9S_5	Tg	5.6	2.5-3
Diopside (P)	$CaMg(SiO_3)_2$	Mo	3.3	6
Dioptase	$CuSiO_3(OH)_2$	Tg	3.31	5
Disthene	Kyanite			
Dolomite (Cb)	$CaMg(CO_3)_2$	Tg	2.84	3.5-4
Dry bone ore	Smithsonite			
Dumortierite	$(Al,Fe)_7(BO_3)(SiO_4)_3(O,OH)_3$	Or	3.34	8.5
Edenite (H)	$Ca_2NaMg_5(AlSi_7O_{22})(OH)_2$	Mo	3.02	6
Electrum	Au-Ag natural alloy			
Eleolite	Nepheline			
Embolite	$Ag(Cl,Br)$	Is	5.6	1-1.5
Emerald	Beryl - green gemstone			
Emery	Corundum with magnetite			
Enargite	Cu_3AsS_4	Or	4.45	3
Endlichite	Vanadinite - arsenic variety			
Enstatite (P)	$MgSiO_3$	Or	3.2	5.5
Epidote	$Ca_2(Al,Fe^{3+})_3(SiO_4)_3(OH)$	Mo	3.3-3.6	7
Epsomite	$MgSO_4 \cdot 7H_2O$ - Epsom salt	Or	1.67	2-2.5
Erythrite	$Co_3(AsO_4)_2 \cdot 8H_2O$	Mo	3.12	1.5-2
Essonite	Grossularite garnet			
Euclase	$BeAlSiO_4(OH)$	Mo	3.04	7.5
Euxenite	$(Y,Ce,Ca,U,Th)(Ti,Nb,Ta,Fe)_2O_6$	Or	4.84	6.5
Fahlore	Tetrahedrite			
Fayalite (Ov)	Fe_2SiO_4	Or	4.39	6.5
Feather ore	Jamesonite			
Feldspar (F)	A group of minerals			
Feldspathoid (Fp)	A group of minerals			
Ferberite	$FeWO_4$	Mo	7.45	4.5
Fergusonite (R)	$(La,Ce,Nd,Y)NbO_4$	Te	4.5-5.7	5.5-6.5
Ferrimolybdite	$Fe^{3+}_2(MoO_4)_3 \cdot 8H_2O$	Or	4-4.5	2.5-3
Ferrosilite (P)	$FeSiO_3$	Or	3.95	5-6
Fibrolite	Sillimanite			
Flint	SiO_2 - cryptocrystalline quartz			
Flos ferri	Aragonite - arborescent			
Fluorite	CaF_2	Is	3.13	4
Fool's gold	Pyrite			
Formanite	Fergusonite with Ta-Nb			
Forsterite (Ov)	Mg_2SiO_4	Or	3.27	6-7
Fowlerite	Rhodonite - zinc bearing			
Franklinite	$(Fe^{2+},Zn,Mn^{2+})(Fe^{3+},Mn^{3+})_2O_4$	Is	5.14	5.5-6
Freibergite	Tetrahedrite - silver bearing			
Gadolinite (R)	$(Y,REE)_2Fe^{2+}Be_2Si_2O_{10}$	Mo	4-4.5	6.5-7
Gahnite (S)	$ZnAl_2O_4$	Is	4-4.6	8
Galaxite (S)	$(Mn,Mg)(Al,Fe^{3+})_2O_4$	Is	4.23	7.5
Galena	PbS	Is	7.2-7.6	2.5

Mineral Tables

Name	Composition	System	Density	Hard
Garnet (G)	A group of minerals			
Garnierite	$(Ni,Mg)_xSi_yO_z$-H_2O	Or	2.41	3-4
Gaylussite	$Na_2Ca(CO_3)_2$-$5H_2O$	Mo	1.96	2.5
Gedrite (A)	Anthophyllite - Al variety			
Geocronite	$Pb_{14}(Sb,As)_6S_{23}$	Mo	6.4	2.5-3
Gersdorffite	NiAsS	Is	6.11	5.5
Geyserite	Opal			
Gibbsite	$Al(OH)_3$	Mo	2.34	2.5-3
Glauberite	$Na_2Ca(SO_4)_2$	Mo	2.77	2.5-3
Glaucodot	Danaite			
Glauconite (M)	$(K,Na)(Al,Fe^{3+},Mg)_2(Al,Si)_4O_{10}(OH)_2$	Mo	2.4-2.95	2
Glaucophane (A)	$Na_2(Mg,Fe^{2+})_3(Al,Si_4O_{11})_2$	Mo	3.07	6-6.5
Gmelinite (Z)	$(Na_2,Ca)(Al_2Si_4O_{12})$-$6H_2O$	Hx	2.09	4.5
Goethite	$FeO(OH)$	Or	3.3-4.3	5-5.5
Gold	Au	Is	17.64	2.5-3
Goslarite	$Zn(SO_4)$-$7H_2O$	Or	2	2-2.5
Graphite	C	Hx	2.16	1.5-2
Greenockite	CdS	Hx	3.98-5	3.5-4
Grossularite (S)	$Ca_3Al_2(SiO_4)_3$	Is	3.42-3.72	6.5-7.5
Gummite	Uraninite			
Gypsum	$CaSO_4$-$2H_2O$	Mo	2.3	2
Halite	NaCl - common salt	Is	2.17	2.5
Halloysite (C)	$Al_2Si_2O_5(OH)_4$	Tr	2-2.6	2
Harmotome	$(Ba,Na,K)_{1-2}(Al,Si)_8O_{16}$-$6H_2O$	Mo	2.46	4-5
Hastingsite (H)	$NaCa_2(Fe^{2+},Fe^{3+})_5Al_2Si_6O_{22}(OH)_2$	Mo	3.17-3.59	6
Hausmanite	$Mn^{2+}Mn^{3+}_2O_4$	Te	4.76	5.5
Hauynite (Fp)	$(Na,Ca)_{4-8}Al_6Si_6(O,S)_{24}$-$(SO_4,Cl)_{1-2}$	Is	2.45	5-6
Hectorite (C)	$Na_{0.3}(Mg,Li)_3Si_4O_{10}(OH)_2$	Mo	2-3	1-2
Hedenbergite	$CaFe^{2+}Si_2O_6$	Mo	3.55	5-6
Heliotrope	Chalcedony - red & green			
Helvite	$(Mn,Fe,Zn)_8Be_6(SiO_4)_6S_2$	Is	3.26	6-6.5
Hematite	Fe_2O_3	Tg	5.3	6.5
Hemimorphite	$Zn_4(Si_2O_7)(OH)_2$-H_2O	Or	3.45	5
Hercynite (S)	$Fe^{2+}Al_2O_4$	Is	3.95	7.5
Hessite	Ag_2Te	Mo	7.2-7.9	1.5-2
Heulandite	$(Ca,Na_2)Al_2Si_7O_{18}$-$6H_2O$	Mo	2.2	3-3.5
Hiddenite	Spodumene - green			
Holmquisite (A)	Glaucophane - Li variety			
Hornblende (H,A)	$NaCa_2(Mg,Fe^{2+})_4(Al,Fe^{3+},Ti)AlSi_6O_{22}(O,OH)_2$	Mo	3-3.47	5-6
Horn Silver	Cerargyrite			
Huebnerite (W)	$MnWO_4$	Mo	7.15	4.5
Humite	$(Mg,Fe^{2+})_7(SiO_4)_3(F,OH)_2$	Or	3.15	6-6.5
Hyacinth	Zircon - brown to orange			
Hyalite	Opal - globular & colorless			
Hyalophane (O)	$(K,Ba)Al(Al,Si)_3O_8$	Mo	2.81	6-6.5
Hydromica	Illite			
Hydrozincite	$Zn_5(CO_3)_2(OH)_6$	Mo	3.2-3.8	2-2.5
Hypersthene (H)	$(Mg,Fe^{2+})SiO_3$	Or	3.2-3.9	5.5-6
Ice	H_2O	Hx	0.99	2.5
Iceland Spar (Cb)	Calcite - clear			
Iddingsite	$H_8Mg_2Fe_2Si_3O_{14}$	Or	2.5-2.8	3

Mineral Tables

Name	Composition	System	Density	Hard
Idocrase	$Ca_{10}(Mg,Fe^{2+})_2Al_4(SiO_4)_5(Si_2O_7)_2(OH)_4$	Te	3.4	6.5
Illite (C)	$(K,H_3O)(Al,Mg,Fe)_2(Si,Al)_4O_{10}(OH)_2 \cdot (H_2O)$	Mo	2.6-2.9	1-2
Ilmenite	$Fe^{2+}TiO_3$	Tg	4.72	5-5.5
Ilvaite	$CaFe^{3+}_2Fe^{2+}(SiO_4)_2(OH)$	Or	4.01	5.5-6
Indicolite	Tourmaline - dark blue			
Iodobromite	$Ag(Cl,Br,I)$	Is	5.7	1-1.5
Iodyrite	AgI	Hx	5.6	1.5-2
Iolite	Cordierite - gemstone			
Iridium	Platinum group metal		22.7	6-7
Iridosmine	Ir, Os platinoid	Tg	19.3-21	6-7
Iron pyrite	Pyrite			
Jacinth	Zircon, hyacinth			
Jacobsite (S)	$(Mn^{2+},Fe^{2+},Mg^{2+},Mn^{3+})_3O_4$	Is	4.75	5.5-6
Jade	Jadeite or nephrite			
Jadeite (P)	$Na(Al,Fe^{3+})Si_2O_6$	Mo	3.3	6.5
Jamesonite (J)	$Pb_4FeSb_6S_{14}$	Mo	5.56	2.5
Jargon	Zircon - clear, yellow or smoky			
Jarosite	$KFe^{3+}_3(SO_4)_2(OH)_6$	Tg	2.9-3.3	2.5-3.5
Jasper	Quartz - red cryptocrystalline			
Kainite	$MgSO_4 \cdot KCl \cdot 3H_2O$	Mo	2.1	3
Kalinite	Alum - potash variety			
Kaliophilite	$KAlSiO_4$	He	2.58	5.5-6
Kalsilite	Nepheline series			
Kaolin group	Clay mineral family			
Kaolinite (C)	$Al_2Si_2O_5(OH)_4$	Mo	2.6	1.5-2
Kernite	$Na_2B_4O_6(OH)_2 \cdot 3H_2O$	Mo	1.91	2.5-3
Krennerite	$AuTe_2$	Or	8.53	2.5
Kunzite	Spodumene - pinko			
Kyanite	Al_2SiO_5	Tr	3.61	4-7
Labradorite (P)	$Ab_{50}An_{50}-Ab_{30}An_{70}$	Tr		
Lapis lazuli	Lazurite - impure			
Langbeinite	$K_2Mg_2(SO_4)_3$	Is	2.83	3.5-4
Larsenite (Ov)	$PbZnSiO_4$	Or	5.9	3
Laumontite (Z)	$(Ca,Na)Al_2Si_4O_{12} \cdot 4H_2O$	Mo	2.29	3.5-4
Lawsonite	$CaAl_2Si_2O_7(OH)_2 \cdot H_2O$	Is	3.09	7.5
Lazulite	$MgAl_2(PO_4)_2(OH)_2$	Mo	3.05	5-6
Lazurite	$Na_3Ca(Al_3Si_3O_{12})S$	Is	2.4	5.5
Lechatelierite	SiO_2 - fused silica	Am	2.5-2.65	6.5
Lepidocrocite	$FeO(OH)$	Or	4	5
Lepidolite (M)	$K(Li,Al)_3(Si,Al)_4O_{10}(F,OH)_2$	Mo	2.84	2.5-3
Leucite (Fp)	$KAlSi_2O_6$	Te	2.47	6
Libethenite	$Cu_2(PO_4)(OH)$	Or	3.8	4
Limonite	$FeO(OH) \cdot nH_2O$	Am	3.3-4	5-5.5
Linarite	$PbCu(SO_4)(OH)_2$	Mo	5.4	2.5
Linnaeite	$Co^{2+}Co^{3+}_2S_4$	Is	4.8	4.5-5.5
Lithium mica	Lepidolite			
Lithiophilite	$LiMnPO_4$	Or	3.34	4-5
Loellingite	$FeAs_2$	Or	7.1-7.4	5
Magnesite (Cb)	$MgCO_3$	Tg	3	4
Magnetite (S)	$Fe^{2+}Fe^{3+}_2O_4$	Is	5.15	5.5-6
Malachite	$Cu_2(CO_3)(OH)_2$	Mo	3.6-4	3.5-4

Mineral Tables

Name	Composition	System	Density	Hard
Manganite	$MnO(OH)$	Mo	4.34	4
Manganosite	MnO	Is	5.18	5-6
Marcasite	FeS_2 - white iron pyrite	Or	4.89	6-6.5
Margarite (M)	$CaAl_2(Al_2Si_2O_{10})(OH)_2$	Mo	3.03	4
Marialite (Sc)	$Na_4Al_3Si_9O_{24}Cl$	Te	2.56	5.5-6
Marmatite	Sphalerite - iron bearing			
Martite	Hematite after magnetite			
Meerschaum	Sepiolite			
Meionite (Sc)	$Ca_4Al_6Si_6O_{24}CO_3$	Te	2.69	5-6
Melaconite	Tenorite			
Melanite (G)	Andradite garnet - black			
Melanterite	$Fe^{2+}SO_4 \cdot 7H_2O$	Mo	1.89	2
Melilite	$(Na,Ca)_2(Mg,Al,Fe^{2+})(Si,Al)_2O_7$	Te	2.95	5-5.5
Menaccanite	Ilmenite			
Menaghinite (J)	$CuPb_{13}Sb_7S_{24}$	Or	6.38	2.5
Mercury	Hg - fluid, quicksilver			
Miargyrite	$AgSbS_2$	Mo	5.19	2-2.5
Mica	A group of minerals			
Microcline (F)	$KAlSi_3O_8$	Tr	2.56	6
Microlite	$(Na,Ca)_2(Ta,Nb)_2O_6(O,OH,F)$	Is	4.2-6.4	5-5.5
Microperthite	Microcline & albite			
Millerite	NiS	Tg	5.5	3-3.5
Mimetite	$Pb_5(AsO_4)_3Cl$	Hx	7.17	3.5-4
Minium	Pb_3O_4	Te	8.2	2.5-3
Mispickel	Arsenopyrite			
Molybdenite	MoS_2	Hx	5.5	1
Monazite	$(La,Ce,Y,Th)(PO_4,SiO_4)$	Mo	4.8-5.5	5-5.5
Monticellite (Ov)	$CaMgSiO_4$	Or	3.2	5
Montmorillonite (C)	$(Na,Ca)_{0.3}(Al,Mg)_2Si_4O_{10}(OH)_2 \cdot nH_2O$	Mo	2-2.7	1.5-2
Moonstone (O)	Opalescent albite or orthoclase			
Morganite	Beryl - rose color			
Mullite	$Al_6Si_2O_{13}$	Or	3.05	6-7
Muscovite (M)	$KAl_2(AlSi_3O_{10})(OH,F)_2$	Mo	2.82	2-2.5
Nacrite (C)	$Al_2(Si_2O_5)(OH)_4$	Mo	2.6	1
Nagyagite	$AuPb(Sb,Bi)Te_{2-3}S_6$	Mo	7.5	1-2
Natroalunite	Alunite with Na-K			
Natrolite (Z)	$Na_2(Al_2Si_3O_{10}) \cdot 2H_2O$	Mo	2.25	5.5-6
Nepheline	$(Na,K)AlSiO_4$	Hx	2.55-2.65	6
Nephrite	Tremolite, similar to jade			
Niccolite	$NiAs$	Hx	7.79	5.5
Nickel bloom	Annabergite			
Nickel iron	Ni, Fe - Meterite alloy			
Ni skutterudite	$(Ni,Co)As_3$	Is	6.5	5.5-6
Nitre	KNO_3 - saltpeter	Or	2.1	2
Nontronite (C)	$Na_{0.3}Fe^{3+}_2(Al,Si)_4O_{10}(OH)_2 \cdot nH_2O$	Mo	2.3	1.5-2
Norbergite	$Mg_3(SiO_4)(F,OH)_2$	Or	3.15	6-6.5
Noselite (Fp)	$Na_8Al_6Si_6O_{24}(SO_4)$	Is	2.34	5.5-6
Octahedrite	Anatase			
Oligoclase	$Ab_{90}An_{10} - Ab_{70}An_{30}$	Tr	2.65	7
Olivine (Ov)	$(Mg,Fe)_2SiO_4$ A group of minerals	Or		
Onyx	Chalcedony - layered structure			

Mineral Tables

Name	Composition	System	Density	Hard
Opal	$SiO_2 \cdot nH_2O$	Am	2.09	5.5-6
Orpiment	As_2S_3	Mo	3.52	1.5-2
Orthite	Allanite			
Orthoclase (F)	$KAlSi_3O_8$	Mo	2.56	6
Osmiridium	Iridosmine			
Ottrelite (M)	$(Mg,Fe^{2+},Mn^{2+})_2Al_2Si_2O_{10}(OH)_4$	Mo	3.52	6-7
Palladium	Platinum group metal	Is	11.55	4.5-5
Paragonite (M)	$NaAl_2(AlSi_3O_{10})(OH)_2$	Mo	2.78	2.5
Pargasite (H)	$NaCa_2(Mg,Fe2+)_4Al_3Si_6O_{22}(OH)_2$	Mo	3.12	6
Peacock ore	Bornite			
Pearceite	$(Ag,Cu)_{16}As_2S_{11}$	Mo	6.13	2.5-3
Pectolite	$NaCa_2Si_3O_8(OH)$	Tr	2.86	5
Penninite	Chlorite			
Pentlandite	$(Fe,Ni)_9S_8$	Is	4.6-5	3.5-4
Peridot (Ov)	Olivine - gemstone			
Perovskite	$CaTiO_3$	Or	4	5.5
Perthite (F)	Microcline & albite mix			
Petalite (Fp)	$LiAlSi_4O_{10}$	Mo	2.42	6-6.5
Petzite	Ag_3AuTe_2	Is	8.7-9.14	2.5
Phenakite	Be_2SiO_4	Tg	2.98	7.5
Phillipsite (Z)	$(K,Na,Ca)_{1-2}(Si,Al)_8O_{16} \cdot 6H_2O$	Mo	2.2	4.5-5
Phlogopite (M)	$K(Mg,Fe^{2+})_3AlSi_3O_{10}(OH,F)_2$	Mo	2.7-2.9	2-2.5
Phosgenite	$Pb_2Cl_2CO_3$	Te	6-6.3	2.5-3
Phosphuranylite	$KCa(H3O)_3(UO_2)_7(PO_4)_4O_4 \cdot 8H_2O$	Or	4.1	2.5
Picotite (S)	Spinel - chromium			
Piedmontite	Epidote - Mn^{3+}	Mo		
Pigeonite (P)	$(Ca,Mg,Fe^{2+})_2Si_2O_6$	Mo	3.3-3.46	6
Pinite (M)	Muscovite mica			
Pitchblende	Uraninite			
Plagioclase (P)	A group of minerals			
Plagionite (J)	$Pb_5Sb_8S_{17}$	Mo	5.4-5.6	2.5
Platinum	Pt, metallic element	Is	14-22	4-4.5
Pleonaste (S)	Spinel - Fe			
Plumbago	Graphite			
Polianite	Pyrolusite			
Pollucite	$(Cs,Na)_2Al_2Si_4O_{12} \cdot H_2O$	Is	2.9	6.5
Polybasite	$(Ag,Cu)_{16}Sb_2S_{11}$	Mo	4.6-5	2.5-3
Polycrase(R)	$(Y,Ca,Ce,U,Th)(Ti,Nb,Ta)_2O_6$	Or	5	5-6
Polyhalite	$K_2Ca_2Mg(SO_4)_4 \cdot 2H_2O$	Tr	2.77	2.5-3.5
Potash alum	$KAl(SO_4)_2 \cdot 11H_2O$	Is	1.75	2-2.5
Potash mica	Muscovite			
Powellite	$CaMoO_4$	Te	4.34	3.5
Prase	Jasper - green			
Prehnite	$Ca_2Al_2(Si_3O_{10})(OH)_2$	Or	2.87	6-6.5
Prochlorite	Chlorite group			
Proustite	Ag_3AsS_3	Tg	5.55	2-2.5
Psilomelane	Mn-mineral group			
Pyrargyrite	Ag_3SbS_3	Tg	5.85	2.5
Pyrite	FeS_2	Is	5.01	6.6
Pyrochlore	$(Na,Ca)_2(Nb,Ta)_2O_6(OH,F)$	Is	4.2-6.4	5.5-5
Pyrolusite	MnO_2	Te	4.4-5.06	6-6.5

Mineral Tables

Name	Composition	System	Density	Hard
Pyromorphite	$Pb_5(PO_4)_3Cl$	Hx	6.7-7	3.5-4
Pyrope (G)	$(Mg,Fe^{2+})_3Al_2(SiO_4)3$	Is	3.65-3.84	7.5
Pyrophyllite	$Al_2Si_4O_{10}(OH)_2$	Tr	2.84	1.5-2
Pyroxene (P,H)	A group of minerals			
Pyrrhotite	$Fe_{1-x}S$, 0<x<0.17	Mo	4.61	3.5-4
Quartz	SiO_2 - a quartz	Tg	2.62	7
Rammelsbergite	$NiAs_2$	Or	7.1	5.5
Rasorite	Kernite			
Realgar	AsS	Mo	3.56	1.5-2
Red ochre	Hematite			
Rhodochrosite (Cb)	$MnCO_3$	Tg	3.69	3
Rhodolite (G)	Pyrope			
Rhodonite	$(Mn^{2+},Fe^{2+},Mg,Ca)SiO_3$	Tr	3.5-3.7	6
Riebeckite (M)	$Na_2(Fe^{2+}_3Fe^{3+}_2)Si_8O_{22}(OH)_2$	Mo	3.4	4
Rock salt	Halite			
Roscoelite (M)	$K(V,Al,Mg)_3AlSi_3O_{10}(OH)_2$	Mo	2.97	2.5
Rubellite	Tourmaline - red or pink			
Ruby	Corundum - red gemstone			
Ruby copper	Cuprite			
Ruby silver	Pyrargyrite or proustite			
Rutile	TiO_2	Te	4.25	6-6.5
Samarskite	$(Ce,Y,U,Ca,Fe,Pb,Th)(Nb,Ta,Ti,Sn)_2O_6$	Or	5.6-5.8	5-6
Sanadine	$(K,Na)AlSi_3O_8$ - high temp. K-feldspar	Mo	2.52	6
Saponite	$(Ca/2,Na)_{0.3}(Mg,Fe^{2+})_3(Si,Al)_4O_{10}(OH)_2 \cdot 4H_2O$	Mo	2.3	1-1.5
Sapphire	Corundum - blue gemstone			
Satin spar	Gypsum - fibrous			
Scapolite	$(Na,Ca)_4Al_3(Al,Si)_3Si_6O_{24}(Cl,CO_3,SO_4)$	Te	2.66	6
Scheelite	$CaWO_4$	Te	6.01	4-5
Schorlite	Tourmaline - black			
Scolecite (Z)	$Ca(Al_2Si_3O_{10}) \cdot 3H_2O$	Mo	2.16-2.4	5-5.5
Scorodite	$Fe^{3+}AsO_4 \cdot 2H_2O$	Or	3.2	3.5-4
Scorzalite	$(Fe^{2+},Mg)Al_2(PO_4)_2(OH)_2$	Mo	3.27	5.5-6
Selenite	Gypsum - clear, crystalline			
Semseyite	$Pb_9Sb_8S_{21}$	Mo	5.8-6.1	2.5
Sepiolite	$Mg_4Si_6O_{15}(OH)_2 \cdot 6H_2O$	Or	2	2
Sericite	Muscovite - fine grained			
Serpentine	$(Mg,Fe)_3Si_2O_5(OH)_4$	Mo	2.53-2.65	2.5-3
Siderite (Cb)	$Fe^{2+}CO_3$	Tg	3.96	3.5
Siegenite	$(Co,Ni)_3S_4$	Is	4.9	5-5.5
Sillimanite	Al_2SiO_5	Or	3.24	7
Silver	Ag	Is	10.5	2.5-3
Silver glance	Argentite			
Sklodowskite	$(H_3O)_2Mg(UO_2)_2(SiO_4)_2 \cdot 4H_2O$	Mo	3.54	2-3
Skutterudite	$(Co,Ni)As_{3-x}$	Is	6.1-6.9	5.5-6
Smaltite	Skutterudite variety			
Smithsonite (Cb)	$ZnCO_3$	Tg	4.45	4.5
Soapstone	Talc			
Sodalite (Fp)	$Na_4Al_3Si_3O_{12}Cl$	Is	2.29	6
Soda nitre	$NaNO_3$	Tg	2.26	1.5-2
Specular iron	Hematite - foliated			
Sperrylite	$PtAs_2$	Is	10.58	6-7

Mineral Tables

Name	Composition	System	Density	Hard
Spessartine (G)	$Mn_3^{2+}Al_2(SiO_4)_3$	Is	4.18	6.5-7.5
Sphalerite	$(Zn,Fe^{2+})S$	Is	4.05	3.5-4
Sphene	$CaTiSiO_5$	Mo	3.48	5-5.5
Spinel group	$MgAl_2O_4$	Is	3.57-3.72	8
Spodumene	$LiAlSi_2O_6$	Mo	3.15	6.5-7
Stannite	Cu_2FeSnS_4	Te	4.3-4.5	3.5-4
Staurolite	$(Fe^{2+},Mg)_2Al_9(Si,Al)_4O_{22}(O,OH)_2$	Mo	3.71	7-7.5
Steatite	Talc			
Stephanite	Ag_5SbS_4	Or	6.25	2-2.5
Sternbergite	$AgFe_2S_3$	Or	4.22	1-1.5
Stibnite	Sb_2S_3	Or	4.63	2
Stilbite (Z)	$NaCa_2Al_5Si_{13}O_{36}\cdot nH_2O$ (n = 28-32)	Mo	2.15	3.5-4
Stillwellite	$(Ce,La,Ca)BSiO_5$	Tg		
Stolzite	$PbWO_4$	Te	7.9-8.2	2.5-3
Stromeyerite	$(Cu,Ag)S$	Or	6-6.3	2.5-3
Strontianite (Cb)	$SrCO_3$	Or	3.78	3.5
Sulphur	S_8	Or	2.06	1.5-2.5
Sunstone (F)	Oligoclase, translucent			
Sylvanite	$(Au,Ag)Te_2$	Mo	7.9-8.3	1.5-2
Sylvite	KCl	Is	1.99	2.5
Talc	$Mg_3Si_4O_{10}(OH)_2$	Mo	2.75	1
Tantalite	$(Fe^{2+},Mn^{2+})Ta_2O_6$	Or	6.2-8	6-6.5
Tennantite	$(Cu,Fe)_{12}As_4S_{13}$	Is	4.6-4.7	3.5-4
Tenorite	CuO	Mo	6.5	3.5-4
Tephroite (Ov)	Mn_2SiO_4	Or	4.11-4.39	6.5
Tetrahedrite	$(Cu,Fe)_{12}Sb_4S_{13}$	Is	4.6-5.2	3.5-4
Thenardite	Na_2SO_4	Or	2.68	2.5
Thomsonite (Z)	$NaCa_2Al_5Si_5O_{20}\cdot 6H_2O$	Or	2.34	5-5.5
Thorianite	ThO_2	Is	10	6
Thorite	$ThSiO_4$	Te	4-6.7	5
Thulite	Zoisite - pink to red			
Tiger's eye	Quartz after crocidolite, yellow			
Tin	Sn	Te	7.28	2
Tinstone	Cassiterite			
Titanite	Sphene			
Topaz	$Al_2SiO_4(F,OH)_2$	Or	3.55	8
Torbernite	$Cu(UO_2)_2(PO_4)_2\cdot nH_2O$ (n = 8-12)	Te	3.2	2-2.5
Tourmaline	$(Na,Ca)(Al,Fe,Li,Mg)_3Al_6(BO_3)_3(Si_6O_{18})(OH)_4$	Tg	3-3.2	7
Tremolite (A)	$Ca_2Mg_5Si_8O_{22}(OH)_2$	Mo	2.9-3.2	5-6
Tridymite	SiO_2 - high temperature quartz	Tr	2.28-2.33	6.5-7
Triphylite	$LiFe^{2+}PO_4$	Or	3.4-3.6	4-5
Troilite	FeS	Hx	4.61	3.5-4
Trona	$Na_3CO_3\cdot NaHCO_3\cdot 2H_2O$	Mo	2.13	2.5
Troostite	Willemite, Manganiferous			
Tungstite	$WO_3\cdot H_2O$	Or	5.5	2.5
Turquoise	$CuAl_6(PO_4)_4(OH)_8\cdot 4H_2O$	Tr	2.6-2.8	5-6
Tyuyamunite	$Ca(UO_2)_2(VO_4)_2\cdot nH_2O$ (n=5-8)	Or	3.3-4.3	1.5-2
Ulexite	$NaCaB_5O_9\cdot 5H_2O$	Tr	1.95	2.5
Uralite (H)	Hornblende after pyroxene			
Uraninite	UO_2	Is	6.5-10.95	5-6
Uranophane	$Ca(UO_2)_2SiO_3(OH)_2\cdot 5H_2O$	Mo	3.9	2.5

Mineral Tables

Name	Composition	System	Density	Hard
Uvarovite (G)	$Ca_3Cr_2(SiO_4)_3$	Is	3.4-3.8	6.5-7
Vanadinite	$Pb_5(VO_4)_3Cl$	Hx	6.8-7.1	3.5-4
Variscite	$Al(PO_4) \cdot 2H_2O$	Or	2.5	4-5
Vermiculite (M)	$(Mg,Fe^{3+},Al)_3(Al,Si)_4O_{10}(OH)_2 \cdot 4H_2O$	Mo	2.3-2.5	1.5-2
Vesuvianite	Idocrase			
Violarite	$Fe^{2+}Ni^{2+}{}_2S_4$	Is	4.5-4.8	4.5-5.5
Vivianite	$Fe^{2+}{}_3(PO_4)_2 \cdot 8H_2O$	Mo	2.65	1.5-2
Wad	Manganese oxides			
Wavellite	$Al_3(OH,F)_3(PO_4)_2 \cdot 5H_2O$	Or	2.34	3.5-4
Wernerite (Sc)	Scapolite			
White pyrite	Marcasite			
White mica	Muscovite			
Willemite	Zn_2SiO_4	Tg	3.9-4.2	5.5
Witherite (Cb)	$BaCO_3$	Or	4.3	3-3.5
Wolframite	$(Fe,Mn)WO_4$	Mo	7.1-7.5	4.5
Wollastonite	$CaSiO_3$	Tr	2.84	5
Wood tin	Cassiterite			
Wulfenite	$PbMoO_4$	Te	6.5-7	3
Wurtzite	$(Zn,Fe)S$	Hx	4.03	3.5-4
Xenotime	YPO_4	Te	4.4-5.1	4-5
Zeolite (Z)	A group of minerals			
Zincite	$(Zn,Mn)O$	Hx	5.43-5.7	4-5
Zinc spinel (S)	Gahnite			
Zinkenite (J)	$Pb_9Sb_{22}S_{42}$	Hx	5.12-5.35	3-3.5
Zinnwaldite	Fe,Li mica			
Zircon	$ZrSiO_4$	Te	4.65	7.5
Zoisite	$Ca_2Al_3Si_3O_{12}(OH)$	Or	3.3	6.5

Element–Oxide Conversion

Element	Multiply by	To get this Oxide
Al	1.889	Al_2O_3
As	1.320	As_2O_3
As	1.534	As_2O_5
B	3.220	B_2O_3
Ba	1.117	BaO
Be	2.775	BeO
Bi	1.115	Bi_2O_3
Ca	1.399	CaO
Ce	1.171	Ce_2O_3
Co	1.271	CoO
Cr	1.462	Cr_2O_3
Cs	1.060	Cs_2O
Cu	1.252	CuO
F	2.055	CaF_2
Fe	1.430	Fe_2O_3
Fe	1.382	Fe_3O_4
Fe	1.286	FeO
K	1.205	K_2O
La	1.172	La_2O_3
Mg	1.658	MgO
Mn	1.291	MnO
Mn	1.582	MnO_2
Mo	1.500	MoO_3
Na	1.348	Na_2O
Nb	1.431	Nb_2O_5
Ni	1.271	NiO
P	2.291	P_2O_5
Pb	1.077	PbO
Rb	1.094	Rb_2O
Sb	1.197	Sb_2O_3
Si	2.139	SiO_2
Sn	1.270	SnO_2
Sr	1.183	SrO
Ta	1.221	Ta_2O_5
Th	1.138	ThO_2
Ti	1.668	TiO_2
U	1.179	U_3O_8
U	1.202	UO_3
U	1.134	UO_2
V	1.785	V_2O_5
W	1.261	WO_3
Y	1.270	Y_2O_3
Zn	1.245	ZnO
Zr	1.351	ZrO_2

Example: It takes 1.245 pounds of zinc oxide to produce 1 pound of zinc.

Minerals Sorted by Density

Name	Density g/cm³	Name	Density g/cm³
Ice	0.99	Brucite	2.39
Carnallite	1.6	Glauconite (M)	2.4-2.95
Epsomite	1.67	Lazurite	2.4
Borax	1.71	Garnierite	2.41
Potash alum	1.75	Chlorite	2.42
Melanterite	1.89	Colemanite	2.42
Allophane (C)	1.9	Petalite (Fp)	2.42
Kernite	1.91	Cancrinite (Fp)	2.45
Ulexite	1.95	Hauynite (Fp)	2.45
Gaylussite	1.96	Harmotome	2.46
Sylvite	1.99	Leucite (Fp)	2.47
Chrysocolla	2-2.4	Iddingsite	2.5-2.8
Goslarite	2	Lechatelierite	2.5-2.65
Halloysite (C)	2-2.6	Variscite	2.5
Hectorite (C)	2-3	Sanadine	2.52
Montmorillonite (C)	2-2.7	Serpentine	2.53-2.65
Sepiolite	2	Cordierite	2.55-2.77
Sulphur	2.06	Nepheline	2.55-2.65
Chabazite (Z)	2.09	Marialite (Sc)	2.56
Gmelinite (Z)	2.09	Microcline (F)	2.56
Opal	2.09	Orthoclase (F)	2.56
Kainite	2.1	Anorthoclase (O)	2.58
Nitre	2.1	Kaliophilite	2.58
Trona	2.13	Alunite	2.59-2.9
Beidellite (C)	2.15	Dickite (C)	2.6
Stilbite (Z)	2.15	Illite (C)	2.6-2.9
Graphite	2.16	Kaolinite (C)	2.6
Scolecite (Z)	2.16-2.4	Nacrite (C)	2.6
Halite	2.17	Turquoise	2.6-2.8
Heulandite	2.2	Albite (F)	2.62
Phillipsite (Z)	2.2	Quartz	2.62
Chalcanthite	2.21	Beryl	2.63-2.9
Natrolite (Z)	2.25	Clinochlore	2.65
Soda nitre	2.26	Oligoclase	2.65
Cristobalite	2.27	Vivianite	2.65
Tridymite	2.28-2.33	Scapolite	2.66
Laumontite (Z)	2.29	Andesine (P)	2.67
Sodalite (Fp)	2.29	Thenardite	2.68
Analcime	2.3	Meionite (Sc)	2.69
Gypsum	2.3	Phlogopite (M)	2.7-2.9
Nontronite (C)	2.3	Bytownite (P)	2.71
Saponite	2.3	Calcite	2.71
Vermiculite (M)	2.3-2.5	Anorthite (P)	2.73
Apophyllite	2.34	Talc	2.75
Gibbsite	2.34	Glauberite	2.77
Noselite (Fp)	2.34	Polyhalite	2.77
Thomsonite (Z)	2.34	Paragonite (M)	2.78
Wavellite	2.34	Biotite (M)	2.8-3.5

Minerals Sorted by Density

Name	Density g/cm³	Name	Density g/cm³
Hyalophane (O)	2.81	Bronzite (E)	3.2-3.9
Muscovite (M)	2.82	Enstatite (P)	3.2
Langbeinite	2.83	Hydrozincite	3.2-3.8
Dolomite (Cb)	2.84	Hypersthene (H)	3.2-3.9
Lepidolite (M)	2.84	Monticellite (Ov)	3.2
Pyrophyllite	2.84	Scorodite	3.2
Wollastonite	2.84	Torbernite	3.2
Anthophyllite (A)	2.85-3.57	Sillimanite	3.24
Pectolite	2.86	Celsian (F)	3.25
Prehnite	2.87	Clinohumite	3.26
Boracite	2.9	Helvite	3.26
Datolite	2.9	Forsterite (Ov)	3.27
Jarosite	2.9-3.3	Scorzalite	3.27
Pollucite	2.9	Axinite	3.28
Tremolite (A)	2.9-3.2	Allanite	3.3-4.2
Aragonite	2.93	Epidote	3.3-3.6
Melilite	2.95	Goethite	3.3-4.3
Anhydrite	2.97	Jadeite (P)	3.3
Cryolite	2.97	Limonite	3.3-4
Roscoelite (M)	2.97	Pigeonite (P)	3.3-3.46
Amblygonite	2.98-3.11	Tyuyamunite	3.3-4.3
Phenakite	2.98	Zoisite	3.3
Danburite	2.99	Dioptase	3.31
Hornblende (H,A)	3-3.47	Clinozoite	3.34
Magnesite (Cb)	3	Dumortierite	3.34
Tourmaline	3-3.2	Lithiophilite	3.34
Edenite (H)	3.02	Cummingtonite (A)	3.35
Boehmite (B)	3.03	Augite	3.4
Margarite (M)	3.03	Clinoenstatite (E)	3.4
Actinolite (A)	3.04	Diaspore	3.4
Euclase	3.04	Diopside (P)	3.4
Ankerite (Cb)	3.05	Idocrase	3.4
Annebergite	3.05	Riebeckite (A)	3.4
Lazulite	3.05	Triphylite	3.4-3.6
Mullite	3.05	Uvarovite (G)	3.4-3.8
Glaucophane (A)	3.07	Grossularite (G)	3.42-3.72
Lawsonite	3.09	Arfvedsonite (A)	3.44
Erythrite	3.12	Hemimorphite	3.45
Pargasite (H)	3.12	Sphene	3.48
Fluorite	3.13	Chrysoberyl	3.5-3.84
Andalusite	3.15	Rhodonite	3.5-3.7
Autunite	3.15	Chloritoid (M)	3.51-3.8
Chondrodite	3.15	Diamond	3.51
Humite	3.15	Acmite (P)	3.52
Norbergite	3.15	Orpiment	3.52
Spodumene	3.15	Ottrelite (M)	3.52
Hastingsite (H)	3.17-3.59	Sklodowskite	3.54
Apatite	3.19	Hedenbergite	3.55

Minerals Sorted by Density

Name	Density g/cm³	Name	Density g/cm³
Topaz	3.55	Clinoclase	4.29
Realgar	3.56	Stannite	4.3-4.5
Spinel group	3.57-3.72	Witherite (Cb)	4.3
Malachite	3.6-4	Manganite	4.34
Kyanite	3.61	Powellite	4.34
Aurichalcite	3.64-3.9	Fayalite (Ov)	4.39
Pyrope (G)	3.65-3.84	Pyrolusite	4.4-5.06
Rhodochrosite (Cb)	3.69	Xenotime	4.4-5.1
Andradite (G)	3.7-4.1	Enargite	4.45
Carnotite	3.7-4.7	Smithsonite (Cb)	4.45
Staurolite	3.71	Barite	4.48
Atacamite	3.76	Brannerite	4.5-6.5
Strontianite (Cb)	3.78	Chromite	4.5-5.09
Libethenite	3.8	Fergusonite (R)	4.5-5.7
Azurite	3.83	Violarite	4.5-4.8
Anatase	3.9	Pentlandite	4.6-5
Antlerite	3.9	Polybasite	4.6-5
Uranophane	3.9	Tennantite	4.6-4.7
Willemite	3.9-4.2	Tetrahedrite	4.6-5.2
Celestite	3.95	Pyrrhotite	4.61
Ferrosilite (P)	3.95	Stillwellite	4.61
Hercynite (S)	3.95	Troilite	4.61
Siderite (Cb)	3.96	Stibnite	4.63
Brochantite	3.97	Zircon	4.65
Greenockite	3.98-5	Covellite	4.68
Alabandite	4	Cubanite	4.7
Ferrimolybdite	4-4.5	Ilmenite	4.72
Gadolinite (R)	4-4.5	Jacobsite (S)	4.75
Gahnite (S)	4-4.6	Braunite	4.76
Lepidocrocite	4	Hausmannite	4.76
Perovskite	4	Linnaeite	4.8
Thorite	4-6.7	Monazite	4.8-5.5
Ilvaite	4.01	Euxenite	4.84
Wurtzite	4.03	Marcasite	4.89
Corundum	4.05	Siegenite	4.9
Sphalerite	4.05	Bastnaesite (R)	4.95
Almandine (G)	4.09-4.31	Polycrase(R)	5
Clinoferrosilite (E)	4.1	Bravoite	5.01
Phosphuranylite	4.1	Pyrite	5.01
Brookite	4.11	Bornite	5.09
Tephroite (Ov)	4.11-4.39	Zinkenite (J)	5.12-5.35
Spessartine (G)	4.18	Franklinite	5.14
Chalcopyrite	4.19	Magnetite (S)	5.15
Microlite	4.2-6.4	Manganosite	5.18
Pyrochlore	4.2-6.4	Miargyrite	5.19
Sternbergite	4.22	Columbite	5.3-7.3
Galaxite (S)	4.23	Hematite	5.3
Rutile	4.25	Linarite	5.4

Minerals Sorted by Density

Name	Density g/cm³	Name	Density g/cm³
Plagionite (J)	5.4-5.6	Wulfenite	6.5-7
Zincite	5.43-5.7	Cerussite (Cb)	6.58
Chalcocite	5.5-5.8	Antimony	6.66
Millerite	5.5	Pyromorphite	6.7-7
Molybdenite	5.5	Vanadinite	6.8-7.1
Tungstite	5.5	Cassiterite	6.9
Cerargyrite	5.55	Loellingite	7.1-7.4
Proustite	5.55	Rammelsbergite	7.1
Jamesonite (J)	5.56	Wolframite	7.1-7.5
Digenite	5.6	Huebnerite (W)	7.15
Embolite	5.6	Mimetite	7.17
Iodyrite	5.6	Acanthite	7.2-7.3
Samarskite	5.6-5.8	Galena	7.2-7.6
Arsenic	5.7	Hessite	7.2-7.9
Boulangerite	5.7-6.3	Tin	7.28
Iodobromite	5.7	Argentite	7.3
Bromargyrite	5.8-6	Ferberite	7.45
Semseyite	5.8-6.1	Nagyagite	7.5
Pyrargyrite	5.85	Niccolite	7.79
Larsenite (Ov)	5.9	Stolzite	7.9-8.2
Crocoite	6	Sylvanite	7.9-8.3
Phosgenite	6-6.3	Awaruite	8
Stromeyerite	6-6.3	Cinnabar	8.1
Scheelite	6.01	Altaite	8.14
Arsenopyrite	6.07	Minium	8.2
Cuprite	6.1	Bismite	8.5-9.5
Skutterudite	6.1-6.9	Krennerite	8.53
Gersdorffite	6.11	Petzite	8.7-9.14
Pearceite	6.13	Copper	8.94
Allemontite	6.15	Calaverite	9.04
Tantalite	6.2-8	Bismuth	9.75
Stephanite	6.25	Thorianite	10
Anglesite	6.3	Silver	10.5
Cobaltite	6.33	Sperrylite	10.58
Menaghinite (J)	6.38	Palladium	11.55
Geocronite	6.4	Platinum	14-22
Calomel	6.45	Gold	17.64
Cervantite	6.5	Iridosmine	19.3-21
Ni skutterudite	6.5	Iridium	22.7
Tenorite	6.5		
Uraninite	6.5-10.95		

Minerals Sorted by Hardness

Name	Hardness	Name	Hardness
Beidellite (C)	1-2	Hydrozincite	2-2.5
Cerargyrite	1-1.5	Melanterite	2
Chlorite	1-2	Miargyrite	2-2.5
Embolite	1-1.5	Muscovite (M)	2-2.5
Hectorite (C)	1-2	Nitre	2
Illite (C)	1-2	Phlogopite (M)	2-2.5
Iodobromite	1-1.5	Potash alum	2-2.5
Molybdenite	1	Proustite	2-2.5
Nacrite (C)	1	Sepiolite	2
Saponite	1-1.5	Sklodowskite	2-3
Sternbergite	1-1.5	Stephanite	2-2.5
Talc	1	Stibnite	2
Bromargyrite	1.5-2	Tin	2
Calomel	1.5-2	Torbernite	2-2.5
Covellite	1.5-2	Altaite	2.5
Dickite (C)	1.5-2	Anglesite	2.5-3
Erythrite	1.5-2	Biotite (M)	2.5-3
Graphite	1.5-2	Boulangerite	2.5-3
Hessite	1.5-2	Brucite	2.5-3
Iodyrite	1.5-2	Calaverite	2.5
Kaolinite (C)	1.5-2	Cancrinite (Fp)	2.5
Montmorillonite (C)	1.5-2	Carnallite	2.5
Nagyagite	1.5-2	Chalcanthite	2.5
Nontronite (C)	1.5-2	Chalcocite	2.5-3
Orpiment	1.5-2	Chrysocolla	2.5-3.5
Pyrophyllite	1.5-2	Clinoclase	2.5-3
Realgar	1.5-2	Copper	2.5-3
Soda nitre	1.5-2	Crocoite	2.5-3
Sulphur	1.5-2.5	Cryolite	2.5-3
Sylvanite	1.5-2	Digenite	2.5-3
Tyuyamunite	1.5-2	Ferrimolybdite	2.5-3
Vermiculite (M)	1.5-2	Galena	2.5
Vivianite	1.5-2	Gaylussite	2.5
Acanthite	2	Geocronite	2.5-3
Annebergite	2	Gibbsite	2.5-3
Argentite	2-2.5	Glauberite	2.5-3
Aurichalcite	2	Gold	2.5-3
Autunite	2-2.5	Halite	2.5
Bismuth	2-2.5	Ice	2.5
Borax	2	Jamesonite (J)	2.5
Carnotite	2	Jarosite	2.5-3.5
Cinnabar	2-2.5	Kernite	2.5-3
Clinochlore	2-2.5	Krennerite	2.5
Epsomite	2-2.5	Lepidolite (M)	2.5-3
Glauconite (M)	2	Linarite	2.5
Goslarite	2-2.5	Menaghinite (J)	2.5
Gypsum	2	Minium	2.5-3
Halloysite (C)	2	Paragonite (M)	2.5

Minerals Sorted by Hardness

Name	Hardness	Name	Hardness
Pearceite	2.5-3	Azurite	3.5-4
Petzite	2.5	Brochantite	3.5-4
Phosgenite	2.5-3	Chalcopyrite	3.5
Phosphuranylite	2.5	Cubanite	3.5
Plagionite (J)	2.5	Cuprite	3.5-4
Polybasite	2.5-3	Dolomite (Cb)	3.5-4
Polyhalite	2.5-3.5	Greenockite	3.5-4
Pyrargyrite	2.5	Langbeinite	3.5-4
Roscoelite (M)	2.5	Laumontite (Z)	3.5-4
Semseyite	2.5	Malachite	3.5-4
Serpentine	2.5-3	Mimetite	3.5-4
Silver	2.5-3	Pentlandite	3.5-4
Stolzite	2.5-3	Powellite	3.5
Stromeyerite	2.5-3	Pyromorphite	3.5-4
Sylvite	2.5	Pyrrhotite	3.5-4
Thenardite	2.5	Scorodite	3.5-4
Trona	2.5	Siderite (Cb)	3.5
Tungstite	2.5	Sphalerite	3.5-4
Ulexite	2.5	Stannite	3.5-4
Uranophane	2.5	Stilbite (Z)	3.5-4
Allemontite	3-4	Strontianite (Cb)	3.5
Allophane (C)	3	Tennantite	3.5-4
Antimony	3-3.5	Tenorite	3.5-4
Antlerite	3	Tetrahedrite	3.5-4
Atacamite	3-3.5	Troilite	3.5-4
Barite	3-3.5	Vanadinite	3.5-4
Boehmite (B)	3	Wavellite	3.5-4
Bornite	3	Wurtzite	3.5-4
Calcite	3	Apophyllite	4-5
Celestite	3-3.5	Bastnaesite (R)	4-5
Cerussite (Cb)	3-3.5	Bismite	4-5
Enargite	3	Brannerite	4-5
Garnierite	3-4	Cervantite	4-5
Heulandite	3-3.5	Chabazite (Z)	4
Iddingsite	3	Fluorite	4
Kainite	3	Harmotome	4-5
Larsenite (Ov)	3	Kyanite	4-7
Millerite	3-3.5	Libethenite	4
Rhodochrosite (Cb)	3	Lithiophilite	4-5
Witherite (Cb)	3-3.5	Magnesite (Cb)	4
Wulfenite	3	Manganite	4
Zinkenite (J)	3-3.5	Margarite (M)	4
Alabandite	3.4-4	Platinum	4-4.5
Alunite	3.5-4	Riebeckite (A)	4
Anhydrite	3.5	Scheelite	4-5
Ankerite (Cb)	3.5-4	Triphylite	4-5
Aragonite	3.5-4	Variscite	4-5
Arsenic	3.5	Xenotime	4-5

Minerals Sorted by Hardness

Name	Hardness	Name	Hardness
Zincite	4-5	Turquoise	5-6
Colemanite	4.5	Uraninite	5-6
Ferberite	4.5	Wollastonite	5
Gmelinite (Z)	4.5	Actinolite (A)	5.5
Huebnerite (W)	4.5	Allanite	5.5
Linnaeite	4.5-5.5	Amblygonite	5.5-6
Palladium	4.5-5	Anatase	5.5-6
Phillipsite (Z)	4.5-5	Arfvedsonite (A)	5.5-6
Smithsonite (Cb)	4.5	Bronzite (E)	5.5-6
Violarite	4.5-5.5	Brookite	5.5-6
Wolframite	4.5	Chromite	5.5
Analcime	5	Cobaltite	5.5
Anthophyllite (A)	5-6	Datolite	5.5
Apatite	5	Enstatite (P)	5.5
Arsenopyrite	5	Fergusonite (R)	5.5-6.5
Augite	5-6.5	Franklinite	5.5-6
Awaruite	5	Gersdorffite	5.5
Clinoenstatite (E)	5-6	Hausmanite	5.5
Clinoferrosilite (E)	5-6	Hypersthene (H)	5.5-6
Cummingtonite (A)	5-6	Ilvaite	5.5-6
Dioptase	5	Jacobsite (S)	5.5-6
Ferrosilite (P)	5-6	Kaliophilite	5.5-6
Goethite	5-5.5	Lazurite	5.5
Hauynite (Fp)	5-6	Magnetite (S)	5.5-6
Hedenbergite	5-6	Marialite (Sc)	5.5-6
Hemimorphite	5	Natrolite (Z)	5.5-6
Hornblende (H,A)	5-6	Niccolite	5.5
Ilmenite	5-5.5	Ni skutterudite	5.5-6
Lazulite	5-6	Noselite (Fp)	5.5-6
Lepidocrocite	5	Opal	5.5-6
Limonite	5-5.5	Perovskite	5.5
Loellingite	5	Rammelsbergite	5.5
Manganosite	5-6	Scorzalite	5.5-6
Meionite (Sc)	5-6	Skutterudite	5.5-6
Melilite	5-5.5	Willemite	5.5
Microlite	5-5.5	Acmite (P)	6-6.5
Monazite	5-5.5	Anorthite (P)	6
Monticellite (Ov)	5	Anorthoclase (O)	6
Pectolite	5	Braunite	6-6.5
Polycrase(R)	5-6	Cassiterite	6-7
Pyrochlore	5-5.5	Celsian (F)	6-6.5
Samarskite	5-6	Chondrodite	6-6.5
Scolecite (Z)	5-5.5	Clinohumite	6
Siegenite	5-5.5	Columbite	6
Sphene	5-5.5	Diopside (P)	6
Thomsonite (Z)	5-5.5	Edenite (H)	6
Thorite	5	Forsterite (Ov)	6-7
Tremolite (A)	5-6	Glaucophane (A)	6-6.5

Minerals Sorted by Hardness

Name	Hardness	Name	Hardness
Hastingsite (H)	6	Jadeite (P)	6.5
Helvite	6-6.5	Lechatelierite	6.5
Humite	6-6.5	Pollucite	6.5
Hyalophane (O)	6-6.5	Spessartine (G)	6.5-7.5
Iridium	6-7	Spodumene	6.5-7
Iridosmine	6-7	Tephroite (Ov)	6.5
Leucite (Fp)	6	Tridymite	6.5-7
Marcasite	6-6.5	Uvarovite (G)	6.5-7
Microcline (F)	6	Zoisite	6.5
Mullite	6-7	Pyrite	6.6
Nepheline	6	Albite (F)	7
Norbergite	6-6.5	Almandine (G)	7-8
Orthoclase (F)	6	Andesine (P)	7
Ottrelite (M)	6-7	Boracite	7
Pargasite (H)	6	Bytownite (P)	7
Petalite (Fp)	6-6.5	Clinozoite	7
Pigeonite (P)	6	Cordierite	7
Prehnite	6-6.5	Danburite	7
Pyrolusite	6-6.5	Epidote	7
Rhodonite	6	Oligoclase	7
Rutile	6-6.5	Quartz	7
Sanadine	6	Sillimanite	7
Scapolite	6	Staurolite	7-7.5
Sodalite (Fp)	6	Tourmaline	7
Sperrylite	6-7	Beryl	7.5-8
Tantalite	6-6.5	Euclase	7.5
Thorianite	6	Galaxite (S)	7.5
Andalusite	6.5-7	Hercynite (S)	7.5
Andradite (G)	6.5-7	Lawsonite	7.5
Axinite	6.5-7	Phenakite	7.5-8
Bravoite	6.5	Pyrope (G)	7.5
Chloritoid (M)	6.5	Zircon	7.5
Cristobalite	6.5	Gahnite (S)	8
Diaspore	6.5-7	Spinel group	8
Euxenite	6.5	Topaz	8
Fayalite (Ov)	6.5	Chrysoberyl	8.5
Gadolinite (R)	6.5-7	Dumortierite	8.5
Grossularite (G)	6.5-7.5	Corundum	9
Hematite	6.5	Diamond	10
Idocrase	6.5		

Distinct Color Minerals

Color	Mineral	Composition
Blue–Gray	Chalcocite	Cu_2S
Brass–Yellow	Chalcopyrite	$CuFeS_2$
Brass–Yellow(pale)	Electrum	Au,Ag
	Marcasite	FeS_2
	Millerite	NiS
	Pentlandite	$(Fe,Ni)S$
	Pyrite	FeS_2
Copper–Pink	Copper	Cu
	Niccolite	$NiAs$
	Breithauptite	$NiSb$
Copper–Pink (pale)	Maucherite	Ni_3As_2
	Melonite	$NiTe_2$
Cream	Emplecite	$Cu_2S \cdot Bi_2S_3$
	Calaverite / Krennerite	$(Au,Ag)Te_2$
Gold–Yellow	Gold	Au
Indigo–Blue	Covellite	CuS
Orange–Red	Crocoite	$PbCrO_4$
	Wulfenite	$PbMoO_4$
Pink	Erythrite	$Co_3(AsO_4)_2 \cdot 8H_2O$
	Kunzite	$LiAl(Si_2O_6)$
	Rhodochrosite	$MnCO_3$
	Rhodonite	$Mn(SiO_3)$
Pink to lilac	Lepidolite	$K_2Li_3Al_3(AlSi_3O_{10})_2$
Pink–Buffish	Bornite	Cu_5FeS_4
Pink–Cream	Cobaltite	$CoAsS$
	Bismuth	Bi
	Pyrrhotite	FeS
	Cubanite	$Cu_2S.Fe_4S_5$
Pink–Gray	Enargite	$Cu_2S \cdot C_uS \cdot As_2S_3$
	Famatinite	$Cu_2S \cdot CuS \cdot Sb_2S_3$
	Coloradote	$HgTe$
Purple	Bornite	Cu_5FeS_4
	Rickardite	Cu_3Te_2
	Umangite	Cu_3Se_3
	Germanite	$Cu_3(Fe,Ge)S_4$
Red	Cinnabar	HgS
	Lepidocrocite	$FeO(OH)$
	Realgar	AsS
	Zoisite (Thulite)	$Ca_2Al_3(SiO_4)_3(OH)$
Violet	Violarite	$(Ni,Fe)_3S_4$
	Bravoite	$(Ni, Fe)S_2$
Yellow	Carnotite	$K_2(UO_2)_2(VO_4)_2 \cdot$ nH_2O
	Orpiment	As_2S_3
	Perovskite	$CaTiO_3$
	Serpentine	$Mg_6(Si_4O_{10})(OH)_8$
	Tyuyamunite	$Ca(UO_2)_2(VO_4)_2$
Yellow–Brown	Jarosite	$KFe_3(OH)_6(SO_4)_2$
Yellow–Green	Autunite	$Ca(UO_2)_2(PO_4)_2 \cdot$ 10 to 12 H_2O
Yellow–Orange	Greenockite	CdS
Yellow–Red	Chondrodite	$Mg_3(SiO_4)_2(F,OH)_2$

Metal Content of Minerals

Name	% Metal
Aluminum	
Bauxite	74
Corundum	53
Spinel	38
Topaz	30
Variscite	17
Wavellite	20
Antimony	
Allemontite	62
Boulangerite	26
Cervantite	79
Jamesonite	29
Meneghinite	19
Miargyrite	41
Niccolite	56
Nickel-Skudderudite	76
Plagionite	38
Polybasite	11
Pyroargyrite	22
Semseyite	27
Stephanite	15
Stibnite	71
Tetrahedrite	30
Zinkenite	45
Arsenic	
Allemontite	38
Arsenopyrite	34
Loellingite	73
Orpiment	61
Proustite	15
Rammelsbergite	72
Realgar	70
Scorodite	32
Skutterudite	76
Sperrylite	43
Tennantite	20
Barite	
Barite	59
Witherite	70
Beryllium	
Beryl	5
Chrysoberyl	7
Phenakite	16
Bismuth	
Bismite	90
Bismuthinite	81
Chromium	
Chromite	46
Cobalt	
Cobaltite	36
Erythrite	30
Linnaeite	58
Siegenite	15
Skutterudite	18
Smaltite	28
Copper	
Antlerite	54
Azurite	55
Bornite	63
Brochantite	56
Chalcocite	80
Chalcopyrite	35
Clinoclase	50
Chrysocolla	36
Covellite	66
Cuprite	89
Digenite	78
Malachite	57
Polybasite	12
Stannite	30
Stromeyerite	31
Tennantite	48
Tetrahedrite	35
Torbernite	6
Gold	
Calaverite	44
Krennerite	44
Petzite	29
Sylvanite	34
Iron	
Hematite	70
Limonite	60
Mangetite	72
Marcasite	46
Pyrite	46
Pyrrhotite	61
Siderite	48
Triphyllite	35
Troilite	64
Violarite	19
Lead	
Anglesite	68
Boulangerite	55
Cerussite	77
Galena	87
Meneghenite	62
Minium	91
Phosgenite	76
Plagionite	40
Pyromorphite	76
Semseyite	53
Stolzite	46
Wulfenite	56
Zinkenite	32

Metal Content of Minerals

Name	% Metal	Name	% Metal
Magnesium		Sylvanite	6
Magnesite	29	**Tantalum**	
Periclase	60	(Ferro)Tantalite	70
Spinel	17	Polycrase	15
Manganese		Samarskite	12
Alabandite	63	**Tin**	
Braunite	64	Cassiterite	79
Hausmanite	72	Stannite	28
Manganoite	77	**Titanium**	
Pyrolusite	63	Anatase	60
Rhodochrosite	48	Brookite	60
Rhodonite	48	Ilmenite	32
Tephroite	54	Perovskite	35
Mercury		Polycrase	15
Calomel	85	Rutile	60
Cinnabar	86	Sphene	24
Metacinnabarite	86	**Tungsten**	
Molybdenum		Ferberite	60
Molybdenite	60	Huebnerite	61
Powellite	48	Scheelite	64
Wulfenite	26	Stolzite	40
Nickel		Woframite	60
Annabergite	29	**Uranium**	
Awaruite	72	U3O8	85
Chloanthite	28	Brannerite	34
Millerite	65	Carnotite	53
Niccolite	44	Phosphuranylite	64
Pentlandite	34	Polycrase	6
Rammelsbergite	28	Samarskite	16
Siegenite	43	Sklodowskite	55
Skutterudite	6	Torbernite	48
Violarite	39	Uraninite	88
Niobium		Uranophane	41
(Ferro)Columbite	55	**Vanadium**	
Polycrase	15	Roscoelite	10
Pyrochlore	52	Vanadite	11
Samarskite	25	V2O5	56
Silver		**Zinc**	
Acanthite	87	Calamine	54
Argentite	87	Franklinite	16
Bromargyrite	57	Gahnite	36
Cerargyrite	75	Hydrozincite	60
Embolite	70	Smithsonite	52
Hessite	46	Sphalerite	64
Miargyrite	37	Willemite	59
Pearceite	77	Wurtzite	61
Petzite	32	Zincite	73
Polybasite	60	**Zirconium**	
Proustite	65	Zircon	50
Pyrargyrite	60		
Stephanite	68		
Sternbergite	34		
Stromeyerite	53		

Gold, Silver, & Diamond Classification

GOLD

Gold purity is rated by the "karat"

24 karat	Very soft, not recommended for jewelry
22 karat	91.7% gold, soft, not recommended for jewelry
18 karat	75.0% gold, recommended for fine jewelry
14 karat	58.3% gold, average jewelry
12 karat	50% gold, not acceptable for jewelry
10 karat	41.7% gold, the lower limit at which a product is considered real gold

Pure gold yellow in color. It is commonly alloyed with silver, copper, nickel and zinc. White gold is an alloy of gold, nickel, copper and zinc.

SILVER

Silver quality is rated by a "fineness" mark. Pure silver is quite soft and unacceptable for most jewelry work. Silver can be alloyed with a variety of metals such as gold and copper.

.999 fine	Nearly pure silver. Used in coins.
.925 fine	When alloyed with 7.5% copper, it is called "sterling silver".

PLATINUM

Unlike gold and silver, platinum in its pure form is very durable. Jewery grade platinum is typically 95% platinum plus 5% iridium or palladium.

DIAMOND

Diamond quality and value are rated by their "Cut", "Color", "Clarity", and "Carat" weight. (Know as the "4 C's")

Cut	Cut refers to the symmetry and proportions of the stone and has a tremendous affect on the brilliance of the diamond. There are many cuts to choose from.
Color	Colorless diamonds are the most desirable. D color · · The best color, almost colorless. The color scale descends from D down through Z with the colors going from clear to yellow and brown
Clarity	Clarity is determined by the number of inclusions (or internal flaws) in the stone. The fewer the number of inclusions, the more valuable the stone. Clarity is graded on the size, location, number and type of flaws
Carat	The weight of a diamond is measured in "carats". Larger diamonds are more rare than smaller diamonds and therefore are worth more. 1 carat (metric) = 0.2 grams

Mineral Crystal System

Xtal System	Xtal Class	Xtal Symmetry
Isometric	Hexoctahedral *	
	C,3A4,4A3,6A2,9P	
	Gyroidal	3A4,4A3,6A2
	Hextetrahedral *	3A2,4A3,6P
	Diploidal *	C,3A2,4A3,3P
	Tetartoidal	3A2,4A3
Hexagonal:		
Hexagonal	Dihexagonal-dipyramidal *	C,1A6,6A2,7P
	Hexagonal-trapezohedral	1A6,6A2
	Dihexagonal-pyramidal *	1A6,6P
	Ditrigonal-dipyramidal *	1A3,3A2,4P
	Hexagonal-dipyramidal *	C,1A6,1P
	Hexagonal-pyramidal	1A6
	Trigonal-dipyramidal	1A3,1P
Trigonal**	Hexagonal-scalenohedral *	C,1A3,3A2,2P
	Trigonal-trapezohedral *	1A3,3A2
	Ditrigonal-pyramidal *	1A3,3P
	Rhombohedral	C,1A3
	Trigonal-pyramidal	1A3
Tetragonal	Ditetragonal-dipyramidal *	C,1A4,4A2,5P
	Tetragonal-trapezohedral	1A4,4A2
	Ditetragonal-pyramidal	1A4,4P
	Tetragonal-scalenohedral *	3A2,2P
	Tetragonal-dipyramidal	C,1A4,1P
	Tetragonal-pyramidal	1A4
	Tetragonal-disphenoidal	1A2
Orthorhombic	Rhombic-dipyramidal *	C,3A2,3P
	Rhombic-disphenoidal	3A2
	Rhombic-pyramidal *	1A2,2P
Monoclinic	Prismatic *	C,1A2,1P
	Sphenoidal	1A2
	Domatic	1P
Triclinic	Pinacoidal *	C
	Pedial	None

Symmetry values are coded as in the following example:
"C,1A4,4A2,3P" is Center of symmetry, **1 A**xis of **4** fold symmetry,
4 Axes of **2** fold symmetry, and **3 P**lanes of symmetry.

**Some references use the term "Rhombohedral"

There are a total of 32 crystal classes, however most minerals
crystallize in only 15 of those classes. The 15 common classes are
marked with an " * " after their name. The above data was obtained from *Danas Manual of Mineralogy*, by James D. Dana, 1959.

Minor Elements in Sed Rock

Average Concentration in parts per million (ppm)
Sedimentary Rocks Types

Element	Earth Crust	Soil	Calcareous	Arenaceous	Argillaceous
Antimony	0.2	2	...	1	3
Arsenic	1.8	7.5	0.5	0.5	20
Barium	425	300	60	250	450
Beryllium	2.8	0.5-4	...	...	3
Bismuth	0.17	0.8	...	0.3	1
Boron	10	29	18	90	220
Cadmium	0.2	0.3	0.05	...	0.2
Chlorine	130	...	200	...	...
Chromium	100	43	4	70	450
Cobalt	25	10	1	1	18
Copper	55	15	5	10	140
Fluorine	625	300	250	...	550
Gold	0.004	0.002	0.003	0.004	0.004
Iodine	0.5	...	4	0.4	1.7
Iron	35000	21000	3800	9700	46000
Lead	0.004	17	7	10	22
Lithium	20	22	10	15	51
Manganese	950	320	400	152	750
Mercury	0.08	0.056	0.03	0.4	0.8
Molybdenum	1.5	2.5	0.4	0.6	3
Nickel	75	17	3	5	44
Niobium	20	...	0.3	...	20
Phosphorus	700	300	200	300	740
Platinum Gp	0.006	...	...	...	...
Potassium	28000	11000	2700	10600	12000
Rare Earths	65	...	22	17	100
Rhenium	0.0004	0.005	...	0.0003	0.0005
Rubidium	90	35	56	40	143
Selenium	0.05	0.31	0.07	1	0.7
Silver	0.07	0.09	0.20	0.4	250
Strontium	375	67	600	20	260
Sulphur	100-2000	100-2000	2000	2400	1850
Tantalum	2	...	...	...	0.8
Tellerium	0.001	...	...	...	...
Thallium	0.45	0.1	...	2	2
Thorium	10	13	2	2	12
Tin	2	10	...	...	40
Titanium	5700	5000	400	1200	4500
Tungsten	1.5	1	0.6	...	3
Uranium	2.7	1	2	0.4	4
Vanadium	135	57	10	20	130
Zinc	70	36	12	15	200
Zirconium	165	270	25	260	160

Minor Elements in Ign Rock

Average Concentration in parts per million (ppm)
Igneous Rocks Types

Element	Granite/ Rhyolite	Syenite/ Trachyte	Diorite/ Andesite	Gabbro/ Basalt	Ultra Mafic
Antimony	0.2	0.5	0.2	0.15	0.1
Arsenic	1.8	3	2.5	1.7	1.1
Barium	600	1100	230	220	1.0
Beryllium	3.5	3.5	2.0	1	0.1
Bismuth	0.02	...	0.008	0.4	1.0
Boron	13	...	16	8	10
Cadmium	0.1	...	0.01	0.15	0.1
Chlorine	300	400	550	230	...
Chromium	30	1.3	55	225	2700
Cobalt	10	1	7	46	140
Copper	13	6	40	90	40
Fluorine	805	...	...	375	60
Gold	0.002	0.003	0.004	0.003	0.006
Iodine	0.17	0.15	0.2	0.11	0.12
Iron	14200	27000	32000	86500	94300
Lead	19	13	15	6	1.2
Lithium	40	30	25	16	0.2
Manganese	425	750	900	1550	1200
Mercury	0.06	...	0.06	0.05	0.008
Molybdenum	1.3	0.6	1.0	1.6	0.3
Nickel	10	4	35	135	2000
Niobium	10	35	15	19	11
Phosphorus	630	1300	1300	2000	1000
Platinum Gp	0.009	...	...	0.15	0.4
Potassium	42000	51000	21000	8300	34
Rare Earths	200	...	40	50	20
Rhenium	0.0006	...	0.0005	0.0006	...
Rubidium	160	200	60	32	0.14
Selenium	0.1	0.07	0.07	0.1	0.1
Silver	0.4	...	0.07	0.1	0.06
Strontium	200	1000	350	460	15
Sulphur	350	...	...	1000	2000
Tantalum	4.0	2	1.7	0.7	0.2
Tellerium	0.007	...	...	...	...
Thallium	2.3	1.5	0.4	0.3	0.02
Thorium	18	13	8.5	3	0.004
Tin	3.1	...	1.4	1.5	0.5
Titanium	1100	...	7400	12300	2700
Tungsten	1.7	1.2	1.5	0.9	0.3
Uranium	3.7	4.0	2.8	0.6	0.02
Vanadium	70	30	106	240	30
Zinc	50	80	55	100	56
Zirconium	180	500	180	130	43

Igneous Rock Classification[1]

Potash (K) Feldspar > 2/3 of Total Feldspar
Accessory Minerals: biotite, hornblende, pyroxene, muscovite

Coarse Grain	Fine Grain	Components
Granite	Rhyolite	Quartz > 10%
Syenite	Trachyte	Quartz & Feldspathoid < 10%
XXX Syenite	Phonolite	XXX Feldspathoid > 10%

Potash (K) Feldspar 1/3 to 2/3 of Total Feldspar
Accessory Minerals: biotite, hornblende, pyroxene

Coarse Grain	Fine Grain	Components
Quartz monzonite	Quartz Latite	Quartz > 10%
Monzonite	Latite	Quartz & Feldspathoid > 10%
XXX Monzonite	XXX Latite	XXX Feldspathoid > 10%

Plagioclase Feldspar > 2/3 of Total Feldspar
Potash (K) Feldspar > 10% of Total Feldspar
Accessory Minerals: hornblende, biotite, pyroxene

Coarse Grain	Fine Grain	Components
Granodiorite	Dacite	Quartz > 10%

Soda Plagioclase, Potash Feldspar<10% of Total Feldspar
Accessory Minerals: hornblende, biotite, pyroxene

Coarse Grain	Fine Grain	Components
Quartz Diorite	Dacite	Quartz > 10%
Diorite	Andesite	Quartz & Feldspathoid<10%

Calcic Plagioclase, Potash Feldspar<10% of Total Feldspar
Accessory Minerals: pyroxene, olivine, uralite

Coarse Grain	Fine Grain	Components
Gabbro, anorthosite	Basalt	Quartz & Feldspathoid<10%
Diabase		Quartz & Feldspathoid<10%
Theralite	Tephrite	Feldspathoid & Pyroxene>10%

Minor or No Feldspar – Mainly Pyroxene and/or Olivine
Accessory Minerals: Serpentine, iron ore

Coarse Grain	Fine Grain	Components
Peridotite, dunite	Limburgite	Pyroxene & olivine

Minor or No Feldspar – Mainly FerroMags & Feldspathoids
Accessory Minerals: hornblende, biotite, iron ore

Coarse Grain	Fine Grain	Components
Fergusite, Missourite	Leucite	FerroMags & Feldspathoids

Trap=Dark aphanitic rock, Felsite=Light aphanitic rock
Porphyry is >50% phenocrysts, porphyritic is <50% phenocrysts.
XXX is a descriptor, such as "biotite latite" for "XXX latite"
[1] *Classification of Rocks, 1955, Russell Travis, Colorado School Mines, Golden, Colorado.* See this book for more detail.

Igneous Rock Class by Color

There is no standard for the classification of igneous rocks by the percentage of dark minerals, however, the following three classes are most common:

S.J. Shand, 1947, Eruptive Rocks, John Wiley, New York

% Dark Minerals	Class Name
0 to 30	Leucocratic
30 to 60	Mesocratic
60 to 90	Melanocratic
> 90	Hypermelanic

S.J. Ellis, 1948, Minerology Magazine, Vol 28, p447-469

% Dark Minerals	Class Name
0 to 10	Holofelsic
10 to 40	Felsic
40 to 70	Mafelsic
> 70	Mafic

I.U.G.S, Anon, 1973, Geotimes, October 1973, p26-30

% Dark Minerals	Class Name
0 to 35	Leucocratic
35 to 65	Mesocratic
65 to 90	Melanocratic
> 90	Ultramafic

Sedimentary Rock Classes[1]

Grain Size < $\frac{1}{256}$ mm – Clastic and Crystalline

Mudstone: Includes claystone and siltstone
Shale: Clay based unit, finely fissile
Argillite: Indurated shale, recrystallized
Bentonite: Clay that swells when wet
Chert: Cryptocrystalline varieties of silica, flint is a variety
Diatomite: Rock made of silica frustules of diatom plants
Limestone: > 80% Calcium carbonate, crystalline
Dolomite: >80% Magnesium carbonate, crystalline
Chalk: Soft lime unit made of microorganism tests, calcite matrix
Caliche: Lime unit formed near surface, calcium carbonate cap
Marlstone: 25 to 75% clay and calcium carbonate
Siderite: Iron carbonate
Coal: Indurated, dense, carbon rock, made from lignite. Types
    range from bituminous to anthracite to graphite.
    8400 btu to 16000+ btu
Phosphorite: Phosphate (Collophane) Rock, massive
Halite (rock salt), Gypsum, & Anhydrite: Massive evaporites

Grain Size $\frac{1}{256}$ – 2 mm – Clastic and Crystalline

Oolite: Spherical with concentric or radial structure
    parts (calcium carbonate)
Limestone: > 80% Calcium carbonate, crystalline
Dolomite: >80% Magnesium carbonate, crystalline
Sandstone: Compacted clastic sediment, usually quartz grains
Arkose: Sandstone with > 25% feldspar grains
Graywacke: Sandstone w/ large quartz and feldspar fragments
    in a clay matrix, angular frags, well indurated
Subgraywacke: Graywacke w/ less feldspar and more quartz
Peat: Residual of partially decomposed vegetation in a bog
Lignite: Consolidated peat, between peat & coal, <8400 btu

Grain Size > 2 mm – Clastic

Conglomerate: Consolidated & rounded parts
Breccia: Consolidated & angular fragments
Gravel: Unconsolidated & rounded fragments
Rubble: Unconsolidated & angular fragments
Till: Unsorted glacial debris, mix of clay, sand, gravel, boulders

Grain Size $\frac{1}{256}$ to >2 mm – Clastic Volcanics

Agglomerate: Consolidated & rounded fragments > 32 mm
Volcanic Breccia: Consolidated & angular fragments > 4mm
Tuff: Consolidated volcanic ash
Ash: Unconsolidated particles < 4 mm

(1) Based in part on classes set up by *Classification of Rocks,
1955, Russell Travis, Colorado School Mines, Golden, CO.*

Metamorphic Rock Classes[1]

Primary Minerals

Quartz, feldspar, calcite, dolomite, talc, muscovite, sericite, chlorite, hornblende, serpentine, biotite, pyroxene, actinolite, epidote, olivine, magnetite

Accessory Minerals

Muscovite, sericite, sillimanite, kyanite, cordierite, tremolite, wollastonite, albite, andalusite, garnet, phlogopite, diopside, enstatite, staurolite, glaucophane, anthophyllite, pyrophyllite, chloritoid, actinolite, tourmaline, epidote, chiastolite, olivine, serpentine, chlorite, biotite, graphite, chondrodite, scapolite

Massive / Granular Structure (Contact Metamorphism)
Nondirectional – Fine, to Medium, to Coarse Grained:

Hornfels (catch–all term for nondirectional metamorphic unit)
Metaquartzite – primarily quartz, with silica cement
Marble – metamorphosed calcite or dolomite
Serpentine – metamorphosed olivine & pyroxene forming
    antigorite or chrysotile (asbestos)
Soapstone – massive talc

Lineate / Foliate Structure (Mechanical Metamorphism)
Cataclastic:

Mylonite - foliated, fine ground
Augen Gneiss – Augen (eye) structures in a gneissic rock of alter–
    nating bands of coarse granular minerals & schist minerals
Flaser Unite – Small lenses of granular material separated by
    wavy ribbons & streaks of fine crystalline, foliated material

Lineate / Foliate Structure (Regional Metamorphism)
Slaty, Phyllitic, Schistose, and Gneissose Structure:

Slate – metamorphosed shale, fissile, slatey cleavage
Phyllite – Argillic unit between slate and schist, silky sheen
Schist – med to coarse grained, mica minerals parallel orientation
Amphibolite – amphibole (hornblende) & plagioclase schist
Gneiss – coarse grained unit of alternating bands of coarse
    granular minerals & schistose minerals
Granulite – alternating coarse & fine bands of hornblende and
    mica, very planar schistosity, high temperature unit

Lineate / Foliate Structure (Plutonic Metamorphism)
Migmatitic Structure:

Migmatites – mixed unit of metamorphic material, this alternating
    layers or lenses of granitic and mafic gneissic material

(1) See previous page footnote for reference.

Geochem Detection Limits [1]

Element	Lower Detection Limit (ppm)	Standard Analysis Method
Aluminum	200	
Antimony	0.1	
Arsenic	0.4	
Barium	1	
Beryllium	0.1	
Bismuth	0.02	
Cadmium	0.04	
Calcium	200	
Cerium	0.02	
Chromium	2	
Cobalt	0.2	
Copper	0.4	
Fluorine	40	Fusion, specific ion electrode
Gold	0.001	Fire assay-atomic absorbtion
Iron	100	
Lanthanum	1	
Lead	1	
Lithium	0.4	
Manganese	10	
Mercury	0.01	Cold vapor- atomic absorbtion
Molybdenum	0.1	
Nickel	0.4	
Niobium	0.2	
Palladium	0.001	Fire assay/ICP-MS
Phosphorus	20	
Platinum	0.005	Fire assay-ICP
Platinum	0.0005	Fire assay/ICP-MS
Potassium	200	
Rhenium	0.004	
Rubidium	0.2	
Selenium	2	
Silver	0.4	
Strontium	0.4	
Sulphur	200	
Tantalum	0.1	
Tellurium	0.1	
Thallium	0.04	
Thorium	0.4	
Tin	0.4	
Titanium	200	
Tungsten	0.2	
Uranium	0.2	
Vanadium	1	
Yttrium	0.2	
Zinc	4	
Zirconium	1	

(1) Data courtesy of *Chemex Labs*.
(2) Unless otherwise indicated, analysis method is 4-acid digestion coupled with ICP-AES or ICP-MS.

Mohs Scale of Hardness

Mohs Index	Rock or Common Item
1	Talc
2	Gypsum
2.5	Fingernail
3	Calcite
3.5	Copper penny
4	Fluorite
5	Apatite
5.5	Glass, steel
6	Orthoclase
6.5	Streak plate
7	Quartz
8	Topaz
9	Corundum
10	Diamond

Particle Size Descriptions

Size Term	Particle Diameter
Sedimentary Units:	
Boulder	>256 mm
Cobble	64 to 256 mm
Pebble	4 to 64 mm
Granule	2 to 4 mm
Very Coarse Sand	1 to 2 mm
Coarse Sand	1/2 to 1 mm
Medium Sand	1/4 to 1/2 mm
Fine Sand	1/8 to 1/4 mm
Very Fine Sand	1/16 to 1/8 mm
Silt	1/256 to 1/16 mm
Clay	< 1/256 mm
Pyroclastic Units:	
Bomb or block	>32 mm
Lapilli	4 to 32 mm
Coarse Ash	1/4 to 4 mm
Fine Ash	< 1/4 mm
Igneous Rocks:	
Pegmatitic	> 30 mm
Coarse Grained	5 to 30 mm
Medium Grained	1 to 5 mm
Fine Grained	< 1 mm

Earthquake Scales

Moment Magnitude	Richter Magnitude	Mercalli Intensity	Description
1.0-3.0	2	I	Usually not felt, detected by instruments.
3.0	2	II	Felt by few, especially on upper floors of buildings, detected by instruments.
3.9	3	III	Felt noticeably indoors, vibration like a passing vehicle, cars may rock.
4.0		IV	Felt indoors by many, outdoors by few, dishes & doors disturbed, like heavy truck nearby, walls-cracking sound.
4.9	4	V	Felt by most people, slight damage; some dishes & windows broken, some cracked plaster, trees disturbed.
5.0	5	VI	Felt by all, many frightened and run outdoors, damage minor to moderate.
5.9	5 to 6	VII	Everyone runs outdoors, much damage to poor design buildings, minor damage to good design buildings, some chimneys broken, noticed by people driving cars.
6.0	6	VIII	Everyone runs outdoors, damage is moderate to major. Damage minor in well designed structures, major in poor designs; chimneys, columns, & walls fall, heavy furniture turned, well water changes; sand & mud ejected.
6.9	7	IX	Major damage in all structures, ground cracked, pipes broken, shift foundation.
7.0 +	7 & 8	X	Major damage, most masonry & frame structures destroyed, ground badly cracked, landslides, water sloshed over river banks, rails bent.
	8	XI	Almost all masonry structures destroyed bridges fall, big fissures in ground, land slumps, rails bent greatly.
	8 & above	XII	Total destruction. Ground surface waves seen, objects thrown up into the air. All construction destroyed.

Richter Magnitudes (ML) are based on the movement of an instrument needle and increases logarithmically, 10 times for each number jump, so ML 8 is not twice as large as ML 4, it is 10,000 times as large! Richter Magnitude is an open-ended scale.

Moment Magnitude (MW) is the modern version of the Richter Magnitudes. Moment Magnitude is based on the energy released by an earthquake and is also logrithmic, but by a factor of 32 not 10. MW 4 releases 65,000,000 Btu while MW8 releases 69,000,000,000,000 Btu. The largest Moment Magnitude recorded to date was 9.5 and occured in Chile on 5/22/1960.

Mercalli Intensity (MM) is based on actual observations of the resulting damage, and therefore can not be measured on instruments.

Core Drill Specs

Core Size	Core Diameter Inch	mm	Core Volume cu inch/foot	Hole Diameter Inch	mm
CONVENTIONAL:					
EX or EWM	0.845	21.5	6.7	1.485	37.7
EXT	0.905	23.0	7.7	1.485	37.7
E17	0.968	24.6	8.8	1.485	37.7
AX or AWM	1.185	30.1	13.2	1.890	48.0
AXT	1.280	32.5	15.4	1.890	48.0
A17	1.310	33.3	16.2	1.890	48.0
BX,BXM,BWM	1.655	42.0	25.8	2.360	59.9
NX, NXM, NXMS, NWM	2.155	54.7	43.8	2.980	75.7
BM	1.281	32.5	15.5	2.360	59.9
BMLC	1.386	35.2	18.1	2.360	59.9
NMLC	2.045	51.9	39.4	2.980	75.7
A19DT	1.156	29.4	12.6	1.890	48.0
A19TT	1.062	27.0	10.6	1.890	48.0
B19DT	1.565	39.8	23.1	2.360	59.9
B19TT	1.500	38.1	21.2	2.360	59.9
N19DT	2.095	53.2	41.4	2.980	75.7
N19TT	2.045	51.9	39.4	2.980	75.7
H19DT	2.500	63.5	58.9	3.783	96.1
H19TT	2.406	61.1	54.6	3.783	96.1
WIRELINE:					
AQ	1.062	27.0	10.6	1.890	48.0
BQ	1.433	36.4	19.3	2.360	59.9
NQ	1.875	47.6	33.1	2.980	75.7
HQ	2.500	63.5	58.9	3.783	96.1
BQ3	1.320	33.5	16.4	2.360	59.9
NQ3	1.775	45.1	29.7	2.980	75.7
HQ3	2.406	61.1	54.6	3.783	96.1
PQ3	3.270	83.1	100.8	4.828	122.6
B18DT	1.565	39.8	23.1	2.360	59.9
B18TT	1.500	38.1	21.2	2.360	59.9
N18DT	2.095	53.2	41.4	2.980	75.7
N18TT	2.045	51.9	39.4	2.980	75.7
H18DT	2.500	63.5	58.9	3.783	96.1
H18TT	2.406	61.1	54.6	3.783	96.1

Geologic Time Scale

Era	Period or System	Epoch, Age or Series	Approximate[1] Million Years Before Present
Phanerozoic Eon:			0 to 543
Cainozoic or Cenozoic:			0 to 65
	Quaternary		0 to 1.8
	Holocene		0 to 0.011
		Iron Age	
		Bronze Age	
		Neolithic	
		Mesolithic	
		Pleistocene	0.011 to 1.8
	Tertiary		2 to 65
	Neogene		1.8 to 23.8
		Pliocene	1.8 to 5.3
		Miocene	5.3 to 23.8
	Paleogene		23.8 to 65
		Oligocene	23.8 to 33.7
		Eocene	33.7 to 54.8
		Paleocene	54.8 to 65
Mesozoic			65 to 248
	Cretaceous		65 to 144
	Jurassic		144 to 206
	Triassic		206 to 248
Paleozoic			248 to 543
	Permian		248 to 290
	Carboniferous		290 to 354
	Pennsylvanian		290 to 323
	Mississippian		323 to 354
	Devonian		354 to 417
	Silurian		417 to 443
	Ordovician		443 to 490
	Cambrian		490 to 543
Proterozoic & Archaen:			543 to start
Neoproterozoic (Precambrian Z)			600 to 900
Mesoproterozoic (Precambrian Y)			800 to 1600
Paleoproterozoic (Precambrian X)			1600 to 2500
Archaean (Precambrian W)			2500 to start

(1) Accepted dates vary greatly, these represent an average set.
(2) Basic data reference Geologic Society of America

Glue, Solvents, Paints & Finishes

Glues & Adhesives, Types & Applications

Acrylic Resin Adhesive

Bonds to anything porous or nonporous, waterproof, very strong, fast setting (3 to 30 minutes), oil and gasoline resistant, good gap and hole filling. Synthetic resin based. 2 part - liquid and powder, expensive, tan. Brands: "3 Ton Adhesive" and "P.A.C. - Plastic Adhesive Cement," Tridox Labs, Philadelphia, PA and "330 Depend No-Mix Adhesive", Loctite Corporation, Rocky Hill, CT.

Acrylonitrile Adhesive

Bonds to anything porous or nonporous, not recommended for wood, flexible, waterproof, similar to rubber cement. Synthetic polymer based. 1 part liquid, flammable, brown. Brand: "Pliobond 1100-2," Ashland Chemical Company, Columbus, OH.

Albumin Glue

Used in interior-type plywood, not as strong as other animal glues, moderately resistant to water and damp atmosphere, high dry strength, applied at room temperature, cured at 250°F, not resistant to mold and fungi. Natural protein based. Made from blood and casein. Dark red to black.

Aliphatic Resin Glue (Yellow glue)

Used mainly for wood; aliphatic resin is a moisture resistant form of polyvinyl acetate glue (PVA glue); not waterproof; very strong; dries translucent; instant sticky but dries in 45 minutes to 24 hours; high resistance to solvents, heat, oil, and grease; sandable; will set at temperatures from 55°F to 110°F; dries hard; glue can be colored with water soluble dyes; not good for bonding over old glues; not good for furniture repair! Synthetic resin based. 1 part liquid, light yellow color, non-toxic, non-flammable, no stain, do not expose to lacquer thinner. Brands: "Titebond Glue," Franklin International, Columbus, OH and "DAP Weldwood Carpenter's Wood Glue," DAP Inc, Baltimore, MD (many others, very common glue).

Anaerobic Adhesive

Bonds metal. Anaerobic adhesives cure only in the absence of air and only in the presence of metal. Used for threadlocking, threadsealing, gasketing, and retaining metal parts; high resistance to chemicals and harsh environmental conditions including vibration; available in a wide range of strengths, flexibilities, viscosities, and gap filling abilities; may be used with either ferrous or non-ferrous metals. Synthetic resin based. 1 part liquid, many colors from purple to green. Brands: "103 Nutlock," Impact Adhesives, Bradford, West Yorkshire, England; "262 Threadlocker Medium to High Strength,"

Loctite Corporation, Rocky Hill, CT; and "Perma-Lok MM115 General Purpose Threadlocker," Permabond Engineering Adhesives, Englewood, NJ.

Bone Glue

Used mostly in making of cartons and paper boxes, there are 15 grades of bone glue based on quality of raw material, method of extraction, and material blend. Green bone glue is used for gummed paper and tapes for cartons. Bone glues are no longer made in the US. Natural protein based. Made from bones. Brand: "Bone Glue," Milligan and Higgins, Johnstown, NY.

Casein Glue

Use mainly for wood; high water resistance (not waterproof); resistant to oil, grease, and gasoline; good gap filling; sets at temperatures above 32°F; high dry strength; clamps recommended; dries in 8 hours. Very good when working with tropical hardwoods, but tough on cutting tools. Natural protein based. Made from milk curd. 1 part powder, mix with water, inexpensive, white to tan color. Brands: "No. 30 Casein Glue," National Casein Company, Chicago, IL and "Casehesive," American Casein Company, Burlington, NJ.

Cellulose Acetate Adhesive

Bonds cellulose acetate plastics, photographic film, balsa wood, porous materials including leather, paper, and fabric.

Cellulose Nitrate Adhesive

Bonds to many porous or nonporous materials, good water resistance (not waterproof), fast setting (2 hours to 24 hours), moderately high strength (up to 3500 psi), shrinks some on drying. 1 part liquid, flammable, clear to amber. Brands: "Ever Fast Liquid Cement," Ambroid Co, Taunton, MA and "Devcon Duco Cement," Chemical Development Corporation, Danvers, MA.

Ceramic Adhesive

Bonds ceramics, glass, and metal. Made with porcelain enamel grit, iron oxide, and stainless steel powder. Heat resistant to 1500°F, shear strength of 1500 psi, must be heated to 1750°F in order to cure. Common in aerospace applications.

Contact Cement (Contact adhesive)

Bonds to many porous or nonporous materials but mainly for laminates to wood, water resistant (not waterproof), requires application of a thin film to both pieces, let dry 40 minutes, then put pieces together for an instant bond, moderate to high strength. Synthetic rubber compound. 1 part liquid, flammable (solvent), adequate ventilation required.

Brands:"DAP Weldwood Original Contact Cement," DAP Inc, Baltimore, MD; "Constantine's Veneer Glue," Constantine's, Bronx, NY; "3M Fastbond Contact Adhesive," Minnesota Mining and Manufacturing Company, St. Paul, MN; and "Devcon Contact Cement," Chemical Development Corporation, Danvers, MA.

Cyanoacrylate Glue (CA glue) (Super Glue)

Bonds many materials including metals, rubber, and most plastics; not a good wood glue; nonporous; oil, water, and chemical resistant; very fast setting (< 5 seconds); low viscosity formulas are not gap fillers, use high viscosity formulas for gaps; poor shock and peel resistance; no clamping needed. Chemically reacts with moisture in the material being glued, may not cure in extremely dry climates. Use extreme care when working with this glue, IT BONDS SKIN INSTANTLY! Acetone clean up. Monomer resin based. 1 part liquid, non-flammable. Brands: "Devcon Premium Super Glue II," Chemical Development Corporation, Danvers, MA; "3M Pronto Instant Adhesive CA-7," Minnesota Mining and Manufacturing Company, St. Paul, MN; "Permabond," Permabond Engineering Adhesives, Englewood, NJ; "Krazy Glue Original," Elmer's Products, Inc, Columbus, OH; "Spectrum Jet Set 41," Holdtite Adhesives Limited, Gateshead, England; and "DAP Super Glue," DAP Inc, Baltimore, MD (many others, very common glue).

Epoxy Adhesive

Bonds to many materials, porous or nonporous; waterproof; resistant to most solvents and acid; setting time ranges from very fast (5 minutes) to very long (weeks); very high dry and wet strength. Some varieties are filled with metal powder (such as steel, aluminum, brass, or titanium) to function as a metal filler. Liquid, gel, and paste formulas usually dry transparent to brown, can be thinned and cleaned with acetone, non-shrinking if no thinner is used. Putty formulas dry to a variety of colors, non-shrinking. Hardens without evaporation (result of chemical reaction and heat). 2 part liquid, gel, paste, or putty; non-flammable; not flexible; liquid, gel, and paste are clear to tan, putty may be green, blue, gray, or black. Brands: "Scotch-Weld Epoxy Adhesive 2158," Minnesota Mining and Manufacturing Company, St. Paul, MN; "Probond Regular Epoxy" and "Elmer's Superfast Epoxy," Elmer's Products, Inc, Columbus, OH; "Fixmaster 4 Minute Epoxy," Loctite Corporation, Rocky Hill, CT; "Devcon 5-Minute Thick Gel Epoxy" and "Devcon Titanium 5 Epoxy," Chemical Development Corporation, Danvers, MA; "VR Epoxy Series," Abatron, Inc, Kenosha, WI; and "J-B Weld,"

"J-B Kwik," "Marineweld," "Waterweld," and "Industro Weld," J-B Weld Company, Sulphur Springs, TX. Extremely common adhesive, most major adhesive manufacturers produce epoxy adhesives.

Ethylene Vinyl Acetate Glue (EVA glue)
Bonds a variety of slick nonporous materials to porous materials, originally developed for overlays such as vinyl and metallic films. High initial tack, dries to a soft, flexible film. Synthetic resin based. 1 part liquid. Brands: "Melamine Glue," Custom-Pak Adhesives, Newark, OH; "Extreme 6001XHM," Adhesive Engineering and Supply, Seabrooke, NH; and "0007 Waterbase Adhesive," Chembond Adhesives, Inc, Tiffin, OH.

Fish Glue
Bonds porous or nonporous materials. Used for woodworking, bellows for organs and player pianos, photographic mounting, gummed paper, household use, and in paints. Natural protein based. Made from the jelly separated from fish oil or skins. The best fish glue is made from Russian isinglass which is produced from sturgeon. High initial tack, long cure time. 1 part paste. Brands: "Fish Glue", Arndt Organ Supply, Ankeny, IA and "Cold Fish Glue", Norland Products, Inc, New Brunswick, NJ.

Furan Cement
Made with synthetic furfural alcohol resins, very strong and highly resistant to chemicals and high temperatures. Commonly used for bonding acid resistant brick and tile.

Hide Glue - Flake
Bonds wood primarily, main glue used in musical instruments and old cabinet work, known as "hot glue" because it is applied while hot, at least 15 grades of hide glue are available, non-staining, fast setting, begins to gel at about 95°F, cures by evaporation, high dry strength (2000 psi), not waterproof. Natural protein (collagen) based. Made mainly from cattle hides. Good quality hide glue has a light clean odor, the cheap stuff stinks! 1 part-dry flakes, mixed with water (about 100 grams of dry glue to 180 grams of water), non-flammable, apply hot (145°F), and be careful of "cold joints" on the work. Brands: "Constantine's Cabinet Flake (Hide) Glue", Constantine's, Bronx, NY; "Hide Glue", Milligan and Higgins, Johnstown, NY; "Hide Glue", Bjorn Industries, Inc, Charlotte, NC; and "Hide Glue", Pianotek Supply Company, Ferndale, MI.

Hide Glue - Liquid (Pearl hide glue)
Bonds wood primarily; similar to flake hide glue but requires no mixing or heating; long setting time; heat resistant; resistant to most sealers, lacquers, water,

mold and varnish; high strength; not flexible but not brittle. Natural protein based. 1 part liquid, non-flammable, honey color. Brand: "Franklin Hide Glue", Franklin International, Columbus, OH.

Hot Melt Glue

Formulations are available to bond most materials, porous or nonporous. Very fast setting time (< 1 minute), moderate to no flexibility, cures by cooling not evaporation, medium strength, waterproof. Sticks of hot melt glue are applied with a special electric hot melt "glue gun", thin materials with hot melt glue backings are applied with an iron. Thermoplastic resin based, a wide variety of resins are available. 1 part solid sticks, pellets, or backings; non-flammable. Brands: "3M Jet-Weld Thermoset Adhesive TE-200", Minnesota Mining and Manufacturing Company, St. Paul, MN; "Hot-Grip", Adhesive Products Corporation, Chicago, IL; "Glue Stix SS6 Slow Set - Woodworking", Arrow Fastener Company, Inc, Saddle Brooke, NJ; and "HM101 Glue Sticks", Chembond Adhesives, Inc, Tiffin, OH (many others, very common adhesive).

Latex Combo Adhesive

Sticks a variety of materials, porous or nonporous, especially good for fabric and paper, water resistant (some are waterproof), moderate to weak strength, very flexible (becomes a synthetic rubber when cured). 1 part liquid or paste, non-flammable. Brand: "Flexible Patch-Stix", Adhesive Products Corporation, Chicago, IL.

Latex Glue

Rub-off latex, used mainly in photographic mounting, does not shrink.

Latex Resin Adhesive

Bonds a wide variety of materials both porous and nonporous such as paper, wood, and metals; use at temperatures above 20°F; cures completely in 24 hours; after cure it is water and heat resistant; high strength; water clean up when wet; mineral spirits clean up when dry. Synthetic latex resin based. 1 part paste, white. Brand: "DAP Easy Bond Do-It-All Adhesive", DAP Inc, Baltimore, MD.

Neoprene Adhesive

Bonds a variety of materials, porous or nonporous, but primarily used to bond paneling to walls; water resistant; moderate to high strength; setting time is two part - apply and separate for 10 minutes to increase tack, then join parts; final set 24 hours. Synthetic rubber based. 1 part viscous liquid, flammable. Brand: "DAP Weldwood Panel Adhesive", DAP Inc, Baltimore, MD.

Polyester Resin Adhesive (Automotive body filler)(Wood filler)

Bonds a variety of materials. Liquid is used mainly

with fiberglass cloth to bond to wood or metal for boat hulls, surf boards, and car bodies; paste is mixed with a filler such as talc and used as an automotive body filler or wood filler. Waterproof, not flexible, high strength, use at temperatures from 70°F to 80°F, setting time < 30 minutes. Color of liquid is usually clear to amber but can be tinted, paste is usually gray or brown; both can be sanded and painted. Synthetic resin based. 2 part liquid or 1 part paste, flammable, amount of catalyst for 2 part liquid is critical so measure precisely. Brands: "Fiberglass Resin Jelly" and "Evercoat Rage Premium Lightweight Body Filler", Fibre Glass-Evercoat, Cincinnati, OH; "Polyester General Purpose Resin ", Fiberglass Coatings, Inc, St. Petersburg, FL; "Automotive Resin ", Kardol Quality Products, Inc, Lebanon, OH; "Bondo Body Filler", Bondo/Mar-Hyde Corporation, Cincinnati, OH; and "Minwax High Performance Wood Filler", Sherwin-Williams Company, Cleveland, OH.

Polysulfide Adhesive

Bonds to a variety of materials but is primarily for sealing seams; basically a caulking type adhesive that, when dry, is completely waterproof; setting time varies from several days to several weeks depending on humidity; medium strength; when cured it becomes a synthetic rubber; flexible. Synthetic elastomer based. 1 or 2 part. Brand: "Exide Polysulfide Caulk", Atlas Minerals and Chemicals, Mertztown, PA.

Polyurethane Glue

Bonds to virtually everything but is superior for wood bonding, pressure and moisture are necessary for optimum bonding, chemically reacts with moisture in the material being glued, expands to fill voids. Expansion can be a problem if too much glue is applied to a joint, use SPARINGLY! Use at temperatures between 40°F and 90°F. 90% cure in 1 to 4 hours, fully cured in 24 hours, clamp pieces together after 15 minutes. Waterproof when dry, accepts stains well, easy to sand, will not dull tools. Wet glue cleans up with denatured alcohol, acetone, or mineral spirits; once dry only mechanical removal (sanding) works. Eye, throat, and skin irritant; use in well ventilated area. Synthetic resin based. 1 part liquid. Amber color when wet, dries to a tan color. Brands: "Gorilla Glue", Lutz File and Tool Company, Cincinnati, OH; "Titebond Polyurethane Glue", Franklin International, Columbus, OH; "Excel One Liquid Polyurethane Adhesive", AmBel Corporation, Cottonport, LA; and "Probond Polyurethane Glue", Elmer's Products, Inc, Columbus, OH.

Polyvinyl Acetate Glue (PVA glue) (Elmer's Glue) (White glue)

Bonds wood, paper products, fabric, leather, and ceramics; not waterproof; very strong if away from moisture; setting times vary from several hours to several days; use at temperatures above 60°F; dries transparent; use for gap filling; do not use where glue must support load; corrodes metal. Does not bond well over old glues, not good for furniture repair! Synthetic resin based. 1 part liquid, non-flammable, white liquid-dries clear. Brands: "DAP Weldwood Hobby and Craft Glue", DAP Inc, Baltimore, MD and "Elmer's Glue-All", Elmer's Products, Inc, Columbus, OH (many more, very common glue).

Polyvinyl Chloride Glue (PVC glue)

Bonds glass, china, porcelain, metal, marble, hard plastics, and other materials including some porous (treat both sides for porous); not generally for wood; waterproof; resistant to gasoline, oil, and alcohol; fast setting (minutes); clean up with lacquer thinner. 1 part liquid, flammable, clear. Brand: "Sheer Magic", Miracle Adhesives Corp, Long Island, NY.

Pyroxylin Cement (Household cement)

Solution of nitrocellulose in a solvent which is sometimes mixed with resin, gum, or synthetic; poor tack but excellent adhesion to almost everything.

Rabbit-skin Glue

Bonds wood but is primarily used for gilding, artwork, and furniture repair. Natural protein based. Made from rabbit skins.

Resorcinol Resin Glue

Bonds a variety of materials but is used mainly as a boat building glue (the main one); completely waterproof; thinning and cleanup before setting with alcohol and water; when cured it is resistant to water, salt water, gasoline, oil, acids, alkalis, and many solvents; setting time varies with temperature - 10 hours at 70°F to 3 hours at 100°F; do not use at temperatures below 70°F; very strong; cures to a very dark color; can be sanded and painted; good gap filler; do not use with copper or copper alloys. Synthetic resin based. 2 part liquid and powder, caustic powder, red. Brand: "DAP Weldwood Waterproof Resorcinol Glue", DAP Inc, Baltimore, MD.

Rice Glue

Bonds to wood, paper, fabric, leather; dry powder must be cooked with water; pre-cooked paste is available; long cure time; good initial tack; dries clear; flexible. Natural starch based. Made from rice. 1 part dry powder or paste.

Rubber Adhesive (Construction adhesive)
(Elastomeric mastic)

Bonds to almost anything, porous or nonporous, will not bond two nonporous materials; water, heat, and alcohol resistant; strong bond; moderately flexible; good gap filling; setting time 24 hours; full strength is reached after 24 hours; use at temperatures above 40°F. Natural or synthetic rubber based, light gray to black color. 1 part viscous liquid, solvents, use adequate ventilation. Brands: "Black Magic Tough Glue", Miracle Adhesives Corporation, Long Island, NY; "DAP Beats The Nail All Purpose Construction Adhesive", DAP Inc, Baltimore, MD; "Devcon Rubber Adhesive", Chemical Development Corporation, Danvers, MA; and "LN-601, Liquid Nails Multi-Purpose Construction Adhesive", Macco Adhesives, Cleveland, OH.

Silicone Adhesive

Although this group is primarily a sealer or caulking compound, it does have adhesive characteristics. Bonds porous or nonporous materials, moderate to weak strength, waterproof, setting time from 2 hours to 2 days, can withstand temperatures of 400°F to 600°F, flexible, will not bond to itself, resists oil and some solvents. 1 part viscous liquid, non-flammable. Brands: "Silicone II Household Glue", General Electric Co, Waterford, NY and "Devcon Premium Silicone Adhesive", Chemical Development Corporation, Danvers, MA.

Soybean Glue

Bonds wood chip layers in interior plywood and paneling, better water resistance than most vegetable pastes and better adhesive power, moderate to low dry strength. Natural protein based. Made from soybean cake. 1 part, yellow powder mixed with water, white to tan paste.

Tapioca Glue

Also known as vegetable glue, used in cheap plywoods, postage stamps, envelopes, and labels. Quick tack and cheap, but deteriorates.

Ultraviolet Curing Adhesive

A variety of synthetic resin and polymer based adhesives that are liquid or paste on application and cure only when exposed to ultraviolet light; typically used for bonding glass to glass, metal, and plastic. Brands: "Solar 7000", Impact Adhesives, West Yorkshire, England and "352 Loctite", Loctite Corporation, Rocky Hill, CT.

Urea-Resin Glue (Plastic resin glue)

Bonds wood primarily; resistant to water, oil, gasoline, and many solvents when cured; do not use with copper or copper alloys; setting time ranges from 3 to 7 hours (less at high temperatures); very high strength (usually stronger than wood); not a gap filler; non-staining; amber or light tan to black color. Synthetic resin based. 1 part powder, mix with water to form cream or 2 part liquid resin and powder catalyst. Brand: "DAP Weldwood Plastic Resin Glue", DAP Inc, Baltimore, MD.

Vinyl Adhesive

Another caulk with adhesive properties. Bonds to a variety of construction materials including wood, concrete, tile, glass, fabric, and metal; water clean up before cure; water resistant after cure; high strength; flexible; paintable; resistant to mildew, oils, paint thinner, gasoline, asphalt, antifreeze, soap, rust, corrosion, salt water, mild acids, and mild alkalis; will bond to itself; will bond damp materials, moisture aids curing. Available in a variety of colors. Synthetic polymer based. 1 part paste, non-toxic, non-flammable. Brand: "Phenoseal Vinyl Adhesive Caulk", Gloucester Company, Franklin, MA.

Water-Phase Epoxy Adhesive

Bonds to many materials but is used primarily with fiberglass as a repair tool and as a surface coat for concrete floors, water soluble when liquid and completely waterproof when hard, medium to high strength, fast setting < 30 minutes, can be sanded and painted. 2 part liquid. Brand: "Dur-A-Poxy High Gloss Water- Based Formula", Dur-A-Flex, East Hartford, CT.

Wheat Glue

Bonds to wood, paper, fabric, and leather; mainly used in paper cartons and bottle labeling; dry powder must be cooked with water; pre-cooked paste is available; long cure time; good initial tack; dries clear; flexible. Natural starch based. Made from wheat. 1 part dry powder or paste.

NOTES:
In all of the glue descriptions, the term "wood" also refers to "wood products" such as plywood, particle board, and aspen board.

Glue Hints and General Rules

1. Apply glues and adhesives to clean, dry surfaces.

2. Drying/curing times can usually be reduced by increasing the temperature. 70°F or higher is generally preferred.

3. Be careful of the solvents and catalysts used in many adhesives, most are toxic and can also hurt your eyes, skin, and lungs. Use adequate ventilation!

4. Hardwoods require less clamping time than softwoods.

5. Domestic hardwoods are usually easier to glue than imported, tropical hardwoods.

6. The end grain of any wood is highly absorbent and will create a weak joint. To prevent this, apply a thin coat of glue to the end grain before the rest of the work and then give it a second coat when doing the normal gluing.

7. Precision alignment of parts glued with contact cement can be obtained by placing a thin sheet of paper between the work pieces after the contact cement has been applied and is no longer tacky, align the work pieces, press together, and then pull out the paper for final bonding.

8. Don't glue green wood. Damp wood may be glued with one of the adhesives that cures by reacting with water.

9. Clamp glue joints whenever possible for increased strength.

10. Don't apply too much glue, this can actually weaken a joint in some cases.

11. When all else fails READ AND FOLLOW DIRECTIONS!

RESOURCES:

Excellent books on common glues and adhesives are:

Adhesives Handbook, 3rd Edition, 1984, J. Shields, Butterworth and Co, London, England.

Home and Workshop Guide to Glues and Adhesives, 1979, George Daniels, Popular Science, Harper and Row, New York, NY.

The Glue Book, 1999, William Tandy Young, The Taunton Press, Newtown, CT.

They contain an abundance of information on glues, gluing techniques, and hints. Any of these books would be a great addition to a reference library!

On the World Wide Web see:

"The Sticky Issue of Adhesives, Glues, and Tapes" at www.naturalhandyman.com

"Adhesive Bonding of Wood Materials" by Charles B. Vick, at www.fpl.fs.fed.us/documnts/fplgtr/fplgtr113/ch09.pdf.

Paints and Finishes

House and Industrial Paints

There are basically 5 groups of house and industrial paints: oil base, alkyd, emulsion, water thinned, and catalytic. Each of these classes is subdivided into exterior and interior.

Oil Base

Interior and exterior, oil vehicle, thinned by solvents such as turpentine and mineral spirits, very slow drying, strong smell. Mainly used as exterior paint. Use in well ventilated area. Good adhesion to chalky surfaces.

Alkyd

Synthetic oil vehicle of a resin known as alkyd. Interior and exterior enamels, easy to apply, fast drying, odorless, and produce a tough coating. Easy cleanup and thinning with mineral spirits. Excellent interior paint, not resistant to chemicals, solvents, or corrosives.

Emulsion

Water based paint mixture. Latex paints fall into this category, the most common latex paints are acrylic and vinyl (PVA). Available as interior and exterior, and as flat, gloss, and semigloss enamels. Very quick drying (sometimes less than 1 hour) but do not wash for 2 to 4 weeks, paints over damp surfaces, odorless, alkali resistant, doesn't usually blister and peel. Excellent cover and blending characteristics, but poor adhesion to chalky surfaces, easy cleanup. Use special latex primers for painting bare wood. Paint at temperatures above 45°F. By far the most popular paint today.

Water-Thinned

Generally a non-emulsion paint such as calcimine, casein, and white wash. These paints are used primarily on masonry surfaces. The most common water thinned paint is Portland Cement paint.

Catalytic

Cures by chemical reaction, not by evaporation of a solvent or water as in the other paints. Catalytic paints are usually two-part paints: you have to mix two parts to start the curing process. Included in this class are the epoxy and polyurethane resins. Extremely tough and durable, they are highly resistant to water, wear, acids, solvents, abrasion, salt water, and chemicals. Drying times are very fast (several hours). Good ventilation is necessary when working with these paints. Catalytic paints can not be applied over other paints. Follow the manufacturer's instructions very closely, these paints are not easy to use.

House paints are further subgrouped into exterior and interior types as described below:

Exterior Paint

Designed to have long life spans, good adhesion, and resistance to moisture, ultraviolet light, mildew, and sulfide and acid fumes. Often includes the varnish and stain groups described later. Never use interior paint in place of exterior paint; it will not hold up under the weather.

Interior Paint

Designed to maximize the hiding ability of the paint with only 1 or 2 coats. Flat paints contain more pigment than high sheen paints but are less durable. Good interior paints can be touched up easily without major changes in the sheen or color.

Wood Finishes

Varnish

Varnish is a solution of a hard resin, a drying oil (linseed oil is most common), metallic dryers, and solvent. There are two types of resin, natural and synthetic. Natural resin varnishes are slow drying (24 to 48 hrs) and are subclassed as "long oil" (meaning high oil content; "spar" varnish is a long oil varnish) and "short oil" (meaning low oil content; "rubbing" varnish is a short oil). Natural resin varnishes are tough and used mainly for exterior and marine applications. Synthetic resin varnishes contain resins such as alkyd (the most common), polyurethane, vinyl, and phenolic. They are more durable and faster drying than natural resin varnishes. Apply with natural bristle brushes; apply 3 to 4 coats total, let dry between coats, and sand with 240 grit sandpaper. Varnishes are usually transparent and are excellent sealers.

Shellac

Shellac is one of the oldest wood finishes. It is made from a mixture of the dry resinous secretions of the lac insect (*laccifer lacca*, southern Asia, mainly northern India) and alcohol. Once mixed, shellac has a very short shelf life, so store it in flake form. Keep water off of shellac! Even a few drops of water will turn shellac cloudy. Shellac is mixed in what is called a "cut." A "3 pound cut" is 3 pounds of shellac in 1 gallon of alcohol. Initial coats are typically 1 or 2 pound cuts. Shellac is applied with a brush. Better finishes use 6 to 8 coats. Each coat should be sanded with 220 to 240 grit sandpaper after it has dried (1 to 2 hours). The final coat is typically rubbed out with a fine 3/0 steel wool.

Lacquer

Lacquer is a fast-drying, high gloss varnish used by

most furniture manufacturers as the top-coat finish. It is very hard, dries crystal clear, and is highly resistant to alcohols, water, heat, and mild acids. Although the original lacquers came from insects and the sap of the sumac tree, almost all lacquers produced today are synthetic and are mixed with some combination of resins (better adhesion), nitrocellulose, linseed or castor oil (improves flexibility), vinyls, acrylics or synthetic polymers. The main problem with lacquer is that it dries so fast that it is sometimes difficult to get a good finish. Use a spray gun if possible; a brush does not work. Multiple coats are usually necessary. Some finishes may react with the solvents in lacquer and may need to be protected with a coat of shellac before applying lacquer.

Oil

Penetrating oils such as linseed oil, tung oil, and Danish rubbing oil make up a class of finishes that protect wood while leaving the grain and natural texture visible. Oils won't crack, chip, or scale off and provide a beautiful surface. The addition of resins such as polyurethane greatly increase the toughness of the surface and still maintain the clear finish. The oils are applied with a soft rag, left to sit for 30 minutes to allow the oil to soak in, then buffed with a soft clean rag. Buffing with fine 4/0 steel wool will improve the sheen.

Water-based Resin

Similar to synthetic resin varnish but uses water as the solvent instead of mineral spirits. Resins include acrylics and urethane. Fast drying - at 35% relative humidity and 70°F will dry to the touch in 15 to 30 minutes and can be sanded and recoated in 2 hours. Apply with natural bristle brushes, 3 to 4 coats total, let dry between coats, and sand with 240 grit sandpaper. Water-based resin finishes are usually transparent. May not be compatible with oil- or solvent-based finishes; use shellac or a clear sealer to separate the two dissimilar finishes.

Other Paints

Primers

Primers are paints intended to produce a good foundation for the overlying coats of paint. Exterior wood primers penetrate deeply into the surface, adhere tightly to the surface, and seal off the wood. Metal primers are specifically designed to adhere to the metal and stop oxidation (rusting). Automotive primers usually contain a lot of resin. Primers typically have an abundance of pigment to allow sanding if necessary.

Fire-Retardant

Paints that decompose by melting into a thick mass of cellular charred material that insulates the material it is painted on. The decomposition begins at a temperature below the combustion point of the substrate; ratings are based on the ability to suppress combustion.

Floor Paint

Specialized coatings that contain hard substances such as epoxy and phenolic modified alkyds, chlorinated rubber, and varnish. The coatings must also be water resistant.

Texture Paint

Interior house coatings for ceilings and walls that produce a matte finish. They can contain sand, styrene fragments, nut shells, perlite, volcanic ash, or any other coarse material to create a texture.

Two Part Paint

This class of paint is generally expensive and includes the epoxies, polyesters, urethanes, and styrene-solubilized polyesters. They are all thermosetting, i.e. they cure by heat once a reactant has been added. These paints are extremely tough and durable and chemically resistant.

Automotive Paints

Urethane Enamel

The best of the car finishes, lasts over 10 years, has the best look, and is the most expensive. Paint jobs can run over $1000 and paint cost alone ranges from $50 to $100 per gallon.

Polyurethane "Clear Coat"

The top coat of a two-part paint, it is applied over a base coat of acrylic enamel or acrylic lacquer producing a beautiful "wet look" finish just like a factory paint job. This type of finish is very difficult to apply and should be done by an expert. Has a life of 8 to 10 years and costs between $400 and $600.

Acrylic Lacquer

Mid-range auto paint, very fast drying, much higher gloss and better durability than the alkyd enamels. Must be machine polished after drying so it is more expensive than the acrylic enamel paints. Acrylic lacquer must not be painted over acrylic enamel. Expect to pay $300 to $500 for this paint job. Life span is 5 to 7 years.

Acrylic Enamel

Mid-range auto paint, very slow drying, much higher gloss and better durability than the alkyd enamels and acrylic lacquer. Acrylic enamel should not be painted over acrylic lacquer. Usually requires a heat

---

Glues, Solvents, Paints & Finishes

booth to aid drying. Expect to pay $200 to $300 for a paint job.

Alkyd Enamel   Cheap paint with low durability (will sometimes loose its gloss in less than 2 months). Paint life will only be 1 to 3 years. The paint job will probably only cost $100 to $200 and is commonly referred to as the "baked enamel" job since the vehicle is baked at 150°F in a heat booth to set the paint.

RESOURCES:

Excellent books and articles on paint and painting techniques include:

The Household Paint Selector, 1975, National Paint and Coatings Association, Barnes and Noble Books, New York, NY;

How To Paint Anything, 1972, Hubbard H. Cobb, Macmillan Publishing Company, Inc, New York, NY;

Paint Handbook, 1981, Guy E. Weismantel, Editor, McGraw-Hill Book Company, New York, NY;

Complete Handbook Of Home Painting, 1975, John L. Scherer, Tab Books, Blue Ridge Summit, PA;

Coloring, Finishing, and Painting Wood, Revised Edition, 1961, A. C. Newell and W. F. Holtrop, Charles A. Bennett Company, Inc, Peoria, IL;

How To Buy A New (Automotive) Paint Job, February 1987, The Family Handyman Magazine, Webb Publishing Company, St. Paul, MN;

Water-based Finishes, 1998, Andy Charron, Taunton Press, Inc, Newtown, CT.

Solvents

A solvent is a material, usually a liquid, that has the power to dissolve another material and form a homogeneous mixture known as a solution. There are literally thousands of solvents available commercially, but most are not readily available to the average consumer. The following solvents are generally available in hardware stores, paint stores, computer stores, and drug stores and provide an excellent range of capabilities. *Note that most of these are toxic, poisonous, and flammable; some are suspected carcinogens; use adequate ventilation with all solvents; exercise caution when using them; and keep out of the reach of children.*

NOTE: The solvents listed below have been arranged in approximate order of "strength," i.e., solvents at the top of the list are stronger than those at the bottom of the list.

Lacquer Thinner

An organic solvent which is a mixture of toluene, isopropanol, methyl isobutyl keytone, acetone, propylene glycol, monomethyl ether acetate, and ethyl acetate. Photochemically reactive. Used to thin lacquers and epoxies but can be used as a general cleaner and degreaser. Highly flammable; poisonous; eye and skin irritant. Dissolves or softens many plastics. **Brands:** "Klean-Strip® Lacquer Thinner," W. M. Barr and Company, Memphis, TN; "Lacquer Thinner R7K22," Sherwin-Williams Company, Cleveland, OH; and "Startex™ Lacquer Thinner," Startex Chemical, Inc, Conroe, TX.

Acetone

A volatile organic solvent for cellulose acetate and nitrocellous. Also known as dimethyl ketone, methyl ketone, dimethlyformaldehyde, ketone propane, or 2-propanone; CH_3COCH_3; soluble in water and alcohol; non-photochemically reactive; used to clean and remove polyester, epoxy resins, ink, adhesives, contact cement, and fiberglass resin. Dissolves or softens many plastics and synthetics. Irritates the eyes, nose, and throat; prolonged contact may cause skin irritation; use with adequate ventilation. **Brands:** "Klean-Strip® Acetone," W. M. Barr and Company, Memphis, TN; "Acetone R6K9," Sherwin-Williams Company, Cleveland, OH; and "Startex™ Acetone," Startex Chemical, Inc, Conroe, TX.

Finger Nail Polish Remover

An organic solvent which is a mixture of acetone, propylene carbonate, dimethyl glutarate, dimethyl succinate, and dimethyl adipate. Good for various applications, dissolves plastics. Extremely flammable; eye, nose, and throat irritant; poisonous; harmful to synthetic fabrics and wood finishes. **Brand:** "Nail Polish Remover," Topco Associates, Inc, Skokie, IL.

Adhesive Cleaners, Thinners, and Removers

Organic solvents which are mixtures of petroleum distillates (mineral spirits) and n-butyl acetate or propylene glycol monomethyl ether acetate. Very powerful solvents that are typically used to clean and thin fresh adhesive, or to clean and remove dried adhesive; also removes oil, grease, and wax. These solvents will clean up brushes and tools that have dried-on adhesives if you let them soak for an hour. Dissolves or softens some plastics, rubber, paint, varnish, and asphalt. Avoid breathing fumes for long periods and use with adequate ventilation. Some are photochemically reactive. **Brands:** "DAP® Weldwood Cleaner and Thinner," DAP, Inc, Baltimore, MD and "Klean-Strip® Adhesive Remover," W. M. Barr and Company, Memphis, TN.

Contact Cement Solvent

An organic solvent which is a mixture of toluene, acetone, and hexane. A very powerful solvent that is typically used with contact cement adhesives, this solvent will clean up brushes and tools that have dried-on contact adhesives if you let them soak for an hour. Dissolves or softens some plastics. Avoid breathing fumes for long periods and use with adequate ventilation. Flammable. **Brand:** "DAP® Weldwood Standard Solvent," DAP, Inc, Baltimore, MD.

Hexane

An organic solvent from petroleum distillation. Also known as n-hexane, hexyl hydride, petroleum ether, and petroleum naphtha; C_6H_{14}. Major solvent and cleaning agent; used in paint thinners, adhesives, degreasing agents, and cleaners. Highly flammable, vapor is explosive. Will soften some plastics, rubber, and synthetic coatings. Toxic; eye, nose, and throat irritant; use with adequate ventilation. **Brands:** "Aktol® Hexane," Aktol Chemicals, Cape Town, South Africa and "Exxsol® Hexane Solvent," Exxon Company USA, Houston, TX.

Toluene

An organic solvent from petroleum distillation or from the tolu tree. Also known as phenyl methane, methyl benzol, toluol, and methyl benzene; $C_6H_5CH_3$. Used as a solvent in paints, inks, adhesives, cleaning agents, and cosmetic nail products; used as a medical agent to expel or destroy roundworms and hookworms. Fast evaporation rate. Flammable; explosive; eye, nose, throat, and skin irritant; use with adequate ventilation.

Brands: "Aktol® Toluene," Aktol Chemicals, Cape Town, South Africa; "Klean-Strip® Toluene," W. M. Barr and Company, Memphis, TN; "Toluene," Exxon Company USA, Houston, TX; "Toluol (Toluene) R2K1," Sherwin-Williams Company, Cleveland, OH; and "Startex™ Toluene," Startex Chemical, Inc, Conroe, TX.

Xylene

An organic solvent from petroleum distillation. A mixture of o-xylene, m-xylene, p-xylene, and ethylbenzene. Also known as dimethylbenzene, xylol, and mixed xylene; $C_6H_4(CH_3)_2$. Moderately soluble in water, slower evaporation rate than toluene. Flammable; eye, nose, and throat irritant; use with adequate ventilation.

Brands: "Aktol® Xylene," Aktol Chemicals, Cape Town, South Africa; "Klean-Strip® Xylol Xylene," W. M. Barr and Company, Memphis, TN; "Xylene," Exxon Company USA, Houston, TX; "Xylol (Xylene) R2K4," Sherwin-Williams Company, Cleveland, OH; and "Startex™ Xylene," Startex Chemical, Inc, Conroe, TX.

Methyl Ethyl Keytone (MEK) (Plastic cement solvent)

An organic solvent which is also known as ethyl methyl keytone, MEK, methyl acetone, or 2-butanone; $CH_3CH_2COCH_3$. Soluble in water, alcohols, ether, acetone, and benzene; dissolves plastic and is typically used in making model airplane cement; will dissolve many plastics, resins, and rubber; used in lacquers, varnishes, polyurethanes, and enamels; used as a solvent for coatings, adhesives, magnetic tape, and printing ink. Very fast evaporation rate. Both liquid and vapor are extremely flammable; poisonous; eye, throat, and skin irritant; strong solvent smell; use with adequate ventilation.

Brands: "Methyl Ethyl Keytone (MEK) R6K10," Sherwin-Williams Company, Cleveland, OH; "Methyl Ethyl Keytone," Wellborn Paint Manufacturing Company, Albuquerque, NM; "Methyl Ethyl Keytone," Mallinckrodt Baker, Inc, Phillipsburg, NJ;

Glues, Solvents, Paints & Finishes **395**

and "Startex™ M.E.K (Methyl Ethyl Ketone),"
Startex Chemical, Inc, Conroe, TX.

Adhesive Remover with Methylene Chloride

An organic solvent which is a mixture of methylene chloride (also known as dichloromethane or methane dichloride; CH_2Cl_2), ethylene glycol monobutyl ether, and methanol. A strong solvent. Dissolves or softens some plastics; do not use with linoleum, rubber, asphalt tile, fiber glass or other synthetics. Use with adequate ventilation. Methylene chloride is a suspected carcinogen.
Brand: "Klean-Strip® Non-flammable Adhesive Remover with Methylene Chloride," W. M. Barr and Company, Memphis, TN.

Naphtha

Petroleum distillate also known as petroleum benzine, or coal tar. Slight odor; non-photochemically reactive; flammable; very fast evaporation rate.
Brands: Ordinary lighter fluid; "Klean-Strip® VM&P Naphtha," W. M. Barr and Company, Memphis, TN; "Naphtha With Benzine and Hexane," Exxon Company USA, Houston, TX; "VM&P Naphtha R1K3," Sherwin-Williams Company, Cleveland, OH; and "Startex™ VM&P Naphtha," Startex Chemical, Inc, Conroe, TX.

Turpentine

An organic solvent distilled from pine trees; also known as "steam distilled spirits" or "gum spirits"; used as a thinner and cleaner for oil based paint, varnish, enamel, and stain. Photochemically reactive.
Brand: "Klean-Strip® Pure Gum Spirits Turpentine," W. M. Barr and Company, Memphis, TN and "Startex™ Gum Turpentine," Startex Chemical, Inc, Conroe, TX.

D-limonene (Citrus terpene)

An organic solvent derived from the evaporation or distillation of citrus fruit oils; also called cajeputene or cinene; $C_{10}H_{16}$. Can also be mixed with petroleum distillates, ethers, and alcohols. Used mainly as a cleaner and degreaser; will dissolve oil, wax, grease, tar, and ink. Eye, throat, and skin irritant; flammable; use with proper ventilation.
Brands: "Citrusolv™ 40," BetCo Corporation, Toledo, OH; "Orange Solvent," CIM Supply, Inc, New Kinsington, PA; and "Orange Asphalt Remover," Orange Products Corporation, Greensboro, NC.

Paint Thinner (Mineral spirits)

An organic solvent from petroleum distillation, used as a

paint thinner and cleaner, also known as Stoddard solvent, white spirits, mineral terpentine, safety solvent naphtha, and petropine. Very slow evaporation rate. Flammable; poisonous; eye and skin irritant; use with adequate ventilation.

Brands: "Klean-Strip® Odorless Mineral Spirits," "Klean-Strip® Paint Thinner," and "Gillespie® Mineral Spirits," W. M. Barr and Company, Memphis, TN; "Startex™ Paint Thinner, 100% Mineral Spirits," Startex Chemical, Inc, Conroe, TX; and "Mineral Spirits R1K4," Sherwin-Williams Company, Cleveland, OH.

Freon® TMS Cleaning Agent

NO LONGER MANUFACTURED; FREON AND OTHER CFC's MUST BE RECYCLED! Trichlortrifluoroethane, Freon® TF, non-flammable, non-conductive, low toxicity, odorless and does not attack plastic, rubber, paints or metal; low surface tension, evaporates fast. Although not commonly seen, freon is an excellent solvent and is typically used to clean electrical connectors and computer components. *Note: Depletes ozone, no longer manufactured.* **Brand:** "DuPont® Freon® TMS Cleaning Agent", DuPont Flurochemicals, Wilmington, DE.

Vetrel® Cleaning Agent

A proprietary hydrofluorocarbon fluid which can be mixed with dichloroethylene, cyclopentane, or methanol. Used mainly for vapor degreasing; can be used on most metals and plastics, and is typically used to clean electrical connectors and computer components. Nonflammable, nontoxic, mild eye and skin irritant.

Brand: "DuPont® Vertrel® Cleaning Agent," DuPont Flurochemicals, Wilmington, DE.

Methyl Alcohol (Methanol) (Solvent alcohol)

An organic solvent also called wood alcohol, CH_3OH. Non-photochemically reactive; used primarily as a thinner for shellac and shellac-based primers and in marine alcohol stoves; soluble in water and other alcohols. Can be mixed with gasoline in a tank to eliminate moisture problems (1/2 pint methanol per 15 gallons gasoline). Good cleaner for computer plastic parts. Do not use with oil or latex paints, stains, or varnishes. Poisonous, flammable ,use in well ventilated area, keep out of the reach of children.

Brands: "Methanol", Methanex Methanol Company, Dallas, TX and "Methanol R6K1," Sherwin-Williams Company, Cleveland, OH.

Denatured Alcohol (Industrial ethanol)

An organic solvent which is a mixture of ethyl alcohol (grain alcohol) and a small amount of methyl alcohol to make it unfit for drinking. Soluble in water and other alcohols; non-photochemically reactive; typically used to thin shellac, clean glass and metal, to clean ink from rubber rollers; and as a fuel in marine stoves. To clean glass, porcelain, and piano keys, mix 1:1 with water. Poisonous, flammable, use in well ventilated area, keep out of the reach of children.

Brands: "Klean-Strip® S-L-X Denatured Alcohol," W. M. Barr and Company, Memphis, TN and "Startex™ Denatured Alcohol," Startex Chemical, Inc, Conroe, TX.

Isopropyl Alcohol (Rubbing alcohol)

An organic solvent also known as 2-propanol, isopropanol, and dimethylcarbinol; $CH_3CHOHCH_3$. Soluble in water and other alcohols; general cleaner and disinfectant; specifically used to clean tape recorder heads and computer disk drive heads. Flammable, poisonous, use in well ventilated area, keep out of the reach of children.

Brands: "TopCare® 70% Isopropyl Alcohol," Topco Associates, Inc, Skokie, IL and "Isopropanol (Isopropyl Alcohol)," Sherwin-Williams Company, Cleveland, OH.

The Universal Solvent

Water (plain old H_2O)

Water is often referred to as the "universal solvent." Water is an excellent solvent due to the polar nature of the water molecule (i.e. electrons are dense on one end of the molecule.) Water is most effective in dissolving other polar materials but when used in conjunction with soaps or detergents, it can be a very effective solvent for some non-polar materials.

Hardware

Steel Bolt & Screw Grades, Types & Classes

INCH Series - SAE Standards		
Grades	ID Mark	Types & Sizes (MTS=Min Tensile Stress)
Grade 60M (SAE J82)		Machine Screws - #4 to 3/4" Carbon steel MTS 60,000 psi Proof Stress - none
Grade 120M (SAE J82)		Machine Screws - #4 to 3/4" Carbon steel, quenched & tempered MTS 120,000 psi Proof Stress - none
Grade 1 (SAE J429)		Bolts, screws, studs - 1/4"-1-1/2" Low or medium carbon steel MTS 60,000psi Proof Stress - 33,000psi
Grade 2 (SAE J429)		Bolts, screws, studs - 1/4"-1-1/2" Low or medium carbon steel MTS 74,000psi: 1/4"- 3/4" MTS 60,000psi: 7/8"- 1-1/2" Proof Stress - 55,000psi: 1/4"- 3/4" Proof Stress - 33,000psi: 7/8"- 1-1/2"
Grade 5 (SAE J429)		Bolts, screws, studs - 1/4"-1-1/2" Med carbon steel, quenched & tempered MTS 120,000psi: 1/4"- 1" MTS 105,000psi: 1-1/8"- 1-1/2" Proof Stress - 85,000psi: 1/4"- 1" Proof Stress - 74,000psi: 1-1/8"- 1-1/2"
Grade 5.1 (SAE J429)		Bolts, screws, studs - #6-5/8" Med carbon steel, quenched & tempered MTS 120,000psi Proof Stress - 85,000psi
Grade 5.2 (SAE J429)		Bolts, screws, studs - 1/4"-1" Low carbon martensite steel, quenched & tempered MTS 120,000psi Proof Stress - 85,000psi
Grade 7 (SAE J429)		Bolts, screws, studs - 1/4"-1-1/2" Med carbon alloy steel, quenched & tempered MTS 133,000psi Proof Stress - 105,000psi
Grade 8 (SAE J429)		Bolts, screws, studs - 1/4"-1-1/2" Med carbon alloy steel, quenched & tempered MTS 150,000psi Proof Stress - 120,000psi
Grade 8.2 (SAE J429)		Bolts, screws, studs - 1/4"-1" Low carbon martensite steel, quenched & tempered MTS 150,000psi Proof Stress - 120,000psi

INCH Series - ASTM Standards		
Grades	ID Mark	Types & Sizes (MTS=Min Tensile Stress)
A307 Grade A	307A	Bolts & studs, 1/4"-4" Low or medium carbon steel MTS 60,000psi Proof Stress - none
A307 Grade B	307B	Bolts & studs, 1/4"-4" Low or medium carbon steel MTS 60,000psi Proof Stress - none
A325 Type 1	A325	Structural & anchor bolts, 1/2"-1-1/2" Medium carbon, carbon-boron, or medium carbon alloy steel MTS - 120,000psi: 1/2"-1" MTS - 105,000psi: 1-1/8"-1-1/2" Proof Stress - 85,000psi: 1/2"-1" Proof Stress - 74,000psi: 1-1/8"-1-1/2"
A325 Type 3	A325	Structural & anchor bolts, 1/2"-1" Atmospheric corrosion resistant steel, quenched & tempered MTS - 120,000psi Proof Stress - 85,000psi
A354 Grade BC	BC	Bolts & studs, 1/4"-4" Medium carbon alloy steel, quenched & tempered MTS - 125,000psi: 1/4" - 2-1/2" MTS - 115,000psi: 2-5/8"-4" Proof Stress - 105,000psi: 1/4"-2-1/2" Proof Stress - 95,000psi: 2-5/8"-4"
A354 Grade BD	BD	Bolts & studs, 1/4"-4" Medium carbon alloy steel, quenched & tempered MTS - 150,000psi: 1/4" - 2-1/2" MTS - 140,000psi: 2-5/8"-4" Proof Stress - 120,000psi: 1/4"-2-1/2" Proof Stress - 105,000psi: 2-5/8"-4"
A449 Type 1		Bolts & studs, 1/4"-4" Medium carbon steel, quenched & tempered MTS - 120,000psi: 1/4" - 1" MTS - 105,000psi: 1-1/8"-1-1/2" MTS - 90,000psi: 1-3/4"-3" Proof Stress - 85,000psi: 1/4"-1" Proof Stress - 74,000psi: 1-1/8"-1-1/2" Proof Stress - 55,000psi: 1-3/4"-3"
A449 Type 2		Bolts & studs, 1/4"-1" Low or medium carbon martensite steel, quenched & tempered MTS - 120,000psi Proof Stress - 85,000psi
A490 Type 1	A490	Structural bolts, 1/2"-1-1/2" Medium carbon alloy steel, quenched & tempered MTS - 150,000psi Proof Stress 120,000psi

INCH Series - ASTM Standards (cont.)		
Grades	ID Mark	Types & Sizes (MTS=Min Tensile Stress)
A490 Type 2	A490	Structural bolts, 1/2"-1" Low carbon martensite steel, quenched & tempered MTS - 150,000psi Proof Stress 120,000psi
A490 Type 3	A490	Structural bolts, 1/2"-1-1/2" Atmospheric corrosion resistant steel, quenched & tempered MTS - 150,000psi Proof Stress - 120,000psi
A574		Hexagon socket-head cap screws #0 - 4" Carbon alloy steel, quenched & tempered MTS - 180,000psi: #0 - 1/2" MTS - 170,000psi: 5/8" - 4" Proof Stress - 140,000psi: #0 - 1/2" Proof Stress - 135,000psi: 5/8" - 4"

METRIC Series - SAE Standards		
Grades	ID Mark	Types & Sizes (MTS=Min Tensile Stress)
Class 4.6 SAE J1199	4.6	Bolts, screws, & studs, 5mm-36mm Low or medium carbon steel MTS - 400 Mpa Proof Stress - 225 MPa
Class 4.8 SAE J1199	4.8	Bolts, screws, & studs, 1.6mm-16mm Low-medium carbon steel, stress relieved MTS - 420 MPa Proof Stress - 310 MPa
Class 5.8 SAE J1199	5.8	Bolts, screws, & studs, 5mm-24mm Low-medium carbon steel, stress relieved MTS - 520 MPa Proof Stress - 380 MPa
Class 8.8 SAE J1199	8.8	Bolts, screws, & studs, 17mm-36mm Medium carbon steel, medium carbon alloy steel, low carbon martensite steel, or medium carbon boron steel, quenched & tempered MTS - 830 MPa Proof Stress - 600 MPa
Class 9.8 SAE J1199	9.8	Bolts, screws, & studs, 1.6mm-16mm Medium carbon steel, low carbon martensite steel, or medium carbon boron steel, quenched & tempered MTS - 900 MPa Proof Stress - 650 MPa
Class 10.9 SAE J1199	10.9	Bolts, screws, & studs, 6mm-36mm Carbon steel, medium carbon alloy steel, low carbon martensite steel, or medium carbon boron steel, quenched & tempered MTS - 1,040 MPa Proof Stress - 830 MPa

METRIC Series - ASTM Standards		
Grades	ID Mark	Types & Sizes (MTS=Min Tensile Stress)
Class 4.6 ASTM F568	4.6	Bolts, screws, & studs, 5mm-100mm Low or medium carbon steel MTS - 400 MPa Proof Stress - 225 MPa
Class 4.8 ASTM F568	4.8	Bolts, screws, & studs, 1.6mm-16mm Low or medium carbon steel, partially or fully annealed MTS - 420 MPa Proof Stress - 310 MPa
Class 5.8 ASTM F568	5.8	Bolts, screws, & studs, 5mm-24mm Low or medium carbon steel, cold worked MTS - 520 MPa Proof Stress - 380 MPa
Class 8.8 ASTM F568	8.8	Bolts, screws, & studs, 16mm-72mm Low or medium carbon steel, quenched & tempered MTS - 830 MPa Proof Stress - 600 MPa
Class 8.8.3 ASTM F568	8.8.3	Bolts, screws, & studs, 16mm-36mm Low carbon martensite steel, quenched & tempered MTS - 830 MPa Proof Stress - 600 MPa
Class 9.8 ASTM F568	9.8	Bolts, screws, & studs, 1.6mm-16mm Medium carbon steel or low carbon martensite steel, quenched & tempered MTS - 900 MPa Proof Stress - 650 MPa
Class 10.9 ASTM F568	10.9	Bolts, screws, & studs, 5mm-100mm Medium carbon, steel, medium carbon alloy steel, or atmospheric corrosion resistant steel, quenched & tempered MTS - 1,040 MPa Proof Stress - 830 MPa
Class 10.9.3 ASTM F568	10.9.3	Bolts, screws, & studs, 16mm-36mm Medium carbon alloy steel, quenched & tempered MTS - 1,040 MPa Proof Stress - 830 MPa
Class 12.9 ASTM F568	12.9	Bolts, screws, & studs, 1.6mm-100mm Alloy steel, quenched & tempered MTS - 1,220 MPa Proof Stress - 970 MPa

METRIC Series - ISO Standards		
Grades	ID Mark	Types & Sizes (MTS=Min Tensile Stress)
Class 3.6 ISO 898-1	3.6	Bolts, screws, & studs, 1mm-300mm Carbon steel MTS - 330 MPa Proof Stress - none
Class 4.6 ISO 898-1	4.6	Bolts, screws, & studs, 1mm-300mm Carbon steel MTS - 400 MPa Proof Stress - none
Class 4.8 ISO 898-1	4.8	Bolts, screws, & studs, 1mm-300mm Carbon steel MTS - 420 MPa Proof Stress - none
Class 5.6 ISO 898-1	5.6	Bolts, screws, & studs, 1mm-300mm Carbon steel MTS - 500 MPa Proof Stress - none
Class 5.8 ISO 898-1	5.8	Bolts, screws, & studs, 1mm-300mm Carbon steel MTS - 520 MPa Proof Stress - none
Class 6.8 ISO 898-1	6.8	Bolts, screws, & studs, 1mm-300mm Carbon steel MTS - 600 MPa Proof Stress - none
Class 8.8 ISO 898-1	8.8	Bolts, screws, & studs, 1mm-300mm Carbon steel, quenched & tempered MTS - 800 MPa: 1mm-16mm MTS - 830 MPa: 16mm-300mm Proof Stress - 640 MPa: 1mm-16mm Proof Stress - 660 MPa: 16mm-300mm
Class 9.8 ISO 898-1	9.8	Bolts, screws, & studs, 1mm-300mm Carbon steel, quenched & tempered MTS - 900 MPa Proof Stress - 720 MPa
Class 10.9 ISO 898-1	10.9	Bolts, screws, & studs, 1mm-300mm Carbon alloy steel, quenched & tempered MTS - 1,040 MPa Proof Stress - 940 MPa
Class 12.9 ISO 898-1	12.9	Bolts, screws, & studs, 1mm-300mm Alloy steel, quenched & tempered MTS - 1,220 MPa Proof Stress - 1,100 MPa

Note:
Abbreviations and symbols:
" = inch, mm = millimeter
psi = pound-force per square inch, MPa = megapascal
ASTM = American Society For Testing And Materials
ISO = International Organization For Standarization,
SAE = Society Of Automotive Engineers

Notes on Clamping Force and Bolt Torque

1. The tables which follow present Clamping Force and Standard Dry Torque for a variety of threaded fasteners. The tables cover a wide variety of material properties and fastener sizes.

2. It should be noted that some combinations of bolt size and proof strength or minimum tensile strength shown in the tables may not be available. Fastener standards written by ANSI, ASME, ASTM, IFI, ISO, and/or SAE can either overlap each other or leave gaps in either material properties or fastener sizes. These overlaps and gaps in information generally occur because each organization is addressing a different aspect of fastener technology. For instance, ASTM deals with the materials used in fastener manufacture and the testing of those materials for acceptability while ANSI/ASME deals with the dimensions of the manufactured fastener.

3. Clamping force and standard dry torque for <u>carbon steel bolts</u> were calculated for clean, dry, non-plated carbon steel with a torque coefficient (also called a friction factor or a nut factor) of 0.20. The clamping force and standard dry torque were calculated to produce a tensile stress in the fastener equal to 70% of the minimum tensile strength or 75% of the proof strength.

4. Standard dry torques for <u>stainless steel and non-ferrous bolts</u> were compiled from test data on fasteners as published by bolt manufacturers, in trade publications, and in fastener textbooks.

5. Clamping force and standard dry torque presented in these tables should be considered approximate because both values are sensitive to many factors which can vary from bolt to bolt. Some of these factors include nominal bolt diameter, material strength, tensile stress area, coefficient of friction at the bearing faces and thread contact surfaces, effective radius of action of frictional forces on the bearing faces and thread contact surfaces, thread half-angle, and helix angle of the thread.

6. Lubricants and Coatings: Lubricants reduce the torque required to produce a given tensile stress or clamping force while coatings (platings or oxidizes) can either increase or decrease the required torque. The table on page 422 presents factors which can be used to approximate the effect of various lubricants and coatings on the torque for <u>carbon steel</u> fasteners only. Lubricants and coatings may have the same effects on <u>stainless steel</u> and <u>non-ferrous</u> fasteners but the authors could not confirm this assumption. Note that lubrication applied to only the external threads is as effective as lubrication being applied to both external and internal threads.

7. Torque Coefficients and Tensile Stress Levels: As stated above, clamping force and standard dry torque presented in the following tables were calculated for a torque coefficient equal to 0.20 and a tensile stress level equal to either 70% of the minimum tensile strength or 75% of the proof strength. The table on page 422 presents factors that can be used to approximate the effect of lowering the torque coefficient to between 0.20 and 0.15 and changing tensile stress level to between 50% and 80% of the proof strength.

8. Bolts with tensile strengths higher than 150,000 psi are not common except in aircraft applications. A few of these special fasteners are:

- NAS 144; 160,000 psi; high carbon alloy steel, quenched and tempered.
- MS2000; 160,000 psi; high carbon alloy steel, quenched and tempered.
- ASTM A574 - Socket Head Cap Screws; #0 to 1/2 " - 180,000 psi; 9/16" to 4" - 170,000 psi; high carbon alloy steel, quenched and tempered.
- NAS 623; 180,000 psi; high carbon alloy steel, quenched and tempered.
- Supertanium®; 180,000 psi; 8 points on head; special steel alloy, quenched and tempered.
- AAS; 200,000 psi; high carbon alloy steel, quenched and tempered.

Clamping forces and standard dry torques for all special alloy bolts should be obtained from the manufacturer.

9. Abbreviations:

AAS - Aircraft Assigned Steel
ANSI - American National Standards Institute
ASME - American Society of Mechanical Engineers
ASTM - American Society for Testing and Materials
IFI - Industrial Fastener Institute
ISO - International Organization for Standardization
MS - Military Standard
NAS - National Aircraft Standard
psi - pound-force per square inch
SAE - Society of Automotive Engineers

Clamping Force and Standard Dry Torque
Coarse INCH-THREADED Carbon Steel Bolts

Grades and Types: SAE J429 - Grade 1

Grade 1 (1/4" to 1-1/2")
Proof Strength = 33,000 pound-force/square inch (lbf/in²)

Bolt Size (inch)	Threads/ Inch	Clamping Force		Standard Dry Torque	
		pound-force (lbf)	kilonewton (kN)	foot pound-force (ft lbf)	newton meter (N m)
1/4	20	787	3.50	3.28	4.45
5/16	18	1,297	5.77	6.75	9.16
3/8	16	1,918	8.53	12.0	16.3
7/16	14	2,631	11.7	19.2	26.0
1/2	13	3,512	15.6	29.3	39.7
9/16	12	4,505	20.0	42.2	57.3
5/8	11	5,594	24.9	58.3	79.0
3/4	10	8,267	36.8	103	140
7/8	9	11,435	50.9	167	226
1	8	14,999	66.7	250	339
1-1/8	7	18,884	84.0	354	480
1-1/4	7	23,983	107	500	677
1-3/8	6	28,586	127	655	888
1-1/2	6	34,774	155	869	1179

Grades and Types: SAE J429- Grade 2

Grade 2 - (1/4" to 3/4")
Proof Strength = 55,000 pound-force/square inch (lbf/in²)

Grade 2 - (7/8" to 1-1/2")
Proof Strength = 33,000 pound-force/square inch (lbf/in²)

Bolt Size (inch)	Threads/ Inch	Clamping Force		Standard Dry Torque	
		pound-force (lbf)	kilonewton (kN)	foot pound-force (ft lbf)	newton meter (Nm)
1/4	20	1,312	5.83	5.47	7.41
5/16	18	2,162	9.61	11.3	15.3
3/8	16	3,197	14.2	20.0	27.1
7/16	14	4,385	19.5	32.0	43.3
1/2	13	5,853	26.0	48.8	66.1
9/16	12	7,508	33.4	70.4	95.4
5/8	11	9,323	41.5	97.1	132
3/4	10	13,778	61.3	172	233
7/8	9	11,435	50.9	167	226
1	8	14,999	66.7	250	339
1-1/8	7	18,884	84.0	354	480
1-1/4	7	23,983	107	500	677
1-3/8	6	28,586	127	655	888
1-1/2	6	34,774	155	869	1,179

Grades and Types: SAE J429 - Grades 5, 5.1, & 5.2

Grade 5 - (1/4" to 1"), Grade 5.1 - (#6 to 5/8"), and Grade 5.2 - (1/4" to 1")
Proof Strength = 85,000 pound-force/square inch (lbf/in²)

Grade 5 - (1-1/8" to 1-1/2")
Proof Strength = 74,000 pound-force/square inch (lbf/in²)

Bolt Size (# or inch)	Threads/ Inch	Clamping Force		Standard Dry Torque	
		pound-force (lbf)	kilonewton (kN)	foot pound-force (ft lbf)	newton meter (Nm)
6	32	579	2.58	1.33	1.81

8	32	893	3.97	2.44	3.31
10	24	1,116	4.96	3.53	4.79
12	24	1,543	6.86	5.55	7.53
1/4	20	2,027	9.02	8.45	11.5
5/16	18	3,341	14.9	17.4	23.6
3/8	16	4,941	22.0	30.9	41.9
7/16	14	6,777	30.1	49.4	67.0
1/2	13	9,046	40.2	75.4	102
9/16	12	11,603	51.6	109	147
5/8	11	14,408	64.1	150	203
3/4	10	21,293	94.7	266	361
7/8	9	29,453	131	430	582
1	8	38,633	172	644	873
1-1/8	7	42,347	188	794	1,077
1-1/4	7	53,780	239	1,120	1,519
1-3/8	6	64,103	285	1,469	1,992
1-1/2	6	77,978	347	1,949	2,643

Grades and Types: SAE J429-Grade 7

Grade 7 - (1/4" to 1-1/2")
Proof Strength = 105,000 pound-force/square inch (lbf/in²)

Bolt Size (inch)	Threads/ Inch	Clamping Force		Standard Dry Torque	
		pound-force (lbf)	kilonewton (kN)	foot pound-force (ft lbf)	newton meter (Nm)
1/4	20	2504	11.1	10.4	14.1
5/16	18	4127	18.4	21.5	29.1
3/8	16	6103	27.1	38.1	51.7
7/16	14	8371	37.2	61.0	82.8
1/2	13	11,175	49.7	93.1	126
9/16	12	14,333	63.8	134	182
5/8	11	17,798	79.2	185	251
3/4	10	26,303	117	329	446
7/8	9	36,383	162	531	719
1	8	47,723	212	795	1,078
1-1/8	7	60,086	267	1,127	1,527
1-1/4	7	76,309	339	1,590	2155
1-3/8	6	90,956	405	2,084	2826
1-1/2	6	110,644	492	2,766	3,750

Grades and Types: SAE J429 - Grades 8 & 8.2

Grade 8 (1/4" to 1-1/2") and Grade 8.2 (1/4" to 1")
Proof Strength = 120,000 pound-force/square inch (lbf/in²)

Bolt Size (inch)	Threads / Inch	Clamping Force		Standard Dry Torque	
		pound- force (lbf)	kilonewton (kN)	foot pound-force (ft lbf)	newton meter (Nm)
1/4	20	2,862	12.7	11.9	16.2
5/16	18	4,716	21.0	24.6	33.3
3/8	16	6,975	31.0	43.6	59.1
7/16	14	9,567	42.6	69.8	94.6
1/2	13	12,771	56.8	106	144
9/16	12	16,380	72.9	154	208
5/8	11	20,340	90.5	212	287
3/4	10	30,060	134	376	509
7/8	9	41,580	185	606	822
1	8	54,540	243	909	1,232
1-1/8	7	68,670	305	1,288	1,746
1-1/4	7	87,210	388	1,817	2,463
1-3/8	6	103,950	462	2,382	3,230
1-1/2	6	126,450	562	3,161	4,286

Grades and Types: ASTM A307 - Grades A & B

Grades A & B (1/4" to 2")
Minimum Tensile Strength = 60,000 pound-force/square inch (lbf/in²)

Bolt Size (inch)	Threads/ Inch	Clamping Force		Standard Dry Torque	
		pound-force (lbf)	kilonewton (kN)	foot pound-force(ft lbf)	newton meter (N m)
1/4	20	1,336	5.94	5.57	7.55
5/16	18	2,201	9.79	11.5	15.5
3/8	16	3,255	14.5	20.3	27.6
7/16	14	4,465	19.9	32.6	44.1
1/2	13	5,960	26.5	49.7	67.3
9/16	12	7,644	34.0	71.7	97.2
5/8	11	9,492	42.2	98.9	134
3/4	10	14,030	62.4	175	234
7/8	9	19,400	86.3	283	384
1	8	25,450	113	424	575
1-1/8	7	32,050	143	601	815
1-1/4	7	40,700	181	848	1,150
1-3/8	6	48,510	216	1,112	1,507
1-1/2	6	59,010	263	1,475	2,000
1-3/4	5	79,800	355	2,328	3,156
2	4-1/2	105,000	467	3,500	4,745

Grades and Types: ASTM A325 - Types 1 & 3

Types 1 & 3 (1/2" to 1")
Proof Strength = 85,000 pound-force/square inch (lbf/in²)
Type 1 (1-1/8" to 1-1/2")
Proof Strength = 74,000 pound-force/square inch (lbf/in²)

Bolt Size (inch)	Threads/ Inch	Clamping Force		Standard Dry Torque	
		pound-force (lbf)	kilonewton (kN)	foot pound-force(ft lbf)	newton meter (Nm)
1/2	13	9,046	40.2	75.4	102
9/16	12	11,603	51.6	109	147
5/8	11	14,408	64.1	150	203
3/4	10	21,293	94.7	266	361
7/8	9	29,453	131	430	582
1	8	38,633	172	644	873
1-1/8	7	42,347	188	794	1,077
1-1/4	7	53,780	239	1,120	1,519
1-3/8	6	64,103	285	1,469	1,992
1-1/2	6	77,978	347	1,949	2,643

Grades and Types: ASTM A354 - Grade BC

Grade BC (1/4" to 2")
Proof Strength = 105,000 pound-force/square inch (lbf/in²)

Bolt Size (inch)	Threads/ Inch	Clamping Force		Standard Dry Torque	
		pound-force (lbf)	kilonewton (kN)	foot pound-force(ft lbf)	newton meter (Nm)
1/4	20	2,504	11.1	10.4	14.1
5/16	18	4,127	18.4	21.5	29.1
3/8	16	6,103	27.1	38.1	51.7
7/16	14	8,371	37.2	61.0	82.8
1/2	13	11,175	49.7	93.1	126
9/16	12	14,333	63.8	134	182
5/8	11	17,798	79.2	185	251
3/4	10	26,303	117	329	446
7/8	9	36,383	162	531	719
1	8	47,723	212	795	1,078

Bolt Size (inch)	Threads/Inch	pound-force	kilonewton	foot pound-force (ft lbf)	newton meter (Nm)
1-1/8	7	60,086	267	1,127	1,527
1-1/4	7	76,309	339	1,590	2,155
1-3/8	6	90,956	405	2,084	2,826
1-1/2	6	110,644	492	2,766	3,750
1-3/4	5	149,625	666	4,364	5,917
2	4-1/2	196,875	876	6,563	8,898

Grades and Types: ASTM A354 - Grade BD

Grade BD (1/4" to 2")
Proof Strength = 120,000 pound-force/square inch (lbf/in²)

Bolt Size (inch)	Threads /Inch	Clamping Force		Standard Dry Torque	
		pound-force (lbf)	kilonewton (kN)	foot pound-force(ft lbf)	newton meter (Nm)
1/4	20	2,862	12.7	11.9	16.2
5/16	18	4,716	21.0	24.6	33.3
3/8	16	6,975	31.0	43.6	59.1
7/16	14	9,567	42.6	69.8	94.6
1/2	13	12,771	56.8	106	144
9/16	12	16,380	72.9	154	208
5/8	11	20,340	90.5	212	287
3/4	10	30,060	134	376	509
7/8	9	41,580	185	606	822
1	8	54,540	243	909	1,232
1-1/8	7	68,670	305	1,288	1,746
1-1/4	7	87,210	388	1,817	2,463
1-3/8	6	103,950	462	2,382	3,230
1-1/2	6	126,450	562	3,161	4,286
1-3/4	5	171,000	761	4,988	6,762
2	4-1/2	225,000	1,001	7,500	10,169

Grades and Types: ASTM A449 - Types 1 & 2

Types 1 & 2 (1/4" to 1")
Proof Strength = 85,000 pound-force/square inch (lbf/in²)

Type 1 (1-1/8"to 1-1/2")
Proof Strength = 74,000 pound-force/square inch (lbf/in²)

Type 1 (1-3/4"to 2")
Proof Strength = 55,000 pound-force/square inch (lbf/in²)

Bolt Size (inch)	Threads/Inch	Clamping Force		Standard Dry Torque	
		pound-force (lbf)	kilonewton (kN)	foot pound-force(ft lbf)	newton meter (Nm)
1/4	20	2,027	9.2	8.45	11.5
5/16	18	3,341	14.9	17.4	23.6
3/8	16	4,941	22.0	30.9	41.9
7/16	14	6,777	30.1	49.4	67.0
1/2	13	9,046	40.2	75.4	102
9/16	12	11,603	51.6	109	147
5/8	11	14,408	64.1	150	203
3/4	10	21,293	94.7	266	361
7/8	9	29,453	131	430	582
1	8	38,633	172	644	873
1-1/8	7	42,347	188	794	1,077
1-1/4	7	53,780	239	1,120	1,519
1-3/8	6	64,103	285	1,469	1,992
1-1/2	6	77,978	347	1,949	2,643
1-3/4	5	78,375	349	2,286	3,099
2	4-1/2	103,125	459	3,438	4,661

Grades and Types: ASTM A490 - Types 1,2 & 3

Types 1 & 3 (1/2" to 1-1/2") & Type 2 (1/2" to 1")
Proof Strength = 120,000 pound-force/square inch (lbf/in²)

Bolt Size (inch)	Threads /Inch	Clamping Force		Standard Dry Torque	
		pound-force (lbf)	kilonewton (kN)	foot pound-force (ft lbf)	newton meter (Nm)
1/2	13	12,771	56.8	106	144
9/16	12	16,380	72.9	154	208
5/8	11	20,340	90.5	212	287
3/4	10	30,060	134	376	509
7/8	9	41,580	185	606	822
1	8	54,540	243	909	1,232
1-1/8	7	68,670	305	1,288	1,746
1-1/4	7	87,210	388	1,817	2,463
1-3/8	6	103,950	462	2,382	3,230
1-1/2	6	126,450	562	3,161	4,286

Grades and Types: ASTM A574

(#1 to 1/2")
Proof Strength = 140,000 pound-force/square inch (lbf/in²)
(9/16" to 2")
Proof Strength = 135,000 pound-force/square inch (lbf/in²)

Bolt Size (# or inch)	Threads/ Inch	Clamping Force		Standard Dry Torque	
		pound-force (lbf)	kilonewton (kN)	foot pound-force (ft lbf)	newton meter (Nm)
1	64	276	1.23	0.336	0.456
2	56	389	1.73	0.557	0.755
3	48	510	2.27	0.842	1.14
4	40	633	2.82	1.18	1.60
5	40	836	3.72	1.74	2.36
6	32	954	4.25	2.20	2.98
8	32	1,470	6.54	4.02	5.45
10	24	1,838	8.17	5.82	7.89
12	24	2,541	11.3	9.15	12.4
1/4	20	3,339	14.9	13.9	18.9
5/16	18	5,502	24.5	28.7	38.9
3/8	16	8,138	36.2	50.9	69.0
7/16	14	11,162	49.6	81.4	110
1/2	13	14,900	66.3	124	168
9/16	12	18,428	82.0	173	234
5/8	11	22,883	102	238	323
3/4	10	33,818	150	423	573
7/8	9	46,778	208	682	925
1	8	61,358	273	1,023	1,386
1-1/8	7	77,254	344	1,449	1,964
1-1/4	7	98,111	436	2,044	2,771
1-3/8	6	116,944	520	2,680	3,634
1-1/2	6	142,256	633	3,556	4,822
1-3/4	5	192,375	856	5,611	7,607
2	4-1/2	253,125	1,126	8,438	11,440

Fine INCH-THREADED Carbon Steel Bolts

Grades and Types: SAE J429 - Grade 1

Grade 1 (1/4" to 1-1/2")
Proof Strength = 33,000 pound-force/square inch (lbf/in²)

Bolt Size (inch)	Threads/ Inch	Clamping Force		Standard Dry Torque	
		pound-force (lbf)	kilonewton (kN)	foot pound-force(lbf)	newton meter (N·m)
1/4	28	901	4.01	3.75	5.09
5/16	24	1,438	6.40	7.49	10.2
3/8	24	2,173	9.67	13.6	18.4
7/16	20	2,938	13.1	21.4	29.0
1/2	20	3,960	17.6	33.0	44.7
9/16	18	5,024	22.3	47.1	63.9
5/8	18	6,336	28.2	66.0	89.5
3/4	16	9,232	41.1	115	156
7/8	14	12,598	56.0	184	249
1	12	16,409	73.0	273	371
1-1/8	12	21,186	94.2	397	539
1-1/4	12	26,557	118	553	750
1-3/8	12	32,546	145	746	1,011
1-1/2	12	39,130	174	978	1,326

Grades and Types: SAE J429 - Grade 2

Grade 2 - (1/4" to 3/4")
Proof Strength = 55,000 pound-force/square inch (lbf/in²)

Grade 2 - (7/8" to 1-1/2")
Proof Strength = 33,000 pound-force/square inch (lbf/in²)

Bolt Size (inch)	Threads/ Inch	Clamping Force		Standard Dry Torque	
		pound-force (lbf)	kilonewton (kN)	foot pound-force (ft lbf)	newton meter (Nm)
1/4	28	1,502	6.68	6.26	8.48
5/16	24	2,397	10.7	12.5	16.9
3/8	24	3,622	16.1	22.6	30.7
7/16	20	4,896	21.8	35.7	48.4
1/2	20	6,600	29.4	55.0	74.6
9/16	18	8,374	37.2	78.5	106
5/8	18	10,560	47.0	110	149
3/4	16	15,366	68.4	192	261
7/8	14	12,598	56.0	184	249
1	12	16,409	73.0	273	371
1-1/8	12	21,186	94.2	397	539
1-1/4	12	26,557	118	553	750
1-3/8	12	32,546	145	746	1,011
1-1/2	12	39,130	174	978	1,326

Grades and Types: SAE J429 - Grades 5, 5.1, & 5.2

Grade 5 - (1/4" to 1"), Grade 5.1 - (#6 to 5/8"), and Grade 5.2 - (1/4" to 1")
Proof Strength = 85,000 pound-force/square inch (lbf/1n²)

Grade 5 - (1-1/8" to 1-1/2")
Proof Strength = 74,000 pound-force/square inch (lbf/in²)

Bolt Size (# or inch)	Threads/ Inch	Clamping Force		Standard Dry Torque	
		pound-force (lbf)	kilonewton (kN)	foot pound-force (ft lbf)	newton meter (Nm)
6	40	646	2.88	1.49	2.02
8	36	939	4.18	2.57	3.48
10	32	1,275	5.67	4.04	5.47
12	28	1,645	7.32	5.92	8.03

Bolt Size (inch)	Threads/Inch	pound-force (lbf)	kilonewton (kN)	foot pound-force (ft lbf)	newton meter (Nm)
1/4	28	2,321	10.3	9.67	13.1
5/16	24	3,704	16.5	19.3	26.2
3/8	24	5,597	24.9	35.0	47.4
7/16	20	7,567	33.7	55.2	74.8
1/2	20	10,200	45.4	85.0	115
9/16	18	12,941	57.6	121	164
5/8	18	16,320	72.6	170	230
3/4	16	23,779	106	297	403
7/8	14	32,449	144	473	642
1	12	42,266	188	704	955
1-1/8	12	47,508	211	891	1,208
1-1/4	12	59,552	265	1,241	1,682
1-3/8	12	72,983	325	1,673	2,268
1-1/2	12	87,746	390	2,194	2,974

Grades and Types: **SAE J429-Grade 7**

Grade 7 - (1/4" to 1-1/2")
Proof Strength = 105,000 pound-force/square inch (lbf/in²)

Bolt Size (inch)	Threads/ Inch	Clamping Force		Standard Dry Torque	
		pound-force (lbf)	kilonewton (kN)	foot pound-force(ft lbf)	newton meter (Nm)
1/4	28	2,867	12.8	11.9	16.2
5/16	24	4,575	20.4	23.8	32.3
3/8	24	6,914	30.8	43.2	58.6
7/16	20	9,348	41.6	68.2	92.4
1/2	20	12,600	56.0	105	142
9/16	18	15,986	71.1	150	203
5/8	18	20,160	89.7	210	285
3/4	16	29,374	131	367	498
7/8	14	40,084	178	585	793
1	12	52,211	232	870	1,180
1-1/8	12	67,410	300	1,264	1,714
1-1/4	12	84,499	376	1,760	2,387
1-3/8	12	103,556	461	2,373	3,218
1-1/2	12	124,504	554	3,113	4,220

Grades and Types: **SAE J429 - Grades 8 & 8.2**

Grade 8 (1/4" to 1-1/2") and Grade 8.2 (1/4" to 1")
Proof Strength = 120,000 pound-force/square inch (lbf/in²)

Bolt Size (inch)	Threads / Inch	Clamping Force		Standard Dry Torque	
		pound- force (lbf)	kilonewton (kN)	foot pound-force(ft lbf)	newton meter (Nm)
1/4	28	3,276	14.6	13.7	18.5
5/16	24	5,229	23.3	27.2	36.9
3/8	24	7,902	35.1	49.4	67.0
7/16	20	10,683	47.5	77.9	106
1/2	20	14,400	64.1	120	163
9/16	18	18,270	81.3	171	232
5/8	18	23,040	102	240	325
3/4	16	33,570	149	420	569
7/8	14	45,810	204	668	906
1	12	59,670	265	995	1,348
1-1/8	12	77,040	343	1,445	1,958
1-1/4	12	96,570	430	2,012	2,728
1-3/8	12	118,350	526	2,712	3,677
1-1/2	12	142,290	633	3,557	4,823

Grades and Types: ASTM A307 - Grades A & B

Grades A & B (1/4" to 1-1/2")
Minimum Tensile Strength = 60,000 pound-force/square inch (lbf/in²)

Bolt Size (inch)	Threads/ Inch	Clamping Force		Standard Dry Torque	
		pound-force (lbf)	kilonewton (kN)	foot pound-force(ft lbf)	newton meter (Nm)
1/4	28	1,529	6.80	6.37	8.64
5/16	24	2,440	10.9	12.7	17.2
3/8	24	3,688	16.4	23.1	31.3
7/16	20	4,985	22.2	36.4	49.3
1/2	20	6,720	29.9	56.0	75.9
9/16	18	8,526	37.9	79.9	108
5/8	18	10,750	47.8	112	152
3/4	16	15,670	69.7	196	266
7/8	14	21,380	95.1	312	423
1	12	27,850	124	464	629
1-1/8	12	35,950	160	674	914
1-1/4	12	45,070	201	939	1,273
1-3/8	12	55,230	246	1,266	1,716
1-1/2	12	66,400	295	1,660	2,251

Grades and Types: ASTM A325 - Types 1 & 3

Types 1 & 3 (1/2" to 1")
Proof Strength = 85,000 pound-force/square inch (lbf/in²)
Type 1 (1-1/8" to 1-1/2")
Proof Strength = 74,000 pound-force/square inch (lbf/in²)

Bolt Size (inch)	Threads/ Inch	Clamping Force		Standard Dry Torque	
		pound-force (lbf)	kilonewton (kN)	foot pound-force(ft lbf)	newton meter (Nm)
1/2	20	10,200	45.4	85.0	115
9/16	18	12,941	57.6	121	164
5/8	18	16,320	72.6	170	230
3/4	16	23,779	106	297	403
7/8	14	32,449	144	473	642
1	12	42,266	188	704	955
1-1/8	12	47,508	211	891	1,208
1-1/4	12	59,552	265	1,241	1,682
1-3/8	12	72,983	325	1,673	2,268
1-1/2	12	87,746	390	2,194	2,974

Grades and Types: ASTM A354 - Grade BC

Grade BC (1/4" to 1-1/2")
Proof Strength = 105,000 pound-force/square inch (lbf/in²)

Bolt Size (inch)	Threads/ Inch	Clamping Force		Standard Dry Torque	
		pound-force (lbf)	kilonewton (kN)	foot pound-force(ft lbf)	newton meter (Nm)
1/4	28	2,867	12.8	11.9	19.2
5/16	24	4,575	20.4	23.8	32.3
3/8	24	6,914	30.8	43.2	58.6
7/16	20	9,348	41.6	68.2	92.4
1/2	20	12,600	56.0	105	142
9/16	18	15,986	71.1	150	203
5/8	18	20,160	89.7	210	285
3/4	16	29,374	131	367	498
7/8	14	40,084	178	585	793
1	12	52,211	232	870	1,180
1-1/8	12	67,410	300	1,264	1,714
1-1/4	12	84,499	376	1,760	2,387

| 1-3/8 | 12 | 103,556 | 461 | 2,373 | 3,218 |
| 1-1/2 | 12 | 124,504 | 554 | 3,113 | 4,220 |

Grades and Types: **ASTM A354 - Grade BD**

Grade BD (1/4" to 1-1/2")
Proof Strength = 120,000 pound-force/square inch (lbf/in²)

| Bolt Size (inch) | Threads/ Inch | Clamping Force | | Standard Dry Torque | |
		pound- force (lbf)	kilonewton (kN)	foot pound-force(ft lbf)	newton meter (Nm)
1/4	28	3,276	14.6	13.7	18.5
5/16	24	5,229	23.3	27.2	36.9
3/8	24	7,902	35.1	49.4	67.0
7/16	20	10,683	47.5	77.9	106
1/2	20	14,400	64.1	120	163
9/16	18	18,270	81.3	171	232
5/8	18	23,040	102	240	325
3/4	16	33,570	149	420	569
7/8	14	45,810	204	668	906
1	12	59,670	265	995	1,348
1-1/8	12	77,040	343	1,445	1,958
1-1/4	12	96,570	430	2,012	2,728
1-3/8	12	118,350	526	2,712	3,677
1-1/2	12	142,290	633	3,557	4,823

Grades and Types: **ASTM A449 - Types 1 & 2**

Types 1 & 2 (1/4" to 1")
Proof Strength = 85,000 pound-force/square inch (lbf/in²)

Type 1 (1-1/8"to 1-1/2")
Proof Strength = 74,000 pound-force/square inch (lbf/in²)

| Bolt Size (inch) | Threads/ Inch | Clamping Force | | Standard Dry Torque | |
		pound-force (lbf)	kilonewton (kN)	foot pound-force(ft lbf)	newton meter (Nm)
1/4	28	2,321	10.3	9.67	13.1
5/16	24	3,704	16.5	19.3	26.2
3/8	24	5,597	24.9	35.0	47.4
7/16	20	7,567	33.7	55.2	74.8
1/2	20	10,200	45.4	85.0	115
9/16	18	12,941	57.6	121	164
5/8	18	16,320	72.6	170	230
3/4	16	23,779	106	297	403
7/8	14	32,449	144	473	642
1	12	42,266	188	704	955
1-1/8	12	47,508	211	891	1,208
1-1/4	12	59,552	265	1,241	1,682
1-3/8	12	72,983	325	1,673	2,268
1-1/2	12	87,746	390	2,194	2,974

Grades and Types: **ASTM A490 - Types 1,2 & 3**

Types 1 & 3 (1/2" to 1-1/2") & Type 2 (1/2" to 1")
Proof Strength = 120,000 pound-force/square inch (lbf/in²)

| Bolt Size (inch) | Threads/ Inch | Clamping Force | | Standard Dry Torque | |
		pound- force (lbf)	kilonewton (kN)	foot pound-force(ft lbf)	newton meter (Nm)
1/2	20	14,400	64.1	120	163
9/16	18	18,270	81.3	170	232
5/8	18	23,040	102	240	325
3/4	16	33,570	149	420	569

7/8	14	45,810	204	668	906
1	12	59,670	265	995	1,348
1-1/8	12	77,040	343	1,445	1,958
1-1/4	12	96,570	430	2,012	2,728
1-3/8	12	118,350	526	2,712	3,677
1-1/2	12	142,290	633	3,557	4,823

Grades and Types: ASTM A574

(#0 to 1/2")
Proof Strength = 140,000 pound-force/square inch (lbf/in²)

(9/16" to 1-1/2")
Proof Strength = 135,000 pound-force/square inch (lbf/in²)

Bolt Size (# or inch)	Threads/ Inch	Clamping Force		Standard Dry Torque	
		pound-force (lbf)	kilonewton (kN)	foot pound-force (ft lbf)	newton meter (Nm)
0	80	189	0.841	0.189	0.256
1	72	292	1.30	0.355	0.482
2	64	413	1.84	0.591	0.802
3	56	549	2.44	0.906	1.23
4	48	693	3.08	1.29	1.75
5	44	873	3.88	1.82	2.46
6	40	1,065	4.74	2.45	3.32
8	36	1,547	6.88	4.23	5.73
10	32	2,100	9.34	6.65	9.02
12	28	2,709	12.1	9.75	13.2
1/4	28	3,822	17.0	15.9	21.6
5/16	24	6,101	27.1	31.8	43.1
3/8	24	9,220	41.0	57.6	78.1
7/16	20	12,460	55.4	90.9	123
1/2	20	16,800	74.7	140	190
9/16	18	20,554	91.4	193	261
5/8	18	25,920	115	270	366
3/4	16	37,766	168	472	640
7/8	14	51,536	229	752	1,019
1	12	67,129	299	1,119	1,517
1-1/8	12	86,670	386	1,625	2,203
1-1/4	12	108,641	483	2,263	3,069
1-3/8	12	133,144	592	3,051	4,137
1-1/2	12	160,076	712	4,002	5,426

Coarse METRIC-THREADED Carbon Steel Bolts

Class or Type: **ASTM F568, Class 4.6** (M5 to M100)
ISO 898/1, Class 4.6 (M5 to M36)

Minimum Tensile Strength = 400 megapascal (MPa) = 58,000 pound-force/square inch (lbf/in²)

Bolt Size (mm)	Thread Pitch (mm)	Clamping Force pound-force (lbf)	Clamping Force kilonewton (kN)	Standard Dry Torque ft. pound-force(ft-lbf)	Standard Dry Torque newton meter (Nm)
1.6	0.35	79.94	0.3556	0.0839	0.1138
1.8	0.35	107.1	0.4763	0.1265	0.1715
2	0.40	130.5	0.5804	0.1712	0.2322
2.2	0.45	156.2	0.6950	0.2255	0.3058
2.5	0.45	213.5	0.9495	0.3502	0.4748
3	0.50	316.8	1.409	0.6235	0.8454
3.5	0.60	426.5	1.897	0.9794	1.328
4	0.70	552.6	2.458	1.450	1.966
4.5	0.75	712.6	3.170	2.104	2.853
5	0.80	892.5	3.970	2.928	3.970
6	1.00	1,267	5.634	4.987	6.761
7	1.00	1,817	8.081	8.344	11.31
8	1.25	2,304	10.25	12.10	16.40
9	1.25	3,028	13.47	17.88	24.25
10	1.50	3,651	16.24	23.96	32.48
11	1.50	4,550	20.24	32.84	44.53
12	1.75	5,305	23.60	41.78	56.64
14	2.00	7,264	32.31	66.73	90.47
16	2.0	9,865	43.88	103.6	140.4
18	2.5	12,120	53.91	143.1	194.0
20	2.5	15,410	68.55	202.2	274.2
22	2.5	19,100	84.96	275.7	373.8
24	3.0	22,190	98.71	349.4	473.8
27	3.0	28,910	128.6	512.2	694.4
30	3.5	35,290	157.0	694.8	942.0
33	3.5	43,660	194.2	945.6	1,282
36	4.0	51,410	228.7	1,215	1,647
39	4.0	61,420	273.2	1,572	2,131
42	4.5	70,570	313.9	1,945	2,637

Class or Type: **ASTM F568, Class 4.8** (M1.6 to M16)
ISO 898/1, Class 4.8 (M1.6 to M16)

Minimum Tensile Strength = 420 MPa = 61,000 lbf/in²

Bolt Size (mm)	Thread Pitch (mm)	Clamping Force pound-force(lbf)	Clamping Force Kilonewton (kN)	Standard Dry Torque ft. pound-force(ft-lbf)	Standard Dry Torque newton meter(Nm)
1.6	0.35	83.94	0.3734	0.0881	0.1195
1.8	0.35	112.4	0.5001	0.1328	0.1800
2	0.40	137.0	0.6095	0.1798	0.2438
2.2	0.45	164.0	0.7297	0.2368	0.3211
2.5	0.45	224.1	0.9970	0.3677	0.4985
3	0.50	332.5	1.479	0.6545	0.8874
3.5	0.60	447.8	1.992	1.028	1.394
4	0.70	580.2	2.581	1.523	2.065
4.5	0.75	748.2	3.328	2.209	2.995
5	0.80	937.2	4.169	3.075	4.169
6	1.00	1,330	5.915	5.235	7.098
7	1.00	1,908	8.485	8.762	11.88
8	1.25	2,419	10.76	12.70	17.22
9	1.25	3,181	14.15	18.79	25.47

10	1.50	3,833	17.05	25.15	34.10
11	1.50	4,777	21.25	34.48	46.75
12	1.75	5,571	24.78	43.86	59.47
14	2.00	7,628	33.93	70.07	95.00
16	2.0	10,360	46.08	108.7	147.4
18	2.5	12,720	56.58	150.3	203.8
20	2.5	16,180	71.97	212.3	287.9
22	2.5	20,050	89.19	289.5	392.5
24	3.0	23,300	103.6	366.9	497.5
27	3.0	30,370	135.1	538.1	729.5
30	3.5	37,050	164.8	729.3	988.8
33	3.5	45,840	203.9	992.8	1,346
36	4.0	53,980	240.1	1,275	1,729
39	4.0	64,500	286.9	1,651	2,238
42	4.5	74,100	329.6	2,042	2,769

Class or Type: ASTM F568, Class 5.8 (M5 to M24)
ISO 898/1, Class 5.8 (M5 to M24)

Minimum Tensile Strength = 520 MPa = 75,000 lbf/in²

Bolt Size (mm)	Thread Pitch (mm)	Clamping Force		Standard Dry Torque	
		pound force(lbf)	Kilonewton (kN)	ft. pound force(ft-lbf)	newton meter (Nm)
1.6	0.35	103.9	0.4623	0.1091	0.1479
1.8	0.35	139.2	0.6192	0.1644	0.2229
2	0.40	169.6	0.7546	0.2226	0.3018
2.2	0.45	203.1	0.9034	0.2932	0.3975
2.5	0.45	277.5	1.234	0.4552	0.6172
3	0.50	411.6	1.831	0.8103	1.099
3.5	0.60	554.4	2.466	1.273	1.726
4	0.70	718.5	3.196	1.886	2.557
4.5	0.75	926.2	4.120	2.735	3.708
5	0.80	1,160	5.162	3.807	5.162
6	1.00	1,647	7.324	6.482	8.789
7	1.00	2,362	10.50	10.85	14.71
8	1.25	2,997	13.33	15.73	21.33
9	1.25	3,939	17.52	23.26	31.54
10	1.50	4,746	21.11	31.14	42.22
11	1.50	5,915	26.31	42.69	57.88
12	1.75	6,895	30.67	54.29	73.61
14	2.00	9,444	42.01	86.76	117.6
16	2.0	12,820	57.03	134.6	182.5
18	2.5	15,750	70.06	186.1	252.3
20	2.5	20,030	89.10	262.9	356.4
22	2.5	24,830	110.4	358.4	485.9
24	3.0	28,850	128.3	454.3	615.9
27	3.0	37,590	167.2	665.9	902.9
30	3.5	45,880	204.1	903.2	1,225
33	3.5	56,760	252.5	1,230	1,667
36	4.0	66,840	297.3	1,579	2,141
39	4.0	79,850	355.2	2,044	2,771
42	4.5	91,720	408.0	2,528	3,427

Class or Type: ISO 898/1, Class 8.8 (up to M16)

Minimum Tensile Strength = 800 MPa = 116,000 lbf/in²

Bolt Size (mm)	Thread Pitch (mm)	Clamping Force		Standard Dry Torque	
		pound force(lbf)	Kilonewton (kN)	ft. pound force(ft-lbf)	newton meter(Nm)
1.6	0.35	159.9	0.7112	0.1679	0.2276
1.8	0.35	214.2	0.9526	0.2529	0.3429

2	0.40	261.0	1.161	0.3425	0.4644
2.2	0.45	312.5	1.390	0.4511	0.6116
2.5	0.45	426.9	1.899	0.7003	0.9495
3	0.50	633.3	2.817	1.247	1.690
3.5	0.60	852.9	3.794	1.959	2.656
4	0.70	1,105	4.916	2.901	3.933
4.5	0.75	1,425	6.339	4.208	5.705
5	0.80	1,785	7.941	5.857	7.941
6	1.00	2,533	11.27	9.972	13.52
7	1.00	3,633	16.16	16.69	22.63
8	1.25	4,609	20.50	24.19	32.80
9	1.25	6,059	26.95	35.78	48.51
10	1.50	7,300	32.47	47.90	64.94
11	1.50	9,098	40.47	65.67	89.03
12	1.75	10,610	47.20	83.53	113.3
14	2.00	14,530	64.63	133.5	180.9
16	2.0	19,730	87.76	207.1	280.8
18	2.5	24,230	107.8	286.2	388.1
20	2.5	30,820	137.1	404.4	548.4
22	2.5	38,200	169.9	551.4	747.6
24	3.0	44,380	197.4	698.9	947.5
27	3.0	57,840	257.3	1,025	1,389
30	3.5	70,570	313.9	1,389	1,883
33	3.5	87,320	388.4	1,890	2,563
36	4.0	102,800	457.3	2,429	3,293
39	4.0	122,800	546.2	3,143	4,262
42	4.5	141,100	627.6	3,890	5,274

Class or Type: **ASTM A325M - Types 1, 2, & 3**
ASTM F568, Class 8.8 (M16 to M36)
ASTM F568 8.8.3 (M16 to M36)
ISO 898/1, Class 8.8 (M16 and over)

Minimum Tensile Strength = 830 MPa = 120,000 lbf / in²

Bolt Size (mm)	Thread Pitch (mm)	Clamping Force		Standard Dry Torque	
		pound force(lbf)	Kilonewton (kN)	ft. pound force(ft-lbf)	newton meter(Nm)
1.6	0.35	165.9	0.7379	0.1742	0.2361
1.8	0.35	222.2	0.9883	0.2624	0.3558
2	0.40	270.8	1.204	0.3553	0.4818
2.2	0.45	324.2	1.442	0.4680	0.6345
2.5	0.45	442.9	1.970	0.7266	0.9851
3	0.50	657.1	2.923	1.294	1.754
3.5	0.60	884.8	3.936	2.032	2.755
4	0.70	1,147	5.101	3.010	4.081
4.5	0.75	1,479	6.577	4.366	5.919
5	0.80	1,852	8.239	6.077	8.239
6	1.00	2,628	11.69	10.35	14.03
7	1.00	3,770	16.77	17.31	23.48
8	1.25	4,782	21.27	25.10	34.03
9	1.25	6,286	27.96	37.12	50.33
10	1.50	7,574	33.69	49.70	67.38
11	1.50	9,440	41.99	68.13	92.38
12	1.75	11,010	48.97	86.67	117.5
14	2.00	15,070	67.03	138.5	187.7
16	2.0	20,470	91.06	214.9	291.3
18	2.5	25,140	111.8	297.0	402.6
20	2.5	31,970	142.2	419.6	568.9
22	2.5	39,630	176.3	572.1	775.6
24	3.0	46,040	204.8	725.1	983.0
27	3.0	60,000	266.9	1,063	1,441

30	3.5	73,220	325.7	1,441	1,954
33	3.5	90,600	403.0	1,962	2,660
36	4.0	106,700	474.6	2,520	3,416
39	4.0	127,400	566.7	3,262	4,422
42	4.0	146,400	651.2	4,035	5,471

Class or Type: ASTM F568, Class 9.8 (M1.6 to M16)
ISO 898/1, Class 9.8 (M1.6 to M16)

Minimum Tensile Strength = 900 MPa = 131,000 lbf/in²

Bolt Size (mm)	Thread Pitch (mm)	Clamping Force		Standard Dry Torque	
		pound-force(lbf)	Kilonewton (kN)	ft.pound-force(ft-lbf)	newton meter(Nm)
1.6	0.35	179.9	0.8001	0.1888	0.2560
1.8	0.35	240.9	1.072	0.2845	0.3858
2	0.40	293.6	1.306	0.3853	0.5224
2.2	0.45	351.5	1.564	0.5075	0.6880
2.5	0.45	480.3	2.136	0.7878	1.068
3	0.50	712.6	3.170	1.403	1.902
3.5	0.60	959.5	4.268	2.204	2.988
4	0.70	1,243	5.531	3.264	4.425
4.5	0.75	1,603	7.132	4.734	6.419
5	0.80	2,008	8.933	6.589	8.933
6	1.00	2,850	12.68	11.22	15.211
7	1.00	4,087	18.18	18.77	25.455
8	1.25	5,184	23.06	27.21	36.896
9	1.25	6,816	30.32	40.25	54.576
10	1.50	8,212	36.53	53.89	73.060
11	1.50	10,240	45.55	73.88	100.2
12	1.75	11,940	53.11	93.98	127.4
14	2.00	16,340	72.68	150.1	203.6
16	2.0	22,190	98.71	233.0	315.9
18	2.5	27,260	121.3	322.0	436.6
20	2.5	34,670	154.2	455.0	616.9
22	2.5	42,970	191.1	620.3	841.0
24	3.0	49,930	222.1	786.2	1,066
27	3.0	65,060	289.4	1,153	1,563
30	3.5	79,400	353.2	1,563	2,119
33	3.5	98,240	437.0	2,127	2,884
36	4.0	115,700	514.7	2,732	3,704
39	4.0	138,200	614.7	3,537	4,795
42	4.5	158,800	706.4	4,375	5,932

Class or Type: ASTM A490M - Types 1, 2, & 3
ASTM F568, Class 10.9 (M5 to M100)
ASTM F568, Class 10.9.3 (M16 to M36)
ISO 898/1, Class 10.9 (M5 to M36)

Minimum Tensile Strength = 1,040 MPa = 151,000 lbf / in²

Bolt Size (mm)	Thread Pitch (mm)	Clamping Force		Standard Dry Torque	
		pound-force(lbf)	Kilonewton (kN)	ft.pound-force(ft-lbf)	newton meter(Nm)
1.6	0.35	207.9	0.9246	0.2182	0.2959
1.8	0.35	278.4	1.238	0.3288	0.4458
2	0.40	339.3	1.509	0.4452	0.6036
2.2	0.45	406.2	1.807	0.5864	0.7950
2.5	0.45	555.0	2.469	0.9104	1.234
3	0.50	823.5	3.663	1.621	2.198
3.5	0.60	1,109	4.932	2.546	3.452
4	0.70	1,437	6.391	3.771	5.113
4.5	0.75	1,853	8.241	5.470	7.417

5	0.80	2,321	10.32	7.614	10.32
6	1.00	3,293	14.65	12.96	17.58
7	1.00	4,723	21.01	21.69	29.41
8	1.25	5,991	26.65	31.45	42.64
9	1.25	7,875	35.03	46.51	63.05
10	1.50	9,491	42.22	62.28	84.44
11	1.50	11,830	52.62	85.37	115.7
12	1.75	13,790	61.34	108.6	147.2
14	2.00	18,890	84.03	173.5	235.2
16	2.0	25,650	114.1	269.3	365.1
18	2.5	31,500	140.1	372.1	504.5
20	2.5	40,060	178.2	525.8	712.8
22	2.5	49,660	220.9	716.8	971.9
24	3.0	57,690	256.6	908.5	1,232
27	3.0	75,180	334.4	1,332	1,806
30	3.5	91,740	408.1	1,806	2,449
33	3.5	113,500	504.9	2,458	3,332
36	4.0	133,700	594.7	3,158	4,281
39	4.0	159,700	710.4	4,087	5,541
42	4.5	183,500	816.2	5,056	6,855

Class or Type: **ASTM F568, Class 12.9** (M1.6 to M100)
ISO 898/1, Class 12.9 (M1.6 to M36)

Minimum Tensile Strength = 1,220 MPa = 177,000 lbf / in²

Bolt Size (mm)	Thread Pitch (mm)	Clamping Force		Standard Dry Torque	
		pound-force(lbf)	Kilonewton (kN)	ft.pound-force(ft-lbf)	newton-meter(Nm)
1.6	0.35	243.8	1.085	0.2560	0.3471
1.8	0.35	326.6	1.453	0.3857	0.5230
2	0.40	398.0	1.770	0.5223	0.7081
2.2	0.45	476.5	2.120	0.6879	0.9326
2.5	0.45	651.0	2.896	1.068	1.448
3	0.50	965.8	4.296	1.901	2.578
3.5	0.60	1,301	5.786	2.987	4.050
4	0.70	1,685	7.497	4.424	5.998
4.5	0.75	2,173	9.667	6.417	8.700
5	0.80	2,722	12.11	8.932	12.11
6	1.00	3,863	17.18	15.21	20.62
7	1.00	5,541	24.65	25.45	34.50
8	1.25	7,028	31.26	36.89	50.02
9	1.25	9,237	41.09	54.55	73.96
10	1.50	11,130	49.51	73.05	99.04
11	1.50	13,880	61.74	100.1	135.8
12	1.75	16,180	71.97	127.4	172.7
14	2.00	22,150	98.53	203.5	275.9
16	2.0	30,080	133.8	315.8	428.2
18	2.5	36,960	164.4	436.5	591.8
20	2.5	47,000	209.1	616.9	836.4
22	2.5	58,250	259.1	840.9	1,140
24	3.0	67,670	301.0	1,066	1,445
27	3.0	88,190	392.3	1,562	2,118
30	3.5	107,600	478.6	2,119	2,873
33	3.5	133,200	592.5	2,883	3,909
36	4.0	156,800	697.5	3,704	5,022
39	4.0	187,300	833.2	4,794	6,500
42	4.5	215,200	957.3	5,931	8,041

Effect of Anti-Seize Compounds, Lubricants, Platings, Coatings, Torque Coefficients, and Stress Levels on Torque for Carbon Steel Bolts

Anti-seize Coumpound, Lubricant, Coating, Torque Coefficient, or Stress Level	Multiply Standard Dry Torque From Tables By:
SAE J429 Grade 1 (1/4" to 1-1/2"), 70% Minimum Tensile Stress	1.70
SAE J429 Grade 2 (5/8" to 1-1/2"), 70% Minimum Tensile Stress	1.70
Zinc plating (hot-dipped galvanized)	1.60
ASTM A449 Type 1 (1-3/4" to 2"), 70% Minimum Tensile Stress	1.53
Steel (oxidized, rusted)	1.50
ASTM A325 Types 1 & 3, 70% Minimum Tensile Stress	1.32
ASTM A449 Type 1 (1/4" to 1-1/2"), 70% Minimum Tensile Stress	1.32
ASTM A449 Type 2 (1/4" to 1"), 70% Minimum Tensile Stress	1.32
SAE J429 Grade 5, 5.1 & 5.2 (all sizes), 70% Minimum Tensile Stress	1.32
SAE J429 Grade 2 (1/4" to 3/4"), 70% Minimum Tensile Stress	1.26
ASTM Type A574 (#0 to ½"), 70% Minimum Tensile Stress	1.20
ASTM Type A574 (5/8" to 2"), 70% Minimum Tensile Stress	1.18
SAE J429 Grade 7 (1/4" to 1-1/2"), 70% Minimum Tensile Stress	1.18
ASTM A354 Grade BD, 70% Minimum Tensile Stress	1.17
ASTM A490 Types 1, 2 & 3, 70% Minimum Tensile Stress	1.17
SAE J429 Grade 8 & 8.2 (all sizes), 70% Minimum Tensile Stress	1.17
ASTM A354 Grade BC, 70% Minimum Tensile Stress	1.11
80% of Proof Strength	1.07
Black oxide	1.00
Steel (clean, dry, non-plated, as-received condition)	1.00
Torque Coefficient = 0.20	1.00
75% of Proof Strength	1.00
Phosphate and oil	0.95
Torque Coefficient = 0.19	0.95
70% of Proof Strength	0.93
Dri-Lock® 204 adhesive coating	0.90
Silver grade anti-seize	0.90
Parkerized and oiled	0.90
Torque Coefficient = 0.18	0.90
65% of Proof Strength	0.87
Corro-Shield® plating (alloy of copper, zinc, and aluminum)	0.85
Grease with copper, graphite and aluminum flakes	0.85
N-1000® anti-seize	0.85

Resistoplate® TF	0.85
Torque Coefficient = 0.17	0.85
Zinc plating (electroplated)	0.85
60% of Proof Strength	0.80
C5A®, copper-graphite based anti-seize	0.80
Cadmium plating	0.80
Grease with copper and graphite flakes	0.80
Grease with graphite flakes and calcium fluoride powder	0.80
Motor oil (SAE 20W)	0.80
N-7000® anti-seize	0.80
Torque Coefficient = 0.16	0.80
WD-40®, light weight oil	0.80
Dri-Lock® 201 adhesive coating	0.75
Grease with nickel and graphite flakes	0.75
Grease with zinc dust	0.75
Motor oil (SAE 40W)	0.75
N-5000® anti-seize	0.75
Torque Coefficient = 0.15	0.75
Zinc anti-seize	0.75
55% of Proof Strength	0.73
Cadmium plating and motor oil (SAE 30W)	0.70
Graphite	0.70
Molybdenum grease	0.70
Motor oil (SAE 30W) with cadmium plating	0.70
White lead grease (lead carbonate)	0.70
50% of Proof Strength	0.67
Dri-Lock® 202 adhesive coating	0.65
Graphite-50® anti-seize	0.65
Grease with graphite flakes	0.65
Grease with graphite flakes and molybdenum disulphide powder	0.65
Moly-50® anti-seize (molybdenum disulphide)	0.65
Nickel based anti-seize	0.65
Dri-Lock® 200 adhesive coating	0.60
Molybdenum film (dry)	0.60
Oil (light weight)	0.60
Dri-Lock® 203 adhesive coating	0.55
Graphite and motor oil	0.55
Grease with molybdenum disulphide powder	0.55
Grease with molybdenum disulphide powder and graphite	0.55
M-702 MOLY® paste lubricant (molybdenum disulphide)	0.55
Moly Paste® (molybdenum disulphide)	0.55
Oil (heavy weight)	0.50
Premier ETP®	0.50
Premier Thread-Eze®	0.50
Wax (extreme pressure)	0.50
Moly-Cote® (molybdenum disulphide)	0.45
Never-sieze®	0.45
Premier® thread lubricant	0.45

Example:

You have a clean, dry, non-plated 1/2-13 coarse threaded SAE J429 Grade 8 bolt. You want the stress in the bolt to be 70% of the minimum tensile stress after you tighten the nut and you want to use WD-40® as the lubricant on the threads, nut and washer.

What is the approximate torque required to develop this stress in the bolt?

From the Clamping Force and Standard Dry Torque Table for coarse threaded bolts you read for a 1/2-13 SAE J429 Grade 8 bolt that a torque of approximately 106 foot pounds-force will develop 75% of the proof strength in this bolt.

From the Effects of Anti-seize Compounds, etc. Table you find that to develop 70% of the minimum tensile stress in an SAE J429 Grade 8 bolt you need to multiply the dry torque by 1.17 to increase the stress level in the bolt. You also find that using WD-40® as a lubricant you need to multiply the dry torque by 0.80 to reduce the torque due to lubrication.

The approximate required torque to give the desired stress level in the bolt is the product of the dry torque and the multipiers that account for different stress levels and lubricants. The approximate required torque is:

106 foot pounds-force x 1.17 x 0.80 = 99 foot pounds-force.

Trademarks:

Premier Industrial Corporation: Corro-Shield®, Resistoplate® TF, Premier ETP®, Premier Thread-Eze®, Moly-Cote® , Never-sieze®, and Premier® thread lubricant.

Locktite Corporation: C5A®, Dri-Lock®, Moly-50®, Graphite-50®, Moly Paste®, N-1000®, N-5000®, and N-7000®.

WD-40 Company: WD-40®

Clover Tool Company: M-702 MOLY®.

Standard Dry Torque for Coarse-Threaded Non-Ferrous and Stainless Steel Bolts

Nylon 6/6 (at 50% relative humidity)

Bolt Size (# or inch)	Threads/ Inch	inch pound-force (in-lbf)	foot pound-force (ft-lbf)	newton meter(Nm)
		Minimum Tensile Strength Approximately 6,500 pound-force / square inch (lbf / in²)		
		Standard Dry Torque		
1	64	0.2280	0.0190	0.0258
2	56	0.3948	0.0329	0.0446
3	48	0.6324	0.0527	0.0715
4	40	0.9552	0.0796	0.1079
5	40	1.381	0.1151	0.1561
6	32	1.924	0.1603	0.2173
8	32	3.431	0.2859	0.3876
10	24	5.617	0.4681	0.6347
12	24	8.634	0.7195	0.9755
1/4	20	14.09	1.174	1.592
5/16	18	29.77	2.481	3.364
3/8	16	54.85	4.571	6.197
7/16	14	91.94	7.662	10.39
1/2	13	143.9	11.99	16.26
9/16	12	213.5	17.79	24.12
5/8	11	303.8	25.32	34.33
3/4	10	559.8	46.65	63.25

Aluminum

Bolt Size (# or inch)	Threads/ Inch	inch pound-force (in-lbf)	foot pound-force (ft-lbf)	newton meter(Nm)
		Minimum Tensile Strength Approximately 55,000 pound-force / square inch (lbf / in²)		
		Standard Dry Torque		
1	64	0.9312	0.0776	0.1052
2	56	1.480	0.1233	0.1672
3	48	2.202	0.1835	0.2488
4	40	3.121	0.2601	0.3526
5	40	4.256	0.3547	0.4809
6	32	5.630	0.4692	0.6361
8	32	9.172	0.7643	1.036
10	24	13.90	1.159	1.571
12	24	19.98	1.665	2.257
1/4	20	45.06	3.755	5.091
5/16	18	83.94	6.995	9.484
3/8	16	139.5	11.63	15.76
7/16	14	214.4	17.87	24.23
1/2	13	311.1	25.93	35.15
9/16	12	432.0	36.00	48.81
5/8	11	579.5	48.29	65.48
3/4	10	963.4	80.28	108.8
7/8	9	1480	123.4	167.3
1	8	2148	179.0	242.7

Yellow Brass, (63% Cu, 37% Zn)

Bolt Size (# or inch)	Threads/ Inch	inch pound-force (in-lbf)	foot pound-force (ft-lbf)	newton meter(Nm)
		Minimum Tensile Strength Approximately 60,000 pound-force / square inch (lbf / in²)		
		Standard Dry Torque		
1	64	1.315	0.1096	0.1486
2	56	2.071	0.1726	0.2340
3	48	3.059	0.2549	0.3456
4	40	4.307	0.3589	0.4866
5	40	5.839	0.4866	0.6597
6	32	7.682	0.6402	0.8679
8	32	12.40	1.033	1.401
10	24	18.64	1.553	2.106
12	24	26.60	2.217	3.005
1/4	20	61.46	5.122	6.944
5/16	18	114.3	9.525	12.91
3/8	16	189.9	15.83	21.46
7/16	14	291.6	24.30	32.95
1/2	13	422.8	35.23	47.77
9/16	12	586.7	48.89	66.29
5/8	11	786.5	65.54	88.86
3/4	10	1,249	104.1	141.1
7/8	9	1,925	160.4	217.5
1	8	2,799	233.3	316.2
1-1/8	7	3,894	324.5	440.0
1-1/4	7	5,232	436.0	591.1
1-3/8	6	6,836	569.7	772.4
1-1/2	6	8,725	727.1	985.8

Silicone Bronze - Type B (98.5% Cu, 1.5% Zn)

Bolt Size (# or inch)	Threads/ Inch	inch pound-force (in-lbf)	foot pound-force (ft-lbf)	newton meter(Nm)
		Minimum Tensile Strength Approximately 70,000 pound-force / square inch (lbf / in²)		
		Standard Dry Torque		
1	64	1.445	0.1204	0.1633
2	56	2.290	0.1908	0.2587
3	48	3.402	0.2835	0.3844
4	40	4.811	0.4009	0.5436
5	40	6.550	0.5458	0.7401
6	32	8.650	0.7208	0.9773
8	32	14.05	1.171	1.587
10	24	21.24	1.770	2.400
12	24	30.46	2.538	3.442
1/4	20	68.77	5.731	7.770
5/16	18	128.6	10.72	14.53
3/8	16	214.5	17.88	24.24
7/16	14	330.5	27.54	37.34
1/2	13	480.7	40.06	54.31
9/16	12	669.0	55.75	75.59
5/8	11	899.1	74.93	101.6
3/4	10	1,416	118.0	160.0

7/8	9	2,180	181.7	246.3
1	8	3,169	264.1	358.0
1-1/8	7	4,408	367.3	498.0
1-1/4	7	5,920	493.3	668.9
1-3/8	6	7,732	644.3	873.6
1-1/2	6	9,865	822.1	1,115

18-8 Stainless Steel (Fe 68%, Cr 18%, Ni 8%)

		Minimum Tensile Strength Approximately 75,000 pound-force / square inch (lbf / in²)		
		Standard Dry Torque		
Bolt Size (# or inch)	Threads/ Inch	inch pound-force (in-lbf)	foot pound-force (ft-lbf)	newton meter(Nm)
1	64	1.575	0.1313	0.1780
2	56	2.490	0.2075	0.2813
3	48	3.691	0.3076	0.4170
4	40	5.212	0.4343	0.5889
5	40	7.085	0.5904	0.8005
6	32	9.344	0.7787	1.056
8	32	15.14	1.262	1.711
10	24	22.85	1.904	2.582
12	24	32.70	2.725	3.695
1/4	20	75.16	6.263	8.492
5/16	18	139.9	11.66	15.81
3/8	16	232.4	19.37	26.26
7/16	14	357.0	29.75	40.34
1/2	13	517.8	43.15	58.50
9/16	12	718.8	59.90	81.21
5/8	11	963.9	80.33	108.9
3/4	10	1,530	127.5	172.9
7/8	9	2,356	196.3	266.2
1	8	3,424	285.3	386.9
1-1/8	7	4,762	396.8	538.0
1-1/4	7	6,396	533.0	722.7
1-3/8	6	8,353	696.1	943.8
1-1/2	6	10,657	888.1	1,204

316 Stainless Steel (Fe 68%, Cr 17%, Ni 12%)

		Minimum Tensile Strength Approximately 75,000 pound-force / square inch (lbf / in²)		
		Standard Dry Torque		
Bolt Size (# or inch)	Threads/ Inch	inch pound-force (in-lbf)	foot pound-force (ft-lbf)	newton meter(Nm)
1	64	1.681	0.1401	0.1899
2	56	2.648	0.2207	0.2992
3	48	3.912	0.3260	0.4420
4	40	5.509	0.4591	0.6224
5	40	7.469	0.6224	0.8439
6	32	9.827	0.8189	1.110
8	32	15.86	1.322	1.792
10	24	23.85	1.988	2.695
12	24	34.04	2.837	3.846
1/4	20	78.75	6.563	8.898
5/16	18	146.6	12.22	16.56
3/8	16	243.6	20.30	27.52
7/16	14	374.2	31.18	42.28

1/2	13	542.8	45.23	61.33
9/16	12	753.5	62.79	85.13
5/8	11	1,010	84.17	114.1
3/4	10	1,582	131.8	178.7
7/8	9	2,443	203.6	276.0
1	8	3,560	296.7	402.2
1-1/8	7	4,961	413.4	560.5
1-1/4	7	6,677	556.4	754.4
1-3/8	6	8,734	727.8	986.8
1-1/2	6	11,162	930.2	1,261

Monel (Ni 67%, Cu 30%, Fe 1.4%)

Minimum Tensile Strength Approximately 82,000 pound-force / square inch (lbf / in²)				
			Standard Dry Torque	
Bolt Size (# or inch)	Threads/ inch	inch pound-force (in-lbf)	foot pound-force (ft-lbf)	newton meter(Nm)
1	64	1.472	0.1227	0.1663
2	56	2.406	0.2005	0.2718
3	48	3.670	0.3058	0.4147
4	40	5.313	0.4428	0.6003
5	40	7.386	0.6155	0.8345
6	32	9.937	0.8281	1.123
8	32	16.68	1.390	1.885
10	24	25.93	2.161	2.930
12	24	38.09	3.174	4.304
1/4	20	85.23	7.103	9.630
5/16	18	158.5	13.21	17.91
3/8	16	263.1	21.93	29.73
7/16	14	403.9	33.66	45.63
1/2	13	585.4	48.78	66.14
9/16	12	812.2	67.68	91.77
5/8	11	1,089	90.75	123.0
3/4	10	1,832	152.7	207.0
7/8	9	2,822	235.2	318.8
1	8	4,101	341.8	463.4
1-1/8	7	5,704	475.3	644.5
1-1/4	7	7,663	638.6	865.8
1-3/8	6	10,008	834.0	1,131
1-1/2	6	12,770	1,064	1,443

Unified Inch Screw Threads - Standard Screw Thread Series

Nominal Size	Basic Major Diameter	Threads Per Inch				
		Coarse	Fine	Extra-Fine	Miniature	Miniature Machine Screw
(# or Inch)	Inch	UNC	UNF	UNEF	UNM	NS
30	0.0118	-	-	-	318	-
35	0.0138	-	-	-	282	-
40	0.0157	-	-	-	254	-
45	0.0177	-	-	-	254	-
50	0.0197	-	-	-	203	-
0000	0.0210	-	-	-	-	160
55	0.0217	-	-	-	203	-
60	0.0236	-	-	-	169	-
70	0.0276	-	-	-	145	-
80	0.0315	-	-	-	127	-
90	0.0354	-	-	-	113	-
100	0.0394	-	-	-	102	-
110	0.0433	-	-	-	102	-
120	0.0472	-	-	-	102	-
140	0.0551	-	-	-	85	-
000	0.0340	-	-	-	-	120
00	0.0470	-	-	-	-	90 & 96
0	0.0600	-	80	-	-	-
1	0.0730	64	72	-	-	-
2	0.0860	56	64	-	-	-
3	0.0990	48	56	-	-	-
4	0.1120	40	48	-	-	-

Unified Inch Screw Threads - Standard Screw Thread Series (cont.)

Nominal Size	Basic Major Diameter	Threads Per Inch				
		Coarse	Fine	Extra-Fine	Miniature	Miniature Machine Screw
(# or Inch)	Inch	UNC	UNF	UNEF	UNM	NS
5 or 1/8	0.1250	40	44	-	-	-
6	0.1380	32	40	-	-	-
8	0.1640	32	36	-	-	-
10	0.1900	24	32	-	-	-
12	0.2160	24	28	32	-	-
1/4	0.2500	20	28	32	-	-
5/16	0.3125	18	24	32	-	-
3/8	0.3750	16	24	32	-	-
-	0.3900	-	-	-	-	-
7/16	0.4375	14	20	28	-	-
1/2	0.5000	13	20	28	-	-
9/16	0.5625	12	18	24	-	-
5/8	0.6250	11	18	24	-	-
11/16	0.6875	-	-	24	-	-
3/4	0.7500	10	16	20	-	-
13/16	0.8125	-	-	20	-	-
7/8	0.8750	9	14	20	-	-
15/16	0.9375	-	-	20	-	-
1	1.0000	8	12	20	-	-
1-1/16	1.0625	-	-	18	-	-
1-1/8	1.1250	7	12	18	-	-

Clearance Holes For Bolts and Screws - Inch Series

Bolt or Screw Size (# or inch)	Nominal Diameter (inch)	Clearance Drills					
		Close Clearance		Normal Clearance		Loose Clearance	
		Drill Size	Diameter (inch)	Drill Size	Diameter (inch)	Drill Size	Diameter (inch)
# 30	0.0118	# 83	0.0120	# 82	0.0125	# 79	0.0145
# 35	0.0138	- - - NA - - -		# 79	0.0145	# 78	0.0160
# 40	0.0157	# 78	0.0160	- - - NA - - -		# 77	0.0180
# 45	0.0177	# 77	0.0180	- - - NA - - -		# 75	0.0210
# 50	0.0197	# 76	0.0200	# 75	0.0210	# 73	0.0240
# 0000	0.0210	- NA-		# 74	0.0225	# 72	0.0250
# 55	0.0217	# 74	0.0225	# 73	0.0240	# 71	0.0260
# 60	0.0236	# 73	0.0240	# 72	0.0250	# 70	0.0280
# 70	0.0276	# 70	0.0280	# 69	0.0292	# 66	0.0330
# 80	0.0316	# 67	0.0320	# 66	0.0330	# 62	0.0380
# 000	0.0340	# 65	0.0350	# 64	0.0360	# 60	0.0400
# 90	0.0354	# 64	0.0360	# 62	0.0380	# 58	0.0420
# 100	0.0394	# 60	0.0400	# 58	0.0420	3/64	0.0469
# 110	0.0433	- - - NA - - -		# 56	0.0465	# 55	0.0520
# 00	0.0470	- - - NA - - -		- - - NA - - -		# 54	0.0550
# 120	0.0472	- - - NA - - -		- - - NA - - -		# 54	0.0550
# 140	0.0551	- - - NA - - -		# 53	0.0595	# 51	0.0670
# 0	0.0600	1/16	0.0625	# 52	0.0635	# 50	0.0700
1/16	0.0625	# 52	0.0635	# 51	0.0670	# 49	0.0730
# 1	0.0730	# 48	0.0760	5/64	0.0781	# 44	0.0860
5/64	0.0781	# 46	0.0810	# 45	0.0820	# 42	0.0935
# 2	0.0860	# 43	0.0890	# 42	0.0935	# 38	0.1015
3/32	0.0938	# 41	0.0960	# 39	0.0995	# 34	0.1110
# 3	0.0990	# 38	0.1015	# 37	0.1040	# 32	0.1160
7/64	0.1094	# 33	0.1130	# 32	0.1160	# 30	0.1285
# 4	0.1120	# 32	0.1160	# 31	0.1200	# 29	0.1360
# 5	0.1250	# 30	0.1285	# 29	0.1360	# 25	0.1490
1/8	0.1250	# 30	0.1285	# 29	0.1360	# 25	0.1490
# 6	0.1380	# 27	0.1440	# 26	0.1470	# 19	0.1660
9/64	0.1406	# 26	0.1470	# 25	0.1490	# 19	0.1660
5/32	0.1563	# 20	0.1610	# 19	0.1660	# 13	0.1850
# 8	0.1640	# 18	0.1695	# 17	0.1730	# 9	0.1960
11/64	0.1719	# 16	0.1770	# 14	0.1820	# 6	0.2040
3/16	0.1875	# 10	0.1935	# 8	0.1990	# 2	0.2210
# 10	0.1900	# 9	0.1960	# 7	0.2010	# 1	0.2280
13/64	0.2031	# 4	0.2090	# 3	0.2130	C	0.2420
# 12	0.2160	# 2	0.2210	# 1	0.2280	F	0.2570
7/32	0.2188	# 1	0.2280	A	0.2340	G	0.2610
15/64	0.2344	C	0.2420	1/4 or E	0.2500	J	0.2770
# 14	0.2420	1/4 or E	0.2500	F	0.2570	L	0.2900
1/4	0.2500	F	0.2570	17/64	0.2656	19/64	0.2969
5/16	0.3125	P	0.3230	Q	0.3320	3/8	0.3750
3/8	0.3750	W	0.3860	X	0.3970	29/64	0.4531
7/16	0.4375	29/64	0.4531	15/32	0.4688	33/64	0.5156
1/2	0.5000	33/64	0.5156	17/32	0.5313	19/32	0.5938
9/16	0.5625	37/64	0.5781	19/32	0.5938	43/64	0.6719
5/8	0.6250	41/64	0.6406	21/32	0.6563	3/4	0.7500
11/16	0.6875	45/64	0.7031	47/64	0.7344	13/16	0.8125

Bolt or Screw Size (# or inch)	Nominal Diameter (inch)	Close Clearance		Normal Clearance		Loose Clearance	
		Drill Size	Diameter (inch)	Drill Size	Diameter (inch)	Drill Size	Diameter (inch)
3/4	0.7500	25/32	0.7813	51/64	0.7969	57/64	0.8906
13/16	0.8125	27/32	0.8438	55/64	0.8594	31/32	0.9688
7/8	0.8750	29/32	0.9063	59/64	0.9219	1-3/64	1.0469
15/16	0.9375	31/32	0.9688	1	1.0000	1-7/64	1.1094
1	1.0000	1-1/32	1.0313	1-1/16	1.0625	1-3/16	1.1875
1-1/16	1.0625	1-3/32	1.0938	1-1/8	1.1250	1-17/64	1.2656
1-1/8	1.1250	1-5/32	1.1563	1-3/16	1.1875	1-11/32	1.3438
1-3/16	1.1875	1-7/32	1.2188	1-17/64	1.2656	1-13/32	1.4063
1-1/4	1.2500	1-19/64	1.2969	1-21/64	1.3281	1-31/64	1.4844
1-5/16	1.3125	1-11/32	1.3438	1-25/64	1.3906	1-9/16	1.5625
1-3/8	1.3750	1-27/64	1.4219	1-29/64	1.4531	1-5/8	1.6250
1-7/16	1.4375	1-31/64	1.4844	1-17/32	1.5313	1-23/32	1.7188
1-1/2	1.5000	1-9/16	1.5625	1-19/32	1.5938	1-25/32	1.7813
1-9/16	1.5625	1-5/8	1.6250	1-21/32	1.6563	1-27/32	1.8438
1-5/8	1.6250	1-11/16	1.6875	1-23/32	1.7188	1-15/16	1.9375

Clearance Holes for Bolts and Screws - Metric Series

Bolt or Screw Size	Nominal Diameter millimeter	Close Clearance		Normal Clearance		Loose Clearance	
		Drill Size	Diameter millimeter	Drill Size	Diameter millimeter	Drill Size	Diameter millimeter
1	1.00	1.05	1.05	1.1	1.10	1.2	1.20
1.1	1.10	1.15	1.15	1.25	1.25	1.3	1.30
1.2	1.20	1.3	1.30	1.35	1.35	1.45	1.45
1.4	1.40	1.5	1.50	1.55	1.55	1.7	1.70
1.6	1.60	1.7	1.70	1.8	1.80	1.9	1.90
1.8	1.80	1.9	1.90	2	2.00	2.15	2.15
2	2.00	2.1	2.10	2.25	2.25	2.4	2.40
2.2	2.20	2.35	2.35	2.45	2.45	2.65	2.65
2.5	2.50	2.65	2.65	2.8	2.80	3	3.00
3	3.00	3.2	3.20	3.35	3.35	3.6	3.60
3.5	3.50	3.7	3.70	3.9	3.90	4.2	4.20
4	4.00	4.25	4.25	4.5	4.50	4.8	4.80
4.5	4.50	4.8	4.80	5	5.00	5.4	5.40
5	5.00	5.3	5.30	5.6	5.60	6	6.00
5.5	5.50	5.8	5.80	6.2	6.20	6.6	6.60
6	6.00	6.4	6.40	6.7	6.70	7.2	7.20
7	7.00	7.4	7.40	7.8	7.80	8.4	8.40
8	8.00	8.5	8.50	9	9.00	9.6	9.60
9	9.00	9.5	9.50	10.1	10.10	10.8	10.80
10	10.00	10.6	10.60	11.2	11.20	12	12.00
11	11.00	11.7	11.70	12.3	12.30	13.2	13.20
12	12.00	12.7	12.70	13.4	13.40	14.5	14.50
14	14.00	14.75	14.75	15.75	15.75	16.75	16.75
15	15.00	16	16.00	16.75	16.75	18	18.00
16	16.00	17	17.00	18	18.00	19	19.00
17	17.00	18	18.00	19	19.00	20	20.00
18	18.00	19	19.00	20	20.00	22	22.00

Clearance Holes for Metric Bolts and Screws (cont.)

Bolt or Screw Size	Nominal Diameter millimeter	Clearance Drills					
		Close Clearance		Normal Clearance		Loose Clearance	
		Drill Size	Diameter millimeter	Drill Size	Diameter millimeter	Drill Size	Diameter millimeter
20	20.00	21	21.00	22	22.00	24	24.00
22	22.00	23	23.00	25	25.00	26	26.00
24	24.00	25	25.00	27	27.00	29	29.00
25	25.00	26	26.00	28	28.00	30	30.00
26	26.00	28	28.00	29	29.00	31	31.00
27	27.00	29	29.00	30	30.00	32	32.00
28	28.00	30	30.00	31	31.00	34	34.00

Notes:
(1) Drill sizes in the table are based on a Clearance Ratio that is defined as: Clearance Ratio = {((Clearance Drill Diameter - Bolt/Screw Diameter)/(Bolt/Screw Diameter)} x 100.
Most drills listed under Close Clearance have Clearance Ratios between 2% and 4% for the Inch Series, and between 4% and 8% for the Metric Series.
Most drills listed under Normal Clearance have Clearance Ratios between 5% and 9% for the Inch Series, and between 10% and 14% for the Metric Series.
Most drills listed under Loose Clearance have Clearance Ratios between 17% and 20% for the Inch Series, and between 18% and 22% for the Metric Series.
(2) - NA - means Not Available. No Inch Series drills are available that provide this clearance.
(3) Similar, but less extensive, tables for the Inch Series may be found in:
IPT's Industrial Fasteners Handbook, IPT Publishing and Training, Inc., Alberta, Canada
www.evergreen.edu/user/serv_res/research/bsi/people/dawn/fabric/fraction.html
bigben.stanford.edu/docs/tapClearanceHoleInfo.html
cfa-www.harvard.edu/~masermri/screws/screw1.html
Similar, but less extensive, tables for the Metric Series may be found in:
IPT's Industrial Fasteners Handbook, IPT Publishing and Training, Inc., Alberta, Canada
Fasteners And Screw Threads, ISO Standards Handbook, ISO, Geneve, Switzerland
Graphics In Engineering Design, 3rd Edition, John Wiley & Sons, New York, NY
(4) Other drill sizes may produce acceptable results. See the Drill Number-Wire Gauge-Screw Size table in the Tools Chapter for additional drill sizes.

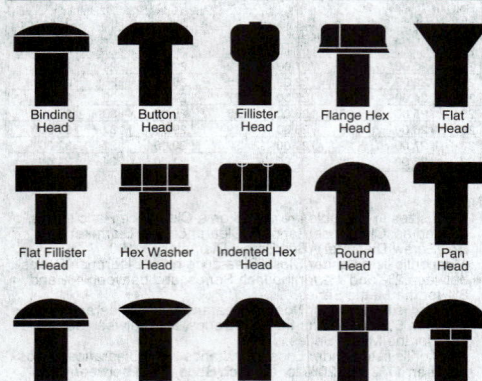

Binding Head   Button Head   Fillister Head   Flange Hex Head   Flat Head

Flat Fillister Head   Hex Washer Head   Indented Hex Head   Round Head   Pan Head

Truss Head   Oval Head   Washer Head   Trimmed Hex   Anchor Head

Bolt Torque Specifications

Whitworth

Bolt Size Inches	Coarse Thread / inch	Grades A & B 62,720 psi Med Carbon Steel	Grade S 112,000 psi Med Carbon Steel	Grade T 123,200 psi Med Carbon Steel
		Standard Dry Torque in Foot–Pounds		
1/4	20	5	7	9
5/16	18	9	15	18
3/8	16	15	27	31
7/16	14	24	43	51
1/2	12	36	64	79
9/16	12	52	94	111
5/8	11	73	128	155
3/4	11	118	213	259
7/8	9	186	322	407
1	8	276	497	611

Whitworth

Bolt Size Inches	Coarse Thread / inch	Grade V 145,600 psi Med Carbon Steel
		Standard Dry Torque in Foot–Pounds
1/4	20	10
5/16	18	21
3/8	16	36
7/16	14	58
1/2	12	89
9/16	12	128
5/8	11	175
3/4	11	287
7/8	9	459
1	8	693

In order to determine the torque for a <u>fine thread</u> bolt increase the above coarse thread ratings by 9%. See first page of Bolt Torque Specifications for information on the Effects of Lubrication on Bolt Torque.

Nails

The "d" listed after each Size Number stands for "penny", which was originally used in old England as a way of describing the number of pennies needed to buy 100 nails. Today, "penny" is used only to define the length of the nail.

COMMON NAILS
For General Construction

Size Number	Length Inches	Shaft Diameter Gauge (inches)	Diameter of Head, inches	Number per Pound
2d	1	15 (0.072)	11/64	840
3d	1-1/4	14 (0.080)	13/64	530
4d	1-1/2	12-1/2 (0.095)	1/4	300
5d	1-3/4	12-1/2 (0.095)	1/4	260
6d	2	11-1/2 (0.113)	17/64	170
7d	2-1/4	11-1/2 (0.113)	17/64	150
8d	2-1/2	10-1/4 (0.131)	9/32	105
9d	2-3/4	10-1/4 (0.131)	9/32	95
10d	3	9 (0.148)	5/16	65
12d	3-1/4	9 (0.148)	5/16	60
16d	3-1/2	8 (0.162)	11/32	44
20d	4	6 (0.192)	13/32	30
30d	4-1/2	5 (0.207)	7/16	22
40d	5	4 (0.225)	15/32	18
50d	5-1/2	3 (0.244)	1/2	14
60d	6	2 (0.263)	17/32	10

BOX NAILS
For Light Construction

Size Number	Length Inches	Shaft Diameter Gauge (inches)	Diameter of Head, inches	Number per Pound
2d	1	15-1/2 (0.067)	11/64	1010
3d	1-1/4	14-1/2 (0.073)	13/64	620
4d	1-1/2	14 (0.080)	1/4	450
5d	1-3/4	14 (0.080)	1/4	375
6d	2	12-1/2 (0.095)	17/64	230
7d	2-1/4	12-1/2 (0.095)	17/64	200
8d	2-1/2	11-1/2 (0.109)	9/32	130
10d	3	10-1/2 (0.128)	5/16	88
12d	3-1/4	10-1/2 (0.128)	5/16	80
16d	3-1/2	10 (0.135)	11/32	70
20d	4	9 (0.148)	13/32	52
30d	4-1/2	9 (0.148)	7/16	45
40d	5	8 (0.162)	15/32	35

Nails (cont.)

COMMON WIRE SPIKES
For Heavy Construction

Size Number	Length Inches	Shaft Diameter Gauge (inches)	Diameter of Head, Gauge	Number per Pound
10d	3	6 (0.192)	3	43
12d	3–1/4	6 (0.192)	3	39
16d	3–1/2	5 (0.207)	2	31
20d	4	4 (0.225)	1	23
30d	4–1/2	3 (0.244)	0	18
40d	5	2 (0.263)	2/0	14
50d	5–1/2	1 (0.283)	3/0	11
60d	6	1 (0.283)	3/0	9
5/6 in	7	(0.312)	0.370 in	7
3/8 in	8–1/2	(0.375)	0.433 in	4

CASING NAILS
For Interior Trim

Size Number	Length Inches	Shaft Diameter Gauge (inches)	Diameter of Head, Gauge	Number per Pound
3d	1–1/4	14–1/2 (0.073)	11–1/2	625
4d	1–1/2	14 (0.080)	11	490
6d	2	12–1/2 (0.095)	9–1/2	250
8d	2–1/2	11–1/2 (0.113)	8–1/2	145
10d	3	10–1/2 (0.128)	7–1/2	95
16d	3–1/2	10 (0.135)	7	70
20d	4	9 (0.148)	6	52

FINISHING NAILS
For Cabinet Work and Interior Trim

Size Number	Length Inches	Shaft Diameter Gauge (inches)	Diameter of Head, Gauge	Number per Pound
2d	1	16–1/2 (0.058)	13–1/2	1350
3d	1–1/4	15–1/2 (0.067)	12–1/2	850
4d	1–1/2	15 (0.072)	12	550
5d	1–3/4	15 (0.072)	12	500
6d	2	13 (0.091)	10	300
8d	2–1/2	12–1/2 (0.095)	9–1/2	190
10d	3	11–1/2 (0.113)	8–1/2	125
16d	3–1/2	11 (0.120)	8	90
20d	4	10 (0.135)	7	60

Nails (cont.)

CONCRETE NAILS
Round, Square, or Fluted
For Fastening to Concrete

Length Inches	Number per Pound
5 Gauge (0.207 inch) Nail with 1/2 inch head:	
1/2	190
5/8	150
3/4	130
7/8	115
1	99
1–1/8	89
1–1/4	80
1–1/2	65
1–3/4	60
2	51
2–1/4	45
2–1/2	40
2–3/4	37
3	34
7 Gauge (0.177 inch) Nail with 3/8 inch head:	
1/2	330
5/8	260
3/4	210
7/8	175
1	155
1–1/8	135
1–1/4	120
1–1/2	100
1–3/4	85
2	75
2–1/4	65
2–1/2	60
2–3/4	55
3	50
9 Gauge (0.148 inch) Nail with 21/64 inch head:	
1/2	440
5/8	350
3/4	285
7/8	240
1	210
1–1/8	185
1–1/4	165
1–1/2	140
1–3/4	120
2	105
2–1/4	90
2–1/2	85
2–3/4	75
3	69
3–3/4	64

Nails (cont.)

ROOFING NAILS

Size Number	Length Inches	Number per Pound
	7/8	250
2d	1	225
3d	1–1/4	190
4d	1–1/2	165
5d	1–3/4	145

SPIRAL FLOORING NAILS

Size Number	Length Inches	Number per Pound
6d	2	177
7d	2–1/4	158
8d	2–1/2	142

FENCE STAPLES

Length Inches	Number per Pound
7/8	125
1	105
1–1/4	88
1–1/2	72
1–3/4	60

WIRE TACKS

Size Oz	Length Inches	Shaft Diameter Gauge
1	3/16	18
1–1/2	7/32	18
2	1/4	17
2–1/2	5/16	17
3	3/8	16
4	7/16	16
6	1/2	15
8	9/16	15
10	5/8	14–1/2
12	11/16	14–1/2
14	3/4	14
16	13/16	14
18	7/8	13–1/2
20	15/16	13–1/2
22	1	13–1/2
24	1–1/8	13

Nails

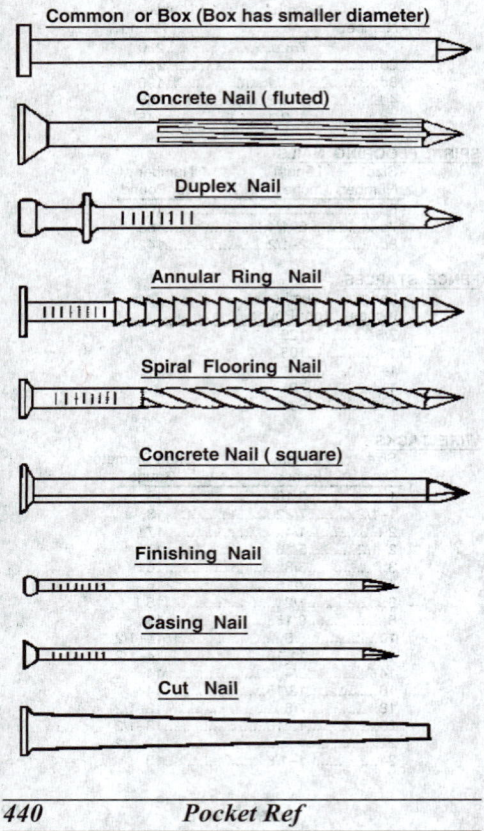

Common or Box (Box has smaller diameter)

Concrete Nail (fluted)

Duplex Nail

Annular Ring Nail

Spiral Flooring Nail

Concrete Nail (square)

Finishing Nail

Casing Nail

Cut Nail

Propane Tank Sizes

Trade Size #	Description	Material	Dimensions Length inch	Dimensions Diameter inch	Water Capacity [A] pound	Water Capacity [A] cubic ft	Tank Weights Empty pound	Tank Weights Full [B] pound
5	Vertical, Acme/Type 1 w/ Overfill Protection Device	Steel	12.0	8.0	13.0	0.208	9.5	14.5
10	Vertical, Acme/Type 1 w/ Overfill Protection Device	Steel	17.4	8.9	26.1	0.418	14.0	24.0
10	Vertical, Acme/Type 1 w/ Overfill Protection Device	Aluminum	16.1	10.4	23.6	0.378	9.0	19.0
11	Vertical, Acme/Type 1 w/ Overfill Protection Device	Steel	12.4	12.2	25.4	0.407	13.0	24.0
20	Vertical, w/ QCC/Type 2 w/ Overfill Protection Device	Steel	17.6	12.2	47.6	0.762	18.0	38.0
20	Vertical, Acme/Type 1 w/ Overfill Protection Device	Steel	17.6	12.2	47.6	0.762	18.0	38.0
20	Vertical, Acme/Type 1 w/ Overfill Protection Device	Aluminum	20.7	12.3	47.6	0.762	13.0	33.0
20	Vertical, Acme/Type 1 w/gauge & Overfill Protection Device	Steel	17.6	12.2	47.6	0.762	19.0	39.0
20	Vertical, Acme/Type 1 w/gauge & Overfill Protection Device	Steel	17.6	12.2	47.6	0.762	19.5	39.5
20	Telephone Cylinder, Acme/Type 1 w/ Overfill Protection Device	Steel	18.9	12.2	47.6	0.762	20.0	40.0
30	Vertical, Acme/Type 1 w/ Overfill Protection Device	Steel	23.4	12.2	71.4	1.14	25.5	55.5
30	Horizontal, Acme/Type 1 w/ Overfill Protection Device	Steel	23.4	12.2	71.4	1.14	26.6	56.6
30	Vertical, Acme/Type 1 w/gauge & Overfill Protection Device	Steel	23.4	12.2	71.4	1.14	27.7	57.7
40	Vertical, Acme/Type 1 w/ Overfill Protection Device	Steel	29.4	12.2	95.2	1.52	30.5	70.5
40	Horizontal, Acme/Type 1 w/ Overfill Protection Device	Steel	29.4	12.2	95.2	1.52	30.5	70.5
40	Telephone Cylinder, Acme/Type 1 w/ Overfill Protection Device	Steel	31.1	12.2	95.2	1.52	34.0	74.0
50	Vertical, w/ Prest-O-Lite Valve, outage, collar type	Steel	28.5	14.5	119	1.91	46.0	96.0
60	Vertical, w/ Prest-O-Lite Valve, less outage, collar type	Steel	43.1	12.2	143	2.29	46.0	106
60	Vertical, w/ Prest-O-Lite Valve, outage, collar type	Steel	43.1	12.2	143	2.29	46.0	106
60	Vertical, w/ Prest-O-Lite Valve, less outage, collar type	Steel	44.6	12.2	143	2.29	45.0	105
60	Vertical, w/ Prest-O-Lite Valve, outage, collar type	Steel	44.6	12.2	143	2.29	45.0	105
100	Vertical, w/ Prest-O-Lite Valve, less outage, collar type	Steel	46.3	15.1	238	3.81	70.0	170
100	Vertical, w/ Prest-O-Lite Valve, outage, collar type	Steel	46.3	15.1	238	3.81	70.0	170
100	Vertical, w/ Prest-O-Lite Valve, less outage, screw type	Steel	47.6	15.1	238	3.81	71.0	171
100	Vertical, w/ Prest-O-Lite Valve, outage, screw type	Steel	47.6	15.1	238	3.81	71.0	171
100	Vertical, w/ Prest-O-Lite Valve, multivalve, collar type	Steel	46.3	15.1	238	3.81	71.0	171
100	Vertical, w/ liquid withdrawal, collar type	Steel	46.3	15.1	238	3.81	71.0	171
100	Vertical, DOT, w/ multivalve & gauge	Steel	42.1	24.0	476	7.62	147	347
200	Vertical, ASME, w/ multivalve, relief & gauge	Steel	42.1	24.0	476	7.62	156	356
420	Vertical, DOT, w/ Prest-O-Lite Valve, outage, fill, relief, & gauge	Steel	53.3	30.0	1,000	16.0	270	690
420	Vertical, ASME, w/ Prest-O-Lite Valve, outage, fill, relief, & gauge	Steel	53.3	30.0	1,000	16.0	309	729
420	Horizontal, ASME, w/QCC & POL type	Steel	42.5	30.0	1,000	16.0	353	773

Notes: [A] = Capacity (volume) of tank when filled with water. [B] = Weight when tank is filled with propane to 80% of water capacity. ASME=American Society of Mechanical Engineers. QCC = Quick Closing Coupling connector valve (quick connect). AGUG = Aboveground/Underground. DOT = U.S. Department of Transportation

Source: Manchester Tank, 1749 Mallory Lane, Suite 400, Brentwood, TN 37027

Approximate Hole Sizes for Wood Screws

Pilot Holes

Nominal Screw Size	Shank Diameter		Hard Wood Twist Drill Size			
	Nominal	Actual	Inch Series		Numbered Series	
	(inch)	(inch)	(fraction)	(decimal)	Number	(decimal)
# 0	0.060	0.064	3/64	0.047	58	0.042
# 1	0.073	0.077	3/64	0.047	55	0.052
# 2	0.086	0.090	1/16	0.063	53	0.060
# 3	0.099	0.103	1/16	0.063	51	0.067
# 4	0.112	0.116	5/64	0.078	48	0.076
# 5	0.125	0.129	5/64	0.078	44	0.086
# 6	0.138	0.142	3/32	0.094	42	0.094
# 7	0.151	0.155	3/32	0.094	38	0.102
# 8	0.164	0.168	7/64	0.109	35	0.110
# 9	0.177	0.181	1/8	0.125	32	0.116
# 10	0.190	0.194	1/8	0.125	30	0.129
# 11	0.203	0.207	1/8	0.125	29	0.136
# 12	0.216	0.220	9/64	0.141	27	0.144
# 14	0.242	0.246	5/32	0.156	20	0.161
# 16	0.268	0.272	3/16	0.188	16	0.177
# 18	0.294	0.298	3/16	0.188	10	0.194
# 20	0.320	0.324	7/32	0.219	3	0.209
# 24	0.372	0.376	1/4	0.250	D	0.246

Nominal Screw Size	Nominal Shank Diameter	Actual Shank Diameter	Soft Wood Twist Drill Size			
			Inch Series		Numbered Series	
	(inch)	(inch)	(fraction)	(decimal)	Number	(decimal)
# 0	0.060	0.064	1/32	0.031	69	0.029
# 1	0.073	0.077	1/32	0.031	65	0.035
# 2	0.086	0.090	3/64	0.047	59	0.041
# 3	0.099	0.103	3/64	0.047	56	0.047
# 4	0.112	0.116	3/64	0.047	55	0.052
# 5	0.125	0.129	1/16	0.063	53	0.060
# 6	0.138	0.142	1/16	0.063	52	0.064
# 7	0.151	0.155	1/16	0.063	50	0.070
# 8	0.164	0.168	5/64	0.078	48	0.076
# 9	0.177	0.181	5/64	0.078	46	0.081
# 10	0.190	0.194	3/32	0.094	44	0.086
# 11	0.203	0.207	3/32	0.094	43	0.089
# 12	0.216	0.220	3/32	0.094	39	0.100
# 14	0.242	0.246	7/64	0.109	34	0.111
# 16	0.268	0.272	1/8	0.125	31	0.120
# 18	0.294	0.298	9/64	0.141	29	0.136
# 20	0.320	0.324	5/32	0.156	26	0.147
# 24	0.372	0.376	11/64	0.172	18	0.170

Shank Clearance Holes

Nominal Screw Size	Shank Diameter		Hard and Soft Woods Twist Drill Size			
	Nominal (inch)	Actual (inch)	Fractional Inch Series (fraction)	(decimal)	Numbered Series Number	(decimal)
# 0	0.060	0.064	1/16	0.063	52	0.064
# 1	0.073	0.077	5/64	0.078	47	0.079
# 2	0.086	0.090	3/32	0.094	42	0.094
# 3	0.099	0.103	7/64	0.109	37	0.104
# 4	0.112	0.116	7/64	0.109	32	0.116
# 5	0.125	0.129	1/8	0.125	30	0.129
# 6	0.138	0.142	9/64	0.141	27	0.144
# 7	0.151	0.155	5/32	0.156	22	0.157
# 8	0.164	0.168	11/64	0.172	18	0.170
# 9	0.177	0.181	3/16	0.188	14	0.182
# 10	0.190	0.194	3/16	0.188	10	0.194
# 11	0.203	0.207	13/64	0.203	4	0.209
# 12	0.216	0.220	7/32	0.219	2	0.221
# 14	0.242	0.246	1/4	0.250	D	0.246
# 16	0.268	0.272	17/64	0.266	I	0.272
# 18	0.294	0.298	19/64	0.297	N	0.302
# 20	0.320	0.324	21/64	0.328	P	0.323
# 24	0.372	0.376	3/8	0.375	V	0.377

82° Countersink Diameter

Nominal Screw Size	Nominal Shank Diameter (inch)	Actual Head Diameter (inch)	Countersink Diameter (fraction)	(decimal)
# 0	0.060	0.119	1/8	0.125
# 1	0.073	0.146	3/16	0.188
# 2	0.086	0.172	3/16	0.188
# 3	0.099	0.199	1/4	0.250
# 4	0.112	0.225	1/4	0.250
# 5	0.125	0.252	1/4	0.250
# 6	0.138	0.279	3/8	0.375
# 7	0.151	0.305	3/8	0.375
# 8	0.164	0.332	3/8	0.375
# 9	0.177	0.358	3/8	0.375
# 10	0.190	0.385	1/2	0.500
# 11	0.203	0.412	1/2	0.500
# 12	0.216	0.438	1/2	0.500
# 14	0.242	0.507	1/2	0.500
# 16	0.268	0.544	5/8	0.625
# 18	0.294	0.635	5/8	0.625
# 20	0.320	0.650	3/4	0.750
# 24	0.372	0.762	3/4	0.750

NOTES:

Pilot hole diameters in the above table are based on thread penetrations of approximately 35% for hard woods and 55% for soft woods. These values were selected as a consensus from drill hole diameters published in various references.

Pilot holes need to be large enough to prevent splitting but small enough to provide adequate holding power.

Pilot holes are strongly recommended for wood screws in hard woods. Pilot holes greatly reduce the possibility of damage to either the wood or the screw.

The total length of the screw should be 1/8 inch shorter than the combined thickness of the two pieces of wood to be joined.

The shank clearance hole should completely pierce the first piece of wood.

The pilot hole should be deep enough into the second piece of wood to accommodate about one half the length of the screw in the second piece of wood.

A countersink is used to make flat or oval head wood screws flush with the wood surface.

SOURCES:

Similar tables have been published in a wide variety of references including:

Woodworker's Pocket Book, Charles H. Hayward, 1957, Evans Brothers Limited, London, England.

Instructions For Selecting And Using Wood Screws and Sheet Metal Screws, A&I Bolt and Nut, Commerce City, CO.

The Visual Handbook of Building And Remodeling, Charlie Wing, 1990, Rodale Press, Emmaus, PA.

Sizes - The Illustrated Encyclopedia, John Lord, 1994, HarperCollins Publishers, Inc, New York, NY.

Benchtop Reference, Fourth Printing, 1986, Popular Science Books, New York, NY.

How To Plan And Build Decks, Fifth Printing, 1983, Sunset Books, Lane Publishing Company, Menlo Park, CA.

WOOD Magazine, www.woodmagazine.com

Pacific Fasteners, www.pacificfasteners.com/catalog/page19.htm

American Fastener, www.americanfastener.com/techref/proper.htm

Bob Vila, www.bobvila.com/screws.htm

Sheet Metal Screw Specs

Screw Diameter # (inch)	Thickness of Metal Gauge #	Diameter of Pierced Hole (inch)	Drilled Hole Size Drill Number
#4 (0.112)	28	0.086	44
	26	0.086	44
	24	0.093	42
	22	0.098	42
	20	0.100	40
#6 (0.138)	28	0.111	39
	26	0.111	39
	24	0.111	39
	22	0.111	38
	20	0.111	36
#7 (0.151)	28	0.121	37
	26	0.121	37
	24	0.121	35
	22	0.121	33
	20	0.121	32
	18	....	31
#8 (0.164)	26	0.137	33
	24	0.137	33
	22	0.137	32
	20	0.137	31
	18	....	30
#10 (0.190)	26	0.158	30
	24	0.158	30
	22	0.158	30
	20	0.158	29
	18	0.158	25
#12 (0.216)	24	....	26
	22	0.185	25
	20	0.185	24
	18	0.185	22
#14 (0.242)	24	....	15
	22	0.212	12
	20	0.212	11
	18	0.212	9

Note: The above values are recommended average values only. Variations in materials and local conditions may require significant deviations from the recommended values.

Drive Styles

Torx ©
external
(6-lobe)

Torx ©
internal
(6-lobe)

Torx - internal
Tamper proof
pin (6-lobe)

Frearson

Clutch

Fluted Socket
4 flutes

Fluted Socket
6 flutes

MorTorq ©

Tri-Wing ©

Square
Socket
(Robertson)

Hex Socket
Allen Head
Internal

Hexagon
External

Hexagon
Internal
Tamper proof

Slotted 6
Lobe Combo

Quadrex ©

Phillips ©

Phillips II ©

Phillips/Slot
Combination
(Combo)

Pozi Drive ©
Phillips 1a

Phillips
Square
Supa Drive©

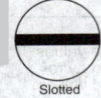
Slotted

Square Slot
Combination

Slotted
Tamper Proof
(One Way)

Spanner
Drilled
Tamper Proof

Spanner
Slotted
Tamper Proof

Phillips ©
Hex Head

5 Node
Security

7 Node
Security

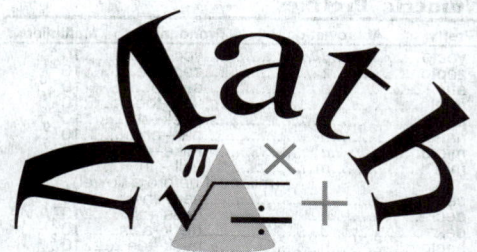

(See also CONSTANTS, page 133)

(See also SURVEYING, page 583)

(See also COMPUTER, page 125)

Numeric Prefixes

Prefix	Abbreviation	Pronounce	Multiplier
yocto	y	yoc–toe	10^{-24}
zepto	z	zep–toe	10^{-21}
atto	a	at–toe	10^{-18}
femto	f	fem–toe	10^{-15}
pico	p	peek–oh	10^{-12}
nano	n	nan–oh	10^{-9}
micro	μ	mike–row	10^{-6}
milli	m	mill – ih	10^{-3}
		(mill-ee if before a vowel)	
centi	c	sent–ih	10^{-2}
deci	d	dess – ih	10^{-1}
deka	da	deck–a	10^{2}
hecto	h	heck–toe	10^{2}
kilo	k	kill–oh	10^{3}
mega	M	meg–a	10^{6}
giga	G	gig–a	10^{9}
tera	T	terr–a	10^{12}
peta	P	pet–a	10^{15}
exa	E	ex–a	10^{18}
zetta	Z	zett–a	10^{21}
yotta	Y	yott–a	10^{24}
octillion			10^{27}
nonillion			10^{30}

Roman Numerals

Roman	Arabic	Roman	Arabic
I	1	LX	60
II	2	LXX	70
III	3	LXXX	80
IV	4	XC	90
V	5	C	100
VI	6	CC	200
VII	7	CCC	300
VIII	8	CD	400
IX	9	D	500
X	10	DC	600
XI	11	DCC	700
XII	12	DCCC	800
XIII	13	CM	900
XIV	14	IM	999
XV	15	M	1,000
XVI	16	MD	1,500
XVII	17	M$\overline{\text{V}}$	4,000
XVIII	18	$\overline{\text{V}}$	5,000
XIX	19	$\overline{\text{X}}$	10,000
XX	20	$\overline{\text{L}}$	50,000
XXX	30	$\overline{\text{C}}$	100,000
XL	40	$\overline{\text{D}}$	500,000
L	50	$\overline{\text{M}}$	1,000,000

Convert Inch–Screw–Foot–MM–Drill

Decimals of Inch	Fraction / Inch or Screw Size	Decimals of Foot	Millimeters	Drill Number
0.001		0.00008	0.0254	
0.002		0.00017	0.0508	
0.003		0.00025	0.0762	
0.004		0.00033	0.1016	
0.005		0.00042	0.1270	
0.006		0.00050	0.1524	
0.007		0.00058	0.1778	
0.0078	1/128	0.00065	0.1981	
0.008		0.00067	0.2032	
0.009		0.00075	0.2286	
0.010		0.00083	0.2540	
0.011		0.00092	0.2794	
0.012	# 30 screw	0.00100	0.3048	
0.013		0.00108	0.3302	
0.0135		0.00113	0.3429	80
0.014	# 35 screw	0.00117	0.3556	79
0.0145		0.00121	0.3683	79
0.015		0.00125	0.3810	
0.0156	1/64	0.00130	0.3962	
0.016	# 40 screw	0.00133	0.4064	78
0.017		0.00142	0.4318	
0.018	# 45 screw	0.00150	0.4572	77
0.019		0.00158	0.4826	
0.020	# 50 screw	0.00167	0.5080	76
0.021	# 0000 screw	0.00175	0.5334	75
0.022	#55 screw	0.00183	0.5588	
0.0225		0.00187	0.5715	74
0.023		0.00192	0.5842	
0.0234	3/128	0.00195	0.5944	
0.024	# 60 screw	0.00200	0.6096	73
0.025		0.00208	0.6350	72
0.026		0.00217	0.6604	71
0.027		0.00225	0.6858	
0.028	# 70 screw	0.00233	0.7112	70
0.029		0.00242	0.7366	
0.0292		0.00243	0.7417	69
0.030		0.00250	0.7620	
0.031		0.00258	0.7874	68
0.0313	1/32	0.00261	0.7950	
0.032	# 80 screw	0.00267	0.8128	67
0.033		0.00275	0.8382	66
0.034	#000 screw	0.00283	0.8636	
0.035	# 90 screw	0.00292	0.8890	65
0.036		0.00300	0.9144	64
0.037		0.00308	0.9398	63
0.038		0.00317	0.9652	62
0.039		0.00325	0.9906	61
0.0391	5/128 #100 screw	0.00326	0.9931	
0.040		0.00333	1.0160	60
0.041		0.00342	1.0414	59
0.042		0.00350	1.0668	58
0.043	#110 screw	0.00358	1.0922	57
0.044		0.00367	1.1176	

Convert Inch–Screw–Foot–MM–Drill

Decimals of Inch	Fraction / Inch or Screw Size	Decimals of Foot	Millimeters	Drill Number
0.045		0.00375	1.1430	
0.046		0.00383	1.1684	
0.0465		0.00388	1.1811	56
0.0469	3/64	0.00391	1.1913	
0.047	#00, # 120 screws	0.00392	1.1938	
0.048		0.00400	1.2192	
0.049		0.00408	1.2446	
0.050		0.00417	1.2700	
0.051		0.00425	1.2954	
0.052		0.00433	1.3208	55
0.053		0.00442	1.3462	
0.054		0.00450	1.3716	
0.0547	7/128	0.00456	1.3894	
0.055	# 140 screw	0.00458	1.3970	54
0.056		0.00467	1.4224	
0.057		0.00475	1.4478	
0.058		0.00483	1.4732	
0.059		0.00492	1.4986	
0.0595		0.00496	1.5113	53
0.060	# 0 screw	0.00500	1.5240	
0.061		0.00508	1.5494	
0.062		0.00517	1.5748	
0.0625	1/16	0.00521	1.5875	
0.063		0.00525	1.6002	
0.0635		0.00529	1.6129	52
0.064		0.00533	1.6256	
0.065		0.00542	1.6510	
0.066		0.00550	1.6764	
0.067		0.00558	1.7018	51
0.068		0.00567	1.7272	
0.069		0.00575	1.7526	
0.070		0.00583	1.7780	50
0.0703	9/128	0.00586	1.7856	
0.071		0.00592	1.8034	
0.072		0.00600	1.8288	
0.073	# 1 screw	0.00608	1.8542	49
0.074		0.00617	1.8796	
0.075		0.00625	1.9050	
0.076		0.00633	1.9304	48
0.077		0.00642	1.9558	
0.078		0.00650	1.9812	
0.0781	5/64	0.00651	1.9837	
0.0785		0.00654	1.9939	47
0.079		0.00658	2.0066	
0.080		0.00667	2.0320	
0.081		0.00675	2.0574	46
0.082		0.00683	2.0828	45
0.083		0.00692	2.1082	
0.084		0.00700	2.1336	
0.085		0.00708	2.1590	
0.0859	11/128 # 2 screw	0.00716	2.1819	
0.086		0.00717	2.1844	44
0.087		0.00725	2.2098	

Convert Inch–Screw–Foot–MM–Drill

Decimals of Inch	Fraction / Inch or Screw Size	Decimals of Foot	Millimeters	Drill Number
0.088		0.00733	2.2352	
0.089		0.00742	2.2606	43
0.090		0.00750	2.2860	
0.091		0.00758	2.3114	
0.092		0.00767	2.3368	
0.093		0.00775	2.3622	
0.0935		0.00779	2.3749	42
0.0938	3/32	0.00782	2.3825	
0.094		0.00783	2.3876	
0.095		0.00792	2.4130	
0.096		0.00800	2.4384	41
0.097		0.00808	2.4638	
0.098		0.00817	2.4892	40
0.099	# 3 screw	0.00825	2.5146	
0.0995		0.00829	2.5273	39
0.100		0.00833	2.5400	
0.101		0.00842	2.5654	
0.1015		0.00846	2.5781	38
0.1016	13/128	0.00847	2.5806	
0.102		0.00850	2.5908	
0.103		0.00858	2.6162	
0.104		0.00867	2.6416	37
0.105		0.00875	2.6670	
0.106		0.00883	2.6924	
0.1065		0.00888	2.7051	36
0.107		0.00892	2.7178	
0.108		0.00900	2.7432	
0.109		0.00908	2.7686	
0.1094	7/64	0.00912	2.7788	
0.110		0.00917	2.7940	35
0.111		0.00925	2.8194	34
0.112	# 4 screw	0.00933	2.8448	
0.113		0.00942	2.8702	33
0.114		0.00950	2.8956	
0.115		0.00958	2.9210	
0.116		0.00967	2.9464	32
0.117		0.00975	2.9718	
0.1172	15/128	0.00977	2.9769	
0.118		0.00983	2.9972	
0.119		0.00992	3.0226	
0.120		0.01000	3.0480	31
0.121		0.01008	3.0734	
0.122		0.01017	3.0988	
0.123		0.01025	3.1242	
0.124		0.01033	3.1496	
0.125	1/8 # 5 screw	0.01042	3.1750	
0.126		0.01050	3.2004	
0.127		0.01058	3.2258	
0.128		0.01067	3.2512	
0.1285		0.01071	3.2639	30
0.129		0.01075	3.2766	
0.130		0.01083	3.3020	
0.131		0.01092	3.3274	

Convert Inch–Screw–Foot–MM–Drill

Decimals of Inch	Fraction / Inch or Screw Size	Decimals of Foot	Millimeters	Drill Number
0.132		0.01100	3.3528	
0.1328	17/128	0.01107	3.3731	
0.133		0.01108	3.3782	
0.134		0.01117	3.4036	
0.135		0.01125	3.4290	
0.136		0.01133	3.4544	29
0.137		0.01142	3.4798	
0.138	# 6 screw	0.01150	3.5052	
0.139		0.01158	3.5306	
0.140		0.01167	3.5560	
0.1405		0.01171	3.5687	28
0.1406	9/64	0.01172	3.5712	
0.141		0.01175	3.5814	
0.142		0.01183	3.6068	
0.143		0.01192	3.6322	
0.144		0.01200	3.6576	27
0.145		0.01208	3.6830	
0.146		0.01217	3.7084	
0.147		0.01225	3.7338	26
0.148		0.01233	3.7592	
0.1484	19/128	0.01237	3.7694	
0.149		0.01242	3.7846	
0.1495		0.01246	3.7973	25
0.150		0.01250	3.8100	
0.151		0.01258	3.8354	
0.152		0.01267	3.8608	24
0.153		0.01275	3.8862	
0.154		0.01283	3.9116	23
0.155		0.01292	3.9370	
0.156		0.01300	3.9624	
0.1563	5/32	0.01303	3.9700	
0.157		0.01308	3.9878	22
0.158		0.01317	4.0132	
0.159		0.01325	4.0386	21
0.160		0.01333	4.0640	
0.161		0.01342	4.0894	20
0.162		0.01350	4.1148	
0.163		0.01358	4.1402	
0.164	# 8 screw	0.01367	4.1656	
0.1641	21/128	0.01368	4.1681	
0.165		0.01375	4.1910	
0.166		0.01383	4.2164	19
0.167		0.01392	4.2418	
0.168		0.01400	4.2672	
0.169		0.01408	4.2926	
0.1695		0.01413	4.3053	18
0.170		0.01417	4.3180	
0.171		0.01425	4.3434	
0.1719	11/64	0.01433	4.3663	
0.172		0.01433	4.3688	
0.173		0.01442	4.3942	17
0.174		0.01450	4.4196	
0.175		0.01458	4.4450	

Convert Inch–Screw–Foot–MM–Drill

Decimals of Inch	Fraction / Inch or Screw Size	Decimals of Foot	Millimeters	Drill Number
0.176		0.01467	4.4704	
0.177		0.01475	4.4958	16
0.178		0.01483	4.5212	
0.179		0.01492	4.5466	
0.1797	23/128	0.01497	4.5644	
0.180		0.01500	4.5720	15
0.181		0.01508	4.5974	
0.182		0.01517	4.6228	14
0.183		0.01525	4.6482	
0.184		0.01533	4.6736	
0.185		0.01542	4.6990	13
0.186		0.01550	4.7244	
0.187		0.01558	4.7498	
0.1875	3/16	0.01563	4.7625	
0.188		0.01567	4.7752	
0.189		0.01575	4.8006	12
0.190	# 10 screw	0.01583	4.8260	
0.191		0.01592	4.8514	11
0.192		0.01600	4.8768	
0.193		0.01608	4.9022	
0.1935		0.01613	4.9149	10
0.194		0.01617	4.9276	
0.195		0.01625	4.9530	
0.1953	25/128	0.01628	4.9606	
0.196		0.01633	4.9784	9
0.197		0.01642	5.0038	
0.198		0.01650	5.0292	
0.199		0.01658	5.0546	8
0.200		0.01667	5.0800	
0.201		0.01675	5.1054	7
0.202		0.01683	5.1308	
0.203		0.01692	5.1562	
0.2031	13/64	0.01697	5.1587	
0.204		0.01700	5.1816	6
0.205		0.01708	5.2070	
0.2055		0.01713	5.2197	5
0.206		0.01717	5.2324	
0.207		0.01725	5.2578	
0.208		0.01733	5.2832	
0.209		0.01742	5.3086	4
0.210		0.01750	5.3340	
0.2109	27/128	0.01758	5.3569	
0.211		0.01758	5.3594	
0.212		0.01767	5.3848	
0.213		0.01775	5.4102	3
0.214		0.01783	5.4356	
0.215		0.01792	5.4610	
0.216	# 12 screw	0.01800	5.4864	
0.217		0.01808	5.5118	
0.218		0.01817	5.5372	
0.2188	7/32	0.01823	5.5575	
0.219		0.01825	5.5626	
0.220		0.01833	5.5880	

Math 453

Convert Inch–Foot–MM–Drill

Decimals of Inch	Fractions of Inch	Decimals of Foot	Millimeters	Drill Number
0.221		0.01842	5.6134	2
0.222		0.01850	5.6388	
0.223		0.01858	5.6642	
0.224		0.01867	5.6896	
0.225		0.01875	5.7150	
0.226		0.01883	5.7404	
0.2266	29/128	0.01888	5.7556	
0.227		0.01892	5.7658	
0.228		0.01900	5.7912	1
0.229		0.01908	5.8166	
0.230		0.01917	5.8420	
0.231		0.01925	5.8674	
0.232		0.01933	5.8928	
0.233		0.01942	5.9182	
0.234		0.01950	5.9436	A
0.2344	15/64	0.01953	5.9538	
0.235		0.01958	5.9690	
0.236		0.01967	5.9944	
0.237		0.01975	6.0198	
0.238		0.01983	6.0452	B
0.239		0.01992	6.0706	
0.240		0.02000	6.0960	
0.241		0.02008	6.1214	
0.242		0.02017	6.1468	C
0.2422	31/128	0.02018	6.1519	
0.243		0.02025	6.1722	
0.244		0.02033	6.1976	
0.245		0.02042	6.2230	
0.246		0.02050	6.2484	D
0.247		0.02058	6.2738	
0.248		0.02067	6.2992	
0.249		0.02075	6.3246	
0.250	1/4	0.02083	6.3500	E
0.251		0.02092	6.3754	
0.252		0.02100	6.4008	
0.253		0.02108	6.4262	
0.254		0.02117	6.4516	
0.255		0.02125	6.4770	
0.256		0.02133	6.5024	
0.257		0.02142	6.5278	F
0.2578	33/128	0.02148	6.5481	
0.258		0.02150	6.5532	
0.259		0.02158	6.5786	
0.260		0.02167	6.6040	
0.261		0.02175	6.6294	G
0.262		0.02183	6.6548	
0.263		0.02192	6.6802	
0.264		0.02200	6.7056	
0.265		0.02208	6.7310	
0.2656	17/64	0.02213	6.7462	
0.266		0.02217	6.7564	H
0.267		0.02225	6.7818	
0.268		0.02233	6.8072	

Convert Inch–Foot–MM–Drill

Decimals of Inch	Fractions of Inch	Decimals of Foot	Millimeters	Drill Number
0.269		0.02242	6.8326	
0.270		0.02250	6.8580	
0.271		0.02258	6.8834	
0.272		0.02267	6.9088	I
0.273		0.02275	6.9342	
0.2734	35/128	0.02278	6.9444	
0.274		0.02283	6.9596	
0.275		0.02292	6.9850	
0.276		0.02300	7.0104	
0.277		0.02308	7.0358	J
0.278		0.02317	7.0612	
0.279		0.02325	7.0866	
0.280		0.02333	7.1120	
0.281		0.02342	7.1374	K
0.2813	9/32	0.02344	7.1450	
0.282		0.02350	7.1628	
0.283		0.02358	7.1882	
0.284		0.02367	7.2136	
0.285		0.02375	7.2390	
0.286		0.02383	7.2644	
0.287		0.02392	7.2898	
0.288		0.02400	7.3152	
0.289		0.02408	7.3406	
0.2891	37/128	0.02409	7.3431	
0.290		0.02417	7.3660	L
0.291		0.02425	7.3914	
0.292		0.02433	7.4168	
0.293		0.02442	7.4422	
0.294		0.02450	7.4676	
0.295		0.02458	7.4930	M
0.296		0.02467	7.5184	
0.2969	19/64	0.02474	7.5413	
0.297		0.02475	7.5438	
0.298		0.02483	7.5692	
0.299		0.02492	7.5946	
0.300		0.02500	7.6200	
0.301		0.02508	7.6454	
0.302		0.02517	7.6708	N
0.303		0.02525	7.6962	
0.304		0.02533	7.7216	
0.3047	39/128	0.02539	7.7394	
0.305		0.02542	7.7470	
0.306		0.02550	7.7724	
0.307		0.02558	7.7978	
0.308		0.02567	7.8232	
0.309		0.02575	7.8486	
0.310		0.02583	7.8740	
0.311		0.02592	7.8994	
0.312		0.02600	7.9248	
0.3125	5/16	0.02604	7.9375	
0.313		0.02608	7.9502	
0.314		0.02617	7.9756	
0.315		0.02625	8.0010	

Math

455

Convert Inch–Foot–MM–Drill

Decimals of Inch	Fractions of Inch	Decimals of Foot	Millimeters	Drill Number
0.316		0.02633	8.0264	O
0.317		0.02642	8.0518	
0.318		0.02650	8.0772	
0.319		0.02658	8.1026	
0.320		0.02667	8.1280	
0.3203	41/128	0.02669	8.1356	
0.321		0.02675	8.1534	
0.322		0.02683	8.1788	
0.323		0.02692	8.2042	P
0.324		0.02700	8.2296	
0.325		0.02708	8.2550	
0.326		0.02717	8.2804	
0.327		0.02725	8.3058	
0.328		0.02733	8.3312	
0.3281	21/64	0.02734	8.3337	
0.329		0.02742	8.3566	
0.330		0.02750	8.3820	
0.331		0.02758	8.4074	
0.332		0.02767	8.4328	Q
0.333		0.02775	8.4582	
0.334		0.02783	8.4836	
0.335		0.02792	8.5090	
0.3359	43/128	0.02799	8.5319	
0.336		0.02800	8.5344	
0.337		0.02808	8.5598	
0.338		0.02817	8.5852	
0.339		0.02825	8.6106	R
0.340		0.02833	8.6360	
0.341		0.02842	8.6614	
0.342		0.02850	8.6868	
0.343		0.02858	8.7122	
0.3438	11/32	0.02865	8.7325	
0.344		0.02867	8.7376	
0.345		0.02875	8.7630	
0.346		0.02883	8.7884	
0.347		0.02892	8.8138	
0.348		0.02900	8.8392	S
0.349		0.02908	8.8646	
0.350		0.02917	8.8900	
0.351		0.02925	8.9154	
0.3516	45/128	0.02930	8.9306	
0.352		0.02933	8.9408	
0.353		0.02942	8.9662	
0.354		0.02950	8.9916	
0.355		0.02958	9.0170	
0.356		0.02967	9.0424	
0.357		0.02975	9.0678	
0.358		0.02983	9.0932	T
0.359		0.02992	9.1186	
0.3594	23/64	0.02995	9.1288	
0.360		0.03000	9.1440	
0.361		0.03008	9.1694	
0.362		0.03017	9.1948	

Convert Inch–Foot–MM–Drill

Decimals of Inch	Fractions of Inch	Decimals of Foot	Millimeters	Drill Number
0.363		0.03025	9.2202	
0.364		0.03033	9.2456	
0.365		0.03042	9.2710	
0.366		0.03050	9.2964	
0.367		0.03058	9.3218	
0.3672	47/128	0.03060	9.3269	
0.368		0.03067	9.3472	U
0.369		0.03075	9.3726	
0.370		0.03083	9.3980	
0.371		0.03092	9.4234	
0.372		0.03100	9.4488	
0.373		0.03108	9.4742	
0.374		0.03117	9.4996	
0.375	3/8	0.03125	9.5250	
0.376		0.03133	9.5504	
0.377		0.03142	9.5758	V
0.378		0.03150	9.6012	
0.379		0.03158	9.6266	
0.380		0.03167	9.6520	
0.381		0.03175	9.6774	
0.382		0.03183	9.7028	
0.3828	49/128	0.03190	9.7231	
0.383		0.03192	9.7282	
0.384		0.03200	9.7536	
0.385		0.03208	9.7790	
0.386		0.03217	9.8044	W
0.387		0.03225	9.8298	
0.388		0.03233	9.8552	
0.389		0.03242	9.8806	
0.390		0.03250	9.9060	
0.3906	25/64	0.03255	9.9212	
0.391		0.03258	9.9314	
0.392		0.03267	9.9568	
0.393		0.03275	9.9822	
0.394		0.03283	10.0076	
0.395		0.03292	10.0330	
0.396		0.03300	10.0584	
0.397		0.03308	10.0838	X
0.398		0.03317	10.1092	
0.3984	51/128	0.03320	10.1194	
0.399		0.03325	10.1448	
0.400		0.03333	10.1600	
0.401		0.03342	10.1854	
0.402		0.03350	10.2108	
0.403		0.03358	10.2362	
0.404		0.03367	10.2616	Y
0.405		0.03375	10.2870	
0.406		0.03383	10.3124	
0.4063	13/32	0.03386	10.3200	
0.407		0.03392	10.3378	
0.408		0.03400	10.3632	
0.409		0.03408	10.3886	

Convert Inch–Foot–MM–Drill

Decimals of Inch	Fractions of Inch	Decimals of Foot	Millimeters	Drill Number
0.410		0.03417	10.4140	
0.411		0.03425	10.4394	
0.412		0.03433	10.4648	
0.413		0.03442	10.4902	Z
0.414		0.03450	10.5156	
0.4141	53/128	0.03451	10.5181	
0.415		0.03458	10.5410	
0.416		0.03467	10.5664	
0.417		0.03475	10.5918	
0.418		0.03483	10.6172	
0.419		0.03492	10.6426	
0.420		0.03500	10.6680	
0.421		0.03508	10.6934	
0.4219	27/64	0.03516	10.7163	
0.422		0.03517	10.7188	
0.423		0.03525	10.7442	
0.424		0.03533	10.7696	
0.425		0.03542	10.7950	
0.426		0.03550	10.8204	
0.427		0.03558	10.8458	
0.428		0.03567	10.8712	
0.429		0.03575	10.8966	
0.4297	55/128	0.03581	10.9144	
0.430		0.03583	10.9220	
0.431		0.03592	10.9474	
0.432		0.03600	10.9728	
0.433		0.03608	10.9982	
0.434		0.03617	11.0236	
0.435		0.03625	11.0490	
0.436		0.03633	11.0744	
0.437		0.03642	11.0998	
0.4375	7/16	0.03646	11.1125	
0.438		0.03650	11.1252	
0.439		0.03658	11.1506	
0.440		0.03667	11.1760	
0.441		0.03675	11.2014	
0.442		0.03683	11.2268	
0.443		0.03692	11.2522	
0.444		0.03700	11.2776	
0.445		0.03708	11.3030	
0.4453	57/128	0.03711	11.3106	
0.446		0.03717	11.3284	
0.447		0.03725	11.3538	
0.448		0.03733	11.3792	
0.449		0.03742	11.4046	
0.450		0.03750	11.4300	
0.451		0.03758	11.4554	
0.452		0.03767	11.4808	
0.453		0.03775	11.5062	
0.4531	29/64	0.03776	11.5087	
0.454		0.03783	11.5316	
0.455		0.03792	11.5570	
0.456		0.03800	11.5824	

Convert Inch–Foot–MM–Drill

Decimals of Inch	Fractions of Inch	Decimals of Foot	Millimeters	Drill Number
0.457		0.03808	11.6078	
0.458		0.03817	11.6332	
0.459		0.03825	11.6586	
0.460		0.03833	11.6840	
0.4609	59/128	0.03841	11.7069	
0.461		0.03842	11.7094	
0.462		0.03850	11.7348	
0.463		0.03858	11.7602	
0.464		0.03867	11.7856	
0.465		0.03875	11.8110	
0.466		0.03883	11.8364	
0.467		0.03892	11.8618	
0.468		0.03900	11.8872	
0.4688	15/32	0.03907	11.9075	
0.469		0.03908	11.9126	
0.470		0.03917	11.9380	
0.471		0.03925	11.9634	
0.472		0.03933	11.9888	
0.473		0.03942	12.0142	
0.474		0.03950	12.0396	
0.475		0.03958	12.0650	
0.476		0.03967	12.0904	
0.4766	61/128	0.03972	12.1056	
0.477		0.03975	12.1158	
0.478		0.03983	12.1412	
0.479		0.03992	12.1666	
0.480		0.04000	12.1920	
0.481		0.04008	12.2174	
0.482		0.04017	12.2428	
0.483		0.04025	12.2682	
0.484		0.04033	12.2936	
0.4844	31/64	0.04037	12.3038	
0.485		0.04042	12.3190	
0.486		0.04050	12.3444	
0.487		0.04058	12.3698	
0.488		0.04067	12.3952	
0.489		0.04075	12.4206	
0.490		0.04083	12.4460	
0.491		0.04092	12.4714	
0.492		0.04100	12.4968	
0.4922	63/128	0.04102	12.5019	
0.493		0.04108	12.5222	
0.494		0.04117	12.5476	
0.495		0.04125	12.5730	
0.496		0.04133	12.5984	
0.497		0.04142	12.6238	
0.498		0.04150	12.6492	
0.499		0.04158	12.6746	
0.500	1/2	0.04167	12.7000	

Squares, Cubes, and Roots

n	Square	Cube	Square Root	Cube Root
1	1	1	1.00000	1.00000
2	4	8	1.41421	1.25992
3	9	27	1.73205	1.44225
4	16	64	2.00000	1.58740
5	25	125	2.23607	1.70998
6	36	216	2.44949	1.81712
7	49	343	2.64575	1.91293
8	64	512	2.82843	2.00000
9	81	729	3.00000	2.08008
10	100	1000	3.16228	2.15443
11	121	1331	3.31662	2.22398
12	144	1728	3.46410	2.28943
13	169	2197	3.60555	2.35133
14	196	2744	3.74166	2.41014
15	225	3375	3.87298	2.46621
16	256	4096	4.00000	2.51984
17	289	4913	4.12311	2.57128
18	324	5832	4.24264	2.62074
19	361	6859	4.35890	2.66840
20	400	8000	4.47214	2.71442
21	441	9261	4.58258	2.75892
22	484	10648	4.69042	2.80204
23	529	12167	4.79583	2.84387
24	576	13824	4.89898	2.88450
25	625	15625	5.00000	2.92402
26	676	17576	5.09902	2.96250
27	729	19683	5.19615	3.00000
28	784	21952	5.29150	3.03659
29	841	24389	5.38516	3.07232
30	900	27000	5.47723	3.10723
31	961	29791	5.56776	3.14138
32	1024	32768	5.65685	3.17480
33	1089	35937	5.74456	3.20753
34	1156	39304	5.83095	3.23961
35	1225	42875	5.91608	3.27107
36	1296	46656	6.00000	3.30193
37	1369	50653	6.08276	3.33222
38	1444	54872	6.16441	3.36198
39	1521	59319	6.24500	3.39121
40	1600	64000	6.32456	3.41995
41	1681	68921	6.40312	3.44822
42	1764	74088	6.48074	3.47603
43	1849	79507	6.55744	3.50340
44	1936	85184	6.63325	3.53035
45	2025	91125	6.70820	3.55689
46	2116	97336	6.78233	3.58305
47	2209	103823	6.85565	3.60883
48	2304	110592	6.92820	3.63424
49	2401	117649	7.00000	3.65931
50	2500	125000	7.07107	3.68403
51	2601	132651	7.14143	3.70843
52	2704	140608	7.21110	3.73251
53	2809	148877	7.28011	3.75629
54	2916	157464	7.34847	3.77976

Squares, Cubes, and Roots

n	Square	Cube	Square Root	Cube Root
55	3025	166375	7.41620	3.80295
56	3136	175616	7.48331	3.82586
57	3249	185193	7.54983	3.84850
58	3364	195112	7.61577	3.87088
59	3481	205379	7.68115	3.89300
60	3600	216000	7.74597	3.91487
61	3721	226981	7.81025	3.93650
62	3844	238328	7.87401	3.95789
63	3969	250047	7.93725	3.97906
64	4096	262144	8.00000	4.00000
65	4225	274625	8.06226	4.02073
66	4356	287496	8.12404	4.04124
67	4489	300763	8.18535	4.06155
68	4624	314432	8.24621	4.08166
69	4761	328509	8.30662	4.10157
70	4900	343000	8.36660	4.12129
71	5041	357911	8.42615	4.14082
72	5184	373248	8.48528	4.16017
73	5329	389017	8.54400	4.17934
74	5476	405224	8.60233	4.19834
75	5625	421875	8.66025	4.21716
76	5776	438976	8.71780	4.23582
77	5929	456533	8.77496	4.25432
78	6084	474552	8.83176	4.27266
79	6241	493039	8.88819	4.29084
80	6400	512000	8.94427	4.30887
81	6561	531441	9.00000	4.32675
82	6724	551368	9.05539	4.34448
83	6889	571787	9.11043	4.36207
84	7056	592704	9.16515	4.37952
85	7225	614125	9.21954	4.39683
86	7396	636056	9.27362	4.41400
87	7569	658503	9.32738	4.43105
88	7744	681472	9.38083	4.44796
89	7921	704969	9.43398	4.46475
90	8100	729000	9.48683	4.48140
91	8281	753571	9.53939	4.49794
92	8464	778688	9.59166	4.51436
93	8649	804357	9.64365	4.53065
94	8836	830584	9.69536	4.54684
95	9025	857375	9.74679	4.56290
96	9216	884736	9.79796	4.57886
97	9409	912673	9.84886	4.59470
98	9604	941192	9.89949	4.61044
99	9801	970299	9.94987	4.62607
100	10000	1000000	10.00000	4.64159
110	12100	1331000	10.48809	4.79142
120	14400	1728000	10.95445	4.93242
130	16900	2197000	11.40175	5.06580
140	19600	2744000	11.83216	5.19249
150	22500	3375000	12.24745	5.31329
160	25600	4096000	12.64911	5.42884
170	28900	4913000	13.03840	5.53966
180	32400	5832000	13.41641	5.64622

Squares, Cubes, and Roots

n	Square	Cube	Square Root	Cube Root
190	36100	6859000	13.78405	5.74890
200	40000	8000000	14.14214	5.84804
210	44100	9261000	14.49138	5.94392
220	48400	10648000	14.83240	6.03681
230	52900	12167000	15.16575	6.12693
240	57600	13824000	15.49193	6.21447
250	62500	15625000	15.81139	6.29961
260	67600	17576000	16.12452	6.38250
270	72900	19683000	16.43168	6.46330
280	78400	21952000	16.73320	6.54213
290	84100	24389000	17.02939	6.61911
300	90000	27000000	17.32051	6.69433
310	96100	29791000	17.60682	6.76790
320	102400	32768000	17.88854	6.83990
330	108900	35937000	18.16590	6.91042
340	115600	39304000	18.43909	6.97953
350	122500	42875000	18.70829	7.04730
360	129600	46656000	18.97367	7.11379
370	136900	50653000	19.23538	7.17905
380	144400	54872000	19.49359	7.24316
390	152100	59319000	19.74842	7.30614
400	160000	64000000	20.00000	7.36806
410	168100	68921000	20.24846	7.42896
420	176400	74088000	20.49390	7.48887
430	184900	79507000	20.73644	7.54784
440	193600	85184000	20.97618	7.60590
450	202500	91125000	21.21320	7.66309
460	211600	97336000	21.44767	7.71944
470	220900	103823000	21.67948	7.77498
480	230400	110592000	21.90890	7.82974
490	240100	117649000	22.13594	7.88374
500	250000	125000000	22.36068	7.93701
510	260100	132651000	22.58318	7.98957
520	270400	140608000	22.80351	8.04145
530	280900	148877000	23.02173	8.09267
540	291600	157464000	23.23790	8.14325
550	302500	166375000	23.45208	8.19321
560	313600	175616000	23.66432	8.24257
570	324900	185193000	23.87467	8.29134
580	336400	195112000	24.08319	8.33955
590	348100	205379000	24.28992	8.38721
600	360000	216000000	24.49490	8.43433
610	372100	226981000	24.69818	8.48093
620	384400	238328000	24.89980	8.52702
630	396900	250047000	25.09980	8.57262
640	409600	262144000	25.29822	8.61774
650	422500	274625000	25.49510	8.66239
660	435600	287496000	25.69047	8.70659
670	448900	300763000	25.88436	8.75034
680	462400	314432000	26.07681	8.79366
690	476100	328509000	26.26785	8.83656
700	490000	343000000	26.45751	8.87904
710	504100	357911000	26.64583	8.92112
720	518400	373248000	26.83282	8.96281

Squares, Cubes, and Roots

n	Square	Cube	Square Root	Cube Root
730	532900	389017000	27.01851	9.00411
740	547600	405224000	27.20294	9.04504
750	562500	421875000	27.38613	9.08560
760	577600	438976000	27.56810	9.12581
770	592900	456533000	27.74887	9.16566
780	608400	474552000	27.92848	9.20516
790	624100	493039000	28.10694	9.24434
800	640000	512000000	28.28427	9.28318
810	656100	531441000	28.46050	9.32170
820	672400	551368000	28.63564	9.35990
830	688900	571787000	28.80972	9.39780
840	705600	592704000	28.98275	9.43539
850	722500	614125000	29.15476	9.47268
860	739600	636056000	29.32576	9.50969
870	756900	658503000	29.49576	9.54640
880	774400	681472000	29.66479	9.58284
890	792100	704969000	29.83287	9.61900
900	810000	729000000	30.00000	9.65489
910	828100	753571000	30.16621	9.69052
920	846400	778688000	30.33150	9.72589
930	864900	804357000	30.49590	9.76100
940	883600	830584000	30.65942	9.79586
950	902500	857375000	30.82207	9.83048
960	921600	884736000	30.98387	9.86485
970	940900	912673000	31.14482	9.89898
980	960400	941192000	31.30495	9.93288
990	980100	970299000	31.46427	9.96655
1000	1000000	1000000000	31.62278	10.00000

Degrees & Trig Functions

n	n Radians	Sine	Cosine	Tangent
0	0.00000	0.00000	1.00000	0.00000
1	0.01745	0.01745	0.99985	0.01746
2	0.03491	0.03490	0.99939	0.03492
3	0.05236	0.05234	0.99863	0.05241
4	0.06981	0.06976	0.99756	0.06993
5	0.08727	0.08716	0.99619	0.08749
6	0.10472	0.10453	0.99452	0.10510
7	0.12217	0.12187	0.99255	0.12278
8	0.13963	0.13917	0.99027	0.14054
9	0.15708	0.15643	0.98769	0.15838
10	0.17453	0.17365	0.98481	0.17633
11	0.19199	0.19081	0.98163	0.19438
12	0.20944	0.20791	0.97815	0.21256
13	0.22689	0.22495	0.97437	0.23087
14	0.24435	0.24192	0.97030	0.24933
15	0.26180	0.25882	0.96593	0.26795
16	0.27925	0.27564	0.96126	0.28675
17	0.29671	0.29237	0.95630	0.30573
18	0.31416	0.30902	0.95106	0.32492
19	0.33161	0.32557	0.94552	0.34433

Degrees & Trig Functions

n	n Radians	Sine	Cosine	Tangent
20	0.34907	0.34202	0.93969	0.36397
21	0.36652	0.35837	0.93358	0.38386
22	0.38397	0.37461	0.92718	0.40403
23	0.40143	0.39073	0.92050	0.42447
24	0.41888	0.40674	0.91355	0.44523
25	0.43633	0.42262	0.90631	0.46631
26	0.45379	0.43837	0.89879	0.48773
27	0.47124	0.45399	0.89101	0.50953
28	0.48869	0.46947	0.88295	0.53171
29	0.50615	0.48481	0.87462	0.55431
30	0.52360	0.50000	0.86603	0.57735
31	0.54105	0.51504	0.85717	0.60086
32	0.55851	0.52992	0.84805	0.62487
33	0.57596	0.54464	0.83867	0.64941
34	0.59341	0.55919	0.82904	0.67451
35	0.61087	0.57358	0.81915	0.70021
36	0.62832	0.58779	0.80902	0.72654
37	0.64577	0.60182	0.79864	0.75355
38	0.66323	0.61566	0.78801	0.78129
39	0.68068	0.62932	0.77715	0.80978
40	0.69813	0.64279	0.76604	0.83910
41	0.71558	0.65606	0.75471	0.86929
42	0.73304	0.66913	0.74314	0.90040
43	0.75049	0.68200	0.73135	0.93252
44	0.76794	0.69466	0.71934	0.96569
45	0.78540	0.70711	0.70711	1.00000
46	0.80285	0.71934	0.69466	1.03553
47	0.82030	0.73135	0.68200	1.07237
48	0.83776	0.74314	0.66913	1.11061
49	0.85521	0.75471	0.65606	1.15037
50	0.87266	0.76604	0.64279	1.19175
51	0.89012	0.77715	0.62932	1.23490
52	0.90757	0.78801	0.61566	1.27994
53	0.92502	0.79864	0.60182	1.32704
54	0.94248	0.80902	0.58779	1.37638
55	0.95993	0.81915	0.57358	1.42815
56	0.97738	0.82904	0.55919	1.48256
57	0.99484	0.83867	0.54464	1.53986
58	1.01229	0.84805	0.52992	1.60033
59	1.02974	0.85717	0.51504	1.66428
60	1.04720	0.86603	0.50000	1.73205
61	1.06465	0.87462	0.48481	1.80405
62	1.08210	0.88295	0.46947	1.88073
63	1.09956	0.89101	0.45399	1.96261
64	1.11701	0.89879	0.43837	2.05030
65	1.13446	0.90631	0.42262	2.14451
66	1.15192	0.91355	0.40674	2.24604
67	1.16937	0.92050	0.39073	2.35585
68	1.18682	0.92718	0.37461	2.47509
69	1.20428	0.93358	0.35837	2.60509
70	1.22173	0.93969	0.34202	2.74748
71	1.23918	0.94552	0.32557	2.90421
72	1.25664	0.95106	0.30902	3.07768
73	1.27409	0.95630	0.29237	3.27085

Degrees & Trig Functions

n	n Radians	Sine	Cosine	Tangent
74	1.29154	0.96126	0.27564	3.48741
75	1.30900	0.96593	0.25882	3.73205
76	1.32645	0.97030	0.24192	4.01078
77	1.34390	0.97437	0.22495	4.33148
78	1.36136	0.97815	0.20791	4.70463
79	1.37881	0.98163	0.19081	5.14455
80	1.39626	0.98481	0.17365	5.67128
81	1.41372	0.98769	0.15643	6.31375
82	1.43117	0.99027	0.13917	7.11537
83	1.44862	0.99255	0.12187	8.14435
84	1.46608	0.99452	0.10453	9.51436
85	1.48353	0.99619	0.08716	11.43005
86	1.50098	0.99756	0.06976	14.30067
87	1.51844	0.99863	0.05234	19.08114
88	1.53589	0.99939	0.03490	28.63625
89	1.55334	0.99985	0.01745	57.28996
90	1.57080	1.00000	0.00000	infinity
91	1.58825	0.99985	-0.01745	-57.28996
92	1.60570	0.99939	-0.03490	-28.63625
93	1.62316	0.99863	-0.05234	-19.08114
94	1.64061	0.99756	-0.06976	-14.30067
95	1.65806	0.99619	-0.08716	-11.43005
96	1.67552	0.99452	-0.10453	-9.51436
97	1.69297	0.99255	-0.12187	-8.14435
98	1.71042	0.99027	-0.13917	-7.11537
99	1.72788	0.98769	-0.15643	-6.31375
100	1.74533	0.98481	-0.17365	-5.67128
101	1.76278	0.98163	-0.19081	-5.14455
102	1.78024	0.97815	-0.20791	-4.70463
103	1.79769	0.97437	-0.22495	-4.33148
104	1.81514	0.97030	-0.24192	-4.01078
105	1.83260	0.96593	-0.25882	-3.73205
106	1.85005	0.96126	-0.27564	-3.48741
107	1.86750	0.95630	-0.29237	-3.27085
108	1.88496	0.95106	-0.30902	-3.07768
109	1.90241	0.94552	-0.32557	-2.90421
110	1.91986	0.93969	-0.34202	-2.74748
111	1.93732	0.93358	-0.35837	-2.60509
112	1.95477	0.92718	-0.37461	-2.47509
113	1.97222	0.92050	-0.39073	-2.35585
114	1.98968	0.91355	-0.40674	-2.24604
115	2.00713	0.90631	-0.42262	-2.14451
116	2.02458	0.89879	-0.43837	-2.05030
117	2.04204	0.89101	-0.45399	-1.96261
118	2.05949	0.88295	-0.46947	-1.88073
119	2.07694	0.87462	-0.48481	-1.80405
120	2.09440	0.86603	-0.50000	-1.73205
121	2.11185	0.85717	-0.51504	-1.66428
122	2.12930	0.84805	-0.52992	-1.60033
123	2.14675	0.83867	-0.54464	-1.53986
124	2.16421	0.82904	-0.55919	-1.48256
125	2.18166	0.81915	-0.57358	-1.42815
126	2.19911	0.80902	-0.58779	-1.37638
127	2.21657	0.79864	-0.60182	-1.32704

Degrees & Trig Functions

n	n Radians	Sine	Cosine	Tangent
128	2.23402	0.78801	−0.61566	−1.27994
129	2.25147	0.77715	−0.62932	−1.23490
130	2.26893	0.76604	−0.64279	−1.19175
131	2.28638	0.75471	−0.65606	−1.15037
132	2.30383	0.74314	−0.66913	−1.11061
133	2.32129	0.73135	−0.68200	−1.07237
134	2.33874	0.71934	−0.69466	−1.03553
135	2.35619	0.70711	−0.70711	−1.00000
136	2.37365	0.69466	−0.71934	−0.96569
137	2.39110	0.68200	−0.73135	−0.93252
138	2.40855	0.66913	−0.74314	−0.90040
139	2.42601	0.65606	−0.75471	−0.86929
140	2.44346	0.64279	−0.76604	−0.83910
141	2.46091	0.62932	−0.77715	−0.80978
142	2.47837	0.61566	−0.78801	−0.78129
143	2.49582	0.60182	−0.79864	−0.75355
144	2.51327	0.58779	−0.80902	−0.72654
145	2.53073	0.57358	−0.81915	−0.70021
146	2.54818	0.55919	−0.82904	−0.67451
147	2.56563	0.54464	−0.83867	−0.64941
148	2.58309	0.52992	−0.84805	−0.62487
149	2.60054	0.51504	−0.85717	−0.60086
150	2.61799	0.50000	−0.86603	−0.57735
151	2.63545	0.48481	−0.87462	−0.55431
152	2.65290	0.46947	−0.88295	−0.53171
153	2.67035	0.45399	−0.89101	−0.50953
154	2.68781	0.43837	−0.89879	−0.48773
155	2.70526	0.42262	−0.90631	−0.46631
156	2.72271	0.40674	−0.91355	−0.44523
157	2.74017	0.39073	−0.92050	−0.42447
158	2.75762	0.37461	−0.92718	−0.40403
159	2.77507	0.35837	−0.93358	−0.38386
160	2.79253	0.34202	−0.93969	−0.36397
161	2.80998	0.32557	−0.94552	−0.34433
162	2.82743	0.30902	−0.95106	−0.32492
163	2.84489	0.29237	−0.95630	−0.30573
164	2.86234	0.27564	−0.96126	−0.28675
165	2.87979	0.25882	−0.96593	−0.26795
166	2.89725	0.24192	−0.97030	−0.24933
167	2.91470	0.22495	−0.97437	−0.23087
168	2.93215	0.20791	−0.97815	−0.21256
169	2.94961	0.19081	−0.98163	−0.19438
170	2.96706	0.17365	−0.98481	−0.17633
171	2.98451	0.15643	−0.98769	−0.15838
172	3.00197	0.13917	−0.99027	−0.14054
173	3.01942	0.12187	−0.99255	−0.12278
174	3.03687	0.10453	−0.99452	−0.10510
175	3.05433	0.08716	−0.99619	−0.08749
176	3.07178	0.06976	−0.99756	−0.06993
177	3.08923	0.05234	−0.99863	−0.05241
178	3.10669	0.03490	−0.99939	−0.03492
179	3.12414	0.01745	−0.99985	−0.01746
180	3.14159	0.00000	−1.00000	0.00000
181	3.15905	−0.01745	−0.99985	0.01746

Degrees & Trig Functions

n	n Radians	Sine	Cosine	Tangent
182	3.17650	−0.03490	−0.99939	0.03492
183	3.19395	−0.05234	−0.99863	0.05241
184	3.21141	−0.06976	−0.99756	0.06993
185	3.22886	−0.08716	−0.99619	0.08749
186	3.24631	−0.10453	−0.99452	0.10510
187	3.26377	−0.12187	−0.99255	0.12278
188	3.28122	−0.13917	−0.99027	0.14054
189	3.29867	−0.15643	−0.98769	0.15838
190	3.31613	−0.17365	−0.98481	0.17633
191	3.33358	−0.19081	−0.98163	0.19438
192	3.35103	−0.20791	−0.97815	0.21256
193	3.36849	−0.22495	−0.97437	0.23087
194	3.38594	−0.24192	−0.97030	0.24933
195	3.40339	−0.25882	−0.96593	0.26795
196	3.42085	−0.27564	−0.96126	0.28675
197	3.43830	−0.29237	−0.95630	0.30573
198	3.45575	−0.30902	−0.95106	0.32492
199	3.47321	−0.32557	−0.94552	0.34433
200	3.49066	−0.34202	−0.93969	0.36397
201	3.50811	−0.35837	−0.93358	0.38386
202	3.52557	−0.37461	−0.92718	0.40403
203	3.54302	−0.39073	−0.92050	0.42447
204	3.56047	−0.40674	−0.91355	0.44523
205	3.57792	−0.42262	−0.90631	0.46631
206	3.59538	−0.43837	−0.89879	0.48773
207	3.61283	−0.45399	−0.89101	0.50953
208	3.63028	−0.46947	−0.88295	0.53171
209	3.64774	−0.48481	−0.87462	0.55431
210	3.66519	−0.50000	−0.86603	0.57735
211	3.68264	−0.51504	−0.85717	0.60086
212	3.70010	−0.52992	−0.84805	0.62487
213	3.71755	−0.54464	−0.83867	0.64941
214	3.73500	−0.55919	−0.82904	0.67451
215	3.75246	−0.57358	−0.81915	0.70021
216	3.76991	−0.58779	−0.80902	0.72654
217	3.78736	−0.60182	−0.79864	0.75355
218	3.80482	−0.61566	−0.78801	0.78129
219	3.82227	−0.62932	−0.77715	0.80978
220	3.83972	−0.64279	−0.76604	0.83910
221	3.85718	−0.65606	−0.75471	0.86929
222	3.87463	−0.66913	−0.74314	0.90040
223	3.89208	−0.68200	−0.73135	0.93252
224	3.90954	−0.69466	−0.71934	0.96569
225	3.92699	−0.70711	−0.70711	1.00000
226	3.94444	−0.71934	−0.69466	1.03553
227	3.96190	−0.73135	−0.68200	1.07237
228	3.97935	−0.74314	−0.66913	1.11061
229	3.99680	−0.75471	−0.65606	1.15037
230	4.01426	−0.76604	−0.64279	1.19175
231	4.03171	−0.77715	−0.62932	1.23490
232	4.04916	−0.78801	−0.61566	1.27994
233	4.06662	−0.79864	−0.60182	1.32704
234	4.08407	−0.80902	−0.58779	1.37638
235	4.10152	−0.81915	−0.57358	1.42815

Degrees & Trig Functions

n	n Radians	Sine	Cosine	Tangent
236	4.11898	−0.82904	−0.55919	1.48256
237	4.13643	−0.83867	−0.54464	1.53986
238	4.15388	−0.84805	−0.52992	1.60033
239	4.17134	−0.85717	−0.51504	1.66428
240	4.18879	−0.86603	−0.50000	1.73205
241	4.20624	−0.87462	−0.48481	1.80405
242	4.22370	−0.88295	−0.46947	1.88073
243	4.24115	−0.89101	−0.45399	1.96261
244	4.25860	−0.89879	−0.43837	2.05030
245	4.27606	−0.90631	−0.42262	2.14451
246	4.29351	−0.91355	−0.40674	2.24604
247	4.31096	−0.92050	−0.39073	2.35585
248	4.32842	−0.92718	−0.37461	2.47509
249	4.34587	−0.93358	−0.35837	2.60509
250	4.36332	−0.93969	−0.34202	2.74748
251	4.38078	−0.94552	−0.32557	2.90421
252	4.39823	−0.95106	−0.30902	3.07768
253	4.41568	−0.95630	−0.29237	3.27085
254	4.43314	−0.96126	−0.27564	3.48741
255	4.45059	−0.96593	−0.25882	3.73205
256	4.46804	−0.97030	−0.24192	4.01078
257	4.48550	−0.97437	−0.22495	4.33148
258	4.50295	−0.97815	−0.20791	4.70463
259	4.52040	−0.98163	−0.19081	5.14455
260	4.53786	−0.98481	−0.17365	5.67128
261	4.55531	−0.98769	−0.15643	6.31375
262	4.57276	−0.99027	−0.13917	7.11537
263	4.59022	−0.99255	−0.12187	8.14435
264	4.60767	−0.99452	−0.10453	9.51436
265	4.62512	−0.99619	−0.08716	11.43005
266	4.64258	−0.99756	−0.06976	14.30067
267	4.66003	−0.99863	−0.05234	19.08114
268	4.67748	−0.99939	−0.03490	28.63625
269	4.69494	−0.99985	−0.01745	57.28996
270	4.71239	−1.00000	0.00000	infinity
271	4.72984	−0.99985	0.01745	−57.28996
272	4.74730	−0.99939	0.03490	−28.63625
273	4.76475	−0.99863	0.05234	−19.08114
274	4.78220	−0.99756	0.06976	−14.30067
275	4.79966	−0.99619	0.08716	−11.43005
276	4.81711	−0.99452	0.10453	−9.51436
277	4.83456	−0.99255	0.12187	−8.14435
278	4.85202	−0.99027	0.13917	−7.11537
279	4.86947	−0.98769	0.15643	−6.31375
280	4.88692	−0.98481	0.17365	−5.67128
281	4.90438	−0.98163	0.19081	−5.14455
282	4.92183	−0.97815	0.20791	−4.70463
283	4.93928	−0.97437	0.22495	−4.33148
284	4.95674	−0.97030	0.24192	−4.01078
285	4.97419	−0.96593	0.25882	−3.73205
286	4.99164	−0.96126	0.27564	−3.48741
287	5.00909	−0.95630	0.29237	−3.27085
288	5.02655	−0.95106	0.30902	−3.07768
289	5.04400	−0.94552	0.32557	−2.90421

Degrees & Trig Functions

n	n Radians	Sine	Cosine	Tangent
290	5.06145	−0.93969	0.34202	−2.74748
291	5.07891	−0.93358	0.35837	−2.60509
292	5.09636	−0.92718	0.37461	−2.47509
293	5.11381	−0.92050	0.39073	−2.35585
294	5.13127	−0.91355	0.40674	−2.24604
295	5.14872	−0.90631	0.42262	−2.14451
296	5.16617	−0.89879	0.43837	−2.05030
297	5.18363	−0.89101	0.45399	−1.96261
298	5.20108	−0.88295	0.46947	−1.88073
299	5.21853	−0.87462	0.48481	−1.80405
300	5.23599	−0.86603	0.50000	−1.73205
301	5.25344	−0.85717	0.51504	−1.66428
302	5.27089	−0.84805	0.52992	−1.60033
303	5.28835	−0.83867	0.54464	−1.53986
304	5.30580	−0.82904	0.55919	−1.48256
305	5.32325	−0.81915	0.57358	−1.42815
306	5.34071	−0.80902	0.58779	−1.37638
307	5.35816	−0.79864	0.60182	−1.32704
308	5.37561	−0.78801	0.61566	−1.27994
309	5.39307	−0.77715	0.62932	−1.23490
310	5.41052	−0.76604	0.64279	−1.19175
311	5.42797	−0.75471	0.65606	−1.15037
312	5.44543	−0.74314	0.66913	−1.11061
313	5.46288	−0.73135	0.68200	−1.07237
314	5.48033	−0.71934	0.69466	−1.03553
315	5.49779	−0.70711	0.70711	−1.00000
316	5.51524	−0.69466	0.71934	−0.96569
317	5.53269	−0.68200	0.73135	−0.93252
318	5.55015	−0.66913	0.74314	−0.90040
319	5.56760	−0.65606	0.75471	−0.86929
320	5.58505	−0.64279	0.76604	−0.83910
321	5.60251	−0.62932	0.77715	−0.80978
322	5.61996	−0.61566	0.78801	−0.78129
323	5.63741	−0.60182	0.79864	−0.75355
324	5.65487	−0.58779	0.80902	−0.72654
325	5.67232	−0.57358	0.81915	−0.70021
326	5.68977	−0.55919	0.82904	−0.67451
327	5.70723	−0.54464	0.83867	−0.64941
328	5.72468	−0.52992	0.84805	−0.62487
329	5.74213	−0.51504	0.85717	−0.60086
330	5.75959	−0.50000	0.86603	−0.57735
331	5.77704	−0.48481	0.87462	−0.55431
332	5.79449	−0.46947	0.88295	−0.53171
333	5.81195	−0.45399	0.89101	−0.50953
334	5.82940	−0.43837	0.89879	−0.48773
335	5.84685	−0.42262	0.90631	−0.46631
336	5.86431	−0.40674	0.91355	−0.44523
337	5.88176	−0.39073	0.92050	−0.42447
338	5.89921	−0.37461	0.92718	−0.40403
339	5.91667	−0.35837	0.93358	−0.38386
340	5.93412	−0.34202	0.93969	−0.36397
341	5.95157	−0.32557	0.94552	−0.34433
342	5.96903	−0.30902	0.95106	−0.32492
343	5.98648	−0.29237	0.95630	−0.30573

Degrees & Trig Functions

n	n Radians	Sine	Cosine	Tangent
344	6.00393	−0.27564	0.96126	−0.28675
345	6.02139	−0.25882	0.96593	−0.26795
346	6.03884	−0.24192	0.97030	−0.24933
347	6.05629	−0.22495	0.97437	−0.23087
348	6.07375	−0.20791	0.97815	−0.21256
349	6.09120	−0.19081	0.98163	−0.19438
350	6.10865	−0.17365	0.98481	−0.17633
351	6.12611	−0.15643	0.98769	−0.15838
352	6.14356	−0.13917	0.99027	−0.14054
353	6.16101	−0.12187	0.99255	−0.12278
354	6.17847	−0.10453	0.99452	−0.10510
355	6.19592	−0.08716	0.99619	−0.08749
356	6.21337	−0.06976	0.99756	−0.06993
357	6.23083	−0.05234	0.99863	−0.05241
358	6.24828	−0.03490	0.99939	−0.03492
359	6.26573	−0.01745	0.99985	−0.01746
360	6.28319	0.00000	1.00000	0.00000

Log, Log e, Circumference & Area

n	Log 10	Log e	Circumference @ Diameter n	Circle Area @ Diameter n
1	0.00000	0.00000	3.1416	0.7854
2	0.30103	0.69315	6.2832	3.1416
3	0.47712	1.09861	9.4248	7.0686
4	0.60206	1.38629	12.5664	12.5664
5	0.69897	1.60944	15.7080	19.6350
6	0.77815	1.79176	18.8496	28.2743
7	0.84510	1.94591	21.9911	38.4845
8	0.90309	2.07944	25.1327	50.2655
9	0.95424	2.19722	28.2743	63.6173
10	1.00000	2.30259	31.4159	78.5398
11	1.04139	2.39790	34.5575	95.0332
12	1.07918	2.48491	37.6991	113.0973
13	1.11394	2.56495	40.8407	132.7323
14	1.14613	2.63906	43.9823	153.9380
15	1.17609	2.70805	47.1239	176.7146
16	1.20412	2.77259	50.2655	201.0619
17	1.23045	2.83321	53.4071	226.9801
18	1.25527	2.89037	56.5487	254.4690
19	1.27875	2.94444	59.6903	283.5287
20	1.30103	2.99573	62.8319	314.1593
21	1.32222	3.04452	65.9734	346.3606
22	1.34242	3.09104	69.1150	380.1327
23	1.36173	3.13549	72.2566	415.4756
24	1.38021	3.17805	75.3982	452.3893
25	1.39794	3.21888	78.5398	490.8739
26	1.41497	3.25810	81.6814	530.9292
27	1.43136	3.29584	84.8230	572.5553
28	1.44716	3.33220	87.9646	615.7522
29	1.46240	3.36730	91.1062	660.5199
30	1.47712	3.40120	94.2478	706.8583

Log–Log e–Circumference–Area

n	Log 10	Log e	Circumference @ Diameter n	Circle Area @ Diameter n
31	1.49136	3.43399	97.3894	754.7676
32	1.50515	3.46574	100.5310	804.2477
33	1.51851	3.49651	103.6726	855.2986
34	1.53148	3.52636	106.8142	907.9203
35	1.54407	3.55535	109.9557	962.1128
36	1.55630	3.58352	113.0973	1017.8760
37	1.56820	3.61092	116.2389	1075.2101
38	1.57978	3.63759	119.3805	1134.1149
39	1.59106	3.66356	122.5221	1194.5906
40	1.60206	3.68888	125.6637	1256.6371
41	1.61278	3.71357	128.8053	1320.2543
42	1.62325	3.73767	131.9469	1385.4424
43	1.63347	3.76120	135.0885	1452.2012
44	1.64345	3.78419	138.2301	1520.5308
45	1.65321	3.80666	141.3717	1590.4313
46	1.66276	3.82864	144.5133	1661.9025
47	1.67210	3.85015	147.6549	1734.9445
48	1.68124	3.87120	150.7964	1809.5574
49	1.69020	3.89182	153.9380	1885.7410
50	1.69897	3.91202	157.0796	1963.4954
51	1.70757	3.93183	160.2212	2042.8206
52	1.71600	3.95124	163.3628	2123.7166
53	1.72428	3.97029	166.5044	2206.1834
54	1.73239	3.98898	169.6460	2290.2210
55	1.74036	4.00733	172.7876	2375.8294
56	1.74819	4.02535	175.9292	2463.0086
57	1.75587	4.04305	179.0708	2551.7586
58	1.76343	4.06044	182.2124	2642.0794
59	1.77085	4.07754	185.3540	2733.9710
60	1.77815	4.09434	188.4956	2827.4334
61	1.78533	4.11087	191.6372	2922.4666
62	1.79239	4.12713	194.7787	3019.0705
63	1.79934	4.14313	197.9203	3117.2453
64	1.80618	4.15888	201.0619	3216.9909
65	1.81291	4.17439	204.2035	3318.3072
66	1.81954	4.18965	207.3451	3421.1944
67	1.82607	4.20469	210.4867	3525.6524
68	1.83251	4.21951	213.6283	3631.6811
69	1.83885	4.23411	216.7699	3739.2807
70	1.84510	4.24850	219.9115	3848.4510
71	1.85126	4.26268	223.0531	3959.1921
72	1.85733	4.27667	226.1947	4071.5041
73	1.86332	4.29046	229.3363	4185.3868
74	1.86923	4.30407	232.4779	4300.8403
75	1.87506	4.31749	235.6194	4417.8647
76	1.88081	4.33073	238.7610	4536.4598
77	1.88649	4.34381	241.9026	4656.6257
78	1.89209	4.35671	245.0442	4778.3624
79	1.89763	4.36945	248.1858	4901.6699
80	1.90309	4.38203	251.3274	5026.5482
81	1.90849	4.39445	254.4690	5152.9973
82	1.91381	4.40672	257.6106	5281.0173
83	1.91908	4.41884	260.7522	5410.6079
84	1.92428	4.43082	263.8938	5541.7694

Log–Log e–Circumference–Area

n	Log 10	Log e	Circumference @ Diameter n	Circle Area @ Diameter n
85	1.92942	4.44265	267.0354	5674.5017
86	1.93450	4.45435	270.1770	5808.8048
87	1.93952	4.46591	273.3186	5944.6787
88	1.94448	4.47734	276.4602	6082.1234
89	1.94939	4.48864	279.6017	6221.1389
90	1.95424	4.49981	282.7433	6361.7251
91	1.95904	4.51086	285.8849	6503.8822
92	1.96379	4.52179	289.0265	6647.6101
93	1.96848	4.53260	292.1681	6792.9087
94	1.97313	4.54329	295.3097	6939.7782
95	1.97772	4.55388	298.4513	7088.2184
96	1.98227	4.56435	301.5929	7238.2295
97	1.98677	4.57471	304.7345	7389.8113
98	1.99123	4.58497	307.8761	7542.9640
99	1.99564	4.59512	311.0177	7697.6874
100	2.00000	4.60517	314.1593	7853.9816
110	2.04139	4.70048	345.5752	9503.3178
120	2.07918	4.78749	376.9911	11309.7336
130	2.11394	4.86753	408.4070	13273.2290
140	2.14613	4.94164	439.8230	15393.8040
150	2.17609	5.01064	471.2389	17671.4587
160	2.20412	5.07517	502.6548	20106.1930
170	2.23045	5.13580	534.0708	22698.0069
180	2.25527	5.19296	565.4867	25446.9005
190	2.27875	5.24702	596.9026	28352.8737
200	2.30103	5.29832	628.3185	31415.9265
210	2.32222	5.34711	659.7345	34636.0590
220	2.34242	5.39363	691.1504	38013.2711
230	2.36173	5.43808	722.5663	41547.5628
240	2.38021	5.48064	753.9822	45238.9342
250	2.39794	5.52146	785.3982	49087.3852
260	2.41497	5.56068	816.8141	53092.9158
270	2.43136	5.59842	848.2300	57255.5261
280	2.44716	5.63479	879.6459	61575.2160
290	2.46240	5.66988	911.0619	66051.9855
300	2.47712	5.70378	942.4778	70685.8347
310	2.49136	5.73657	973.8937	75476.7635
320	2.50515	5.76832	1005.3096	80424.7719
330	2.51851	5.79903	1036.7256	85529.8600
340	2.53148	5.82895	1068.1415	90792.0277
350	2.54407	5.85793	1099.5574	96211.2750
360	2.55630	5.88610	1130.9734	101787.6020
370	2.56820	5.91350	1162.3893	107521.0086
380	2.57978	5.94017	1193.8052	113411.4948
390	2.59106	5.96615	1225.2211	119459.0607
400	2.60206	5.99146	1256.6371	125663.7061
410	2.61278	6.01616	1288.0530	132025.4313
420	2.62325	6.04025	1319.4689	138544.2360
430	2.63347	6.06379	1350.8848	145220.1204
440	2.64345	6.08677	1382.3008	152053.0844
450	2.65321	6.10925	1413.7167	159043.1281
460	2.66276	6.13123	1445.1326	166190.2514
470	2.67210	6.15273	1476.5485	173494.4543
480	2.68124	6.17379	1507.9645	180955.7368

Log–Log e–Circumference–Area

n	Log 10	Log e	Circumference @ Diameter n	Circle Area @ Diameter n
490	2.69020	6.19441	1539.3804	188574.0990
500	2.69897	6.21461	1570.7963	196349.5408
510	2.70757	6.23441	1602.2123	204282.0623
520	2.71600	6.25383	1633.6282	212371.6634
530	2.72428	6.27288	1665.0441	220618.3441
540	2.73239	6.29157	1696.4600	229022.1044
550	2.74036	6.30992	1727.8760	237582.9444
560	2.74819	6.32794	1759.2919	246300.8640
570	2.75587	6.34564	1790.7078	255175.8633
580	2.76343	6.36303	1822.1237	264207.9422
590	2.77085	6.38012	1853.5397	273397.1007
600	2.77815	6.39693	1884.9556	282743.3388
610	2.78533	6.41346	1916.3715	292246.6566
620	2.79239	6.42972	1947.7874	301907.0540
630	2.79934	6.44572	1979.2034	311724.5311
640	2.80618	6.46147	2010.6193	321699.0877
650	2.81291	6.47697	2042.0352	331830.7240
660	2.81954	6.49224	2073.4512	342119.4400
670	2.82607	6.50728	2104.8671	352565.2355
680	2.83251	6.52209	2136.2830	363168.1108
690	2.83885	6.53669	2167.6989	373928.0656
700	2.84510	6.55108	2199.1149	384845.1001
710	2.85126	6.56526	2230.5308	395919.2142
720	2.85733	6.57925	2261.9467	407150.4079
730	2.86332	6.59304	2293.3626	418538.6813
740	2.86923	6.60665	2324.7786	430084.0343
750	2.87506	6.62007	2356.1945	441786.4669
760	2.88081	6.63332	2387.6104	453645.9792
770	2.88649	6.64639	2419.0263	465662.5711
780	2.89209	6.65929	2450.4423	477836.2426
790	2.89763	6.67203	2481.8582	490166.9938
800	2.90309	6.68461	2513.2741	502654.8246
810	2.90849	6.69703	2544.6900	515299.7350
820	2.91381	6.70930	2576.1060	528101.7251
830	2.91908	6.72143	2607.5219	541060.7948
840	2.92428	6.73340	2638.9378	554176.9441
850	2.92942	6.74524	2670.3538	567450.1731
860	2.93450	6.75693	2701.7697	580880.4816
870	2.93952	6.76849	2733.1856	594467.8699
880	2.94448	6.77992	2764.6015	608212.3377
890	2.94939	6.79122	2796.0175	622113.8852
900	2.95424	6.80239	2827.4334	636172.5124
910	2.95904	6.81344	2858.8493	650388.2191
920	2.96379	6.82437	2890.2652	664761.0055
930	2.96848	6.83518	2921.6812	679290.8715
940	2.97313	6.84588	2953.0971	693977.8172
950	2.97772	6.85646	2984.5130	708821.8425
960	2.98227	6.86693	3015.9289	723822.9474
970	2.98677	6.87730	3047.3449	738981.1319
980	2.99123	6.88755	3078.7608	754296.3961
990	2.99564	6.89770	3110.1767	769768.7399
1000	3.00000	6.90776	3141.5927	785398.1634

Right Triangle Trig Formulas

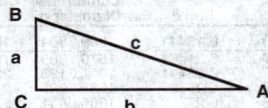

A, B, C = Angles   a, b, c = Distances

$$\sin A = \frac{a}{c} \quad , \quad \cos A = \frac{b}{c} \quad , \quad \tan A = \frac{a}{b}$$

$$\cot A = \frac{b}{a} \quad , \quad \sec A = \frac{c}{b} \quad , \quad \csc A = \frac{c}{a}$$

Area = (a b) / 2

Given a and b, Find A, B, and c

$$\tan A = \frac{a}{b} = \cot B \quad , \quad c = \sqrt{a^2 + b^2} = a\sqrt{1 + \frac{b^2}{a^2}}$$

Given a and c, Find A, B, b

$$\sin A = \frac{a}{c} = \cos B \; , \; b = \sqrt{(c + a)(c - a)} = c\sqrt{1 - \frac{a^2}{c^2}}$$

Given A and a, Find B, b, c

$$B = 90° - A \; , \; b = a \, \cot A \; , \; c = \frac{a}{\sin A}$$

Given A and b, Find B, a, c

$$B = 90° - A \quad , \quad a = b \, \tan A \quad , \quad c = \frac{b}{\cos A}$$

Given A and c, Find B, a, b

$$B = 90° - A \quad , \quad a = c \, \sin A \quad , \quad b = c \, \cos A$$

Oblique Triangle Formulas

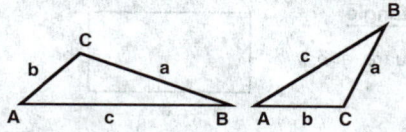

Given A, B and a, Find b, C and c

$$b = \frac{a \sin B}{\sin A} \ , \ C = 180^\circ - (A + B) \ , \ c = \frac{a \sin C}{\sin A}$$

Given A, a and b, Find B, C and c

$$\sin B = \frac{b \sin A}{a} \ , C = 180^\circ - (A + B) \ , c = \frac{a \sin C}{\sin A}$$

Given a, b and C, Find A, B and c

$$\tan A = \frac{a \sin C}{b - (a \cos C)} \ , \ B = 180^\circ - (A + C)$$

$$c = \frac{a \sin C}{\sin A}$$

Given a, b and c, Find A, B and C

$$\cos A = \frac{b^2 + c^2 - a^2}{2 \, bc} \ , \ \cos B = \frac{a^2 + c^2 - b^2}{2 \, ac}$$

$$C = 180^\circ - (A + B)$$

Given a, b, c, A, B and C Find Area

$$s = \frac{a + b + c}{2} \ , \ Area = \sqrt{s(s-a)(s-b)(s-c)}$$

$$Area = \frac{bc \sin A}{2} \ , \quad Area = \frac{a^2 \sin B \sin C}{2 \sin A}$$

Plane Figure Formulas

Rectangle

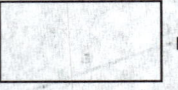

If square, a=b

$$Area = ab$$
$$Perimeter = 2(a + b) \ , \ Diagonal = \sqrt{a^2 + b^2}$$

Parallelogram

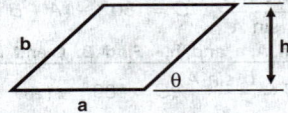

All sides are parallel
θ = degrees

$$Area = ah = ab \sin\theta \ , \ Perimeter = 2(a + b)$$

Trapezoid

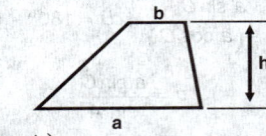

$$Area = \frac{(a+b)}{2}h$$
$$Perimeter = Sum\ of\ lengths\ of\ sides$$

Quadrilateral

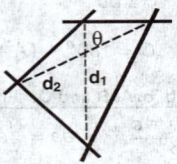

θ = degrees

$$Area = \frac{d_1 \times d_2 \times \sin\theta}{2}$$

Plane Figure Formulas

Trapezium

a to g = lengths

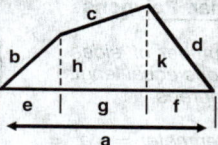

$Perimeter = a + b + c + d$

$$Area = \frac{(h+k)\,g + e\,h + f\,k}{2}$$

Equilateral Triangle

a = all sides equal

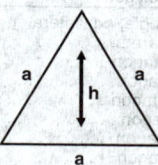

$Perimeter = 3\,a$, $h = \dfrac{a}{2}\sqrt{3} = 0.866\,a$

$$Area = a^2\,\frac{\sqrt{3}}{4} = 0.433\,a^2$$

Annulus

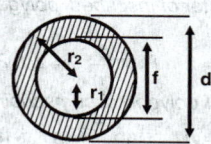

$$Area = 0.7854\left(d^2 - f^2\right)$$

$$Area = \pi\left(r_1 + r_2\right)\left(r_2 - r_1\right)$$

Regular Polygons

n = number of sides
(all sides equal length)
θ = degrees

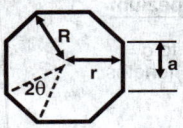

Perimeter = $n\,a$

Area = $\dfrac{n\,a\,r}{2} = n r^2 \tan\theta = \dfrac{n R^2}{2} \sin 2\theta$

Polygon	Number of Sides	Area
Triangle, equilateral	3	$0.4330\ a^2$
Square	4	$1.0000\ a^2$
Pentagon	5	$1.7205\ a^2$
Hexagon	6	$2.5981\ a^2$
Heptagon	7	$3.6339\ a^2$
Octagon	8	$4.8284\ a^2$
Nonagon	9	$6.1818\ a^2$
Decagon	10	$7.6942\ a^2$
Undecagon	11	$9.3656\ a^2$
Dodecagon	12	$11.1962\ a^2$

Area of inscribed polygon in a circle of radius R:

$$A = \tfrac{1}{2} n R^2 \sin\frac{2\pi}{n} = \tfrac{1}{2} n R^2 \sin\frac{360^\circ}{n}$$

Perimeter of inscribed polygon in circle of radius R:

$$P = 2nR \sin\frac{\pi}{n} = 2nR \sin\frac{180^\circ}{n}$$

Area of polygon circumscribing a circle of radius r:

$$A = nr^2 \tan\frac{\pi}{n} = nr^2 \tan\frac{180^\circ}{n}$$

Perimeter of polygon circumscribing a circle of

radius r: $P = 2nr \tan\frac{\pi}{n} = 2nr \tan\frac{180^\circ}{n}$

Note: In all equations, π radians = 180°
1 radian = 57.29578°

Plane Figure Formulas

Circle

Z = point
X = point
θ = degrees
c,d,r,m = lengths
π = 3.14159
c = cord
r = radius

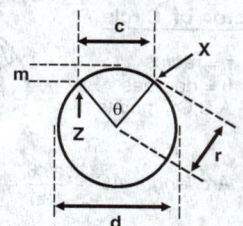

$$Circumference = 2\pi r = \pi d = 3.14159\,d$$

$$Area = \pi r^2 = \pi\,\frac{d^2}{4} = 0.78539\,d^2$$

$$Area = \frac{Perimeter^2}{4\pi} = 0.07958\,Perimeter^2$$

$$Length\ of\ arc\ XZ = \theta\,\frac{\pi}{180}\,r = 0.017453\,\theta\,r$$

$$r = \frac{m^2 + \frac{1}{4}c^2}{2m} = \frac{\frac{1}{2}c}{\sin\frac{1}{2}\theta}$$

$$c = 2\sqrt{2\,mr - m^2} = 2r\,\sin\frac{1}{2}\theta$$

$$m = r \pm \sqrt{r^2 - \frac{c^2}{4}} \quad (use\ +\ if\ arc \geq 180°,$$
$$use\ -\ if\ arc < 180°\,)$$

$$m = \frac{1}{2}c\,\tan\frac{1}{4}\theta = 2r\,\sin^2\frac{1}{4}\theta$$

Plane Figure Formulas

Sector of Circle

r = radius
θ = degrees
A,B,C = points

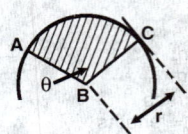

$$Arc\ length\ AC = \frac{\pi r \theta}{180} = 0.01745\ r\ \theta$$

$$Area\ ABCA = \frac{\pi \theta r^2}{360} = 0.008727\ \theta\ r^2$$

$$Area\ ABCA = \frac{Arc\ length\ AC \times r}{2}$$

Segment of Circle

r = radius
θ = degrees
A,B,C,D = points

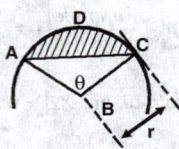

$$Area\ ACDA = \frac{r^2}{2}\left(\frac{\pi\theta}{180} - \sin\theta\right)$$

Circular Zone

Area ACDFA =
Circle Area –
   Segment Area ABCA –
   Segment Area FDEF

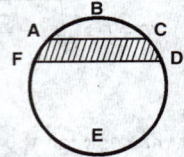

Plane Figure Formulas

Hollow Circle Sector

θ = degrees
A,B,C,D = points
r = radius

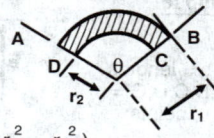

$$Area\ ABCDA = \frac{\pi\ \theta\ (r_1^2 - r_2^2)}{360}$$

$$Area\ ABCDA = \frac{r_1 - r_2}{2}\ (Arc\ length\ AB + Arc\ length\ CD)$$

Fillet

r = radius
Area of fillet = $0.215\ r^2$

Parabola

A,B,C = points
a,b = lengths

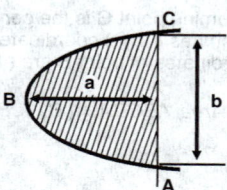

$$Area\ ABCA = \frac{2}{3}\ ab$$

$$Arc\ Length\ ABC = \frac{b}{2}\sqrt{1 + \left(\frac{4a}{b}\right)^2}\ +$$

(approximation!)

$$\frac{b^2}{8\ a}\log_e\left[\frac{4a}{b} + \sqrt{1 + \left(\frac{4a}{b}\right)^2}\right]$$

Ellipse

a,b = lengths
A,B,C,D,G = points

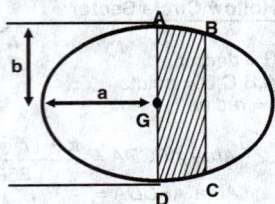

Area of ellipse $= \pi\, a\, b$

Perimeter of ellipse $= \pi\left[\, 1.5\,(a+b) - \sqrt{ab}\,\right]$

  (approximate)

Assuming point G is the center of the ellipse, which has (x, y) coordinates of (0, 0), and the coordinates of point B are (B_x, B_y) :

$$\text{Area ABCDA} = (B_x \times B_y) + ab\,\sin^{-1}\left(\frac{B_x}{a}\right)$$

Solid Figure Formulas

Parallelopiped and Cube

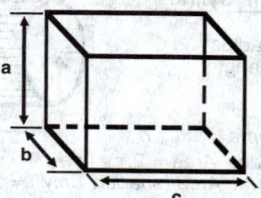

a,b,c = lengths

If a Cube:

Volume = a^3 Surface area = $6 a^2$

If a Parallelopiped (a, b, and c can be different):

Volume = $a b c$ Area = $2 (ab + bc + ac)$

Prism – Right, or oblique, regular or irregular

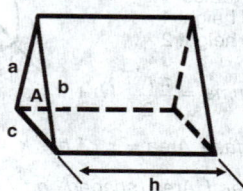

A = area
h = length
a,b,c = length

Volume = $A h$ where A is the area of the end plate abca. If the end plate has 3 or more sides, see page 478 for rules of calculating areas

of polygons.

Surface area = $h (a + b + c + ... n \text{ sides})$

If end planes are parallel but not at $90°$ to h, the same formulas apply but a slice at $90°$ through the prism must be used to determine a, b, and c.

Solid Figure Formulas

Right Cylinder

r = radius
h = length

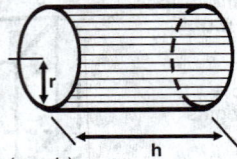

$Volume = \pi r^2 h$

$Surface\ Area = 2 \pi r (r + h)$

$Lateral\ Area\ (shaded\ only) = 2 \pi r h$

If end planes are parallel but not at 90° to h, the same formulas apply but a slice at 90° through the cylinder must be used to determine r. Surface area includes the ends, lateral area is shaded.

Frustum of a Right Cylinder

r = radius
h = height 1
k = height 2

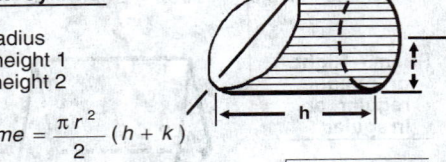

$Volume = \dfrac{\pi r^2}{2} (h + k)$

$Surface\ Area = \pi r \left[h + k + r + \sqrt{r^2 + \left(\dfrac{h-k}{2}\right)^2} \right]$

$Lateral\ Area\ (shaded\ only) = \pi r (h + k)$

Right Cone

r = radius
h = height
k = side length

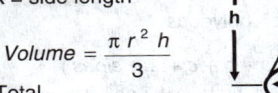

$Volume = \dfrac{\pi r^2 h}{3}$

Total
$Surface\ Area = \pi r (r + k)$
$Lateral\ Area$ (outer surface of the cone without the circular base area) $= \pi r k$

Solid Figure Formulas

Right Pyramid

A = base plane
h = height
k = side length

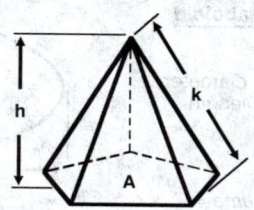

$$Volume = \frac{(Area\ of\ base\ A)\,h}{3}$$

Surface Area (no base) = Perimeter of base $A \times \dfrac{k}{2}$

Use polygon areas on page 478, if you want to include the base area

Sphere

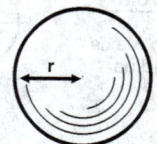

r = radius

$$Volume = \frac{4\,\pi\,r^3}{3}$$

Surface Area = $4\,\pi\,r^2$

Circular Ring

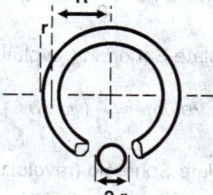

r = cross section radius
R = ring radius

$$Volume = 2\,\pi^2\,R\,r^2$$

$$Surface\ Area = 4\,\pi^2\,R\,r$$

Solid Figure Formulas

Paraboloid

d = diameter
h = length

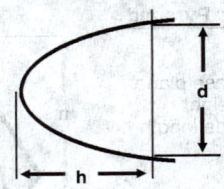

Volume $= \dfrac{\pi}{8} \times d^2 \times h$

Surface Area (*no base*) =

$$\frac{2}{3} \times \pi \times \frac{d}{h^2} \left[\left(\frac{d^2}{16} + h^2 \right)^{\frac{3}{2}} - \left(\frac{d}{4} \right)^3 \right]$$

Ellipsoid and Spheroid

a, b, c = axis radius

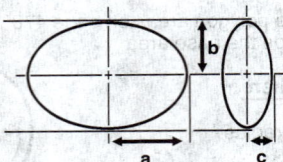

Volume $= \dfrac{4}{3} \times \pi \times a \times b \times c$

Prolate Spheroid (revolution about major axis b)

Volume $= \dfrac{4}{3} (\pi \, a b^2)$

Oblate Spheroid (revolution about minor axis a)

Volume $= \dfrac{4}{3} (\pi \, b \, a^2)$

(See also WEIGHTS OF MATERIALS, p. 655, for
Angle of Repose, Rock Densities, etc)

NOTE: Two pocket sized handbooks are available that deal with
roadway and milling equipment specifications and other general
data: (a) *Pioneer Facts and Figures*, Portec Pioneer Division, Minneapolis, MN and (b) *Cedarapids Reference Book*, Iowa Mfg Co,
Cedar Rapids, Iowa.

US Standard Test Sieve Series

Tyler Inch/Mesh #	Sieve Designation Inch/Sieve #	Nominal Sieve Opening Inches	Millimeters
	5 inch	5.0	125
	4.24 inch	4.24	106
	4 inch	4.0	100
	3–1/2 inch	3.5	90
2.97 inch	3 inch	3.0	75
	2–1/2 inch	2.5	63
	2.12 inch	2.12	53
2.10 inch	2 inch	2.00	50
	1–3/4 inch	1.75	45
1.48 inch	1–1/2 inch	1.50	37.5
	1–1/4 inch	1.25	31.5
1.05 inch	1.06 inch	1.06	26.5
	1 inch	1.00	25.0
0.883 inch	7/8 inch	0.875	22.4
0.742 inch	3/4 inch	0.750	19.0
0.624 inch	5/8 inch	0.625	16.0
0.525 inch	0.530 inch	0.530	13.2
	1/2 inch	0.500	12.5
0.441 inch	7/16 inch	0.438	11.2
0.371 inch	3/8 inch	0.375	9.5
2 1/2	5/16 inch	0.312	8.0
3	0.265 inch	0.265	6.7
	1/4 inch	0.250	6.3
3 1/2	3–1/2	0.223	5.6
4	4	0.187	4.75
5	5	0.157	4.00
6	6	0.132	3.35
7	7	0.11	2.80
8	8	0.0937	2.36
9	10	0.0787	2.00
10	12	0.0661	1.70
12	14	0.0555	1.40
14	16	0.0469	1.18
16	18	0.0394	1.00
20	20	0.0331	0.85
24	25	0.0278	0.71
28	30	0.0234	0.60
32	35	0.0197	0.50
35	40	0.0165	0.425
42	45	0.0139	0.355
48	50	0.0117	0.300
60	60	0.0098	0.250
65	70	0.0083	0.212
80	80	0.0070	0.180
100	100	0.0059	0.150
115	120	0.0049	0.125
150	140	0.0041	0.106
170	170	0.0035	0.090
200	200	0.0029	0.075
250	230	0.0025	0.063
270	270	0.0021	0.053
325	325	0.0017	0.045
400	400	0.0015	0.038
450	450	0.0012	0.032
500	500	0.0010	0.025
635	635	0.0008	0.020

Mineral Dressing Sizing Scale

Size	Mineral Dressing Method
+4 inch to 400 mesh	Screening
+4 inch to 65 mesh	Magnetic Separator (dry)
+4 inch to 325 mesh	Magnetic Separator (wet)
+4 inch to 4 mesh	Sink – Float
+4 inch to 65 mesh	Hammer Mill – Jaw Crusher
+4 inch to 65 mesh	Gyratory Crusher
+4 inch to 28 mesh	Rolls
4 inch to 20 mesh	Jigging
2 inch to 3 mesh	Rod Mill
1 inch to 325 mesh	Ball Mill
0.5 inch to 26 micron	Pulverizer
3 mesh to 48 mesh	Weinig Jig
4 mesh to 100 mesh	Humphreys Spiral
8 mesh to 200 mesh	Shaking Table
10 mesh to 18.5 micron	Isodynamic Separator
35 mesh to 4.6 micron	Classification
35 mesh to 6.5 micron	Flotation
48 mesh to 3.25 micron	Turbidimetry
65 mesh to 9.25 micron	Superpanner
100 mesh to 6.5 micron	Infrasizer
0.81 micron to 0.25 micron	Centrifuge
400 mesh to 0.2 micron	Normal Microscope Range
± 0.5 micron	Brownian Movement and the wavelength of visible light
0.41 micron to 0.001 micron	Normal Electron Microscope
± 0.025 micron	Thinnest files visible by light interference
0.004 micron	Large Molecules
0.0007 micron	Average Crystal Unit

NOTE: The above size ranges are approximations only and the actual size range can vary considerably depending on the material and current technology.

Stockpile Volume & Weight

The following formula is used to calculate the volume of a stockpile if the diameter and height are known:

Volume in cubic feet = 0.2618 x D^2 x h
D = Diameter of the base of the cone in feet
h = Height of the cone in feet

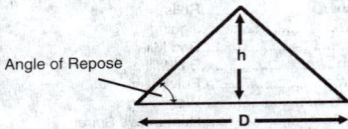

Angle of Repose

In order to calculate the actual weight of material in the stockpile, determine the density or weight/cubic foot (or look up an approximation of the density in the WEIGHTS OF MATERIALS chapter.)

Weight (tons) = Volume (ft^3) x Density ($\frac{lb}{ft^3}$) x $\frac{1\ ton}{2000\ lb}$

1 cubic yard = 27 cubic feet
1 cubic foot = 0.037037 cubic yards

CONICAL STOCKPILE VOLUMES (37° Angle of Repose)

Diameter in feet	Height in feet	Volume in Cu Yds	Weight in Tons at 100 lbs/cu foot
26.54	10	68	92
39.81	15	230	310
53.08	20	545	740
66.35	25	1065	1440
79.62	30	1845	2490
92.89	35	2930	3955
106.16	40	4370	5900
132.70	50	8540	11525
159.25	60	14755	19920
185.79	70	23430	31630
212.33	80	34970	47210
238.87	90	49790	67220
265.41	100	68300	92210

To find volumes and weights of stockpiles with other angles of repose, multiply those values in the table by the factor computed as follows:

Factor=[1865.4686/ (Angle of Repose)^2] – [0.000014*(Angle of Repose)^2] – 0.3819

Material Dumping Angles

Material	Dumping Angle in Degrees
Ashes, dry	33
Ashes, moist	36
Ashes, wet	30
Asphalt	45
Cinders, dry	33
Cinders, moist	34
Cinders, wet	31
Cinders and Clay	30
Clay	45
Coal, hard	24
Coal, soft	30
Coke	23
Concrete	30
Earth, loose	28
Earth, compact	50
Garbage	30
Gravel	40
Ore, dry	30
Ore, damp	37
Rubble	45
Sand, dry	35
Sand, damp	40
Sand, with crushed stone	27
Stone	30
Stone, broken	27
Stone, crushed	30

Rock Bulking Factors

Material	Density In Place	Density After Mined	Percent Expansion
Basalt	3.00	1.72	75 to 80%
Clay	1.86	1.49	20 to 30%
Dolomite	2.56	1.73	50 to 60%
Gneiss	2.69	1.54	75 to 80%
Granite	2.72	1.55	75 to 80%
Gravel, dry	1.80	1.40	20 to 30%
Gravel, wet	2.00	1.60	20 to 30%
Gravel, wet w/clay	1.92	1.28	50 to 60%
Limestone	2.69	1.54	75 to 80%
Quartz	2.64	1.51	75 to 80%
Sand, dry	1.60	1.28	20 to 30%
Sand, wet	1.95	1.56	20 to 30%
Sandstone	2.42	1.38	75 to 80%
Slate	2.80	1.52	85 to 90%
Soil, w/clay	1.76	1.41	20 to 30%

Length Of Belt In a Roll

In order to calculate the number of feet of conveyor belt in a tightly coiled roll, use the following equations:

A = Diameter of coil in inches + Diameter of coil hole in inches

Belt length in feet = A x Number of coils x 0.131

Conveyor Slope Maximums

Material	Maximum Slope Degrees
Cement, loose	22
Coke, screened	18
Coke, breeze	20
Concrete, 6 inch slump	12
Concrete, 4 inch slump	20
Concrete, 2 inch slump	24 to 26
Coal, +4 inch lump, soft	15
Coal, – 4 inch lump, soft	16
Coal, anthracite	16
Coal, unsized	18
Coal, soft, fine	20 to 22
Earth, loose	20
Earth, sluggish	22
Glass batch	21
Gravel, sized, washed	12
Gravel, sized, unwashed	15
Gravel, unsized	18 to 20
Grain, whole	15
Gypsum, powdered	23
Lime, powdered	23
Logs, no bark	10
Ore, +4 inch	18
Ore, – 4 inch	20
Ore, sized	16
Packages, paper wrapped, smooth belt	16
Packages, paper wrapped, ribflex belt	25 to 45
Salt	20
Sand, dry	16
Sand, moist, bank run	20
Sand, foundry	24
Sulphur, powdered	21
Stone, sized, +4 inch	15
Stone, sized, – 4 inch	16
Stone, unsized, +4 inch	16
Stone, unsized, – 4 inch	18
Stone, – 3/8 inch	20
Wood chips	25

Conveyor Capacities

Belt Width Inches	Material Size Inches	Belt Speed Feet/min	Tons/hour capacity @ lbs/cu ft material weight with 22° idlers.
12	2 to 3	200	14 @ 30, 44 @ 100, 70 @ 150
16	3 to 5	300	36 @ 30, 123 @ 100, 183 @ 150
18	4 to 6	300	39 @ 30, 156 @ 100, 231 @ 150
24	6 to 8	300	84 @ 30, 276 @ 100, 414 @ 150
30	7 to 12	350	150 @ 30, 504 @ 100, 756 @ 150
36	8 to 16	350	228 @ 30, 728 @ 100, 1088 @ 150
42	10 to 20	400	340 @ 30, 1128 @ 100, 1692 @ 150
48	12 to 24	400	452 @ 30, 1512 @ 100, 2248 @ 150

Note: For capacities with 35° idlers, multiply 22° capacity by 1.15

Conveyor Horsepower vs. Load

Conv Length Feet	Horsepower Required for <u>Transporting</u> Material on Level Ground at the given Tons/Hour Capacity					
	100	200	400	600	800	1000
25	2.0	2.5	3.5	4.5	5.5	6.5
50	2.4	3.0	4.2	5.4	6.6	7.8
100	3.0	3.8	5.3	6.8	8.3	9.8
200	4.3	5.3	7.5	9.7	11.9	14.1
300	5.6	7.0	9.8	12.6	15.4	18.2
400	6.8	8.5	11.9	15.3	18.7	22.1
500	8.0	10.1	14.3	18.5	22.7	26.9

Conv Lift Feet	<u>Extra</u> Horsepower Required in addition to above HP For <u>Lifting</u> at the given Tons/Hour Capacity					
	100	200	400	600	800	1000
10	1	2	4	6	8	10
20	2	4	8	12	16	20
30	3	6	12	18	24	30
40	4	8	16	24	32	40
50	5	10	20	30	40	50
60	6	12	24	36	48	60
80	8	16	32	48	64	80
100	10	20	40	60	80	100

The above data is for equipment manufactured by *Portec Pioneer Division, Minneapolis, MN 55414.*

Jaw Crusher Hp vs. Tons/Hour

The following data is for *Pioneer, Portec Division Jaw Crushers.*
Contact Pioneer in Minneapolis, MN, for current, exact specs.

Model Size[1]	Horsepower Elec/Diesel	Tons/Hr Capacity @ given Feed Size(in)						
		3/4	1	1-1/4	1-1/2	2	2-1/2	3
1016	15/25	7	10	12	14	19	24	28
1020	20/30	8	12	15	18	24	30	36
1024	25/40	10	15	18	22	29	36	44
1036	40/60	...	22	27	33	44	55	67
1524	40/60	...	...	...	...	36	45	54
1536	75/110	...	...	...	...	54	68	81
1830	60/90	...	...	...	...	...	61	74
2036	100/140	...	...	...	...	...	...	93
2148	125/170	...	...	...	...	...	...	124
2854	150/190	3-1/2 inch feed = 178 TPH						

Model Size[1]	Horsepower Elec/Diesel	Tons/Hr Capacity @ given Feed Size(in)						
		4	5	6	7	8	9	10
1524	40/60	72	...	...	...	...	...	...
1536	75/110	109	136	...	...	...	...	...
1830	60/90	98	123	...	...	...	...	...
2036	100/140	124	156	187	...	...	...	...
2436	100/150	136	171	205	239	273	...	...
2148	125/170	165	207	248	...	...	...	...
2854	150/190	204	256	308	360	410	...	...
3042	150/190	178	223	268	313	357	...	...
3546	200/250	210	275	318	370	423	475	...
4248	250/310	...	315	365	425	485	546	607
4248	250/310	11 inch feed = 668 TPH						
4248	250/310	12 inch feed = 730 TPH						

(1) Model Size values in column 1 describe the dimensions at the top of the jaw opening. The first two digits, e.g. "15" in Model 1524, are the number of inches between the jaw plates. The second two digits, e.g. "24" in Model 1524, are the number of inches between the side plates.

Capacities in the above tables are based on material that weighs 2700 lbs/cu. yard (100 lbs/cu. foot) and the Jaw Crusher has closed side plates.

Money

Currency Exchange Rates September 2007

EXAMPLE: 1 US Dollar = 49.60 Afghanistan Afgani		

Country	Currency	Value	Country	Currency	Value
Afghanistan	Afgani	49.60	Kazakhstan	Tenge	121.31
Algeria	Alg. Dinar	68.04	Kenya	Ken. Shilling	67.15
Argentina	Arg. Peso	3.15	Kiribati	Aus. Dollar	1.15
Australia	Aus. Dollar	1.15	Kuwait	Kuw. Dinar	0.28
Austria*	Euro	0.71	Kyrgyzstan	Som	37.18
Bahamas	Bah. Dollar	1.00	Laos	New Kip	9,612
Bahrain	Bhr. Dinar	0.38	Lebanon	Leb. Pound	1,512
Barbados	Bar. Dollar	2.00	Lithuania	Litas	2.45
Belgium*	Euro	0.71	Malta	Malt. Lira	0.30
Belize	Bel. Dollar	1.97	Mexico	Mex. Peso	10.93
Bermuda	Ber. Dollar	1.00	Morocco	Dirham	8.00
Brazil	Real	1.87	Mozambique	Metical	25.79
Bulgaria	Lev	1.39	Myanmar-Burma	Kyat	6.42
Cameroon	CFA Franc	465.47	Netherlands*	Euro	0.71
Canada	Can. Dollar	1.00	New Zealand	N.Z. Dollar	1.34
Cayman Is.	Cay. Dollar	0.85	Norway	Nor. Krone	5.52
Chad	CFA Franc	465.47	Oman	Om. Rial	0.38
Chile	Chl. Peso	512.85	Pakistan	Pak. Rupee	60.60
China	Yuan-Renminbi	7.51	Panama	Balboa	1.00
Colombia	Col. Peso	2,021	Papua N.G.	Kina	2.89
Costa Rica	Colon	518.54	Paraguay	Guarani	4,980
Cuba	Cub. Peso	1.00	Peru	New Sol	3.11
Cyprus	Cyp. Pound	0.41	Philippines	Phl. Peso	45.16
Czech Rep.	Koruna	19.55	Poland	Zloty	2.67
Denmark	Den. Krone	5.29	Portugal*	Euro	0.71
Dominican R.	Dom. Peso	33.65	Puerto Rico	US Dollar	1.00
Ecuador	Sucre	25,000	Romania	New Leu	2.40
Egypt	Egy. Pound	5.59	Russia	Ruble	25.01
El Salvador	Colon	8.75	Saudi Arabia	Saudi Riyal	3.74
EU*	Euro	0.71	Singapore	Sing. Dollar	1.50
Fiji	Fiji Dollar	1.58	South Africa	Rand	6.97
Finland*	Euro	0.71	South Korea	S.K. Won	921.05
France*	Euro	0.71	Spain*	Euro	0.71
Gambia	Dalasi	21.90	Swaziland	Lilangeni	6.97
Germany*	Euro	0.71	Sweden	Swd. Krona	6.51
Ghana	Cedi	0.94	Switzerland	Sw. Franc	1.17
Greece*	Euro	0.71	Syria	Syr. Pound	51.25
Guatemala	Quetzal	7.71	Taiwan	N.T. Dollar	32.93
Haiti	Gourde	35.65	Thailand	Baht	34.20
Hong Kong	H.K. Dollar	7.78	Tunisia	Tun. Dinar	1.26
Hungary	Forint	177.66	Turkmenistan	Manat	5,200
Iceland	Ice. Krona	62.15	Uganda	Ug. Shilling	1,749
India	Ind. Rupee	39.77	Ukraine	Hryvnia	5.00
Indonesia	Rupiah	9,310	United Kingdom	Pound	0.49
Iran	Ir. Rial	9,125	Uruguay	Uru. Peso	23.13
Iraq(New Iq.	Dinar)	1,234	Vanuatu	Vatu	102.73
Ireland*	Euro	0.71	Venezuela	Bolivar	2,147
Israel	Shekel	4.04	Vietnam	Dong	16,143
Italy*	Euro	0.71	Yemen	Ym. Rial	198.95
Jamaica	Jam. Dollar	69.78	Zambia	Kwacha	3,785
Japan	Yen	114.98	Zimbabwe	Zim. Dollar	30,000

Some exchange rates are very VOLATILE, use these exchange rates only as a general guide. For current rates see the Business/Finance section of most major daily newspapers or on the World Wide Web see www.bloomberg.com, www.xe.com or www.ft.com.

* All countries in the European Union use the Euro. Coins and bank notes of individual countries in the EU were withdrawn on February 28, 2002

Discount Factors / Present Val

Year	Rate of Interest per Year in Percent						
	5	6	7	8	9	10	11
1	0.952	0.943	0.935	0.926	0.917	0.909	0.901
2	0.907	0.890	0.873	0.857	0.842	0.826	0.812
3	0.864	0.840	0.816	0.794	0.772	0.751	0.731
4	0.823	0.792	0.763	0.735	0.708	0.683	0.659
5	0.784	0.747	0.713	0.681	0.650	0.621	0.593
6	0.746	0.705	0.666	0.630	0.596	0.564	0.535
7	0.711	0.665	0.623	0.583	0.547	0.513	0.482
8	0.677	0.627	0.582	0.540	0.502	0.467	0.434
9	0.645	0.592	0.544	0.500	0.460	0.424	0.391
10	0.614	0.558	0.508	0.463	0.422	0.386	0.352
11	0.585	0.527	0.475	0.429	0.388	0.350	0.317
12	0.557	0.497	0.444	0.397	0.356	0.319	0.286
13	0.530	0.469	0.415	0.368	0.326	0.290	0.258
14	0.505	0.442	0.388	0.340	0.299	0.263	0.232
15	0.481	0.417	0.362	0.315	0.275	0.239	0.209
20	0.377	0.312	0.258	0.215	0.178	0.149	0.124

Year	Rate of Interest per Year in Percent						
	12	13	14	15	16	17	18
1	0.893	0.885	0.877	0.870	0.862	0.855	0.847
2	0.797	0.783	0.769	0.756	0.743	0.731	0.718
3	0.712	0.693	0.675	0.658	0.641	0.624	0.609
4	0.636	0.613	0.592	0.572	0.552	0.534	0.516
5	0.567	0.543	0.519	0.497	0.476	0.456	0.437
6	0.507	0.480	0.456	0.432	0.410	0.390	0.370
7	0.452	0.425	0.400	0.376	0.354	0.333	0.314
8	0.404	0.376	0.351	0.327	0.305	0.285	0.266
9	0.361	0.333	0.308	0.284	0.263	0.243	0.225
10	0.322	0.295	0.270	0.247	0.227	0.208	0.191
11	0.287	0.261	0.237	0.215	0.195	0.178	0.162
12	0.257	0.231	0.208	0.187	0.168	0.152	0.137
13	0.229	0.204	0.182	0.163	0.145	0.130	0.116
14	0.205	0.181	0.160	0.141	0.125	0.111	0.099
15	0.183	0.160	0.140	0.123	0.108	0.095	0.084
20	0.104	0.087	0.073	0.061	0.051	0.043	0.037

EXAMPLE:

What is the present value of $100 in 12 years at a 14% discount?

Net Present Value = $100 x 0.208 = $20.80

Simple Interest on $100

| Days | \multicolumn{7}{c}{Rate of Interest in Percent} |
	5	6	7	8	9	10	11
1	0.014	0.016	0.019	0.022	0.025	0.027	0.030
2	0.027	0.033	0.038	0.044	0.049	0.055	0.060
3	0.041	0.049	0.058	0.066	0.074	0.082	0.090
4	0.055	0.066	0.077	0.088	0.099	0.110	0.121
5	0.069	0.082	0.096	0.110	0.123	0.137	0.151
6	0.082	0.099	0.115	0.132	0.148	0.164	0.181
7	0.096	0.115	0.134	0.153	0.173	0.192	0.211
8	0.110	0.132	0.153	0.175	0.197	0.219	0.241
9	0.123	0.148	0.173	0.197	0.222	0.247	0.271
10	0.137	0.164	0.192	0.219	0.247	0.274	0.301
20	0.274	0.329	0.384	0.438	0.493	0.548	0.603
30	0.411	0.493	0.575	0.658	0.740	0.822	0.904
40	0.548	0.658	0.767	0.877	0.986	1.10	1.21
50	0.685	0.822	0.959	1.10	1.23	1.37	1.51
60	0.822	0.986	1.15	1.32	1.48	1.64	1.81
70	0.959	1.15	1.34	1.53	1.73	1.92	2.11
80	1.10	1.32	1.53	1.75	1.97	2.19	2.41
90	1.23	1.48	1.73	1.97	2.22	2.47	2.71
100	1.37	1.64	1.92	2.19	2.47	2.74	3.01
200	2.74	3.29	3.84	4.38	4.93	5.48	6.03

| Days | \multicolumn{7}{c}{Rate of Interest in Percent} |
	12	13	14	15	16	17	18
1	0.033	0.036	0.038	0.041	0.044	0.047	0.049
2	0.066	0.071	0.077	0.082	0.088	0.093	0.099
3	0.099	0.107	0.115	0.123	0.132	0.140	0.148
4	0.132	0.142	0.153	0.164	0.175	0.186	0.197
5	0.164	0.178	0.192	0.205	0.219	0.233	0.247
6	0.197	0.214	0.230	0.247	0.263	0.279	0.296
7	0.230	0.249	0.268	0.288	0.307	0.326	0.345
8	0.263	0.285	0.307	0.329	0.351	0.373	0.395
9	0.296	0.321	0.345	0.370	0.395	0.419	0.444
10	0.329	0.356	0.384	0.411	0.438	0.466	0.493
20	0.658	0.712	0.767	0.822	0.877	0.932	0.986
30	0.986	1.07	1.15	1.23	1.32	1.40	1.48
40	1.32	1.42	1.53	1.64	1.75	1.86	1.97
50	1.64	1.78	1.92	2.05	2.19	2.33	2.47
60	1.97	2.14	2.30	2.47	2.63	2.79	2.96
70	2.30	2.49	2.68	2.88	3.07	3.26	3.45
80	2.63	2.85	3.07	3.29	3.51	3.73	3.95
90	2.96	3.21	3.45	3.70	3.95	4.19	4.44
100	3.29	3.56	3.84	4.11	4.38	4.66	4.93
200	6.58	7.12	7.67	8.22	8.77	9.32	9.86

EXAMPLE: If you put $100 in savings for 30 days at 12% simple interest, how much interest do you earn during that period?
30 days = $0.986 (98.6¢)   130 days = 3.29 + 0.986 = $4.27

Compound Interest

Year	Rate of Interest per Year in Percent						
	5	6	7	8	9	10	11
1	1.05	1.06	1.07	1.08	1.09	1.10	1.11
2	1.10	1.12	1.14	1.17	1.19	1.21	1.23
3	1.16	1.19	1.22	1.26	1.30	1.33	1.37
4	1.22	1.26	1.31	1.36	1.41	1.46	1.52
5	1.28	1.34	1.40	1.47	1.54	1.61	1.68
6	1.34	1.42	1.50	1.59	1.68	1.77	1.86
7	1.41	1.50	1.60	1.71	1.83	1.95	2.07
8	1.48	1.59	1.72	1.86	1.99	2.14	2.30
9	1.55	1.69	1.84	2.00	2.17	2.36	2.55
10	1.63	1.79	1.97	2.16	2.37	2.59	2.83
11	1.71	1.90	2.10	2.33	2.58	2.85	3.14
12	1.80	2.01	2.25	2.52	2.81	3.14	3.49
13	1.89	2.13	2.41	2.72	3.07	3.45	3.87
14	1.98	2.26	2.58	2.94	3.34	3.79	4.29
15	2.08	2.40	2.76	3.17	3.64	4.17	4.77
20	2.65	3.21	3.86	4.66	5.60	6.72	8.03

Year	Rate of Interest per Year in Percent						
	12	13	14	15	16	17	18
1	1.12	1.13	1.14	1.15	1.16	1.17	1.18
2	1.25	1.28	1.30	1.32	1.34	1.37	1.39
3	1.40	1.44	1.48	1.52	1.56	1.60	1.64
4	1.57	1.63	1.69	1.75	1.81	1.87	1.94
5	1.76	1.84	1.93	2.01	2.10	2.19	2.29
6	1.97	2.08	2.20	2.31	2.44	2.56	2.70
7	2.21	2.35	2.51	2.66	2.83	3.00	3.19
8	2.47	2.65	2.86	3.05	3.28	3.51	3.76
9	2.77	3.00	3.26	3.51	3.80	4.10	4.44
10	3.10	3.39	3.71	4.04	4.41	4.80	5.24
11	3.47	3.83	4.24	4.65	5.12	5.62	6.18
12	3.89	4.33	4.83	5.35	5.94	6.57	7.29
13	4.35	4.89	5.50	6.15	6.89	7.69	8.60
14	4.87	5.53	6.27	7.07	7.99	9.00	10.15
15	5.46	6.25	7.15	8.13	9.26	10.52	11.98
20	9.63	11.51	13.77	16.35	19.45	23.07	27.39

EXAMPLE (compounded annually):
If you put $100 in savings for 8 years at 12% compound interest,
how much interest do you earn during that period?

[$100 x 2.47] – $100 = $147 interest

Numbered Days of the Year

Date	#	Date	#	Date	#	Date	#	Date	#
Jan 1	1	Mar 15	74	May 27	147	Aug 8	220	Oct 20	293
Jan 2	2	Mar 16	75	May 28	148	Aug 9	221	Oct 21	294
Jan 3	3	Mar 17	76	May 29	149	Aug 10	222	Oct 22	295
Jan 4	4	Mar 18	77	May 30	150	Aug 11	223	Oct 23	296
Jan 5	5	Mar 19	78	May 31	151	Aug 12	224	Oct 24	297
Jan 6	6	Mar 20	79	Jun 1	152	Aug 13	225	Oct 25	298
Jan 7	7	Mar 21	80	Jun 2	153	Aug 14	226	Oct 26	299
Jan 8	8	Mar 22	81	Jun 3	154	Aug 15	227	Oct 27	300
Jan 9	9	Mar 23	82	Jun 4	155	Aug 16	228	Oct 28	301
Jan 10	10	Mar 24	83	Jun 5	156	Aug 17	229	Oct 29	302
Jan 11	11	Mar 25	84	Jun 6	157	Aug 18	230	Oct 30	303
Jan 12	12	Mar 26	85	Jun 7	158	Aug 19	231	Oct 31	304
Jan 13	13	Mar 27	86	Jun 8	159	Aug 20	232	Nov 1	305
Jan 14	14	Mar 28	87	Jun 9	160	Aug 21	233	Nov 2	306
Jan 15	15	Mar 29	88	Jun 10	161	Aug 22	234	Nov 3	307
Jan 16	16	Mar 30	89	Jun 11	162	Aug 23	235	Nov 4	308
Jan 17	17	Mar 31	90	Jun 12	163	Aug 24	236	Nov 5	309
Jan 18	18	Apr 1	91	Jun 13	164	Aug 25	237	Nov 6	310
Jan 19	19	Apr 2	92	Jun 14	165	Aug 26	238	Nov 7	311
Jan 20	20	Apr 3	93	Jun 15	166	Aug 27	239	Nov 8	312
Jan 21	21	Apr 4	94	Jun 16	167	Aug 28	240	Nov 9	313
Jan 22	22	Apr 5	95	Jun 17	168	Aug 29	241	Nov 10	314
Jan 23	23	Apr 6	96	Jun 18	169	Aug 30	242	Nov 11	315
Jan 24	24	Apr 7	97	Jun 19	170	Aug 31	243	Nov 12	316
Jan 25	25	Apr 8	98	Jun 20	171	Sep 1	244	Nov 13	317
Jan 26	26	Apr 9	99	Jun 21	172	Sep 2	245	Nov 14	318
Jan 27	27	Apr 10	100	Jun 22	173	Sep 3	246	Nov 15	319
Jan 28	28	Apr 11	101	Jun 23	174	Sep 4	247	Nov 16	320
Jan 29	29	Apr 12	102	Jun 24	175	Sep 5	248	Nov 17	321
Jan 30	30	Apr 13	103	Jun 25	176	Sep 6	249	Nov 18	322
Jan 31	31	Apr 14	104	Jun 26	177	Sep 7	250	Nov 19	323
Feb 1	32	Apr 15	105	Jun 27	178	Sep 8	251	Nov 20	324
Feb 2	33	Apr 16	106	Jun 28	179	Sep 9	252	Nov 21	325
Feb 3	34	Apr 17	107	Jun 29	180	Sep 10	253	Nov 22	326
Feb 4	35	Apr 18	108	Jun 30	181	Sep 11	254	Nov 23	327
Feb 5	36	Apr 19	109	Jul 1	182	Sep 12	255	Nov 24	328
Feb 6	37	Apr 20	110	Jul 2	183	Sep 13	256	Nov 25	329
Feb 7	38	Apr 21	111	Jul 3	184	Sep 14	257	Nov 26	330
Feb 8	39	Apr 22	112	Jul 4	185	Sep 15	258	Nov 27	331
Feb 9	40	Apr 23	113	Jul 5	186	Sep 16	259	Nov 28	332
Feb 10	41	Apr 24	114	Jul 6	187	Sep 17	260	Nov 29	333
Feb 11	42	Apr 25	115	Jul 7	188	Sep 18	261	Nov 30	334
Feb 12	43	Apr 26	116	Jul 8	189	Sep 19	262	Dec 1	335
Feb 13	44	Apr 27	117	Jul 9	190	Sep 20	263	Dec 2	336
Feb 14	45	Apr 28	118	Jul 10	191	Sep 21	264	Dec 3	337
Feb 15	46	Apr 29	119	Jul 11	192	Sep 22	265	Dec 4	338
Feb 16	47	Apr 30	120	Jul 12	193	Sep 23	266	Dec 5	339
Feb 17	48	May 1	121	Jul 13	194	Sep 24	267	Dec 6	340
Feb 18	49	May 2	122	Jul 14	195	Sep 25	268	Dec 7	341
Feb 19	50	May 3	123	Jul 15	196	Sep 26	269	Dec 8	342
Feb 20	51	May 4	124	Jul 16	197	Sep 27	270	Dec 9	343
Feb 21	52	May 5	125	Jul 17	198	Sep 28	271	Dec 10	344
Feb 22	53	May 6	126	Jul 18	199	Sep 29	272	Dec 11	345
Feb 23	54	May 7	127	Jul 19	200	Sep 30	273	Dec 12	346
Feb 24	55	May 8	128	Jul 20	201	Oct 1	274	Dec 13	347
Feb 25	56	May 9	129	Jul 21	202	Oct 2	275	Dec 14	348
Feb 26	57	May 10	130	Jul 22	203	Oct 3	276	Dec 15	349
Feb 27	58	May 11	131	Jul 23	204	Oct 4	277	Dec 16	350
Feb 28	59	May 12	132	Jul 24	205	Oct 5	278	Dec 17	351
Mar 1	60	May 13	133	Jul 25	206	Oct 6	279	Dec 18	352
Mar 2	61	May 14	134	Jul 26	207	Oct 7	280	Dec 19	353
Mar 3	62	May 15	135	Jul 27	208	Oct 8	281	Dec 20	354
Mar 4	63	May 16	136	Jul 28	209	Oct 9	282	Dec 21	355
Mar 5	64	May 17	137	Jul 29	210	Oct 10	283	Dec 22	356
Mar 6	65	May 18	138	Jul 30	211	Oct 11	284	Dec 23	357
Mar 7	66	May 19	139	Jul 31	212	Oct 12	285	Dec 24	358
Mar 8	67	May 20	140	Aug 1	213	Oct 13	286	Dec 25	359
Mar 9	68	May 21	141	Aug 2	214	Oct 14	287	Dec 26	360
Mar 10	69	May 22	142	Aug 3	215	Oct 15	288	Dec 27	361
Mar 11	70	May 23	143	Aug 4	216	Oct 16	289	Dec 28	362
Mar 12	71	May 24	144	Aug 5	217	Oct 17	290	Dec 29	363
Mar 13	72	May 25	145	Aug 6	218	Oct 18	291	Dec 30	364
Mar 14	73	May 26	146	Aug 7	219	Oct 19	292	Dec 31	365

Plumbing and Pipe

(See also TOOLS, p. 597 for pipe thread data)

(See also WATER, p. 617 for Friction Loss Values)

Copper Pipe & Tubing

When measuring copper pipe, sweat fittings are measured by their inside diameter (ID) and compression fittings are measured by their outside diameter (OD). Hard temper comes in 20 foot straight lengths and soft temper comes in 20 foot straight lengths or 60 foot coils. Copper tubing is normally designed to conform with ASTM Designation B88. See the code for specific information on each type.

Use 50/50 solid core solder (NOT ROSIN CORE) and a high quality flux when soldering sweat fittings.

TYPES OF COPPER PIPE

Type	Characteristics
DWV	DWV stands for "Drain, Waste and Vent" and is recommended for above ground use only and no pressure applications. Sweat fittings only. Available only in hard type and in sizes from 1–1/4 inch to 6 inch.
K	A thick walled, flexible copper tubing. Much thicker wall than Type L and M and is required for all underground installations. Typical uses include water services, plumbing, heating, steam, gas, oil, oxygen, and other applications where thick walled tubing is required. Can be used with sweat, flared, and compression fittings. Available in hard and soft types.
L	Standard tubing used for interior, above ground plumbing. Uses include heating, air-conditioning, steam, gas and oil and for underground drainage lines. This is a flexible tubing but be very careful not to crimp the line when bending it. Special tools (inexpensive) are readily available to make bending much easier and safer. Although sweat, compression and flare fittings are available, only sweat and flare fittings are legal for gas lines. Available in hard and soft types.
M	Typically used with interior heating and pressure line applications. Wall thickness is slightly less than types K and L. Normally used with sweat fittings. Available in hard and soft types.

Copper Pipe & Tubing

Nominal Size Inches	Actual OD Inches	Type K Wall Th. Inch	Weight Lbs/foot	Type L Wall Th. Inch	Weight Lbs/foot
1/4	0.375	0.035	0.145	0.030	0.126
3/8	0.500	0.049	0.269	0.035	0.198
1/2	0.625	0.049	0.344	0.040	0.285
5/8	0.750	0.049	0.418	0.042	0.362
3/4	0.875	0.065	0.641	0.045	0.455
1	1.125	0.065	0.839	0.050	0.655
1-1/4	1.375	0.065	1.040	0.055	0.884
1-1/2	1.625	0.072	1.360	0.060	1.140
2	2.125	0.083	2.060	0.070	1.750
2-1/2	2.625	0.095	2.930	0.080	2.480
3	3.125	0.109	4.000	0.090	3.330
3-1/2	3.625	0.120	5.120	0.100	4.290
4	4.125	0.134	6.510	0.110	5.380
5	5.125	0.160	9.670	0.125	7.610
6	6.125	0.192	13.90	0.140	10.20
8	8.125	0.271	25.90	0.200	19.30
10	10.125	0.338	40.30	0.250	30.10
12	12.125	0.405	57.80	0.280	40.40

Nominal Size Inches	Actual OD Inches	Type M Wall Th. Inch	Weight Lbs/foot	Type DWV Wall Th. Inch	Weight Lbs/foot
1-1/4	1.375	0.042	0.682	0.040	0.65
1-1/2	1.625	0.049	0.940	0.042	0.81
2	2.125	0.058	1.460	0.042	1.07
2-1/2	2.625	0.065	2.030	...	...
3	3.125	0.072	2.680	0.045	1.69
3-1/2	3.625	0.083	3.580	...	...
4	4.125	0.095	4.660	0.058	2.87
5	5.125	0.109	6.660	0.072	4.43
6	6.125	0.122	8.920	0.083	6.10
8	8.125	0.170	16.50	...	...
10	10.125	0.212	25.60	...	...
12	12.125	0.254	36.70	...	...

"Wall Th." stands for Wall Thickness
"OD" stands for Outside Diameter

Data included in this table is courtesy of *ITT–Grinnell Corporation, Providence, Rhode Island.*

Plastic Pipe

Although there are many plastic pipe types listed below, PVC and ABS are by far the most common types. It is imperative that the correct primers and solvents be used on each type of pipe or the joints will not seal properly and the overall strength will be weakened.

TYPES OF PLASTIC PIPE

Type	Characteristics
PVC	Polyvinyl Chloride, Type 1, Grade 1. This pipe is strong, rigid and resistant to a variety of acids and bases. Some solvents and chlorinated hydro-carbons may damage the pipe. PVC is very common, easy to work with and readily available at most hardware stores. Maximum useable temperature is 140°F (60°C) and pressure ratings start at a minimum of 125 to 200 psi (check for specific ratings on the pipe or ask the seller). PVC can be used with water, gas, and drainage systems but NOT with hot water systems.
ABS	Acrylonitrile Butadiene Styrene, Type 1. This pipe is strong and rigid and resistant to a variety of acids and bases. Some solvents and chlorinated hydro-carbons may damage the pipe. ABS is very common, easy to work with and readily available at most hardware stores. Maximum useable temperature is 160°F (71°C) at low pressures. It is most common as a DWV pipe.
CPVC	Chlorinated polyvinyl chloride. Similar to PVC but designed specifically for piping water at up to 180°F (82°C) (can actually withstand 200°F for a limited time). Pressure rating is 100 psi.
PE	Polyethylene. A flexible pipe for pressurized water systems such as sprinklers. Not for hot water.
PEX	Polyethylene cross-Inked. A flexible pipe for pressurized water systems such as sprinklers.
PB	Polybutylene. A flexible pipe for pressurized water systems both hot and cold. ONLY compression and banded type joints can be used.
Polypropylene	Low pressure, lightweight material that is good up to 180°F (82°C). Highly resistant to acids, bases, and many solvents. Good for laboratory plumbing.
PVDF	Polyvinylidene fluoride. Strong, very tough, and resistant to abrasion, acids, bases, solvents, and much more. Good to 280°F (138°C). Good in lab.
FRP Epoxy	A thermosetting plastic over fiberglass. Very high strength and excellent chemical resistance. Good to 220°F (105°C). Excellent for labs.

Plastic Pipe

Nominal Size Inches	Actual OD Inches	PVC Sched. 40 Wall Th. Inch	Weight Lbs/foot	PVC Sched. 80 Wall Th. Inch	Weight Lbs/foot
1/4	0.540	...	...	0.119	0.10
1/2	0.840	0.109	0.16	0.147	0.21
3/4	1.050	0.113	0.22	0.154	0.28
1	1.315	0.133	0.32	0.179	0.40
1–1/4	1.660	0.140	0.43	0.191	0.57
1–1/2	1.900	0.145	0.52	0.200	0.69
2	2.375	0.154	0.70	0.218	0.95
2–1/2	2.875	0.203	1.10	0.276	1.45
3	3.500	0.216	1.44	0.300	1.94
4	4.500	0.237	2.05	0.337	2.83
6	6.625	0.280	3.61	0.432	5.41
8	8.625	0.322	5.45	0.500	8.22
10	10.750	0.365	7.91	0.593	12.28
12	12.750	0.406	10.35	0.687	17.10

Nominal Size Inches	Actual OD Inches	CPVC Sched. 40 Wall Th. Inch	Weight Lbs/foot	CPVC Sched. 80 Wall Th. Inch	Weight Lbs/foot
1/4	0.540	...	...	0.119	0.12
1/2	0.840	0.109	0.19	0.147	0.24
3/4	1.050	0.113	0.25	0.154	0.33
1	1.315	0.133	0.38	0.179	0.49
1–1/4	1.660	0.140	0.51	0.191	0.67
1–1/2	1.900	0.145	0.61	0.200	0.81
2	2.375	0.154	0.82	0.218	1.09
2–1/2	2.875	0.203	1.29	0.276	1.65
3	3.500	0.216	1.69	0.300	2.21
4	4.500	0.237	2.33	0.337	3.23
6	6.625	0.280	4.10	0.432	6.17
8	8.625	...	...	0.500	9.06

Nominal Size Inches	Actual OD Inches	PVDF Sched. 80 Wall Th. Inch	Weight Lbs/foot	Polypropylene 80 Wall Th. Inch	Weight Lbs/foot
1/2	0.840	0.147	0.24	0.147	0.14
3/4	1.050	0.154	0.33	0.154	0.19
1	1.315	0.179	0.49	0.179	0.27
1–1/4	1.660	0.191	...	0.191	0.38
1–1/2	1.900	0.200	0.81	0.200	0.45
2	2.375	0.218	1.13	0.218	0.62

$$\text{Pipe Schedule Number} = 1000 \times \frac{\text{psi internal pressure}}{\text{psi allowable fiber stress}}$$

Steel Pipe

Nominal Size & OD Inches	Schedule Numbers[1] a – b – c	Wall Thick Inches	Inside Diameter Inches	Pipe Weight Lbs/foot
1/8 0.405	...–...–10S	0.049	0.307	0.186
	40–Std–40S	0.068	0.269	0.245
	80–XS–80S	0.095	0.215	0.315
1/4 0.540	...–...–10S	0.065	0.410	0.330
	40–Std–40S	0.088	0.364	0.425
	80–XS–80S	0.119	0.302	0.535
3/8 0.675	...–...–5S	0.065	0.710	0.538
	...–...–10S	0.065	0.545	0.428
	40–Std–40S	0.091	0.493	0.568
	80–XS–80S	0.126	0.423	0.739
1/2 0.840	...–...–5S	0.065	0.710	0.538
	...–...–10S	0.083	0.674	0.671
	40–Std–40S	0.109	0.622	0.851
	80–XS–80S	0.147	0.546	1.088
	160–...–...	0.187	0.466	1.304
	...–XXS–...	0.294	0.252	1.714
3/4 1.050	...–...–5S	0.065	0.920	0.684
	...–...–10S	0.083	0.884	0.857
	40–Std–40S	0.113	0.824	1.131
	80–XS–80S	0.154	0.742	1.474
	160–...–...	0.218	0.614	1.937
	...–XXS–...	0.308	0.434	2.441
1 1.315	...–...–5S	0.065	1.185	0.868
	...–...–10S	0.109	1.097	1.404
	40–Std–40S	0.133	1.049	1.679
	80–XS–80S	0.179	0.957	2.172
	160–...–...	0.250	0.815	2.844
	...–XXS–...	0.358	0.599	3.659
1–1/4 1.660	...–...–5S	0.065	1.530	1.107
	...–...–10S	0.109	1.442	1.805
	40–Std–40S	0.140	1.380	2.273
	80–XS–80S	0.191	1.278	2.997
	160–...–...	0.250	1.160	3.765
	...–XXS–...	0.382	0.896	5.214
1–1/2 1.900	...–...–5S	0.065	1.770	1.274
	...–...–10S	0.109	1.682	2.085
	40–Std–40S	0.145	1.610	2.718
	80–XS–80S	0.200	1.500	3.631
	160–...–...	0.281	1.338	4.859
	...–XXS–...	0.400	1.100	6.408
	...–...–...	0.525	0.850	7.710
	...–...–...	0.650	0.600	8.678
2 2.375	...–...–5S	0.065	2.245	1.604
	...–...–10S	0.109	2.157	2.638
	40–Std–40S	0.154	2.067	3.653
	80–XS–80S	0.218	1.939	5.022
	160–...–...	0.343	1.689	7.444
	...–XXS–...	0.436	1.503	9.029
	...–...–...	0.562	1.251	10.882
	...–...–...	0.687	1.001	12.385

Steel Pipe

Nominal Size & OD Inches	Schedule Numbers [1] a – b – c	Wall Thick Inches	Inside Diameter Inches	Pipe Weight Lbs/foot
2-1/2 2.875	...–...–5S	0.083	2.709	2.475
	...–...–10S	0.120	2.635	3.531
	40–Std–40S	0.203	2.469	5.793
	80–XS–80S	0.276	2.323	7.661
	160–...–...	0.375	2.125	10.01
	...–XXS–...	0.552	1.771	143.70
	...–...–...	0.675	1.525	15.860
	...–...–...	0.800	1.275	17.729
3 3.500	...–...–5S	0.083	3.334	3.03
	...–...–10S	0.120	3.260	4.33
	40–Std–40S	0.216	3.068	7.58
	80–XS–80S	0.300	2.900	10.25
	160–...–...	0.437	2.626	14.32
	...–XXS–...	0.600	2.300	18.58
	...–...–...	0.725	2.050	21.487
	...–...–...	0.850	1.800	24.057
3-1/2 4.000	...–...–5S	0.083	3.834	3.47
	...–...–10S	0.120	3.760	4.97
	40–Std–40S	0.226	3.548	9.11
	80–XS–80S	0.318	3.364	12.51
	...–XXS–...	0.636	2.728	22.850
4 4.500	...–...–5S	0.083	4.334	3.92
	...–...–10S	0.120	4.260	5.61
	...–...–...	0.188	4.124	8.560
	40–Std–40S	0.237	4.026	10.79
	80–XS–80S	0.337	3.826	14.98
	120–...–...	0.437	3.626	18.96
	...–...–...	0.500	3.500	21.360
	160–...–...	0.531	3.438	22.51
	...–XXS–...	0.674	3.152	27.54
	...–...–...	0.800	2.900	31.613
	...–...–...	0.925	2.650	35.318
5 5.563	...–...–5S	0.109	5.345	6.35
	...–...–10S	0.134	5.295	7.77
	40–Std–40S	0.258	5.047	14.62
	80–XS–80S	0.375	4.813	20.78
	120–...–...	0.500	4.563	27.04
	160–...–...	0.625	4.313	32.96
	...–XXS–...	0.750	4.063	38.55
	...–...–...	0.875	3.813	43.810
	...–...–...	1.000	3.563	47.734
6 6.625	...–...–5S	0.109	6.407	7.59
	...–...–10S	0.134	6.357	9.29
	...–...–...	0.219	6.187	15.020
	40–Std–40S	0.280	6.065	18.97
	80–XS–80S	0.432	5.761	28.57
	120–...–...	0.562	5.501	36.39
	160–...–...	0.718	5.189	45.30
	...–XXS–...	0.864	4.897	53.16
	...–...–...	1.000	4.625	60.076

Steel Pipe

Nominal Size & OD Inches	Schedule Numbers [1] a – b – c	Wall Thick Inches	Inside Diameter Inches	Pipe Weight Lbs/foot
6 / 6.625	...–...–...	1.125	4.375	66.084
	...–...–5S	0.109	8.407	9.91
	...–...–10S	0.148	8.329	13.40
	...–...–...	0.219	8.187	19.640
	20–...–...	0.250	8.125	22.36
	30–...–...	0.277	8.071	24.70
	40–Std–40S	0.322	7.981	28.55
8	60–...–...	0.406	7.813	35.64
8.625	80–XS–80S	0.500	7.625	43.39
	100–...–...	0.593	7.439	50.87
	120–...–...	0.718	7.189	60.63
	140–...–...	0.812	7.001	67.76
	...–XXS–...	0.875	6.875	72.42
	160–...–...	0.906	6.813	74.69
	...–...–...	1.000	6.625	81.437
	...–...–...	1.125	6.375	90.114
	...–...–5S	0.134	10.482	15.15
	...–...–10S	0.165	10.420	18.70
	...–...–...	0.219	10.312	24.63
	20–...–...	0.250	10.250	28.04
	30–...–...	0.307	10.136	34.24
	40–Std–40S	0.365	10.020	40.48
	60–XS–80S	0.500	9.750	54.74
10	80–...–...	0.593	9.564	64.33
10.750	100–...–...	0.718	9.314	76.93
	120–...–...	0.843	9.064	89.20
	...–...–...	0.875	9.000	92.28
	140–...–...	1.000	8.750	104.13
	160–...–...	1.125	8.500	115.65
	...–...–...	1.250	8.250	126.832
	...–...–...	1.500	7.750	148.19
	...–...–5S	0.156	12.438	20.99
	...–...–10S	0.180	12.390	24.20
	20–...–...	0.250	12.250	33.38
	30–...–...	0.330	12.090	43.77
	...–Std–40S	0.375	12.000	49.56
	40–...–...	0.406	11.938	53.53
	...–XS...80S	0.500	11.750	65.42
12	60–...–...	0.562	11.626	73.16
12.750	80–...–...	0.687	11.376	88.51
	...–...–...	0.750	11.250	96.2
	100–...–...	0.843	11.064	107.20
	...–...–...	0.875	11.000	110.9
	120–...–...	1.000	10.750	125.49
	140–...–c	1.125	10.500	139.68
	...–...–...	1.250	10.250	153.6
	160–...–...	1.312	10.126	160.27
	...–...–5S	0.156	13.688	23.0
14	...–...–10S	0.188	13.624	27.7
14.000	...–...–...	0.210	13.580	30.9

Steel Pipe

Nominal Size & OD Inches	Schedule Numbers [1] a – b – c	Wall Thick Inches	Inside Diameter Inches	Pipe Weight Lbs/foot
	...–...–...	0.219	13.562	32.2
	10–...–...	0.250	13.500	36.71
	...–...–...	0.281	13.438	41.2
	20–...–...	0.312	13.376	45.68
	...–...–...	0.344	13.312	50.2
	30–Std–...	0.375	13.250	54.57
	40–...–...	0.437	13.126	63.37
14	...–...–...	0.469	13.062	67.8
14.000	...–XS–...	0.500	13.000	72.09
	60–...–...	0.593	12.814	84.91
	...–XXS–...	0.625	12.750	89.28
	80–...–...	0.750	12.500	106.13
	100–...–...	0.937	12.126	130.73
	120–...–...	1.093	11.814	150.67
	140–...–...	1.250	11.500	170.22
	160–...–...	1.406	11.188	189.12
	...–...–5S	0.165	15.670	28
	...–...–10S	0.188	15.624	32
	10–...–...	0.250	15.500	42.05
	20–...–...	0.312	15.376	52.36
	30–Std–...	0.375	15.250	62.58
16	40–XS–...	0.500	15.000	82.77
16.000	60–...–...	0.656	14.688	107.50
	80–...–...	0.843	14.314	136.46
	100–...–...	1.031	13.938	164.83
	120–...–...	1.218	13.564	192.29
	140–...–...	1.437	13.126	223.64
	160–...–...	1.593	12.814	245.11
	...–...–5S	0.165	17.670	31
	...–...–10S	0.188	17.624	36
	10–...–...	0.250	17.500	47.39
	20–...–...	0.312	17.376	59.03
	...–Std–...	0.375	17.250	70.59
	30–...–...	0.437	17.126	82.06
18	...–XS–...	0.500	17.000	93.45
18.000	40–...–...	0.562	16.876	104.75
	60–...–...	0.750	16.500	138.17
	80–...–...	0.937	16.126	170.75
	100–...–...	1.156	15.688	207.96
	120–...–...	1.375	15.250	244.14
	140–...–...	1.562	14.876	274.23
	160–...–...	1.781	14.438	308.51
	...–...–5S	0.188	19.634	40
	...–...–10S	0.218	19.564	46
	10–...–...	0.250	19.500	52.73
20	20–Std–...	0.375	19.250	78.60
20.000	30–XS–...	0.500	19.000	104.13
	40–...–...	0.593	18.814	122.91
	60–...–...	0.812	18.376	166.40
	...–...–...	0.875	18.250	178.73

Steel Pipe

Nominal Size & OD Inches	Schedule Numbers [1] a – b – c	Wall Thick Inches	Inside Diameter Inches	Pipe Weight Lbs/foot
20 20.000	80–...–...	1.031	17.938	208.87
	100–...–...	1.281	17.438	256.10
	120–...–...	1.500	17.000	296.37
	140–...–...	1.750	16.500	341
	160–...–...	1.968	16.064	379.01
22 22.000	...–...–5S	0.188	21.624	44
	...–...–10S	0.218	21.564	51
	10–...–...	0.250	21.500	58
	20–Std–...	0.375	21.250	87
	30–XS–...	0.500	21.000	115
	...–...–...	0.625	20.750	143
	...–...–...	0.750	20.500	170
	60–...–...	0.875	20.250	197
	80–...–...	1.125	19.750	251
	100–...–...	1.375	19.250	303
	120–...–...	1.625	18.750	354
	140–...–...	1.875	18.250	403
	160–...–...	2.125	17.750	451
24 24.000	...–...–5S	0.218	23.564	55
	10–...–...	0.250	23.500	63.41
	20–Std–...	0.375	23.250	94.62
	...–XS–...	0.500	23.000	125.49
	30–...–...	0.562	22.876	140.80
	...–...–...	0.625	22.750	156.03
	40–...–...	0.687	22.626	171.17
	...–...–...	0.750	22.500	186.24
	...–...–...	0.875	22.250	216
	60–...–...	0.968	22.064	238.11
	80–...–...	1.218	21.564	296.36
	100–...–...	1.531	20.938	367.40
	120–...–...	1.812	20.376	429.39
	140–...–...	2.062	19.876	483.13
	160–...–...	2.343	19.314	541.94
26 26.000	...–...–...	0.250	25.500	67
	10–...–...	0.312	25.376	86
	...–Std–...	0.375	25.250	103
	20–XS–...	0.500	25.000	136
	...–...–...	0.625	24.750	169
	...–...–...	0.750	24.500	202
	...–...–...	0.875	24.250	235
	...–...–...	1.000	24.000	267
	...–...–...	1.125	23.750	299
28 28.000	...–...–...	0.250	27.500	74
	10–...–...	0.312	27.376	92
	...–Std–...	0.375	27.250	111
	20–XS–...	0.500	27.000	147
	30–...–...	0.625	26.750	183
	...–...–...	0.750	26.500	218
	...–...–...	0.875	26.250	253
	...–...–...	1.000	26.000	288

Steel Pipe

Nominal Size & OD Inches	Schedule Numbers [1] a – b – c	Wall Thick Inches	Inside Diameter Inches	Pipe Weight Lbs/foot
	...–...–...	1.125	25.750	323
	...–...–5S	0.250	29.500	79
	10–...–10S	0.312	29.376	99
	...–Std–...	0.375	29.250	119
30	20–XS–...	0.500	29.000	158
30.000	30–...–...	0.625	28.750	196
	40–...–...	0.750	28.500	234
	...–...–...	0.875	28.250	272
	...–...–...	1.000	28.000	310
	...–...–...	1.125	27.750	347
	...–...–...	0.250	31.500	85
	10–...–...	0.312	31.376	106
	...–Std–...	0.375	31.250	127
	20–XS–...	0.500	31.000	168
32	30–...–...	0.625	30.750	209
32.000	40–...–...	0.688	30.624	230
	...–...–...	0.750	30.500	250
	...–...–...	0.875	30.250	291
	...–...–...	1.000	30.000	331
	...–...–...	1.125	29.750	371
	...–...–...	0.250	33.500	90
	10–...–...	0.312	33.376	112
	...–Std–...	0.375	33.250	135
	20–XS–...	0.500	33.000	179
34	30–...–...	0.625	32.750	223
34.000	40–...–...	0.688	32.624	245
	...–...–...	0.750	32.500	266
	...–...–...	0.875	32.250	310
	...–...–...	1.000	32.000	353
	...–...–...	1.125	31.750	395
	...–...–...	0.250	35.500	96
	10–...–...	0.312	35.376	119
	...–Std–...	0.375	35.250	143
36	20–XS–...	0.500	35.000	190
36.000	30–...–...	0.625	34.750	236
	40–...–...	0.750	34.500	282
	...–...–...	0.875	34.250	328
	...–...–...	1.000	34.000	374
	...–...–...	1.125	33.750	419
	...–...–...	0.250	41.500	112
	...–Std–...	0.375	41.250	167
	20–XS–...	0.500	41.000	222
42	30–...–...	0.625	40.750	276
42.000	40–...–...	0.750	40.500	330
	...–...–...	1.000	40.000	438
	...–...–...	1.250	39.500	544
	...–...–...	1.500	39.000	649

Steel Pipe

(1) In the preceding tables, column 2 contains information on the schedules of various types of pipe. Specifically, these types of pipe for the a–b–c spec are as follows:

    a – ANSI B36.10, Steel Pipe Schedule numbers
    b – ANSI B36.10, Steel Pipe nominal wall thickness
    c – ANSI B36.19, Stainless Steel Schedule numbers

(2) Std = Standard XS = Extra strong XXS = Double Extra Strong

STEEL PIPE FORMULAS

Additional values pertaining to each steel pipe size can be calculated with the following formulas:

    d = Inside diameter of pipe in inches
    D = Outside diameter of pipe in inches
    T = Thickness of pipe wall in inches
    x = multiply

Weight of pipe in pounds per foot = $10.6802 \times T \times (D - T)$

Outside surface area in sq feet per foot = $0.2618 \times D$

Inside surface area in sq feet per foot = $0.2618 \times d$

Inside area of pipe in square inches = $0.785 \times d^2$

Total area of metal in square inches = $0.785 \times (D^2 - d^2)$

Moment of Inertia in inches^4 = $0.0491 \times (D^4 - d^4)$

Radius of Gyration in inches = $0.25 \times \sqrt{D^2 + d^2}$

Section Modulus in inches^3 = $(0.0982 \times (D^4 - d^4)) / D$

Weight of water in a pipe in pounds = $0.3405 \times d^2$

Pressure Ratings of Standard Schedule 40 Steel Pipe

1/8 to 1 inch continuous weld or seamless = 700 psi
1–1/4 to 3 inch continuous weld = 800 psi
3–1/2 to 4 inch continuous weld = 1200 psi
2 to 12 inch electric weld = 1000 to 1300 psi
1–1/4 to 3 inch seamless = 1000 psi
3 to 12 inch seamless = 1000 to 1300 psi

The basic steel data and formulas listed above are courtesy of *ITT–Grinnell Corporation, Providence, Rhode Island.*

Rope, Cable & Chain

Cable Clips for Wire Rope

U-Bolt Clips

Wire Rope & Clip Size	U-Bolt Diam.	Number of Clips	Clip Spacing	Rope Turn Back	Bolt Torque	Approx. Weight
inch	inch		inch	inch	ft-lbf	lbm
1/8	7/32	2	1-5/8	3-1/4	4.5	0.05
3/16	1/4	2	2	3-3/4	7.5	0.08
1/4	5/16	2	2-3/8	4-3/4	15	0.17
5/16	3/8	2	2-5/8	5-1/4	30	0.30
3/8	7/16	2	3-1/4	6-1/2	45	0.41
7/16	1/2	2	3-1/2	7	65	0.65
1/2	1/2	3	3-3/4	11-1/2	65	0.75
9/16	9/16	3	4	12	95	1.00
5/8	5/8	3	4	12	95	1.00
3/4	5/8	4	4-1/2	18	130	1.40
7/8	3/4	4	5-1/4	19	225	2.40
1	3/4	5	6	26	225	2.50
1-1/8	3/4	6	6-3/4	34	225	3.00
1-1/4	7/8	7	7-1/2	44	360	4.50
1-3/8	7/8	7	8-1/4	44	360	5.20
1-1/2	7/8	8	9	54	360	5.90
1-5/8	1	8	9-3/4	58	43s0	7.30
1-3/4	1-1/8	8	10-1/2	61	590	9.80
2	1-1/4	8	12	71	750	13.40
2-1/4	1-1/4	8	13-1/2	73	750	15.70
2-1/2	1-1/4	9	15	84	750	17.90
2-3/4	1-1/4	10	19	100	750	23.00
3	1-1/2	10	21	106	1,200	31.00
3-1/2	1-1/2	12	35	149	1,200	40.00

Notes:
(1) Wire rope clips are about 80% efficient.
(2) The correct usage of wire rope clips is illustrated on the next page.
(3) References: Similar tables can be found in the following sources:

General Purpose Catalog, Bethlehem Wire Rope, Williamsport Wirerope Works, Inc, Williamsport, PA, 2000 (see www.wwwrope.com)
Wire Rope Users Manual, Third Edition, Wire Rope Technical Board, 1993. Crosby Clips, The Crosby Group, Inc, Tulsa, OK (see www.thecrosbygroup.com)
Materials Handling Handbook, Second Edition, John Wiley & Sons, 1985. CooperTools Materials Handling Products Catalog, CooperTools, Apex, NC, 1995.

Twin-base Clips (Double-saddle, Chair, or Fist Grip Clips)

Wire Rope & Clip Size	Nut Size or Stud Diam.	Number of Clips	Clip Spacing	Rope Turn Back	Bolt Torque	Approx. Weight
inch	inch		inch	inch	ft-lbf	lbm
3/16	3/8	2	1-7/8	4	30	0.23
1/4	3/8	2	1-7/8	4	30	0.23
5/16	3/8	2	2-1/8	5	30	0.28
3/8	7/16	2	2-1/4	5-1/4	45	0.40
7/16	1/2	2	2-5/8	6-1/2	65	0.62
1/2	1/2	3	3	11	65	0.62
9/16	5/8	3	3-3/8	12-3/4	130	1.03
5/8	5/8	3	3-3/4	13-1/2	130	1.03
3/4	3/4	3	4-1/2	16	225	1.75
7/8	3/4	4	5-1/4	26	225	2.25
1	3/4	5	6	37	225	3.00
1-1/8	7/8	5	6-3/4	41	360	4.00
1-1/4	7/8	6	7-1/2	55	360	4.00
1-3/8	1	6	8-1/4	62	500	7.00
1-1/2	1	7	9	78	500	7.00

When placing cable clamps on the wire, the U–bolt side of the clip MUST be placed on the short, turn–back side while the saddle goes on the long side (the "live" end). Torque the nuts down to the specified torque for the particular U–bolt diameter, place a load on the wire, and then re-torque the clamps.

U-bolt Clip

Correct Attachment

Incorrect Attachment

Incorrect Attachment

Twin-base Clip

Chain - Strength and Weight

Chain Size or Trade Size		Material Diameter		Strength		Weight	
Fractional inch	mm	inch	mm	Working Load			
				lbf	kN	lbm/ft	kg/m
Grade 100 Steel Chain (Alloy Steel Heat Treated)							
7/32	5.5	0.217	5.5	2,700	12.0	0.32	0.47
9/32	7	0.276	7	4,300	19.1	0.74	1.10
5/16	8.0	0.315	8.0	5,700	25.4	0.89	1.33
3/8	10	0.394	10	8,800	39.1	1.48	2.20
1/2	13	0.512	13	15,000	66.7	2.50	3.72
5/8	16	0.630	16	22,600	101	3.79	5.64
3/4	20	0.787	20	35,300	157	5.98	8.90
7/8	22	0.866	22	42,700	190	7.05	10.49
Grade 80 Steel Chain (Alloy Steel Heated Treated)							
7/32	5.5	0.217	5.5	2,100	9.34	0.43	0.64
9/32	7	0.276	7	3,500	15.6	0.70	1.04
5/16	8.0	0.315	8.0	5,100	22.7	0.92	1.37
3/8	10	0.394	10	7,100	31.6	1.42	2.11
1/2	13	0.512	13	12,000	53.4	2.44	3.63
5/8	16	0.630	16	18,100	80.5	3.56	5.30
3/4	20	0.787	20	28,300	126	5.62	8.36
7/8	22	0.866	22	34,200	152	7.50	11.16
1	26	1.024	26	47,700	212	9.65	14.36
1-1/4	32	1.260	32	72,300	322	15.25	22.69
1-1/2	38	1.500	38	80,000	356	21.40	31.85
Grade 70 Steel Chain (Transport Chain) (Carbon Steel Heat Treated)							
1/4	7	0.31	8	3,150	14.0	0.94	1.40
5/16	8	0.34	9	4,700	20.9	1.11	1.65
3/8	10	0.39	10	6,600	29.4	1.42	2.11
7/16	12	0.47	12	8,750	38.9	2.12	3.15
1/2	13	0.51	13	11,300	50.3	2.38	3.54
Grades 40 & 43 Steel Chain (High Test Chain) (Carbon Steel)							
1/4	7	0.28	7	2,600	11.6	0.68	1.01
5/16	9	0.34	9	3,900	17.3	1.06	1.58
3/8	10	0.39	10	5,400	24.0	1.53	2.27
7/16	12	0.47	12	7,200	32.0	2.11	3.14
1/2	13	0.51	13	9,200	40.9	2.47	3.68
5/8	17	0.66	17	11,500	51.2	3.69	5.49
3/4	20	0.78	20	16,200	72.1	5.67	8.43
Grade 30 Steel Chain (Proof Coil Chain) (Low Carbon Steel)							
1/8	4	0.16	4	375	1.67	0.21	0.31
3/16	6	0.22	6	800	3.56	0.38	0.57
1/4	7	0.28	7	1,300	5.78	0.64	0.95
5/16	8	0.32	8	1,900	8.45	0.91	1.35
7/16	12	0.47	12	3,500	15.6	2.10	3.13
1/2	13	0.51	13	4,500	20.0	2.51	3.74
3/8	10	0.39	10	2,650	11.8	1.37	2.03

Chain Size or Trade Size		Material Diameter		Strength Working Load		Weight	
fractional inch	mm	inch	mm	lbf	kN	lbm/ft	kg/m
Grade 30 Steel Chain (Proof Coil Chain) (Low Carbon Steel)							
5/8	17	0.66	17	6,900	30.7	3.86	5.74
3/4	20	0.78	20	10,600	47.2	5.44	8.10
7/8	23	0.91	23	12,800	56.9	7.48	11.12
1	26	1.02	26	17,900	79.6	10.25	15.25
Stainless Steel Chain							
1/8	4	0.16	4	410	1.82	0.21	0.31
7/32	5	0.22	5	1,200	5.34	0.41	0.61
9/32	7	0.28	7	2,000	8.90	0.75	1.12
5/16	8	0.31	8	2,400	10.7	0.95	1.41
3/8	10	0.38	10	3,550	15.8	1.38	2.05
1/2	13	0.50	13	6,500	28.9	2.45	3.65
Aluminum Chain							
17/64	7	0.26	7	550	2.45	0.19	0.28
5/16	9	0.34	9	850	3.78	0.36	0.54
3/8	10	0.41	10	1,200	5.34	0.54	0.80
Straight Link Machine Chain (Low Carbon Steel)							
4	3	0.12	3	215	0.96	0.11	0.16
3	3	0.14	3	270	1.20	0.15	0.22
2	4	0.15	4	325	1.45	0.19	0.28
1	4	0.16	4	390	1.73	0.23	0.34
1/0	4	0.18	4	465	2.07	0.27	0.40
2/0	5	0.19	5	545	2.42	0.33	0.49
3/0	5	0.21	5	635	2.82	0.37	0.55
4/0	6	0.23	6	700	3.11	0.44	0.65
5/0	6	0.25	6	925	4.11	0.53	0.79
Twisted Link Machine Chain (Low Carbon Steel)							
4	3	0.12	3	205	0.91	0.13	0.19
3	3	0.14	3	255	1.13	0.16	0.24
2	4	0.15	4	310	1.38	0.20	0.30
1	4	0.16	4	370	1.65	0.25	0.37
1/0	4	0.18	4	440	1.96	0.29	0.43
2/0	5	0.19	5	520	2.31	0.34	0.51
3/0	5	0.21	5	605	2.69	0.36	0.54
4/0	6	0.23	6	670	2.98	0.45	0.67
5/0	6	0.25	6	880	3.91	0.56	0.83
Straight Link Coil Chain (Low Carbon Steel)							
4	3	0.12	3	205	0.91	0.10	0.15
3	3	0.14	3	255	1.13	0.13	0.19
2	4	0.15	4	310	1.38	0.15	0.22
1	4	0.16	4	370	1.65	0.19	0.28
1/0	4	0.18	4	440	1.96	0.22	0.33
2/0	5	0.19	5	520	2.31	0.27	0.40

Chain Size or Trade Size		Material Diameter		Strength		Weight	
fractional				Working Load			
inch	mm	inch	mm	lbf	kN	lbm/ft	kg/m
Straight Link Coil Chain (Low Carbon Steel) (cont.)							
3/0	5	0.21	5	605	2.69	0.31	0.46
4/0	6	0.23	6	670	2.98	0.35	0.52
5/0	6	0.25	6	880	3.91	0.46	0.68
Twisted Link Coil Chain (Low Carbon Steel)							
4	3	0.12	3	195	0.87	0.10	0.15
3	3	0.14	3	240	1.07	0.13	0.19
2	4	0.15	4	295	1.31	0.16	0.24
1	4	0.16	4	350	1.56	0.20	0.30
1/0	4	0.18	4	415	1.85	0.23	0.34
2/0	5	0.19	5	495	2.20	0.28	0.42
3/0	5	0.21	5	575	2.56	0.33	0.49
4/0	6	0.23	6	635	2.82	0.37	0.55
5/0	6	0.25	6	835	3.71	0.49	0.73
Passing Link Chain (Low Carbon Steel)							
2/0	5	0.19	5	450	2.00	0.32	0.48
4/0	6	0.22	6	600	2.67	0.43	0.64
End Welded Sash Chain (Low Carbon Steel)							
14	2	0.08	2	75	0.33	0.04	0.07
Handy Link Utility Chain (Low Carbon Steel)							
135	3	0.14	3	255	1.13	0.10	0.15
Lock Link, Single Loop Chain (Low Carbon Steel)							
2	2	0.09	2	155	0.69	0.09	0.13
1/0	3	0.12	3	265	1.18	0.16	0.24
2/0	3	0.14	3	340	1.51	0.23	0.34
3/0	4	0.15	4	405	1.80	0.26	0.39
4/0	4	0.16	4	485	2.16	0.29	0.43
5/0	4	0.18	4	580	2.58	0.34	0.51
Double Loop Chain (Inco or Tenso Chain) (Low Carbon Steel)							
5	2	0.06	2	55	0.24	0.04	0.06
4	2	0.07	2	70	0.31	0.05	0.07
3	2	0.08	2	90	0.40	0.06	0.09
2	2	0.09	2	115	0.51	0.08	0.12
1	3	0.11	3	155	0.69	0.10	0.15
1/0	3	0.12	3	200	0.89	0.13	0.19
2/0	3	0.14	3	255	1.13	0.16	0.24
3/0	4	0.15	4	305	1.36	0.20	0.30
4/0	4	0.16	4	365	1.62	0.25	0.37
8/0	6	0.23	6	705	3.14	0.51	0.76
Single Jack Chain (Low Carbon Steel or Brass)							
20	1	0.03	1	3	0.013	0.01	0.01
18	1	0.05	1	5	0.022	0.02	0.03
16	2	0.06	2	10	0.044	0.03	0.04
14	2	0.08	2	16	0.071	0.04	0.06

Chain Size or Trade Size		Material Diameter		Strength		Weight	
fractional inch	mm	inch	mm	Working Load			
				lbf	kN	lbm/ft	kg/m
Single Jack Chain (Low Carbon Steel or Brass) (cont.)							
12	3	0.11	3	29	0.13	0.09	0.13
10	3	0.14	3	43	0.19	0.14	0.21
8	4	0.16	4	60	0.27	0.21	0.31
6	5	0.19	5	80	0.36	0.30	0.45
Double Jack Chain (Low Carbon Steel or Brass)							
16	2	0.06	2	11	0.049	0.04	0.05
Sash Chain (Low Carbon Steel or Stainless Steel)							
8	1	0.04	1	75	0.334	0.04	0.06
25	1	0.04	1	94	0.418	0.05	0.07
30	1	0.03	1	81	0.360	0.05	0.07
35	1	0.04	1	106	0.472	0.06	0.09
40	1	0.04	1	131	0.58	0.07	0.10
45	1	0.05	1	175	0.78	0.09	0.13
50	2	0.06	2	225	1.00	0.11	0.16
Sash Chain (Bronze)							
8	1	0.04	1	68	0.302	0.04	0.06
25	1	0.04	1	80	0.356	0.05	0.07
30	1	0.03	1	75	0.334	0.05	0.07
35	1	0.04	1	100	0.445	0.06	0.09
40	1	0.04	1	125	0.56	0.07	0.10
45	1	0.05	1	163	0.73	0.09	0.13
50	2	0.06	2	210	0.93	0.11	0.16
Safety Chain (Plumber's Chain) (Brass)							
2/0	1	0.02	1	23	0.102	0.02	0.02
1/0	1	0.02	1	35	0.156	0.02	0.03
1	1	0.03	1	45	0.200	0.04	0.05
2	1	0.03	1	50	0.222	0.04	0.05

Notes:

(1) Abbreviations used: lbf = pound-force, lbm/ft = pound-mass/foot, kg/m = kilogram/meter, kN = kilonewton, mm = millimeter
(2) Conversions: 2,000 pounds-force = 1 short ton-force and 1 short ton-force = 0.90718474 metric ton-force.
(3) Only Grade 100 and Grade 80 Alloy Steel Chain should be used for overhead lifting.
(4) References: Similar tables may be found in:

ASTM A 391/A 391M - 98, Grade 80 Alloy Steel Chain, American Society For Testing And Materials, West Conshohocken, PA, 1998.
ASTM A 973M A 973M - 00, Grade 100 Alloy Steel Chain, American Society For Testing And Materials, West Conshohocken, PA, 2000.
Materials Handling Products Catalog, CooperTools, Apex, NC, 1995.
Acco Chain And Accessories, Acco Chain & Lifting Products Division, York, PA, 1996.

Feet of Wire Rope on a Drum or Reel

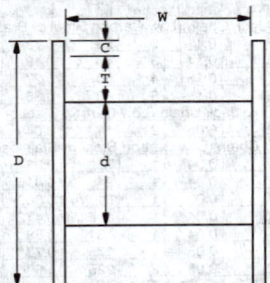

Values in the table can be used in the equation:
L = (T + d) x T x W x K
Where:
L = length of wire rope (feet)
T = thickness of wire rope on drum or reel (inches), T = ½(D - d) - C
W = width of drum or reel (inches)
d = diameter of drum or reel barrel (inches)
K = constant = 0.2618/wire rope diameter squared
D = diameter of drum or reel flange (inches)
C = clearance (inches)

Wire Rope Diameter		Value of K For wire rope Manufactured		Wire Rope Diameter		Value of K For wire rope Manufactured	
Fractional inch	inch	After 1993	Before 1993	Fractional inch	inch	After 1993	Before 1993
1/16	0.0625	57.5	29.8	13/16	0.8125	0.360	0.354
3/32	0.0938	25.5	16.8	7/8	0.8750	0.310	0.308
1/8	0.1250	14.4	10.7	1	1.0000	0.237	0.239
5/32	0.1563	9.37	7.45	1-1/8	1.1250	0.188	0.191
3/16	0.1875	6.50	5.47	1-1/4	1.2500	0.152	0.152
7/32	0.2188	4.87	4.19	1-3/8	1.3750	0.126	0.127
1/4	0.2500	3.73	3.31	1-1/2	1.5000	0.106	0.107
5/16	0.3125	2.39	2.22	1-5/8	1.6250	0.0899	0.0886
3/8	0.3750	1.69	1.59	1-3/4	1.7500	0.0775	0.0770
7/16	0.4375	1.24	1.19	1-7/8	1.8750	0.0675	0.0675
1/2	0.5000	0.950	0.928	2	2.0000	0.0594	0.0597
9/16	0.5625	0.750	0.743	2-1/8	2.1250	0.0526	0.0532
5/8	0.6250	0.608	0.608	2-1/4	2.2500	0.0469	0.0477
11/16	0.6875	0.502	0.507	2-3/8	2.3750	0.0421	0.0419
3/4	0.7500	0.422	0.429	2-1/2	2.5000	0.0380	0.0380

NOTES:

(1) Values of K are based on the maximum allowable oversize for wire rope. Prior to 1993 oversize was specified as a fixed fraction of an inch, such as +1/32" for wire rope smaller than 3/4" diameter.

In 1993 the oversize specifications were changed to percentages of the wire rope diameter, such as +8% for wire rope 1/8" and smaller.

(2) Clearance should be about 2 inches unless wire rope end fittings require more space.

(3) Equation is based on uniform wire rope winding on the drum or reel. It will not give correct lengths if the winding is non-uniform.

(4) Values calculated using the above method are approximate.

(5) References: Similar tables can be found in:

Wire Rope Users Manual, Third Edition, Wire Rope Technical Board, 1993.

Riggers Bible, R.P. Leach, Moore Printing, 1976.

Load Capacity Loss due to Line Angle

Line angle with load degrees		Load Loss Factor
α	β	K
0	90	1.0000
5	85	0.9962
10	80	0.9848
15	75	0.9659
20	70	0.9397
25	65	0.9063
30	60	0.8660
35	55	0.8192
40	50	0.7660
45	45	0.7071
50	40	0.6428
55	35	0.5736
60	30	0.5000
65	25	0.4226
70	20	0.3420
75	15	0.2588
80	10	0.1736
85	5	0.0872

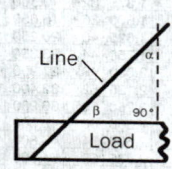

Notes:

(1) Tension load in a line (cable, rope, sling or wire rope) increases by the Tension Load Factor, K, as the Line Angle with the horizontal (β) decreases or with the vertical (α) increases.

(2) Based on the equation
$$K = [\, 1/\sin\beta \,] \text{ or } K = [\, 1/\cos\alpha \,]$$
$$\alpha + \beta = 90°$$

(3) Tension Load on Line = $K \times [\text{Load}/2]$

(4) Example:
Tension Load = 2000# $\alpha = 30°$ $\beta = 60°$
K = 1.155
Tension Load = 1.155 x (2000# / 2)
Tension Load = 1.155 x 1000# = 1,155#

Synthetic and Natural Fiber Rope

Manila Rope, 3-Strand

Rope Diameter		Minimum Breaking Strength		Safe Load FS = 12		Weight	
inch	mm	lbf	kN	lbf	kN	lbm/ft	kg/m
3/16	0.188 5	405	1.80	33.8	0.150	0.014	0.020
1/4	0.250 6	540	2.40	45.0	0.200	0.018	0.027
5/16	0.313 8	900	4.00	75.0	0.334	0.026	0.039
3/8	0.375 10	1,215	5.40	101	0.450	0.038	0.056
7/16	0.438 11	1,575	7.01	131	0.584	0.049	0.072
1/2	0.500 12	2,385	10.6	199	0.884	0.070	0.104
9/16	0.563 14	3,105	13.8	259	1.15	0.096	0.143
5/8	0.625 16	3,960	17.6	330	1.47	0.127	0.189
3/4	0.750 18	4,860	21.6	405	1.80	0.159	0.237
13/16	0.813 20	5,850	26.0	488	2.17	0.186	0.277
7/8	0.875 22	6,930	30.8	578	2.57	0.214	0.318
1	1.000 24	8,100	36.0	675	3.00	0.257	0.382
1-1/16	1.063 26	9,450	42.0	788	3.50	0.298	0.443
1-1/8	1.125 28	10,800	48.0	900	4.00	0.343	0.510
1-1/4	1.250 30	12,150	54.0	1,010	4.49	0.397	0.591
1-3/8	1.375 32	13,500	60.1	1,130	5.03	0.456	0.679
1-1/2	1.500 36	16,650	74.1	1,390	6.18	0.570	0.848
1-5/8	1.625 40	20,250	90.1	1,690	7.52	0.711	1.06
1-3/4	1.750 42	23,850	110	1,990	8.85	0.850	1.26
2	2.000 48	27,900	120	2,330	10.4	1.02	1.52
2-1/8	2.125 52	32,400	140	2,700	12.0	1.20	1.79
2-1/4	2.250 56	36,900	160	3,080	13.7	1.39	2.07
2-1/2	2.500 60	42,300	190	3,530	15.7	1.64	2.44
2-5/8	2.625 64	46,800	210	3,900	17.3	1.82	2.71
2-7/8	2.875 68	54,900	240	4,580	20.4	2.15	3.20
3	3.000 72	57,500	260	4,790	21.3	2.30	3.42
3-5/16	3.313 80	69,500	310	5,790	25.8	2.84	4.23
3-5/8	3.625 88	81,900	360	6,830	30.4	3.49	5.19
4	4.000 96	94,500	420	7,880	35.1	4.14	6.16

Nylon Rope, 3-Strand and 8-Strand

Rope Diameter		Minimum Breaking Strength		Safe Load FS = 12		Weight	
inch	mm	lbf	kN	lbf	kN	lbm/ft	kg/m
3/16	0.19 5	880	3.91	73.3	0.326	0.009	0.013
1/4	0.25 6	1,486	6.61	124	0.551	0.016	0.023
5/16	0.31 8	2,295	10.2	191	0.851	0.025	0.036
3/8	0.38 10	3,240	14.4	270	1.20	0.036	0.053

Nylon Rope, 3-Strand and 8-Strand (cont.)

Rope Diameter			Strength				Weight	
			Minimum Breaking Strength		Safe Load FS = 12			
inch		mm	lbf	kN	lbf	kN	lbm/ft	kg/m
7/16	0.44	11	4,320	19.2	360	1.60	0.048	0.071
1/2	0.50	12	5,670	25.2	473	2.10	0.063	0.094
9/16	0.56	14	7,200	32.0	600	2.67	0.080	0.119
5/8	0.63	16	8,910	39.6	743	3.30	0.099	0.147
3/4	0.75	18	12,780	56.8	1,070	4.76	0.143	0.213
7/8	0.88	22	17,280	76.9	1,440	6.41	0.195	0.290
1	1.00	24	22,230	98.9	1,850	8.23	0.253	0.377
1-1/16	1.06	26	25,200	112	2,100	9.34	0.287	0.427
1-1/8	1.13	28	28,260	126	2,360	10.5	0.322	0.479
1-1/4	1.25	30	34,830	155	2,900	12.9	0.397	0.591
1-5/16	1.31	32	38,250	170	3,190	14.2	0.437	0.650
1-1/2	1.50	36	48,600	216	4,050	18.0	0.570	0.848
1-5/8	1.63	40	57,375	255	4,780	21.3	0.673	1.00
1-3/4	1.75	44	66,150	294	5,510	24.5	0.780	1.16
2	2.00	48	84,600	376	7,050	31.4	1.00	1.49
2-1/8	2.13	52	95,400	424	7,950	35.4	1.13	1.68
2-1/4	2.25	56	107,100	476	8,930	39.7	1.27	1.89
2-1/2	2.50	60	131,400	584	11,000	48.9	1.57	2.34
2-5/8	2.63	64	144,000	641	12,000	53.4	1.73	2.57
2-3/4	2.75	68	171,000	761	14,300	63.6	2.08	3.10
3	3.00	72	185,400	825	15,500	68.9	2.26	3.36
3-1/4	3.25	80	224,100	1,000	18,700	83.2	2.75	4.09
3-1/2	3.50	88	267,300	1,190	22,300	99.2	3.29	4.90
4	4.00	96	324,000	1,440	27,000	120	4.00	5.95
4-1/4	4.25	104	369,000	1,640	30,800	137	4.60	6.85
4-1/2	4.50	112	418,500	1,860	34,900	155	5.25	7.81
5	5.00	120	480,600	2,140	40,100	178	6.10	9.08
5-5/16	5.31	128	532,800	2,370	44,400	198	6.85	10.2
5-5/8	5.63	136	589,500	2,620	49,100	218	7.67	11.4
6	6.00	144	660,600	2,940	55,100	245	8.70	12.9

Polyester Rope, 3-Strand and 8-Strand

Rope Diameter			Strength				Weight	
			Minimum Breaking Strength		Safe Load FS = 12			
inch		mm	lbf	kN	lbf	kN	lbm/ft	kg/m
3/16	0.19	5	765	3.40	63.8	0.284	0.011	0.016
1/4	0.25	6	1,315	5.85	110	0.487	0.020	0.029
5/16	0.31	8	2,050	9.1	171	0.760	0.031	0.045
3/8	0.38	10	2,900	12.9	242	1.07	0.044	0.065
7/16	0.44	11	3,915	17.4	326	1.45	0.059	0.088

Polyester Rope, 3-Strand and 8-Strand (cont.)

Rope Diameter			Strength Minimum Breaking Strength		Safe Load FS = 12		Weight	
inch		mm	lbf	kN	lbf	kN	lbm/ft	kg/m
1/2	0.50	12	5,085	22.6	424	1.88	0.077	0.115
9/16	0.56	14	6,435	28.6	536	2.39	0.098	0.146
5/8	0.63	16	7,825	34.8	652	2.90	0.120	0.179
3/4	0.75	18	11,200	49.8	933	4.15	0.172	0.256
7/8	0.88	22	15,225	67.7	1,270	5.65	0.234	0.348
1	1.00	24	19,775	88.0	1,650	7.34	0.304	0.452
1-1/16	1.06	26	22,225	99	1,850	8.23	0.342	0.509
1-1/8	1.13	28	24,800	110	2,070	9.21	0.385	0.573
1-1/4	1.25	30	29,800	133	2,480	11.0	0.465	0.692
1-5/16	1.31	32	32,500	145	2,710	12.1	0.51	0.759
1-1/2	1.50	36	42,200	188	3,520	15.7	0.67	0.997
1-5/8	1.63	40	49,250	219	4,100	18.2	0.78	1.16
1-3/4	1.75	44	57,000	254	4,750	21.1	0.91	1.35
2	2.00	48	72,000	320	6,000	26.7	1.17	1.74
2-1/8	2.13	52	81,000	360	6,750	30.0	1.33	1.98
2-1/4	2.25	56	90,500	403	7,540	33.5	1.49	2.22
2-1/2	2.50	60	110,000	489	9,170	40.8	1.84	2.74
2-5/8	2.63	64	121,000	538	10,100	44.9	2.03	3.02
2-3/4	2.75	68	144,000	641	12,000	53.4	2.43	3.62
3	3.00	72	156,000	694	13,000	57.8	2.64	3.93
3-1/4	3.25	80	188,500	838	15,700	69.8	3.23	4.81
3-1/2	3.50	88	225,000	1,000	18,800	83.6	3.87	5.76
4	4.00	96	270,000	1,200	22,500	100	4.70	6.99
4-1/4	4.25	104	310,000	1,380	25,800	115	5.47	8.14
4-1/2	4.50	112	355,000	1,580	29,600	132	6.30	9.38
5	5.00	120	410,000	1,820	34,200	152	7.32	10.9
5-5/16	5.31	128	459,000	2,040	38,300	170	8.25	12.3
5-5/8	5.63	136	508,500	2,260	42,400	189	9.25	13.8
6	6.00	144	567,000	2,520	47,300	210	10.5	15.6

Polyester/Polyolefin Dual Fiber Rope, 3-Strand

Rope Diameter			Strength Minimum Breaking Strength		Safe Load FS = 12		Weight	
inch		mm	lbf	kN	lbf	kN	lbm/ft	kg/m
1/4	0.25	6	1,200	5.34	100	0.445	0.016	0.024
5/16	0.31	8	1,870	8.3	156	0.693	0.025	0.037
3/8	0.38	10	2,700	12.0	225	1.00	0.036	0.054
7/16	0.44	11	3,500	15.6	292	1.30	0.048	0.071
1/2	0.50	12	4,400	19.6	367	1.63	0.062	0.092

Polyester/Polyolefin Dual Fiber Rope, 3-Strand(cont.)

Rope Diameter			Strength				Weight	
			Minimum Breaking Strength		Safe Load FS = 12			
inch		mm	lbf	kN	lbf	kN	lbm/ft	kg/m
9/16	0.56	14	5,200	23.1	433	1.93	0.079	0.118
5/8	0.63	16	6,100	27.1	508	2.26	0.095	0.141
3/4	0.75	18	8,400	37.4	700	3.11	0.135	0.201
7/8	0.88	22	11,125	49.5	927	4.12	0.180	0.268
1	1.00	24	13,175	58.6	1,100	4.89	0.218	0.324
1-1/16	1.06	26	14,775	66	1,230	5.47	0.245	0.365
1-1/8	1.13	28	16,325	73	1,360	6.05	0.271	0.403
1-1/4	1.25	30	19,900	89	1,660	7.38	0.334	0.497
1-5/16	1.31	32	21,950	98	1,830	8.14	0.365	0.543
1-1/2	1.50	36	28,250	126	2,350	10.5	0.470	0.699
1-5/8	1.63	40	32,950	147	2,750	12.2	0.550	0.818
1-3/4	1.75	44	36,850	164	3,070	13.7	0.620	0.923
2	2.00	48	48,050	214	4,000	17.8	0.810	1.21
2-1/8	2.13	52	53,950	240	4,500	20.0	0.910	1.35
2-1/4	2.25	56	59,950	267	5,000	22.2	1.01	1.50
2-1/2	2.50	60	73,550	327	6,130	27.3	1.24	1.85
2-5/8	2.63	64	80,650	359	6,720	29.9	1.36	2.02
2-3/4	2.75	68	95,400	424	7,950	35.4	1.61	2.40
3	3.00	72	102,900	458	8,580	38.2	1.74	2.59
3-1/4	3.25	80	122,800	546	10,200	45.4	2.12	3.15
3-1/2	3.50	88	144,800	644	12,100	53.8	2.50	3.72
4	4.00	96	171,000	761	14,300	63.6	3.00	4.46
4-1/4	4.25	104	195,800	871	16,300	72.5	3.45	5.13
4-1/2	4.50	112	224,800	1,000	18,700	83.2	3.95	5.88
5	5.00	120	254,700	1,130	21,200	94.3	4.55	6.77
5-5/16	5.31	128	282,600	1,260	23,500	105	5.06	7.53
5-5/8	5.63	136	312,300	1,390	26,000	116	5.62	8.36
6	6.00	144	351,000	1,560	29,300	130	6.35	9.45

Polypropylene Fiber Rope, 3-Strand and 8-Strand

Rope Diameter			Strength				Weight	
			Minimum Breaking Strength		Safe Load FS = 12			
inch		mm	lbf	kN	lbf	kN	lbm/ft	kg/m
3/16	0.19	5	650	2.89	54.2	0.241	0.01	0.01
1/4	0.25	6	1,125	5.00	93.8	0.417	0.01	0.02
5/16	0.31	8	1,710	7.61	143	0.634	0.02	0.03
3/8	0.38	10	2,430	10.8	203	0.90	0.03	0.04
7/16	0.44	11	3,150	14.0	263	1.17	0.04	0.05
1/2	0.50	12	3,780	16.8	315	1.40	0.05	0.07

Polypropylene Fiber Rope, 3-Strand and 8-Strand (cont.)

Rope Diameter			Strength Minimum Breaking Strength		Safe Load FS = 12		Weight	
inch		mm	lbf	kN	lbf	kN	lbm/ft	kg/m
9/16	0.56	14	4,590	20.4	383	1.70	0.06	0.09
5/8	0.63	16	5,580	24.8	465	2.07	0.07	0.11
3/4	0.75	18	7,650	34.0	638	2.84	0.10	0.15
7/8	0.88	22	10,350	46.0	863	3.84	0.14	0.21
1	1.00	24	12,825	57.0	1,070	4.76	0.18	0.27
1-1/16	1.06	26	14,400	64.1	1,200	5.34	0.20	0.30
1-1/8	1.13	28	16,000	71.2	1,330	5.92	0.23	0.34
1-1/4	1.25	30	19,350	86.1	1,610	7.16	0.28	0.41
1-5/16	1.31	32	21,150	94.1	1,760	7.83	0.30	0.45
1-1/2	1.50	36	27,350	122	2,280	10.1	0.39	0.59
1-5/8	1.63	40	31,950	142	2,660	11.8	0.46	0.68
1-3/4	1.75	44	36,900	164	3,080	13.7	0.53	0.79
2	2.00	48	46,800	208	3,900	17.3	0.69	1.03
2-1/8	2.13	52	52,650	234	4,390	19.5	0.78	1.16
2-1/4	2.25	56	59,400	264	4,950	22.0	0.88	1.31
2-1/2	2.50	60	72,000	320	6,000	26.7	1.07	1.59
2-5/8	2.63	64	80,500	358	6,710	29.8	1.20	1.79
2-3/4	2.75	68	94,500	420	7,880	35.1	1.41	2.10
3	3.00	72	102,600	456	8,550	38.0	1.53	2.28
3-1/4	3.25	80	121,500	540	10,100	44.9	1.86	2.77
3-1/2	3.50	88	144,000	641	12,000	53.4	2.23	3.32
4	4.00	96	171,900	765	14,300	63.6	2.72	4.05
4-1/4	4.25	104	198,000	881	16,500	73.4	3.15	4.69
4-1/2	4.50	112	223,200	993	18,600	82.7	3.60	5.36
5	5.00	120	256,500	1,140	21,400	95.2	4.20	6.25
5-5/16	5.31	128	287,100	1,280	23,900	106	4.74	7.05
5-5/8	5.63	136	319,500	1,420	26,600	118	5.31	7.90
6	6.00	144	358,200	1,590	29,900	133	6.03	8.97

Sisal Rope, 3-Strand

Nominal Rope Diameter			Strength Minimum Breaking Strength		Safe Load FS = 12		Weight	
inch		mm	lbf	kN	lbf	kN	lbm/ft	kg/m
3/16	0.19	5	290	1.29	24.2	0.11	0.01	0.02
1/4	0.25	6	385	1.71	32.1	0.14	0.02	0.03
5/16	0.31	8	640	2.85	53.3	0.24	0.03	0.04
3/8	0.38	10	865	3.85	72.1	0.32	0.04	0.06
7/16	0.44	11	1,120	4.98	93.3	0.42	0.05	0.07
1/2	0.50	12	1,700	7.56	142	0.63	0.07	0.10
9/16	0.56	14	2,210	9.83	184	0.82	0.10	0.14

Sisal Rope, 3-Strand (cont.)

Nominal Rope Diameter			Strength					Weight	
			Minimum Breaking Strength		Safe Load FS = 12				
inch		mm	lbf	kN	lbf	kN		lbm/ft	kg/m
5/8	0.63	16	2,815	12.5	235	1.04		0.13	0.19
3/4	0.75	18	3,455	15.4	288	1.28		0.16	0.24
7/8	0.88	22	4,930	21.9	411	1.83		0.21	0.32
1	1.00	24	5,760	25.6	480	2.14		0.27	0.40
1-1/16	1.06	26	6,720	29.9	560	2.49		0.30	0.44
1-1/8	1.13	28	7,680	34.2	640	2.85		0.34	0.51
1-1/4	1.25	30	8,640	38.4	720	3.20		0.40	0.59
1-5/16	1.31	32	9,600	42.7	800	3.56		0.46	0.68
1-1/2	1.50	36	11,840	52.7	987	4.39		0.57	0.85
1-5/8	1.63	40	14,440	64.2	1,200	5.34		0.71	1.06
1-3/4	1.75	44	16,960	75.4	1,410	6.27		0.85	1.26
2	2.00	48	19,840	88.3	1,650	7.34		1.02	1.52
2-1/4	2.25	56	26,240	117	2,190	9.74		1.39	2.07
2-5/8	2.63	64	33,280	148	2,770	12.3		1.82	2.71
3	3.00	72	40,960	182	3,410	15.2		2.30	3.42

Notes:
(1) Abbreviations used:
   lbf = pound-force, lbm/ft = pound-mass/foot, kg/m = kilogram/meter,
   kN = kilonewton, mm = millimeter, FS = Factor of Safety
(2) Conversions: 2,000 pounds-force = 1 short ton-force and
   1 short ton-force = 0.90718474 metric ton-force.
(3) Safe Load = Minimum Breaking Strength divided by Factor of Safety.
   The appropriate Factor of Safety should be determined by the user. Sequoia
   Publishing recommends a Factor of Safety of 12. Factors of Safety below 12
   should only be used by those with expert knowledge of the conditions and risks
   of use. The load applied to the rope should never exceed the Safe Load.
(4) Manila rope is made from the fibers of the abaca plant (musa testilus,
   Manila hemp).
   Nylon rope is made from continuous filiment polyamide (nylon 6 or nylon 6.6).
   Polyester rope is made from continuous filiment polyester.
   Polypropylene rope is made from monofilament or film polypropylene.
   Sisal rope is made from the fibers of the sisal hemp plant (agave sisalana,
   hemp plant).

References: Similar tables may be found in:
Columbian Rope, Guntown, MS (see www.columbianrope.com)
*Federal Specification T-R-605B, Rope, Manila and Sisal, General Service
Administration, Washington, DC, 1973.*
*Rope Standards, CIS-1, Cordage Institute, Wayne, PA, 1999 (see
www.ropecord.com).*
Rope Specifications, Wall Industries, Inc., Granite Quarry, NC, 1988.
*Feeney Wire Rope & Rigging, Inc., Oakland, CA, (see
www.feeneywire.com)*
*Handbook Of Rigging, Second Edition, W.E. Rossnagel, McGraw-Hill Book
Company, 1957.*

Strength and Weight of Wire Rope
6 strand x 19 wire (6x19)

Bright wire, uncoated, fiber core (FC)
Improved Plow Steel (IPS)

Wire Diameter			Strength Nominal Strength		Safe Load		Weight	
inch		mm	lbf	kN	lbf	kN	lbm/ft	kg/m
1/4	0.25	6.4	5,480	24.4	1,100	4.89	0.11	0.16
5/16	0.31	8	8,520	37.9	1,700	7.56	0.16	0.24
3/8	0.38	9.5	12,200	54.3	2,440	10.9	0.24	0.36
7/16	0.44	11.5	16,540	73.6	3,310	14.7	0.32	0.48
1/2	0.50	13	21,400	95.2	4,280	19.0	0.42	0.63
9/16	0.56	14.5	27,000	120	5,400	24.0	0.53	0.79
5/8	0.63	16	33,400	149	6,680	29.7	0.66	0.98
3/4	0.75	19	47,600	212	9,520	42.3	0.95	1.41
7/8	0.88	22	64,400	286	12,900	57.4	1.29	1.92
1	1.00	26	83,600	372	16,700	74.3	1.68	2.50
1-1/8	1.13	29	105,200	468	21,000	93.4	2.13	3.17
1-1/4	1.25	32	129,200	575	25,800	115	2.63	3.91
1-3/8	1.38	35	155,400	691	31,100	138	3.18	4.73
1-1/2	1.50	38	184,000	818	36,800	164	3.78	5.63
1-5/8	1.63	42	214,000	952	42,800	190	4.44	6.61
1-3/4	1.75	45	248,000	1,100	49,600	221	5.15	7.66
1-7/8	1.88	48	282,000	1,250	56,400	251	5.91	8.80
2	2.00	52	320,000	1,420	64,000	285	6.72	10.0
2-1/8	2.13	54	358,000	1,590	71,600	318	7.59	11.3
2-1/4	2.25	57	400,000	1,780	80,000	356	8.51	12.7
2-3/8	2.38	60	444,000	1,980	88,800	395	9.48	14.1
2-1/2	2.50	64	488,000	2,170	97,600	434	10.5	15.6
2-5/8	2.63	67	536,000	2,380	107,000	476	11.6	17.3
2-3/4	2.75	70	584,000	2,600	117,000	520	12.7	18.9

Bright Wire, Uncoated, Independent Wire Rope Core (IWRC)
Improved Plow Steel (IPS)

Wire Diameter			Strength Nominal Strength		Safe Load		Weight	
inch		mm	lbf	kN	lbf	kN	lbm/ft	kg/m
1/4	0.250	6.4	5,880	26.2	1,180	5.25	0.12	0.18
5/16	0.313	8	9,160	40.7	1,830	8.14	0.18	0.27
3/8	0.375	9.5	13,120	58.4	2,620	11.7	0.26	0.39
7/16	0.438	11.5	17,780	79.1	3,560	15.8	0.35	0.52
1/2	0.500	13	23,000	102	4,600	20.5	0.46	0.68
9/16	0.563	14.5	29,000	129	5,800	25.8	0.59	0.88
5/8	0.625	16	35,800	159	7,160	31.8	0.72	1.07
3/4	0.750	19	51,200	228	10,200	45.4	1.04	1.55

Bright Wire, Uncoated, Independent Wire Rope Core (IWRC)

Improved Plow Steel (IPS) (cont.)

Wire Diameter			Strength				Weight	
inch		mm	Nominal Strength		Safe Load			
			lbf	kN	lbf	kN	lbm/ft	kg/m
7/8	0.875	22	69,200	308	13,800	61.4	1.42	2.11
1	1.000	26	89,800	399	18,000	80.1	1.85	2.75
1-1/8	1.125	29	113,000	503	22,600	101	2.34	3.48
1-1/4	1.250	32	138,800	617	27,800	124	2.89	4.30
1-3/8	1.375	35	167,000	743	33,400	149	3.50	5.21
1-1/2	1.500	38	197,800	880	39,600	176	4.16	6.19
1-5/8	1.625	42	230,000	1,020	46,000	205	4.88	7.26
1-3/4	1.750	45	266,000	1,180	53,200	237	5.67	8.44
1-7/8	1.875	48	304,000	1,350	60,800	271	6.5	9.67
2	2.000	51	344,000	1,530	68,800	306	7.39	11.0
2-1/8	2.125	54	384,000	1,710	76,800	342	8.35	12.4
2-1/4	2.250	57	430,000	1,910	86,000	383	9.36	13.9
2-3/8	2.375	60	478,000	2,130	95,600	425	10.4	15.5
2-1/2	2.500	64	524,000	2,330	105,000	467	11.6	17.3
2-5/8	2.625	67	576,000	2,560	115,000	512	12.8	19.0
2-3/4	2.750	70	628,000	2,790	126,000	560	14.0	20.8
2-7/8	2.875	73	682,000	3,030	136,000	605	15.3	22.8
3	3.000	76	740,000	3,290	148,000	658	16.6	24.7
3-1/8	3.125	79	798,000	3,550	160,000	712	18.0	26.8
3-1/4	3.250	83	858,000	3,820	172,000	765	19.5	29.0
3-3/8	3.375	86	918,000	4,080	184,000	818	21.0	31.3
3-1/2	3.500	89	982,000	4,370	196,000	872	22.7	33.8
3-5/8	3.625	92	1,046,000	4,650	209,000	930	24.3	36.2
3-3/4	3.750	95	1,114,000	4,960	223,000	992	26.0	38.7
3-7/8	3.875	98	1,182,000	5,260	236,000	1,050	27.7	41.2
4	4.000	102	1,254,000	5,580	251,000	1,120	29.6	44.0
4-1/8	4.125	105	1,316,000	5,850	263,000	1,170	31.7	47.2
4-1/4	4.250	108	1,388,000	6,170	278,000	1,240	33.3	49.6
4-3/8	4.375	111	1,468,000	6,530	294,000	1,310	35.4	52.7

Extra-Improved Plow Steel (EIPS)

Wire Diameter			Strength				Weight	
inch		mm	Nominal Strength		Safe Load			
			lbf	kN	lbf	kN	lbm/ft	kg/m
1/4	0.250	6.4	6,800	30.2	1,360	6.05	0.12	0.18
5/16	0.313	8	10,540	46.9	2,110	9.39	0.18	0.27
3/8	0.375	9.5	15,100	67.2	3,020	13.4	0.26	0.39
7/16	0.438	11.5	20,400	90.7	4,080	18.1	0.35	0.52
1/2	0.500	13	26,600	118	5,320	23.7	0.46	0.68
9/16	0.563	14.5	33,600	149	6,720	29.9	0.59	0.88
5/8	0.625	16	41,200	183	8,240	36.7	0.72	1.07
3/4	0.750	19	58,800	262	11,800	52.5	1.04	1.55

Bright Wire, Uncoated, Independent Wire Rope Core (IWRC)

Extra Improved Plow Steel (EIPS)

Wire Diameter			Strength				Weight	
inch		mm	Nominal Strength		Safe Load			
			lbf	kN	lbf	kN	lbm/ft	kg/m
7/8	0.875	22	79,600	354	15,900	70.7	1.42	2.11
1	1.000	26	103,400	460	20,700	92.1	1.85	2.75
1-1/8	1.125	29	130,000	578	26,000	116	2.34	3.48
1-1/4	1.250	32	159,800	711	32,000	142	2.89	4.30
1-3/8	1.375	35	192,000	854	38,400	171	3.50	5.21
1-1/2	1.500	38	228,000	1,010	45,600	203	4.16	6.19
1-5/8	1.625	42	264,000	1,170	52,800	235	4.88	7.26
1-3/4	1.750	45	306,000	1,360	61,200	272	5.67	8.44
1-7/8	1.875	48	348,000	1,550	69,600	310	6.50	9.67
2	2.000	52	396,000	1,760	79,200	352	7.39	11.0
2-1/8	2.125	54	442,000	1,970	88,400	393	8.35	12.4
2-1/4	2.250	57	494,000	2,200	98,800	439	9.36	13.9
2-3/8	2.375	60	548,000	2,440	110,000	489	10.4	15.5
2-1/2	2.500	64	604,000	2,690	121,000	538	11.6	17.3
2-5/8	2.625	67	662,000	2,940	132,000	587	12.8	19.0
2-3/4	2.750	70	722,000	3,210	144,000	641	14.0	20.8
2-7/8	2.875	73	784,000	3,490	157,000	698	15.3	22.8
3	3.000	76	850,000	3,780	170,000	756	16.6	24.7
3-1/8	3.125	79	916,000	4,070	183,000	814	18.0	26.8
3-1/4	3.250	83	984,000	4,380	197,000	876	19.5	29.0
3-3/8	3.375	86	1,058,000	4,710	212,000	943	21.0	31.3
3-1/2	3.500	89	1,128,000	5,020	226,000	1,010	22.7	33.8
3-5/8	3.625	92	1,204,000	5,360	241,000	1,070	24.3	36.2
3-3/4	3.750	95	1,282,000	5,700	256,000	1,140	26.0	38.7
3-7/8	3.875	98	1,360,000	6,050	272,000	1,210	27.7	41.2
4	4.000	102	1,440,000	6,410	288,000	1,280	29.6	44.0
4-1/8	4.125	105	1,514,000	6,730	303,000	1,350	31.7	47.2
4-1/4	4.250	108	1,598,000	7,110	320,000	1,420	33.3	49.6
4-3/8	4.375	111	1,688,000	7,510	338,000	1,500	35.4	52.7

Extra-Extra-Improved Plow Steel (EEIPS)

Wire Diameter			Strength				Weight	
inch		mm	Nominal Strength		Safe Load			
			lbf	kN	lbf	kN	lbm/ft	kg/m
3/8	0.375	9.5	16,600	73.8	3,320	14.8	0.26	0.39
7/16	0.438	11.5	22,400	99.6	4,480	19.9	0.35	0.52
1/2	0.500	13	29,200	130	5,840	26.0	0.46	0.68
9/16	0.563	14.5	37,000	165	7,400	32.9	0.59	0.88
5/8	0.625	16	45,400	202	9,080	40.4	0.72	1.07
3/4	0.750	19	64,800	288	13,000	57.8	1.04	1.55
7/8	0.875	22	87,600	390	17,500	77.8	1.42	2.11
1	1.000	26	113,800	506	22,800	101.4	1.85	2.75
1-1/8	1.125	29	143,000	636	28,600	127	2.34	3.48
1-1/4	1.250	32	175,800	782	35,200	157	2.89	4.30
1-3/8	1.375	35	212,000	943	42,400	189	3.50	5.21

Bright Wire, Uncoated, Independent Wire Rope Core (IWRC)
Extra-Extra-Improved Plow Steel (EEIPS)

Wire Diameter			Strength				Weight	
inch		mm	Nominal Strength		Safe Load			
			lbf	kN	lbf	kN	lbm/ft	kg/m
1-1/2	1.500	38	250,000	1,110	50,000	222	4.16	6.19
1-5/8	1.625	42	292,000	1,300	58,400	260	4.88	7.26
1-3/4	1.750	45	338,000	1,500	67,600	301	5.67	8.44
1-7/8	1.875	48	384,000	1,710	76,800	342	6.50	9.67
2	2.000	52	434,000	1,930	86,800	386	7.39	11.0
2-1/8	2.125	54	486,000	2,160	97,200	432	8.35	12.4
2-1/4	2.250	57	544,000	2,420	108,800	484	9.36	13.9
2-3/8	2.375	60	602,000	2,680	120,000	534	10.4	15.5
2-1/2	2.500	64	664,000	2,950	133,000	592	11.6	17.3
2-5/8	2.625	67	728,000	3,240	146,000	649	12.8	19.0
2-3/4	2.750	70	794,000	3,530	159,000	707	14.0	20.8
2-7/8	2.875	74	862,000	3,830	172,000	765	15.3	22.8
3	3.000	77	936,000	4,160	187,000	832	16.6	24.7

Compacted Strand Wire Rope
Bright wire, uncoated, fiber core (FC)

Wire Diameter			Strength				Weight	
inch		mm	Nominal Strength		Safe Load			
			lbf	kN	lbf	kN	lbm/ft	kg/m
3/8	0.375	9.5	14,780	65.7	2,960	13.2	0.26	0.39
7/16	0.438	11.5	20,000	89.0	4,000	17.8	0.35	0.52
1/2	0.500	13	26,000	116	5,200	23.1	0.46	0.68
9/16	0.563	14.5	32,800	146	6,560	29.2	0.57	0.85
5/8	0.625	16	40,400	180	8,080	35.9	0.71	1.06
3/4	0.750	19	57,600	256	11,500	51.2	1.03	1.53
7/8	0.875	22	78,000	347	15,600	69.4	1.40	2.08
1	1.000	26	101,400	451	20,300	90.3	1.82	2.71
1-1/8	1.125	29	127,200	566	25,400	113	2.31	3.44
1-1/4	1.250	32	156,400	696	31,300	139	2.85	4.24
1-3/8	1.375	35	188,200	837	37,600	167	3.45	5.13
1-1/2	1.500	38	222,000	988	44,400	198	4.10	6.10
1-5/8	1.625	42	260,000	1,160	52,000	231	4.80	7.14
1-3/4	1.750	45	300,000	1,330	60,000	267	5.56	8.27
1-7/8	1.875	48	342,000	1,520	68,400	304	6.38	9.49
2	2.000	52	386,000	1,720	77,200	343	7.26	10.8

Compacted Strand Wire Rope (cont.)

Bright Wire, Uncoated, Independent Wire Rope Core (IWRC)

Wire Diameter			Strength				Weight	
inch		mm	Nominal Strength		Safe Load			
			lbf	kN	lbf	kN	lbm/ft	kg/m
3/8	0.375	9.5	16,600	73.8	3,320	14.8	0.31	0.46
7/16	0.438	11.5	22,400	99.6	4,480	19.9	0.39	0.58
1/2	0.500	13	29,200	130	5,840	26.0	0.49	0.73
9/16	0.563	14.5	37,000	165	7,400	32.9	0.63	0.94
5/8	0.625	16	45,400	202	9,080	40.4	0.78	1.16
3/4	0.750	19	64,800	288	13,000	57.8	1.13	1.68
7/8	0.875	22	87,600	390	17,500	77.8	1.54	2.29
1	1.000	26	113,800	506	22,800	101	2.00	2.98
1-1/8	1.125	29	143,000	636	28,600	127	2.54	3.78
1-1/4	1.250	32	175,800	782	35,200	157	3.14	4.67
1-3/8	1.375	35	212,000	943	42,400	189	3.80	5.66
1-1/2	1.500	38	250,000	1,110	50,000	222	4.50	6.70
1-5/8	1.625	42	292,000	1,300	58,400	260	5.27	7.84
1-3/4	1.750	45	338,000	1,500	67,600	301	6.12	9.11
1-7/8	1.875	48	384,000	1,710	76,800	342	7.02	10.4
2	2.000	52	434,000	1,930	86,800	386	7.98	11.9

6 Strand x 37 Wire (6 X 37)

Bright wire, uncoated, fiber core (FC)

Improved Plow Steel (IPS)

Wire Diameter			Strength				Weight	
inch		mm	Nominal Strength		Safe Load			
			lbf	kN	lbf	kN	lbm/ft	kg/m
1/4	0.250	6.4	5,480	24.4	1,100	4.89	0.11	0.16
5/16	0.313	8	8,520	37.9	1,700	7.56	0.16	0.24
3/8	0.375	9.5	12,200	54.3	2,440	10.9	0.24	0.36
7/16	0.438	11.5	16,540	73.6	3,310	14.7	0.32	0.48
1/2	0.500	13	21,400	95.2	4,280	19.0	0.42	0.63
9/16	0.563	14.5	27,000	120	5,400	24.0	0.53	0.79
5/8	0.625	16	33,400	149	6,680	29.7	0.66	0.98
3/4	0.750	19	47,600	212	9,520	42.3	0.95	1.41
7/8	0.875	22	64,400	286	12,900	57.4	1.29	1.92
1	1.000	26	83,600	372	16,700	74.3	1.68	2.50
1-1/8	1.125	29	105,200	468	21,000	93.4	2.13	3.17
1-1/4	1.250	32	129,200	575	25,800	115	2.63	3.91
1-3/8	1.375	35	155,400	691	31,100	138	3.18	4.73
1-1/2	1.500	38	184,000	818	36,800	164	3.78	5.63
1-5/8	1.625	42	214,000	952	42,800	190	4.44	6.61
1-3/4	1.750	45	248,000	1,100	49,600	221	5.15	7.66
1-7/8	1.875	48	282,000	1,250	56,400	251	5.91	8.80
2	2.000	52	320,000	1,420	64,000	285	6.72	10.0
2-1/8	2.125	54	358,000	1,590	71,600	318	7.59	11.3

Improved Plow Steel (IPS) (cont.)

Wire Diameter			Strength					Weight	
inch	mm		Nominal Strength		Safe Load				
			lbf	kN	lbf	kN		lbm/ft	kg/m
2-1/4	2.250	57	400,000	1,780	80,000	356		8.51	12.7
2-3/8	2.375	60	444,000	1,980	88,800	395		9.48	14.1
2-1/2	2.500	64	488,000	2,170	97,600	434		10.5	15.6
2-5/8	2.625	67	536,000	2,380	107,000	476		11.6	17.3
2-3/4	2.750	70	584,000	2,600	117,000	520		12.7	18.9
2-7/8	2.875	74	634,000	2,820	127,000	565		13.9	20.7
3	3.000	77	688,000	3,060	138,000	614		15.1	22.5
3-1/8	3.125	80	742,000	3,300	148,000	658		16.4	24.4
3-1/4	3.250	83	798,000	3,550	160,000	712		17.7	26.3

Bright wire, Uncoated, Independent Wire Rope Core (IWRC)

Improved Plow Steel (IPS)

Wire Diameter			Strength				Weight	
inch	mm		Nominal Strength		Safe Load			
			lbf	kN	lbf	kN	lbm/ft	kg/m
1/4	0.250	6.4	5,880	26.2	1,180	5.25	0.12	0.18
5/16	0.313	8	9,160	40.7	1,830	8.14	0.18	0.27
3/8	0.375	9.5	13,120	58.4	2,620	11.7	0.26	0.39
7/16	0.438	11.5	17,780	79.1	3,560	15.8	0.35	0.52
1/2	0.500	13	23,000	102	4,600	20.5	0.46	0.68
9/16	0.563	14.5	29,000	129	5,800	25.8	0.59	0.88
5/8	0.625	16	35,800	159	7,160	31.8	0.72	1.07
3/4	0.750	19	51,200	228	10,200	45.4	1.04	1.55
7/8	0.875	22	69,200	308	13,800	61.4	1.42	2.11
1	1.000	26	89,800	399	18,000	80.1	1.85	2.75
1-1/8	1.125	29	113,000	503	22,600	101	2.34	3.48
1-1/4	1.250	32	138,800	617	27,800	124	2.89	4.30
1-3/8	1.375	35	167,000	743	33,400	149	3.50	5.21
1-1/2	1.500	38	197,800	880	39,600	176	4.16	6.19
1-5/8	1.625	42	230,000	1,020	46,000	205	4.88	7.26
1-3/4	1.750	45	266,000	1,180	53,200	237	5.67	8.44
1-7/8	1.875	48	304,000	1,350	60,800	270	6.50	9.67
2	2.000	52	344,000	1,530	68,800	306	7.39	11.0
2-1/8	2.125	54	384,000	1,710	76,800	342	8.35	12.4
2-1/4	2.250	57	430,000	1,910	86,000	383	9.36	13.9
2-3/8	2.375	60	478,000	2,130	95,600	425	10.4	15.5
2-1/2	2.500	64	524,000	2,330	105,000	467	11.6	17.3
2-5/8	2.625	67	576,000	2,560	115,000	512	12.8	19.1
2-3/4	2.750	70	628,000	2,790	126,000	560	14.0	20.8
2-7/8	2.875	74	682,000	3,030	136,000	605	15.3	22.8
3	3.000	77	740,000	3,290	148,000	658	16.6	24.7
3-1/8	3.125	80	798,000	3,550	160,000	712	18.0	26.8
3-1/4	3.250	83	858,000	3,820	172,000	765	19.5	29.0
3-3/8	3.375	86	918,000	4,080	184,000	818	21.0	31.3
3-1/2	3.500	90	982,000	4,370	196,000	872	22.7	33.8

Improved Plow Steel (IPS) (cont.)

Wire Diameter			Strength		Safe Load		Weight	
inch		mm	Nominal Strength					
			lbf	kN	lbf	kN	lbm/ft	kg/m
3-5/8	3.625	92	1,046,000	4,650	209,000	930	24.3	36.2
3-3/4	3.750	95	1,114,000	4,960	223,000	992	26.0	38.7
3-7/8	3.875	98	1,182,000	5,260	236,000	1,050	27.7	41.2
4	4.000	102	1,254,000	5,580	251,000	1,120	29.6	44.0
4-1/8	4.125	105	1,316,000	5,850	263,000	1,170	31.7	47.2
4-1/4	4.250	108	1,388,000	6,170	278,000	1,240	33.3	49.6
4-3/8	4.375	111	1,468,000	6,530	294,000	1,310	35.4	52.7

Bright Wire, Uncoated, Independent Wire Rope Core (IWRC)
Extra-Improved Plow Steel (EIPS)

Wire Diameter			Strength		Safe Load		Weight	
inch		mm	Nominal Strength					
			lbf	kN	lbf	kN	lbm/ft	kg/m
1/4	0.250	6.4	6,800	30.2	1,360	6.05	0.12	0.18
5/16	0.313	8	10,540	46.9	2,110	9.39	0.18	0.27
3/8	0.375	9.5	15,100	67.2	3,020	13.4	0.26	0.39
7/16	0.438	11.5	20,400	90.7	4,080	18.1	0.35	0.52
1/2	0.500	13	26,600	118	5,320	23.7	0.46	0.68
9/16	0.563	14.5	33,600	149	6,720	29.9	0.59	0.88
5/8	0.625	16	41,200	183	8,240	36.7	0.72	1.07
3/4	0.750	19	58,800	262	11,800	52.5	1.04	1.55
7/8	0.875	22	79,600	354	15,900	70.7	1.42	2.11
1	1.000	26	103,400	460	20,700	92.1	1.85	2.75
1-1/8	1.125	29	130,000	578	26,000	116	2.34	3.48
1-1/4	1.250	32	159,800	711	32,000	142	2.89	4.30
1-3/8	1.375	35	192,000	854	38,400	171	3.50	5.21
1-1/2	1.500	38	228,000	1,010	45,600	203	4.16	6.19
1-5/8	1.625	42	264,000	1,170	52,800	235	4.88	7.26
1-3/4	1.750	45	306,000	1,360	61,200	272	5.67	8.44
1-7/8	1.875	48	348,000	1,550	69,600	310	6.50	9.67
2	2.000	52	396,000	1,760	79,200	352	7.39	11.0
2-1/8	2.125	54	442,000	1,970	88,400	393	8.35	12.4
2-1/4	2.250	57	494,000	2,200	98,800	439	9.36	13.9
2-3/8	2.375	60	548,000	2,440	110,000	489	10.4	15.5
2-1/2	2.500	64	604,000	2,690	121,000	538	11.6	17.3
2-5/8	2.625	67	662,000	2,940	132,000	587	12.8	19.0
2-3/4	2.750	70	722,000	3,210	144,000	641	14.0	20.8
2-7/8	2.875	73	784,000	3,490	157,000	698	15.3	22.8
3	3.000	77	850,000	3,780	170,000	756	16.6	24.7
3-1/8	3.125	80	916,000	4,070	183,000	814	18.0	26.8
3-1/4	3.250	83	984,000	4,380	197,000	876	19.5	29.0
3-3/8	3.375	86	1,058,000	4,710	212,000	943	21.0	31.3
3-1/2	3.500	89	1,128,000	5,020	226,000	1,010	22.7	33.8
3-5/8	3.625	92	1,204,000	5,360	241,000	1,070	24.3	36.2
3-3/4	3.750	95	1,282,000	5,700	256,000	1,140	26.0	38.7

Extra-Improved Plow Steel (EIPS)

Wire Diameter			Strength				Weight	
inch		mm	Nominal Strength		Safe Load			
			lbf	kN	lbf	kN	lbm/ft	kg/m
3-7/8	3.875	98	1,360,000	6,050	272,000	1,210	27.7	41.2
4	4.000	102	1,440,000	6,410	288,000	1,280	29.6	44.0
4-1/8	4.125	105	1,514,000	6,730	303,000	1,350	31.7	47.2
4-1/4	4.250	108	1,598,000	7,110	320,000	1,420	33.3	49.6
4-3/8	4.375	111	1,688,000	7,510	338,000	1,500	35.4	52.7

Bright Wire, Uncoated, Independent Wire Rope Core (IWRC)
Extra-Extra-Improved Plow Steel (EEIPS)

Wire Diameter			Strength				Weight	
inch		mm	Nominal Strength		Safe Load			
			lbf	kN	lbf	kN	lbm/ft	kg/m
3/8	0.375	9.5	16,600	73.8	3,320	14.8	0.26	0.39
7/16	0.438	11.5	22,400	99.6	4,480	19.9	0.35	0.52
1/2	0.500	13	29,200	130	5,840	26.0	0.61	0.68
9/16	0.563	14.5	37,000	165	7,400	32.9	0.59	0.88
5/8	0.625	16	45,400	202	9,080	40.4	0.72	1.07
3/4	0.750	19	64,800	288	13,000	57.8	1.04	1.55
7/8	0.875	22	87,600	390	17,500	77.8	1.42	2.11
1	1.000	26	113,800	506	22,800	101.4	1.85	2.75
1-1/8	1.125	29	143,000	636	28,600	127	2.34	3.48
1-1/4	1.250	32	175,800	782	35,200	157	2.89	4.30
1-3/8	1.375	35	212,000	943	42,400	189	3.50	5.21
1-1/2	1.500	38	250,000	1,110	50,000	222	4.16	6.19
1-5/8	1.625	42	292,000	1,300	58,400	260	4.88	7.26
1-3/4	1.750	45	338,000	1,500	67,600	301	5.67	8.44
1-7/8	1.875	48	384,000	1,710	76,800	342	6.50	9.67
2	2.000	52	434,000	1,930	86,800	386	7.39	11.0
2-1/8	2.125	54	486,000	2,160	97,200	432	8.35	12.4
2-1/4	2.250	57	544,000	2,420	108,800	484	9.36	13.9
2-3/8	2.375	60	602,000	2,680	120,000	534	10.4	15.5
2-1/2	2.500	64	664,000	2,950	133,000	592	11.6	17.3
2-5/8	2.625	67	728,000	3,240	146,000	649	12.8	19.0
2-3/4	2.750	70	794,000	3,530	159,000	707	14.0	20.8
2-7/8	2.875	74	862,000	3,830	172,000	765	15.3	22.8
3	3.000	77	936,000	4,160	187,000	832	16.6	24.7

Compacted Strand Wire Rope

Bright wire, Uncoated, Fiber Core (FC)

Wire Diameter			Strength				Weight	
inch		mm	Nominal Strength		Safe Load			
			lbf	kN	lbf	kN	lbm/ft	kg/m
3/8	0.375	9.5	14,780	65.7	2,960	13.2	0.26	0.39
7/16	0.438	11.5	20,000	89.0	4,000	17.8	0.35	0.52
1/2	0.500	13	26,000	116	5,200	23.1	0.46	0.68
9/16	0.563	14.5	32,800	146	6,560	29.2	0.57	0.85
5/8	0.625	16	40,400	180	8,080	35.9	0.71	1.06
3/4	0.750	19	57,600	256	11,500	51.2	1.03	1.53
7/8	0.875	22	78,000	347	15,600	69.4	1.40	2.08
1	1.000	26	101,400	451	20,300	90.3	1.82	2.71
1-1/8	1.125	29	127,200	566	25,400	113	2.31	3.44
1-1/4	1.250	32	156,400	696	31,300	139	2.85	4.24
1-3/8	1.375	35	188,200	837	37,600	167	3.45	5.13
1-1/2	1.500	38	222,000	988	44,400	198	4.10	6.10
1-5/8	1.625	42	260,000	1,160	52,000	231	4.80	7.14
1-3/4	1.750	45	300,000	1,330	60,000	267	5.56	8.27
1-7/8	1.875	48	342,000	1,520	68,400	304	6.38	9.49
2	2.000	52	386,000	1,720	77,200	343	7.26	10.8

Bright wire, uncoated, Independent Wire Rope Core (IWRC)

3/8	0.375	9.5	16,600	73.8	3,320	14.8	0.31	0.46
7/16	0.438	11.5	22,400	99.6	4,480	19.9	0.39	0.58
1/2	0.500	13	29,200	130	5,840	26.0	0.49	0.73
9/16	0.563	14.5	37,000	165	7,400	32.9	0.63	0.94
5/8	0.625	16	45,400	202	9,080	40.4	0.78	1.16
3/4	0.750	19	64,800	288	13,000	57.8	1.13	1.68
7/8	0.875	22	87,600	390	17,500	77.8	1.54	2.29
1	1.000	26	113,800	506	22,800	101	2.00	2.98
1-1/8	1.125	29	143,000	636	28,600	127	2.54	3.78
1-1/4	1.250	32	175,800	782	35,200	157	3.14	4.67
1-3/8	1.375	35	212,000	943	42,400	189	3.80	5.66
1-1/2	1.500	38	250,000	1,110	50,000	222	4.50	6.70
1-5/8	1.625	42	292,000	1,300	58,400	260	5.27	7.84
1-3/4	1.750	45	338,000	1,500	67,600	301	6.12	9.11
1-7/8	1.875	48	384,000	1,710	76,800	342	7.02	10.4
2	2.000	52	434,000	1,930	86,800	386	7.98	11.9

Notes:
(1) Abbreviations used:
  lbf = pound-force, lbm/ft = pound-mass/foot,
  kg/m = kilogram/meter, kN = kilonewton, mm = millimeter
(2) Conversions: 2,000 pounds-force = 1 short ton-force and
  1 short ton-force = 0.90718474 metric ton-force.
(3) Factor of safety = 5; Safe Load = Nominal Strength divided by 5.
(4) References: Similar tables may be found in:

Wire Rope Users Manual, Third Edition, Wire Rope Technical Board, 1993.
Southwest Wire Rope, Houston, TX (see www.southwestwirerope.com)
Wire Rope Corporation of America, Chillicothe, MO (see www.wrca.com)
Standard Handbook For Mechanical Engineers, Tenth Edition, McGraw-Hill, 1996.
Materials Handling Handbook, Second Edition, John Wiley & Sons, 1985.

Knots & Bends

Blackwall Hitch
A fast way to secure a rope to a hook. Temporary hitch

Blood Knot
A common fishing knot which joins two lines of equal diameter together. Do not use if lines are different diameters.

Bowline
One of the most used knot due to its no slip design. Can be tied around objects into any size loop. Used for a rescue sling.

Bowline on the Bight
This is a double loop knot that is easy to tie and untie and does not readily jam. A good knot when you need to pull on a rope.

Butterfly Knot
This knot is used when you need an attachment loopin a bight of a
loaded rope. The knot is perpendicular to the loop.

Carrick Bend (also called a sailor's knot or anchor bend)
This knot is very strong, easy to tie, does not slip when wet, does
not jam, and is readily untied.

Cats Paw or Racking Hitch
Used for hitching a rope to a hook so that the rope will not slip
through the hook.

Chain Knot
Used to shorten a rope or extension cord. Very quick release.
This knot is also used in crocheting.

Clinch Knot - Improved
One of the most common knots for securing a fish hook to a fishing line. Not recommended for braided lines. Difficult if line > 30lb

Clove Hitch - An all purpose hitch that is <u>not</u> totally secure. Good for poles and cleats but not recommended with square post as it comes loose. Hard to undo under heavy load.

Constrictor Hitch
Used to clamp a rope tightly around an object. In the configuration shown above, it is quick release. If the black tip end is pulled to the right, out of the loop, it is more secure but not quick release.

Crabbers Eye Knot (aka a running knot with crossed ends)
Knot will not slip with a steady pull load. Large top loop will slip <u>until knot is taught</u>. Bottom loop will not slip. Not a well known knot.

Double Back Knot
A knot used in beading. Can be used as an end knot or as a
separator knot.

Dropper Loop
Used to form a loop anywhere on a line so another line or hook can
be attached.

Figure 8 or Flemish Knot
One of the strongest knots. Mountain climbers use it as a "tie-in"
knot. Also used to keep rope ends from fraying.

Fishermans Bend or Anchor Bend
Used to attach a rope to an anchor or climbers carabiner ring. The
above version shows it with an additional half-hitch for security.

Fisherman's Eye (Running Knot + Overhand Knot)
A good non-slip bight. A commonly used fishing knot when you need to make an eye.

Fisherman's Knot (two Overhand Knots)
Used to tie two fishing lines together. It can be secured further by using a tripple overhand. Easy to make, difficult to untie.

Flemish 2 Ropes
Used to join two ropes together. Not used very often because it is a thicker knot.

Fourfold Overhand (Threefold has three laps instead of four)
Good sewing knot. The Threefold Knot version was also called a blood knot (used at a whips end to inflict more pain and draw blood)

Granny Knot or Lubbeis Knot or Slip Knot
Knot slips easily and is only usefull for wrapping a package or
magic tricks. If 4 ends are pulled tight, it creates 4 right angles.

Half Hitch - Double
A very basic knot which is typically used in conjunction with making
other knots more secure.

Killick Knot (a Timber Hitch + Half Hitch
Used for towing large, heavy items like a log. Also used to fasten a
stone to the end of the rope to make a boat anchor.

Lark's Head
Used to tie a tarpaulin when holes exist. Easy to make but the
ends need to be loaded or the knot will slip.

Lark's Head - Double

Lark's Head - Trebble

Lark's Head with Crossed Ends

Midshipman's Hitch
Used to attach a tail-block to a rope.

Morring Hitch aka Slippery Hitch
A quick release knot used to temporarily moor a small boat. Knot will hold fast under tension.

Overhand Knot
The simplest of all knots and a key component of other knots. Keeps ends from fraying or keeps other knots from slipping.

Overhand Rosette
Two ropes tied in a simple Overhand Knot. A simple, quick way to join two ropes together. The Flemish Knot adds more security.

Palomar Knot
A fishing knot used to secure a hook. Ok with braided lines. Ring above represents the eye of the fish hook.

Perfection Loop
A fishing knot used to form a loop at the end of a line. Will not slip and is a very neat and compact knot.

Rolling Hitch aka Mangus Hitch. Easy to tie, very secure. Fastens a rope to a post. Also used on sail boats when a side pull is needed to hold fast in the direction of the standing line.

Running Knot
Used as a sailors neck handkerchief and whenever you need a bight to enlarge or decrease.

Sheepshank
Used to shorten the length of a rope and give the rope strength. Use the knotted version below for more security.

Sheepshank Knotted
A more secure Sheepshank. Used to shorten the length of a rope and giving the rope strength.

Knots & Bends (cont.)

Sheet Bend
A strong, easy to make and release, knot used to secure a sail (with a sails clew). Can also be used to join two ropes together.

Sheet Bend - More secure. A strong, easy to make and release, knot used to secure a sail (with a sails clew). Can also be used to join two ropes together. Works well with ropes of different diameters. A double will even hold nylon rope.

Slippery Ring Knot
Used to moor a small boat for short periods of time. Easy to tie and quick to release.

Square Knot or Sailor's Knot or Reef Knot
Most common knot for securing 2 ropes. <u>Warning</u>: it will capsize or jam under heavy load and untie with movement.

Surgeon's Knot
A fishing knot which forms a loop at the end of the line. This knot is much thicker than the Perfection Loop.

Tautline Hitch
A common hitch used to secure a tent rope to a stake

Timber Hitch
A quick way to secure or tow logs. The more weight, the tighter it holds.

Topsail Halliard Bend
Used on yachts as a non-slip knot that secures a line to an object. Note that line comes off at a right angle.

Knots & Bends (cont.)

 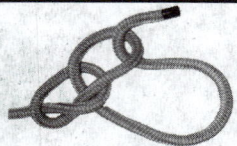

Tripple Crown Knot
Each loop is loaded; there is no communication between loops

Truckers Hitch
Slip knot version of the knot shown below.

Trucker's Hitch - no slip knot
Used to cinch down a load. Easy to adjust tightness. Can be made more secure finishing with one or two half hitches.

Uni Knot
A basic fishing knot that will not slip on any line or rope when pulled taunt. The ring above represents the eye of a fish hook.

Uni Knot - Double
A fishing knot used for joining 2 fishing lines of the same diameter. Good with braided lines. Fast, easy, no slip when pulled tight.

Steel & Metals

(See also PLUMBING AND PIPE, page 501)
(See also Rebar on page 102)

Steel Wire Gauges

Gauge Number	American or Brown & Sharpe	Birming-ham or Stubs Iron	US Steewire or Washburn & Moen	W & M Music Wire	British Imperial Std Wire
7/0	...	...	0.4900	0.0087	0.500
6/0	0.580000	...	0.4615	0.0095	0.464
5/0	0.516500	...	0.4305	0.010	0.432
4/0	0.460000	0.454	0.3938	0.011	0.400
3/0	0.409642	0.425	0.3625	0.012	0.372
2/0	0.364796	0.380	0.3310	0.0133	0.348
0	0.324861	0.340	0.3065	0.0144	0.324
1	0.289297	0.300	0.2830	0.0156	0.300
2	0.257627	0.284	0.2625	0.0166	0.276
3	0.229423	0.259	0.2437	0.0178	0.252
4	0.204307	0.238	0.2253	0.0188	0.232
5	0.181940	0.220	0.2070	0.0202	0.212
6	0.162023	0.203	0.1920	0.0215	0.192
7	0.144285	0.180	0.1770	0.0230	0.176
8	0.128490	0.165	0.1620	0.0243	0.160
9	0.114423	0.148	0.1483	0.0256	0.144
10	0.101897	0.134	0.1350	0.0270	0.128
11	0.090742	0.120	0.1205	0.0284	0.116
12	0.080808	0.109	0.1055	0.0296	0.104
13	0.071962	0.095	0.0915	0.0314	0.092
14	0.064084	0.083	0.0800	0.0326	0.080
15	0.057068	0.072	0.0720	0.0345	0.072
16	0.050821	0.065	0.0625	0.0360	0.064
17	0.045257	0.058	0.0540	0.0377	0.056
18	0.040303	0.049	0.0475	0.0395	0.048
19	0.035890	0.042	0.0410	0.0414	0.040
20	0.031961	0.035	0.0348	0.0434	0.036
21	0.028462	0.032	0.03175	0.0460	0.032
22	0.025346	0.028	0.0286	0.0483	0.028
23	0.022572	0.025	0.0258	0.0510	0.024
24	0.020101	0.022	0.0230	0.0550	0.022
25	0.017900	0.020	0.0204	0.0586	0.020
26	0.015941	0.018	0.0181	0.0626	0.018
27	0.014195	0.016	0.0173	0.0658	0.0164
28	0.012641	0.014	0.0162	0.0720	0.0148
29	0.011257	0.013	0.0150	0.0760	0.0136
30	0.010025	0.012	0.0140	0.0800	0.0124
31	0.008928	0.010	0.0132	...	0.0116
32	0.007950	0.009	0.0128	...	0.0108
33	0.007080	0.008	0.0118	...	0.0100
34	0.006305	0.007	0.0104	...	0.0092
35	0.005615	0.005	0.0095	...	0.0084
36	0.005000	0.004	0.0090	...	0.0076
37	0.004453	...	0.0085	...	0.0068
38	0.003965	...	0.0080	...	0.0060
39	0.003531	...	0.0075	...	0.0052
40	0.003144	...	0.0070	...	0.0048
41	0.00280	...	...	...	...
42	0.00249	...	...	...	...
43	0.00222	...	...	...	...
44	0.00198	...	...	...	...
45	0.00176	...	...	...	...
46	0.00157	...	...	...	...
47	0.00140	...	...	...	...
48	0.00124	...	...	...	...
49	0.00111	...	...	...	...
50	0.00099	...	...	...	...

Steel Sheet Gauges

Gauge Number	Steel Weight lbs per sq foot	Thickness Inches		Weight lbs/sq ft	
		US Standard Gauge	Manufacturers Standard	Galvanized Sheet	Stainless Steel
7/0	20.00	0.5000	...	...	...
6/0	18.75	0.4687	...	...	...
5/0	17.50	0.4375	...	...	...
4/0	16.25	0.4062	...	...	...
3/0	15.00	0.3750	...	...	...
2/0	13.75	0.3437	...	...	...
0	12.50	0.3125	...	...	...
1	11.25	0.2812	...	...	...
2	10.62	0.2656	...	...	...
3	10.00	0.2500	0.2391	...	...
4	9.37	0.2344	0.2242	...	...
5	8.75	0.2187	0.2092	...	...
6	8.12	0.2031	0.1943	...	...
7	7.50	0.1875	0.1793	...	...
8	6.87	0.1719	0.1644	...	...
9	6.25	0.1562	0.1495	...	...
10	5.62	0.1406	0.1345	5.7812	5.7937
11	5.00	0.1250	0.1196	5.1562	5.1500
12	4.37	0.1094	0.1046	4.5312	4.5063
13	3.75	0.0937	0.0897	3.9062	3.8625
14	3.12	0.0781	0.0747	3.2812	3.2187
15	2.81	0.0703	0.0673	2.9687	2.8968
16	2.50	0.0625	0.0598	2.6562	2.5750
17	2.25	0.0562	0.0538	2.4062	2.3175
18	2.00	0.0500	0.0478	2.1562	2.0600
19	1.75	0.0437	0.0418	1.9062	1.8025
20	1.50	0.0375	0.0359	1.6562	1.5450
21	1.37	0.0344	0.0329	1.5312	1.4160
22	1.25	0.0312	0.0299	1.4062	1.2875
23	1.12	0.0281	0.0269	1.2812	1.1587
24	1.00	0.0250	0.0239	1.1562	1.0300
25	0.875	0.0219	0.0209	1.0312	0.9013
26	0.750	0.0187	0.0179	0.9062	0.7725
27	0.687	0.0172	0.0164	0.8437	0.7081
28	0.625	0.0156	0.0149	0.7812	0.6438
29	0.562	0.0141	0.0135	0.7187	0.5794
30	0.500	0.0125	0.0120	0.6562	0.5150
31	0.437	0.0109	0.0105	...	...
32	0.406	0.0102	0.0097	...	...
33	0.375	0.0094	0.0090	...	...
34	0.344	0.0086	0.0082	...	...
35	0.312	0.0078	0.0075	...	...
36	0.281	0.0070	0.0067	...	...
37	0.266	0.0066	0.0064	...	...
38	0.250	0.0062	0.0060	...	...
39	0.234	0.0059	...	...	...
40	0.219	0.0055	...	...	...
41	0.211	0.0053	...	...	...
42	0.203	0.0051	...	...	...
43	0.195	0.0049	...	...	...
44	0.187	0.0047	...	...	...

Steel Plate Sizes

Thickness Inches	Weight Lbs/sq foot	Thickness Inches	Weight Lbs/sq foot
3/16	7.65	2–1/8	86.70
1/4	10.20	2–1/4	91.80
5/16	12.75	2–1/2	102.00
3/8	15.30	2–3/4	112.20
7/16	17.85	3	122.40
1/2	20.40	3–1/4	132.60
9/16	22.95	3–1/2	142.80
5/8	25.50	3–3/4	153.00
11/16	28.05	4	163.20
3/4	30.60	4–1/4	173.40
13/16	33.15	4–1/2	183.60
7/8	35.70	5	204.00
1	40.80	5–1/2	224.40
1–1/8	45.90	6	244.80
1–1/4	51.00	6–1/2	265.20
1–3/8	56.10	7	285.60
1–1/2	61.20	7–1/2	306.00
1–5/8	66.30	8	326.40
1–3/4	71.40	9	367.20
1–7/8	76.50	10	408.00
2	81.60		

WIRE and SHEET SPECIFICATIONS

Weight values listed on the previous three pages are based on a theoretical specific gravity of 7.7 for Iron (480 lbs/cubic foot) and 7.854 for Steel (489.6 lbs/cubic foot). B.W. gauge weights are based on a steel weight of 40.8 lbs/ square foot.

US Standard Gauge was established by Congress in 1893 and establishes that the weight determines the gauge, not the thickness. Galvanized Sheet Gauge is customarily assumed to be based on the US Standard Gauge except 2.5 ounces per square foot is added to the gauge weight of the same US Standard Gauge number.

Channel STEEL Specs

Size (Bar) Inches	Weight Lbs/foot
3/4 x 5/16 x 1/8	0.50
3/4 x 3/8 x 1/8	0.56
7/8 x 3/8 x 1/8	0.61
7/8 x 7/16 x 1/8	0.69
1 x 3/8 x 1/8	0.68
1 x 1/2 x 1/8	0.84
1–1/8 x 9/16 x 3/16	1.16
1–1/4 x 1/2 x 1/8	1.01
1–1/2 x 1/2 x 1/8	1.12
1–1/2 x 9/16 x 3/16	1.44
1–1/2 x 3/4 x 1/8	1.17
1–1/2 x 1–1/2 x 3/16	2.65
1–3/4 x 1/2 x 3/16	1.55
2 x 1/2 x 1/8	1.43
2 x 9/16 x 3/16	1.86
2 x 5/8 x 1/4	2.28
2 x 1 x 1/8	1.59
2 x 1 x 3/16	2.32
2–1/2 x 5/8 x 3/16	2.27

STRUCTURAL CHANNEL

C = Standard Channel
MC = Miscellaneous Channel

Size Inches	Weight Lbs/foot
C 3 x 1-3/8 x 0.170	4.1
x 1–1/2 x 0.258	5.0
x 1–5/8 x 0.356	6.0
MC 3 x 1–7/8 x 0.312	7.1
x 0.500	9.0
C 4 x 1–5/8 x 0.184	5.4
x 1–5/8 x 0.247	6.25
x 1–3/4 x 0.321	7.25
MC 4 x 2–1/2 x 0.500	13.8
C 5 x 1–3/4 x 0.190	6.7
x 1–7/8 x 0.325	9.0
C 6 x 1–7/8 x 0.200	8.2
x 2 x 0.314	10.5
x 2–1/8 x 0.437	13.0
MC 6 x 2–1/2 x 0.310	12.0
MC 6 x 3 x 0.316	15.1
x 0.375	16.3
MC 6 x 3–1/2 x 0.340	15.3

STRUCTURAL CHANNEL

Size Inches	Weight Lbs/foot
MC 6 x 3–1/2 x 0.379	18.0
C 7 x 2–1/8 x 0.210	9.8
x 2–1/4 x 0.314	12.25
x 2–1/4 x 0.419	14.75
MC 7 x 3 x 0.375	17.6
x 3–1/2 x 0.352	19.1
x 3–5/8 x 0.503	22.7
MC 8 x 1–7/8 x 0.179	8.50
C 8 x 2–1/4 x 0.220	11.5
x 2–3/8 x 0.303	13.75
x 2–1/2 x 0.487	18.75
MC 8 x 3 x 0.353	18.7
x 0.400	20.0
x 3–1/2 x 0.377	21.4
x 0.427	22.8
C 9 x 2–3/8 x 0.233	13.4
x 2–1/2 x 0.285	15.0
x 2–5/8 x 0.448	20.0
MC 9 x 3–1/2 x 0.400	23.9
x 0.450	25.4
MC 10 x 1–1/8 x 0.152	6.5
x 1–1/2 x 0.170	8.4
x 3–3/8 x 0.290	22.0
x 0.380	25.0
C 10 x 2–5/8 x 0.240	15.3
x 2–3/4 x 0.379	20.0
x 2–7/8 x 0.526	25.0
x 3 x 0.673	30.0
MC 10 x 4 x 0.425	28.5
x 4–1/8 x 0.575	33.6
x 4–3/8 x 0.796	41.1
C 12 x 3 x 0.282	20.7
x 0.387	25.0
x 3–1/8 x 0.510	30.0
MC 12 x 1–1/2 x 0.190	10.6
x 3–5/8 x 0.370	31.0
x 3–3/4 x 0.467	35.0
x 3–7/8 x 0.590	40.0
x 4 x 0.712	45.0
x 4–1/8 x 0.835	50.0
MC 13 x 4 x 0.375	31.8
x 4–1/8 x 0.447	35.0

Channel & Angle STEEL Specs

STRUCTURAL CHANNEL

Size Inches	Weight Lbs/ foot
MC 13 x 4–1/8 x 0.560	40.0
x 4–3/8 x 0.787	50.0
C 15 x 3–3/8 x 0.400	33.9
x 3–1/2 x 0.520	40.0
x 3–3/4 x 0.716	50.0
MC 18 x 4 x 0.450	42.7
x 4 x 0.500	45.8
x 4–1/8 x 0.600	51.9
x 4–1/8 x 0.700	58.0

ANGLE STEEL

Size Inches	Weight Lbs/ foot
1/2 x 1/2 x 1/8	0.38
5/8 x 5/8 x 1/8	0.48
3/4 x 3/4 x 1/8	0.59
x 3/32	0.463
x 3/16	0.84
7/8 x 7/8 x 1/8	0.70
1 x 5/8 x 1/8	0.64
1 x 3/4 x 1/8	0.70
1 x 1 x 1/8	0.80
x 3/16	1.16
x 1/4	1.49
1–1/8 x 1–1/8 x 1/8	0.90
1–1/4 x 1–1/4 x 1/8	1.01
x 3/16	1.48
x 1/4	1.92
1–3/8 x 7/8 x 1/8	0.91
x 3/16	1.32
1–1/2 x 1–1/4 x 3/16	1.64
1–1/2 x 1–1/2 x 1/8	1.23
x 3/16	1.80
x 1/4	2.34
x 5/16	2.86
x 3/8	3.35
1–3/4 x 1–1/4 x 1/8	1.23
x 1/4	2.34
1–3/4 x 1–3/4 x 1/8	1.44
x 3/16	2.12
x 1/4	2.77
x 5/16	3.39

ANGLE STEEL

Size Inches	Weight Lbs/ foot
1–3/4 x 1–3/4 x 3/8	3.99
2 x 1–1/4 x 3/16	1.96
2 x 1–1/4 x 1/4	2.55
2 x 1–1/2 x 1/8	1.44
x 3/16	2.12
x 1/4	2.77
2 x 2 x 1/8	1.65
x 3/16	2.44
x 1/4	3.19
x 5/16	3.92
x 3/8	4.70
x 1/2	6.00
2–1/4 x 1–1/2 x 3/16	2.28
x 1/4	2.98
2–1/4 x 2–1/4 x 3/16	2.75
x 1/4	3.62
x 5/16	4.50
2–1/4 x 2–1/4 x 3/8	5.30
2–1/2 x 1–1/2 x 3/16	2.44
x 1/4	3.19
x 5/16	3.92
2–1/2 x 2 x 1/8	1.86
x 3/16	2.75
x 1/4	3.62
x 5/16	4.50
x 3/8	5.30
x 1/2	6.74
2–1/2 x 2–1/2 x 3/16	3.07
x 1/4	4.10
x 5/16	5.00
x 3/8	5.90
x 1/2	7.70
3 x 2 x 3/16	3.07
x 1/4	4.1
x 5/16	5.0
x 3/8	5.9
x 1/2	7.7
3 x 2–1/2 x 3/16	3.4
x 1/4	4.5
x 5/16	5.6
x 3/8	6.6
x 1/2	8.5
3 x 3 x 3/16	3.7
x 1/4	4.9

Angle STEEL Specs

Size Inches	Weight Lbs/ foot
3 x 3 x 5/16	6.1
x 3/8	7.2
x 7/16	8.3
x 1/2	9.4
3-1/2 x 2-1/2 x 1/4	4.9
x 5/16	6.1
x 3/8	7.2
x 1/2	9.4
3-1/2 x 3 x 1/4	5.4
x 5/16	6.6
x 3/8	7.9
x 1/2	10.2
3-1/2 x 3-1/2 x 1/4	5.8
x 5/16	7.2
x 3/8	8.5
x 7/16	9.8
x 1/2	11.1
4 x 3 x 1/4	5.8
x 5/16	7.2
x 3/8	8.5
x 7/16	9.8
x 1/2	11.1
x 5/8	13.6
4 x 3-1/2 x 1/4	6.2
x 5/16	7.7
x 3/8	9.1
x 7/16	10.6
x 1/2	11.9
4 x 4 x 1/4	6.6
x 5/16	8.2
x 3/8	9.8
x 7/16	11.3
x 1/2	12.8
x 5/8	15.7
x 3/4	18.5
5 x 3 x 1/4	6.6
x 5/16	8.2
x 3/8	9.8
x 7/16	11.3
x 1/2	12.8
5 x 3-1/2 x 1/4	7.0
x 5/16	8.7
x 3/8	10.4
x 7/16	12.0
x 1/2	13.6

Size Inches	Weight Lbs/ foot
5 x 3-1/2 x 5/8	16.8
x 3/4	19.8
5 x 5 x 5/16	10.3
x 3/8	12.3
x 7/16	14.3
x 1/2	16.2
x 5/8	20.0
x 3/4	23.6
x 7/8	27.2
6 x 3-1/2 x 5/16	9.8
x 3/8	11.7
x 1/2	15.3
6 x 4 x 5/16	10.3
x 3/8	12.3
x 7/16	14.3
x 1/2	16.2
x 5/8	20.0
x 3/4	23.6
x 7/8	27.2
x 9/16	18.1
6 x 6 x 5/16	12.50
x 3/8	14.9
x 7/16	17.2
x 1/2	19.6
x 9/16	21.9
x 5/8	24.2
x 3/4	28.7
x 7/8	33.1
x 1	37.4
7 x 4 x 3/8	13.6
x 7/16	15.8
x 1/2	17.9
x 5/8	22.1
x 3/4	26.2
8 x 4 x 7/16	17.2
x 1/2	19.6
x 9/16	21.9
x 5/8	24.2
x 3/4	28.7
x 7/8	33.1
x 1	37.4
8 x 6 x 7/16	20.4
x 1/2	23.0
x 9/16	25.7
x 5/8	28.5

Angle, Tee, & Round STEEL Specs

ANGLE STEEL

Size Inches	Weight Lbs/ foot
8 x 6 x 3/4	33.8
x 7/8	39.1
x 1	51.0
8 x 8 x 1/2	26.4
x 9/16	29.6
x 5/8	32.7
x 3/4	38.9
x 7/8	45.0
x 1	51.0
x 1–1/8	56.9
9 x 4 x 1/2	21.3

TEE BAR

Size Inches Flange x Stem	Weight Lbs/ foot
3/4 x 3/4 x 1/8	0.61
1 x 1 x 1/8	0.85
x 3/16	1.20
1–1/4 x 1–1/4 x 1/8	1.09
x 3/16	1.55
x 1/4	1.93
1–1/2 x 1–1/2 x 3/16	1.90
x 1/4	2.43
1–3/4 x 1–3/4 x 3/16	2.26
x 1/4	2.90
2 x 1–1/2 x 1/4	3.12
2 x 2 x 1/4	3.62
x 5/16	4.30
2–1/4 x 2–1/4 x 1/4	4.10
2–1/2 x 2–1/2 x 1/4	4.60
x 3/8	6.40

ROUND BAR

Size Inches	Weight Lbs/ foot
1/8	0.042
3/16	0.094
1/4	0.167
5/16	0.261
3/8	0.376
7/16	0.511
1/2	0.668

ROUND BAR

Size Inches	Weight Lbs/ foot
9/16	0.845
5/8	1.043
11/16	1.262
3/4	1.502
13/16	1.763
7/8	2.045
15/16	2.347
1	2.670
1–1/16	3.015
1–1/8	3.380
1–3/16	3.766
1–1/4	4.172
1–5/16	4.600
1–3/8	5.049
1–7/16	5.518
1–1/2	6.008
1–9/16	6.520
1–5/8	7.051
1–11/16	7.604
1–3/4	8.178
1–13/16	8.773
1–7/8	9.388
1–15/16	10.024
2	10.682
2–1/16	11.360
2–1/8	12.058
2–3/16	12.778
2–1/4	13.519
2–5/16	14.280
2–3/8	15.063
2–7/16	15.866
2–1/2	16.690
2–9/16	17.535
2–5/8	18.401
2–11/16	19.287
2–3/4	20.195
2–13/16	21.123
2–7/8	22.072
2–15/16	23.043
3	24.034
3–1/16	25.045
3–1/8	26.078
3–3/16	27.132
3–1/4	28.206
3–5/16	28.301
3–3/8	30.417
3–7/16	31.554
3–1/2	32.712
3–9/16	33.891
3–5/8	35.091
3–11/16	36.311

Round & Square STEEL BAR Specs

ROUND BAR

Size Inches	Weight Lbs/ foot
3–3/4	37.552
3–13/16	38.815
3–7/8	40.098
3–15/16	41.401
4	42.726
4–1/16	44.072
4–1/8	45.438
4–3/16	46.826
4–1/4	48.234
4–5/16	49.663
4–3/8	51.113
4–7/16	52.584
4–1/2	54.075
4–9/16	55.588
4–5/8	57.121
4–11/16	58.676
4–3/4	60.251
4–13/16	61.847
4–7/8	63.463
4–15/16	65.101
5	66.760
5–1/16	68.439
5–1/8	70.139
5–3/16	71.861
5–1/4	73.603
5–5/16	75.365
5–3/8	77.149
5–7/16	78.954
5–1/2	80.779
5–9/16	82.626
5–5/8	84.493
5–11/16	86.381
5–3/4	88.290
5–13/16	90.220
5–7/8	92.170
5–15/16	94.142
6	96.13
6–1/8	100.18
6–1/4	104.31
6–1/2	112.82
6–5/8	117.21
6–3/4	121.67
7	130.85
7–1/8	135.56
7–1/4	140.36
7–1/2	150.21
8	170.91

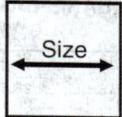

Size

SQUARE BAR

Size Inches	Weight Lbs/ foot
1/8	0.053
3/16	0.120
1/4	0.213
5/16	0.332
3/8	0.478
7/16	0.651
1/2	0.850
9/16	1.076
5/8	1.328
11/16	1.607
3/4	1.913
13/16	2.245
7/8	2.603
15/16	2.988
1	3.400
1–1/16	3.838
1–1/8	4.303
1–3/16	4.795
1–1/4	5.313
1–5/16	5.857
1–3/8	6.428
1–7/16	7.026
1–1/2	7.650
1–9/16	8.301
1–5/8	8.978
1–11/16	9.682
1–3/4	10.413
1–13/16	11.170
1–7/8	11.953
1–15/16	12.763
2	13.600
2–1/16	14.463
2–1/8	15.353
2–3/16	16.270
2–1/4	17.213
2–5/16	18.182
2–3/8	19.178
2–7/16	20.201
2–1/2	21.250
2–9/16	22.326
2–5/8	23.428

Square & Hex STEEL BAR Specs

SQUARE BAR

Size Inches	Weight Lbs/ foot
2–11/16	24.557
2–3/4	25.713
2–13/16	26.895
2–7/8	28.103
2–15/16	29.339
3	30.600
3–1/16	31.889
3–1/8	33.204
3–3/16	34.545
3–1/4	35.913
3–5/16	37.308
3–3/8	38.729
3–7/16	40.176
3–1/2	41.651
3–9/16	43.151
3–5/8	44.679
3–11/16	46.233
3–3/4	47.813
3–13/16	49.420
3–7/8	51.054
3–15/16	52.714
4	54.401
4–1/16	56.114
4–1/8	57.854
4–3/16	59.620
4–1/4	61.413
4–5/16	63.233
4–3/8	65.079
4–7/16	66.952
4–1/2	68.851
4–9/16	70.777
4–5/8	72.729
4–11/16	74.708
4–3/4	76.714
4–13/16	78.746
4–7/8	80.804
4–15/16	82.889
5	85.001
5–1/16	87.139
5–1/8	89.304
5–3/16	91.496
5–1/4	93.714
5–5/16	95.958
5–3/8	98.229
5–7/16	100.527
5–1/2	102.851
5–9/16	105.202
5–5/8	107.580
5–11/16	109.983
5–3/4	112.414
5–13/16	114.871
5–7/8	117.355
5–15/16	119.865
6	122.40

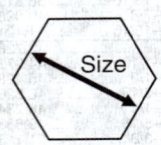

Size

HEXAGONAL BAR

Size Inches	Weight Lbs/ foot
1/8	0.046
3/16	0.104
1/4	0.184
5/16	0.288
3/8	0.414
7/16	0.564
1/2	0.736
9/16	0.932
5/8	1.150
11/16	1.392
3/4	1.656
13/16	1.944
7/8	2.254
15/16	2.588
1	2.945
1–1/16	3.324
1–1/8	3.727
1–3/16	4.152
1–1/4	4.601
1–5/16	5.072
1–3/8	5.567
1–7/16	6.085
1–1/2	6.625
1–9/16	7.189
1–5/8	7.775
1–11/16	8.385
1–3/4	9.018
1–13/16	9.673
1–7/8	10.352
1–15/16	11.053
2	11.778
2–1/16	12.526
2–1/8	13.296
2–3/16	14.090
2–1/4	14.907

Hex & Octagonal STEEL Bar Specs

HEXAGONAL BAR

Size Inches	Weight Lbs/ foot
2–5/16	15.746
2–3/8	16.609
2–7/16	17.495
2–1/2	18.403
2–9/16	19.335
2–5/8	20.290
2–11/16	21.267
2–3/4	22.268
2–13/16	23.292
2–7/8	24.338
2–15/16	25.408
3	26.501
3–1/16	27.616
3–1/8	28.755
3–3/16	29.917
3–1/4	31.102
3–5/16	32.309
3–3/8	33.540
3–7/16	34.794
3–1/2	36.070
3–9/16	37.370
3–5/8	38.693
3–11/16	40.039
3–3/4	41.407
3–13/16	42.799
3–7/8	44.214
3–15/16	45.652
4	47.112
4–1/16	48.596
4–1/8	50.103
4–3/16	51.633
4–1/4	53.185
4–5/16	54.761
4–3/8	56.360
4–7/16	57.982
4–1/2	59.627
4–9/16	61.294
4–5/8	62.985
4–11/16	64.699
4–3/4	66.436
4–13/16	68.196
4–7/8	69.978
4–15/16	71.784
5	73.613
5–1/16	75.465
5–1/8	77.340
5–3/16	79.238
5–1/4	81.158
5–5/16	83.102
5–3/8	85.069
5–7/16	87.059
5–1/2	89.072
5–9/16	91.108
5–5/8	93.167
5–11/16	95.248
5–3/4	97.353
5–13/16	99.481
5–7/8	101.63
5–15/16	103.81
6	106.00

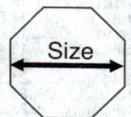

OCTAGONAL BAR

Size Inches	Weight Lbs/ foot
1/8	0.044
3/16	0.099
1/4	0.176
5/16	0.275
3/8	0.396
7/16	0.539
1/2	0.704
9/16	0.891
5/8	1.100
11/16	1.331
3/4	1.584
13/16	1.859
7/8	2.157
15/16	2.476
1	2.817
1–1/16	3.180
1–1/8	3.565
1–3/16	3.972
1–1/4	4.401
1–5/16	4.852
1–3/8	5.325
1–7/16	5.820
1–1/2	6.338
1–9/16	6.877
1–5/8	7.438
1–11/16	8.021
1–3/4	8.626
1–13/16	9.253
1–7/8	9.902

Octagonal & Flat STEEL Bar Specs

OCTAGONAL BAR

Size Inches	Weight Lbs/ foot
1–15/16	10.574
2	11.267
2–1/16	11.982
2–1/8	12.719
2–3/16	13.478
2–1/4	14.259
2–5/16	15.063
2–3/8	15.888
2–7/16	16.735
2–1/2	17.604
2–9/16	18.496
2–5/8	19.409
2–11/16	20.344
2–3/4	21.301
2–13/16	22.280
2–7/8	23.282
2–15/16	24.305
3	25.350
3–1/16	26.417
3–1/8	27.507
3–3/16	28.618
3–1/4	29.751
3–5/16	30.907
3–3/8	32.084
3–7/16	33.283
3–1/2	34.504
3–9/16	35.748
3–5/8	37.013
3–11/16	38.300
3–3/4	39.610
3–13/16	40.941
3–7/8	42.294
3–15/16	42.670
4	45.067
4–1/16	46.486
4–1/8	47.928
4–3/16	49.391
4–1/4	50.876
4–5/16	52.384
4–3/8	53.913
4–7/16	55.465
4–1/2	57.038
4–9/16	58.633
4–5/8	60.251
4–11/16	61.890
4–3/4	63.552
4–13/16	65.235
4–7/8	66.940
4–15/16	68.668
5	70.417
5–1/16	72.189
5–1/8	73.982
5–3/16	75.798
5–1/4	77.635
5–5/16	79.494
5–3/8	81.376
5–7/16	83.279
5–1/2	85.205
5–9/16	87.152
5–5/8	89.122
5–11/16	91.113
5–3/4	93.127
5–13/16	95.162
5–7/8	97.220
5–15/16	99.299
6	101.40

FLAT STEEL BAR

Size Inches	Weight Lbs/ foot
1/8 x 5/16	0.133
x 3/8	0.159
x 7/16	0.186
x 1/2	0.213
x 9/16	0.239
x 5/8	0.266
x 11/16	0.292
x 3/4	0.319
x 7/8	0.372
x 1	0.425
x 1–1/8	0.478
x 1–1/4	0.531
x 1–3/8	0.584
x 1–1/2	0.638
x 1–5/8	0.691
x 1–3/4	0.744
x 1–7/8	0.797
x 2	0.850
x 2–1/4	0.956
x 2–1/2	1.063
x 2–3/4	1.169
x 3	1.275
x 3–1/2	1.488
x 4	1.700
x 5	2.125
x 6	2.550
3/16 x 5/16	0.199
x 3/8	0.239
x 7/16	0.279
x 1/2	0.319
x 9/16	0.359
x 5/8	0.398
x 11/16	0.438
x 3/4	0.478
x 7/8	0.558
x 1	0.638
x 1–1/8	0.717

Flat STEEL Bar Specs

FLAT STEEL BAR

Size Inches	Weight Lbs/foot		Size Inches	Weight Lbs/foot
3/16 x 1-1/4	0.797		5/16 x 3	3.188
x 1-3/8	0.877		x 3-1/2	3.719
x 1-1/2	0.956		x 4	4.250
x 1-5/8	1.036		x 4-1/2	4.781
x 1-3/4	1.116		x 5	5.313
x 1-7/8	1.195		x 6	6.375
x 2	1.275		3/8 x 7/16	0.558
x 2-1/4	1.434		x 1/2	0.638
x 2-1/2	1.594		x 9/16	0.717
x 2-3/4	1.753		x 5/8	0.797
x 3	1.913		x 11/16	0.877
x 3-1/2	2.231		x 3/4	0.956
x 4	2.550		x 7/8	1.116
x 4-1/2	2.869		x 1	1.275
x 5	3.188		x 1-1/8	1.434
x 6	3.825		x 1-1/4	1.594
1/4 x 5/16	0.266		x 1-3/8	1.753
x 3/8	0.319		x 1-1/2	1.913
x 7/16	0.372		x 1-5/8	2.072
x 1/2	0.425		x 1-3/4	2.231
x 9/16	0.478		x 1-7/8	2.391
x 5/8	0.531		x 2	2.550
x 11/16	0.584		x 2-1/4	2.869
x 3/4	0.638		x 2-1/2	3.188
x 7/8	0.744		x 2-3/4	3.506
x 1	0.850		x 3	3.825
x 1-1/8	0.956		x 3-1/2	4.463
x 1-1/4	1.063		x 4	5.100
x 1-3/8	1.169		x 4-1/2	5.738
x 1-1/2	1.275		x 5	6.375
x 1-5/8	1.381		x 6	7.650
x 1-3/4	1.488		1/2 x 9/16	0.956
x 1-7/8	1.594		x 5/8	1.063
x 2	1.700		x 11/16	1.169
x 2-1/4	1.913		x 3/4	1.275
x 2-1/2	2.125		x 13/16	1.381
x 2-3/4	2.338		x 7/8	1.488
x 3	2.550		x 1	1.700
x 3-1/2	2.975		x 1-1/8	1.913
x 4	3.400		x 1-1/4	2.125
x 4-1/2	3.825		x 1-3/8	2.338
x 5	4.250		x 1-1/2	2.550
x 6	5.100		x 1-5/8	2.763
5/16 x 3/8	0.398		x 1-3/4	2.975
x 7/16	0.465		x 2	3.400
x 1/2	0.531		x 2-1/4	3.825
x 9/16	0.598		x 2-1/2	4.250
x 5/8	0.664		x 2-3/4	4.675
x 3/4	0.797		x 3	5.100
x 7/8	0.930		x 3-1/2	5.950
x 1	1.063		x 4	6.800
x 1-1/8	1.195		x 5	8.500
x 1-1/4	1.328		x 6	10.200
x 1-3/8	1.461		5/8 x 11/16	1.461
x 1-1/2	1.594		x 3/4	1.594
x 1-5/8	1.727		x 13/16	1.727
x 1-3/4	1.859		x 7/8	1.859
x 2	2.125		x 1	2.125
x 2-1/4	2.391		x 1-1/8	2.391
x 2-1/2	2.656		x 1-1/4	2.656
x 2-3/4	2.922		x 1-3/8	2.922
			x 1-1/2	3.188
			x 1-5/8	3.453

Flat STEEL Bar Specs

FLAT STEEL BAR

Size Inches	Weight Lbs/ foot
5/8 x 1–3/4	3.719
x 1–7/8	3.984
x 2	4.250
x 2–1/4	4.781
x 2–1/2	5.313
x 2–3/4	5.844
x 3	6.375
x 3–1/2	7.438
x 4	8.500
x 5	10.625
x 6	12.750
3/4 x 7/8	2.231
x 1	2.550
x 1–1/8	2.869
x 1–1/4	3.188
x 1–3/8	3.506
x 1–1/2	3.825
x 1–5/8	4.144
x 1–3/4	4.463
x 1–7/8	4.781
x 2	5.100
x 2–1/4	5.738
x 2–1/2	6.375
x 2–3/4	7.013
x 3	7.650
x 3–1/2	8.925
x 4	10.200
x 5	12.750
x 6	15.300
7/8 x 1	2.975
x 1–1/8	3.347
x 1–1/4	3.719
x 1–3/8	4.091
x 1–1/2	4.463
x 1–5/8	4.834
x 1–3/4	5.206
x 1–7/8	5.578
x 2	5.950
x 2–1/4	6.694
x 2–1/2	7.438
x 2–3/4	8.181
x 3	8.925
x 3–1/2	10.413
x 4	11.900
x 5	14.875
x 6	17.850
1 x 1–1/8	3.825
x 1–1/4	4.250
x 1–3/8	4.675
x 1–1/2	5.100
x 1–5/8	5.525
x 1–3/4	5.950
x 1–7/8	6.375
x 2	6.800
x 2–1/4	7.650
x 2–1/2	8.500
x 2–3/4	9.350
x 3	10.200
x 3–1/2	11.900
x 4	13.600
x 5	17.000

Size Inches	Weight Lbs/ foot
1 x 6	20.400
1–1/4 x 1–3/8	5.844
x 1–1/2	6.375
x 1–5/8	6.906
x 1–3/4	7.438
x 1–7/8	7.969
x 2	8.500
x 2–1/4	9.563
x 2–1/2	10.625
x 2–3/4	11.688
x 3	12.750
x 3–1/2	14.875
x 4	17.000
x 5	21.250
x 6	25.500
1–1/2 x 1–3/4	8.925
x 1–7/8	9.563
x 2	10.200
x 2–1/4	11.475
x 2–1/2	12.750
x 2–3/4	14.025
x 3	15.300
x 3–1/2	17.850
x 4	20.400
x 5	25.500
x 6	30.600
2 x 2–1/4	15.300
x 2–1/2	17.000
x 2–3/4	18.700
x 3	20.400
x 3–1/2	23.800
x 4	27.200
x 5	34.000
x 6	40.800
3 x 4	40.800
x 5	51.000
x 6	61.200

Square STEEL Tubing Specs

OD Size Inches (gauge)	Weight Lbs/ foot	OD Size Inches (gauge)	Weight Lbs/ foot
1/2 x 0.035 (20)	0.221	2–1/2 x 0.188 (3/16)	5.59
x 0.049 (18)	0.301	x 0.250 (1/4)	7.11
x 0.065 (16)	0.385	3 x 0.083 (14)	3.29
5/8 x 0.035 (20)	0.281	x 0.120 (11)	4.70
x 0.049 (18)	0.384	x 0.188 (3/16)	6.87
x 0.065 (16)	0.495	x 0.250 (1/4)	8.81
3/4 x 0.035 (20)	0.340	3–1/2 x 0.120 (11)	5.52
x 0.049 (18)	0.467	x 0.188 (3/16)	8.15
x 0.065 (16)	0.606	x 0.250 (1/4)	10.51
x 0.083 (14)	0.753	x 0.313 (5/16)	12.70
x 0.120 (11)	1.03	4 x 0.120 (11)	6.33
7/8 x 0.035 (20)	0.400	x 0.188 (3/16)	9.42
x 0.049 (18)	0.550	x 0.250 (1/4)	12.21
x 0.065 (16)	0.716	x 0.313 (5/16)	14.83
1 x 0.035 (20)	0.459	x 0.375 (3/8)	17.27
x 0.049 (18)	0.634	x 0.500 (1/2)	21.63
x 0.065 (16)	0.827	5 x 0.188 (3/16)	11.97
x 0.073	0.910	x 0.250 (1/4)	15.62
x 0.083 (14)	1.04	x 0.313 (5/16)	19.08
x 0.095 (13)	1.17	x 0.375 (3/8)	22.37
x 0.109 (12)	1.32	x 0.500 (1/2)	28.43
x 0.120 (11)	1.44	6 x 0.188 (3/16)	14.53
1–1/4 x 0.035 (20)	0.578	x 0.250 (1/4)	19.02
x 0.049 (18)	0.800	x 0.313 (5/16)	23.34
x 0.065 (16)	1.05	x 0.375 (3/8)	27.48
x 0.083 (14)	1.32	x 0.500 (1/2)	35.24
x 0.120 (11)	1.84	7x 0.188 (3/16)	17.08
x 0.135	2.03	x 0.250 (1/4)	22.42
x 0.188 (3/16)	2.61	x 0.313 (5/16)	27.59
1–1/2 x 0.035 (20)	0.698	x 0.375 (3/8)	32.58
x 0.049 (18)	0.967	x 0.500 (1/2)	42.05
x 0.065 (16)	1.27	8 x 0.188 (3/16)	19.63
x 0.083 (14)	1.60	x 0.250 (1/4)	25.82
x 0.120 (11)	2.25	x 0.313 (5/16)	31.84
x 0.188 (3/16)	3.04	x 0.375 (3/8)	37.69
1–3/4 x 0.065 (16)	1.49	x 0.500 (1/2)	48.85
x 0.083 (14)	1.88	10 x 0.188 (3/16)	24.73
x 0.120 (11)	2.66	x 0.250 (1/4)	32.63
2 x 0.065 (16)	1.71	x 0.313 (5/16)	40.35
x 0.083 (14)	2.16	x 0.375 (3/8)	47.90
x 0.095 (13)	2.46	x 0.500 (1/2)	62.46
x 0.120 (11)	3.07	12 x 0.188 (3/16)	29.84
x 0.188 (3/16)	4.32	x 0.250 (1/4)	39.43
x 0.250 (1/4)	5.41	x 0.313 (5/16)	48.86
2–1/2 x 0.083 (14)	2.73	x 0.375 (3/8)	58.10
x 0.120 (11)	3.88	x 0.500 (1/2)	76.07
		x 0.625 (5/8)	93.34

Rectangle STEEL Tubing Specs

OD Size Inches (gauge)	Weight Lbs/foot	OD Size Inches (gauge)	Weight Lbs/foot
1–1/2 x 1 x 0.083 (14)	1.32	7 x 5 x 0.188 (3/16)	14.53
x 0.120 (11)	1.84	x 0.250 (1/4)	19.02
2 x 1 x 0.083 (14)	1.60	x 0.313 (5/16)	23.34
2 x 1–1/4 x 0.083 (14)	1.74	x 0.375 (3/8)	27.48
2 x 1–1/2 x 0.120 (11)	2.66	x 0.500 (1/2)	35.24
2–1/2 x 1 x 0.083 (14)	1.88	8 x 2 x 0.188 (3/16)	11.97
2–1/2 x 1–1/4 x 0.083(14)	2.02	8 x 3 x 0.188 (3/16)	13.25
2–1/2 x 1–1/2 x 0.083(14)	2.16	x 0.250 (1/4)	17.32
x 0.180 (7)	4.45	8 x 4 x 0.188 (3/16)	14.53
x 0.250	5.40	x 0.250 (1/4)	19.02
3 x 1 x 0.083 (14)	2.16	x 0.313 (5/16)	23.34
3 x 1–1/2 x 0.083 (14)	2.45	x 0.375 (3/8)	27.48
x 0.120 (11)	3.48	x 0.500 (1/2)	35.24
x 0.180 (7)	5.07	8 x 6 x 0.188 (3/16)	17.08
3 x 2 x 0.083 (14)	2.73	x 0.250 (1/4)	22.42
x 0.120 (11)	3.88	x 0.313 (5/16)	27.59
x 0.188 (3/16)	5.59	x 0.375 (3/8)	32.58
x 0.250 (1/4)	7.11	x 0.500 (1/2)	42.05
4 x 2 x 0.083 (14)	3.29	10 x 2 x 0.188 (3/16)	14.53
x 0.120 (11)	4.70	10 x 4 x 0.188 (3/16)	17.08
x 0.188 (3/16)	6.87	x 0.250 (1/4)	22.42
x 0.250 (1/4)	8.81	10 x 5 x 0.250 (1/4)	24.12
4 x 2–1/2 x 0.120 (11)	5.11	10 x 6 x 0.250 (1/4)	25.82
4 x 3 x 0.120 (11)	5.52	x 0.313 (5/16)	31.84
x 0.188 (3/16)	8.15	x 0.375 (3/8)	37.69
x 0.250 (1/4)	10.51	x 0.500 (1/2)	48.85
x 0.313 (5/16)	12.70	10 x 8 x 0.250 (1/4)	29.23
5 x 2 x 0.188 (3/16)	8.15	x 0.375 (3/8)	42.79
x 0.250 (1/4)	10.51	x 0.500 (1/2)	55.66
5 x 2–1/2 x 0.120 (11)	5.92	12 x 2 x 0.188 (3/16)	17.08
x 0.180 (7)	8.74	12 x 4 x 0.250 (1/4)	25.82
5 x 3 x 0.188 (3/16)	9.42	x 0.375 (3/8)	37.69
x 0.250 (1/4)	12.21	12 x 6 x 0.250 (1/4)	29.23
x 0.313 (5/16)	14.83	x 0.375 (3/8)	42.97
x 0.375 (3/8)	17.27	x 0.500 (1/2)	55.66
x 0.500 (1/2)	21.63	12 x 8 x 0.250 (1/4)	32.63
6 x 2 x 0.188 (3/16)	9.42	x 0.313 (5/16)	40.35
x 0.250 (1/4)	12.21	x 0.375 (3/8)	47.90
6 x 3 x 0.188 (3/16)	10.70	x 0.500 (1/2)	62.46
x 0.250 (1/4)	13.91		
x 0.313 (5/16)	16.96		
x 0.375 (3/8)	19.82		
6 x 4 x 0.188 (3/16)	11.97		
x 0.250 (1/4)	15.62		
x 0.313 (5/16)	19.08		
x 0.375 (3/8)	22.37		
x 0.500 (1/2)	28.43		

Round STEEL Tubing Specs

OD Size Inches (gauge)	Weight Lbs/ foot	OD Size Inches (gauge)	Weight Lbs/ foot
1/8 x 0.028(22)	0.0290	7/8 x 0.083(14)	0.7021
x 0.035(20)	0.0336	x 0.095(13)	0.7914
5/32 x 0.028(22)	0.0384	x 0.109(12)	0.8917
x 0.035(20)	0.0452	x 0.120(11)	0.9676
3/16 x 0.022(24)	0.0390	15/16 x 0.049(18)	0.4652
x 0.028(22)	0.0478	x 0.095(13)	0.8553
x 0.035(20)	0.0572	1 x 0.035(20)	0.3607
x 0.049(18)	0.0727	x 0.049(18)	0.4977
x 0.065(16)	0.0854	x 0.065(16)	0.6491
1/4 x 0.028(22)	0.0664	x 0.083(14)	0.8129
x 0.035(20)	0.0804	x 0.095(13)	0.9182
x 0.049(18)	0.1052	x 0.109(12)	1.037
x 0.065(16)	0.1284	x 0.120(11)	1.128
5/16 x 0.028(22)	0.0852	x 0.250(1/4)	2.003
x 0.035(20)	0.1039	1–1/4 x 0.049(18)	0.6285
x 0.049(18)	0.1382	x 0.065(16)	0.8226
3/8 x 0.028(22)	0.1038	x 0.109(12)	1.328
x 0.035(20)	0.1271	x 0.120(11)	1.448
x 0.049(18)	0.1706	1–1/2 x 0.049(18)	0.7593
x 0.065(16)	0.2152	x 0.065(16)	0.9962
7/16 x 0.049(18)	0.2036	x 0.095(13)	1.426
x 0.065(16)	0.2589	x 0.109(12)	1.619
x 0.095(13)	0.3480	x 0.250(1/4)	3.338
1/2 x 0.035(20)	0.1738	x 0.500(1/2)	5.340
x 0.042(19)	0.2054	2 x 0.049(18)	1.021
x 0.049(18)	0.2360	x 0.065(16)	1.343
x 0.065(16)	0.3020	x 0.095(13)	1.933
x 0.083(14)	0.3696	x 0.120(11)	2.409
x 0.095(13)	0.4109	x 0.250(1/4)	4.673
9/16 x 0.049(18)	0.2690	x 0.500(1/2)	8.010
x 0.065(16)	0.3457	2–1/2 x 0.065(16)	1.690
x 0.120(11)	0.5677	x 0.095(13)	2.440
5/8 x 0.035(20)	0.2205	x 0.120(11)	3.050
x 0.049(18)	0.3014	x 0.250(1/4)	6.008
x 0.065(16)	0.3888	x 0.500(1/2)	10.68
x 0.095(13)	0.5377	3 x 0.065(16)	2.038
x 0.120(11)	0.6472	x 0.109(12)	3.366
11/16 x 0.049(18)	0.3344	x 0.120(11)	3.691
x 0.083(14)	0.5363	x 0.250(1/4)	7.343
x 0.109(12)	0.6740	x 0.500(1/2)	13.35
3/4 x 0.035(20)	0.2673	4 x 0.065(16)	2.732
x 0.049(18)	0.3668	x 0.109(12)	4.530
x 0.065(16)	0.4755	x 0.120(11)	4.973
x 0.083(14)	0.5913	x 0.250(1/4)	10.01
x 0.109(12)	0.7462	x 0.500(1/2)	18.69
x 0.120(11)	0.8074	5 x 0.109(12)	5.694
x 0.250(1/4)	1.3350	x 0.120(11)	6.254
13/16 x 0.035(20)	0.2908	x 0.250(1/4)	12.68
x 0.049(18)	0.3998	x 0.500(1/2)	24.03
x 0.120(11)	0.8881	6 x 0.120(11)	7.536
7/8 x 0.035(20)	0.3140	x 0.250(1/4)	15.35
x 0.049(18)	0.4323	x 0.500(1/2)	29.37
x 0.065(16)	0.5623	x 1.000(1)	53.40

Wrought Aluminum Tempering

Designation	Description
F	As fabricated, temper from shaping process only.
O	Annealed, recrystallized, softest temper for wrought.
H1*	Strain hardened only.
H2*	Strain hardened and then partially annealed.
H3*	Strain hardened and then stabilized.
W	Solution heat–treated.
T	Thermally treated to produce tempers other than F,O, or H.
T1	Cooled from elevated temperature and then naturally aged.
T2	Cooled from elevated temperature, cold worked, and then naturally aged.
T3	Solution heat–treated, cold worked, and then naturally aged, improved strength.
T4	Solution heat–treated and then naturally aged to a sub–stantially stable condition. Not cold worked.
T5	Artificially aged only. Rapid cool process like casting.
T6	Solution heat–treated and then artificially aged. Not cold worked after heat treated. Common class.
T7	Solution heat–treated and then stabilized, good growth control and residual stress.
T8	Solution heat–treated, cold worked, and then artificially aged. Cold worked to improve strength.
T9	Solution heat–treated, artificially aged, and then cold worked to improve strength.
T10	Cold worked and then artificially aged. Rapid cooling after heat treatment then cold worked for strength.
T51	Stress–relieved by stretching.
T52	Stress–relieved by compressing.
T53	Stress–relieved by combined stretching and compressing.
T42	Wrought only, properties of T4.
T62	Wrought only, properties of T6.

* One or two additonal numbers may follow these designa-
tions such as H111 or H323. The additonal numbers indicate the
amount of strain hardening remaining after partial annealing or the
degree f strain hardening before stabilization.

Density & Melting Points of Metals, Alloys, & Elements

Name of Material	Symbol	Density of Solid (gas g/l lbm/ft³) lb/in³	g/cm³	Melting Point °F	°C
Actinium	Ac	0.364	10.07	1,924	1,051
Aluminum (99.996%)	Al	0.098	2.70	1,221	660
Aluminum bronze	- - -	0.281	7.78	- - -	- - -
Aluminum bronze	- - -	0.274	7.58	- - -	- - -
Aluminum bronze, 5% Al	- - -	0.295	8.17	- - -	- - -
Aluminum bronze alloy, 9A	- - -	0.282	7.80	- - -	- - -
Aluminum bronze alloy, 9B	- - -	0.273	7.55	- - -	- - -
Aluminum bronze alloy, 9C	- - -	0.271	7.50	- - -	- - -
Aluminum bronze alloy, 9D	- - -	0.278	7.70	- - -	- - -
Aluminum silicon bronze	- - -	0.278	7.69	- - -	- - -
Aluminum, casting, 108, A108	- - -	0.101	2.79	- - -	- - -
Aluminum, casting, 138	- - -	0.107	2.95	- - -	- - -
Aluminum, casting, 142	- - -	0.102	2.81	- - -	- - -
Aluminum, casting, 195, B195	- - -	0.102	2.81	- - -	- - -
Aluminum, casting, 214	- - -	0.096	2.65	- - -	- - -
Aluminum, casting, 220	- - -	0.093	2.57	- - -	- - -
Aluminum, casting, 319	- - -	0.101	2.79	- - -	- - -
Aluminum, casting, 355	- - -	0.098	2.71	- - -	- - -
Aluminum, casting, 356	- - -	0.097	2.68	- - -	- - -
Aluminum, casting, 360	- - -	0.095	2.64	- - -	- - -
Aluminum, casting, 380	- - -	0.098	2.71	- - -	- - -
Aluminum, casting, 40E	- - -	0.102	2.81	- - -	- - -
Aluminum, casting, 43	- - -	0.097	2.69	- - -	- - -
Aluminum, casting, 750	- - -	0.104	2.88	- - -	- - -
Aluminum, casting, A13	- - -	0.096	2.66	- - -	- - -
Aluminum, casting, A132	- - -	0.098	2.72	- - -	- - -
Aluminum, casting, D132	- - -	0.100	2.76	- - -	- - -
Aluminum, casting, F132	- - -	0.099	2.74	- - -	- - -
Aluminum, wrought, 1100	- - -	0.098	2.71	- - -	- - -
Aluminum, wrought, 2011	- - -	0.102	2.82	- - -	- - -
Aluminum, wrought, 2014	- - -	0.101	2.80	- - -	- - -
Aluminum, wrought, 2017	- - -	0.101	2.80	- - -	- - -
Aluminum, wrought, 2024	- - -	0.100	2.77	- - -	- - -
Aluminum, wrought, 2218	- - -	0.102	2.81	- - -	- - -
Aluminum, wrought, 3003	- - -	0.099	2.73	- - -	- - -
Aluminum, wrought, 4032	- - -	0.097	2.69	- - -	- - -
Aluminum, wrought, 5005	- - -	0.098	2.70	- - -	- - -
Aluminum, wrought, 5050	- - -	0.097	2.69	- - -	- - -
Aluminum, wrought, 5052	- - -	0.097	2.68	- - -	- - -
Aluminum, wrought, 5056	- - -	0.095	2.64	- - -	- - -
Aluminum, wrought, 5083	- - -	0.096	2.66	- - -	- - -
Aluminum, wrought, 5086	- - -	0.096	2.65	- - -	- - -
Aluminum, wrought, 5154	- - -	0.096	2.65	- - -	- - -
Aluminum, wrought, 5357	- - -	0.098	2.70	- - -	- - -
Aluminum, wrought, 5456	- - -	0.096	2.66	- - -	- - -
Aluminum, wrought, 6061, 6063	- - -	0.098	2.70	- - -	- - -
Aluminum, wrought, 6101, 6151	- - -	0.098	2.70	- - -	- - -
Aluminum, wrought, 7075	- - -	0.101	2.80	- - -	- - -
Aluminum, wrought, 7079	- - -	0.099	2.74	- - -	- - -
Aluminum, wrought, 7178	- - -	0.102	2.82	- - -	- - -
Aluminum, wrought, EC, 1060	- - -	0.098	2.70	- - -	- - -
Americium	Am	0.429	11.87	2,149	1,176
Antimony	Sb	0.239	6.62	1,167	631
Argon - gas	A	[1.784]	[0.111]	- - -	- - -
Arsenic	As	0.207	5.72	-309	-189
Astatine	At	0.207	5.73	576	302
Barium	Ba	0.130	3.60	1,344	729
Berkelium	Bk	0.506	14.00	1,801	983
Beryllium	Be	0.067	1.85	2,352	1,289
Beryllium copper	- - -	0.297	8.23	- - -	- - -
Bismuth	Bi	0.354	9.80	521	271
Boron	B	0.089	2.45	3,798	2,092
Brass, cartridge, 70%	- - -	0.308	8.53	- - -	- - -
Brass, extra-high-leaded	- - -	0.307	8.50	- - -	- - -
Brass, forging	- - -	0.305	8.44	- - -	- - -
Brass, free-cutting	- - -	0.307	8.50	- - -	- - -
Brass, high-leaded	- - -	0.307	8.50	- - -	- - -

Density & Melting Points (cont.) Name of Material	Symbol	Density of Solid [gas g/l & lbm/ft³] lb/in³	g/cm³	Melting Point °F	°C
Brass, high-leaded (tube)	---	0.308	8.53	---	---
Brass, leaded naval	---	0.305	8.44	---	---
Brass, low, 80%	---	0.313	8.67	---	---
Brass, low-lead (tube)	---	0.307	8.50	---	---
Brass, medium-leaded	---	0.306	8.47	---	---
Brass, naval	---	0.304	8.41	---	---
Brass, red, 85%	---	0.316	8.75	---	---
Brass, yellow	---	0.306	8.47	---	---
Bromine	Br	0.113	3.12	19	-7
Bronze, architectural	---	0.306	8.47	---	---
Bronze, commercial, 90%	---	0.318	8.80	---	---
Bronze, jewelry, 87.5%	---	0.317	8.78	---	---
Bronze, leaded commercial	---	0.319	8.83	---	---
Cadmium	Cd	0.313	8.65	610	321
Calcium	Ca	0.056	1.55	1,544	840
Californium	Cf	---	---	1,724	940
Carbon, graphite	C	0.081	2.25	6,919	3,826
Carpenter 20-Cb3	---	0.291	8.06	2,597	1,425
Cerium	Ce	0.245	6.77	1,468	798
Cesium	Cs	0.068	1.87	83	28
Chlorine - Gas	Cl	[3.214]	[0.201]	---	---
Chromium	Cr	0.260	7.19	3,380	1,860
Chromium copper, 1% Cr	---	0.314	8.70	---	---
Cobalt	Co	0.320	8.85	2,723	1,495
Conatantan	---	0.322	8.90	---	---
Copper alloy, 61% Cu - 1% Sn - 1% Pb - 37% Zn	---	0.303	8.40	---	---
Copper alloy, 70% Cu - 1% Sn - 3% Pb - 29% Zn	---	0.305	8.45	---	---
Copper alloy, 70% Cu - 5% Sn - 25% Pb	---	0.336	9.30	---	---
Copper alloy, 72% Cu - 1% Sn - 3% Pb - 24% Zn	---	0.307	8.50	---	---
Copper alloy, 76% Cu - 2.5% Sn - 6.5% Pb - 15% Zn	---	0.317	8.77	---	---
Copper alloy, 78% Cu - 7% Sn - 15% Pb	---	0.334	9.25	---	---
Copper alloy, 80% Cu - 10% Sn - 10% Pb	---	0.323	8.95	---	---
Copper alloy, 81% Cu - 3% Sn - 7% Pb - 9% Zn	---	0.314	8.70	---	---
Copper alloy, 83% Cu - 4% Sn - 6% Pb - 7% Zn	---	0.311	8.60	---	---
Copper alloy, 83% Cu - 7% Sn - 7% Pb - 3% Zn	---	0.323	8.93	---	---
Copper alloy, 85% Cu - 5% Sn - 5% Pb - 5% Zn	---	0.318	8.80	---	---
Copper alloy, 85% Cu - 5% Sn - 9% Pb - 1% Zn	---	0.320	8.87	---	---
Copper alloy, 87% Cu - 10% Sn - 1% Pb - 2% Zn	---	0.318	8.80	---	---
Copper alloy, 87% Cu - 8% Sn - 1% Pb - 4% Zn	---	0.318	8.80	---	---
Copper alloy, 88% Cu - 10% Sn - 2% Zn	---	0.314	8.70	---	---
Copper alloy, 88% Cu - 6% Sn - 1.5% Pb - 4% Zn	---	0.314	8.70	---	---
Copper alloy, 88% Cu - 8% Sn - 4% Zn	---	0.323	8.93	---	---
Copper alloy, 89% Cu - 11% Sn	---	0.317	8.78	---	---
Copper, deoxidized high residual phosphorus (DHP)	---	0.323	8.94	---	---
Copper, electrolytic tough pitch (ETP)	---	0.321	8.89	---	---
Copper, free-machining, 0.5% Te	---	0.323	8.94	---	---
Copper, free-machining, 1.0% Pb	---	0.323	8.94	---	---
Copper, pure	Cu	0.324	8.96	1,985	1,085
Copper, wrough, gilding, 95%	---	0.320	8.86	---	---
Cupro-nickel, 10%	---	0.323	8.94	---	---
Cupro-nickel, 30%	---	0.323	8.94	---	---
Curium	Cm	0.253	7.00	2,444	1,340
Duranickel	---	0.298	8.26	---	---
Dysprosium	Dy	0.309	8.55	2,574	1,412
Erbium	Er	0.331	9.15	2,784	1,529
Europium	Eu	0.189	5.24	1,512	822
Fermium	Fm	---	---	2,781	1,527
Fluorine - Gas	F	[1.696]	[0.106]	-363	-220
Francium	Fr	---	---	81	27
Gadolinium	Gd	0.284	7.86	2,395	1,313
Gallium	Ga	0.213	5.91	86	30
Germanium	Ge	0.192	5.32	1,721	938
GMR-235	---	0.290	8.03	---	---
Gold	Au	0.698	19.32	1,948	1,064
Hafnium	Hf	0.473	13.10	4,048	2,231
Hastelloy B	---	0.334	9.24	---	---
Hastelloy B-2	---	0.333	9.21	---	---
Hastelloy C	---	0.323	8.94	---	---
Hastelloy C-276	---	0.322	8.90	2,500	1,371
Hastelloy C-4	---	0.312	8.64	---	---
Hastelloy D	---	0.282	7.80	---	---
Hastelloy F	---	0.295	8.17	---	---

Density & Melting Points (cont.)		Density of Solid [gas g/l & lbm/ft³]		Melting Point	
Name of Material	Symbol	lb/in³	g/cm³	°F	°C
Hastelloy N	---	0.323	8.93	---	---
Hastelloy S	---	0.316	8.76	2,516	1,380
Hastelloy W	---	0.326	9.03	2,399	1,315
Hastelloy X	---	0.297	8.23	2,354	1,290
Haynes 188	---	0.330	9.13	2,548	1,398
Haynes 25 (L-605)	---	0.330	9.13	2,570	1,410
Haynes 556	---	0.297	8.23	---	---
Helium - Gas	He	[0.1785]	[0.011]	-452	-269
Hipernik, 50% Ni	---	0.298	8.25	---	---
Holmium	Ho	0.245	6.79	2,685	1,474
Hydrogen - Gas	H	[0.0899]	[0.006]	-435	-259
Illium G	---	0.310	8.58	---	---
Illium R	---	0.310	8.58	---	---
Incoloy	---	0.290	8.02	---	---
Incoloy 800	---	0.287	7.94	2,525	1,385
Incoloy 801	---	0.287	7.94	2,525	1,385
Incoloy 825	---	0.294	8.14	2,552	1,400
Incoloy 901	---	0.297	8.23	---	---
Incoloy T	---	0.288	7.98	---	---
Inconel	---	0.307	8.51	---	---
Inconel 600	---	0.304	8.42	2,579	1,415
Inconel 625	---	0.305	8.44	2,462	1,350
Inconel 671	---	0.284	7.86	2,462	1,350
Inconel 690	---	0.290	8.03	2,507	1,375
Inconel 700	---	0.295	8.17	---	---
Inconel 713C	---	0.286	7.91	---	---
Inconel X 550	---	0.300	8.30	---	---
Inconel X 750	---	0.298	8.25	2,597	1,425
Inconel, cast	---	0.300	8.30	---	---
Indium	In	0.264	7.31	314	157
Inhibited admiralty	---	0.308	8.53	---	---
Invar, 36% Ni	---	0.289	8.00	---	---
Iodine	I	0.178	4.94	236	114
Iridium	Ir	0.818	22.65	4,437	2,447
Iron alloy, 16-25-6	---	0.292	8.08	---	---
Iron alloy, A-286	---	0.287	7.94	---	---
Iron alloy, RA-330	---	0.290	8.03	---	---
Iron, gray cast	---	0.258	7.15	---	---
Iron, ingot	---	0.284	7.87	---	---
Iron, malleable	---	0.263	7.27	---	---
Iron, pure	Fe	0.284	7.87	2,795	1,535
Iron, wrought	---	0.278	7.70	---	---
Krypton - Gas	Kr	[3.743]	[0.234]	-251	-157
Lanthanum	La	0.222	6.15	1,684	918
Lead (99.90%+ Pb)	Pb	0.410	11.34	622	328
Lead babbitt alloy, 8	---	0.363	10.04	---	---
Lead babbitt alloy, G	---	0.365	10.10	---	---
Lead babbitt alloy, SAE 13	---	0.370	10.24	---	---
Lead babbitt alloy, SAE 14	---	0.352	9.73	---	---
Lead babbitt alloy, SAE 15	---	0.365	10.10	---	---
Lead, 1% antimonial	---	0.407	11.27	---	---
Lead, 8% antimonial	---	0.388	10.74	---	---
Lead, 9% antimonial	---	0.385	10.66	---	---
Lead, arsenical	---	0.410	11.34	---	---
Lead, calcium	---	0.410	11.34	---	---
Lead, corroding	---	0.410	11.36	---	---
Lead, hard, 94% Pb - 6% Sb	---	0.393	10.88	---	---
Lead, hard, 96% Pb - 4% Sb	---	0.399	11.04	---	---
Lithium	Li	0.019	0.53	357	181
Lutetium (99.8%)	Lu	0.356	9.85	3,025	1,663
Magnesium (99.8%)	Mg	0.063	1.74	1,200	649
Magnesium, aerospace alloy, AZ91C-T6	---	0.065	1.81	---	---
Magnesium, aerospace alloy, AZ91E-T6	---	0.065	1.81	---	---
Magnesium, aerospace alloy, EA55B-T6	---	0.070	1.94	---	---
Magnesium, aerospace alloy, EA55RS-T4	---	0.070	1.94	---	---
Magnesium, aerospace alloy, EA65B-T6	---	0.069	1.92	---	---
Magnesium, aerospace alloy, EA55RS-T4	---	0.069	1.92	---	---
Magnesium, aerospace alloy, WE54-T6	---	0.069	1.90	---	---
Magnesium, casting alloy, AM100A	---	0.065	1.81	---	---
Magnesium, casting alloy, AZ63A	---	0.066	1.84	---	---
Magnesium, casting alloy, AZ81A	---	0.065	1.80	---	---
Magnesium, casting alloy, AZ91A, B, C	---	0.065	1.81	---	---

Density & Melting Points (cont.)	Symbol	Density of Solid [gas g/l & lbm/ft³] lb/in³	g/cm³	Melting Point °F	°C
Name of Material					
Magnesium, casting alloy, AZ92A	---	0.066	1.82	---	---
Magnesium, casting alloy, EK30A	---	0.065	1.79	---	---
Magnesium, casting alloy, EK41A	---	0.065	1.81	---	---
Magnesium, casting alloy, EZ33A	---	0.066	1.83	---	---
Magnesium, casting alloy, HK31A	---	0.065	1.79	---	---
Magnesium, casting alloy, HZ32A	---	0.066	1.83	---	---
Magnesium, casting alloy, ZE41A	---	0.066	1.82	---	---
Magnesium, casting alloy, ZH42, ZH62A	---	0.067	1.86	---	---
Magnesium, casting alloy, ZK51A	---	0.065	1.81	---	---
Magnesium, wrought alloy, A3A	---	0.064	1.77	---	---
Magnesium, wrought alloy, AZ31B	---	0.064	1.77	---	---
Magnesium, wrought alloy, AZ61A	---	0.065	1.80	---	---
Magnesium, wrought alloy, AZ80A	---	0.065	1.80	---	---
Magnesium, wrought alloy, HM21A	---	0.064	1.78	---	---
Magnesium, wrought alloy, HM31A	---	0.065	1.81	---	---
Magnesium, wrought alloy, M1A	---	0.064	1.76	---	---
Magnesium, wrought alloy, PE	---	0.064	1.76	---	---
Magnesium, wrought alloy, ZE10A	---	0.064	1.76	---	---
Magnesium, wrought alloy, ZK60A, B	---	0.066	1.83	---	---
Manganese	Mn	0.268	7.43	2,275	1,246
Manganese bronze	---	0.302	8.36	---	---
Manganese bronze, 110 ksi	---	0.278	7.70	---	---
Manganese bronze, 60 ksi	---	0.296	8.20	---	---
Manganese bronze, 65 ksi	---	0.300	8.30	---	---
Manganese bronze, 90 ksi	---	0.285	7.90	---	---
Mercury	Hg	0.489	13.55	-38	-39
Molybdenum	Mo	0.369	10.22	4,753	2,623
Monel	---	0.319	8.84	---	---
Monel, cast	---	0.312	8.63	---	---
Monel, cast, H	---	0.307	8.50	---	---
Monel, cast, S	---	0.302	8.36	---	---
Monel, K	---	0.306	8.47	---	---
Muntz metal	---	0.303	8.39	---	---
Muntz metal, leaded	---	0.304	8.41	---	---
Neodymium	Nd	0.253	7.00	1,870	1,021
Neon - Gas	Ne	[0.8999]	[0.056]	-415	-249
Neptunium	Np	0.741	20.50	1,179	637
Ni-o-nel	---	0.284	7.86	---	---
Nickel (99.95%)	Ni	0.322	8.90	2,651	1,455
Nickel alloy, 35% Ni - 45% Fe - 20.0% Cr	---	0.287	7.95	---	---
Nickel alloy, 60% Ni - 24% Fe - 16.0% Cr	---	0.298	8.25	---	---
Nickel alloy, 80% Ni - 20.0% Cr	---	0.303	8.40	---	---
Nickel silver, 12% Ni	---	0.323	8.95	---	---
Nickel silver, 16% Ni	---	0.323	8.95	---	---
Nickel silver, 20% Ni	---	0.320	8.85	---	---
Nickel silver, 25% Ni	---	0.318	8.80	---	---
Nickel silver, 55-18	---	0.314	8.70	---	---
Nickel silver, 65-18	---	0.315	8.73	---	---
Nickel, A	---	0.321	8.89	---	---
Nickel, cast	---	0.301	8.34	---	---
Nickel, D	---	0.317	8.78	---	---
Nimonic 80A	---	0.298	8.25	---	---
Nimonic 90	---	0.299	8.27	---	---
Niobium	Nb	0.310	8.57	4,476	2,469
Nitrogen - Gas	N	[1.25]	[0.078]	-346	-210
Nobelium	No	---	---	1,521	827
Osmium	Os	0.817	22.61	5,491	3,033
Oxygen - Gas	O	[1.429]	[0.089]	-362	-219
Palladium	Pd	0.434	12.02	2,831	1,555
Pewter	---	0.263	7.28	---	---
Phosphor bronze, 1.25%	---	0.321	8.89	---	---
Phosphor bronze, 10%	---	0.317	8.78	---	---
Phosphor bronze, 5%	---	0.320	8.86	---	---
Phosphor bronze, 8%	---	0.318	8.80	---	---
Phosphor bronze, free-cutting	---	0.321	8.89	---	---
Phosphorus, white	P	0.065	1.83	111	44
Platinum	Pt	0.775	21.45	3,216	1,769
Plutonium	Pu	0.717	19.84	1,184	640
Polonium	Po	0.340	9.40	489	254
Potassium	K	0.031	0.86	146	63
Praseodymium	Pr	0.245	6.77	1,708	931
Promethium	Pm	0.262	7.26	1,908	1,042

| Density & Melting Points (cont.) | | Density of Solid [gas g/l lbm/ft³] | | Melting Point | |
Name of Material	Symbol	lb/in³	g/cm³	°F	°C
Protactinium	Pa	0.556	15.40	2,867	1,575
Radium	Ra	0.181	5.00	1,292	700
Radon - Gas	Rn	[9.96]	[0.622]	-96	-71
René 41	---	0.298	8.26	2,500	1,371
Rhenium	Re	0.760	21.04	5,767	3,186
Rhodium	Rh	0.448	12.41	3,565	1,963
Rubidium	Rb	0.055	1.53	103	39
Ruthenium	Ru	0.450	12.45	4,233	2,334
Samarium	Sm	0.271	7.49	1,965	1,074
Scandium	Sc	0.108	2.99	2,806	1,541
Selenium	Se	0.173	4.80	430	221
Silicon	Si	0.084	2.33	2,577	1,414
Silicon brass	---	0.300	8.30	---	---
Silicon bronze	---	0.300	8.30	---	---
Silicon bronze, high-silicon	---	0.308	8.53	---	---
Silicon bronze, low-silicon	---	0.316	8.75	---	---
Silver	Ag	0.379	10.49	1,763	962
Sodium	Na	0.035	0.97	208	98
Solder, lead-silver, 2.5S, 97.5% Pb - 2.5% Ag	---	---	---	1,074	579
Solder, lead-silver, 5.5S, 94.5% Pb - 5.5% Ag	---	0.408	11.30	649	343
Solder, lead-tin-silver, 1.5S, 97.5% Pb - 1.0% Sn - 1.5% Ag	---	0.408	11.30	595	313
Solder, lead-tin-silver, 36.0% Pb - 62.0% Sn - 2.0% Ag	---	---	---	374	190
Solder, lead-tin-silver, 94.5% Pb - 5.0% Sn - 0.5% Ag	---	---	---	574	301
Solder, lead-tin-silver, 96TS, 96.0% Pb - 4.0% Ag	---	0.376	10.40	430	221
Solder, lead-tin-silver, 97.0% Pb - 2.5% Sn - 0.5% Ag	---	---	---	590	310
Solder, lead-antimony, 95TA, 95.0% Sn - 5.0% Sb	---	0.282	7.80	464	240
Solder, tin-lead, 10B, 90.0% Pb - 10.0% Sn	---	0.390	10.80	574	301
Solder, tin-lead, 15B, 85.0% Pb - 15.0% Sn	---	0.379	10.50	554	290
Solder, tin-lead, 20A, 80.0% Pb - 20.0% Sn	---	0.368	10.20	536	280
Solder, tin-lead, 25A, 75.0% Pb - 25.0% Sn	---	0.361	9.99	513	267
Solder, tin-lead, 30A, 70.0% Pb - 30.0% Sn	---	0.350	9.69	491	255
Solder, tin-lead, 35A, 65.0% Pb - 35.0% Sn	---	0.350	9.69	477	247
Solder, tin-lead, 40A, 60.0% Pb - 40.0% Sn	---	0.335	9.27	455	235
Solder, tin-lead, 45A, 55.0% Pb - 45.0% Sn	---	0.324	8.97	442	228
Solder, tin-lead, 50A, 50.0% Pb - 50.0% Sn	---	0.319	8.83	423	217
Solder, tin-lead, 5A, 95.0% Pb - 5.0% Sn	---	0.408	11.30	594	312
Solder, tin-lead, 60A, 40.0% Pb - 60.0% Sn	---	0.312	8.64	374	190
Solder, tin-lead, 63A, 37.0% Pb - 63.0% Sn	---	0.303	8.40	361	183
Solder, tin-lead, 70A, 30.0% Pb - 70.0% Sn	---	0.301	8.32	378	192
Solder, tin-lead-antimony, 20C, 79.0% Pb - 20.0% Sn - 1.0% Sb	---	0.368	10.20	518	270
Solder, tin-lead-antimony, 25C, 73.7% Pb - 25.0% Sn - 1.3% Sb	---	0.359	9.94	504	262
Solder, tin-lead-antimony, 30C, 68.4% Pb - 30.0% Sn - 1.6% Sb	---	0.348	9.63	482	250
Solder, tin-lead-antimony, 35C, 63.2% Pb - 35.0% Sn - 1.8% Sb	---	0.341	9.44	469	243
Solder, tin-lead-antimony, 40C, 58.0% Pb - 40.0% Sn - 2.0% Sb	---	0.333	9.22	448	231
Steel, 10.27% Si	---	0.252	6.97	---	---
Steel, 20% W - 4.0% Cr - 2.0% V - 12.0% Co	---	0.321	8.89	---	---
Steel, 4% Si	---	0.275	7.60	---	---
Steel, ANSI-SAE 1008	---	0.284	7.87	---	---
Steel, ANSI-SAE 1024	---	0.284	7.86	---	---
Steel, ANSI-SAE 1042	---	0.283	7.84	---	---
Steel, ANSI-SAE 18Ni250	---	0.289	8.00	---	---
Steel, ANSI-SAE 5130	---	0.283	7.84	---	---
Steel, ANSI-SAE 52100	---	0.282	7.81	---	---
Steel, carbon, 0.06% C	---	0.284	7.87	---	---
Steel, carbon, 0.23% C	---	0.284	7.86	---	---
Steel, carbon, 0.435% C	---	0.283	7.84	---	---
Steel, carbon, 1.22% C	---	0.283	7.83	---	---
Steel, cobalt alloy, HS-21	---	0.300	8.30	---	---
Steel, cobalt alloy, HS-25	---	0.330	9.13	---	---
Steel, cobalt alloy, HS-31	---	0.311	8.61	---	---
Steel, cobalt alloy, HS-36	---	0.327	9.04	---	---
Steel, cobalt alloy, S-816	---	0.314	8.68	---	---
Steel, cobalt alloy, V-36	---	0.311	8.60	---	---
Steel, cobalt-chromium-nickel alloy, N-155 (HS-95)	---	0.297	8.23	---	---
Steel, cobalt-chromium-nickel alloy, S-590	---	0.302	8.36	---	---
Steel, heat-resistant, HA	---	0.279	7.72	---	---
Steel, heat-resistant, HC	---	0.272	7.53	---	---
Steel, heat-resistant, HD	---	0.274	7.58	---	---
Steel, heat-resistant, HE	---	0.277	7.67	---	---
Steel, heat-resistant, HF	---	0.280	7.75	---	---
Steel, heat-resistant, HH	---	0.279	7.72	---	---
Steel, heat-resistant, HI	---	0.279	7.72	---	---

Name of Material	Symbol	Density of Solid [gas g/l] lb/in³	Density of Solid [gas g/l & lbm/ft³] g/cm³	Melting Point °F	Melting Point °C
Steel, heat-resistant, HK	---	0.280	7.75	---	---
Steel, heat-resistant, HL	---	0.279	7.72	---	---
Steel, heat-resistant, HN	---	0.283	7.83	---	---
Steel, heat-resistant, HT	---	0.286	7.92	---	---
Steel, heat-resistant, HU	---	0.290	8.04	---	---
Steel, heat-resistant, HW	---	0.294	8.14	---	---
Steel, heat-resistant, HX	---	0.294	8.14	---	---
Steel, low-carbon chromium-molybdenun, 0.5% Mo	---	0.284	7.86	---	---
Steel, low-carbon chromium-molybdenun, 1.0% Cr - 0.5% Mo	---	0.284	7.86	---	---
Steel, low-carbon chromium-molybdenun, 1.25% Cr - 0.5% Mo	---	0.284	7.86	---	---
Steel, low-carbon chromium-molybdenun, 2.25% Cr - 1.0% Mo	---	0.284	7.86	---	---
Steel, low-carbon chromium-molybdenun, 5.0% Cr - 0.5% Mo	---	0.281	7.78	---	---
Steel, low-carbon chromium-molybdenun, 7.0% Cr - 0.5% Mo	---	0.281	7.78	---	---
Steel, low-carbon chromium-molybdenun, 9.0% Cr - 1.0% Mo	---	0.277	7.67	---	---
Steel, medium-carbon, 1.0% Cr - 0.35% Mo - 0.25% V	---	0.284	7.86	---	---
Steel, medium-carbon, die, H11, 5.0% Cr - 1.5% Mo - 0.4% V	---	0.281	7.79	---	---
Steel, molybdenum alloy, Mo - 0.5% Ti	---	0.368	10.20	---	---
Steel, nickel-alloy, D-979	---	0.299	8.27	---	---
Steel, nickel-alloy, M-252	---	0.299	8.27	---	---
Steel, stainless, 15-5 PH	---	0.282	7.80	2,588	1,420
Steel, stainless, 17-4 PH	---	0.282	7.80	2,588	1,420
Steel, stainless, 17-7 PH	---	0.282	7.81	2,588	1,420
Steel, stainless, CA-15	---	0.275	7.61	---	---
Steel, stainless, CA-40	---	0.275	7.61	---	---
Steel, stainless, CB-30	---	0.272	7.53	---	---
Steel, stainless, CC-50	---	0.272	7.53	---	---
Steel, stainless, CE-30	---	0.277	7.67	---	---
Steel, stainless, CF-16F	---	0.280	7.75	---	---
Steel, stainless, CF-20	---	0.280	7.75	---	---
Steel, stainless, CF-8	---	0.280	7.75	---	---
Steel, stainless, CF-8C	---	0.280	7.75	---	---
Steel, stainless, CF-8M, CF-12M	---	0.280	7.75	---	---
Steel, stainless, CH-20	---	0.279	7.72	---	---
Steel, stainless, CK-20	---	0.280	7.75	---	---
Steel, stainless, CN-7M	---	0.289	8.00	---	---
Steel, stainless, PH13-8 Mo	---	0.282	7.80	2,588	1,420
Steel, stainless, PH15-7 Mo	---	0.282	7.80	---	---
Steel, tool, A2	---	0.284	7.86	---	---
Steel, tool, A6	---	0.283	7.84	---	---
Steel, tool, A7	---	0.277	7.66	---	---
Steel, tool, A8	---	0.284	7.87	---	---
Steel, tool, A9	---	0.281	7.78	---	---
Steel, tool, D2	---	0.278	7.70	---	---
Steel, tool, D3	---	0.278	7.70	---	---
Steel, tool, D4	---	0.278	7.70	---	---
Steel, tool, H10	---	0.282	7.81	---	---
Steel, tool, H11	---	0.280	7.75	---	---
Steel, tool, H13	---	0.280	7.76	---	---
Steel, tool, H14	---	0.285	7.89	---	---
Steel, tool, H19	---	0.288	7.98	---	---
Steel, tool, H21	---	0.299	8.28	---	---
Steel, tool, H22	---	0.302	8.36	---	---
Steel, tool, H26	---	0.313	8.67	---	---
Steel, tool, H41	---	0.285	7.88	---	---
Steel, tool, H42	---	0.294	8.15	---	---
Steel, tool, L2	---	0.284	7.86	---	---
Steel, tool, L6	---	0.284	7.86	---	---
Steel, tool, M1	---	0.285	7.89	---	---
Steel, tool, M10	---	0.285	7.88	---	---
Steel, tool, M2	---	0.295	8.16	---	---
Steel, tool, M3, class1	---	0.294	8.15	---	---
Steel, tool, M3, class2	---	0.295	8.16	---	---
Steel, tool, M30	---	0.289	8.01	---	---
Steel, tool, M33	---	0.290	8.03	---	---
Steel, tool, M36	---	0.296	8.18	---	---
Steel, tool, M4	---	0.288	7.97	---	---
Steel, tool, M41	---	0.295	8.17	---	---
Steel, tool, M42	---	0.288	7.98	---	---
Steel, tool, M46	---	0.283	7.83	---	---
Steel, tool, M47	---	0.288	7.96	---	---
Steel, tool, M7	---	0.287	7.95	---	---
Steel, tool, O1	---	0.284	7.85	---	---

Density & Melting Points (cont.)		Density of Solid [gas g/l & lbm/ft³]		Melting Point	
Name of Material	Symbol	lb/in³	g/cm³	°F	°C
Steel, tool, O2	---	0.277	7.66	---	---
Steel, tool, O7	---	0.282	7.80	---	---
Steel, tool, P2	---	0.284	7.86	---	---
Steel, tool, P20	---	0.284	7.85	---	---
Steel, tool, P5	---	0.282	7.80	---	---
Steel, tool, P6	---	0.284	7.85	---	---
Steel, tool, S1	---	0.285	7.88	---	---
Steel, tool, S2	---	0.281	7.79	---	---
Steel, tool, S5	---	0.280	7.76	---	---
Steel, tool, S6	---	0.280	7.75	---	---
Steel, tool, S7	---	0.280	7.76	---	---
Steel, tool, T1	---	0.313	8.67	---	---
Steel, tool, T15	---	0.296	8.19	---	---
Steel, tool, T2	---	0.313	8.67	---	---
Steel, tool, T4	---	0.314	8.68	---	---
Steel, tool, T5	---	0.316	8.75	---	---
Steel, tool, T6	---	0.321	8.89	---	---
Steel, tool, T8	---	0.305	8.43	---	---
Steel, tool, W1	---	0.284	7.84	---	---
Steel, tool, W2	---	0.284	7.85	---	---
Steel, wrought stainless, 19-9DL	---	0.288	7.97	---	---
Steel, wrought stainless, type 201	---	0.282	7.80	2,597	1,425
Steel, wrought stainless, type 202	---	0.282	7.80	2,597	1,425
Steel, wrought stainless, type 205	---	0.282	7.80	---	---
Steel, wrought stainless, type 301	---	0.285	7.90	2,570	1,410
Steel, wrought stainless, type 302	---	0.285	7.90	2,570	1,410
Steel, wrought stainless, type 302B	---	0.289	8.00	2,530	1,388
Steel, wrought stainless, type 303	---	0.285	7.90	2,570	1,410
Steel, wrought stainless, type 304	---	0.285	7.90	2,597	1,425
Steel, wrought stainless, type 304L	---	0.289	8.00	2,597	1,425
Steel, wrought stainless, type 304N	---	0.289	8.00	2,597	1,425
Steel, wrought stainless, type 305	---	0.289	8.00	2,597	1,425
Steel, wrought stainless, type 308	---	0.289	8.00	2,550	1,400
Steel, wrought stainless, type 309	---	0.289	8.00	2,570	1,410
Steel, wrought stainless, type 310	---	0.285	7.90	2,597	1,425
Steel, wrought stainless, type 314	---	0.279	7.72	---	---
Steel, wrought stainless, type 316	---	0.289	8.00	2,530	1,388
Steel, wrought stainless, type 316L	---	0.289	8.00	2,530	1,388
Steel, wrought stainless, type 316N	---	0.289	8.00	2,530	1,388
Steel, wrought stainless, type 317	---	0.289	8.00	2,530	1,388
Steel, wrought stainless, type 317L	---	0.289	8.00	2,530	1,388
Steel, wrought stainless, type 321	---	0.285	7.90	2,575	1,413
Steel, wrought stainless, type 329	---	0.282	7.80	---	---
Steel, wrought stainless, type 330	---	0.289	8.00	2,575	1,413
Steel, wrought stainless, type 347	---	0.289	8.00	2,575	1,413
Steel, wrought stainless, type 384	---	0.289	8.00	2,597	1,425
Steel, wrought stainless, type 403	---	0.278	7.70	---	---
Steel, wrought stainless, type 405	---	0.278	7.70	2,741	1,505
Steel, wrought stainless, type 409	---	0.282	7.80	2,741	1,505
Steel, wrought stainless, type 410	---	0.278	7.70	2,741	1,505
Steel, wrought stainless, type 414	---	0.282	7.80	2,647	1,453
Steel, wrought stainless, type 416	---	0.278	7.70	2,741	1,505
Steel, wrought stainless, type 420	---	0.278	7.70	2,696	1,480
Steel, wrought stainless, type 422	---	0.282	7.80	2,687	1,475
Steel, wrought stainless, type 429	---	0.282	7.80	2,696	1,480
Steel, wrought stainless, type 430	---	0.278	7.70	2,674	1,468
Steel, wrought stainless, type 430F	---	0.278	7.70	2,674	1,468
Steel, wrought stainless, type 431	---	0.278	7.70	---	---
Steel, wrought stainless, type 434	---	0.282	7.80	2,674	1,468
Steel, wrought stainless, type 436	---	0.282	7.80	2,674	1,468
Steel, wrought stainless, type 440A, 440B, 440C	---	0.278	7.70	2,597	1,425
Steel, wrought stainless, type 444	---	0.282	7.80	---	---
Steel, wrought stainless, type 446	---	0.275	7.60	2,674	1,468
Steel, wrought stainless, type 501	---	0.278	7.70	---	---
Steel, wrought stainless, type 502	---	0.282	7.80	---	---
Steel, wrought stainless, type S30430	---	0.289	8.00	2,597	1,425
Stellite 6B	---	0.303	8.38	2,469	1,354
Strontium	Sr	0.094	2.60	1,416	769
Sulfur, yellow	S	0.075	2.07	239	115
Tantalum	Ta	0.600	16.60	5,468	3,020
Technetium	Tc	0.415	11.50	3,999	2,204
Tellurium	Te	0.225	6.24	841	450

Name of Material	Symbol	Density of Solid [gas g/l] & lbm/ft³ lb/in³	g/cm³	Melting Point °F	°C
Terbium	Tb	0.298	8.25	2,473	1,356
Thalium	Tl	0.428	11.85	579	304
Thorium	Th	0.423	11.72	3,196	1,758
Thulium	Tm	0.336	9.31	2,813	1,545
Tin (pure)	Sn	0.264	7.30	450	232
Tin babbitt, alloy 1	---	0.265	7.34	---	---
Tin babbitt, alloy 2	---	0.267	7.39	---	---
Tin babbitt, alloy 3	---	0.272	7.46	---	---
Tin babbitt, alloy 4	---	0.272	7.53	---	---
Tin babbitt, alloy 5	---	0.280	7.75	---	---
Titanium (99.0%)	---	0.163	4.52	---	---
Titanium (99.1%)	---	0.163	4.51	---	---
Titanium (99.2%)	---	0.163	4.51	---	---
Titanium (99.5%)	---	0.163	4.51	---	---
Titanium (99.9%)	Ti	0.163	4.51	3,038	1,670
Titanium, 99.2% Ti - 0.2% Pd	---	0.163	4.51	---	---
Titanium alloy, Ti - 0.8% Ni - 0.3% Mo	---	0.164	4.54	---	---
Titanium alloy, Ti - 10.0% V - 2.0% Fe - 3.0% Al	---	0.168	4.65	---	---
Titanium alloy, Ti-11.0% Sn-1.0% Mo-2.25% Al-5.0% Zr-1.0% Mo-0.2% Si	---	0.174	4.82	---	---
Titanium alloy, Ti - 13.0% V - 11.0% Cr - 3.0% Al	---	0.175	4.84	---	---
Titanium alloy, Ti - 2.0% Fe - 2.0% Cr - 2.0% Mo	---	0.168	4.65	---	---
Titanium alloy, Ti - 2.5% Al - 16.0% V	---	0.168	4.65	---	---
Titanium alloy, Ti - 3.0% Al - 2.5% V	---	0.162	4.48	---	---
Titanium alloy, Ti-3.0% Al-8.0% V-6.0% Cr-4.0% Mo-4.0% Zr	---	0.174	4.82	---	---
Titanium alloy, Ti - 4.0% Al - 3.0% Mo - 1.0% V	---	0.163	4.51	---	---
Titanium alloy, Ti - 4.0% Al - 4.0% Mn	---	0.163	4.52	---	---
Titanium alloy, Ti - 5.0% Al - 2.5% Sn	---	0.161	4.47	---	---
Titanium alloy, Ti - 5.0% Al - 2.5% Sn (low O2)	---	0.161	4.47	---	---
Titanium alloy, Ti-5.0% Al-5.0% Sn-2.0% Zr-2.0% Mo-0.25% Si	---	0.163	4.51	---	---
Titanium alloy, Ti - 6.0% Al - 2.0% Nb - 1.0% Ta - 1.0% Mo	---	0.162	4.48	---	---
Titanium alloy, Ti - 6.0% Al - 2.0% Sn - 2.0% Zr - 2.0% Mo - 2.0% Cr - 0.25% Si	---	0.165	4.57	---	---
Titanium alloy, Ti - 6.0% Al - 2.0% Sn - 4.0% Zr - 2.0% Mo	---	0.164	4.54	---	---
Titanium alloy, Ti - 6.0% Al - 2.0% Sn - 4.0% Zr - 6.0% Mo	---	0.168	4.65	---	---
Titanium alloy, Ti - 6.0% Al - 4.0% V	---	0.160	4.43	---	---
Titanium alloy, Ti - 6.0% Al - 4.0% V (low O2)	---	0.160	4.43	---	---
Titanium alloy, Ti - 6.0% Al - 6.0% V - 2.0% Sn	---	0.164	4.54	---	---
Titanium alloy, Ti - 7.0% Al - 4.0% Mo	---	0.162	4.48	---	---
Titanium alloy, Ti - 8.0% Al - 1.0% Mo - 1.0% V	---	0.158	4.37	---	---
Titanium alloy, Ti - 8.0% Mn	---	0.171	4.72	---	---
Titanium alloy, Ti - 8.0% Mo - 8.0% V - 2.0% Fe - 3.0% Al	---	0.175	4.84	---	---
Tungsten	W	0.697	19.30	6,192	3,422
Udimet 500	---	0.293	8.10	2,453	1,345
Udimet 700	---	0.286	7.92	2,453	1,345
UMCo 50	---	0.291	8.05	2,543	1,395
Uranium	U	0.689	19.07	2,073	1,134
Vanadium	V	0.221	6.11	3,504	1,929
Waspaloy	---	0.297	8.22	2,471	1,355
White metal	---	0.263	7.28	---	---
Xenon - Gas	Xe	[5.896]	[0.368]	-169	-112
Ytterbium	Yb	0.251	6.96	1,506	819
Yttrium	Y	0.161	4.47	2,772	1,522
Zinc (pure)	Zn	0.258	7.13	787	420
Zinc alloy, AC41A	---	0.242	6.70	---	---
Zinc alloy, AG40A	---	0.238	6.60	---	---
Zinc alloy, rolled, 1.0% Cu - 0.010% Mg	---	0.259	7.18	---	---
Zinc alloy, Zn - Cu - Ti, 0.8% Cu - 0.15% Ti	---	0.259	7.18	---	---
Zinc, commercial rolled, 0.03% Pb - 0.03% Cd	---	0.258	7.14	---	---
Zinc, commercial rolled, 0.06% Pb - 0.06% Cd	---	0.258	7.14	---	---
Zinc, commercial rolled, 0.08% Pb	---	0.258	7.14	---	---
Zinc, rolled, copper-hardened, 1.0% Cu	---	0.259	7.18	---	---
Zirconium	Zr	0.235	6.51	3,371	1,855

SOURCE: ASM Metals Reference Book, 3rd Edition, ASM (American Society for Metals) International, Materials Park, OH.

Hardness Number Conversions

Brinell Hardness Scale - For Carbon And Alloy Steel

Brinell Indentation dia mm	Brinell Hardness 3000 kg load 10 mm dia ball — Standard Ball	Tungsten Carbide ball	Vickers Hardness	Rockwell Hardness Scales — A scale 60 kg load Brale Indenter	B scale 100 kg load 1/16 in dia ball	C scale 150 kg load Brale Indenter	D scale 100 kg load Brale Indenter	Rockwell Superficial Hardness Brale Indenter — 15N scale 15 kg load	30N scale 30 kg load	45N scale 45 kg load	Knoop Hardness 500 g load and greater	Scleroscope Hardness	Approximate Tensile Strength of Steel (ksi)
2.25	- - -	(745)	840	84.1	- - -	65.3	74.8	93.2	82.2	72.2	852	91	- - -
2.30	- - -	(712)	783	83.1	- - -	63.4	73.4	91.6	80.5	70.4	808	- - -	- - -
2.35	- - -	(682)	737	82.2	- - -	61.7	72.0	91.0	79.0	68.5	768	84	- - -
2.40	- - -	(653)	697	81.2	- - -	60.0	70.7	90.2	77.5	66.5	732	81	- - -
2.45	- - -	627	667	80.5	- - -	58.7	69.7	89.6	76.3	65.1	703	79	347
2.50	- - -	601	640	79.8	- - -	57.3	68.7	89.0	75.1	63.5	677	77	328
2.55	- - -	578	615	79.1	- - -	56.0	67.7	88.4	73.9	62.1	652	75	313
2.60	- - -	555	591	78.4	- - -	54.7	66.7	87.8	72.7	60.6	626	73	298
2.65	- - -	534	569	77.8	- - -	53.5	65.8	87.2	71.6	59.2	604	71	288
2.70	- - -	514	547	76.9	- - -	52.1	64.7	86.5	70.3	57.6	579	70	273
2.75	(495)	- - -	539	76.7	- - -	51.6	64.3	86.3	69.9	56.9	571	- - -	269
2.80	(477)	- - -	528	76.3	- - -	51.0	63.8	85.9	69.4	56.1	558	68	263
2.85	(461)	- - -	516	75.9	- - -	50.3	63.2	85.6	68.7	55.2	545	66	257
2.90	444	444	508	75.6	- - -	49.6	62.7	85.3	68.2	54.5	537	- - -	252
2.95	429	429	495	75.1	- - -	48.8	61.9	84.9	67.4	53.5	523	65	244
3.00	415	415	491	74.9	- - -	48.5	61.7	84.7	67.2	53.2	518	- - -	242
3.05	401	401	474	74.3	- - -	47.2	60.8	84.1	66.0	51.7	499	63	231
3.10	388	388	472	74.2	- - -	47.1	60.8	84.0	65.8	51.5	496	61	229
3.15	375	375	455	73.4	- - -	45.7	59.7	83.4	64.6	49.9	476	59	220
3.20	363	363	440	72.8	- - -	44.5	58.8	82.8	63.5	48.4	459	58	212
3.25	352	352	425	72.0	- - -	43.1	57.8	82.0	62.3	46.9	441	56	202
3.30	341	341	410	71.4	- - -	41.8	56.8	81.4	61.1	45.3	423	54	193
3.35	331	331	396	70.6	- - -	40.4	55.7	80.6	59.9	43.6	407	54	184
3.40	321	321	383	70.0	- - -	39.1	54.6	80.0	58.7	42.0	392	52	177
3.45	311	311	372	69.3	(110.0)	37.9	53.8	79.3	57.6	40.5	379	51	172
3.50	302	302	360	68.7	(109.0)	36.6	52.8	78.6	56.4	39.1	367	50	164

Brinell Indentation dia, mm	Brinell Hardness 3000 kg load 10 mm dia. ball		Vickers Hardness	Rockwell Hardness Scales				Rockwell Superficial Hardness Superficial Brale Indenter			Knoop Hardness	Scleroscope Hardness	Approximate Strength of Steel (ksi)
	Standard Ball	Tungsten Carbide ball		A scale 60 kg load Brale Indenter	B scale 100 kg load 1/16-in dia. ball	C scale 150 kg load Brale Indenter	D scale 100 kg load Brale Indenter	15N scale 15 kg load	30N scale 30 kg load	45N scale 45 kg load	500 g load and greater		
3.35	331	331	350	68.1	(108.5)	35.5	51.9	78.0	55.4	37.8	356	48	159
3.40	321	321	339	67.5	(108.0)	34.3	51.0	77.3	54.3	36.4	345	47	154
3.45	311	311	328	66.9	(107.5)	33.1	50.0	76.7	53.3	34.4	336	46	149
3.50	302	302	319	66.3	(107.0)	32.1	49.3	76.1	52.2	33.8	327	45	146
3.55	293	293	309	65.7	(106.0)	30.9	48.3	75.5	51.2	32.4	318	43	142
3.60	285	285	301	65.3	(105.5)	29.9	47.6	75.0	50.3	31.2	310	42	138
3.65	277	277	292	64.6	(104.5)	28.8	46.7	74.4	49.3	29.9	302	41	134
3.70	269	269	284	64.1	(104.0)	27.6	45.9	73.7	48.3	28.5	294	40	131
3.75	262	262	276	63.6	(103.0)	26.6	45.0	73.1	47.3	27.3	286	39	127
3.80	255	255	269	63.0	(102.0)	25.4	44.2	72.5	46.2	26.0	279	38	123
3.85	248	248	261	62.5	(101.1)	24.2	43.2	71.7	45.1	24.5	272	37	120
3.90	241	241	253	61.8	100.0	22.8	42.0	70.9	43.9	22.8	265	36	116
3.95	235	235	247	61.4	99.0	21.7	41.4	70.3	42.9	21.5	259	35	114
4.00	229	229	241	60.8	98.2	20.5	40.5	69.7	41.9	20.1	253	34	111
4.05	223	223	234	---	97.3	(19.0)	---	---	---	---	247	---	107
4.10	217	217	228	---	96.4	(17.7)	---	---	---	---	242	33	105
4.15	212	212	222	---	95.5	(16.4)	---	---	---	---	237	32	102
4.20	207	207	218	---	94.6	(15.2)	---	---	---	---	232	31	100
4.25	201	201	212	---	93.7	(13.8)	---	---	---	---	227	---	98
4.30	197	197	207	---	92.8	(12.7)	---	---	---	---	222	30	95
4.35	192	192	202	---	91.9	(11.5)	---	---	---	---	217	29	93
4.40	187	187	196	---	90.9	(10.2)	---	---	---	---	212	---	90
4.45	183	183	192	---	90.0	(9.0)	---	---	---	---	207	28	89
4.50	179	179	188	---	89.0	(8.0)	---	---	---	---	202	27	87
4.55	174	174	182	---	88.0	(6.7)	---	---	---	---	198	---	85
4.60	170	170	178	---	87.0	(5.4)	---	---	---	---	194	26	83

| Brinell Hardness 3000 kg load 10 mm dia. ball | | | Vickers Hardness | Rockwell Hardness Scales | | | | Rockwell Superficial Hardness- Superficial Brale Indenter | | | Knoop Hardness 500 g load and greater | Scleroscope Hardness | Approximate Tensile Strength of Steel (ksi) |
Brinell Indentation dia, mm	Standard Ball	Tungsten Carbide ball		A scale 60 kg load Brale Indenter	B scale 100 kg load 1/16-in dia. ball	C scale 150 kg load Brale Indenter	D scale 100 kg load Brale Indenter	15N scale 15 kg load	30N scale 30 kg load	45N scale 45 kg load			
4.65	167	167	175	---	86.0	(4.4)	---	---	---	---	190	---	81
4.70	163	163	171	---	85.0	(3.3)	---	---	---	---	186	25	79
4.75	159	159	167	---	83.9	(2.0)	---	---	---	---	182	---	78
4.80	156	156	163	---	82.9	(0.9)	---	---	---	---	178	24	76
4.85	152	152	159	---	81.9	---	---	---	---	---	174	---	75
4.90	149	149	156	---	80.8	---	---	---	---	---	170	23	73
4.95	146	146	153	---	79.7	---	---	---	---	---	166	---	72
5.00	143	143	150	---	78.6	---	---	---	---	---	163	22	71
5.10	137	137	143	---	76.4	---	---	---	---	---	157	21	67
5.20	131	131	137	---	74.2	---	---	---	---	---	151	---	65
5.30	126	126	132	---	72.0	---	---	---	---	---	145	20	63
5.40	121	121	127	---	69.8	---	---	---	---	---	140	19	60
5.50	116	116	122	---	67.6	---	---	---	---	---	135	18	58
5.60	111	111	117	---	65.4	---	---	---	---	---	131	17	56

NOTES: Numbers in parentheses are outside the normal range of the test and are only given for information.

SOURCES: ASM Metals Reference Book, 3rd Edition, ASM International, Materials Park, OH, 1993

Thermal Expansion Coefficients

Linear Thermal Expansion Coefficient - CL (See Note 1)		
Material	per °C	per °F
Acetal	0.0001065	0.0000592
Acrylic, extruded	0.0002340	0.0001300
Acrylic, sheet, cast	0.0000810	0.0000450
Acrylonitrile butadiene styrene (ABS)	0.0000738	0.0000410
Allyl diglycol carbonate (ADC), cast sheet	0.0001120	0.0000622
Aluminum	0.0000231	0.0000128
Aluminum, alloy 2014, annealed	0.0000230	0.0000128
Aluminum, alloy 3003, rolled	0.0000232	0.0000129
Aluminum, alloy 306	0.0000210	0.0000117
Antimony	0.0000110	0.0000061
Arsenic	0.0000047	0.0000026
Barium	0.0000206	0.0000114
Beryllium	0.0000113	0.0000063
Bismuth	0.0000134	0.0000074
Brass	0.0000188	0.0000104
Brass, red, 85%	0.0000187	0.0000104
Brass, yellow or high	0.0000203	0.0000113
Brick masonary	0.0000055	0.0000031
Bronze	0.0000175	0.0000097
Bronze, aluminum	0.0000164	0.0000091
Bronze, cast	0.0000180	0.0000100
Cadmium	0.0000300	0.0000167
Calcium	0.0000223	0.0000124
Cellulose acetate (CA)	0.0001300	0.0000722
Cellulose acetate butyrate (CAB)	0.0002520	0.0000140
Cellulose nitrate (CN)	0.0001000	0.0000556
Cerium	0.0000052	0.0000029
Chlorinated polyvinyl chloride (CPVC)	0.0000666	0.0000370
Chromium	0.0000062	0.0000034
Clay tile structure	0.0000059	0.0000033
Cobalt	0.0000125	0.0000069
Concrete	0.0000143	0.0000079
Concrete structure	0.0000098	0.0000055
Constantan	0.0000188	0.0000104
Copper	0.0000168	0.0000093
Copper, beryllium 25	0.0000178	0.0000099
Corundum, sintered	0.0000065	0.0000036
Cupronickel 30%	0.0000162	0.0000090
Cupronickel 55-45	0.0000188	0.0000104
Diamond	0.0000011	0.0000006
Dysprosium	0.0000099	0.0000055
Ebonite	0.0000700	0.0000389
Epoxy, casting resins & compounds, unfilled	0.0000550	0.0000306
Erbium	0.0000122	0.0000068
Ethylene ethyl acrylate (EEA)	0.0002050	0.0001139
Ethylene vinyl acetate (EVA)	0.0001800	0.0001000
Europium	0.0000350	0.0000194

Linear Thermal Expansion Coefficient - CL (See Note 1)		
Material	per °C	per °F
Fluoroethylene propylene (FEP)	0.0001350	0.0000750
Gadolinium	0.0000090	0.0000050
Germanium	0.0000061	0.0000034
Glass, ordinary	0.0000090	0.0000050
Glass, pyrex	0.0000032	0.0000018
Glass, quartz	0.0000005	0.0000003
Glass, sheet	0.0000085	0.0000047
Glass, window	0.0000080	0.0000044
Gold	0.0000142	0.0000079
Granite	0.0000084	0.0000047
Graphite, pure	0.0000078	0.0000043
Hafnium	0.0000059	0.0000033
Hard alloy K20	0.0000060	0.0000033
Hastelloy C	0.0000113	0.0000063
Holmium	0.0000112	0.0000062
Ice	0.0000510	0.0000283
Inconel	0.0000115	0.0000064
Indium	0.0000330	0.0000183
Invar	0.0000015	0.0000008
Iridium	0.0000064	0.0000036
Iron	0.0000120	0.0000067
Iron, cast	0.0000106	0.0000059
Iron, cast gray	0.0000105	0.0000058
Iron, ingot	0.0000117	0.0000065
Iron, wrought	0.0000120	0.0000067
Lanthanum	0.0000121	0.0000067
Lead	0.0000293	0.0000163
Lead, antimonial or hard lead	0.0000265	0.0000147
Limestone	0.0000080	0.0000044
Lithium	0.0000460	0.0000256
Lutetium	0.0000099	0.0000055
Magnesium	0.0000269	0.0000150
Magnesium, alloy AZ31B	0.0000260	0.0000144
Manganese	0.0000217	0.0000121
Marble	0.0000100	0.0000056
Mica	0.0000030	0.0000017
Molybdenum	0.0000052	0.0000029
Monel	0.0000140	0.0000078
Neodymium	0.0000096	0.0000053
Nickel	0.0000130	0.0000072
Nickel silver (CuNi12Zn24)	0.0000180	0.0000100
Niobium	0.0000073	0.0000041
Nylon, general purpose	0.0000720	0.0000400
Nylon, Type 11, molding and extruding compound	0.0001000	0.0000556
Nylon, Type 12, molding and extruding compound	0.0000805	0.0000447
Nylon, Type 6, cast	0.0000850	0.0000472
Nylon, Type 6/6, molding compound	0.0000800	0.0000444

Linear Thermal Expansion Coefficient - CL (See Note 1)		
Material	per °C	per °F
Osmium	0.0000061	0.0000034
Palladium	0.0000118	0.0000066
Phenolic resin without fillers	0.0000800	0.0000444
Plaster	0.0000166	0.0000092
Platinum	0.0000090	0.0000050
Plutonium	0.0000467	0.0000259
Polyallomer	0.0000915	0.0000508
Polyamide (PA)	0.0001100	0.0000611
Polyaryletherketone (PAEK), unfilled	0.0004442	0.0002046
Polyarylsulfone (PASU)	0.0000400	0.0000222
Polybutylene (PB), extrusion compound	0.0001390	0.0000772
Polybutylene terephthalate (PBT), unfilled	0.0000810	0.0000450
Polycarbonate (PC)	0.0000702	0.0000390
Polychlorotrifluoroethylene (PCTFE)	0.0000530	0.0000294
Polyetheretherketone (PEEK)	0.0000468	0.0000260
Polyetherimide (PEI)	0.0000558	0.0000310
Polyethersulfone (PES)	0.0000558	0.0000310
Polyethylene (PE)	0.0002000	0.0001111
Polyethylene terephthalate (PET)	0.0000594	0.0000330
Polyethylene, high density (HDPE)	0.0002250	0.0001250
Polyethylene, low density (LDPE)	0.0002898	0.0001610
Polyethylene, ultrahigh-molecular-weight (UHMW-PE)	0.0001296	0.0000720
Polyethylene-chlorotrifluoroethylene (PE-CTFE)	0.0000800	0.0000444
Polyimide (PI), unfilled	0.0000505	0.0000281
Polymethyl pentene (PMP), unfilled	0.0000660	0.0000361
Polyphenylene oxide (PPO)	0.0000594	0.0000330
Polyphenylene sulfide (PPS)	0.0000504	0.0000280
Polypropylene (PP), unfilled	0.0000905	0.0000503
Polystyrene (PS)	0.0000700	0.0000389
Polysulfone (PSO)	0.0000558	0.0000310
Polyurethane (PUR), rigid	0.0000576	0.0000320
Polyvinyl chloride (PVC)	0.0001100	0.0000611
Polyvinylidene chloride (PVDC), injection molding	0.0001900	0.0001056
Polyvinylidene fluoride (PVDF)	0.0001278	0.0000710
Porcelain	0.0000045	0.0000025
Potassium	0.0000830	0.0000461
Praseodymium	0.0000067	0.0000037
Promethium	0.0000110	0.0000061
Quartz, parallel to axis	0.0000080	0.0000044
Quartz, perpendicular to axis	0.0000146	0.0000081
Resistance alloy (CuNi44)	0.0000152	0.0000084
Rhenium	0.0000067	0.0000037
Rhodium	0.0000083	0.0000046
Rubber, hard	0.0000800	0.0000444
Ruthenium	0.0000091	0.0000051
Samarium	0.0000127	0.0000071

Linear Thermal Expansion Coefficient - CL (See Note 1)		
Material	per °C	per °F
Scandium	0.0000102	0.0000057
Selenium	0.0000038	0.0000021
Silicon	0.0000051	0.0000028
Silicone, casting resin, flexible	0.0000145	0.0000081
Silver	0.0000197	0.0000109
Silver, German	0.0000180	0.0000100
Sodium	0.0000710	0.0000394
Solder 50-50	0.0000234	0.0000130
Steatite	0.0000085	0.0000047
Steel	0.0000115	0.0000064
Steel, carbon	0.0000117	0.0000065
Steel, chromium	0.0000110	0.0000061
Steel, galvanized	0.0000116	0.0000065
Steel, high speed	0.0000115	0.0000064
Steel, mild	0.0000120	0.0000067
Steel, nickel (36% Ni)	0.0000015	0.0000008
Steel, sintered	0.0000115	0.0000064
Steel, stainless, type 304	0.0000173	0.0000096
Strontium	0.0000225	0.0000125
Styrene maleic anhydride (SMA), molding and extrusion	0.0000800	0.0000444
Styrene methyl methacrylate	0.0000560	0.0000311
Tantalum	0.0000065	0.0000036
Tellurium	0.0000369	0.0000205
Terbium	0.0000103	0.0000057
Terne	0.0000116	0.0000065
Tetrafluoroethylene (TFE), fluorocarbon	0.0001170	0.0000650
Tetrafluoroethylene (TFE), fluoropolymer, bearing grade	0.0000882	0.0000490
Thallium	0.0000299	0.0000166
Thorium	0.0000125	0.0000069
Thulium	0.0000133	0.0000074
Tin	0.0000230	0.0000128
Titanium	0.0000085	0.0000047
Tungsten	0.0000045	0.0000025
Uranium	0.0000139	0.0000077
Vanadium	0.0000097	0.0000054
Wood, fir	0.0000037	0.0000021
Wood, oak	0.0000049	0.0000027
Wood, parallel to fibers	0.0000035	0.0000019
Wood, perpendicular to fibers	0.0000325	0.0000181
Wood, pine	0.0000054	0.0000030
Ytterbium	0.0000263	0.0000146
Yttrium	0.0000106	0.0000059
Zinc	0.0000302	0.0000168
Zirconium	0.0000057	0.0000032

Volume Thermal Expansion Coefficient

Volume Thermal Expansion Coefficient - CV - (See Note 2)		
Material	per °C	per °F
Alcohol	0.001100	0.000611
Benzene	0.001250	0.000694
Bromine	0.001100	0.000611
Ethanol (ethyl alcohol)	0.001100	0.000611
Ether	0.001600	0.000889
Gasoline	0.001000	0.000556
Glycerin	0.000500	0.000278
Kerosene	0.001000	0.000556
Mercury	0.000180	0.000100
Paraffin oil	0.000764	0.000424
Petroleum	0.001000	0.000556
Sulphuric acid, concentrated	0.000550	0.000306
Toluene	0.001080	0.000600
Trichloroethylene	0.001170	0.000650
Turpentine	0.001000	0.000556
Water	0.000180	0.000100

NOTES:
1. - Calculate linear thermal expansion as follows:
     $LF - LI = CL \times LI \times (TF - TI)$
     where:
     LF = final length
     LI = initial length
     CL = linear thermal expansion coefficient from table
     TF = final temperature
     TI = initial temperature
2. - Calculate volume thermal expansion as follows:
     $VF - VI = CV \times VI \times (TF - TI)$
     where:
     VF = final volume
     VI = initial volume
     CV = volume thermal expansion coefficient from table
     TF = final temperature
     TI = initial temperature

Surveying and Mapping

(See also MATH, page 447, for Trig Functions)

Percent Grade to Degrees

slope degrees	gradient 1:X	% grade
0.1	573.0	0.2
0.2	286.5	0.3
0.3	191.0	0.5
0.4	143.2	0.7
0.5	114.6	0.9
0.6	95.5	1.0
0.7	81.8	1.2
0.8	71.6	1.4
0.9	63.7	1.6
1.0	57.3	1.7
2.0	28.6	3.5
3.0	19.1	5.2
4.0	14.3	7.0
5.0	11.4	8.7
6.0	9.5	10.5
7.0	8.1	12.3
8.0	7.1	14.1
9.0	6.3	15.8
10.0	5.7	17.6
11.0	5.1	19.4
12.0	4.7	21.3
13.0	4.3	23.1
14.0	4.0	24.9
15.0	3.7	26.8
16.0	3.5	28.7
17.0	3.3	30.6
18.0	3.1	32.5
19.0	2.9	34.4
20.0	2.7	36.4
21.0	2.6	38.4
22.0	2.5	40.4
23.0	2.4	42.4
24.0	2.2	44.5
25.0	2.1	46.6
26.0	2.1	48.8
27.0	2.0	51.0
28.0	1.9	53.2
29.0	1.8	55.4
30.0	1.7	57.7
31.0	1.7	60.1
32.0	1.6	62.5
33.0	1.5	64.9
34.0	1.5	67.5
35.0	1.4	70.0
36.0	1.4	72.7
37.0	1.3	75.4
38.0	1.3	78.1
39.0	1.2	81.0
40.0	1.2	83.9
41.0	1.2	86.9
42.0	1.1	90.0
43.0	1.1	93.3
44.0	1.0	96.6
45.0	1.0	100.0
46.0	1.0	103.6
47.0	0.9	107.2
48.0	0.9	111.1

Percent Grade to Degrees

slope degrees	gradient 1:X	% grade
49.0	0.9	115.0
50.0	0.8	119.2
51.0	0.8	123.5
52.0	0.8	128.0
53.0	0.8	132.7
54.0	0.7	137.6
55.0	0.7	142.8
56.0	0.7	148.3
57.0	0.6	154.0
58.0	0.6	160.0
59.0	0.6	166.4
60.0	0.6	173.2
61.0	0.6	180.4
62.0	0.5	188.1
63.0	0.5	196.2
64.0	0.5	205.0
65.0	0.5	214.5
66.0	0.4	224.6
67.0	0.4	235.6
68.0	0.4	247.5
69.0	0.4	260.5
70.0	0.4	274.7
71.0	0.3	290.4
72.0	0.3	307.8
73.0	0.3	327.1
74.0	0.3	348.7
75.0	0.3	373.2
76.0	0.2	401.1
77.0	0.2	433.1
78.0	0.2	470.5
79.0	0.2	514.5
80.0	0.2	567.1
81.0	0.2	631.4
82.0	0.1	711.5
83.0	0.1	814.4
84.0	0.1	951.4
85.0	0.1	1143.0
86.0	0.1	1430.1
87.0	0.1	1908.1
88.0	0.0	2863.6
89.0	0.0	5729.0
90.0	0.0	∞

$$Tan\left[Slope\ Degrees\right] = \frac{Vertical\ Rise\ Distance}{Horizontal\ Distance}$$

$$Gradient = 1\ unit\ in\ \frac{Horizontal\ Distance}{Vertical\ Rise\ Distance}\ units\ or\ 1{:}\frac{H}{V}$$

$$\%\ Grade\ is\ 100\ x\ Tan\left[Slope\right]\ or\ \frac{100\ x\ Vertical\ Rise}{Horizontal\ Distance}$$

Stadia Formula

Most theodolites have an internal set of cross hairs that when used with a stadia rod, allows the calculation of slope distance. (magnification is normally 100 and slope distance = 100 x Stadia Rod Vertical Intercept). If angles are involved, the formula is:

D = HI + [Slope Distance x Sin (2V)/2] – M

D = Elevation difference between survey points
HI = Instrument height above survey point
V = Vertical angle (degrees) at the theodolite
M = Mid point cross hair reading on stadia rod

Stadia Table

	Assume stadia slope distance of 100	
Slope Angle (°)	Vertical Distance	Horizontal Distance
0.0	0.00	100.00
0.5	0.87	99.99
1.0	1.74	99.97
1.5	2.62	99.93
2.0	3.49	99.88
2.5	4.36	99.81
3.0	5.23	99.73
3.5	6.09	99.63
4.0	6.96	99.51
4.5	7.82	99.38
5.0	8.68	99.24
5.5	9.54	99.08
6.0	10.40	98.91
6.5	11.25	98.72
7.0	12.10	98.51
7.5	12.94	98.30
8.0	13.78	98.06
8.5	14.62	97.82
9.0	15.45	97.55
9.5	16.28	97.28
10.0	17.10	96.98
10.5	17.92	96.68
11.0	18.73	96.36
11.5	19.54	96.03
12.0	20.34	95.68
12.5	21.13	95.32
13.0	21.92	94.94
13.5	22.70	94.55
14.0	23.47	94.15

Stadia Table

Assume stadia slope distance of 100

Slope Angle (°)	Vertical Distance	Horizontal Distance
14.5	24.24	93.73
15.0	25.00	93.30
15.5	25.75	92.86
16.0	26.50	92.40
16.5	27.23	91.93
17.0	27.96	91.45
17.5	28.68	90.96
18.0	29.39	90.45
18.5	30.09	89.93
19.0	30.78	89.40
19.5	31.47	88.86
20.0	32.14	88.30
20.5	32.80	87.74
21.0	33.46	87.16
21.5	34.10	86.57
22.0	34.73	85.97
22.5	35.36	85.36
23.0	35.97	84.73
23.5	36.57	84.10
24.0	37.16	83.46
24.5	37.74	82.80
25.0	38.30	82.14
25.5	38.86	81.47
26.0	39.40	80.78
26.5	39.93	80.09
27.0	40.45	79.39
27.5	40.96	78.68
28.0	41.45	77.96
28.5	41.93	77.23
29.0	42.40	76.50
29.5	42.86	75.75
30.0	43.30	75.00
30.5	43.73	74.24
31.0	44.15	73.47
31.5	44.55	72.70
32.0	44.94	71.92
32.5	45.32	71.13
33.0	45.68	70.34
33.5	46.03	69.54
34.0	46.36	68.73
34.5	46.68	67.92
35.0	46.98	67.10
35.5	47.28	66.28
36.0	47.55	65.45
36.5	47.82	64.62
37.0	48.06	63.78
37.5	48.30	62.94
38.0	48.51	62.10
38.5	48.72	61.25
39.0	48.91	60.40

Stadia Table

Assume stadia slope distance of 100

Slope Angle (°)	Vertical Distance	Horizontal Distance
39.5	49.08	59.54
40.0	49.24	58.68
40.5	49.38	57.82
41.0	49.51	56.96
41.5	49.63	56.09
42.0	49.73	55.23
42.5	49.81	54.36
43.0	49.88	53.49
43.5	49.93	52.62
44.0	49.97	51.74
44.5	49.99	50.87
45.0	50.00	50.00
45.5	49.99	49.13
46.0	49.97	48.26
46.5	49.93	47.38
47.0	49.88	46.51
47.5	49.81	45.64
48.0	49.73	44.77
48.5	49.63	43.91
49.0	49.51	43.04
49.5	49.38	42.18
50.0	49.24	41.32
50.5	49.08	40.46
51.0	48.91	39.60
51.5	48.72	38.75
52.0	48.51	37.90
52.5	48.30	37.06
53.0	48.06	36.22
53.5	47.82	35.38
54.0	47.55	34.55
54.5	47.28	33.72
55.0	46.98	32.90
55.5	46.68	32.08
56.0	46.36	31.27
56.5	46.03	30.46
57.0	45.68	29.66
57.5	45.32	28.87
58.0	44.94	28.08
58.5	44.55	27.30
59.0	44.15	26.53
59.5	43.73	25.76
60.0	43.30	25.00

Horizontal Distance = Slope Distance x Cos²(Slope Degrees)

Vertical Distance = (Slope Distance/2) x Sin(2 x Slope Degrees)

Mapping Scales & Areas

scale 1:X	Feet/ Inch	Inch/ Mile	Acres/ Sq Inch	Sq Miles/ Sq Inch
100	8.3	633.60	0.0016	0.000002
120	10.0	528.00	0.0023	0.000004
200	16.7	316.80	0.0064	0.000010
240	20.0	264.00	0.0092	0.000014
250	20.8	253.44	0.0100	0.000016
300	25.0	211.20	0.0143	0.000022
400	33.3	158.40	0.0255	0.000040
480	40.0	132.00	0.0367	0.000057
500	41.7	126.72	0.0399	0.000062
600	50.0	105.60	0.0574	0.000090
1000	83.3	63.36	0.1594	0.000249
1200	100.0	52.80	0.2296	0.000359
1500	125.0	42.24	0.3587	0.000560
2000	166.7	31.68	0.6377	0.000996
2400	200.0	26.40	0.9183	0.001435
2500	208.3	25.34	0.9964	0.001557
3000	250.0	21.12	1.4348	0.002242
3600	300.0	17.60	2.0661	0.003228
4000	333.3	15.84	2.5508	0.003986
4800	400.0	13.20	3.6731	0.005739
5000	416.7	12.67	3.9856	0.006227
6000	500.0	10.56	5.7392	0.008968
7000	583.3	9.05	7.8117	0.012206
7200	600.0	8.80	8.2645	0.012913
7920	660.0	8.00	10.0000	0.015625
8000	666.7	7.92	10.2030	0.015942
8400	700.0	7.54	11.2489	0.017576
9000	750.0	7.04	12.9132	0.020177
9600	800.0	6.60	14.6924	0.022957
10000	833.3	6.34	15.9423	0.024910
10800	900.0	5.87	18.5950	0.029055
12000	1000.0	5.28	22.9568	0.035870
13200	1100.0	4.80	27.7778	0.043403
14400	1200.0	4.40	33.0579	0.051653
15000	1250.0	4.22	35.8701	0.056047
15600	1300.0	4.06	38.7971	0.060620
15840	1320.0	4.00	40.0000	0.062500
16000	1333.3	3.96	40.8122	0.063769
16800	1400.0	3.77	44.9954	0.070305
18000	1500.0	3.52	51.6529	0.080708
19200	1600.0	3.30	58.7695	0.091827
20000	1666.7	3.17	63.7690	0.099639
20400	1700.0	3.11	66.3453	0.103664

Mapping Scales & Areas

scale 1:X	Feet/ Inch	Inch/ Mile	Acres/ Sq Inch	Sq Miles/ Sq Inch
21120	1760.0	3.00	71.1111	0.111111
21600	1800.0	2.93	74.3802	0.116219
22800	1900.0	2.78	82.8742	0.129491
24000	2000.0	2.64	91.8274	0.143480
25000	2083.3	2.53	99.6391	0.155686
30000	2500.0	2.11	143.4803	0.224188
31680	2640.0	2.00	160.0000	0.250000
40000	3333.3	1.58	255.0760	0.398556
45000	3750.0	1.41	322.8306	0.504423
48000	4000.0	1.32	367.3095	0.573921
50000	4166.7	1.27	398.5563	0.622744
60000	5000.0	1.06	573.9210	0.896752
62500	5208.3	1.01	622.7442	0.973038
63360	5280.0	1.00	640.0000	1.000000
80000	6666.7	0.79	1020.3041	1.594225
90000	7500.0	0.70	1291.3223	2.017691
96000	8000.0	0.66	1469.2378	2.295684
100000	8333.3	0.63	1594.2251	2.490977
125000	10416.7	0.51	2490.9767	3.892151
126720	10560.0	0.50	2560.0000	4.000000
200000	16666.7	0.32	6376.9003	9.963907
250000	20833.3	0.25	9963.9067	15.568604
253440	21120.0	0.25	10240.0000	16.000000
380160	31680.0	0.17	23040.0000	36.000000
500000	41666.7	0.13	39855.6270	62.274417
760320	63360.0	0.08	92160.0000	144.000000
1000000	83333.3	0.06	159422.5079	249.097669

Feet / Inch = Scale / 12

Meters / Inch = Scale / 39.37

Miles / Inch = Scale / 63,291.14

Chains / Inch = Scale / 792.08

Inch / Mile = 63360 / Scale

Acres / Square Inch = $Scale^2$ / 6,272,640

Square Miles / Square Inch = $Scale^2$ / 4,014,489,600

Apparent Dip Table

True Dip	Angle between Strike and direction of Cross Section				
	5°	10°	15°	20°	25°
5°	0.4	0.9	1.3	1.7	2.1
10°	0.9	1.8	2.6	3.5	4.3
15°	1.3	2.7	4.0	5.2	6.5
20°	1.8	3.6	5.4	7.1	8.7
25°	2.3	4.6	6.9	9.1	11.1
30°	2.9	5.7	8.5	11.2	13.7
35°	3.5	6.9	10.3	13.5	16.5
40°	4.2	8.3	12.3	16.0	19.5
45°	5.0	9.9	14.5	18.9	22.9
50°	5.9	11.7	17.1	22.2	26.7
55°	7.1	13.9	20.3	26.0	31.1
60°	8.6	16.7	24.1	30.6	36.2
65°	10.6	20.4	29.0	36.3	42.2
70°	13.5	25.5	35.4	43.2	49.3
75°	18.0	32.9	44.0	51.9	57.6
80°	26.3	44.6	55.7	62.7	67.4
85°	44.9	63.3	71.3	75.7	78.3

True Dip	Angle between Strike and direction of Cross Section				
	30°	35°	40°	45°	50°
5°	2.5	2.9	3.2	3.5	3.8
10°	5.0	5.8	6.5	7.1	7.7
15°	7.6	8.7	9.8	10.7	11.6
20°	10.3	11.8	13.2	14.4	15.6
25°	13.1	15.0	16.7	18.2	19.7
30°	16.1	18.3	20.4	22.2	23.9
35°	19.3	21.9	24.2	26.3	28.2
40°	22.8	25.7	28.3	30.7	32.7
45°	26.6	29.8	32.7	35.3	37.5
50°	30.8	34.4	37.5	40.1	42.4
55°	35.5	39.3	42.6	45.3	47.6
60°	40.9	44.8	48.1	50.8	53.0
65°	47.0	50.9	54.0	56.6	58.7
70°	53.9	57.6	60.5	62.8	64.6
75°	61.8	65.0	67.4	69.2	70.7
80°	70.6	72.9	74.7	76.0	77.0
85°	80.1	81.3	82.2	82.9	83.5

Apparent Dip Table

True Dip	Angle between Strike and direction of Cross Section				
	55°	60°	65°	70°	75°
5°	4.1	4.3	4.5	4.7	4.8
10°	8.2	8.7	9.1	9.4	9.7
15°	12.4	13.1	13.6	14.1	14.5
20°	16.6	17.5	18.3	18.9	19.4
25°	20.9	22.0	22.9	23.7	24.2
30°	25.3	26.6	27.6	28.5	29.1
35°	29.8	31.2	32.4	33.3	34.1
40°	34.5	36.0	37.3	38.3	39.0
45°	39.3	40.9	42.2	43.2	44.0
50°	44.3	45.9	47.2	48.2	49.0
55°	49.5	51.0	52.3	53.3	54.1
60°	54.8	56.3	57.5	58.4	59.1
65°	60.3	61.7	62.8	63.6	64.2
70°	66.0	67.2	68.1	68.8	69.4
75°	71.9	72.8	73.5	74.1	74.5
80°	77.9	78.5	79.0	79.4	79.7
85°	83.9	84.2	84.5	84.7	84.8

When a cross section cuts across the plane of a bedding sur-face, fault or topography (at any angle less than 90°), the observed dip (apparent dip) at the cross section intersection will always be less than the true dip. In order to use the above table, first, determine the "Angle Between Strike" value by subtracting the true strike (bearing) of the unit from the bearing of the cross sec-tion; second, measure the observed dip and locate that number in the body of the table; third, follow the row across to the left in order to determine the true dip. If you need a more precise value than listed in the table, use the following formula to calculate the answer:

Tan (Apparent Dip) = Tan (True Dip) x Sin (Angle Between)

Note that if the "Angle between Strike" value is 80° to 90°, the value of the true dip and apparent dip are nearly identical.

Three Point Problem

A common problem in both surveying and geology is the determination of the strike (bearing) of a bedding surface, fault, topographic surface, etc. when the location and elevation of three points on the surface are known.

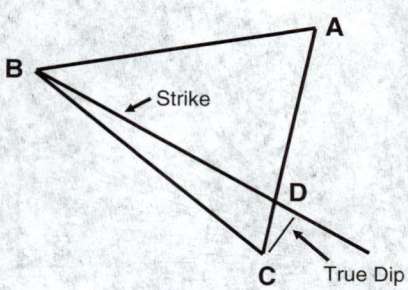

The elevation and location of points A, B, and C are known. If the elevation of point B is between the elevations of points A (the highest point) and C (the lowest point), then the strike (bearing) of the plane defined by ABC is determined by locating point D, on the line between A and C, and then drawing a strike line between B and D. Since strike is defined as the bearing of a horizontal line on the plane of ABC, the elevations of point B and D must be the same. The exact location of point D can be calculated from the following equation:

$$\text{Length CD} = \text{Length AC} \times \frac{\text{BC elevation difference}}{\text{AC elevation difference}}$$

Note that the true dip must always be at a right angle to the strike. The value of the true dip can be calculated with the following equation:

$$\text{Dip Angle }(°) = \text{Arc Tan}\left((\text{Elev D–C}) / \text{Length True Dip Line}\right)$$

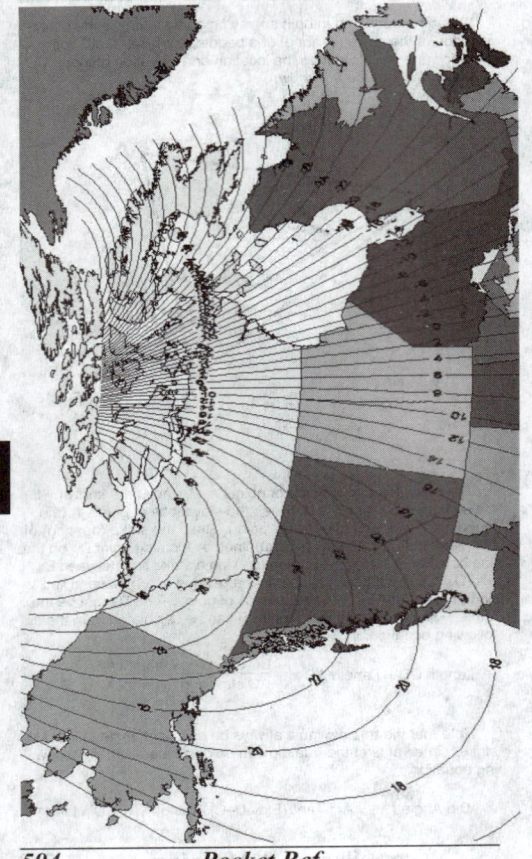

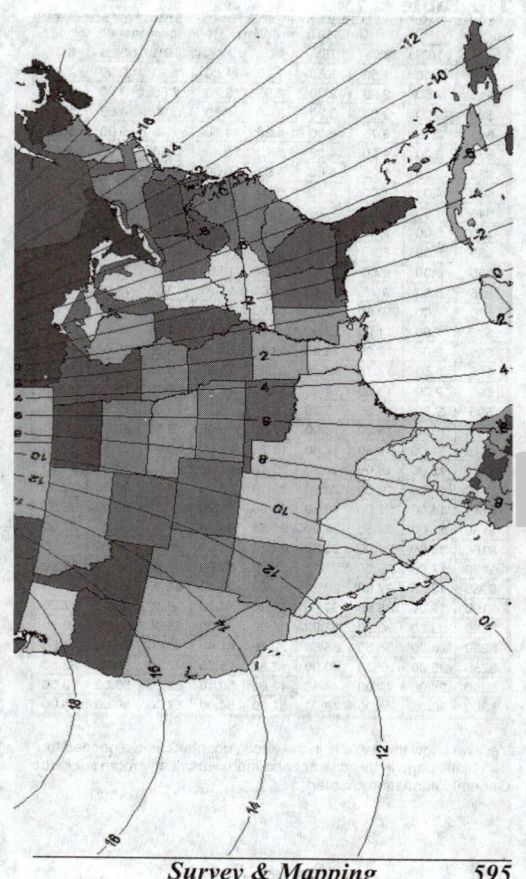

Tip Table

Bill	Dollar Tip at a Given Tip Percentage							
	10%	15%	16%	17%	18%	19%	20%	25%
$10	1.00	1.50	1.60	1.70	1.80	1.90	2.00	2.50
$15	1.50	2.25	2.40	2.55	2.70	2.85	3.00	3.75
$20	2.00	3.00	3.20	3.40	3.60	3.80	4.00	5.00
$25	2.50	3.75	4.00	4.25	4.50	4.75	5.00	6.25
$30	3.00	4.50	4.80	5.10	5.40	5.70	6.00	7.50
$35	3.50	5.25	5.60	5.95	6.30	6.65	7.00	8.75
$40	4.00	6.00	6.40	6.80	7.20	7.60	8.00	10.00
$45	4.50	6.75	7.20	7.65	8.10	8.55	9.00	11.25
$50	5.00	7.50	8.00	8.50	9.00	9.50	10.00	12.50
$55	5.50	8.25	8.80	9.35	9.90	10.45	11.00	13.75
$60	6.00	9.00	9.60	10.20	10.80	11.40	12.00	15.00
$65	6.50	9.75	10.40	11.05	11.70	12.35	13.00	16.25
$70	7.00	10.50	11.20	11.90	12.60	13.30	14.00	17.50
$75	7.50	11.25	12.00	12.75	13.50	14.25	15.00	18.75
$80	8.00	12.00	12.80	13.60	14.40	15.20	16.00	20.00
$85	8.50	12.75	13.60	14.45	15.30	16.15	17.00	21.25
$90	9.00	13.50	14.40	15.30	16.20	17.10	18.00	22.50
$95	9.50	14.25	15.20	16.15	17.10	18.05	19.00	23.75
$100	10.00	15.00	16.00	17.00	18.00	19.00	20.00	25.00
$110	11.00	16.50	17.60	18.70	19.80	20.90	22.00	27.50
$120	12.00	18.00	19.20	20.40	21.60	22.80	24.00	30.00
$130	13.00	19.50	20.80	22.10	23.40	24.70	26.00	32.50
$140	14.00	21.00	22.40	23.80	25.20	26.60	28.00	35.00
$150	15.00	22.50	24.00	25.50	27.00	28.50	30.00	37.50
$160	16.00	24.00	25.60	27.20	28.80	30.40	32.00	40.00
$170	17.00	25.50	27.20	28.90	30.60	32.30	34.00	42.50
$180	18.00	27.00	28.80	30.60	32.40	34.20	36.00	45.00
$190	19.00	28.50	30.40	32.30	34.20	36.10	38.00	47.50
$200	20.00	30.00	32.00	34.00	36.00	38.00	40.00	50.00
$230	23.00	34.50	36.80	39.10	41.40	43.70	46.00	57.50
$250	25.00	37.50	40.00	42.50	45.00	47.50	50.00	62.50
$280	28.00	42.00	44.80	47.60	50.40	53.20	56.00	70.00
$300	30.00	45.00	48.00	51.00	54.00	57.00	60.00	75.00

Yes, we know this table is in the wrong chapter, but we needed to fill a blank page in this chapter and there wasn't any room left in the General Information chapter!

(See WELDING, p. 667 for more tools & soldering)

(See also MATH, p.449 for drill number table)

(See also HARDWARE for clearance fit drill sizes)

American National Taps & Dies

Thread	Fine Threads			Coarse Threads		
	Threads / inch	Tap Drill	Tap Decimal inch	Threads / inch	Tap Drill	Tap Decimal inch
#0	80	3/64	0.0469	...	...	...
#1	72	#53	0.0595	64	#53	0.0595
#2	64	#50	0.0700	56	#50	0.0700
#3	56	#46	0.0810	48	#47	0.0785
#4	48	#42	0.0935	40	#43	0.0890
1/8	40	#38	0.1015	32	3/32	0.0938
#5	44	#37	0.1040	40	#38	0.1015
#6	40	#33	0.1130	32	#36	0.1065
#8	36	#29	0.1360	32	#29	0.1360
3/16	32	#22	0.1570	24	#26	0.1470
#10	32	#21	0.1590	24	#25	0.1495
#12	28	#14	0.1820	24	#16	0.1770
1/4	28	#3	0.2130	20	#7	0.2010
5/16	24	I	0.2720	18	F	0.2570
3/8	24	Q	0.3320	16	5/16	0.3125
7/16	20	25/64	0.3906	14	U	0.3680
1/2	20	29/64	0.4531	13	27/64	0.4219
9/16	18	33/64	0.5156	12	31/64	0.4844
5/8	18	37/64	0.5781	11	17/32	0.5313
3/4	16	11/16	0.6875	10	21/32	0.6563
7/8	14	13/16	0.8125	9	49/64	0.7656
1	12	59/64	0.9219	8	7/8	0.8750
1-1/8	12	1-3/64	1.0469	7	63/64	0.9844
1-1/4	12	1-11/64	1.1719	7	1-7/64	1.1094
1-3/8	12	1-19/64	1.2969	6	1-7/32	1.2188
1-1/2	12	1-27/64	1.4219	6	1-11/32	1.3438
1-3/4	...	...	...	5	1-35/64	1.5469
2	...	...	...	4-1/2	1-25/32	1.7813
2-1/4	...	...	...	4-1/2	2-1/32	2.0313
2-1/2	...	...	...	4	2-1/4	2.2500
2-3/4	...	...	...	4	2-1/2	2.5000
3	...	...	...	4	2-3/4	2.7500
3-1/4	...	...	...	4	3	3.0000
3-1/2	...	...	...	4	3-1/4	3.2500
3-3/4	...	...	...	4	3-1/2	3.5000
4	...	...	...	4	3-3/4	3.7500

Note that there are literally hundreds of other sizes and thread per inch taps and dies available, e.g. 1/4 inch can have 10,12,14, 16,18,22,23,24,25,26,27,30,32,34,36,38,40,42,44,48,50,52,56,60, 64,72, and 80 threads/inch depending on the standard. Threads shown in the table above are simply the most common.

Metric Taps and Dies

Thread Size mm	Thread Size Inches	Pitch in mm French	Pitch in mm International	Tap Drill Size mm	Tap Drill Size Inches
1.5	0.0591	0.35	...	1.10	0.0433
2	0.0787	0.45	...	1.50	0.0591
2	0.0787	...	0.40	1.60	0.0630
2.3	0.0906	...	0.40	1.90	0.0748
2.5	0.0984	0.45	...	2.00	0.0787
2.6	0.1024	...	0.45	2.10	0.0827
3	0.1181	...	0.5	2.50	0.0984
3	0.1181	0.60	...	2.40	0.0945
3.5	0.1378	0.60	0.60	2.90	0.1142
4	0.1575	0.75	...	3.25	0.1280
4	0.1575	...	0.70	3.30	0.1299
4.5	0.1772	0.75	0.75	3.75	0.1476
5	0.1969	0.90	...	4.10	0.1614
5	0.1969	...	0.80	4.20	0.1654
5.5	0.2165	0.90	0.90	4.60	0.1811
6	0.2362	1.00	1.00	5.00	0.1969
7	0.2756	1.00	1.00	6.00	0.2362
8	0.3150	1.00	...	7.00	0.2756
8	0.3150	...	1.25	6.80	0.2677
9	0.3543	1.00	...	8.00	0.3150
9	0.3543	...	1.25	7.80	0.3071
10	0.3937	1.50	1.50	8.80	0.3386
11	0.4331	...	1.50	9.60	0.3780
12	0.4724	1.50	...	10.50	0.4134
12	0.4724	...	1.75	10.50	0.4134
14	0.5512	2.00	2.00	12.00	0.4724
16	0.6299	2.00	2.00	14.00	0.5512
18	0.7087	2.50	2.50	15.50	0.6102
20	0.7874	2.50	2.50	17.50	0.6890
22	0.8661	2.50	2.50	19.50	0.7677
24	0.9449	3.00	3.00	21.00	0.8268
26	1.0236	3.00	...	23.00	0.9055
27	1.0630	...	3.00	24.00	0.9449
28	1.1024	3.00	...	25.00	0.9843
30	1.1811	3.50	3.50	26.50	1.0433
32	1.2598	3.50	...	28.50	1.1220
33	1.2992	...	3.50	29.50	1.1614
34	1.3386	3.50	...	30.50	1.2008
36	1.4173	4.00	4.00	32.00	1.25
38	1.4961	4.00	...	34.00	1.
39	1.5354	...	4.00	35.00	
40	1.5748	4.00	...	36.00	
42	1.6535	4.50	4.50	37.	

Tools

British Taps & Dies

Thread	British Std Whitworth		British Standard Fine	
	Threads / inch	Tap Drill	Threads / inch	Tap Drill
1/8	40	2.55mm	...	..
3/16	24	3.70mm	32	5/32
7/32	...	...	28	4.65mm
1/4	20	5.10mm	26	5.3mm
9/32	...	...	26	...
5/16	18	6.50mm	22	6.75mm
3/8	16	5/16	20	8.25mm
7/16	14	9.25mm	18	9.70mm
1/2	12	10.5mm	16	7/16
9/16	12	12.1mm	16	1/2
5/8	11	13.5mm	14	14mm
11/16	11	...	14	...
3/4	10	41/64	12	16.75mm
7/8	9	19.25mm	11	25/32
1	8	22.00mm	10	22.75
1-1/8	7	24.75mm	9	25.50mm
1-1/4	7	1-3/32	9	28.75mm
1-3/8	...	...	8	31.50mm
1-1/2	6	33.50mm	8	1-23/64
1-3/4	5	39.00mm	...	...
2	4.5	44.50mm	...	...

British Assoc Std Thread (B.A.)

Thread	Threads / inch	Pitch mm	Major Diameter mm
0	25.4	1.00	6.0
1	28.2	0.90	5.3
2	31.4	0.81	4.7
3	34.8	0.73	4.1
4	38.5	0.66	3.6
5	43.0	0.59	3.2
6	47.9	0.53	2.8
7	52.9	0.48	2.5
8	59.1	0.43	2.2
9	65.1	0.39	1.9
10	72.6	0.35	1.7
11	82.0	0.31	1.5
12	90.7	0.28	1.3
13	102.0	0.25	1.2
14	110.0	0.23	1.0
15	121.0	0.21	0.9
16	134.0	0.19	0.79

American Std Taper Pipe

Pipe Size inch	Threads per inch	Pipe Diameter inch	Tap Drill
1/8	27	0.405	R
1/4	18	0.540	7/16
3/8	18	0.675	37/64
1/2	14	0.840	23/32
3/4	14	1.050	59/64
1	11.5	1.315	1-5/32
1-1/4	11.5	1.660	1-1/2
1-1/2	11.5	1.900	1-47/64
2	11.5	2.375	2-7/32
2-1/2	8	2.875	2-5/8
3	8	3.500	3-1/4
3-1/2	8	4.000	3-3/4
4	8	4.500	4-1/4
4-1/2	8	5.000	4-3/4
5	8	5.563	5-9/32
6	8	6.625	6-11/32
7	8	7.625	...
8	8	8.625	...
9	8	9.625	...
10	8	10.750	...
12	8	12.750	...
>14 OD	8	Same as Col 1	...

American Std Straight Pipe

Pipe Size inch	Threads per inch	Pipe Diameter inch	Tap Drill
1/8	27	0.405	S
1/4	18	0.540	29/64
3/8	18	0.675	19/32
1/2	14	0.840	47/64
3/4	14	1.050	15/16
1	11.5	1.315	1-3/16
1-1/4	11.5	1.660	1-33/64
1-1/2	11.5	1.900	1-3/4
2	11.5	2.375	2-7/32
2-1/2	8	2.875	2-21/32
3	8	3.500	3-9/32
3-1/2	8	4.000	3-25/32
4	8	4.500	4-9/32
4-1/2	8	5.000	4-25/32
5	8	5.563	5-11/32
6	8	6.625	6-13/32

Drill & Cutting Lubricants

Material to be Worked	Machine Process		
	Drilling	Threading	Lathe
Aluminum	Soluble oil Kerosene Lard oil	Soluble oil, Kerosene, & Lard oil	Soluble oil
Brass	Dry Soluble oil Kerosene Lard Oil	Soluble oil Lard oil	Soluble oil
Bronze	Dry Soluble oil Mineral oil Lard oil	Soluble oil Lard oil	Soluble oil
Cast Iron	Dry Air jet Soluble oil	Dry Sulphurized oil Mineral lard oil	Dry Soluble oil
Copper	Dry Soluble oil Mineral lard oil Kerosene	Soluble oil Lard oil	Soluble
Malleable Iron	Dry Soda water	Lard oil Soda water	Soluble oil Soda water
Monel metal	Soluble oil Lard oil	Lard oil	Soluble oil
Steel alloys	Soluble oil Sulphurized oil Mineral lard oil	Sulphurized oil Lard oil	Soluble oil
Steel, machine	Soluble oil Sulphurized oil Lard oil Mineral lard oil	Soluble oil Mineral lard oil	Soluble oil
Steel, tool	Soluble oil Sulphurized oil Mineral lard oil	Sulphurized oil Lard oil	Soluble oil

The above table of cutting fluids is courtesy of Cincinnati Milacron.

Drilling Speeds vs. Material

Material	Speed rpm	Description
Cast Iron	6000 to 6500	1/16 inch drill
	3500 to 4500	1/8 inch drill
	2500 to 3000	3/16 inch drill
	2000 to 2500	1/4 inch drill
	1500 to 2000	5/16 inch drill
	1500 to 2000	3/8 inch drill
	1000 to 1500	> 7/16 inch drill
Glass	700	Special metal tube drilling
Plastics	6000 to 6500	1/16 inch drill
	5000 to 6000	1/8 inch drill
	3500 to 4000	3/16 inch drill
	3000 to 3500	1/4 inch drill
	2000 to 2500	5/16 inch drill
	1500 to 2000	3/8 inch drill
	500 to 1000	> 7/16 inch drill
Soft Metals (copper)	6000 to 6500	1/16 inch drill
	6000 to 6500	1/8 inch drill
	5000 to 6000	3/16 inch drill
	4500 to 5000	1/4 inch drill
	3500 to 4000	5/16 inch drill
	3000 to 3500	3/8 inch drill
	1500 to 2500	> 7/16 inch drill
Steel	5000 to 6500	1/16 inch drill
	3000 to 4000	1/8 inch drill
	2000 to 2500	3/16 inch drill
	1500 to 2000	1/4 inch drill
	1000 to 1500	5/16 inch drill
	1000 to 1500	3/8 inch drill
	500 to 1000	> 7/16 inch drill
Wood	4000 to 6000	Carving and routing
	3800 to 4000	All woods, 0 to 1/4 inch drills
	3100 to 3800	All woods, 1/4 to 1/2 inch drills
	2300 to 3100	All woods, 1/2 to 3/4 inch drills
	2000 to 2300	All woods, 3/4 to 1 inch drills
	700 to 2000	All woods, >1 inch drills, fly cutters,
	< 700	and multi-spur bits

If in doubt about what speed to use, always select the slower speeds. Speeds for drill sizes not listed above can be estimated by looking at speeds for sizes one step over and one step under.

Fire Extinguishers

Fire extinguishers are an absolute must in any shop, garage, home, automobile, or business. Fire extinguishers are classified by the types of fires they will put out and the size of the fire they will put out. The basic types are as follows:

TYPE A: For wood, cloth, paper, trash and other common materials. These fires are put out by "heat absorbing" water or water based materials or smothered by dry chemicals.

TYPE B: For oil, gasoline, grease, paints & other flammable liquids. These fires are put out by smothering, preventing the release of combustible vapors, or stopping the combustion chain. Use Halon, dry chemicals, carbon dioxide, or foam.

TYPE C: For "live" electrical equipment. These fires are put out by the same process as TYPE B, but the extinguishing material <u>must be electrically non-conductive</u>. Use halon, dry chemicals, or carbon dioxide.

TYPE D: For combustible metals such as magnesium. These fires must be put out by heat absorption and smothering. Obtain specific information on these requirements from the fire department.

Combinations of the above letters indicate the extinguisher will put out more than one type of fire. For example, a Type ABC unit will put out all three types of fires. The "size" of the fire an extinguisher will put out is shown by a number in front of the Type, such as "10B". The base line numbers are as follows:

Fire Extinguishers

Class "1A": Will put out a stack of 50 burning sticks that are 20 inches long each.

Class "1B": Will put out an area of burning naptha that is 2.5 square feet in size.

Any number other than the "1" simply indicates the extinguisher will put out a fire that many times larger, for example "10A" will put out a fire 10 times larger than "1A".

Some general recommendations when purchasing a fire extinguisher are as follows:

1. Buy TYPE ABC so that you never have to think about what type of fire you are using it on.

2. For electronic equipment buy an inert gas extinguisher-no equipment damage, less mess. Until 1993, Halon was the gas of choice. Due to EPA regulations, Halon has been replaced with products such as Halotron-I, Inergen, Dupont FE-36, and FM-200. Carbon dioxide can also be used and is less expensive than the other inert gasses.

3. Relative costs of ABC extinguishers are:
FOAM- very expensive-special use, i.e., aircraft fires;
INERT GAS- very expensive-leaves no mess;
CARBON DIOXIDE-expensive-leaves no mess;
DRY CHEMICAL-inexpensive-leaves a mess.

4. Buy units with metal components and a gauge and are approved by Underwriters Labs or other testing group. Plastic units are generally poorly constructed and break easily; buy good extinguishers, your life and property may depend on it !

5. Buy more than one extinguisher and mount them on the wall near escape routes so that children can reach them.

6. Study the instructions when you get the unit, there may not be time after a fire has started.

Sandpaper & Abrasives

Grit Current System	Grit Old System	Word Description	Use
12	4-1/2	Very Coarse	Very rough work,
16	4	Very Coarse	usually requires
20	3-1/2	Very Coarse	high speed, heavy
24	3	Very Coarse	machines. For
30	2-1/2	Coarse	unplaned woods,
36	2	Coarse	wood floors, rough cut.
40	1-1/2	Coarse	Rough wood work,
50	1	Coarse	#1 is coarsest for
60	1/2	Medium	use with pad sander.
80	1/0	Medium	General wood work,
100	2/0	Medium	plaster patches, 1st
120	3/0	Fine	smooth of old paint.
150	4/0	Fine	Hardwood prep, final for
180	5/0	Fine	softwoods, old paint.
220	6/0	Very Fine	Final sanding or between
240	7/0	Very Fine	coats, won't show sand
280	8/0	Very Fine	marks, dry sanding.
320	9/0	Extra Fine	Polish final coats, between
360	10/0	Extra Fine	coats, wet sand paints
400	10/0	Extra Fine	& varnishes, top coats.
500		Super Fine	Sand metal, plastic, &
600		Super Fine	ceramics, wet sanding.

COATING TYPES:

Open coat: Grains cover 50% to 70% of the backing, which leaves a lot of space between each grain. The open space is necessary in applications where the material being sanded has a tendency to clog up or "load" the abrasive surface. The clogging drastically reduces the cutting ability of the abrasive and reduces the life of the abrasive. Less common than Closed coat.

Closed coat: Grains cover all of the backing. This type is much more efficient (removes material faster) than Open coat since there are more abrasion grains per square inch. Closed coat is the preferred coating type as long as grain clogging is not a problem.

GLUE TYPES

Glues are generally restricted to a combination of "Hide" glues and resin based glues, depending on the application. Glues are usually

Sandpaper & Abrasives

applied as a two part process, the base coat and the top grain holding coat.

BACKING TYPES:

Paper: Weights range from "A" through "F". "A" is the most flexible and is used mainly for finishing jobs and with small grain sizes abrasives. "A" is primarily used for hand sanding. "C" and "D" weights are stronger, less flexible, and used for both hand sanding and power sanders. "E" is much stronger, very tear resistant and much less flexible than "C" and "D" and is used mainly in belt and disc applications. "F" is the strongest paper and is used mainly for rolls and belts.

Cloth: Weights are "J" (jeans) and "X" (drills). "J" is used for finishing and polishing operations, particularly where contours are involved. "X" is less flexible than "J" but is stronger. "X" is used for heavy belt, disk and drum grinding and polishing.

Fiber: Composed of multiple layers of paper that has been chemically treated. These backings are very tough, heat resistant and used mostly for drum and disc applications, particularly high speed.

Combination: Composed of both paper and cloth or cloth and fiber, producing a very strong, flexible, non-stretching, and tear resistant backing. They are used mostly in high speed, drum sanding applications

ABRASIVE TYPES:

Silicon Carbide: The hardest and sharpest of all abrasives but is more brittle than aluminum oxide. Color is blue-black and it is a manufactured abrasive. Typically used in applications such as finishing of soft metals, glass, ceramics, hard wood floors and plastics. It is very fast cutting and is therefore good for both material removal as well as polishing. This abrasive is very popular for sanding lacquered and enameled surfaces such as car paints. Durite by Norton is a common brand name. Grain sizes normally range from 600 to 12.

Aluminum Oxide: Extremely tough, grit is very sharp and much harder than flint, garnet and emery. Color is red to brown and it is a manufactured abrasive. More expensive than most other types but its toughness results in a longer lasting abrasive so its cost is actually equivalent. Recommended for metals and hard woods and is the preferred choice for power sanding. Norton brand names – Adalox or Metalite. Grain sizes normally range from 500 to 16.

Sandpaper & Abrasives

Garnet: Much softer than the synthetic abrasives listed above but harder and sharper than flint. Garnet is a crushed natural mineral, red to brown in color. Used mainly in furniture finishing and woodworking. Yields an excellent wood finish. Grain sizes normally range from 280 to 20.

Flint: Generally poor cutting strength and durability so it is not used in production environments. Used in the leather industry and as a good non-clogging abrasive in paint removal and some woodwork. Flint is gray to white colored natural quartz mineral. Flint is non-conductive and therefore is also useful as an abrasive in the electronics industry. Inexpensive. Grain sizes normally range from 4/0 to 3.

Emery: Good polishing features but poor for material removal. Grains are round and black in color. Poor penetration but good for polishing metals. Poor for wood use. Grain sizes normally range from 3/0 to 3.

Crocus: Soft and short lived. Made of ferrous oxide (red color). Good for polishing, particularly soft metals like gold.

Pumice: Powdered volcanic glass that is commonly used to tone down a glossy finish to a satin, smooth surface. Grades range from 4–F (the finest) through #7 (the coarsest). Frequent inspections of the work surface should be made in order to prevent breaking through the surface.

Cork: Cork is sometimes used as a wet polishing media.

Rottenstone: Also referred to as diatomaceous earth. It is much softer and finer grained than pumice and is used in combination with water, solvents, or oils to produce a satin finish on woods.

Rubbing Compounds: Sometimes also referred to as "rouge" is normally used as a polish for enamel and lacquer paints. It is not for use on bare woods.

Steel Wool: Although not technically an abrasive, it is commonly used to remove rust, old finishes, and to smooth rough surfaces. Sizes range from 4/0 (the finest) through #5 (the coarsest). With steel wool, it is important to rub the wood in the direction of the grain, not across it, so that the surface is not scratched.

Some of the above abrasive data is courtesy of *Norton, Coated Abrasives Division, Troy, New York.*

Saws

Chain Saw Classification

Chain saws can be broadly grouped into the following four categories, based on ruggedness and size:

1. **Mini–saw:** Light weight (6 to 9 pounds), small engine size (1.8 to 2.5 cubic inches or electric), and short bar lengths (8 to 12 inches, 1/4 inch pitch). Good for <3 cords per year.

2. **Light–Duty:** Light weight (9 to 13 pounds), small engine size (2.5 to 3.8 cubic inches or electric), and medium bar lengths (14 to 16 inches, 3/8 inch pitch). Good for 3 to 6 cords per year.

3. **Medium–Duty:** Medium weight (13 to 18 pounds), medium engine size (3.5 to 4.8 cubic inches), and medium–long bar lengths (16 to 24 inches, 3/8 to 0.404 inch pitch). Good for 6 to 10 cords per year. If money permits, this class of saw is probably the best choice for the average wood cutter, even if he does not cut the 6 to 10 cords per year. It is heavy duty enough to last a long time under light use.

4. **Heavy–Duty:** Heavy weight (over 18 pounds), large engine size (over 4.8 cubic inches), and long bar lengths (over 24 inches, 0.404 to 1/2 inch pitch). These heavy duty units are generally for the professional. They are heavy, expensive, and require more strength to use. They can be used continuously.

Depth Capacity of Std Circular Power Handsaws

Blade Diameter	Capacity @ 90°	Capacity @ 45°
4-1/2	1-5/16	1-1/16 to 1-1/14
6-1/2	2-1/16	1-5/8
6-3/4	2-7/32	1-3/4
7-1/4	2-3/8 to 2-7/16	1-7/8 to 1-29/32
7-1/2	2-17/22	2-1/16
8-1/4	2-15/16	2-1/4
10-1/4	3-5/8	2-3/4
12	4-3/8	3-5/16

Circular Power Handsaws

Abrasive Wheel

Abrasive blade made of aluminum oxide (metal cutting) or silicon carbide (masonry cutting). Comes in standard sizes of 6, 7, and 8 inch diameter and with 1/2 or 5/8 diameter arbor. No teeth. Also called a cut-off wheel

Combination Blade

Quiet, accurate and leaves a very smooth finish. Designed especially for crosscuts and miters across wood grain. Acceptable for ripping, but it's not as fast as ripping blades. Hollow ground combination blades minimize chipping.

Ripping Blade

These blades have large, set teeth with deep gullets. Designed especially for cutting fast in the direction of the wood grain. Minimum binding of blade. Very rough finish.

Chisel–Tooth Combination Blade

General purpose, settooth blade. Good for both ripping and crosscuts and it cuts fast but leaves a rough cut. This is the most common blade used by contractors. Bevel–ground, carbide–tipped blades of the same basic design are among the most durable of the blades.

Circular Power Handsaws

Crosscut, Fine–Tooth, & Paneling Blades

All of these blades have a large number of small teeth that are very sharp. Crosscut has the least teeth, fine–tooth has more and paneling has the most. Crosscut, as the name implies, was designed for cutting across the wood grain and leaving a smooth edge. It is also good for plywood. Fine–tooth blades are also good for plywood, but are also used on fiber boards (Celotex), veneers, and thin plastics. Paneling blades have many, extra fine teeth. It is particularly useful in cutting paneling and laminates since the cut edge usually does not have to be touched up.

Flattop–Ground Carbide Tipped Blade

A fast cutting, long lasting blade used as a combination blade in construction. Good for ripping, crosscutting and mitering but does not leave a good smooth edge.

Steel Cutting Blade

An unusual blade design that is used to cut ferrous (iron and steel) sheetmetal that is up to 3/32 inch thick. This blade actually "burns" its way through the metal, leaving a clean edge.

Saber Saw Blades

Teeth per inch	Blade Usage
3	Lumber up to 6 inches thick, fast cutting, very rough cut, good ripping blade.
5 or 6	Lumber up to 2 inches thick, fast cutting, rough cut, good ripping blade.
7 or 8	Best general purpose blade, relatively smooth cut. Good for lumber and fiber insulation board.
10	Good general purpose blade, smoother cut than the 7 or 8 blade. Use 10 through 14 for cutting hardwoods under 1/2 inch thick and for plastics, composition board, drywall, and plywood when a smooth edge is needed. If hard, abrasive materials are to be cut, such as laminates, use the metal cutting H.S.S. types. Good for some scrollwork.
12 or 14	Very smooth cutting blade but is also very slow cutting. Good for hardwoods, plywood, fiberglass, plastics, rubber, linoleum, laminates, and plexiglass. As with the 10 tpi blades, if the material is particularly hard or abrasive, use the metal cutting H.S.S. types instead.
Knife	These blades have either a knife edge or a sharp edge with an abrasive grit bonded to the blade. No grit blades are useful for cutting rubber, cork, leather, cardboard, styrofoam, & silicones. Grit blades come in fine, medium and coarse and can be used on fiberglass, epoxies, ceramic tile, stone, clay pipe, brick, steel, & veneer.
	H.S.S. METAL CUTTING BLADES
6 to 10	Rough cutting for aluminum, brass, copper, laminates, hardwoods and other soft materials. Good up to 1/2 inch thickness.
14	Cuts same materials as 6 to 10 tpi plus mild steels and hardboards. Leaves a much smoother edge. Thickness should be 1/4 to 1/2 inch thick.
18	Same as 14 tpi but maximum thickness 1/8 inch.
24	Smooth edge cutting for steel and sheet metal. Also good for other hard materials such as plastics, tile, and Bakelite. Maximum thickness should be 1/8 inch.
32	Very fine cuts for steel and thin wall tubing up to 1/16 inch thick.

Capacities of Hydraulic Rams in Tons

Diameter (inch)	Hydraulic Pressure in pound-force/square inch				
	300	500	1000	1500	2000
1.0	0.12	0.20	0.39	0.59	0.79
1.5	0.27	0.44	0.88	1.33	1.77
2.0	0.47	0.79	1.57	2.36	3.14
2.5	0.74	1.23	2.45	3.68	4.91
3.0	1.06	1.77	3.53	5.30	7.07
3.5	1.44	2.41	4.81	7.22	9.62
4.0	1.88	3.14	6.28	9.42	12.6
4.5	2.39	3.98	7.95	11.9	15.9
5.0	2.95	4.91	9.82	14.7	19.6
5.5	3.56	5.94	11.9	17.8	23.8
6.0	4.24	7.07	14.1	21.2	28.3
6.5	4.98	8.30	16.6	24.9	33.2
7.0	5.77	9.62	19.2	28.9	38.5
7.5	6.63	11.0	22.1	33.1	44.2
8.0	7.54	12.6	25.1	37.7	50.3
8.5	8.51	14.2	28.4	42.6	56.7
9.0	9.54	15.9	31.8	47.7	63.6
9.5	10.6	17.7	35.4	53.2	70.9
10	11.8	19.6	39.3	58.9	78.5
11	14.3	23.8	47.5	71.3	95.0
12	17.0	28.3	56.5	84.8	113
13	19.9	33.2	66.4	99.5	133
14	23.1	38.5	77.0	115	154
15	26.5	44.2	88.4	133	177
16	30.2	50.3	101	151	201
17	34.0	56.7	113	170	227
18	38.2	63.6	127	191	254
19	42.5	70.9	142	213	284
20	47.1	78.5	157	236	314
21	52.0	86.6	173	260	346
22	57.0	95.0	190	285	380
23	62.3	104	208	312	415
24	67.9	113	226	339	452
25	73.6	123	245	368	491
30	106	177	353	530	707
35	144	241	481	722	962
40	188	314	628	942	1257
50	295	491	982	1473	1963
60	424	707	1414	2121	2827

Capacities of Hydraulic Rams in tons

Diameter (inch)	Hydraulic Pressure in pound-force/square inch				
	3000	4000	5000	6000	7000
1.0	1.18	1.57	1.96	2.36	2.75
1.5	2.65	3.53	4.42	5.30	6.19
2.0	4.71	6.28	7.85	9.42	11.0
2.5	7.36	9.82	12.3	14.7	17.2
3.0	10.6	14.1	17.7	21.2	24.7
3.5	14.4	19.2	24.1	28.9	33.7
4.0	18.8	25.1	31.4	37.7	44.0
4.5	23.9	31.8	39.8	47.7	55.7
5.0	29.5	39.3	49.1	58.9	68.7
5.5	35.6	47.5	59.4	71.3	83.2
6.0	42.4	56.5	70.7	84.8	99.0
6.5	49.8	66.4	83.0	99.5	116
7.0	57.7	77.0	96.2	115	135
7.5	66.3	88.4	110	133	155
8.0	75.4	101	126	151	176
8.5	85.1	113	142	170	199
9.0	95.4	127	159	191	223
9.5	106	142	177	213	248
10	118	157	196	236	275
11	143	190	238	285	333
12	170	226	283	339	396
13	199	265	332	398	465
14	231	308	385	462	539
15	265	353	442	530	619
16	302	402	503	603	704
17	340	454	567	681	794
18	382	509	636	763	891
19	425	567	709	851	992
20	471	628	785	942	1100
21	520	693	866	1039	1212
22	570	760	950	1140	1330
23	623	831	1039	1246	1454
24	679	905	1131	1357	1583
25	736	982	1227	1473	1718
30	1060	1414	1767	2121	2474
35	1443	1924	2405	2886	3367
40	1885	2513	3142	3770	4398
50	2945	3927	4909	5890	6872
60	4241	5655	7069	8482	9896

Tons of Force Required to Punch Structural Steel
(60,000 psi shear strength, ASTM-A36)

Diameter Hole (inch)	Material Thickness (inch)					
	0.0625	0.1250	0.1875	0.2500	0.3125	0.3750
0.2500	1.5	2.9	4.4	5.9	7.4	8.8
0.3125	1.8	3.7	5.5	7.4	9.2	11.0
0.3750	2.2	4.4	6.6	8.8	11.0	13.3
0.4375	2.6	5.2	7.7	10.3	12.9	15.5
0.5000	2.9	5.9	8.8	11.8	14.7	17.7
0.5625	3.3	6.6	9.9	13.3	16.6	19.9
0.6250	3.7	7.4	11.0	14.7	18.4	22.1
0.6875	4.0	8.1	12.1	16.2	20.2	24.3
0.7500	4.4	8.8	13.3	17.7	22.1	26.5
0.8125	4.8	9.6	14.4	19.1	23.9	28.7
0.8750	5.2	10.3	15.5	20.6	25.8	30.9
0.9375	5.5	11.0	16.6	22.1	27.6	33.1
1.0000	5.9	11.8	17.7	23.6	29.5	35.3
1.0625	6.3	12.5	18.8	25.0	31.3	37.6
1.1250	6.6	13.3	19.9	26.5	33.1	39.8
1.1875	7.0	14.0	21.0	28.0	35.0	42.0
1.2500	7.4	14.7	22.1	29.5	36.8	44.2
1.3125	7.7	15.5	23.2	30.9	38.7	46.4
1.3750	8.1	16.2	24.3	32.4	40.5	48.6
1.5000	8.8	17.7	26.5	35.3	44.2	53.0
1.7500	10.3	20.6	30.9	41.2	51.5	61.9
2.0000	11.8	23.6	35.3	47.1	58.9	70.7
2.2500	13.3	26.5	39.8	53.0	66.3	79.5
2.5000	14.7	29.5	44.2	58.9	73.6	88.4
2.7500	16.2	32.4	48.6	64.8	81.0	97.2
3.0000	17.7	35.3	53.0	70.7	88.4	106.0

Tons of Force Required to Punch Structural Steel
(60,000 psi shear strength, ASTM-A36)

Diameter Hole (inch)	Material Thickness (inch)					
	0.6250	0.7500	0.8750	1.0000	1.1250	1.2500
0.5000	29.5					
0.5625	33.1					
0.6250	36.8	44.2				
0.6875	40.5	48.6				
0.7500	44.2	53.0	61.9			
0.8125	47.9	57.4	67.0	76.6		
0.8750	51.5	61.9	72.2	82.5		
0.9375	55.2	66.3	77.3	88.4	99.4	
1.0000	58.9	70.7	82.5	94.2	106.0	
1.0625	62.6	75.1	87.6	100.1	112.7	125.2
1.1250	66.3	79.5	92.8	106.0	119.3	132.5
1.1875	69.9	83.9	97.9	111.9	125.9	139.9
1.2500	73.6	88.4	103.1	117.8	132.5	147.3
1.3125	77.3	92.8	108.2	123.7	139.2	154.6
1.3750	81.0	97.2	113.4	129.6	145.8	162.0
1.5000	88.4	106.0	123.7	141.4	159.0	176.7
1.7500	103.1	123.7	144.3	164.9	185.6	206.2
2.0000	117.8	141.4	164.9	188.5	212.1	235.6
2.2500	132.5	159.0	185.6	212.1	238.6	
2.5000	147.3					

The previous two charts can also be used to determine tonnage values for materials other than ASTM-A36 Structural Steel. Simply use the multiplier value below times the table values above.

Chart Multipliers for Other Materials

Material	psi Shear Strength	Chart Multiplier
Aluminum, 1.2 hard	19,000	0.32
Copper, rolled	28,000	0.47
Steel, mild,HR plate	50,000	0.83
Boiler plate	55,000	0.92
Steel (ASTM-A242)	66,000	1.10
Steel(ASTM-A572)	70,000	1.17
Steel, 50 carbon HP	70,000	1.17
Steel, stainless	70,000	1.17
Steel, structural T1	90,000	1.50

(See also AIR chapter, p. 22 for more pollution data)

Friction Loss in Various Pipe

Values in this table are Friction Loss Constants (C) for Various Pipe Materials - use these values to plug in to the next 11 pages of tables ("Des" in the column head below is for "Design or In-service.")

Pipe material or surface coating	C Range High	C Range Low	C New, Clean	C Des
Acrylonite butadiene styrene (ABS)	150	120	140	130
Aluminum	150	130		100
Asbestos cement	160	140	150	140
Asphalt lining	140	130		...
Brass	150	120	140	130
Brick sewer				100
Cast iron, asphalt coated	140	90	130	100
Cast iron, bitumastic enamel lined	150	140		...
Cast iron, bituminous lined	160	130	150	140
Cast iron, cement lined	150	100	140	120
Cast iron, new, unlined	150	110	130	120
Cast iron, old, unlined	120	60		80
Cast iron, sea-coated	140	100	130	120
Cement lining	140	130		...
Concrete	150	90	120	100
Concrete lined, steel forms	140			...
Concrete lined, wooden forms	120			...
Concrete, old	110	100		...
Concrete, steel forms	140			...
Concrete, wooden forms	120			...
Copper	150	120	140	130
Ductile iron, cement-lined	140	100		120
Fiber	150	140		...
Galvanized iron	150	120	140	130
Glass	120	110		130
Lead	150	120	140	130
Plastic	150	120	140	130
Polyethylene	150	140	150	140
Polyvinyl chloride (PVC)	150	120	140	130
Steel, coal-tar enamel lined	150	140		...
Steel, corrugated			60	60
Steel, interior riveted, no projecting rivets	140	100	130	110
projecting girth and horz. rivets			120	110
projecting girth rivets			130	100
Steel, welded and seamless	150	100	140	120
Tin	150	120	140	130
Vitrified clay	140	100		110
Wrought iron, plain	150	80	130	100

Notes:
1. Values shown above are used in the Hazen-Williams equation for flow in pipes. *Feet of Head Loss* values shown on the next 11 *pages* were developed using the Hazen-Williams equation and the constants from the above table.
2. Feet of Head Loss values are subject to the following conditions:
  a) Pipes carrying water at approximately 60° F (15.6°C).
  b) Pipes are flowing full.
  c) Velocities of water are generally less than 10 feet per second.

Head Loss/100 Feet Pipe Due To Friction : C=60

See page 618

Flow (gpm)	1/2	3/4	1	1-1/4	1-1/2	2	2-1/2
0.5	4.4	0.6	0.2	0.1			
1	15.9	2.2	0.5	0.2	0.1		
2	57.2	7.9	2.0	0.7	0.3	0.1	
3		16.8	4.1	1.4	0.6	0.1	
4		28.6	7.1	2.4	1.0	0.2	0.1
5		43.3	10.7	3.6	1.5	0.4	0.1
10			38.4	13.0	5.3	1.3	0.4
15			81.3	27.4	11.3	2.8	0.9
20				46.7	19.2	4.7	1.6
30				98.9	40.7	10.0	3.4
40					69.3	17.1	5.8
50						25.8	8.7
60						36.1	12.2
70						48.1	16.2
80						61.6	20.8
90						76.5	25.8
100						93.0	31.4
150							66.4
200							
250							
300							
400							

Flow (gpm)	3	4	5	6	8	10	12
5	0.1						
10	0.2						
15	0.4	0.1					
20	0.7	0.2	0.1				
30	1.4	0.3	0.1				
40	2.4	0.6	0.2	0.1			
50	3.6	0.9	0.3	0.1			
60	5.0	1.2	0.4	0.2			
70	6.7	1.6	0.6	0.2	0.1		
80	8.5	2.1	0.7	0.3	0.1		
90	10.6	2.6	0.9	0.4	0.1		
100	12.9	3.2	1.1	0.4	0.1		
150	27.3	6.7	2.3	0.9	0.2	0.1	
200	46.5	11.5	3.9	1.6	0.4	0.1	0.1
250	70.3	17.3	5.8	2.4	0.6	0.2	0.1
300	98.5	24.3	8.2	3.4	0.8	0.3	0.1
400		41.3	13.9	5.7	1.4	0.5	0.2
500		62.5	21.1	8.7	2.1	0.7	0.3
600		87.5	29.5	12.1	3.0	1.0	0.4
700			39.3	16.2	4.0	1.3	0.6
800			50.3	20.7	5.1	1.7	0.7
900			62.5	25.7	6.3	2.1	0.9
1000			76.0	31.3	7.7	2.6	1.1
1200				43.8	10.8	3.6	1.5
1500				66.2	16.3	5.5	2.3
2000					27.8	9.4	3.9
3000					58.8	19.8	8.2
4000						33.8	13.9
5000						51.0	21.0

Head Loss/100 Feet Pipe Due To Friction : C=70

See page 618

Flow (gpm)	Inside Pipe Diameter (inch)						
	1/2	3/4	1	1-1/4	1-1/2	2	2-1/2
0.5	3.3	0.5	0.1				
1	11.9	1.7	0.4	0.1	0.1		
2	43.0	6.0	1.5	0.5	0.2	0.1	
3	91.1	12.6	3.1	1.1	0.4	0.1	
4		21.5	5.3	1.8	0.7	0.2	
5		32.5	8.0	2.7	1.1	0.3	0.1
10			28.9	9.7	4.0	1.0	0.3
15			61.2	20.6	8.5	2.1	0.7
20				35.1	14.5	3.6	1.2
30				74.4	30.6	7.5	2.5
40					52.1	12.8	4.3
50					78.7	19.4	6.5
60						27.2	9.2
70						36.1	12.2
80						46.3	15.6
90						57.5	19.4
100						69.9	23.6
150							49.9
200							85.0
250							
300							
400							

Flow (gpm)	3	4	5	6	8	10	12
5							
10	0.1						
15	0.3	0.1					
20	0.5	0.1					
30	1.0	0.3	0.1				
40	1.8	0.4	0.1	0.1			
50	2.7	0.7	0.2	0.1			
60	3.8	0.9	0.3	0.1			
70	5.0	1.2	0.4	0.2			
80	6.4	1.6	0.5	0.2	0.1		
90	8.0	2.0	0.7	0.3	0.1		
100	9.7	2.4	0.8	0.3	0.1		
150	20.6	5.1	1.7	0.7	0.2	0.1	
200	35.0	8.6	2.9	1.2	0.3	0.1	
250	52.9	13.0	4.4	1.8	0.4	0.2	0.1
300	74.1	18.3	6.2	2.5	0.6	0.2	0.1
400		31.1	10.5	4.3	1.1	0.4	0.1
500		47.0	15.8	6.5	1.6	0.5	0.2
600		65.8	22.2	9.1	2.3	0.8	0.3
700		87.5	29.5	12.1	3.0	1.0	0.4
800			37.8	15.6	3.8	1.3	0.5
900			47.0	19.3	4.8	1.6	0.7
1000			57.1	23.5	5.8	2.0	0.8
1200			80.0	32.9	8.1	2.7	1.1
1500				49.8	12.3	4.1	1.7
2000				84.7	20.9	7.0	2.9
3000					44.2	14.9	6.1
4000					75.2	25.4	10.4
5000						38.4	15.8

Head Loss/100 Feet Pipe Due To Friction : C=80

See page 618

Flow (gpm)	Inside Pipe Diameter (inch)						
	1/2	3/4	1	1-1/4	1-1/2	2	2-1/2
0.5	2.6	0.4	0.1				
1	9.3	1.3	0.3	0.1			
2	33.6	4.7	1.1	0.4	0.2		
3	71.1	9.9	2.4	0.8	0.3	0.1	
4		16.8	4.1	1.4	0.6	0.1	
5		25.4	6.3	2.1	0.9	0.2	0.1
10		91.6	22.6	7.6	3.1	0.8	0.3
15			47.8	16.1	6.6	1.6	0.6
20			81.3	27.4	11.3	2.8	0.9
30				58.1	23.9	5.9	2.0
40				98.9	40.7	10.0	3.4
50					61.5	15.2	5.1
60					86.2	21.2	7.2
70						28.2	9.5
80						36.1	12.2
90						45.0	15.2
100						54.6	18.4
150							39.0
200							66.4
250							
300							
400							

	3	4	5	6	8	10	12
5							
10	0.1						
15	0.2	0.1					
20	0.4	0.1					
30	0.8	0.2	0.1				
40	1.4	0.3	0.1				
50	2.1	0.5	0.2	0.1			
60	2.9	0.7	0.2	0.1			
70	3.9	1.0	0.3	0.1			
80	5.0	1.2	0.4	0.2			
90	6.2	1.5	0.5	0.2	0.1		
100	7.6	1.9	0.6	0.3	0.1		
150	16.1	4.0	1.3	0.5	0.1		
200	27.3	6.7	2.3	0.9	0.2	0.1	
250	41.3	10.2	3.4	1.4	0.3	0.1	
300	57.9	14.3	4.8	2.0	0.5	0.2	0.1
400	98.5	24.3	8.2	3.4	0.8	0.3	0.1
500		36.7	12.4	5.1	1.3	0.4	0.2
600		51.4	17.3	7.1	1.8	0.6	0.2
700		68.4	23.1	9.5	2.3	0.8	0.3
800		87.5	29.5	12.1	3.0	1.0	0.4
900			36.7	15.1	3.7	1.3	0.5
1000			44.6	18.4	4.5	1.5	0.6
1200			62.5	25.7	6.3	2.1	0.9
1500			94.4	38.9	9.6	3.2	1.3
2000				66.2	16.3	5.5	2.3
3000					34.5	11.6	4.8
4000					58.8	19.8	8.2
5000					88.8	30.0	12.3

Head Loss/100 Feet Pipe Due To Friction : C=90

Flow	Inside Pipe Diameter (inch)						See page 618
(gpm)	1/2	3/4	1	1-1/4	1-1/2	2	2-1/2
0.5	2.1	0.3	0.1				
1	7.5	1.0	0.3	0.1			
2	27.0	3.8	0.9	0.3	0.1		
3	57.2	7.9	2.0	0.7	0.3	0.1	
4	97.4	13.5	3.3	1.1	0.5	0.1	
5		20.4	5.0	1.7	0.7	0.2	0.1
10		73.7	18.1	6.1	2.5	0.6	0.2
15			38.4	13.0	5.3	1.3	0.4
20			65.4	22.1	9.1	2.2	0.8
30				46.7	19.2	4.7	1.6
40				79.5	32.7	8.1	2.7
50					49.5	12.2	4.1
60					69.3	17.1	5.8
70					92.2	22.7	7.7
80						29.1	9.8
90						36.1	12.2
100						43.9	14.8
150						93.0	31.4
200							53.4
250							80.7
300							
400							

	3	4	5	6	8	10	12
5							
10	0.1						
15	0.2						
20	0.3	0.1					
30	0.7	0.2	0.1				
40	1.1	0.3	0.1				
50	1.7	0.4	0.1	0.1			
60	2.4	0.6	0.2	0.1			
70	3.2	0.8	0.3	0.1			
80	4.0	1.0	0.3	0.1			
90	5.0	1.2	0.4	0.2			
100	6.1	1.5	0.5	0.2	0.1		
150	12.9	3.2	1.1	0.4	0.1		
200	22.0	5.4	1.8	0.8	0.2	0.1	
250	33.2	8.2	2.8	1.1	0.3	0.1	
300	46.5	11.5	3.9	1.6	0.4	0.1	0.1
400	79.2	19.5	6.6	2.7	0.7	0.2	0.1
500		29.5	10.0	4.1	1.0	0.3	0.1
600		41.3	13.9	5.7	1.4	0.5	0.2
700		55.0	18.5	7.6	1.9	0.6	0.3
800		70.4	23.7	9.8	2.4	0.8	0.3
900		87.5	29.5	12.1	3.0	1.0	0.4
1000			35.9	14.8	3.6	1.2	0.5
1200			50.3	20.7	5.1	1.7	0.7
1500			76.0	31.3	7.7	2.6	1.1
2000				53.2	13.1	4.4	1.8
3000					27.8	9.4	3.9
4000					47.3	15.9	6.6
5000					71.4	24.1	9.9

See page 618

Head Loss/100 Feet Pipe Due To Friction : C=100

Flow (gpm)	1/2	3/4	1	1-1/4	1-1/2	2	2-1/2
0.5	1.7	0.2	0.1				
1	6.2	0.9	0.2	0.1			
2	22.2	3.1	0.8	0.3			
3	47.1	6.5	1.6	0.5	0.2	0.1	
4	80.2	11.1	2.7	0.9	0.4	0.1	
5		16.8	4.1	1.4	0.6	0.1	
10		60.6	14.9	5.0	2.1	0.5	0.2
15			31.6	10.7	4.4	1.1	0.4
20			53.8		7.5	1.8	0.6
30				38.4	15.8	3.9	1.3
40				65.5	26.9	6.6	2.2
50				98.9	40.7	10.0	3.4
60					57.0	14.1	4.7
70					75.9	18.7	6.3
80					97.1	23.9	8.1
90						29.7	10.0
100						36.1	12.2
150						76.5	25.8
200							44.0
250							66.4
300							93.1
400							

Flow (gpm)	3	4	5	6	8	10	12
5							
10	0.1						
15	0.2						
20	0.3	0.1					
30	0.5	0.1					
40	0.9	0.2	0.1				
50	1.4	0.3	0.1				
60	2.0	0.5	0.2	0.1			
70	2.6	0.6	0.2	0.1			
80	3.3	0.8	0.3	0.1			
90	4.1	1.0	0.3	0.1			
100	5.0	1.2	0.4	0.2			
150	10.6	2.6	0.9	0.4	0.1		
200	18.1	4.5	1.5	0.6	0.2	0.1	
250	27.3	6.7	2.3	0.9	0.2	0.1	
300	38.3	9.4	3.2	1.3	0.3	0.1	
400	65.2	16.1	5.4	2.2	0.5	0.2	0.1
500	98.5	24.3	8.2	3.4	0.8	0.3	0.1
600		34.0	11.5	4.7	1.2	0.4	0.2
700		45.2	15.3	6.3	1.5	0.5	0.2
800		57.9	19.5	8.0	2.0	0.7	0.3
900		72.0	24.3	10.0	2.5	0.8	0.3
1000		87.5	29.5	12.1	3.0	1.0	0.4
1200			41.4	17.0	4.2	1.4	0.6
1500			62.5	25.7	6.3	2.1	0.9
2000				43.8	10.8	3.6	1.5
3000				92.7	22.8	7.7	3.2
4000					38.9	13.1	5.4
5000					58.8	19.8	8.2

Head Loss/100 Feet Pipe Due To Friction : C=110

Flow (gpm)	Inside Pipe Diameter (inch) See page 618						
	1/2	3/4	1	1-1/4	1-1/2	2	2-1/2
0.5	1.4	0.2					
1	5.2	0.7	0.2	0.1			
2	18.6	2.6	0.6	0.2	0.1		
3	39.5	5.5	1.3	0.5	0.2		
4	67.2	9.3	2.3	0.8	0.3	0.1	
5		14.1	3.5	1.2	0.5	0.1	
10		50.8	12.5	4.2	1.7	0.4	0.1
15			26.5	8.9	3.7	0.9	0.3
20			45.1	15.2	6.3	1.5	0.5
30			95.5	32.2	13.3	3.3	1.1
40				54.9	22.6	5.6	1.9
50				82.9	34.1	8.4	2.8
60					47.8	11.8	4.0
70					63.6	15.7	5.3
80					81.4	20.1	6.8
90						24.9	8.4
100						30.3	10.2
150						64.2	21.6
200							36.9
250							55.7
300							78.0
400							

Flow (gpm)	3	4	5	6	8	10	12
5							
10	0.1						
15	0.1						
20	0.2	0.1					
30	0.5	0.1					
40	0.8	0.2	0.1				
50	1.2	0.3	0.1				
60	1.6	0.4	0.1	0.1			
70	2.2	0.5	0.2	0.1			
80	2.8	0.7	0.2	0.1			
90	3.5	0.9	0.3	0.1			
100	4.2	1.0	0.3	0.1			
150	8.9	2.2	0.7	0.3	0.1		
200	15.2	3.7	1.3	0.5	0.1		
250	22.9	5.6	1.9	0.8	0.2	0.1	
300	32.1	7.9	2.7	1.1	0.3	0.1	
400	54.7	13.5	4.5	1.9	0.5	0.2	0.1
500	82.6	20.4	6.9	2.8	0.7	0.2	0.1
600		28.5	9.6	4.0	1.0	0.3	0.1
700		37.9	12.8	5.3	1.3	0.4	0.2
800		48.6	16.4	6.7	1.7	0.6	0.2
900		60.4	20.4	8.4	2.1	0.7	0.3
1000		73.4	24.7	10.2	2.5	0.8	0.3
1200			34.7	14.3	3.5	1.2	0.5
1500			52.4	21.6	5.3	1.8	0.7
2000			89.2	36.7	9.0	3.1	1.3
3000				77.1	19.1	6.5	2.7
4000					32.6	11.0	4.5
5000					49.3	16.6	6.8

See page 618

Head Loss/100 Feet Pipe Due To Friction : C=120							
Flow	Inside Pipe Diameter (inch)						
(gpm)	1/2	3/4	1	1-1/4	1-1/2	2	2-1/2
0.5	1.2	0.2					
1	4.4	0.6	0.2	0.1			
2	15.9	2.2	0.5	0.2	0.1		
3	33.6	4.7	1.1	0.4	0.2		
4	57.2	7.9	2.0	0.7	0.3	0.1	
5	86.4	12.0	3.0	1.0	0.4	0.1	
10		43.3	10.7	3.6	1.5	0.4	0.1
15		91.6	22.6	7.6	3.1	0.8	0.3
20			38.4	13.0	5.3	1.3	0.4
30			81.3	27.4	11.3	2.8	0.9
40				46.7	19.2	4.7	1.6
50				70.6	29.1	7.2	2.4
60				98.9	40.7	10.0	3.4
70					54.1	13.3	4.5
80					69.3	17.1	5.8
90					86.2	21.2	7.2
100						25.8	8.7
150						54.6	18.4
200						93.0	31.4
250							47.4
300							66.4
400							

Flow	3	4	5	6	8	10	12
5							
10	0.1						
15	0.1						
20	0.2						
30	0.4	0.1					
40	0.7	0.2	0.1				
50	1.0	0.2	0.1				
60	1.4	0.3	0.1				
70	1.9	0.5	0.2	0.1			
80	2.4	0.6	0.2	0.1			
90	2.9	0.7	0.2	0.1			
100	3.6	0.9	0.3	0.1			
150	7.6	1.9	0.6	0.3	0.1		
200	12.9	3.2	1.1	0.4	0.1		
250	19.5	4.8	1.6	0.7	0.2	0.1	
300	27.3	6.7	2.3	0.9	0.2	0.1	
400	46.5	11.5	3.9	1.6	0.4	0.1	0.1
500	70.3	17.3	5.8	2.4	0.6	0.2	0.1
600	98.5	24.3	8.2	3.4	0.8	0.3	0.1
700		32.3	10.9	4.5	1.1	0.4	0.2
800		41.3	13.9	5.7	1.4	0.5	0.2
900		51.4	17.3	7.1	1.8	0.6	0.2
1000		62.5	21.1	8.7	2.1	0.7	0.3
1200		87.5	29.5	12.1	3.0	1.0	0.4
1500			44.6	18.4	4.5	1.5	0.6
2000			76.0	31.3	7.7	2.6	1.1
3000				66.2	16.3	5.5	2.3
4000					27.8	9.4	3.9
5000					41.9	14.1	5.8

Head Loss/100 Feet Pipe Due To Friction : C=130

See page 618

Flow (gpm)	1/2	3/4	1	1-1/4	1-1/2	2	2-1/2
			Inside Pipe Diameter (inch)				
0.5	1.1	0.1					
1	3.8	0.5	0.1				
2	13.7	1.9	0.5	0.2	0.1		
3	29.0	4.0	1.0	0.3	0.1		
4	49.3	6.8	1.7	0.6	0.2	0.1	
5	74.5	10.3	2.5	0.9	0.4	0.1	
10		37.3	9.2	3.1	1.3	0.3	0.1
15		79.0	19.5	6.6	2.7	0.7	0.2
20			33.1	11.2	4.6	1.1	0.4
30			70.1	23.7	9.7	2.4	0.8
40				40.3	16.6	4.1	1.4
50				60.9	25.1	6.2	2.1
60				85.3	35.1	8.6	2.9
70					46.7	11.5	3.9
80					59.8	14.7	5.0
90					74.3	18.3	6.2
100					90.3	22.2	7.5
150						47.1	15.9
200						80.2	27.1
250							40.9
300							57.3
400							97.5

Flow (gpm)	3	4	5	6	8	10	12
5							
10							
15	0.1						
20	0.2						
30	0.3	0.1					
40	0.6	0.1					
50	0.9	0.2	0.1				
60	1.2	0.3	0.1				
70	1.6	0.4	0.1	0.1			
80	2.0	0.5	0.2	0.1			
90	2.5	0.6	0.2	0.1			
100	3.1	0.8	0.3	0.1			
150	6.5	1.6	0.5	0.2	0.1		
200	11.1	2.7	0.9	0.4	0.1		
250	16.8	4.1	1.4	0.6	0.1		
300	23.6	5.8	2.0	0.8	0.2	0.1	
400	40.1	9.9	3.3	1.4	0.3	0.1	
500	60.7	14.9	5.0	2.1	0.5	0.2	0.1
600	85.0	20.9	7.1	2.9	0.7	0.2	0.1
700		27.8	9.4	3.9	1.0	0.3	0.1
800		35.6	12.0	4.9	1.2	0.4	0.2
900		44.3	15.0	6.2	1.5	0.5	0.2
1000		53.9	18.2	7.5	1.8	0.6	0.3
1200		75.5	25.5	10.5	2.6	0.9	0.4
1500			38.5	15.8	3.9	1.3	0.5
2000			65.5	27.0	6.6	2.2	0.9
3000				57.1	14.1	4.7	2.0
4000				97.2	23.9	8.1	3.3
5000					36.2	12.2	5.0

Head Loss/100 Feet Pipe Due To Friction : C=140

See page 618

Flow (gpm)	Inside Pipe Diameter (inch)						
	1/2	3/4	1	1-1/4	1-1/2	2	2-1/2
0.5	0.9	0.1					
1	3.3	0.5	0.1				
2	11.9	1.7	0.4	0.1	0.1		
3	25.3	3.5	0.9	0.3	0.1		
4	43.0	6.0	1.5	0.5	0.2	0.1	
5	65.0	9.0	2.2	0.7	0.3	0.1	
10		32.5	8.0	2.7	1.1	0.3	0.1
15		68.9	17.0	5.7	2.4	0.6	0.2
20			28.9	9.7	4.0	1.0	0.3
30			61.2	20.6	8.5	2.1	0.7
40				35.1	14.5	3.6	1.2
50				53.1	21.8	5.4	1.8
60				74.4	30.6	7.5	2.5
70				98.9	40.7	10.0	3.4
80					52.1	12.8	4.3
90					64.8	16.0	5.4
100					78.7	19.4	6.5
150						41.1	13.9
200						69.9	23.6
250							35.6
300							49.9
400							85.0

Flow (gpm)	3	4	5	6	8	10	12
5							
10							
15	0.1						
20	0.1						
30	0.3	0.1					
40	0.5	0.1					
50	0.7	0.2	0.1				
60	1.0	0.3	0.1				
70	1.4	0.3	0.1				
80	1.8	0.4	0.1	0.1			
90	2.2	0.5	0.2	0.1			
100	2.7	0.7	0.2	0.1			
150	5.7	1.4	0.5	0.2			
200	9.7	2.4	0.8	0.3	0.1		
250	14.7	3.6	1.2	0.5	0.1		
300	20.6	5.1	1.7	0.7	0.2	0.1	
400	35.0	8.6	2.9	1.2	0.3	0.1	
500	52.9	13.0	4.4	1.8	0.4	0.2	0.1
600	74.1	18.3	6.2	2.5	0.6	0.2	0.1
700	98.5	24.3	8.2	3.4	0.8	0.3	0.1
800		31.1	10.5	4.3	1.1	0.4	0.1
900		38.6	13.0	5.4	1.3	0.4	0.2
1000		47.0	15.8	6.5	1.6	0.5	0.2
1200		65.8	22.2	9.1	2.3	0.8	0.3
1500		99.4	33.5	13.8	3.4	1.1	0.5
2000			57.1	23.5	5.8	2.0	0.8
3000				49.8	12.3	4.1	1.7
4000				84.7	20.9	7.0	2.9
5000					31.5	10.6	4.4

Head Loss/100 Feet Pipe Due To Friction : C=150

See page 618

Flow (gpm)	1/2	3/4	1	1-1/4	1-1/2	2	2-1/2
0.5	0.8	0.1					
1	2.9	0.4	0.1				
2	10.5	1.5	0.4	0.1			
3	22.2	3.1	0.8	0.3	0.1		
4	37.9	5.3	1.3	0.4	0.2		
5	57.2	7.9	2.0	0.7	0.3	0.1	
10		28.6	7.1	2.4	1.0	0.2	0.1
15		60.6	14.9	5.0	2.1	0.5	0.2
20			25.4	8.6	3.5	0.9	0.3
30			53.8	18.2	7.5	1.8	0.6
40			91.7	30.9	12.7	3.1	1.1
50				46.7	19.2	4.7	1.6
60				65.5	26.9	6.6	2.2
70				87.1	35.8	8.8	3.0
80					45.9	11.3	3.8
90					57.0	14.1	4.7
100					69.3	17.1	5.8
150						36.1	12.2
200						61.6	20.8
250						93.0	31.4
300							44.0
400							74.8

	3	4	5	6	8	10	12
5							
10							
15	0.1						
20	0.1						
30	0.3	0.1					
40	0.4	0.1					
50	0.7	0.2	0.1				
60	0.9	0.2	0.1				
70	1.2	0.3	0.1				
80	1.6	0.4	0.1	0.1			
90	2.0	0.5	0.2	0.1			
100	2.4	0.6	0.2	0.1			
150	5.0	1.2	0.4	0.2			
200	8.5	2.1	0.7	0.3	0.1		
250	12.9	3.2	1.1	0.4	0.1		
300	18.1	4.5	1.5	0.6	0.2	0.1	
400	30.8	7.6	2.6	1.1	0.3	0.1	
500	46.5	11.5	3.9	1.6	0.4	0.1	0.1
600	65.2	16.1	5.4	2.2	0.5	0.2	0.1
700	86.7	21.4	7.2	3.0	0.7	0.2	0.1
800		27.4	9.2	3.8	0.9	0.3	0.1
900		34.0	11.5	4.7	1.2	0.4	0.2
1000		41.3	13.9	5.7	1.4	0.5	0.2
1200		57.9	19.5	8.0	2.0	0.7	0.3
1500		87.5	29.5	12.1	3.0	1.0	0.4
2000			50.3	20.7	5.1	1.7	0.7
3000				43.8	10.8	3.6	1.5
4000				74.6	18.4	6.2	2.6
5000					27.8	9.4	3.9

Head Loss/100 Feet Pipe Due To Friction : C=160

Flow (gpm)	Inside Pipe Diameter (inch)					See page 618	
	1/2	3/4	1	1-1/4	1-1/2	2	2-1/2
0.5	0.7	0.1					
1	2.6	0.4	0.1				
2	9.3	1.3	0.3	0.1			
3	19.7	2.7	0.7	0.2	0.1		
4	33.6	4.7	1.1	0.4	0.2		
5	50.8	7.0	1.7	0.6	0.2	0.1	
10		25.4	6.3	2.1	0.9	0.2	0.1
15		53.8	13.3	4.5	1.8	0.5	0.2
20		91.6	22.6	7.6	3.1	0.8	0.3
30			47.8	16.1	6.6	1.6	0.6
40			81.3	27.4	11.3	2.8	0.9
50				41.5	17.1	4.2	1.4
60				58.1	23.9	5.9	2.0
70				77.3	31.8	7.8	2.6
80				98.9	40.7	10.0	3.4
90					50.6	12.5	4.2
100					61.5	15.2	5.1
150						32.1	10.8
200						54.6	18.4
250						82.5	27.8
300							39.0
400							66.4

Flow	3	4	5	6	8	10	12
5							
10							
15	0.1						
20	0.1						
30	0.2	0.1					
40	0.4	0.1					
50	0.6	0.1					
60	0.8	0.2	0.1				
70	1.1	0.3	0.1				
80	1.4	0.3	0.1				
90	1.7	0.4	0.1	0.1			
100	2.1	0.5	0.2	0.1			
150	4.5	1.1	0.4	0.2			
200	7.6	1.9	0.6	0.3	0.1		
250	11.5	2.8	1.0	0.4	0.1		
300	16.1	4.0	1.3	0.5	0.1		
400	27.3	6.7	2.3	0.9	0.2	0.1	
500	41.3	10.2	3.4	1.4	0.3	0.1	
600	57.9	14.3	4.8	2.0	0.5	0.2	0.1
700	77.0	19.0	6.4	2.6	0.6	0.2	0.1
800	98.5	24.3	8.2	3.4	0.8	0.3	0.1
900		30.2	10.2	4.2	1.0	0.3	0.1
1000		36.7	12.4	5.1	1.3	0.4	0.2
1200		51.4	17.3	7.1	1.8	0.6	0.2
1500		77.7	26.2	10.8	2.7	0.9	0.4
2000			44.6	18.4	4.5	1.5	0.6
3000			94.4	38.9	9.6	3.2	1.3
4000				66.2	16.3	5.5	2.3
5000					24.6	8.3	3.4

Friction Loss in Pipe Fittings

Steel/Copper	Equivalent feet of pipe caused by joint @ diam. inch						
Fitting	1/2	3/4	1	1–1/4	1–1/2	2	2–1/2
90° Std Elbow	1.6	2.1	2.6	3.5	4.0	5.2	6.2
90° Long Elbow	0.9	1.2	1.6	2.1	2.4	3.1	3.7
90° Street Elbow	2.6	3.4	4.4	5.8	6.7	8.6	10.3
45° Std Elbow	0.8	1.0	1.3	1.7	2.0	2.6	3.1
45° Street Elbow	1.4	1.8	2.3	3.0	3.5	4.5	5.4
Square Elbow	3	3.9	5.0	6.6	7.7	9.8	11.7
Std T Flow Run	1	1.4	1.8	2.3	2.7	3.5	4.1
Std T Flow Branch	3.1	4.1	5.3	6.9	8.1	10.3	12.3
Gate Valve–open	0.5	0.7	0.9	1.2	1.3	1.8	2.1

Friction Loss in Pipe Fittings

Plastic	Equivalent feet of pipe caused by joint @ diam. inch						
Fitting	1/2	3/4	1	1–1/4	1–1/2	2	2–1/2
90° Std Elbow	1.6	2.1	2.6	3.5	4.0	5.5	6.2
Std T Flow Run	1.0	1.4	1.7	2.3	2.7	4.3	5.1
Std T Flow Branch	4.0	5.1	6.0	6.9	8.1	13.0	19.3

Suction, Head, Vapor Pressure

Water Temp °F	Vapor Pressure	Suction Lift or Head @ Altitude in Feet				
		0	2000	4000	8000	12000
60	0.6 ft water	20	17.5	15.5	11.5	7.5
70	0.8 ft water	19.5	17	15	11	7
80	1.2 ft water	19.5	17	15	11	7
90	1.6 ft water	19	16.5	14.5	10.5	6.5
100	2.2 ft water	18.5	16	14	10	6
110	2.9 ft water	17.5	15	13	9	5
120	3.9 ft water	16.5	14	12	8	4
130	5.1 ft water	15.5	13	11	7	3
140	6.7 ft water	14	11.5	9.5	5.5	1.5
150	8.6 ft water	12	9.5	7.5	3.5	–0.5
160	10.9 ft water	9.5	7	5	1	...
170	13.8 ft water	6.5	4	2	–2	...
180	17.3 ft water	3	0.5	–1.5	...	...
190	21.6 ft water	–1	–3.5	–5.5	...	...
200	26.6 ft water	–6	–8.5	...	...	...
210	32.6 ft water	–12	...	...	...	...
212	34.0 ft water	–13.5	...	...	...	...

+ values indicate suction lift, – values indicate suction head
See also Air and Water table on page 13.

Horizontal Pipe Discharge

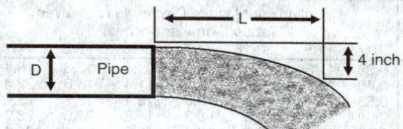

L Distance inches	Gallons per Minute Discharge for a given Nominal Pipe Diameter D (Inches)						
	1	1–1/4	1–1/2	2	2–1/2	3	4
4	6	10	13	22	31	48	83
5	7	12	17	27	39	61	104
6	8	15	20	33	47	73	125
7	10	17	23	38	55	85	146
8	11	20	26	44	62	97	166
9	13	22	30	49	70	110	187
10	14	24	33	55	78	122	208
11	16	27	36	60	86	134	229
12	17	29	40	66	94	146	250
13	18	31	43	71	102	158	270
14	20	34	46	77	109	170	292
15	21	36	50	82	117	183	312
16	23	39	53	88	125	196	334
17	...	41	56	93	133	207	355
18	...	...	60	99	144	220	375
19	...	...	...	110	148	232	395
20	...	...	...	...	156	244	415
21	...	...	...	...	...	256	435
22	...	...	...	...	...	...	460

L Distance inches	Gallons per Minute Discharge for a given Nominal Pipe Diameter D (Inches)				
	5	6	8	10	12
5	163	...	...	...	...
6	195	285	...	...	...
7	228	334	580	...	...
8	260	380	665	1060	...
9	293	430	750	1190	1660
10	326	476	830	1330	1850
11	360	525	915	1460	2020
12	390	570	1000	1600	2220
13	425	620	1080	1730	2400
14	456	670	1160	1860	2590
15	490	710	1250	2000	2780
16	520	760	1330	2120	2960
17	550	810	1410	2260	3140
18	590	860	1500	2390	3330
19	620	910	1580	2520	3500
20	650	950	1660	2660	3700
21	685	1000	1750	2800	3890
22	720	1050	1830	2920	4060
23	750	1100	1910	3060	4250
24	...	1140	2000	3200	4440

Nozzle Discharge

Nozzle Pressure lbs/sq in	Gallons per Minute Discharge for a given Nozzle Diameter (Inches)						
	1/16	1/8	3/16	1/4	5/16	3/8	7/16
10	0.38	1.48	3.3	5.9	9.24	13.3	18.1
15	0.45	1.81	4.1	7.2	11.4	16.3	22.4
20	0.53	2.09	4.7	8.3	13.1	18.7	25.6
25	0.59	2.34	5.3	9.3	14.6	21.0	28.7
30	0.64	2.56	5.8	10.2	16.0	23.1	31.4
35	0.69	2.78	6.2	11.1	17.1	25.0	33.8
40	0.74	2.96	6.7	11.7	18.4	26.6	36.2
45	0.79	3.14	7.1	12.6	19.5	28.2	38.3
50	0.83	3.30	7.4	13.2	20.6	29.9	40.5
60	0.90	3.62	8.2	14.5	22.6	32.6	44.3
70	0.98	3.91	8.8	15.7	24.4	35.3	47.9
80	1.05	4.19	9.4	16.8	26.1	37.6	51.2
90	1.11	4.43	10.0	17.7	27.8	40.1	54.5
100	1.17	4.67	10.4	18.7	29.2	42.2	57.3
120	1.23	5.17	11.5	20.4	31.8	46.0	62.4
140	1.28	5.70	12.4	22.1	34.4	49.8	67.6
160	1.32	6.30	13.3	23.6	36.9	53.3	72.3
180	1.36	6.92	14.1	25.0	39.0	56.4	76.5
200	1.38	7.52	14.9	26.4	41.1	59.5	81.6

Nozzle Pressure lbs/sq in	Gallons per Minute Discharge for a given Nozzle Diameter (Inches)						
	1/2	9/16	5/8	3/4	7/8	1	1–1/8
10	23.6	30.2	36.9	53.3	72.5	94.8	120
15	28.9	36.7	45.2	65.1	88.7	116	147
20	33.4	42.4	52.2	75.4	102	134	169
25	37.3	47.3	58.2	84.0	115	149	189
30	40.9	51.9	63.9	92.2	126	164	208
35	44.2	56.1	69.0	99.8	136	177	224
40	47.3	59.9	73.8	106	145	189	239
45	50.1	63.4	78.2	113	153	200	254
50	52.8	67.0	82.5	119	162	211	268
60	57.9	73.3	90.4	130	177	232	293
70	62.6	79.3	97.8	141	192	251	317
80	66.8	84.8	105	151	205	268	339
90	70.8	90.3	111	160	218	285	360
100	74.9	95.0	117	169	229	300	379
120	81.8	103	128	184	250	327	413
140	88.3	112	138	199	271	354	447
160	94.6	120	148	213	289	378	478
180	100	127	156	225	306	400	506
200	106	134	165	238	323	423	535

NOTE: The above discharge rates are theoretical. Actual values will only be 95% of the above values, depending on such factors as shape of the nozzle, bore smoothness, etc.

Vertical Pipe Discharge

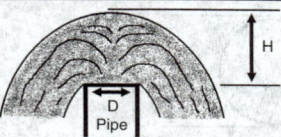

The following formula is an approximation of the output of a vertical pipe.

$$GPM = \sqrt{H} \times K \times D^2 \times 5.68$$

GPM = gallons per minute
H = height in inches
D = diameter of pipe in inches
K = constant from 0.87 to 0.97 for diameters of 2 to 6 inches and heights (H) up to 24 inches.

Example: K=0.97, 6 inch diameter with 10 inch height ≅ 626 gpm

Weir Discharge Volumes

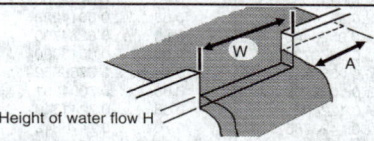

Height of water flow H

Head Inches	GPM for Width of Weir in Feet			gpm/foot over 5 feet wide
	1	3	5	
1	35	107	179	36
1.5	64	197	329	66
2	98	302	506	102
2.5	136	421	705	142
3	178	552	926	187
4	269	845	1420	288
5	369	1174	1978	402
6	476	1534	2592	529
7	...	1922	3255	667
8	...	2335	3963	814
9	...	2769	4713	972
10	...	3225	5501	1138
12	...	4189	7181	1496

Based on the Francis formula:
Cu ft/sec water = $3.33 (W - 0.2 H) H^{1.5}$ Where H=height in feet, W=width in feet and distance "A" should be at least 3 H.

Horizontal Cylinder Fillage

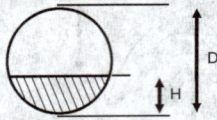

The following equation can be used to calculate the number of gallons remaining in a horizontal tank if the height of the liquid remaining in the tank and the diameter of the tank are known.

Gallons Remaining = Depth Factor × Total Tank Gallons

Use the formula $Ratio = \dfrac{H}{D}$ and then the following table in order to calculate the Depth Factor.

Ratio	Depth Factor	Ratio	Depth Factor
0.02	0.0047728	0.52	0.5254580
0.04	0.0134171	0.54	0.5508752
0.06	0.0244963	0.56	0.5762106
0.08	0.0374780	0.58	0.6014229
0.10	0.0520440	0.60	0.6264700
0.12	0.0679724	0.62	0.6513090
0.14	0.0850946	0.64	0.6758962
0.16	0.1032755	0.66	0.7001861
0.18	0.1224023	0.68	0.7241318
0.20	0.1423785	0.70	0.7476842
0.22	0.1631194	0.72	0.7707919
0.24	0.1845494	0.74	0.7934001
0.26	0.2065999	0.76	0.8154506
0.28	0.2292081	0.78	0.8368806
0.30	0.2523158	0.80	0.8576215
0.32	0.2758682	0.82	0.8775977
0.34	0.2998139	0.84	0.8967245
0.36	0.3241038	0.86	0.9149054
0.38	0.3486910	0.88	0.9320276
0.40	0.3735300	0.90	0.9479560
0.42	0.3985771	0.92	0.9625220
0.44	0.4237894	0.94	0.9755037
0.46	0.4491248	0.96	0.9865829
0.48	0.4745420	0.98	0.9952272
0.50	0.5000000	1.00	1.0000000

Steam Table

Gauge psi	Temp °F	Gauge psi	Temp °F	Gauge psi	Temp °F	Gauge psi	Temp °F
5	227	55	303	110	344	210	392
6	230	56	304	112	345	212	392
7	232	57	305	114	347	214	393
8	235	58	306	116	348	216	394
9	237	59	306	118	349	218	395
10	240	60	307	120	350	220	395
11	242	61	308	122	351	222	396
12	244	62	309	124	352	224	397
13	246	63	310	126	353	226	398
14	248	64	311	128	355	228	398
15	250	65	312	130	356	230	399
16	252	66	313	132	357	232	400
17	254	67	314	134	358	234	400
18	255	68	314	136	359	235	401
19	257	69	315	138	360	237	402
20	259	70	316	140	361	239	402
21	261	71	317	142	362	241	403
22	262	72	318	144	363	243	404
23	264	73	319	146	364	245	404
24	265	74	319	148	365	247	405
25	267	75	320	150	366	249	406
26	268	76	321	152	367	251	407
27	270	77	322	154	368	253	407
28	271	78	322	156	369	255	408
29	273	79	323	158	370	257	408
30	274	80	324	160	371	259	409
31	276	81	325	162	372	261	410
32	277	82	326	164	372	263	410
33	278	83	326	166	373	265	411
34	280	84	327	168	374	267	412
35	281	85	328	170	375	269	412
36	282	86	328	172	376	271	413
37	283	87	329	174	377	273	414
38	285	88	330	176	378	275	414
39	286	89	331	178	379	277	415
40	287	90	331	180	380	279	415
41	288	91	332	182	380	281	416
42	289	92	333	184	381	283	417
43	290	93	333	186	382	285	417
44	291	94	334	188	383	295	420
45	293	95	335	190	384	305	423
46	294	96	335	192	385	355	437
47	295	97	336	194	385	375	442
48	296	98	337	196	386	385	445
49	297	99	337	198	387	405	449
50	298	100	338	200	388	455	461
51	299	102	339	202	389	510	472
52	300	104	341	204	389	560	482
53	301	106	342	206	390	585	486
54	302	108	343	208	391		

Water Pollution

Drinking water standards as adopted by the EPA, Safe Drinking Water Act, and US Public Health Service in (1974 as amended in 1986 and 1996) and adopted by the American Water Works Association are summarized below:

Pollutant	Maximum Contaminant Level (MCL) mg/liter or ppm
Alpha particle activity (gross)	15 pCi/L
Arsenic	0.01
Bacteria	4/100mL
Barium	2.00
Benzene (organic)	0.005
Beta particle and photon radioactivity	4 mrem/yr
Cadmium	0.005
Carbon tetrachloride (organic)	0.005
Chloride	250.0
Coliform	5% *
Color (platinum–cobalt scale)	15 units
Copper	1.3
Chromium (hexavalent)	0.01
Cyanide	0.02
1,1 Dichloroethylene (organic)	0.007
1,2 Dichloroethylene (organic)	0.005
Dioxin (2,3,7,8-TCDD)	0.00000003
Endrin (organic)	0.002
Fluoride	4.0
Foaming agents	0.5
Iron (>0.3 makes red water)	0.3
Lead	0.015
Lindane (organic)	0.0002
Manganese (>0.1 forms brown-black stain)	0.05
Mercury	0.002
Methoxychlor (organic)	0.04
Nitrate	10.0
Odor (threshold odor)	3
p-Dichlorobenzene (organic)	0.075
pH	6.5 - 8.5
Radium–226 and –228	5 pCi/L
Selenium	0.05
Silver	0.1
Sulfate (SO_4)(>500 has a laxative effect)	250.0
Total Dissolved Solids	500.0
Toxaphene (organic)	0.003
1,1,1 Trichloroethane (organic)	0.2
Trichloroethylene (organic)	0.005
Trihalomethanes (organic)	1 to 5 TU
Turbidity (silica scale)	30 μg/L
Uranium	0.002
Vinyl chloride (organic)	5.0
Zinc	0.07
2, 4 – D (organic)	

Exposures over safe limits can result in a variety of serious health problems. For specific information, refer to the National Primary Drinking Water Standards, EPA 810-F-94-001, December 1999, EPA, Washington, DC.

* No more than 5% of samples for a month may be positive.
See also the AIR Chapter for more on pollution, page 22.

Water Hardness

Water hardness is a function of the amount of dissolved calcium salts, magnesium salts, iron and aluminum. The salts occur in a variety of forms but are typically calcium and magnesium bicarbonates (referred to as "temporary hardness") and sulphates and chlorides (referred to as "permanent hardness").

Although the most obvious effect of hard water is in preventing soap from lathering, most people cannot tolerate drinking water that exceeds 300 ppm carbonate, or 1500 ppm chloride, or 2000 ppm sulphate and more than 500 ppm sulphate can produce a laxative effect in the body. Livestock can usually tolerate much higher levels of hardness, but total dissolved solids >10,000 ppm will create problems.

The following formula is used to calculate total hardness:

Total Hardness in ppm Carbonate = (ppm Calcium x 2.497)
+ (ppm Magnesium x 4.115) + (ppm Iron x 1.792)
+ (ppm Manganese x 1.822)

Hard water is treated by either a zeolite process (home water softeners) or a lime–soda ash process (large operations).

Hardness is also measured in "grains per gallon" and "degrees". Equivalents are as follows:

1 ppm = 0.058 grains/US gallon
1 ppm = 0.07 Clark degrees
1 ppm = 0.10 French degrees
1 ppm = 0.056 German degrees
1 French degree = 1 hydrotimetric degree
1 Clark degree = 1 grain / Imperial gallon as calcium carbonate
1 French degree = 1 part / 100,000 calcium carbonate
1 German degree = 1 part / 100,000 calcium oxide
1 grain / US gallon = 17.1 ppm
1 grain / US gallon = 1.20 Clark degrees
1 grain / US gallon = 1.71 French degrees
1 grain / US gallon = 0.958 German degrees

Water Data & Formulas

1 gallon water = 231 cubic inches = 8.333 pounds (@ 65° F)
1 pound of water = 27.72 cubic inches (@ 65° F)
1 cubic foot water = 7.5 gallons = 62.4 pounds (salt water
  weighs approximately 64.3 pounds per cubic foot)
pounds per square inch at bottom of a column of water = height
  of column in feet x 0.434 (@ 39° F)
1 miner's inch = 9 to 12 gallons per minute

Horsepower to Raise Water

$$Horsepower = \frac{gallons\ per\ minute \times Total\ Head\ in\ feet}{3960}$$

(if pumping a liquid other than water, multiply the gallons per
minute above by the liquids specific gravity)

Gallons Per Minute through a Pipe

$GPM = 2.448 \times (Pipe\ Diameter\ in\ inches)^2 \times (Feet\ /\ second\ of\ water\ velocity)$

Weight of Water in a Pipe

$Pounds\ Water = Pipe\ Length\ feet \times Pipe\ diameter\ inches^2 \times 0.34$

Gallons per Minute of a Slurry

$$GPM\ Slurry = GPM\ Water + \frac{4 \times Tons\ of\ per\ hour\ of\ solids}{Specific\ Gravity\ of\ Solids}$$

Cost to Pump Water – Electric

$$\$\ per\ hour = \frac{gpm \times Head\ in\ feet \times 0.746 \times Rate\ per\ KWH}{3960 \times Pump\ Efficiency \times Electric\ Motor\ Efficiency}$$

(70% Pump and 90% Motor Efficiency is a good average)

Cost to Pump Water – Gasoline and Diesel

$$\$\ per\ hour = \frac{GPM \times Head\ in\ feet \times K \times \$\ per\ gallon\ fuel}{3960 \times Pump\ Efficiency}$$

K = 0.110 for gasoline or 0.065 for diesel
  (K is actually gallons of fuel per horsepower)

(70% Pump Efficiency is a good average value)

Weather

(See page 320 for Temperature Conversions)

Beaufort Wind Strength Scale

Beaufort Number or "Force"	Wind Speed Knots (Mile/hour) [km/hour]	Description
0	0–1 (< 1) [< 2]	**Calm:** Still. Smoke will rise vertically. The sea is mirror smooth.
1	1–3 (1–3) [2–6]	**Light Air:** Rising smoke drifts, weather vane is inactive. Scale-like ripples on sea, no foam on wave crests.
2	4–6 (4–7) [7–11]	**Light Breeze: Leaves rustle, can feel wind** on your face, weather vane is active. Short wavelets, glassy wave crests.
3	7–10 (8–12) [12–19]	**Gentle Breeze:** Leaves and twigs move around. Light weight flags extend. Long wavelets, glassy wave crests.
4	11–16 (13–18) [20–30]	**Moderate Breeze:** Moves thin branches, raises dust and paper. Fairly frequent whitecaps occur.
5	17–21 (19–24) [31–39]	**Fresh Breeze:** Small trees sway. Moderate waves, many white foam crests.
6*	22–27 (25–31) [40–50]	**Strong Breeze:** Large tree branches move, open wires begin to "whistle", umbrellas are difficult to control. Some spray on the sea surface.
7	28–33 (32–38) [51–61]	**Moderate Gale:** Large trees begin to sway, noticeably difficult to walk. Foam from waves blown in streaks.
8	34–40 (39–46) [62–74]	**Fresh Gale: Small branches broken** from trees, walking in wind is very difficult. Long streaks of foam appear on sea.
9	41–47 (47–54) [75–87]	**Strong Gale:** Slight damage occurs to buildings, shingles are blown off roofs. High waves, crests start to roll over.
10	48–55 (55–63) [88–102]	**Whole Gale:** Large trees are uprooted, building damage is considerable. The sea takes on a white appearance.
11	56–63 (64–72) [103–117]	**Storm:** Extensive widespread damage. Exceptionally high waves, visibility affected.
12	64+ (>73) [>118]	**Hurricane:** Extreme destruction. Storm waves at sea. Air is filled with spray and foam.

* Small craft advisories are usually issued when force 6 is reached.

Fujita-Pearson Tornado Intensity Scale

Scale	Tornado Strength Name	Tornado	Maximum Wind Speed (mile/hour)	Path Length (mile)	Average Path Length (yard)	Damage	Description of Damage
F0	Weak	Gale	< 73	< 1.0	< 18	Light	Damage to tree branches, billboards, and chimneys. Some small trees uprooted.
F1	Weak	Moderate	73 - 112	1.0 - 3.1	18 - 55	Moderate	Roofing materials peeled off, mobile home pushed off foundations or overturned, moving automobiles pushed off road.
F2	Strong	Significant	113 - 157	3.2 - 9.9	56 - 175	Considerable	Roofs torn off wood-frame homes, mobile homes demolished, railroad boxcars pushed over, large trees uprooted or snapped-off.
F3	Strong	Severe	158 - 206	10 - 31	176 - 556	Severe	Roofs and some walls torn off well-built wood-frame homes, locomotives over-turned, most trees in forested areas up rooted, automobiles lifted and moved.
F4	Violent	Devastating	207 - 260	32 - 99	557 - 1759	Devastating	Well-built homes leveled, automobiles thrown about, heavy objects become missiles.
F5	Violent	Incredible	261 - 318	100 - 315	1760 - 5456	Incredible	Structures are lifted off foundations and carried away, reinforced concrete structures damaged. Less than 2% of all tornadoes reach this intensity.
F6	-	-	319 - 380	-	-	-	Not expected to occur on Earth.

Hurricane Intensity Scale

Saffir-Simpson Damage Potential Scale For Hurricanes

Category	Central Pressure (in of Hg)	Wind Speed (mile/hour)	Storm Surge (feet)	Damage Level	Description of Damage
1	≥28.94	74-95	4-5	Minimal	Damage to trees, shrubs, foliage and unanchored mobile homes. Well-built structures undamaged. Low-lying coastal roads may flood.
2	28.91-28.50	96-110	6-8	Moderate	Some trees blown down; major damage to mobile homes. Some damage to roofing materials, doors and windows. Major damage to piers.Evacuation of low-lying homes on coast may be required.
3	28.47-27.91	111-130	9-12	Extensive	Leaves torn from trees; some large trees blown down. Mobile homes destroyed; some structural damage to small homes and utility buildings, minor damage to non-load bearing walls. Piers destroyed. Serious flooding near the coast damages structures, and structures 5 ft. above sea level may flood as far as 6 miles inland.

Hurricane Intensity Scale (con't)

Category	Central Pressure (in of Hg)	Wind Speed (mile/hour)	Storm Surge (feet)	Damage	Description of Damage Level
4	27.88-27.17	131-155	13-18	Extreme	Extensive damage to roofing materials and non-load bearing walls. Complete structural failure of roofs on small homes. Major damage to lower floors of structures near the coast. Major erosion of beaches. Land less than 10 ft. above sea level require massive evacuation up to 6 miles inland.
5	≤27.15	≥156	>18	Catastrophic	Complete roof structure failure on many buildings. Some complete building failures, small utility buildings blown over or away. Major damage to lower floors of all structures less than 15 ft. above sea level within 500 yards of the coast. Massive evacuation of areas on low ground within 5-10 miles of the coast may be required.

Wind Chill Factors

In order to determine a "Wind Chill Factor", locate the measured outside temperature row and then the wind speed column and then read the corresponding "Wind Chill Factor" at the intersection of the row and column. "Wind Chill Factor" is the combined effect of actual temperature and wind speed that increases heat loss in the body and makes the measured outside temperature "feel" colder. **Based on new equation: NOAA 2001**

Outside Temp °F	Wind Speed - miles/hour											
	5	10	15	20	25	30	35	40	45	50	55	60
50	48	46	45	44	43	42	41	41	40	40	40	39
45	42	40	38	37	36	35	35	34	33	33	32	32
40	36	34	32	30	29	28	28	27	26	26	25	25
35	31	27	25	24	23	22	21	20	19	19	18	17
30	25	21	19	17	16	15	14	13	12	12	11	10
25	19	15	13	11	9	8	7	6	5	4	4	3
20	13	9	6	4	3	1	0	-1	-2	-3	-3	-4
15	7	3	0	-2	-4	-5	-7	-8	-9	-10	-11	-11
10	1	-4	-7	-9	-11	-12	-14	-15	-16	-17	-18	-19
5	-5	-10	-13	-15	-17	-19	-21	-22	-23	-24	-25	-26
0	-11	-16	-19	-22	-24	-26	-27	-29	-30	-31	-32	-33
-5	-16	-22	-26	-29	-31	-33	-34	-36	-37	-38	-39	-40
-10	-22	-28	-32	-35	-37	-39	-41	-43	-44	-45	-46	-48
-15	-28	-35	-39	-42	-44	-46	-48	-50	-51	-52	-54	-55
-20	-34	-41	-45	-48	-51	-53	-55	-57	-58	-60	-61	-62
-25	-40	-47	-51	-55	-58	-60	-62	-64	-65	-67	-68	-69
-30	-46	-53	-58	-61	-64	-67	-69	-71	-72	-74	-75	-76
-35	-52	-59	-64	-68	-71	-73	-76	-78	-79	-81	-82	-84
-40	-57	-66	-71	-74	-78	-80	-82	-84	-86	-88	-89	-91
-45	-63	-72	-77	-81	-84	-87	-89	-91	-93	-95	-97	-98

Light grey shaded area indicates frostbite occurs in 15 minutes or less and presents a serious health hazard.

Wind Chill (°F) = $35.74 + 0.6215 (T) - 35.75 (V^{0.16}) + 0.4275 (T) (V^{0.16})$
where T=air temperature in °F and V=wind speed (mph)
Source: National Weather Service, http://www.srh.noaa.gov

Wind Chill	Possible Effects
30°F or higher	Generally unpleasant
30° to 15 °F	Unpleasant
14° to 0°F	Very unpleasant
- 01° to - 20°F	Frostbite possible
- 21° to - 60°F	Frostbite likely; outdoor activity dangerous
- 61° or lower	Exposed flesh freezes within 30 seconds.

Heat – Humidity Factor

Rel. Hum. %	Air Temperature (°F)										
	70	75	80	85	90	95	100	105	110	115	120
0%	64	69	73	78	83	87	91	95	99	103	107
10%	65	70	75	80	85	90	95	100	105	111	116
20%	66	72	77	82	87	93	99	105	112	120	130
30%	67	73	78	84	90	96	104	113	123	135	148
40%	68	74	79	86	93	101	110	123	137	151	
50%	69	75	81	88	96	107	120	135	150		
60%	70	76	82	90	100	114	132	149			
70%	70	77	85	93	106	124	144				
80%	71	78	86	97	113	136					
90%	71	79	88	102	122						
100%	72	80	91	108							

WARNING: The light grey shaded area above identifies the "danger zones" where the Heat/Humidity Index is 90 or above.

Heat/Humidity Index Danger Zones

- 90°-104° Heat cramps or heat exhaustion possible
- 105°-130° Heat cramps or heat exhaustion likely, heatstroke possible
- 130°- more Heat stroke highly likely

See page 221 for information on treating heat-related health problems.

Safe Loads For Clear Solid Ice

Thickness of Ice	Load or Activity
3 inches	Cross Country Skiers
4 inches	1 person ice fishing
5 inches	1 snowmobile
6 inches	1 ice boat
7 inches	Group activities
8 inches	1 car or truck
9 inches	Several vehicles

Ice thickness may vary within a small area
- New (black) ice is stronger than old (milky) ice
- Ice closer to shore is weaker than ice farther out
- Obstructions i.e., rocks, logs and plants, weaken ice
- Underground springs weaken ice
- Waterfowl and schools of fish prevent ice formation
- Water currents weaken ice
- Ice covered by snow and/or water weakens the ice.

Survival equipment for each person
- Ice awls
- Life Jacket
- 25 feet of rope
- Whistle

Because ice strength is influenced by so many factors, this information should be used only as a general guide. If you're not sure - stay off the ice.

Cold Water Survival Times

Water Temperature	Exhaustion	Death
80° F (27°C)	indefinite	indefinite
70-80° (21-27°C)	3-12 hrs	3 hrs - indefinite
60-70° (16-21°C)	2-7 hrs	2-40 hrs
50-60° (10-16°C)	1-2 hrs	1-6 hrs
40-50° (4-10°C)	30-60 min	1-3 hrs
32.5-40° (0-4°C)	15-30 min	30-90 min
32.5° (0°C)	<15 min	15 - 45 min

Weather Map Symbols

Thunderstorm	$\lceil\mathfrak{F}$	Hail	△
Severe Thunderstorm	$\mathfrak{F}$	Rain and Snow Mixture	● ✳
Thunderstorm with Hail	△⃠	Light Hail Shower	△▽
Thunderstorm with Rain and/or Snow	•/✳	Dust Storm	$\mathcal{G}$
Thunderstorm no precipitation at station	⌐⃗	Sleet	⊿●
Severe Thunderstorm Watch Box (290 is the Watch Number)	S290	Drifting or Blowing Snow	┿
		Snow Grains	⊸△
Hurricane	𝟞	Ice Crystals	↔
Tropical Storm	𝟞	Ground Fog	==
		Fog	=
Tornado or Funnel Cloud	)(	Dense Fog	≡
Tornado Watch Box (300 is the Watch Number)	T300	Fog with Rain	••
		Smoke	⌿⌿⌿
Lightning	⟨	Haze	∞
Showers	▽	High Pressure	H
		Low Pressure	L

Weather Map Symbols (cont.)

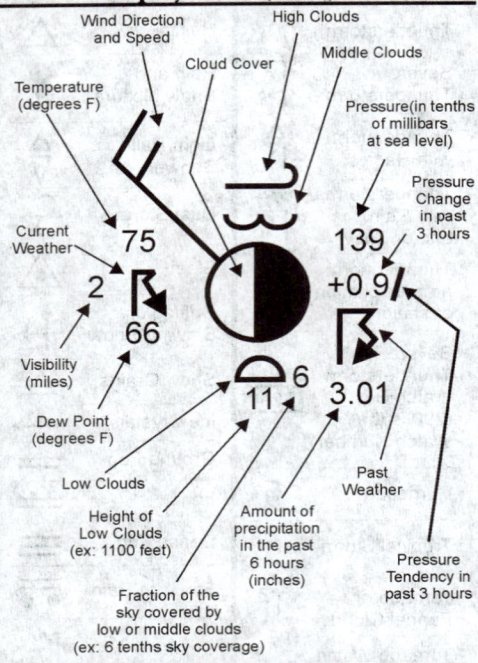

Wind Direction and Speed
High Clouds
Cloud Cover
Middle Clouds
Temperature (degrees F)
Pressure (in tenths of millibars at sea level)
Pressure Change in past 3 hours
Current Weather
Visibility (miles)
Dew Point (degrees F)
Low Clouds
Height of Low Clouds (ex: 1100 feet)
Amount of precipitation in the past 6 hours (inches)
Fraction of the sky covered by low or middle clouds (ex: 6 tenths sky coverage)
Past Weather
Pressure Tendency in past 3 hours

Cold Front (Surface)	▲▲▲
Warm Front (Surface)	●●●
Occluded Front (Surface)	▲▲
Stationary Front (Surface)	▲●▲
Low Pressure Trough	▬ ▬ ▬

	Symbol	Light	Intensity Moderate	Heavy
Rain	●	● ●	●● / ●	●● / ●●
Snow	✳	✳ ✳	✳✳	✳✳✳
Drizzle	،	، ،	،،	،،
Rain Shower	▽̇	▽̇	▽̈	
Snow Shower	✻▽	✻▽	✻▽	
Freezing Rain	∿	∿	∿	
Freezing Drizzle	∿	∿	∿	

Sky Cover Symbols

○	No Clouds	◓	Six-tenths
◍	One-tenth or less	◑	Seven-tenths to Eight-tenths
◔	Two-tenths to Three-tenths	◎	Nine-tenths or slightly overcast
◕	Four-tenths	●	Overcast or Ten-tenths
◑	Five-tenths	⊗	Sky Obscured

Pressure Tendency Symbols

⌃	Increasing, then decreasing - total change positive or zero	∨	Decreasing, then increasing - total change negative or zero
/	Increasing, then steady	\	Decreasing, then steady
/	Increasing	\	Decreasing
✓	Decreasing, then increasing - total change positive or zero	⌄	Increasing, then decreasing - total change negative or zero
—	Steady - no change		

Cloud Symbols

Low Clouds:

Cumulus or Fair weather Cumulus

Cumulus with domes or towers

Cumulus with summits

Stratocumulus (formed from spreading out of Cumulus)

Stratocumulus (not formed from spreading out of Cumulus)

Fair weather Stratus

Bad weather Stratus

Cumulus & Stratocumulus

Cumulonimbus or Thunderheads

Middle Clouds:

Thin Altostratus

Thick Altostratus or Nimbostratus

Thin Altocumulus

Patchy Altocumulus

Thin Altocumulus in bands, gradually thickening

Altocumulus (formed from spreading out of Cumulus)

Altocumulus in thick or multiple layers

Altocumulus with Cumuliform turrets

Altocumulus in a chaotic sky

High Clouds:

Scattered Cirrus

Patches of Dense Cirrus

Dense Cirrus

Cirrus, hook shaped, gradually thickening

Bands of Cirrus or Cirrostratus, in the lower part of the sky

Bands of Cirrus or Cirrostratus, in the upper part of the sky

Cirrostratus, covering the entire sky

Partial Cirrostratus cover

Cirrocumulus

Wind Direction & Speed

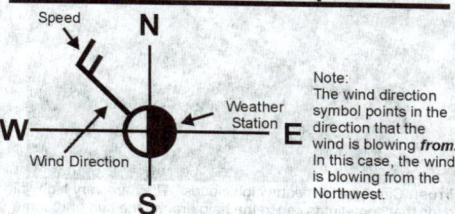

Note:
The wind direction symbol points in the direction that the wind is blowing *from.* In this case, the wind is blowing from the Northwest.

Wind Speed	Miles/hour	Knots
◎	Calm	Calm
	1-2	1-2
	3-8	3-7
	9-14	8-12
	15-20	13-17
	21-25	18-22
	26-31	23-27
	32-37	28-32
	38-43	33-37
	44-49	38-42
	50-54	43-47
	55-60	48-52
	61-66	53-57
	67-71	58-62
	72-77	63-67
	78-83	68-72
	84-89	73-77
	119-123	103-107

Cloud Types - In order highest to lowest

Cirrus: "Cirro" prefix means high clouds. They are very high, thin clouds that sometimes cause the halo around the sun or moon. Halos are ice crystals and indicate cold weather to follow. Hair-like versions of these clouds are called "horsetail clouds".

Cirrocummulus: Another very high cloud that has a patchy or wave like appearance. These clouds are not precipitation clouds.

Cumulonimbus: These are the largest of all the clouds and can span several layers vertically. They are heavy, large, dark clouds that bring rain, lightening, hail, strong winds, and tornadoes.

Altocumulus: "Alto" prefix means mid-level clouds. These middle clouds are usually light, fluffy clouds and are not associated with precipitation.

Altostratus: These clouds are gray or bluish-gray and do not allow enough sun to break through to have a shadow on the ground. Snow falls from these clouds.

Stratocumulus: This is a layer located on the top of a cumulus cloud and rarely has precipitation, even though the color can be dark gray. These clouds can be scattered or in layers or clusters. They have very little vertical development and lack sharp edges.

Cumulus: These clouds are large, puffy clouds with distinct edges. They are the kind of clouds artists like to paint and rarely produce precipitation.

Nimbostratus: "Nimbo" prefix implies a precipitation producing cloud. They are the dark gray clouds that are usually below 6,000 feet and are associated with a light to moderate rain.

Stratus: Precipitation rarely falls from these clouds because the upward vertical motion needed for precipitation is weak, but a light mist or drizzle can happen. When fog lifts it becomes a stratus.

Weights & Properties of Materials

See also GEOLOGY on page 339 for minerals, CARPENTRY on page 64 for woods and STEEL on page 549.
See powder and granulated material notes at end of chapters.

Material	Specific Gravity	Weight lbs per cu foot	Weight lbs per cu yard	Weight kgs per cu meter	Angle of Repose
ABS (acrylonitrile butadiene styrene)	1.05	65.5	1769.8	1050.0	
Acetal	1.58	98.3	2654.8	1575.0	
Acetic acid, 90%	1.06	66.3	1790	1062.0	
Acetone	0.79	49.3	1331.6	790.0	
Acetylene (gas, 68°F, 14.7 psia, air = 1)	0.907	0.068	1.84	1.09	
Acetylene (liquid, -121°F)	0.62	38.4	1,037	615	
Acetylene (liquid, 70°F)	0.38	23.6	637	378	
Acrylic (cast)	1.19	74.0	1997.4	1185.0	
Acrylonitrile	1.15	71.8	1938.4	1150.0	
ADC (Allyl diglycol carbonate,cast sheet)	1.35	84.3	2275.5	1350.0	
ADI fluid	0.90	56.1	1514.8	898.7	
Adipic acid	0.72	45.0	1,215	721	
Air (gas, 68°F, 14.7 psia, air = 1)	1.000	0.075	2.03	1.20	
Alcohol, ethyl	0.789	49	1329	788.5	
Alcohol, methyl	0.791	49	1333	790.9	
Alder wood, red (12% moisture content)	0.41	28.7	774	459	
Alfalfa, ground	0.26	16	432	256.3	+45
Almonds, broken	0.46	29.0	783	465	
Alum, lumpy	0.88	55	1485	881.0	30-45
Alum, pulverized	0.75	47	1269	752.9	30-45
Alumina	0.96	60	1620	961.1	30-45
Aluminum oxide	1.52	95	2565	1521.8	30
Aluminum, solid	2.64	165	4455	2643.1	
Ammonia gas	0.00	0.048	1.29	0.8	
Ammonia (gas, 68°F, 14.7 psia, air = 1)	0.060	0.004	0.12	0.07	

Material	Specific Gravity	Weight lbs per cu foot	Weight lbs per cu yard	Weight kgs per cu meter	Angle of Repose
Ammonia (liquid, -28°F, 14.7 psia)	0.63	39.3	1,062	630	
Ammonium sulfate	0.83	52	1404	833.0	
Andesite, solid	2.77	173	4671	2771.2	
Antimony, cast	6.70	418	11286	6695.7	
Apple wood, dry	0.71	44	1188	704.8	
Apples	0.64	40	1080	640.7	
Argon (gas, 68°F, 14.7 psia, air = 1)	1.379	0.104	2.80	1.66	
Argon (liquid, -303°F, 14.7 psia)	1.39	87.0	2,349	1,394	
Arsenic	5.67	354	9558	5670.5	
ASA (Acrylate styrene acrylonitrile)	1.06	66.2	1786.7	1060.0	
Asbestos, shredded	0.35	22	594	352.4	30
Asbestos, solid	2.45	153	4131	2450.8	
Ash wood, black, dry	0.54	34	918	544.6	
Ash wood, white, dry	0.67	42	1134	672.8	
Ash wood, black (12% moisture content)	0.49	34.3	925	549	
Ash wood, blue (12% moisture content)	0.58	40.6	1,095	650	
Ash wood, green (12% moisture content)	0.56	39.2	1,057	627	
Ash wood, Oregon (12% moisture content)	0.55	38.5	1,038	616	
Ash wood, white (12% moisture content)	0.60	42.0	1,133	672	
Ashes	0.66	41	1107	656.8	
Aspen wood	0.42	26	702	416.5	
Aspen wood, bigtooth (12% moisture content)	0.39	27.3	736	437	
Aspen wood, quaking (12% moisture content)	0.38	26.6	717	426	
Asphalt, compacted	2.36	147	3977	2359	
Asphalt, crushed	0.72	45	1215	720.8	30-45
Aviation gasoline	0.72	44.9	1213.6	720.0	
Babbitt	7.28	454	12258	7272.4	
Bagasse	0.12	7.5	202	120.1	45
Bakelite, solid	1.36	85	2295	1361.6	
Baking powder	0.72	45	1215	720.8	30-45
Barite, crushed	2.88	180	4860	2883.3	
Barium	3.78	236	6372	3780.4	
Bark, wood refuse	0.24	15	405	240.3	45
Barley	0.61	38	1026	608.7	
Basalt, broken	1.96	122	3294	1954.3	
Basalt, solid	3.01	188	5076	3011.5	
Basswood, American (12% moisture content)	0.37	25.9	698	414	
Bauxite, crushed	1.28	80	2160	1281.5	30-45
Beans, castor	0.58	36	972	576.7	
Beans, cocoa	0.59	37	999	592.7	

Material	Specific Gravity	Weight lbs per cu foot	Weight lbs per cu yard	Weight kgs per cu meter	Angle of Repose
Beans, navy	0.80	50	1350	800.9	
Beans, soy	0.72	45	1215	720.8	
Beech wood, American (12% moisture content)	0.64	44.7	1,208	717	
Beeswax	0.96	60	1620	961.1	
Beets	0.72	45	1215	720.8	
Bentonite	0.59	37	999	592.7	45
Benzene	0.88	54.9	1483.3	880.0	
Bicarbonate of Soda	0.69	43	1161	688.8	42
Birch wood, yellow	0.71	44	1188	704.8	
Birch wood, paper (12% moisture content)	0.55	38.5	1,038	616	
Birch wood, sweet (12% moisture content)	0.65	45.4	1,227	728	
Birch wood, yellow (12% moisture content)	0.62	43.4	1,170	694	
Bismuth	9.79	611	16497	9787.3	
Bones, pulverized	0.88	55	1485	881.0	
Borax, fine	0.85	53	1431	849.0	30-45
Bran	0.26	16	432	256.3	30-45
Brass, cast	8.56	534	14418	8553.9	
Brass, rolled	8.56	534	14418	8553.9	
Brewers grain	0.43	27	729	432.5	45
Brick, chrome	2.80	175	4725	2803.2	
Brick, common red	1.92	120	3240	1922.2	
Brick, fire clay	2.40	150	4050	2402.8	
Brick, magnesia	2.56	160	4320	2563.0	
Brick, silica	2.05	128	3456	2050.4	
Bronze	8.16	509	13743	8153.4	
Buckwheat	0.66	41	1107	656.8	
Butane (gas, 68°F, 14.7 psia, air = 1)	2.067	0.155	4.20	2.49	
Butane (liquid, 70°F)	0.58	36.2	978	580	
Butter	0.87	54	1458	865.0	
Butternut wood (12% moisture content)	0.38	26.6	717	426	
Cadmium	8.65	540	14580	8650.0	
Calcium carbide	1.20	75	2025	1201.4	30-45
Caliche	1.44	90	2430	1441.7	
Carbon dioxide	0.00	0.1234	3.3318	2.0	
Carbon dioxide (gas, 68°F, 14.7 psia, gas = 1)	1.529	0.115	3.10	1.84	
Carbon dioxide (liquid, 2°F, 60.3 psia)	1.01	63.3	1,709	1,014	
Carbon monoxide	0.00	0.0781	2.1087	1.3	
Carbon monoxide (gas, 68°F, 14.7 psia, air = 1)	0.967	0.073	1.96	1.16	
Carbon, powdered	0.08	5	135	80.1	
Carbon, solid	2.15	134	3618	2146.5	
Cardboard	0.69	43	1161	688.8	
Cedar, red	0.38	24	648	384.4	
Cellulose nitrate	1.38	85.8	2317.6	1375.0	

Material	Specific Gravity	Weight lbs per cu foot	Weight lbs per cu yard	Weight kgs per cu meter	Angle of Repose
Cement, also see Concrete					
Cement, Portland, mix design only	3.15	197	5309	3150.0	
Cement, Portland 1 cu. ft. sack	1.51	94	2538	1506	
Cement, slurry	1.44	90	2430	1441.7	
Chalk, fine	1.12	70	1890	1121.3	45
Chalk, lumpy	1.44	90	2430	1441.7	45
Chalk, solid	2.50	156	4212	2498.9	
Charcoal	0.21	13	351	208.2	
Cherry wood, dry	0.56	35	945	560.6	
Chestnut wood, dry	0.48	30	810	480.6	
Chlorine (gas, 68°F, 14.7 psia, air = 1)	2.486	0.187	5.05	2.99	
Chloroform	1.52	95	2565	1521.8	
Chocolate, powder	0.64	40	1080	640.7	
Chromic acid, flake	1.20	75	2025	1201.4	25
Chromium	6.86	428	11556	6855.9	
Chromium ore	2.16	135	3645	2162.5	30-45
Cinders, Coal, ash	0.64	40	1080	640.7	25-40
Cinders, Furnace	0.91	57	1539	913.1	
Clay, compacted	1.75	109	2943	1746.0	
Clay, Dry excavated	1.09	68	1836	1089.3	
Clay, Dry lump	1.07	67	1809	1073.2	25-45
Clay, fire	1.36	85	2295	1361.6	
Clay, Wet excavated	1.83	114	3078	1826.1	
Clay, Wet lump	1.60	100	2700	1601.8	
Clover seed	0.77	48	1296	768.9	28
Coal, Anthracite, broken	1.11	69	1863	1105.3	30-45
Coal, Anthracite, solid	1.51	94	2538	1505.7	
Coal, Bituminous, broken	0.83	52	1404	833.0	30-45
Coal, Bituminous, solid	1.35	84	2268	1345.6	
Cobalt	8.75	546	14742	8746.1	
Coconut, meal	0.51	32	864	512.6	
Coconut, shredded	0.35	22	594	352.4	45
Coffee, fresh beans	0.56	35	945	560.6	35-45
Coffee, roast beans	0.43	27	729	432.5	
Coke	0.42	26	702	416.5	
Concrete, Asphaltic	2.24	140	3780	2242.6	
Concrete, Gravel	2.40	150	4050	2402.8	
Concrete, heavy w/ baryte aggregate	3.20	200	5400	3204	
Concrete, lightweight w/ expanded clay agg.	1.09	68	1836	1089	
Concrete, Limestone agg. w/Portland cement	2.37	148	3996	2370.7	
Copper sulphate, ground	3.60	225	6073	3603.0	
Copper, cast	8.69	542	14634	8682.0	
Copper, rolled	8.91	556	15012	8906.3	
Copra, expeller cake chopped	0.46	29	783	464.5	20
Copra, expeller					

Material	Specific Gravity	Weight lbs per cu foot	Weight lbs per cu yard	Weight kgs per cu meter	Angle of Repose
cake ground	0.51	32	864	512.6	30
Copra, meal, ground	0.64	40	1080	640.7	39
Copra, medium size	0.53	33	891	528.6	20
Cork, natural bark	0.24	15	405	240.3	
Cork, ground, commercial	0.08	5	135	80.1	45
Cork, solid, commercial	0.18	11.5	311	184.2	
Corn, grits	0.67	42	1134	672.8	30-45
Corn, on the cob (ear)		28	756	448.5	
Corn, shelled	0.72	45	1215	720.8	
Cottonseed, cake, lumpy	0.67	42	1134	672.8	30-45
Cottonseed, dry, de-linted	0.56	35	945	560.6	30-45
Cottonseed, dry, not de-linted	0.32	20	540	320.4	45
Cottonseed, hulls	0.19	12	324	192.2	45
Cottonseed, meal	0.59	37	999	592.7	30-45
Cottonseed, meats	0.64	40	1080	640.7	30-45
Cottonwood	0.42	26	702	416.5	
CPVC (Chlorinated polyvinyl chloride)	1.54	95.8	2587.3	1535.0	
Crude oil	0.85	53.1	1432.7	850.0	
Cryolite	1.60	100	2700	1601.8	30-45
Cullet	1.60	100	2700	1601.8	30-45
Culm	0.75	47	1269	752.9	
Cypress wood	0.51	32	864	512.6	
Diesel fuel	0.84	52.1	1407.4	835.0	
Dolomite, lumpy	1.52	95	2565	1521.8	30-45
Dolomite, pulverized	0.74	46	1242	736.9	
Dolomite, solid	2.90	181	4887	2899.3	
Down, goose & duck very best	0.002	0.14	3.9	2.3	
good	0.003	0.18	4.9	2.9	
poor	0.006	0.36	9.7	5.8	
Dry ice (solid carbon di-oxide,-109.1°F,14.7 psia)	1.56	97.4	2,630	1,560	
Earth, dense	2.00	125	3375	2002.3	30-45
Earth, Fullers, raw	0.67	42	1134	672.8	35
Earth, loam, dry, excavated	1.25	78	2106	1249.4	30-45
Earth, moist, excavated	1.44	90	2430	1441.7	30-45
Earth, packed	1.52	95	2565	1521.8	
Earth, soft loose mud	1.73	108	2916	1730.0	
Earth, wet, excavated	1.60	100	2700	1601.8	30-45
Ebony wood	0.96	60	1620	961.1	
EC (Ethyl cellulose)	1.13	70.5	1904.7	1130.0	
Elm, dry	0.56	35	945	560.6	
Emery	4.01	250	6750	4004.6	
Epoxy	1.26	78.3	2115.4	1255.0	
Ethane (gas, 68°F, 14.7 psia, air = 1)	1.049	0.079	2.13	1.26	
Ether	0.74	46	1242	736.9	
Ethyl chloride	0.90	56.2	1517.0	900.0	
Ethyl ether	0.71	44.3	1196.7	710.0	

Material	Specific Gravity	Weight lbs per cu foot	Weight lbs per cu yard	Weight kgs per cu meter	Angle of Repose
Ethylene (gas, 68°F, 14.7 psia, air = 1)	0.975	0.073	1.98	1.17	
Ethylene glycol	1.11	69.5	1877.7	1114.0	
EVOH (Ethylene vinyl alcohol)	1.16	72.4	1955.2	1160.0	
Feathers, goose & duck unwashed in bale	0.04	2.5	67.5	40.0	
Feldspar, pulverized	1.23	77	2079	1233.4	45
Feldspar, solid	2.56	160	4320	2563.0	
Fertilizer, acid phosphate	0.96	60	1620	961.1	
Fir, Douglas	0.53	33	891	528.6	
Fish, meal	0.59	37	999	592.7	45
Fish, scrap	0.72	45	1215	720.8	
Flaxseed, whole	0.72	45	1215	720.8	
Flour, wheat	0.59	37	999	592.7	45
Fluorine (gas, 68°F, 14.7 psia, air = 1)	1.304	0.098	2.65	1.57	
Fluorspar, lumps	1.60	100	2700	1601.8	45
Fluorspar, pulverized	1.44	90	2430	1441.7	45
Fluorspar, solid	3.21	200	5400	3203.7	
Furan	1.75	109.2	2949.7	1750.0	
Garbage	0.48	30	810	480.6	
Gasoline	0.74	45.9	1238.9	735.0	
Glass, window	2.58	161	4347	2579.0	
Glue, animal, flaked	0.56	35	945	560.6	
Glue, vegetable, glue powdered	0.64	40	1080	640.7	
Gluten, meal	0.63	39	1053	624.7	30-45
Glycerin	1.26	78.7	2123.8	1260.0	
Gneiss, bed in place	2.87	179	4833	2867.3	
Gneiss, broken	1.86	116	3132	1858.1	
Gold, pure 24 kt	19.29	1204	32508	19286.3	
Granite, broken	1.65	103	2781	1649.9	
Granite, solid	2.69	168	4536	2691.1	
Graphite, flake	0.64	40	1080	640.7	30-45
Gravel, dry, 1/4 to 2 inch	1.68	105	2835	1681.9	
Gravel, loose, dry	1.52	95	2565	1521.8	30-45
Gravel, w/ sand, natural	1.92	120	3240	1922.2	
Gravel, wet, 1/4 to 2 inch	2.00	125	3375	2002.3	
Gypsum board	0.85	52.8	1425.6	845.8	
Gypsum, broken	1.81	113	3051	1810.1	
Gypsum, crushed	1.60	100	2700	1601.8	
Gypsum, pulverized	1.12	70	1890	1121.3	45
Gypsum, solid	2.79	174	4698	2787.2	
Halite (salt), broken	1.51	94	2538	1505.7	
Halite (salt), solid	2.32	145	3915	2322.7	
Hay, loose	0.08	5	135	80.1	
Hay, pressed	0.38	24	648	384.4	
HDPE (High-density polyethylene)	0.96	59.8	1615.6	958.5	
Helium (gas, 68°F, 14.7 psia, air = 1)	0.138	0.010	0.28	0.17	

Material	Specific Gravity	Weight lbs per cu foot	Weight lbs per cu yard	Weight kgs per cu meter	Angle of Repose
Helium (liquid, -452°F, 14.7 psia)	0.13	7.80	211	125	
Hematite, broken	3.22	201	5427	3219.7	
Hematite, solid	4.90	306	8262	4901.7	
Hemlock, dry	0.40	25	675	400.5	
Hickory, dry	0.85	53	1431	849.0	
Hops, moist	0.56	35	945	560.6	45
Hydraulic fluid	0.86	53.9	1454.2	862.7	
Hydrochloric acid 40%	1.20	75	2025	1201.4	
Hydrogen (gas, 68°F, 14.7 psia, air = 1)	0.070	0.005	0.14	0.08	
Hydrogen (liquid, -423°F, 14.7 psia)	0.07	4.43	120	71.0	
Hydrogen chloride (gas, 68°F, 14.7 psia, air = 1)	1.268	0.095	2.57	1.53	
Hydrogen sulphide (gas, 68°F, 14.7 psia, air = 1)	1.190	0.089	2.42	1.43	
Ice, crushed	0.59	37	999	592.7	
Ice, solid	0.92	57.4	1549.8	919.5	
Ilmenite	2.31	144	3888	2306.7	30-45
Iridium	22.16	1383	37341	22153.6	
Iron oxide pigment	0.40	25	675	400.5	40
Iron, cast	7.21	450	12150	7208.3	
Iron, wrought	7.77	485	13095	7769.0	
Ivory	1.84	115	3105	1842.1	
Jet fuel, JP-4	0.78	48.6	1312.8	778.9	
Kaolin, green crushed	1.03	64	1728	1025.2	35
Kaolin, pulverized	0.35	22	594	352.4	45
Kerosene	0.80	49.9	1348.4	800.0	
LDPE (Low-density polyethylene)	0.92	57.7	1558.3	924.5	
Lead, cast, 20°C (68°F)	11.34	708	19114	11340.0	
Lead, just liquid, 327.4°C	10.69	667	18,012	10,686	
Lead, just solid, 327.4°C	11.01	687	18,550	11,005	
Lead, red	3.69	230	6210	3684.3	
Lead, rolled, 20°C (68°F)	11.36	709	19148	11360.0	
Lead, white pigment	4.09	255	6885	4084.7	
Leather	0.95	59	1593	945.1	
Lignite, dry	0.80	50	1350	800.9	30-45
Lignum Vitae, dry	1.28	80	2160	1281.5	
Lime, hydrated	0.48	30	810	480.6	30-45
Lime, quick, fine	1.20	75	2025	1201.4	
Lime, quick, lump	0.85	53	1431	849.0	
Lime, stone, large	2.69	168	4536	2691.1	
Lime, stone, lump	1.54	96	2592	1537.8	
Limestone, broken	1.55	97	2619	1553.8	
Limestone, pulverized	1.39	87	2349	1393.6	
Limestone, solid	2.61	163	4401	2611.0	45
Limonite, broken	2.47	154	4158	2466.8	
Limonite, solid	3.80	237	6399	3796.4	
Linseed, meal	0.51	32	864	512.6	30-45
Linseed, whole	0.75	47	1269	752.9	

Material	Specific Gravity	Weight lbs per cu foot	Weight lbs per cu yard	Weight kgs per cu meter	Angle of Repose
Locust, dry	0.71	44	1188	704.8	
Magnesite, solid	3.01	188	5076	3011.5	
Magnesium sulfate, crystal	1.12	70	1890	1121.3	
Magnesium, solid	1.75	109	2943	1746.0	
Magnetite, broken	3.29	205	5535	3283.8	
Magnetite, solid	5.05	315	8505	5045.8	
Mahogany, Honduras, dry	0.54	34	918	544.6	
Mahogany, Spanish, dry	0.85	53	1431	849.0	
Malt	0.34	21	567	336.4	30-45
Manganese oxide	1.92	120	3240	1922.2	
Manganese, solid	7.61	475	12825	7608.8	
Manure	0.40	25	675	400.5	
Maple, dry	0.71	44	1188	704.8	
Marble, broken	1.57	98	2646	1569.8	30-45
Marble, solid	2.56	160	4320	2563.0	
Marl, wet, excavated	2.24	140	3780	2242.6	
Medium Density Fiberboard (MDF)	0.75	46.6	1268	746.5	
Mercury @ 0°C (32°F)	13.61	849	22923	13599.7	
Methane (gas, 68°F, 14.7 psia, air = 1)	0.554	0.042	1.12	0.67	
Methyl chloride	0.99	61.8	1668.7	990.0	
Methyl chloride (gas, 68°F, 14.7 psia, air = 1)	1.785	0.134	3.62	2.15	
Mica, broken	1.60	100	2700	1601.8	30-45
Mica, solid	2.88	180	4860	2883.3	
Milk, powdered	0.45	28	756	448.5	45
Molybdenum	10.19	636	17172	10187.8	
Mortar, sand & cement, set.	2.16	135	3645	2162.5	
Mortar, sand & cement, wet.	2.40	150	4050	2402.8	
Mud, fluid	1.73	108	2916	1730.0	
Mud, packed	1.91	119	3213	1906.2	
Natural gas (gas, 68°F, 14.7 psia, air = 1)	0.667	0.050	1.35	0.80	
Natural gas (liquid, 60°F)	0.42	26.5	715	424	
Nickel silver	8.45	527	14229	8441.7	
Nickel, rolled	8.67	541	14607	8666.0	
Nitric acid, 91%	1.51	94	2538	1505.7	
Nitric oxide (gas, 68°F, 14.7 psia, air = 1)	1.037	0.078	2.11	1.25	
Nitrogen (gas, 68°F, 14.7 psia, air = 1)	0.967	0.073	1.96	1.16	
Nitrogen (liquid, -321°F)	0.81	50.5	1,364	809	
Nitrous oxide (gas, 68°F, 14.7 psia, air = 1)	1.530	0.115	3.11	1.84	
Nylon, Type 11	1.04	64.9	1753.0	1040.0	
Nylon, Type 12	1.02	63.7	1719.3	1020.0	
Nylon, Type 6	1.13	70.5	1904.7	1130.0	
Nylon, Type 6/12	1.08	67.4	1820.4	1080.0	

Material	Specific Gravity	Weight lbs per cu foot	Weight lbs per cu yard	Weight kgs per cu meter	Angle of Repose
Nylon, Type 6/6	1.14	71.2	1921.5	1140.0	
Nylon, Type 6/9	1.09	68.0	1837.3	1090.0	
Oak, live, dry	0.95	59	1593	945.1	
Oak, red	0.71	44	1188	704.8	
Oats	0.43	27	729	432.5	32
Oats, rolled	0.30	19	513	304.4	30-45
Oil Cake	0.79	49	1323	784.9	
Oil, linseed	0.94	58.8	1587.6	941.9	
Oil, lubricating	0.91	56.8	1533.9	910.0	
Oil, petroleum	0.88	55	1485	881.0	
Oil, transformer	0.88	54.9	1483.3	880.0	
Oriented Strand Board (OSB)	0.57	35.5	959	568.7	
Oxygen (gas, 68°F, 14.7 psia, air = 1)	1.105	0.083	2.24	1.33	
Oxygen (liquid, -297°F, 14.7 psia)	1.14	71.2	1,923	1,141	
Oyster shells, ground	0.85	53	1431	849.0	30-45
PAI (Polyamide-imide)	1.42	88.6	2393.5	1420.0	
Paper, standard	1.20	75	2025	1201.4	
Paraffin	0.72	45	1215	720.8	
Particle Board	0.73	45.7	1234	732	
PAS (Polyarylsulfone)	1.33	83.0	2241.8	1330.0	
PBT (Polybutylene terephthalate)	1.34	83.7	2258.6	1340.0	
PC (Polycarbonate)	1.20	74.9	2022.7	1200.0	
PCTFE (Polychlorotri-fluoroethylene)	2.14	133.6	3607.1	2140.0	
PE-CTFE (Polyethylene-chlorotrifluoroethylene)	1.69	105.5	2848.6	1690.0	
PE-TFE (Polyethylene-polytetrafluoroethylene), modified	1.70	106.1	2865.4	1700.0	
Peanuts, not shelled	0.27	17	459	272.3	30-45
Peanuts, shelled	0.64	40	1080	640.7	30-45
Peat, dry	0.40	25	675	400.5	
Peat, moist	0.80	50	1350	800.9	
Peat, wet	1.12	70	1890	1121.3	
Pecan wood	0.75	47	1269	752.9	
PEEK (Polyetheretherketone)	1.31	81.8	2208.1	1310.0	
PEI (Polyetherimide)	1.27	79.3	2140.7	1270.0	
PES (Polyethersulfone)	1.42	88.3	2385.1	1415.0	
PET (Polyethylene terephthalate)	1.35	84.0	2267.1	1345.0	
PETG (Polyethylene terephthalate glycol)	1.25	78.0	2106.9	1250.0	
Petroleum ethyl	0.66	41.2	1112.5	660.0	
PFA (Perfluoroalkoxy resin)	2.15	133.9	3615.5	2145.0	
Phenolic casting resin	1.28	79.9	2157.5	1280.0	
Phosphate Rock, broken	1.76	110	2970	1762.0	
Phosphorus	2.34	146	3942	2338.7	

Material	Specific Gravity	Weight lbs per cu foot	Weight lbs per cu yard	Weight kgs per cu meter	Angle of Repose
PI (Polyimide)	1.40	87.1	2351.4	1395.0	
Pine, White, dry	0.42	26	702	416.5	
Pine, Yellow Northern, dry	0.54	34	918	544.6	
Pine, Yellow Southern, dry	0.72	45	1215	720.8	
Pitch	1.15	72	1935.9	1148.5	
Plaster	0.85	53	1431	849.0	
Platinum	21.51	1342	36234	21496.8	
Plywood	0.62	38.4	1036.8	615.1	
PMP (Polymethylpentene)	0.83	52.1	1405.8	834.0	
Polyallomer	0.90	56.0	1512.8	897.5	
Polyaryletherketone	1.30	81.2	2191.2	1300.0	
Polybutadiene	0.97	60.6	1635.0	970.0	
Polybutylene	0.92	57.3	1546.5	917.5	
Polyester, cast	1.25	78.0	2106.9	1250.0	
Polyolefin (High hardness)	0.94	58.7	1584.4	940.0	
Polyolefin (Low hardness)	0.93	58.1	1567.6	930.0	
Polysulfone	1.25	78.0	2106.9	1250.0	
Porcelain	2.40	150	4050	2402.8	
Porphyry, broken	1.65	103	2781	1649.9	
Porphyry, solid	2.55	159	4293	2546.9	
Potash	1.28	80	2160	1281.5	
Potassium chloride	2.00	125	3375	2002.3	30-45
Potatoes, white	0.77	48	1296	768.9	
PP (Polypropylene)	0.91	56.5	1525.4	905.0	
PPS (Polyphenylene sulfide)	1.35	84.3	2275.5	1350.0	
Prop alcohol	0.81	50.9	1373.4	814.8	
Propane (gas, 68°F, 14.7 psia, air = 1)	1.562	0.117	3.17	1.88	
Propane (liquid, -44°F, 14.7 psia)	0.58	36.3	980	581	
Propane (liquid, 70°F)	0.50	31.1	840	498	
Propylene or Propene (gas, 68°F, 14.7 psia, air = 1)	1.451	0.109	2.95	1.75	
PS (Polystyrene)	1.05	65.5	1769.8	1050.0	
Pulverized Asphalt Concrete (PAC, @ 5.5% moisture)	2.46	154	4146	2460	
Pumice stone	0.64	40	1080	640.7	
PVC (Polyvinyl chloride)	1.30	81.2	2191.2	1300.0	
PVDC (Polyvinylidene chloride)	1.69	105.2	2840.2	1685.0	
PVDF (Polyvinylidene fluoride)	1.78	110.8	2991.9	1775.0	
Quartz sand	1.20	75	2025	1201.4	
Quartz, lump	1.55	97	2619	1553.8	
Quartz, solid	2.64	165	4455	2643.1	
Raps oil	0.91	56.8	1533.9	910.0	
Reclaimed Asphalt Pavement (RAP)	2.08	130	3510	2082	
Reclaimed Concrete Material (RCM)	2.07	129	3483	2066	

Material	Specific Gravity	Weight lbs per cu foot	Weight lbs per cu yard	Weight kgs per cu meter	Angle of Repose
Redwood, Calif, dry	0.45	28	756	448.5	
Resin, synthetic, crshd	0.56	35	945	560.6	
Rice grits	0.69	43	1161	688.8	30-45
Rice, hulled	0.75	47	1269	752.9	
Rice, rough	0.58	36	972	576.7	30-45
Rip-rap	1.60	100	2700	1601.8	
Rosin	1.07	67	1809	1073.2	
Rubber, caoutchouc	0.95	59	1593	945.1	
Rubber, ground scrap	0.48	30	810	480.6	45
Rubber, mfged	1.52	95	2565	1521.8	
Rye	0.71	44	1188	704.8	
Salt cake	1.44	90	2430	1441.7	30-45
Salt, coarse	0.80	50	1350	800.9	30-45
Salt, fine	1.20	75	2025	1201.4	30-45
Saltpeter	1.20	75	2025	1201.4	30-45
SAN (Styrene acrylonitrile)	1.07	66.8	1803.5	1070.0	
Sand and Gravel, dry	1.73	108	2916	1730.0	
Sand and Gravel, wet	2.00	125	3375	2002.3	
Sand, damp	1.92	120	3240	1922.2	
Sand, dry	1.60	100	2700	1601.8	34
Sand, loose	1.44	90	2430	1441.7	30-45
Sand, rammed	1.68	105	2835	1681.9	
Sand, water filled	1.92	120	3240	1922.2	15-30
Sand, wet	1.92	120	3240	1922.2	45
Sand, wet (2nd source)	2.08	130	3510	2082.4	
Sand, wet packed	2.08	130	3510	2082.4	
Sandstone, broken	1.51	94	2538	1505.7	
Sandstone, solid	2.32	145	3915	2322.7	
Sawdust	0.27	17	459	272.3	
Sewage, sludge	0.72	45	1215	720.8	
Shale, broken	1.59	99	2673	1585.8	30-45
Shale, solid	2.68	167	4509	2675.1	
Silicone epoxy	1.52	94.9	2562.0	1520.0	
Silver	10.46	653	17631	10461.1	
Slag, broken	1.76	110	2970	1762.0	
Slag, crushed 1/4 inch	1.19	74	1998	1185.4	
Slag, furn. granulated	0.96	60	1620	961.1	
Slag, solid	2.12	132	3564	2114.4	
Slate, broken	1.67	104	2808	1665.9	
Slate, pulverized	1.36	85	2295	1361.6	30-45
Slate, solid	2.69	168	4536	2691.1	
Snow, compacted	0.48	30	810	480.6	
Snow, freshly fallen	0.16	10	270	160.2	
Soap, chips	0.16	10	270	160.2	30-45
Soap, flakes	0.16	10	270	160.2	30-45
Soap, powder	0.37	23	621	368.4	30-45
Soap, solid	0.80	50	1350	800.9	
Soda Ash, heavy	0.96	60	1620	961.1	30-45
Soda Ash, light	0.43	27	729	432.5	30-45
Sodium	0.98	61	1647	977.1	
Sodium Aluminate ground	1.15	72	1944	1153.3	
Sodium Nitrate, grnd	1.20	75	2025	1201.4	

Weights of Materials

Material	Specific Gravity	Weight lbs per cu foot	Weight lbs per cu yard	Weight kgs per cu meter	Angle of Repose
Soybeans, whole	0.75	47	1269	752.9	
Spruce, Calif, dry	0.45	28	756	448.5	
Starch, powdered	0.56	35	945	560.6	
Steel, cast	7.85	490	13230	7849.1	
Steel, rolled	7.93	495	13365	7929.2	
Stone, crushed	1.60	100	2700	1601.8	
Sugar, brown	0.72	45	1215	720.8	
Sugar, granulated	0.85	53	1431	849.0	30-45
Sugar, powdered	0.80	50	1350	800.9	
Sugar, raw cane	0.96	60	1620	961.1	45
Sugarbeet pulp, dry	0.21	13	351	208.2	
Sugarbeet pulp, wet	0.56	35	945	560.6	
Sugarcane	0.27	17	459	272.3	45
Sulfur, lump	1.31	82	2214	1313.5	30-45
Sulfur, pulverized	0.96	60	1620	961.1	30-45
Sulfur, solid	2.00	125	3375	2002.3	
Sulphur dioxide (gas, 68°F, 14.7 psia)	2.264	0.170	4.60		
2.73Sulfuric acid, 87%	1.79	112	3024	1794.1	
Sycamore, dry	0.59	37	999	592.7	
Taconite	2.80	175	4725	2803.2	
Talc, broken	1.75	109	2943	1746.0	
Talc, solid	2.69	168	4536	2691.1	
Tanbark, ground	0.88	55	1485	881.0	
Tankage	0.96	60	1620	961.1	
Tar	1.15	72	1935.9	1148.5	
Tin, cast	7.36	459	12393	7352.5	
Tobacco	0.32	20	540	320.4	45
Toluene	0.87	54.3	1466.4	870.0	
Trap rock, broken	1.75	109	2943	1746.0	
Trap rock, solid	2.88	180	4860	2883.3	
Trichloroethylene	1.47	91.8	2477.8	1470.0	
Tungsten	19.62	1224	33048	19606.6	
Turf	0.40	25	675	400.5	
Turpentine	0.87	54	1458	865.0	
Vanadium	5.50	343	9261	5494.3	
Walnut, black, dry	0.61	38	1026	608.7	
Water, pure	1.00	62.4	1684.8	999.6	
Water, sea	1.03	64.08	1730.16	1026.5	
Wheat	0.77	48	1296	768.9	28
Wheat, cracked	0.67	42	1134	672.8	30-45
Willow wood	0.42	26	702	416.5	
Wool	1.31	82	2214	1313.5	
Zinc oxide	0.40	25	675	400.5	45
Zinc, cast	7.05	440	11880	7048.1	

Note on powders & granular materials: The specific gravity shown for powders and granular materials is NOT the absolute specific gravity of the mineral particles but the apparent specific gravity of the powder derived from the bulk density. For example, hydrated limes absolute specific gravity is between 2.2 and 2.6, however, the spcific gravity of powdered lime is between 0.50 and 0.64.

Welding

Arc Electrodes - Mild Steel

Electrode #	Description
⇓	This digit indicates the following:
Exx1z	All positions of welding
Exx2z	Flat and horizontal positions
Exx3z	Flat welding positions only

⇓⇓	These digits indicate the following:
Exx10	DC, reverse polarity
Exx11	AC or DC, reverse polarity
Exx12	DC, straight polarity or AC
Exx13	AC or DC, straight polarity
Exx14	DC, either polarity or AC, iron powder
Exx15	DC, reverse polarity, low hydrogen
Exx16	AC or DC, reverse polarity, low hydrogen
Exx18	AC or DC, reverse, iron powder, low hydrogen
Exx20	DC, straight polarity, or AC for horizontal fillet welds; and DC either polarity, or AC, for flat position welding
Exx24	DC, either polarity, or AC, iron powder
Exx27	DC, straight polarity, or AC for horizontal fillet welding; and DC, either polarity, or AC, for flat position welding, iron powder
Exx28	AC or DC, reverse polarity, iron powder, low hydrogen

The "xx" shown above is a two digit number indicating the weld metal tensile strength in 1000psi increments. For example, E**7018** is 70,000 psi weld metal.

Electrode Amperages

Type	Amperage Per Rod Diameter (inches)				
	1/16	5/64	3/32	1/8	5/32
E6010			60-90	80-120	110-160
E6011			50-90	80-130	120-180
E6012			40-90	80-120	120-190
E6013	20-40	25-60	30-80	80-120	120-190
E7010-A1			30-80	70-120	100-160
E7014			80-110	110-150	140-190
E7016			75-105	100-150	140-190
E7018 (& -A1)			70-120	100-150	120-200
E7020-A1					
E7024			90-120	120-150	180-230
E7028					175-250
E8016-B2			60-100	80-120	140-190
E8018-C3			70-120	100-150	120-200
Stainless:					
3xx AC-DC	20-40	30-60	60-90	90-120	120-160
4xx AC-DC	20-40	30-60	60-90	90-120	120-160
5xx AC-DC	20-40	30-60	60-90	90-120	120-160

Electrode Amperages (cont.)

Type	Amperage Per Rod Diameter (inches)				
	3/16	7/32	1/4	5/16	3/8
E6010	150-200	175-250	225-300		
E6011	140-220	170-250	225-325		
E6012	140-240	180-315	225-350		
E6013	140-240	225-300	250-350		
E6020	175-250	225-325	250-350	325-450	450-600
E6027	225-300	275-375	350-450		
E7010-A1	130-200				
E7014	180-260	250-325	300-400	400-500	
E7016	190-250	250-300	300-375		
E7018	200-275	275-350			
E7020-A1	225-350				
E7024	250-300	300-350	350-400	400-500	
E7028	175-250	250-325	300-400		
E8016-B2	180-250	300-425			
E8018-C3	200-275				
Stainless:					
3xx AC-DC	150-190	225-300			
4xx AC-DC	150-190				
5xx AC-DC	150-190		225-300		

Note: All of the above ratings are estimates and you should always verify amperages with the manufacturer before you start a job.

Electrodes - Low Alloy Steel

Low Alloy Steel Specifications (American Welding Society Specification A 5.5-69) are coded the same as the Mild Steel Specification of two pages ago, except that the specification number is followed by a dash and then a letter-number code indicating the chemical composition of the weld metal.   For example, **E8016–C1**

The composition codes are as follows:

–A .... Carbon-molybdenum steel
–B .... Chromium-molybdenum steel
–C .... Nickel steel
–D .... Manganese-molybdenum steel
–G .... All other Low Alloy Steel Electrodes, with minimums of
        0.2% molybdenum, 0.3%chromium, 1% manganese,
        0.8% silicon, 0.5% nickel, and 0.1% vanadium.
–M .... Military specification

The final digit of the composition code specifies the exact composition of the weld metal.

Electrodes - Stainless Steel

Stainless electrode specifications (AWS A5.4-62T) are coded with the American Iron and Steel Institute alloy type number followed by a dash and two digit number (either 15 or 16) indicating usability or a set of letters (AC, DC, AC–DC or ELC AC–DC) indicating the type of current to be used. For example, **E308–15** or **308 ELC AC–DC**

Electrode Brand Conversion

Make	E6010	E6011	E6012
Airco	6010	6011,C,LOC	6012,C
Air Products	6010IP	6011,C	6012GP,SF,IP
Arc Products	SW610,AP100	SW14,IMP	SW612,PFA
Gen. Dynamics	610,IP	611,A	612,A
Hobart Bros.	10,IP	335A	12,212A,12A
Lincoln (Fleetweld)	5,5P	35,180,35LS	7
McKay Co	6010,IP	6011,IP	6012
Murex Weld Prod	Speedex 610	Type A,611C	Type N13
Reid Avery (Raco)	6010	6011,IP	6012,IP
Westinghouse	XL610,A	ACP611	FP612,2-612

Make	E6013	E6020	E6027
Airco	6013,C	6020	Easyarc 6027
Air Products	6013GP,SF	6020	6027IP
Arc Products	SW16		DH27
Gen. Dynamics	613,A	620	IP627
Hobart Bros.	13A,447A,413	27	
Lincoln (Fleetweld)	37,57		Jetweld 2
McKay Co	6013	6020	
Murex Weld Prod	Type U,U13	Type D,FHP	Speedex 27
Reid Avery Co	6013		ZIP 27
Westinghouse	SW613,2M-613	DH620	ZIP 27

Make	E7014	E7016	E7018
Airco	Easyarc 7014	7016,M	7018MR,C
Air Products	7014IP	7016,A	7018,IP
Arc Products	SW15IP	70LA-2	170LA,SW47
Gen. Dynamics	IP714	716,A	IP718,A
Hobart Bros.	14A	16	LH718
Lincoln (Fleetweld)	47		Jetweld-LH70
McKay Co	7014	Puralloy 70AC	7018
Murex Weld Prod	Speedex U	Type HTS,18,180	
HTS,M,718			
Reid Avery Co	7014	7016	7018
Westinghouse	ZIP 14	LOH-2-716	WIZ-18

Make	E7024	E7028
Airco	Easyarc 7024	Easyarc 7028
Air Products	7024IP	7028
Arc Products	SW44	DH170
Gen. Dynamics	IP724	IP728
Hobart Bros.	24	
Lincoln	Jetweld 3,1	Jetweld HL3800
McKay Co	7024	
Murex Weld Prod	Speedex 24	Speedex 28
Reid Avery Co		
Westinghouse	ZIP 24	WIZ 28

Gas Welding Rods

Rod Diameter	Rods per Pound (36 inch long)			
	Steel	Brass	Aluminum	Cast Iron
1/16	31	29	91	NA
3/32	14	13	41	NA
1/8	8	7	23	NA
5/32	5	NA	NA	NA
3/16	3-1/2	3	9	5-1/2
1/4	2	2	6	2-1/4
5/16	1-1/3	NA	NA	1/2
3/8	1	1	NA	1/4

Welding Gases

Gas	Tank Sizes Cubic Ft	Comments
Acetylene	300 100 75 40 10	Formula – C_2H_2, explosive Colorless, flammable gas, garlic–like odor, explosion danger if used in welding with gage pressures over 15 psig (30 psig absolute).
Oxygen	244, 122, 80, 40, 20 4500 liquid	Formula – O_2, non-explosive Colorless, odorless, tasteless. Supports combustion in welding.
Nitrogen	225, 113 80, 40, 20	Formula – N_2, non-explosive Colorless, odorless, tasteless, inert.
Argon	330, 131 4754 liquid	Formula – Ar, non-explosive Colorless, odorless, tasteless, inert.
Carbon Dioxide	50 lbs 20 lbs	Formula – CO_2, non-explosive Toxic in large quantities Colorless, odorless, tasteless, inert.
Hydrogen	191	Formula – H_2, explosive Colorless, odorless, tasteless Lightest gas known.
Helium	221	Formula – He, non-explosive Colorless, odorless, tasteless, inert.

Hard & Soft Solder Alloys

Metal to be Soldered	Alloy Component Percentage				
	Tin	Lead	Zinc	Copper	Other
SOFT SOLDER:					
Aluminum	70	..	25	...	Al=3,Pho=2
Bismuth	33	33	..	...	Bi=34
Block tin	99	1	..	...	
Brass	66	34	..	...	
Copper	60	40	..	...	
Gold	67	33	..	...	
Gun metal	63	37	..	...	
Iron & Steel	50	50	..	...	
Lead	33	67	..	...	
Pewter	25	25	..	...	Bi=50
Silver	67	33	..	...	
Steel, galvanized	58	42	..	...	
Steel, tinned	64	36	..	...	
Zinc	55	45	..	...	
HARD SOLDER:					
Brass, soft	..	..	78	22	
Brass, hard	..	..	55	45	
Copper	..	..	50	50	
Iron, cast	..	..	45	55	
Iron & Steel	..	..	36	64	
Gold	..	..	..	22	Ag=11,
				...	Au=67
Silver	..	..	10	20	Ag=70

FLUX	Use on this Metal
Ammonia Chloride	Galvanized iron, iron, nickel, tin, zinc, brass, copper, gun metal
Borax	For hard solders, brass, copper, gold, iron & steel, silver
Cuprous oxide	Cast iron
Hydrochloric Acid	Galvanized iron and steel, tin, zinc
Organic	Lead, pewter
Rosin	Brass, bronze, cadmium, copper, lead, silver, gun metal, tinned steel
Stainless Steel Flux	Special for stainless steel only
Sterling	Silver
Tallow	Lead, pewter
Zinc Chloride	Bismuth, tin, brass, copper, gold, silver, gun metal, tinned steel

Tempering Color for Steel

Heated Color of Carbon Steel	Temperature °F	Temper Item or Comment
Faint yellow	420	Knives, hammers
Very pale yellow	430	Reamers
Light yellow	440	Lathe tools, scrapers, milling cutters, reamers
Pale straw–yellow	450	Twist drills for hard use
Straw–yellow	460	Dies, punches, bits, reamers
Deep straw–yellow	470	
Dark yellow	480	Twist drills, large taps
	485	Knurls
Yellow–brown	490	
Brown–yellow	500	Axes, wood chisels, drifts, taps 1/2 inch or over, nut taps, thread dies
Spotted red–brown	510	
Brown–purple	520	Taps 1/4 inch and under
Light purple	530	
Full purple	540	Cold chisels, center punches
Dark purple	550	
Full blue	560	Screwdrivers, springs, gears
Dark blue	570	
Medium blue	600	Scrapers, spokeshaves
Light blue	640	
Red-visible at night	750	
Red-visible at twilight	885	
Red-visible in daylight	975	
Red-visible in sunlight	1075	
Dark red	1290	
Dull cherry red	1475	
Cherry red	1650	
Bright cherry red	1830	
Orange–red	2010	
Orange–yellow	2190	
Yellow–white	2370	
White	2550	
Brilliant white	2730	
Blue–white	2900	
Acetylene flame	4080	
Induction furnace	5450	
Electric arc light	7200	

Tempering is commonly a two step process. Step 1: To harden the tool, heat the tool end to a bright red, quench tool end in cold water until it is cool to the touch, then sharpen or polish tool end. At this point the tool has been hardened but it is now brittle. Step 2: To temper the tool, heat the tool to the temperature indicated by its color in the above table, then quench it in water. The amount of temper is a function of what type of work the tool will be doing, so if your tool is not listed above, simply select one of the above tools that does similar work.

Structure of a Welding Symbol

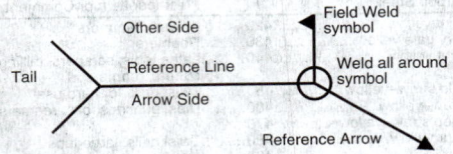

Main Elements:

The **Reference Arrow** connects the reference line to a joint that is to be welded.

The **Reference line** is the core of the weld symbol. The area below it contains information about the weld to be made on the arrow side of the joint. Information above the reference line describes the weld to be made on the ide opposite the arrow.

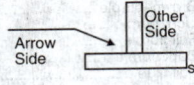

Optional Elements:

The **Field Weld** symbol is included only if the weld is to be done in the field. If no symbol is present, the weld is to be done in the shop.

The **open circle** at the junction of the reference line and arrow is present if the weld is to be made all the way around the joint.

When the Reference Line has a **tail**, it usually contains special instructions.

Joint Types

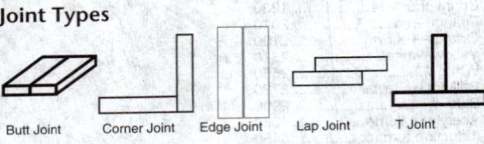

Butt Joint   Corner Joint   Edge Joint   Lap Joint   T Joint

Weld Types

The four main types of welds are

- Fillet welds
- Groove welds
- Plug or slot welds
- Flange welds

Groove Welds
Bevel Groove

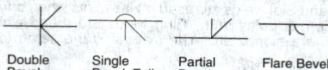

Double
Bevel

Single
Bevel, Full

Partial
Bevel

Flare Bevel

May be used on all 5 joint types.

Square Groove

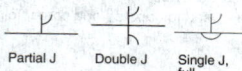

Partial
square

Double
square

May be used on butt, tee, edge and corner joints

J-Groove

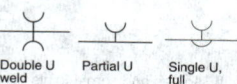

Partial J

Double J

Single J,
full

May be used on all 5 joint types

U-Groove

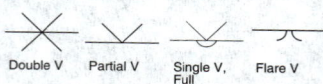

Double U
weld

Partial U

Single U,
full

Used with butt, edge and corner joints

V-Groove

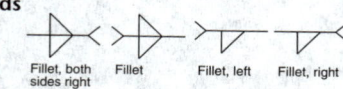

Double V

Partial V

Single V,
Full

Flare V

Used on butt, edge and corner welds

Fillet Welds
Fillet

Fillet, both
sides right

Fillet

Fillet, left

Fillet, right

Fillet welds may be used on lap, tee and corner joints.

Plug and Slot Welds

Plug and Slot welds are used on lap joints when one of the pieces has holes in it. Plug welds are round while slot welds are elongated. The symbol is the same for both types.

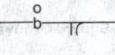

Plug or slot weld

Flange Welds

Flange Welds are used for joining two rounded bjects, such as pipes. Edge Flange welds may e used for butt or edge joints; Corner Flange welds are used for Edge or corner joints.

Edge Flange   Corner Flange

Other types of Welds

Spot or Projection - Used for lap, tee and corner joints

Spot or projection weld

Seam - used for lap, tee, edge and corner joints

Seam Weld

Braze- used for butt, lap, tee and corner joints -

BRAZE

Braze

Conversion Tables

The tables that follow contain some of the most commonly used conversion factors. If you can not locate the conversion you need (such as "Feet" to "Inches"), try looking up the reverse conversion ("Inches" to "Feet") and if it exists, divide that number into 1 to get your conversion. In order to save space, only one direction of conversion is listed in some cases. Additional sources include *Handbook of Chemistry and Physics* and *C.R.C Standard Math Tables* by The Chemical Rubber Publishing Co, *Scientific Tables* by Ciba-Geigy Ltd, *Websters Desk Encyclopedia* by Grisewood & Dempsey, *Field Geologists Manual* by The Australian Institute of Mining & Metallurgy, *Conversion Factors* by Forney's Inc, *Conversions* by Cahn Instruments, and *Technical Reference Handbook* by E.P Rasis. See page 320 for temperature conversions.

ABBREVIATIONS USED IN CONVERSION TABLES

abs ......absolute	g...........gram
apoth ....apothecary	H₂O......water
atm ......atmosphere	Hg ....Mercury
avdp ....avoirdupois	hr ....hour
Avogad.Avogadro's Number	in ....inch
Brit........British	Int ....International
Btu........British thermal unit	IST ....Int Steam Table
Cal........calorie	kg ....kilogram
cgs ....centime-	km ....kilometer
ter-gram-second	kw ....kilowatt
chem ....chemical	lb ....pound
chg ......charge	lbf ....pound-force
circ ....circular	liq ....liquid
cm ....centimeter	ln ....logarithm (natural)
cp ....candle power	log ....logarithm (common)
cu ....cubic	mech .....mechanical
db ....decibel	min ....minute
dm ....decimeter	Mks ......me-
°C ....Degrees Celsius	ter-kilogram-second
°F ....Degrees Fahrenheit	mm ....millimeter
K ....Kelvin	Naut ......nautical
°R ....Degrees Rankine	oz ....ounce
elec ......electrical	petro......petroleum
equiv ....equivalent	sec ....second
flu ....fluid	spher .....spherical
ft ....feet	sq ....square
gal ....gallon	US ....United States

Conversion Tables   677

Convert From	Into	Multiply By
Abamperes	Amperes	10
	Faradays/sec (chem)	1.03638×10^{-4}
	Statamperes	2.99793×10^{10}
Abcoulombs	Ampere–hours	0.00278
	Coulombs	10
	Electronic charges	6.24196×10^{19}
	Faradays (chem)	1.03638×10^{-4}
	Statcoulombs	2.99793×10^{10}
Abfarads	Farads	1×10^{9}
	Microfarads	1×10^{15}
	Statfarads	8.98758×10^{20}
Abhenries	Henries	1×10^{-9}
Abmhos	Megamhos	1000
	Mhos	1×10^{9}
	Statmhos	8.98758×10^{20}
Abohms	Megohms	1×10^{-15}
	Microhms	0.001
	Ohms	1×10^{-9}
Abohm–cm	Ohm–cm	1×10^{-9}
Abvolts	Microvolts	0.01
	Millivolts	1×10^{-5}
	Volts	1×10^{-8}
Abvolts/cm	Volts/cm	1×10^{-8}
	Volts/inch	2.54×10^{-8}
Acres	Hectare or sq hectometer	0.404687
	Sq chains (Gunters)	10
	Sq cm	4.04686×10^{7}
	Sq feet	43560
	Sq feet (US Survey)	43559.826
	Sq inches	6.27264×10^{6}
	Sq kilometers	4.04686×10^{-3}
	Sq links (Gunter)	1×10^{5}
	Sq meters	4046.856421
	Sq miles (statute)	1.5625×10^{-3}
	Sq perches	160
	Sq rods	160
	Sq yards	4840
Acre–feet	Cu feet	43560
	Cu meters	1233.482
	Cu yards	1613.33
	Gallons (US)	3.259×10^{5}
Acre–inches	Cu feet	3630
	Cu meters	102.7901531
	Cu yards	134.44
	Gallons (US)	27154.286
Almude (Portugal)	Liters	16.7
Almude (Spain)	Liters	4.625
Amma (Ancient Greece)	Orguias	10
	Stadion	0.1
Amma (Ancient Rome)	Digiti	4
Amperes	Abamperes	0.1
	Amperes (Int)	1.00016
	Coulombs/sec	1
	Faradays/sec (Chem)	1.03638×10^{-5}
Amperes	Microamperes	1×10^{6}
	Milliamperes	1000
	Statamperes	2.99793×10^{9}
Amperes (Int)	Amperes	0.99984

Convert From	Into	Multiply By
Ampere–hours	Abcoulombs	360
	Coulombs	3600
	Faradays (Chem)	0.03731
Amperes/meter	Amps/inch	0.0254
	Oersteds	0.012566
	Newton/weber	1.0
Amperes/sq cm	Amps/sq inch	6.452
	Amps/sq meter	10^4
Amperes/sq inch	Amps/sq cm	0.1550
	Amps/sq meter	1550.0
Amperes/sq meter	Amps/sq cm	10^{-4}
	Amps/sq inch	6.452×10^{-4}
Ampere–turns	Gilberts	1.25664
Ångstrom	Centimeters	1×10^{-8}
	Inches	3.9370×10^{-9}
	Meters	1×10^{-10}
	Micrometers	1×10^{-4}
	Microns	0.0001
	Millimicrons	0.1
Anker (Latvia)	Liters	38.256
Anoman (Ceylon)	Bushels, US	5.83
Archin (Turkey)	Meters	1
Ares	Acres	0.024711
	Sq dekameters	1
	Sq feet	1076.39
	Sq meters	100
	Sq miles	3.86102×10^{-5}
	Sq yards	119.60
Arpent (French)	Acre	=0.85
	Meter	=58.6
Arroba (Spain)	Liters of wine	16.14
Artaba (Iran)	Liters	66
Astronomical Unit	Kilometers	1.496×10^8
Atmospheres	Bars	1.01325
	Cm of Hg @ 0°C	76
	Cm of H_2O @ 4°C	1033.29
	Dynes/sq cm	1.01325×10^6
	Ft of H_2O @ 39.2°F	33.8995
	Grams–force/sq cm	1033.23
	In of Hg @ 32°F	29.9213
	Kg–force/sq cm	1.0332
	Kg–force/sq meter	10332
	Kilopascals	101.325
	Mm of Hg @ 0°C	760
	Newtons/sq meter	1.01325×10^5
	Pascals	101325
	Pounds–force/sq inch	14.6960
	Tons–force(short)/sq inch	0.00735
	Tons-force(short)/sq foot	1.05811
	Torrs	760
Baht (Thailand)	Grams	15
Barile (Rome)	Liters	58.34
Barns	Sq cm	1×10^{-24}
Barrels (Brit)	Bags (Brit)	1.5
	Barrels (US dry)	1.41541
	Barrels (US liq)	1.37251
	Bushels (Brit)	4.5
	Bushels (US)	4.64426

Convert From	Into	Multiply By
	Cu feet	5.77957
	Cu meters	0.16366
	Gallons (Brit)	36
	Liters	163.6592
Barrels (US oil)	Cu feet	5.61458
	Gallons (US)	42
	Liters	158.9873
Barrels (US dry)	Barrels (US liq)	0.969696
	Bushels (US)	3.28122
	Cu feet	4.08333
	Cu inches	7056
	Cu meters	0.11563
	Quarts (US dry)	105
Barrels (US liq)	Barrels (US dry)	1.03125
	Barrels (wine)	1
	Cu feet	4.2109
	Cu inches	7276.5
	Cu meters	0.11924
	Gallons (Brit)	26.22924
	Gallons (US liq)	31.5
	Liters	119.240
Bars	Atmospheres	0.98692
	Baryes	1×10^6
	Cm of Hg @ 0°C	75.0062
	Dynes/sq cm	1×10^6
	Ft of H$_2$O @ 60°F	33.4883
	Grams–force/sq cm	1019.72
	In of Hg @ 32°F	29.530
	Kg–force/sq cm	1.01972
	Millibars	1000
	Newtons/sq meter	1×10^5
	Pascals	1×10^5
	Pounds–force/sq foot	2088.54
	Pounds–force/sq inch	14.5038
Barye	Dynes/sq cm	1.0
	Newtons/sq meter	0.10
	Pascals	0.10
Baryl	Atmospheres	9.8692×10^{-7}
	Bars	1×10^{-6}
	Dynes/sq cm	1
	Grams–force/sq cm	0.00102
	Millibars	0.001
Bath (Old Testament)	Liters	22
Becquerels	Curie	2.7027×10^{-11}
	Disintegrations/sec	1.0
Bekahs (Old Testament)	Grams	5.67
	Shekel (Old Testament)	0.5
Bels	Decibels	10
Biot	Amperes	10
Bit	Byte (computers)	1/8
Board feet	Cu cm	2359.74
	Cu feet	0.08333
	Cu inches	144
Bolts of cloth	Ells	32
	Linear feet	120
	Meters	36.576
Bougie decimales	Candles (Int)	1.0
Btu	Btu (Int Steam Tab)	0.999331

Convert From	Into	Multiply By
	Btu (mean)	0.998560
	Btu @ 60°F	0.999687
	Cal, g	251.996
	Cal, g (Int Steam Tab)	251.827
	Cal, g (mean)	251.634
	Cal, g @ 20°C	252.122
	Ergs	1.0544 x 10^{10}
	Foot–poundals	25020.1
	Foot pound–force	777.649
	Gram–force cm	1.0751 x 10^7
	Hp–hours	0.000393
	Joules	1054.35
	Joules (Int)	1054.18
	Kg–calories	0.2520
	Kg–force meters	107.514
	Kw–hours	0.000292875
	Kw–hours (Int)	0.00029283
	Liter–atm	10.4056
	Therm	0.00001
	Watt–seconds	1054.35
	Watt–seconds (Int)	1054.18
Btu (IST)	Btu	1.00067
Btu (Mean)	Btu	1.00144
Btu @ 60°F	Btu	1.00031
Btu/hr	Calorie–kg/hr	0.252
	Ergs/sec	2.92875 x 10^6
	Foot pound–force/hr	777.649
	Gram–cal/sec	0.07
	Horsepower	0.000393
	Kilowatts	0.00029
	Watts	0.29287
Btu/min	Foot pound–force/sec	12.97
	Horsepower	0.02358
	Kilowatts	0.01758
	Watts	17.576
Btu/lb	Cal, g/gram	0.55555
	Foot pound–force/lb	777.649
	Joules/gram	2.326
Btu/sq ft/min	Watts/sq inch	0.1221
Buckets (Brit)	Cu cm	18184.35
	Gallons (Brit)	4
Bushels (Brit)	Bags (Brit)	0.3333
Bushels (Brit)	Bushels (US)	1.03206
	Cu cm	36368.7
	Cu feet	1.28435
	Cu inches	2219.36
	Gallons (Brit)	8
	Liters	36.3687
Bushels (US)	Barrels (US dry)	0.30476
	Bushels (Brit)	0.96894
	Cu cm	35239.07
	Cu feet	1.24446
	Cu inches	2150.42
	Cu meters	0.03524
	Cu yards	0.04609
	Gallons (US dry)	8
	Gallons (US liq)	9.30918
	Liters	35.23907

Convert From	Into	Multiply By
	Ounces (US fluid)	1191.57
	Pecks (US)	4
	Pints (US dry)	64
	Quarts (US dry)	32
	Quarts (US liq)	37.23671
Butts (US liq)	Bushels (US)	13.54574
	Cu feet	16.85708
	Cu meters	0.47734
	Gallons (US)	126
Byte	Bit (computers)	8
Cable (English)	Degrees latitude	1/600th
	Meter	185.37
Cable lengths(US Surv)	Fathoms (US Survey)	120
	Feet (US Survey)	720
	Meters	219.456
Calories, g	Btu	0.003971
	Btu (IST)	0.003968
	Btu (mean)	0.003965
	Btu @ 60°F	0.00397
	Cal, g (IST)	0.99933
	Cal, g (mean)	0.99856
	Cal, g @ 20°C	1.00050
	Cu cm–atm	41.2929
	Cu ft–atm	0.00146
	Ergs	4.184×10^7
	Foot–poundals	99.2878
	Foot pound–force	3.08596
	Gram–force cm	42664.9
	Hp–hours	1.558×10^{-6}
	Joules	4.184
	Joules (Int)	4.1833
	Kg–force meter	0.42665
	Kw–hours	1.162×10^{-6}
	Liter–atm	0.04129
	Watt–hours	0.00116
	Watt–hours (Int)	0.001162
	Watt–seconds	4.184
Cal, g (mean)	Btu	0.00397
Cal, g (mean)	Cal, g	1.00144
Cal, g @ 20°C	Btu	0.00397
	Cal, g	0.99949
Calories, kg	Btu	3.96832
	Btu (IST)	3.96567
	Btu (mean)	3.96261
	Btu @ 60°F	3.96708
	Cal, g	1000
	Cal, kg (mean)	0.99856
	Cal, kg @ 20°C	1.0005
	Cu cm–atm	41292.9
	Ergs	4.184×10^{10}
	Foot–poundals	99288
	Foot pound–force	3085.96
	Gram–force cm	4.266×10^7
	Hp–hours	0.00156
	Joules	4184
	Kw–hours	0.00116
	Liter–atm	41.292
	Watt–hours	1.1622

Convert From	Into	Multiply By
Cal, kg (mean)	Btu	3.974
	Cal, g	1001.4
Cal, g/gram	Btu/lb	1.8
	Foot pound–force/lb	1400.7
	Joules/gram	4.1868
Cal, g/hr	Btu/hr	0.00397
	Ergs/sec	11630
	Watts	0.001163
Cal, kg/hr	Watts	1.1630
Cal, g/min	Btu/min	0.00397
	Ergs/sec	697333
	Watts	0.0697
Cal, kg/min	Watts	69.767
Cal, g/sec	Btu/sec	0.00397
	Foot pound–force/sec	3.0875
	Horsepower	0.0056
	Watts	4.186
Cal, g–sec	Planck's constant	6.315×10^{33}
Candelas	Hefner units	1.11
	Lumen/steradian	1.00
Candelas/sq cm	Candelas/sq inch	6.4516
	Lamberts	3.1416
Candelas/sq ft	Candelas/sq inch	6.944×10^{-3}
	Candelas/sq meter	10.7639
	Lamberts	3.3816×10^{-3}
Candelas/sq meter	Candelas/sq foot	0.09290304
	Lamberts	3.1416×10^{-4}
Candles (Engl)	Candles (Int)	1.042
Candles (Germ)	Candles (Int)	1.053
Candles (Int)	Candles (Engl)	0.96
	Candles (Germ)	0.95
	Candles (pentane)	1.00
	Carcel units	0.104
	Hefner units	1.11
Candles (Int)	Lumens/steradian	1
Candles/sq cm	Candles/sq in	6.452
	Candles/sq meter	10000
	Foot–lamberts	2918.6
	Lamberts	3.1416
Candles/sq in	Candles/sq cm	0.155
	Candles/sq ft	144
	Foot–lamberts	452.39
	Lamberts	0.4869
Candle power	Lumens	12.566
Cape foot (S. Africa)	Meter	0.315
Cape rood (S. Africa)	Meter	3.788
Carats (gold)	Milligrams/gram	41.666
Carats (metric)	Grains	3.0865
	Grams	0.2
	Milligrams	200
Carcel units	Candles (Int)	9.61
Centals	Kilograms	45.359
	Pounds	100
Centares	Ares	0.01
	Sq feet	10.764
	Sq inches	1550
	Sq meters	1
	Sq yards	1.19599

Convert From	Into	Multiply By
Centigrams	Grains	0.15432
	Grams	0.01
Centiliters	Cu cm	10.0
	Cu inches	0.610254
	Drams	2.705
	Liters	0.01
	Ounces (US fluid)	0.33814
Centimeters	Angstrom	1×10^8
	Feet	0.03281
	Hands	0.0984
	Inches	0.3937
	Kilometers	1×10^{-5}
	Links (Gunter's)	0.0497
	Links (Ramden's)	0.0328
	Meters	0.01
	Micrometers	1×10^4
	Microns	10000
	Miles (Naut)	5.3996×10^{-6}
	Miles (statute)	6.2137×10^{-6}
	Millimeters	10
	Millimicrons	1×10^7
	Mils	393.7
	Picas (printers)	2.371
	Points (printers)	28.4528
	Rods	0.00199
	Yards	0.01094
Cm–dynes	Cm gram–force	1.02×10^{-3}
	Foot pound–force	7.376×10^{-8}
	Meter kg–force	1.02×10^{-8}
Cm gram–force	Cm–dynes	980.7
Cm gram–force	Foot pound–force	7.23×10^{-5}
	Meter kg–force	1×10^{-5}
Cm of Hg 0°C	Atmospheres	0.01316
	Bars	0.01333
	Dynes/sq cm	13332
	Ft of H_2O @ 4°C	0.446
	In Hg @ 0°C	0.3937
	Kg–force/sq meter	135.95
	Newtons/sq meter	1.333×10^3
	Pascals	1.333×10^3
	Pound–force/sq ft	27.845
	Pound–force/sq in	0.1934
	Torrs	10
Cm of H_2O 4°C	Atmospheres	0.00097
	Newtons/sq meter	98.0606
	Pascals	98.0606
	Pound–force/sq in	0.014223
Cm/sec	Feet/min	1.9685
	Feet/sec	0.0328
	Km/hr	0.036
	Km/min	0.0006
	Knots (Int)	0.0194
	Meters/min	0.6
	Miles/hr	0.02237
	Miles/min	0.000373
Cm/sec/sec	Ft/sec/sec	0.0328
	Km/hr/sec	0.036
	Meters/sec/sec	0.01

Convert From	Into	Multiply By
	Miles/hr/sec	0.0224
Cm/year	Inches/year	0.3937
Centipoises	Grams/cm/sec.	0.01
	Poises	0.01
	Lbs/ft/hr	2.4191
	Lbs/ft/sec	0.00067
Chains (Gunter or US Survey)		
	Centimeters	2011.7
	Chains-Ramden or Engineer	0.66000132
	Feet	66.000132
	Feet (US Survey)	66
	Furlongs (US Survey)	0.1
	Inches (US Survey)	792
	Links (Gunter)	100
	Links (Ramden)	66.000132
	Meters	20.117
	Miles (US Survey)	0.0125
	Rods (US Survey)	4
	Yards (US Survey)	22
Chains (Ramden)	Chains (Gunter)	1.515152
	Feet	100
Chaldron (dry, English)	Bushels	36
Cheval vapeur	Horsepower	0.98632
Circles	Degrees	360
	Grades	400
	Minutes	21600
Circles	Radians	6.2832
	Signs	12
Circular inches	Circular mm	645.16
	Sq cm	5.067
	Sq inches	0.7854
Circular mm	Sq cm	0.00785
	Sq inches	0.00122
	Sq mm	0.7854
Circular mils	Circular inches	1×10^{-6}
	Sq cm	5.06707×10^{-6}
	Sq inches	7.85398×10^{-7}
	Sq mm	0.000507
	Sq mills	0.7854
Circumference	Degrees	360
	Radians	6.28318
Cords	Cord feet	8
	Cu feet	128
	Cu meters	3.6246
Cord–feet	Cords	0.125
	Cu feet	16
Coulombs	Abcoulombs	0.1
	Ampere–hours	0.000278
	Ampere–seconds	1
	Coulombs (Int)	1.000165
	Faradays (Chem)	1.0364×10^{-5}
	Faradays (Phys)	1.0361×10^{-5}
	Mks elec chg unit	1
	Statcoulombs	2.9979×10^{9}
Coulombs/cu meter	Abcoulombs/cu cm	1×10^{-7}
	Abcoulombs/cu in	1.6387×10^{-6}
	Abcoulombs/cu meter	0.10
	Coulombs/cu cm	1×10^{-6}

Convert From	Into	Multiply By
	Coulombs/cu in	1.6387×10^{-5}
Coulombs/sq cm	Coulombs/sq in	6.4516
	Coulombs/sq meter	10000
Coulombs/sq in	Coulombs/sq cm	0.1550
	Coulombs/sq meter	1550
Coulombs/sq meter	Coulombs/sq cm	10^{-4}
	Coulombs/sq inch	6.452×10^{-4}
Cu centimeters	Board feet	0.00042
	Bushels (Brit)	2.7496×10^{-5}
	Bushels (US)	2.8378×10^{-5}
	Cu feet	3.5315×10^{-5}
	Cu inches	0.06102
	Cu meters	1×10^{-6}
	Cu yards	1.308×10^{-6}
	Drachms (Brit)	0.28156
	Drams (US fluid)	0.27051
	Gallons (Brit)	0.00022
	Gallons (US dry)	0.00023
	Gallons (US liq)	0.00026
	Gills (Brit)	0.00704
	Gills (US)	0.00845
	Liters	0.001
Cu centimeters	Ounces (Brit liq)	0.03519
	Ounces (US liq)	0.03381
	Pints (US dry)	0.00182
	Pints (US liq)	0.00211
	Quarts (Brit)	0.00088
	Quarts (US dry)	0.00091
	Quarts (US liq)	0.00106
Cu cm/gram	Cu ft/lb	0.01602
Cu cm/sec	Cu ft/min	0.00212
	Gallons (US)/min	0.01585
	Gallons (US)/sec	0.00026
Cu cm–atm	Btu	9.61×10^{-5}
	Cal, g	0.02422
	Joules	0.101325
	Watt–hours	2.815×10^{-5}
Cu decimeters	Cu cm	1000
	Cu feet	0.035314
	Cu inches	61.0237
	Cu meters	0.001
	Cu yards	0.00131
	Liters	1.0
Cu dekameters	Cu decimeters	1×10^{6}
	Cu feet	35314.7
	Cu inches	6.102×10^{7}
	Cu meters	1000
	Liters	1×10^{6}
Cu feet	Acre–feet	2.296×10^{-5}
	Board–feet	12
	Bushels (Brit)	0.7786
	Bushels (US)	0.8036
	Cords of wood	0.00781
	Cord–feet	0.0625
	Cu centimeters	28316.8
	Cu inches	1728.0
	Cu meters	0.02832
	Cu yards	0.03704

Convert From	Into	Multiply By
	Gallons (US dry)	6.42851
	Gallons (US liq)	7.48052
	Liters	28.31687
	Ounces (Brit fluid)	996.614
	Ounces (US fluid)	957.506
	Pints (US dry)	51.4281
	Pints (US liq)	59.8442
Cu feet	Quarts (US dry)	25.714
	Quarts (US liq)	29.922
Cu ft H_2O 60°F	Lbs of H_2O	62.366
Cu ft/hour	Acre–feet/hr	2.2957 x 10^{-5}
	Cu cm/sec	7.8658
	Cu ft/min	0.0167
	Gallons (US)/hr	7.4805
	Liters/hr	28.317
Cu ft/minute	Acre–feet/hr	0.00138
	Acre–feet/min	2.2957 x 10^{-5}
	Cu cm/sec	471.95
Cu ft/minute	Cu ft/hr	60
	Gallons (US)/min	7.48052
	Gallons (US)/sec	0.1247
	Liters/sec	0.47195
	Pounds of H_2O/min (32°F)	62.43
Cu ft/pound	Cu cm/gram	62.428
	Milliliter/gram	62.428
Cu ft/sec	Acre–inches/hr	0.99174
	Cu cm/sec	28316.8
	Cu yards/min	2.2222
	Gallons (US)/min	448.83
	Liters/min	1699.01
	Liters/sec	28.317
	Million gallons/day	0.64632
Cu ft H_2O/sec	Lbs H_2O/min	3741.97
Cu ft–atm	Btu	2.7213
	Cal, g	685.76
	Foot pound–force	2116.2
	Hp–hours	0.00107
	Joule	2869.205
	Kg–force meter	292.58
	Kw–hours	0.000797
	Newton meter	2869.205
Cubic inches	Barrels (Brit)	0.0001
	Barrels (US dry)	0.0001417
	Board feet	0.00694
	Bushels (Brit)	0.00045
	Bushels (US)	0.00047
	Cu cm	16.3871
	Cu feet	0.000579
	Cu meters	1.639 x 10^{-5}
	Cu yards	2.143 x 10^{-5}
	Drams (US fluid)	4.43290
	Gallons (Brit)	0.00360
	Gallons (US dry)	0.00372
	Gallons (US liq)	0.00433
	Liters	0.01639
	Milliliters	16.3871
	Ounces (Brit fluid)	0.57674
	Ounces (US fluid)	0.55411

Convert From	Into	Multiply By
	Pecks	0.00186
	Pints (US dry)	0.02976
	Pints (US liq)	0.03463
	Quarts (US dry)	0.01488
	Quarts (US liq)	0.01732
Cu in H_2O 60°F	Lbs of H_2O	0.03609
Cu meters	Acre–feet	0.00081
	Barrels (Brit)	6.11026
	Barrels (US dry)	8.64849
	Barrels (US liq)	8.38641
	Bushels (Brit)	27.4962
	Bushels (US)	28.3776
	Cu cm	1×10^6
	Cu feet	35.3147
Cu meters	Cu inches	61023.7
	Cu yards	1.30795
	Gallons (Brit)	219.969
	Gallons (US liq)	264.172
	Hogshead	4.1932
	Liters	1000
	Pints (US liq)	2113.38
	Quarts (US liq)	1056.69
	Steres	1
Cu meters/kg	Liters/kg	1000
	Liters/gram	1.0
	Cu feet/lb	16.01846
	Cu feet/kg	35.31467
	Cu cm/gram	1000
Cu meters/min	Gallons (Brit)/min	219.969
	Gallons (US)/min	264.172
	Liters/min	1000
Cu mm	Cu cm	0.001
	Cu inches	6.102×10^{-5}
	Cu meters	1×10^{-9}
	Minims (Brit)	0.01689
	Minims (US)	0.01623
Cu yards	Bushels (Brit)	21.0223
	Bushels (US)	21.6962
	Cu cm	764554.9
	Cu feet	27
	Cu inches	46656
	Cu meters	0.76455
	Gallons (Brit)	168.179
	Gallons (US dry)	173.569
	Gallons (US liq)	201.974
	Liters	764.5549
	Prospecting dishes	112
	Quarts (Brit)	672.9149
	Quarts (US dry)	694.279
	Quarts (US liq)	807.896
Cu yards/min	Cu ft/sec	0.45
	Gallons (US)/sec	3.3662
	Liters/sec	12.742
Cubits	Centimeters	45.72
	Feet	1.5
	Inches	18
Cubit (the distance from the elbow to the finger tip):		
Bible	Inches	21.8

Convert From	Into	Multiply By
Egypt 2650BC	Inches	20.6
Babylon 1500BC	Inches	20.9
Assyrian 700 BC	Inches	21.6
Jerusalem (1 AD	Inches	20.6
Druid Eng 1AD	Inches	20.4
Black, Arabia, 800 AD.	Inches	21.3
Mexico–Aztec	Inches	20.7
Ancient China	Inches	20.9
Ancient Greece	Inches	18.2
England	Inches	18.0
Northern 3000BC to 1800AD.	Inches	26.6
Cup	Gallons	0.0625
	Gills	2
	Pint	0.5
	Milliliters	236.588
	Ounces, fluid	8
	Quarts	0.25
	Tablespoons	16
	Teaspoons	48
Cup, metric	Milliliters	200
Cup, tea	Pint	0.25
	Milliliters	142.06
Daltons (Chem)	Grams	1.66×10^{-24}
Daltons (Phys)	Grams	1.659×10^{-24}
Day (mean solar)	Day (sidereal)	1.0027379
	Hours (mean solar)	24
	Hours (sidereal)	24.06571
	Years (calendar)	0.0027397
	Years (sidereal)	0.002738
	Years (tropical)	0.002738
Days (sidereal)	Days (mean solar)	0.9972696
	Hours (mean solar)	23.93447
	Hours (sidereal)	24
	Min (mean solar)	1436.068
	Min (sidereal)	1440
	Second (sidereal)	86400
	Years (calendar)	0.002732
	Years (sidereal)	0.00273
	Years (tropical)	0.00273
Decibels	Bels	0.1
Decigrams	Grams	0.1
Deciliters	Liters	0.1
Decimeters	Centimeters	10
	Feet	0.32808
	Inches	3.937
	Meters	0.1
Decisteres	Cu meters	0.1
Degrees	Circles	0.00278
	Minutes	60
	Quadrants	0.01111
	Radians	0.01745
	Seconds	3600
Degrees/cm	Radians/cm	0.01745
Degrees/foot	Radians/cm	0.0005726
Degrees/inch	Radians/cm	0.00687
Degrees/min.	Degrees/sec	0.01667
	Radians/sec	0.00029
	Revolutions/sec	4.6296×10^{-5}

Convert From	Into	Multiply By
Degrees/sec	Radians/sec	0.01745
	Revolutions/min	0.16667
	Revolutions/sec	0.00278
Dekagrams	Grams	10.0
Dekaliters	Liters	10.0
	Pecks	1.1351
Dekaliters	Pints (US dry)	18.162
Dekameters	Centimeters	1000
	Feet	32.8084
	Inches	393.7008
	Kilometers	0.01
	Meters	10
	Yards	10.9361
Demals	Gram–equiv/cu dm	1
Digit (Ancient Greece)	Centimeters	1.84
	Inches	0.72
	Orguia	0.01
Digitus (Ancient Rome)	Centimeters	1.84
	Inches	0.73
	Palmus	0.25
Drachms (apoth)	Drams	1.0
	Grams	3.8879
	Scruples	3
Drachms (fluid)	Cu centimeter	3.55163
	Cu inches	0.21673
	Minims	60
	Milliliters	3.55163
Drams (troy)	Drams (avdp)	2.19429
	Grains	60
	Grams	3.8879346
	Ounces (troy)	0.125
Drams (avdp)	Drams (troy)	0.455729
	Grains	27.3437
	Grams	1.771845
	Ounces (troy)	0.056966
	Ounces (avdp)	0.0625
	Pennyweights	1.13932
	Pounds (troy)	0.004747
	Pounds (avdp)	0.00391
	Scruples (apoth)	1.36719
Drams (US fluid)	Cu cm	3.6967
	Cu inches	0.225586
	Drachms (fluid)	1.04084
	Gills (US)	0.03125
	Milliliter	3.69669
	Minims	60
	Ounces (US fluid)	0.125
	Pints (US liq)	0.00781
Dynes	Grain–force	0.015737
	Gram–force	0.0010197
	Joules/cm	10^{-7}
	Joules/meter	10^{-5}
	Kilogram–force	1.02×10^{-6}
	Newtons	0.00001
	Poundals	7.233×10^{-5}
	Pound–force	2.248×10^{-6}
Dynes/cm	Ergs/sq cm	1
	Ergs/sq mm	0.01

Convert From	Into	Multiply By
	Gram-force/cm	0.0010197
	Poundals/inch	0.0001837
Dynes/cu cm	Gram-force/cu cm	0.0010197
	Poundals/cu inch	0.001185
Dynes/sq cm	Atmospheres	9.869×10^{-7}
	Bars	1×10^{-6}
	Baryes	1
	Cm of Hg @ 0°C	7.500617×10^{-5}
	Cm of H_2O @ 4°C	0.00101978
	Gram-force/sq cm	0.00101972
	In of Hg @ 32°F	2.953×10^{-5}
	In of H_2O @ 4°C	0.0004015
	Kg-force/sq meter	0.0101972
	Newton/sq meter	0.10
	Pascals	0.10
	Poundals/sq in	0.0004666
	Pound-force/sq in	1.450×10^{-6}
Dyne-cm	Ergs	1
	Foot-poundals	2.373×10^{-6}
	Foot pound-force	7.376×10^{-8}
	Gram-force cm	0.00102
	Inch pound-force	8.8508×10^{-7}
	Joules	1×10^{-7}
	Kg-force meter	1.0197×10^{-8}
	Newton-meters	1×10^{-7}
Electron volts	Ergs	1.6021×10^{-12}
	Joules	1.602189×10^{-19}
Electronic charges	Abcoulombs	1.6022×10^{-20}
	Coulombs	1.6022×10^{-19}
	Statcoulombs	4.803×10^{-10}
Ells (cloth)	Cm	114.3
	Inches	45
Em (Pica-printer)	Inch	0.167
	Cm	0.4233
Ephahs (Old Testament)	Liters	22
	Omers (Old Testament)	10
Ergs	Btu	9.4845×10^{-11}
	Cu cm-atmospheres	9.8692×10^{-7}
	Cu ft-atmospheres	3.4853×10^{-9}
	Cu ft lb-force/sq in	5.122×10^{-10}
	Dyne-cm	1
	Electron Volts	6.241×10^{11}
	Foot-poundals	2.373×10^{-6}
	Foot pound-force	7.376×10^{-8}
	Gram-calories	2.3885×10^{-8}
	Gram-force cm	0.0010197
	Horsepower-hours	3.725×10^{-14}
	Joules	1×10^{-7}
	Joules (Int)	9.998×10^{-8}
	Kw-hours	2.778×10^{-14}
	Kg-calories	2.3901×10^{-11}
	Kg-force meter	1.0197×10^{-8}
	Liter-atmospheres	9.869×10^{-10}
	Watt-hours	0.278×10^{-10}
	Watt-sec	1×10^{-7}
Ergs/sec	Btu/min	5.691×10^{-9}
Ergs/sec	Gram-calorie/min	1.4331×10^{-6}
	Dyne-cm/sec	1

Convert From	Into	Multiply By
	Foot pound–force/min	4.425×10^{-6}
	Foot pound–force/sec	7.376×10^{-8}
	Gram–force cm/sec.	0.0010197
	Horsepower	1.341×10^{-10}
	Joules/sec	1×10^{-7}
	Kg–calories/minute	1.43×10^{-9}
	Kilowatts	1×10^{-10}
	Watts	1×10^{-7}
Ergs/sq cm	Dynes/cm	1
	Ergs/sq mm	0.01
Ergs/sq mm	Dynes/cm	100
	Ergs/sq cm	100
Erg–sec	Planck's constant	1.5093×10^{26}
Faraday	Ampere–hours	26.8
	Coloumbs	9.649×10^{4}
Faraday/sec	Ampere (absolute)	9.65×10^{4}
Farads	Abfarads	1×10^{-9}
	Farads (Int)	1.00049
	Microfarads	1×10^{6}
	Statfarads	8.98758×10^{11}
Farads (Int)	Farads	0.9995
Fathoms (US Survey)	Centimeters	182.88
	Feet (US Survey)	6
	Furlongs (US Survey)	0.0090909
	Inches (US Survey)	72
	Meters	1.8288
	Miles (naut,Int)	0.00098747
	Miles (statute)	0.0011363
	Yards (US Survey)	2
Feet	Centimeters	30.48
	Chains (Gunter's)	0.015151
	Fathoms	0.166667
	Feet (US Survey)	0.999998
	Furlongs	0.001515
	Inches	12
	Kilometers	3.048×10^{-4}
	Meters	0.3048
	Microns	304800
	Miles (naut,Int)	0.000165
	Miles (statute or US Surv.)	0.000189
	Millimeters	304.8
	Mils	1.2×10^{4}
	Rods	0.060606
	Ropes (Brit)	0.05
	Yards	0.333333
Feet (US Survey)	Centimeters	30.48006
	Chains (Gunter's)	0.015152
	Chains (Ramden's)	0.01000002
	Feet	1.000002
	Inches	12.000024
	Links (Gunter's)	1.515155
	Links (Ramden's)	1.000002
	Meters	0.304801
	Miles (statute or US Surv.)	0.00018939
	Rods (US Survey)	0.06060618
	Yards	0.333334
Feet (Athens History)	Inches	12.44
Feet (Aegina History)	Inches	12.36

Convert From	Into	Multiply By
Feet (Miletus History)	Inches	12.52
Feet (Olympia History)	Inches	12.64
Feet (Etruria History)	Inches	12.44
Feet (Rome History)	Inches	11.66
Feet (North History)	Inches	13.19
Feet (England History)	Inches	13.19
Feet (France History)	Inches	12.79
Feet (Moscow History)	Inches	13.17
Feet of Air @ 60°F	Atmospheres	3.608×10^{-5}
	Ft of Hg @ 32°F	0.0009
	Ft of H_2O @ 60°F	0.00122
	In of Hg @ 32°F	0.00108
	Pound–force/sq in	0.00053
Feet of Hg @ 32°F	Cm of Hg @ 0°C	30.48
	Ft of H_2O @ 60°F	13.6086
	In of H_2O @ 60°F	163.30
	Ounce–force/sq in	94.302
	Pound–force/sq in	5.8938
Feet of H_2O @ 4°C	Atmospheres	0.0295
	Cm of Hg @ 0°C	2.2419
	Dynes/sq cm	29888.9
	Gram–force/sq cm	30.479
	In of Hg @ 32°F	0.8826
	Kg–force/sq meter	304.78
	Newtons/sq meter	2988.888
	Pascals	2988.888
	Pound–force/sq foot	62.424
	Pound–force/sq inch	0.433501
Feet/hour	Cm/hr	30.48
	Cm/minute	0.508
	Cm/second	0.008467
	Feet/minute	0.016667
	Inches/hour	12
	Kilometers/hr	0.0003048
	Kilometers/min	5.08×10^{-6}
	Knots (Int)	0.00016458
	Miles/hr	0.0001894
	Miles/min	3.15656×10^{-6}
	Miles/sec	5.2609×10^{-8}
Feet/minute	Cm/sec	0.508
	Feet/sec	0.016667
	Kilometers/hr	0.018288
	Meters/min	0.3048
	Meters/sec	0.00508
	Miles/hr	0.011364
Feet/second	Cm/sec	30.48
	Kilometers/hr	1.09728
	Kilometers/min	0.01829
Feet/second	Knots	0.5921
	Meters/min	18.288
	Miles/hr	0.681818
	Miles/min	0.011364
Feet/(sec x sec)	Cm/(sec x sec)	30.48
	Km/(hr x sec)	1.0973
	Meters/(sec x sec)	0.3048
	Miles/(hr x sec)	0.681818
Feet/100 feet	Percent grade	1
Fifth	Jiggers	17.067

Convert From	Into	Multiply By
	Ounces, fluid	25.6
	Pints	1.6
	Pony	25.6
	Quart	0.80
	Shots	25.6
Firkins (Brit)	Bushels (Brit)	1.125
	Cu cm	40914.8
	Cu feet	1.44489
	Firkins (US)	1.2009
	Gallons (Brit)	9
	Liters	40.91481
	Pints (Brit)	72
Firkins (US)	Barrels (US dry)	0.294643
	Barrels (US liq)	0.285714
	Bushels (US)	0.966788
	Cu feet	1.203125
	Firkins (Brit)	0.832674
	Gallons (US liq)	9
	Liters	34.0687
	Pints (US liq)	72
Flask of mercury	Kilograms	34.473
Foot–candles	Lumens/sq ft	1
	Lumens/sq meter	10.7639
	Lux	10.7639
	Milliphots	1.07639
Foot–lamberts	Candles/sq cm	0.00034
	Candles/sq ft	0.31831
	Millilamberts	1.07639
	Lamberts	0.0010764
	Lumens/sq ft	1
Foot–poundals	Btu	3.9968×10^{-5}
	Btu (IST)	3.9941×10^{-5}
	Btu (mean)	3.991×10^{-5}
	Cal, gram	0.010072
	Cal, gram (IST)	0.010065
	Cal, gram (mean)	0.010057
	Cu cm–atmospheres	0.41589
	Cu ft–atmospheres	1.4687×10^{-5}
	Dyne–cm	4.21401×10^{5}
	Ergs	4.21401×10^{5}
	Foot pound–force	0.03108
	Hp–hours	1.5697×10^{-8}
	Joules	0.0421401
	Joules (Int)	0.042133
Foot–poundals	Kg–force meter	0.004297
	Kw–hours	1.1706×10^{-8}
	Liter–atmospheres	0.0004159
Foot pound–force	Btu (thermochemical)	0.0012859
	Btu (IST)	0.0012851
	Btu (mean)	0.0012841
	Cal, gram (thermochemical)	0.3240483
	Cal, gram (IST)	0.3238316
	Cal, gram (mean)	0.3235827
	Cal, gram @ 20°C	0.32421
	Cal, kg (IST)	0.0003238
	Cu ft–atmospheres	0.0004725
	Dyne–cm	1.3558179×10^{7}
	Ergs	1.3558179×10^{7}

Convert From	Into	Multiply By
	Foot–poundals	32.174049
	Gram–calories	0.3238316
	Gram–force cm	13825.5
	Hp–hours	5.0505051×10^{-7}
	Joules	1.3558179
	Kg–calories	3.24×10^{-4}
	Kg–force meter	0.13825495
	Kw–hours	3.766161×10^{-7}
	Kw–hours (Int)	3.765544×10^{-7}
	Liter–atmospheres	0.01338088
	Newton–meters	1.3558179
	Watt–hours	0.0003766160
Foot pound–force/hr	Btu/min	2.1433×10^{-5}
	Btu (mean)/min	2.1401×10^{-5}
	Cal, gram/min	0.0054
	Cal, gram (mean)/min	0.00539
	Ergs/min	2.2597×10^{5}
	Foot pound–force/min	0.016667
	Horsepower	5.0505×10^{-7}
	Horsepower (metric)	5.1205×10^{-7}
	Kilowatts	3.7662×10^{-7}
	Watts	0.0003766
	Watts (Int)	0.0003765
Foot pound–force/min	Btu/minute	1.284×10^{-3}
	Btu/sec	2.1433×10^{-5}
	Btu (mean)/sec	2.1401×10^{-5}
	Cal, g/sec	0.0054
	Cal, g (mean)/sec	0.00539
	Ergs/sec	2.2597×10^{5}
	Foot pound–force/sec	0.01667
	Horsepower	3.0303×10^{-5}
	Horsepower (metric)	3.0723×10^{-5}
	Joules/sec	0.0226
	Joules (Int)/sec	0.02259
	Kilogram–calories/min	3.24×10^{-4}
	Kilowatts	2.2597×10^{-5}
	Watts	0.022597
Foot pound–force/lb	Btu/lb	0.001286
	Btu (IST)/lb	0.001285
	Btu (mean)/lb	0.001284
Foot pound–force/lb	Cal, g/gram	0.00071441
	Cal, g (IST)/gram	0.00071392
	Cal, g (mean)/gram	0.00071337
	Hp–hr/lb	5.0505×10^{-7}
	Joules/gram	0.002989
	Kg–force meter/gram	0.0003
	Kw–hr/gram	8.303×10^{-10}
Foot pound–force/sec	Btu/hour	4.6262
	Btu/min	0.077104
	Btu (mean)/min	0.077045
	Btu/sec	0.001286
	Btu (mean)/sec	0.001284
	Cal, g/sec	0.32405
	Cal, g (mean)/sec	0.32358
	Ergs/sec	1.3558×10^{7}
	Gram–force cm/sec	13825.5
	Horsepower	0.001818
	Joules/sec	1.3558

Convert From	Into	Multiply By
	Kg–calories/min	0.019433
	Kilowatts	0.001356
	Watts	1.3558
	Watts (Int)	1.3556
Furlongs (US Survey)	Centimeters	20116.8
	Chains (Gunter's)	10
	Chains (Ramden's)	6.6
	Feet (US Survey)	660
	Inches (US Survey)	7920
	Meters	201.17
	Miles (naut,Int)	0.1086
	Miles (statute)	0.125
	Rods (US Survey)	40
	Yards (US Survey)	220
Gallons (Brit)	Barrels (Brit)	0.02778
	Bushels (Brit)	0.125
	Cu centimeters	4546.09
	Cu feet	0.1605
	Cu inches	277.419
	Drachms (Brit flu)	1280
	Firkins (Brit)	0.1111
	Gallons (US liq)	1.2009
	Gills (Brit)	32
	Liters	4.546
	Minims (Brit)	76800
	Ounces (Brit flu)	160
	Ounces (US flu)	153.722
	Pecks (Brit)	0.5
	Lbs of H₂O @ 62°F	10.0092
Gallons (US dry)	Barrels (US dry)	0.038096
	Barrels (US liq)	0.03694
	Bushels (US)	0.125
	Cu centimeters	4404.88
	Cu feet	0.15556
	Cu inches	268.8
	Gallons (US liq)	1.163647
Gallons (US dry)	Liters	4.4049
Gallons (US liq)	Acre–feet	3.0689 x 10⁻⁶
	Barrels (US liq)	0.031746
	Barrels (US petro)	0.0238095
	Bushels (US)	0.10742
	Cu centimeters	3785.41
	Cu feet	0.13368
	Cu inches	231
	Cu meters	0.003785
	Cu yards	0.00495
	Gallons (Brit)	0.83267
	Gallons (US dry)	0.85937
	Gallons (wine)	1
	Gills (US)	32
	Liters	3.7854
	Minims (US)	61440
	Ounces (US flu)	128
	Pints (US liq)	8
	Quarts (US liq)	4
Gallons(US)H₂O @4°C	Lb of H₂O	8.345196
Gallons(US)H₂O@60°F	Lb of H₂O	8.337134
Gallons(US)/day	Cu feet/hr	0.00557

Convert From	Into	Multiply By
Gallons (Brit)/hour	Cu meters/min	7.5768×10^{-5}
Gallons (US)/hour	Acre–feet/hr	3.0689×10^{-6}
	Cu meters/min	6.309×10^{-6}
	Cu feet/hr	0.13368
	Cu yards/min	8.2519×10^{-5}
	Liters/hr	3.7854
Gallons (US)/min	Liters/sec	0.06309
	Cu feet/sec	2.228×10^{-3}
	Cu feet/hour	8.0208
Gallons (Brit)/sec	Cu cm/sec	4546.09
Gallons (US)/sec	Cu cm/sec	3785.4
	Cu feet/min	8.0208
	Cu yards/min	0.29707
	Liters/min	227.124
Gammas	Gauss	1×10^{-5}
	Grams	1×10^{-6}
	Micrograms	1
	Teslas	1×10^{-9}
Gausses	Gausses (Int)	0.9997
	Gammas	1×10^{5}
	Gilberts/cm	1
	Maxwells/sq cm	1
	Lines/sq cm	1
	Lines/sq inch	6.4516
	Teslas	1×10^{-4}
	Webers/sq cm	1×10^{-8}
	Webers/sq inch	6.452×10^{-8}
	Webers/sq meter	1×10^{-4}
Gausses (Int)	Gausses	1.00033
Geepounds	Slugs	1
	Kilograms	14.594
	Pound–force sq sec/ft	1
Geepounds	Pounds	32.174
Gerahs (Old Testament)	Bekahs (Old Testament)	0.1
	Grams	0.567
	Shekels (Old Testament)	0.05
Gigameters	Meters	1×10^{9}
Gilberts	Abampere–turns	0.07958
	Ampere–turns	0.79577
	Gilberts (Int)	1.00016
Gilberts (Int)	Gilberts	0.99983
Gilberts/cm	Ampere–turns/cm	0.79577
	Ampere–turns/in	2.02127
	Ampere–turns/meter	79.58
	Oersteds	1
	Teslas	1×10^{-4}
Gilberts/maxwell	Ampere–turns/weber	7.958×10^{7}
Gills (Brit)	Cu centimeters	142.065
	Gallons (Brit)	0.03125
	Gills (US)	1.20095
	Liters	0.142
	Ounces (Brit flu)	5
	Ounces (US flu)	4.8038
	Pints (Brit)	0.25
Gills (US)	Cu centimeters	118.29
	Cu inches	7.2188
	Drams (US flu)	32
	Gallons (US liq)	0.03125

Convert From	Into	Multiply By
	Gills (Brit)	0.8327
	Liters	0.1183
	Minims (US)	1920
	Ounces (US flu)	4
	Pints (US liq)	0.25
	Quarts (US liq)	0.125
Grades	Circles	0.0025
	Circumferences	0.0025
	Degrees	0.9
	Minutes	54
	Radians	0.01571
	Revolutions	0.0025
	Seconds	3240
Grains	Carats (metric)	0.32399
	Drams (troy)	0.01667
	Drams (avdp)	0.03657
	Grams	0.0648
	Milligrams	64.7989
	Ounces (troy)	0.00208
	Ounces (avdp)	0.00229
	Pennyweights	0.04167
	Pounds (troy)	0.00017
	Pounds (avdp)	0.00014
	Scruples (apoth)	0.05
	Tons (metric)	6.4799×10^{-8}
Grain–force	Dynes	63.546
	Newtons	6.3546×10^{-4}
	Poundals	0.0046
Grains/cu ft	Grams/cu meter	2.28835
Grains/gal (US)	Parts/million	17.118
	Pounds/million gal	142.86
Grains/gal (Brit)	Parts/million	14.254
Grams	Carats (metric)	5
	Decigrams	10
	Dekagrams	0.1
	Drams (troy)	0.2572
	Drams (avdp)	0.5644
	Grains	15.432
	Kilograms	0.001
	Micrograms	1×10^{6}
	Milligrams	1000
	Myriagrams	0.0001
	Ounces (troy)	0.03215
	Ounces (avdp)	0.03527
	Pennyweights	0.64301
	Pounds (troy)	0.00268
	Pounds (avdp)	0.002205
	Scruples (apoth)	0.77162
	Tons (metric)	1×10^{-6}
Gram–force	Dynes	980.665
	Joules/cm	9.807×10^{-5}
	Joules/meter	9.807×10^{-3}
	Newtons	9.807×10^{-3}
	Poundals	0.07093
Grams/cm	Grams/inch	2.54
	Kg/km	100
	Kg/meter	0.1
	Pounds/ft	0.067197

Convert From	Into	Multiply By
	Pounds/inch	0.0056
	Tons (metric)/km	0.1
Gram–force/cm	Dynes/cm	980.665
	Poundals/inch	0.18017
Grams/(cm x sec)	Poises	1
	Lb/(ft x sec)	0.0672
Grams/cu cm	Grains/milliliter	15.4324
	Grams/milliliter	1.0
	Pounds/cu foot	62.428
	Pounds/cu inch	0.0361
	Pounds/gal (Brit)	10.022
	Pounds/gal (US dry)	9.7111
	Pounds/gal (US liq)	8.3454
Gram–force/cu cm	Dynes/cu cm	980.665
	Poundals/cu cm	1.16236
Grams/cu meter	Grains/cu ft	0.437
Grams/liter	Grains/gallon	58.4178
	Parts/million	1000
	Lbs/cu foot	0.0624
	Lbs/1000 gal (US)	8.3454
Grams/milliliter	Grams/cu cm	1.0
	Pounds/cu foot	62.428
	Pounds/gallon (US)	8.34540
Gram–force/sq cm	Atmospheres	0.00097
Gram–force/sq cm	Bars	0.00098
	Cm of Hg @ 0°C	0.07356
	Dynes/sq cm	980.665
	In of Hg @ 32°F	0.02896
	Kg–force/sq meter	10
	Mm of Hg @ 0°C	0.73556
	Pascals	98.0665
	Poundals/sq inch	0.45762
	Pound–force/sq inch	0.01422
	Pound–force/sq foot	2.0482
Grams/ton (long)	Milligrams/kg	0.9842
Grams/ton (short)	Milligrams/kg	1.1023
Gram–calories	Btu	3.968×10^{-3}
	Ergs	4.1868×10^{7}
	Foot/pound–force	3.088
	Horsepower–hours	1.5596×10^{-6}
	Kilowatt–hours	1.163×10^{-6}
	Watt–hours	1.163×10^{-3}
Gram–calories/sec	Btu/hr	14.286
Gram–force cm	Btu	9.3×10^{-5}
	Btu (IST)	9.295×10^{-8}
	Btu (mean)	9.288×10^{-5}
	Cal, gram	2.344×10^{-5}
	Cal, gram (IST)	2.342×10^{-5}
	Cal, gram (mean)	2.34×10^{-5}
	Cal, gram (15°C)	2.343×10^{-5}
	Cal, gram (20°C)	2.345×10^{-5}
	Cal, kg	2.344×10^{-8}
	Cal, kg (IST)	2.342×10^{-8}
	Cal, kg (mean)	2.34×10^{-8}
	Dyne–cm	980.665
	Ergs	980.665
	Foot–poundals	0.00233
	Foot pound–force	7.233×10^{-5}

Convert From	Into	Multiply By
	Hp–hours	3.653×10^{-11}
	Joules	9.807×10^{-5}
	Kw–hours	2.724×10^{-11}
	Kw–hours (Int)	2.724×10^{-11}
	Newton–meters	9.807×10^{-5}
	Watt–hours	2.724×10^{-11}
Gram–force cm/sec	Btu/sec	9.301×10^{-8}
	Cal, gram/sec	2.344×10^{-5}
	Ergs/sec	980.665
	Foot pound–force/sec	7.233×10^{-5}
	Horsepower	1.315×10^{-7}
	Joules/sec	9.807×10^{-5}
	Kilowatts	9.807×10^{-8}
	Kilowatts (Int)	9.805×10^{-8}
	Watts	9.807×10^{-5}
Grams–sq cm	Pounds–sq inch	0.00034
Gram–force sec/sq cm	Poises	980.665
Gravity constant	Cm/(sec x sec)	980.665
	Ft/(sec x sec)	32.17405
Gray	Joules/kg	1.0
Gray	Rad	100
	Ergs/gram	1×10^4
Gray/sec	Joules/kg sec	1.0
	Rad/sec	100
	Ergs/gram sec	1×10^4
Hands	Centimeters	10.16
	Feet	0.3333
	Inches	4
Hectares	Acres	2.471
	Ares	100
	Sq cm	1×10^8
	Sq feet	107639.1
	Sq meters	10000
	Sq miles	0.00386
	Sq rods	395.369
Hectograms	Grams	100
	Pounds (apoth or troy)	0.2679
	Pounds (avdp)	0.2205
Hectogram–force	Poundals	7.0932
Hectoliters	Bushels (Brit)	2.7497
	Bushels (US)	2.8378
	Cu cm	1.0×10^5
	Cu feet	3.5316
	Gallons (US liq)	26.418
	Liters	100
	Ounces (US flu)	3381.4
	Pecks (US)	11.351
Hectometers	Centimeters	10000
	Decimeters	1000
	Dekameters	10
	Feet	328.08
	Meters	100
	Rods	19.88
	Yards	109.36
Hectowatts	Watts	100
Hefner units	Candles (English)	0.864
	Candles (German)	0.855
	Candles (Int)	0.9

Convert From	Into	Multiply By
Henries...............	10cp pentane candles............	0.09
	Abhenries...............	1×10^9
	Henries (Int)...............	0.9995
	Millihenries...............	1000
	Mks (r or nr) units...............	1
	Stathenries...............	1.113×10^{-12}
Henries (Int)...............	Henries...............	1.0005
Henries/meter...............	Gausses/oersted...............	795775
	Mks (nr) units...............	0.0796
	Mks (r) units...............	1
Hertz...............	Cycles/sec...............	1.0
Hins (Old Testament)......	Liters...............	3.667
Hogsheads...............	Butts (Brit)...............	0.5
	Cu feet...............	8.4219
	Cu inches...............	14553
	Cu meters...............	0.238
Hogsheads...............	Gallons (Brit)...............	52.458
	Gallons (US)...............	63
	Gallons (wine)...............	63
	Liters...............	238.47
Hogshead (Brit)............	Cu feet...............	10.11
Homers (Old Testament)	Liters...............	220
Horsepower (mech)........	Btu (mean)/hr...............	2542.47
	Btu (mean)/min...............	42.375
	Btu (mean)/sec...............	0.7062
	Cal, gram/hr...............	6.416×10^5
	Cal, gram (IST)/hr...............	6.412×10^5
	Cal, gram (mean)/hr...............	6.4069×10^5
	Cal, gram/min...............	10694
	Cal, gram (IST)/min...............	10686
	Cal, gram (mean)/min...............	10678
	Ergs/sec...............	7.457×10^9
	Foot pound–force/hr...............	1980000
	Foot pound–force/min...............	33000
	Foot pound–force/sec...............	550
	Horsepower (boiler)...............	0.076
	Horsepower (electric)...............	0.9996
	Horsepower (metric)...............	1.0139
	Joules/sec...............	745.7
	Kg–calories/min...............	10.686
	Kilowatts...............	0.7457
	Kilowatts (Int)...............	0.7456
	Tons of refrigeration...............	0.212
	Watts...............	745.7
Horsepower (boiler)........	Btu (mean)/hr...............	33445.7
	Cal, gram/min...............	140671.6
	Cal, gram (mean)/min...............	140469.4
	Cal, gram (20°C)/min...............	140742.2
	Ergs/sec...............	9.8097×10^{10}
	Foot pound–force/min...............	434107
	Horsepower (mech)...............	13.155
	Horsepower (electric)...............	13.1497
	Horsepower (metric)...............	13.337
	Horsepower (water)...............	13.149
	Joules/sec...............	9809.5
	Kilowatts...............	9.8095
Horsepower (electric)......	Btu/hr...............	2547.16
	Btu (IST)/hr...............	2545.5

Convert From	Into	Multiply By
	Btu (mean)/hr	2543.5
	Cal, gram/sec	178.298
	Cal, kg/hr	641.87
	Ergs/sec	7.46×10^9
	Foot pound-force/min	33013
	Foot pound-force/sec	550.2
	Horsepower (mech)	1.0004
	Horsepower (boiler)	0.07605
	Horsepower (metric)	1.01428
	Horsepower (water)	0.99994
	Joules/sec	746
	Kilowatts	0.746
Horsepower (electric)	Watts	746
Horsepower (metric)	Btu/hr	2511.3
	Btu (IST)/hr.	2509.7
	Btu (mean)/hr	2507.7
	Cal, gram/hr	6.328×10^5
	Cal, gram (IST)/hr	6.324×10^5
	Cal, gram (mean)/hr	6.319×10^5
	Ergs/sec	7.355×10^9
	Foot pound-force/min	32548.6
	Foot pound-force/sec	542.476
	Horsepower (mech)	0.9863
	Horsepower (boiler)	0.07498
	Horsepower (electric)	0.9859
	Horsepower (water)	0.98587
	Kg-force meter/sec	75
	Kilowatts	0.7355
	Watts	735.499
Horsepower (water)	Foot pound-force/min	33015
	Horsepower (mech)	1.00046
	Horsepower (boiler)	0.076
	Horsepower (electric)	1.00006
	Horsepower (metric)	1.0143
	Kilowatts	0.746043
Horsepower-hours	Btu	2546.1
	Btu (IST)	2544.4
	Btu (mean)	2542.5
	Cal, gram	641616
	Cal, gram (IST)	641187
	Cal, gram (mean)	640694
	Ergs	2.685×10^{13}
	Foot pound-force	1.98×10^6
	Gram-calories	641187
	Joules	2.685×10^6
	Kg-calories	641.2
	Kg-force meter	273745
	Kw-hours	0.7457
	Watt-hours	745.7
Horsepower-hr/lb	Btu/lb	2546
	Cal, gram/gram	1414.5
	Cu ft-(lb/sq in)/lb	13750
	Foot pound-force/lb	1980000
	Joules/gram	5918.35
Hours (mean solar)	Days (mean solar)	0.04167
	Days (sidereal)	0.04178
	Hours (sidereal)	1.002738
	Minutes (mean solar)	60

Convert From	Into	Multiply By
	Minutes (sidereal)	60.164
	Seconds (mean solar)	3600
	Seconds (sidereal)	3609.86
	Weeks (mean calendar)	0.00595
Hours (sidereal)	Days (mean solar)	0.41553
	Days (sidereal)	0.04167
	Hours (mean solar)	0.99727
	Minutes (mean solar)	59.836
Hours (sidereal)	Minutes (sidereal)	60
Hundredweights (long)	Kilograms	50.802
	Pounds	112
	Quarters (Brit long)	4
	Quarters (US long)	0.2
	Tons (long)	0.05
Hundredweights (short)	Kilograms	45.359
	Ounces (avdp)	1600
	Pounds (avdp)	100
	Quarters (Brit short)	4
	Quarters (US short)	0.2
	Tons (long)	0.04464
	Tons (metric)	0.04536
	Tons (short)	0.05
Inches	Ångström	2.54×10^8
	Centimeters	2.54
	Chains (Gunter's)	0.001263
	Cubits	0.05556
	Fathoms (US Survey)	0.013889
	Feet	0.08333
	Feet (US Survey)	0.083333167
	Links (Gunter's)	0.12626
	Links (Ramden's)	0.08333
	Meters	0.0254
	Miles	1.578×10^{-5}
	Millimeters	25.40
	Mils	1000
	Picas (printer)	6.0225
	Points (printer)	72.27
	Yards	0.0278
Inches of Hg @ 32°F	Atmospheres	0.03342
	Bars	0.03386
	Dynes/sq cm	33864
	Ft of air @ 1atm,60°F	926.27
	Ft of H_2O @ 39.2°F	1.13299
	Gram–force/sq cm	34.532
	Kg–force/sq meter	345.32
	Mm of Hg @ 0°C	25.4
	Newtons/sq meter	3386.389
	Ounce–force/sq inch	7.858
	Pascals	3386.389
	Pound–force/sq ft	70.726
Inches of Hg @ 60°F	Atmospheres	0.033327
	Dynes/sq cm	33768
	Gram–force/sq cm	34.434
	Mm of Hg @ 60°F	25.4
	Newtons/sq meter	3376.85
	Ounce–force/sq inch	7.8363
	Pascals	3376.85
	Pound–force/sq ft	70.5267

Conversion Tables 703

Convert From	Into	Multiply By
Inches of H$_2$O @ 4°C	Atmospheres	0.002458
	Dynes/sq cm	2490.8
	Inch of Hg @ 32°F	0.07355
	Kg–force/sq meter	25.398
Inches of H$_2$O @ 4°C	Ounce–force/sq foot	83.232
	Ounce–force/sq inch	0.578002
	Pound–force/sq foot	5.202018
	Pound–force/sq inch	0.03613
Inch pound–force	Foot pound–force	0.0833
Inches/hour	Cm/hour	2.54
	Feet/hour	0.0833
	Miles/hour	1.5783 x 10^{-5}
Inches/minute	Cm/hour	152.4
	Feet/hour	5
	Miles/hour	0.000947
Jiggers	Fifths	0.059
	Ounces, fluid	1.5
	Pints	0.09375
	Pony	1.5
	Shots	1.5
Joules (abs)	Btu	0.0009485
	Btu (IST)	0.0009478
	Btu (mean)	0.0009471
	Cal, gram	0.23901
	Cal, gram (IST)	0.23885
	Cal, gram (mean)	0.23866
	Cal, gram @ 20°C	0.23913
	Cal, kg (mean)	0.000239
	Cu ft–atmosphere	0.0003485
	Ergs	1 x 10^7
	Foot–poundals	23.73
	Foot pound–force	0.7376
	Gram–force cm	10197.2
	Horsepower–hours	3.7251 x 10^{-7}
	Joules (Int)	0.9998
	Kg–calories	2.390 x 10^{-4}
	Kg–force meter	0.10197
	Kw–hours	2.78 x 10^{-7}
	Liter–atmospheres	0.009869
	Volt–coulombs (Int)	0.999835
	Watt–hours (abs)	0.0002778
	Watt–hours (Int)	0.0002777
	Watt–seconds	1
	Watt–seconds (Int)	0.9998
Joules (Int)	Btu	0.000949
	Btu (IST)	0.000948
	Btu (mean)	0.000947
	Cal, gram	0.239045
	Cal, gram (IST)	0.23889
	Cal, gram (mean)	0.2387
	Cu cm–atmosphere	9.87086
	Cu ft–atmosphere	0.000349
	Dyne–cm	1.000165 x 10^7
	Ergs	1.000165 x 10^7
	Foot–poundals	23.734
	Foot pound–force	0.7377
	Gram–force cm	10199
	Joules (abs)	1.000165

Convert From	Into	Multiply By
Joules (Int)	Kw–hours	2.778 x 10⁻⁷
	Liter–atmosphere	0.00987
	Volt–coulombs	1.000165
	Volt–coulombs (Int)	1
	Watt–second	1.000165
	Watt–second (Int)	1
Joules/ampere–hour	Joules/abcoulomb	0.00278
	Joules/statcoulomb	9.266 x 10⁻¹⁴
Joules/coulomb	Joules/abcoulomb	10
	Volts	1
Joules/cm	Dynes	10⁷
	Gram–force	1.020 x 10⁴
	Joules/meter	100
	Newtons	100
	Poundals	723.3
	Pound–force	22.48
Joules/cu meter	Btu (IST)/cu ft	2.6839 x 10⁻⁶
	Dyne cm/cu meter	1 x 10⁷
	Foot pound–force/cu ft	0.020885
	Watt hr/cu ft	7.86578 x 10⁻⁶
Joules/kilogram K	Btu/lb °R	2.38846 x 10⁻⁴
	Calories/gram °C	2.38846 x 10⁻⁴
	Joules/kg °C	1.0
	Kilocalories/kg °C	2.38846 x 10⁻⁴
	Kilojoules/kg °C	1 x 10⁻³
Joules (abs)/second	Btu/min	0.0569
	Cal, gram/min	14.33
	Cal, kg/min	0.01434
	Cal, kg (mean)/min	0.01432
	Dyne–cm/sec	1 x 10⁷
	Ergs/sec	1 x 10⁷
	Foot pound–force/sec	0.73756
	Gram–force cm/sec	10197
	Horsepower	0.00134
	Watts	1
	Watts (Int)	0.9998
Joules (Int)/sec	Btu/min	0.05692
	Btu (mean)/min	0.05683
	Cal, gram/min	14.343
	Cal, kg/min	0.01434
	Dyne–cm/sec	1.000165 x 10⁷
	Ergs/sec	1.000165 x 10⁷
	Foot pound–force/min	44.26
	Foot pound–force/sec	0.73768
	Gram–force cm/sec	10198.8
	Horsepower	0.00134
	Watts	1
	Watts (Int)	1.000165
Kabs (Old Testament)	Liters	1.22
Kantar (Egypt)	Pounds (avdp)	99.094
Kati (Malaysia)	Kilograms	0.605
	Pounds	1.333
Kilderkins (Brit)	Cu cm	81829.6
	Cu feet	2.8898
Kilderkins (Brit)	Cu inches	4993.5
	Cu meters	0.0818
	Gallons (Brit)	18
	Liters	72.7 to 81.8

Convert From	Into	Multiply By
Kilograms	Drams (apoth or troy)	257.21
	Drams (avdp)	564.38
	Grains	15432.36
	Grams	1000
	Hundredweights (long)	0.019684
	Hundredweights (short)	0.022046
	Joules/cm	0.09807
	Ounces (apoth or troy)	32.1507
	Ounces (avdp)	35.27396
	Pennyweights	643.0149
	Pounds (apoth or troy)	2.67923
	Pounds (avdp)	2.20462
	Quarters (Brit long)	0.078736
	Quarters (US long)	0.003937
	Scruples (apoth)	771.6179
	Slugs	0.06852
	Tons (long)	0.00098
	Tons (metric)	0.001
	Tons (short)	0.001102
Kilogram–force	Dynes	980665
	Joules/meter	9.80665
	Newtons	9.80665
	Poundals	70.9316
	Gram–force	1000
	Kips	0.002205
	Pound–force	2.20462
	Sthenes	0.009807
Kilograms/cu meter	Grams/cu cm	0.001
	Lb/cu ft	0.0624
	Lb/cu inch	3.6127×10^{-5}
	Lb/mil-foot	3.405×10^{-10}
Kilograms/meter	Pounds/ft	0.672
Kilogram–force/sq cm	Atmospheres	0.9678
	Bars	0.980665
	Cm of Hg @ 0°C	73.556
	Dynes/sq cm	980665
	Ft of H₂O @ 39.2°F	32.8104
	In of Hg @ 32°F	28.959
	Newtons/sq meter	98066.5
	Pascals	98066.5
	Pound–force/sq inch	14.223
Kilogram–force/sq meter	Atmospheres	9.678×10^{-5}
	Bars	9.80665×10^{-5}
	Dynes/sq cm	98.0665
	Ft of H₂O @ 39.2°F	0.00328
	Gram–force/sq cm	0.1
	In of Hg @ 32°F	0.0029
	Mm of Hg @ 0°C	0.07356
	Newtons/sq meter	9.80665
	Pascals	9.80665
Kilogram–force/sq meter	Pound–force/sq foot	0.20482
	Pound–force/sq inch	0.00142
Kilogram–force/sq mm	Pound–force/sq ft	204816
	Pound–force/sq in	1422.3
	Tons–force (short)/sq in	0.71117
Kilogram sq cm	Pounds sq ft	0.00237
	Pounds sq in	0.34172
Kilogram–force meter	Btu (mean)	0.00929

Convert From	Into	Multiply By
	Cal, gram (mean)	2.3405
	Cal, kg (mean)	0.0023405
	Cu ft–atmospheres	0.003418
	Dyne–cm	9.807×10^7
	Ergs	9.807×10^7
	Foot–poundals	232.715
	Foot pound–force	7.233
	Gram–force cm	100000
	Horsepower–hours	3.653×10^{-6}
	Joules	9.80665
	Joules (Int)	9.8053
	Kw–hours	2.724×10^{-6}
	Liter–atmospheres	0.0968
	Newton–meters	9.80665
	Watt–hours	0.002724
	Watt–hours (Int)	0.0027236
Kilogram–force m/sec	Watts	9.80665
Kilolines	Maxwells	1000
	Webers	1×10^{-5}
Kiloliters	Cu centimeters	1.0×10^6
	Cu feet	35.315
	Cu inches	61023.7
	Cu meters	1.0
	Cu yards	1.30795
	Gallons (Brit)	219.969
	Gallons (US dry)	227.021
	Gallons (US liq)	264.172
	Liters	1000
Kilometers	Astronomical units	6.685×10^{-9}
	Centimeters	100000
	Feet	3280.84
	Feet (US Survey)	3280.83
	Inches	3.937×10^4
	Light years	1.057×10^{-13}
	Meters	1000
	Miles (naut, Int)	0.53996
	Miles (statute)	0.62137
	Millimeters	10^6
	Myriameters	0.1
	Rods	198.839
	Yards	1093.61
Kilometers/hr	Cm/sec	27.778
	Feet/hr	3280.84
	Feet/min	54.6807
	Knots (Int)	0.53996
	Meters/sec	0.2778
Kilometers/hr	Miles (statute)/hr	0.62137
Kilometers/hr/sec	Cm/sec/sec	27.78
	Ft/sec/sec	0.9113
	Meters/sec/sec	0.2778
	Miles/hr/sec	0.6214
Kilometers/liter	Miles/gallon (UK or Can)	2.824811
	Miles/gallon (US)	2.352146
Kilometers/min	Cm/sec	1666.67
	Feet/min	3280.8
	Kilometers/hr	60
	Knots (Int)	32.397
	Miles/hr	37.2823

Convert From	Into	Multiply By
	Miles/min	0.62137
Kilonewtons	Dynes	1×10^8
	Pound–force	224.8089
	Poundals	7233.014
	Ton–force	0.112404
Kilopascals	Atmospheres	9.8692×10^{-3}
	Bars	1×10^{-2}
	Pound–force/sq inch	0.1450377
	Pound–force/sq ft	20.88542
	Pascals	1×10^3
	Newtons/sq meter	1×10^3
	Kilogram–force/sq cm	0.010197
	Inch of Hg @ 0°C	0.2952
	Inch of H_2O @ 68°F	4.021
Kilovolts/cm	Abvolts/cm	1×10^{11}
	Microvolts/meter	1×10^{11}
	Millivolts/meter	1×10^8
	Statvolts/cm	3.336
	Volts/inch	2540
Kilowatts	Btu/hr	3414.4
	Btu (IST)/hr	3412.14
	Btu (mean)/hr	3409.5
	Btu (mean)/min	56.825
	Btu (mean)/sec	0.9471
	Cal, gram(mean)/hr	859184
	Cal, gram(mean)/min	14319.7
	Cal, gram(mean)/sec	238.66
	Cal, kg (mean)/hr	859.18
	Cal, kg (mean)/min	14.32
	Cal, kg (mean)/sec	0.23866
	Cu ft–atm/hr	1254.7
	Ergs/sec	1×10^{10}
	Foot–poundals/min	1.424×10^6
	Foot pound–force/hr	2.655×10^6
	Foot pound–force/min	44253.7
	Foot pound–force/sec	737.56
	Gram–force cm/sec	1.0197×10^7
	Horsepower	1.341
	Horsepower (boiler)	0.1019
	Horsepower (electric)	1.34
	Horsepower (metric)	1.3596
	Joules/hr	3.6×10^6
Kilowatts	Joules (IST)/hr	3.599×10^6
	Joules/sec	1000
	Kg–force meter/hr	3.671×10^5
	Kilowatts (Int)	999.835
	Watts (Int)	999.835
Kilowatts (Int)	Btu/hr	3414.99
	Btu (IST)/hr	3412.76
	Btu (mean)/hr	3410.08
	Btu (mean)/min	56.835
	Btu (mean)/sec	0.9472
	Cal, gram (mean)/hr	859326
	Cal, gram (mean)/min	14322
	Cal, kg/hr	860.56
	Cal, kg (IST)/hr	860
	Cal, kg (mean)/hr	859.3
	Cu cm–atm/hr	3.55×10^7

Convert From	Into	Multiply By
	Cu ft–atm/hr	1254.9
	Ergs/sec	1.000165 x 10^10
	Foot–poundals/min	1.424 x 10^6
	Foot pound–force/min	44261
	Foot pound–force/sec	737.68
	Gram–force cm/sec	1.0199 x 10^7
	Horsepower	1.341
	Horsepower (boiler)	0.102
	Horsepower (electric)	1.341
	Horsepower (metric)	1.35985
	Joules/hr	3.6006 x 10^6
	Joules (Int)/hr	3.6 x 10^6
	Kg–force meter/hr	367158
	Kilowatts	1.000165
Kilowatt–hours	Btu (mean)	3409.5
	Cal, gram (mean)	859184
	Ergs	3.6 x 10^13
	Foot pound–force	2.655 x 10^6
	Gram–calories	859845
	Hp–hours	1.341
	Joules	3.6 x 10^6
	Kg–calories	859.845
	Kg–force meter	367098
	Lb H$_2$O evaporated from and at 212°F	3.5169
	Lb H$_2$O raised from 62°F to 212°F	22.728
	Watt–hours	1000
	Watt–hours (Int)	999.8
Kilowatt–hours (Int)	Btu (mean)	3410.1
	Cal, gram (IST)	860000
	Cal, gram (mean)	859326
	Cu cm–atm	3.5535 x 10^7
	Cu ft–atm	1254.9
	Foot pound–force	2.656 x 10^6
	Hp–hours	1.3412
	Joules	3.6006 x 10^6
	Joules (Int)	3.6 x 10^6
	Kg–force meter	367158
Kw–hr/gram	Btu/lb	1.549 x 10^6
Kw–hr/gram	Btu (IST)/lb	1.548 x 10^6
	Btu (mean)/lb	1.5465 x 10^6
	Cal, gram/gram	860421
	Cal, gram (mean)/gram	859184
	Cu cm–atm/gram	3.553 x 10^7
	Cu ft–atm/gram	1254.703
	Hp–hr/lb	608.28
	Joules/gram	3.6 x 10^6
Kin (Japan)	Kilograms	0.600
Knots (Int)	Cm/sec	51.44
	Feet/hr	6076.1
	Feet/min	101.269
	Feet/sec	1.688
	Kilometers/hr	1.852
	Meters/min	30.867
	Meters/sec	0.5144
	Miles (naut,Int)/hr	1
	Miles (statute)/hr	1.1508

Convert From	Into	Multiply By
	Yards/hour	2025.4
Koku (Japan)	Liters	180.39
Kotyle (Greece)	Deciliters	2.92
Kwan (Japan)	Kilograms	3.75
	Pounds (avdp)	8.267
Lamberts	Candles/sq cm	0.31831
	Candles/sq ft	295.72
	Candles/sq inch	2.0536
	Foot-lamberts	929.03
	Lumens/sq cm	1
Lasts (Brit)	Liters (dry)	2909.4
Lb	see Pound	
Leagues (naut, Brit)	Feet	18240
	Kilometers	5.5595
	Leagues (naut, Int)	1.0006
	Leagues (statute)	1.1515
	Miles (statute)	3.4545
Leagues (naut, Int)	Fathoms	3038.06
	Feet	18228
	Kilometers	5.556
	Leagues (statute)	1.1508
	Miles (statute)	3.4523
Leagues (statute)	Fathoms (US Survey)	2640
	Feet (US Survey)	15840
	Kilometers	4.828
	Leagues (naut, Int)	0.86898
	Miles (naut, Int)	2.607
	Miles (statute)	3
Li (China)	Miles	0.333
Libbra (Italy)	Kilograms	1
Light years	Astronomical units	63241.07
	Kilometers	9.46073×10^{12}
	Miles (statute)	5.8785×10^{12}
	Parsecs	0.306601
Lines	Maxwells	1
Lines (Brit)	Centimeters	0.2117
	Inches	0.0833
Lines/sq cm	Gausses	1
	Teslas	1×10^{-4}
Lines/sq inch	Gausses	0.155
	Teslas	1.55×10^{-5}
	Webers/sq cm	1.55×10^{-8}
	Webers/sq inch	1×10^{-8}
	Webers/sq meter	1.55×10^{-5}
Liniya (Russia)	Inches	0.1
Links (Gunters)	Chains (Gunters)	0.01
	Feet	0.66000132
	Feet (US Survey)	0.66
	Inches	7.9200158
	Meters	0.2012
	Miles (statute)	0.000125
	Rods (US Survey)	0.04
Links (Ramdens)	Centimeters	30.48
	Chains (Ramdens)	0.01
	Feet	1
	Inches	12
Liters	Baths (Old Testament)	0.0454545
	Bushels (Brit)	0.0275

Convert From	Into	Multiply By
	Bushels (US)	0.02838
	Cu cm	1000
	Cu feet	0.03531
	Cu inches	61.0237
	Cu meters	0.001
	Cu yards	0.00131
	Drams (US flu)	270.512
	Ephahs (Old Testament)	0.0454545
	Gallons (Brit)	0.21997
	Gallons (US dry)	0.22702
	Gallons (US liq)	0.26417
	Gills (Brit)	7.03902
	Gills (US)	8.4535
	Hins (Old Testament)	0.2727
	Hogsheads	0.00419
	Homers (Old Testament)	0.004545
	Kabs (Old Testament)	0.8182
	Logs (Old Testament)	3.27
	Milliliters	1000
	Minims (US)	16230.73
	Omers (Old Testament)	0.454545
	Ounces (Brit flu)	35.195
	Ounces (US flu)	33.81402
	Pecks (Brit)	0.10998
	Pecks (US)	0.1135
	Pints (Brit)	1.7598
	Pints (US dry)	1.8162
	Pints (US liq)	2.1134
	Quarts (Brit)	0.8799
	Quarts (US dry)	0.9081
	Quarts (US liq)	1.0567
Liters/min	Cu ft/min	0.0353
	Cu ft/sec	0.0005886
	Gal (US liq)/min	0.26417
	Gal (US liq)/sec	4.403×10^{-3}
Liters/sec	Cu ft/min	2.1189
	Cu ft/sec	0.0353
	Cu yards/min	0.07848
	Gal (US liq)/min	15.8503
	Gal (US liq)/sec	0.26417
Liter–atmospheres	Btu	0.0961
	Btu (IST)	0.09604
	Btu (mean)	0.09596
	Cal, gram	24.2173
	Cal, gram (IST)	24.201
	Cal, gram (mean)	24.182
	Cu ft–atm	0.0353
	Foot–poundals	2404.5
	Foot pound–force	74.733
	Hp–hours	3.774×10^{-5}
	Joules	101.33
	Joules (Int)	101.31
	Kg–force meter	10.33
	Kw–hours	2.815×10^{-5}
Load (Brit)	Cu yards of alluvium	1
Logs (Old Testament)	Liters	0.3056
Lumens	Candela steradian	1.0
	Candle power (spherical)	0.07958

Convert From	Into	Multiply By
	Watt	0.0015
Lumens/sq cm	Lamberts	1
	Lux	1 x 10⁴
	Phots	1
Lumens/sq ft	Foot-candles	1
	Foot-lamberts	1
	Lumens/sq meter	10.76391
	Lux	10.76391
Lumens/sq meter	Foot-candles	0.0929
	Lumens/sq ft	0.0929
	Phots	0.0001
	Lux	1
Lux	Foot-candles	0.0929
	Lumens/sq meter	1
	Phots	0.0001
Maass (Germany)	Liters	0.859
Mace (China)	Grains	58.33
Magnum	Bottles of wine	2
	Quarts	1.6
Marc (France)	Kilograms	0.2448
Maxwells	Gauss-sq cm	1
	Lines	1
	Maxwells (Int)	0.99967
	Volt-seconds	1 x 10⁻⁸
	Webers	1 x 10⁻⁸
Maxwells (Int)	Maxwells	1.00033
Maxwells/sq cm	Maxwells/sq in	6.4516
Maxwells/sq in.	Maxwells/sq cm	0.155
Megabyte	Bytes (computers)	1048576
Meganewtons	Dynes	1 x 10¹¹
	Pound-force	224808.9
	Poundals	7.233014 x 10⁶
	Ton-force	112.404
Megmhos/cm	Abmhos/cm	0.001
	Megmhos/inch	2.54
	(Microhm-cm)⁻¹	
Megmhos/inch.	Megmhos/cm	0.3937
Megohms	Microhms	1 x 10¹²
	Ohms	1 x 10⁶
	Statohms	1.1126 x 10⁻⁶
Meters	Angstrom	1 x 10¹⁰
	Centimeters	100
	Chains (Gunter's)	0.04971
	Chains (Ramden's)	0.03281
	Fathoms	0.54681
	Feet	3.28084
	Feet (US Survey)	3.28083
	Furlongs	0.00497
	Inches	39.3701
	Kilometers	0.001
	Links (Gunter's)	4.97097
	Links (Ramden's)	3.28084
	Megameters	1 x 10⁻⁶
	Miles (Brit, naut)	0.00053996
	Miles (Int, naut)	0.00053996
	Miles (statute)	0.000621
	Millimeters	1000
	Millimicrons	1 x 10⁹

Convert From	Into	Multiply By
	Mils	39370.08
	Rods	0.1988
	Yards	1.0936
Meters/hr	Feet/hr	3.2808
	Feet/min	0.05468
	Knots (Int)	0.00054
	Miles (statute)/hr	0.000621
Meters/min	Cm/sec	1.66667
	Feet/min	3.2808
	Feet/sec	0.05468
	Kilometers/hr	0.06
	Knots (Int)	0.032397
	Miles (statute)/hr	0.03728
Meters/sec	Feet/min	196.85
	Feet/sec	3.2808
	Kilometers/hr	3.6
	Kilometers/min	0.06
	Miles (statute)/hr	2.2369
	Miles (statute)/sec	6.2137×10^{-4}
Meters/(sec x sec)	Cm/(sec x sec)	100
	Feet/(sec x sec)	3.281
	Kilometers/(hr x sec)	3.6
	Miles/(hr x sec)	2.2369
Meter–candles	Lumens/sq meter	1
	Lux	1
Meter kg–force	Cm–dynes	9.807×10^7
	Cm gram–force	10^5
	Foot pound–force	7.233
Mhos	Abmhos	1×10^{-9}
	Mhos (Int)	1.000495
	Mks units	1
	Siemens	1
	Statmhos	8.9876×10^{11}
Mhos (Int)	Abmhos	9.995×10^{-10}
	Mhos	0.9995
Mhos/meter	Abmhos/cm	1×10^{-11}
	Mhos (Int)/meter	1.000495
	Siemens/meter	0.010
Microamperes	Amperes	1×10^{-6}
	Milliamperes	0.001
Microfarads	Abfarads	1×10^{-15}
	Farads	1×10^{-6}
	Statfarads	8.988×10^5
	Picofarads	1×10^6
Micrograms	Grams	1×10^{-6}
	Milligrams	0.001
Microhenries	Henries	1×10^{-6}
	Stathenries	1.113×10^{-18}
Microhms	Abohms	1000
	Megohms	1×10^{-12}
	Ohms	1×10^{-6}
	Statohms	1.113×10^{-18}
Microhm–cm	Abohm–cm	1000
	Circ mil–ohms/ft	6.015
	Microhm–inches	0.3937
	Ohm–cm	1×10^{-6}
Microhm–inches	Circ mil–ohms/ft	15.279
	Microhm–cm	2.54

Convert From	Into	Multiply By
Micrometers	Ångstroms	1×10^4
	Centimeters	1×10^{-4}
	Feet	3.2808×10^{-6}
	Inches	3.9370×10^{-5}
	Microns	1
	Mils	3.93701×10^{-2}
Micromicrofarads	Farads	1×10^{-12}
Micromicrons	Ångstrom	0.01
	Centimeters	1×10^{-10}
	Inches	3.937×10^{-11}
	Meters	1×10^{-12}
	Micrometers	1×10^{-6}
	Microns	1×10^{-6}
Microns	Ångstrom	10000
	Centimeters	0.0001
	Feet	3.2808×10^{-6}
	Inches	3.937×10^{-5}
	Meters	1×10^{-6}
Microns	Micrometers	1.0
	Millimeters	0.001
	Millimicrons	1000
Miglio (Rome)	Miles	0.925
Miles (Naut,Brit)	Cable lengths (Brit)	8.444
	Fathoms	1013.33
	Feet	6080
	Meters	1853.18
	Miles (Naut,Int)	1.00064
	Miles (statute)	1.1515
Miles (Naut,Int)	Cable lengths	8.439
	Fathoms	1012.69
	Feet	6076.12
	Feet (US survey)	6076.10
	Kilometers	1.852
	Leagues (Naut,Int)	0.3333
	Meters	1852
	Miles (Naut,Brit)	0.99936
	Miles (Statute)	1.15078
Miles (International)	Centimeters	160934
	Chains (Ramden's)	52.8
	Feet	5280
	Feet (US Survey)	5279.9894
	Inches	63360
	Kilometers	1.609344
	Light years	1.701×10^{-13}
	Meters	1609.344
	Miles (Naut,Brit)	0.8684
	Miles (Naut,Int)	0.86898
	Myriameters	0.16093
	Parsecs	5.21552×10^{-14}
Miles (Statute or US Surv)	Chains (Gunter's)	80
	Furlongs (US Survey)	8
	Links (Gunter's)	8000
	Rods (US Survey)	320
	Yards (US Survey)	1760
Miles/gallon (UK or Can)	Kilometers/liter	0.354006
	Kilometers/liter	0.425154
Miles/hr	Cm/second	44.704
	Feet/hour	5280

Convert From	Into	Multiply By
	Feet/minute	88
	Feet/second	1.4667
	Kilometers/hour	1.6093
	Kilometers/min	0.0268
	Knots (Int)	0.868976
	Meters/min	26.822
	Miles/min	0.01667
Miles/(hr x min)	Cm/(sec x sec)	0.74507
Miles/(hr x sec)	Cm/(sec x sec)	44.704
	Ft/(sec x sec)	1.4667
	Kilometers/(hr x sec)	1.6093
	Meters/(sec x sec)	0.4470
Miles/min	Cm/second	2682.2
	Feet/hr	316800
Miles/min	Feet/min	88
	Kilometers/min	1.6093
	Knots (Int)	52.1386
	Meters/min	1609.34
	Miles/hr	60
Milion (New Testament)	Meters	1478
	Yards	1618
Milliamperes	Amperes	0.001
	Microamperes	1000
Milliar (Ancient Rome)	Miles	0.92
	Stadia	8
Millibars	Atmospheres	0.000987
	Bars	0.001
	Baryes	1000
	Dynes/sq cm	1000
	Gram-force/sq cm	1.0197
	In of Hg @ 32°F	0.0295
	Newtons/sq meter	100
	Pascals	100
	Pound-force/sq ft	2.0885
	Pound-force/sq inch	0.0145
Milligrams	Carats (1877 defn)	0.00487
	Carats (metric)	0.005
	Drams (troy)	0.000257
	Drams (avdp)	0.00056
	Grains	0.01543
	Grams	0.001
	Kilograms	1×10^{-6}
	Ounces (troy)	3.215×10^{-5}
	Ounces (avdp)	3.527×10^{-5}
	Pennyweights	0.000643
	Pounds (troy)	2.679×10^{-6}
	Pounds (avdp)	2.205×10^{-6}
	Scruples (apoth)	0.000772
Milligrams/assay ton	Milligrams/kg	34.2857
	Ounces (troy)/ton (short)	1
Milligrams/gm	Carats	0.024
	Grams/ton (short)	907.185
	Milligrams/assay ton	29.16667
	Ounces (avdp)/ton (long)	35.84
	Ounces (avdp)/ton (short)	32
	Ounces (troy)/ton (long)	32.66667
	Ounces (troy)/ton (short)	29.16667
Milligram-force/inch	Dynes/cm	0.38609

Convert From	Into	Multiply By
	Dynes/inch	0.980665
	Gram–force/cm	0.000394
	Gram–force/inch	0.001
	Newton/meter	3.8609×10^{-4}
Milligrams/kg	Pounds (avdp)/ton (short)	0.002
Milligrams/liter	Grains/gallon	0.05842
	Grams/liter	0.001
	Parts/million	1
	Lb/cu ft	6.2428×10^{-5}
Milligrams/ton (metric)	Parts/billion	1.0
Milligram–force/mm	Dynes/cm	9.80665
Millihenries	Abhenries	1×10^6
	Henries	0.001
	Stathenries	1.11265×10^{-15}
Millilamberts	Candles/sq cm	0.000318
	Candles/sq inch	0.002054
	Foot–lamberts	0.929
	Lamberts	0.001
	Lumens/sq cm	0.001
	Lumens/sq ft	0.929
Milliliters	Cu cm	1.0
	Cu inches	0.06102
	Drams (US fluid)	0.27052
	Gills (US)	0.00845
	Liters	0.001
	Minims (US)	16.231
	Ounces (Brit,flu)	0.035195
	Ounces (US,flu)	0.0338
	Pints (Brit)	0.00176
	Pints (US liq)	0.00211
Millimeters	Ångstrom	1×10^7
	Centimeters	0.1
	Decimeters	0.01
	Dekameters	0.0001
	Feet	0.00328
	Inches	0.03937
	Kilometers	10^{-6}
	Meters	0.001
	Micrometers	1000
	Microns	1000
	Mils	39.37
	Yards	1.094×10^{-3}
Millimeters Hg @ 0°C	Atmospheres	0.001316
	Bars	0.00133
	Dynes/sq cm	1333.2
	Gram–force/sq cm	1.3595
	Kg–force/sq meters	13.595
	Newton/sq meter	133.3224
	Pascals	133.3224
	Pound–force/sq ft	2.7845
	Pound–force/sq in	0.0193
	Torrs	1
Millimicrons	Ångstrom	10
	Centimeters	1×10^{-7}
	Inches	3.937×10^{-8}
	Meters	1×10^{-9}
	Micrometers	0.001
	Microns	0.001

Convert From	Into	Multiply By
	Millimeters	1 x 10⁻⁶
Million gal/day	Cu ft/sec.	1.547
Milliphots	Foot–candles	0.929
	Lumens/sq ft.	0.929
	Lumens/sq meter	10
	Lux	10
	Phots	0.001
Millivolts	Statvolts	3.336 x 10⁻⁶
	Volts	0.001
Mils	Centimeters	2.540 x 10⁻³
	Feet	8.333 x 10⁻⁵
	Inches	0.001
	Kilometers	2.540 x 10⁻⁸
	Millimeter	0.0254
	Yards	2.778 x 10⁻⁵
Mina	Pounds	0.95 to 2.32
Miners inch	Cu feet/min	1.2 to 1.56
	Cu feet/sec.	0.02 to 0.026
	Liters/sec.	0.57 to 0.74
Minims (Brit)	Cu cm	0.0592
	Cu inches	0.0036
	Milliliters	0.05919
	Ounces (Brit,flu)	0.00208
	Scruples (Brit,flu)	0.05
Minims (US)	Cu cm	0.06161
	Cu inches	0.00376
	Drams (US,flu)	0.01667
	Gallons (US,liq)	1.628 x 10⁻⁵
	Gills (US)	0.00052
	Liters	6.1612 x 10⁻⁵
	Milliliters	0.061612
	Ounces (US,flu)	0.002083
	Pints (US,liq)	0.00013
Minutes (angle)	Degrees	0.016667
	Quadrants	0.000185
	Radians	0.0002909
	Seconds (angle)	60
Minutes (solar time)	Days (mean solar)	0.000694
	Days (sideral)	0.000696
	Hours (mean solar)	0.016667
	Hours (sideral)	0.016712
	Minutes (sideral)	1.002738
Minutes (sidereal)	Days (mean solar)	0.000693
	Minutes (mean solar)	0.99727
	Months (mean calendar)	2.2769 x 10⁻⁵
	Seconds (sideral)	60
Minutes(angle)/cm	Radians/cm	0.0002909
Mna (Greece)	Kilograms	1.5
Moles/cu meter	Kilomoles/cu meter	1 x 10⁻³
	Millimoles/cu meter	1 x 10³
	Moles/liter	1 x 10⁻³
	Units/cu meter	6.022137 x 10²³
Moles/liter	Moles/cu meter	1000
	Moles/cu decimeter	1.0
Moles/cu decimeters	Moles/liter	1.0
Momme (Japan)	Grams	3.75
	Kwan	0.001
Months (lunar)	Days (mean solar)	29.5306

Convert From	Into	Multiply By
	Hours (mean solar)	708.734
	Minutes (mean solar)	42524.05
	Second (mean solar)	2.551×10^6
	Weeks (mean calendar)	4.21866
Months (mean calend.)	Days (mean solar)	30.4167
	Hours (mean solar)	730
	Months (lunar)	1.030005
	Weeks (mean calendar)	4.34524
	Years (calendar)	0.08333
	Years (sidereal)	0.08327
	Years (tropical)	0.08328
Morgen (S. Africa)	Acres	2.1165
Mou (China)	Square yards	806.67
Myriagrams	Grams	10000
	Kilograms	10
	Pounds (avdp)	22.046
Myriawatts	Kilowatts	10
Nail (Old English)	Inches	2.25
Nepers	Decibels	8.686
Newtons	Dynes	100000
	Joules/meter	1.0
	Kilogram–force	0.10197
	Kilogram–meter/sq sec	1.0
	Poundals	7.233
	Pound–force	0.2248089
Newton–meters	Dyne–cm	1×10^7
	Foot Pound–force	0.73756
	Gram–force cm	10197
	Kg–force meter	0.10197
	Pound–force inch	8.8507
Newtons/sq meter	Atmospheres	9.8692×10^{-6}
	Bars	1×10^{-5}
	Baryes	10
	Dynes/sq cm	10
	Cm of Hg (0°C)	0.00075
	Cm of H_2O (4°C)	0.0101972
	Kg–force/sq cm	1.01972×10^{-5}
	Kg–force/sq meter	0.101972
	Pascal	1
	Poundals/sq ft	0.67197
	Pound–force/sq foot	0.0208854
	Pound–force/sq in	0.00014504
	Torr (0°C)	7.50062×10^{-3}
Noggins (Brit)	Cubic cm	142.065
	Gallons (Brit)	0.03125
	Gills (Brit)	1
Obolos (Greece)	Grams	0.6 to 11.2
Oersteds	Ampere–turns/inch	2.0213
	Ampere–turns/meter	79.5775
	Ampere/meter	79.5775
	Gilberts/cm	1
	Oersteds (Int)	1.000165
Oersteds (Int)	Oersteds	0.999835
Ohms	Abohms	1×10^9
	Megohms	1×10^{-6}
	Microhms	1×10^6
Ohms	Ohms (Int)	0.999505

Convert From	Into	Multiply By
	Statohms	1.1126 x 10⁻¹²
Ohms (Int)	Ohms	1.000495
Ohm–cm	Circ mil–ohms/ft	6.015 x 10⁶
	Microhm–cm	1 x 10⁶
Ohm–cm	Ohm–inches	0.3937
Ohm–inches	Ohm–cm	2.54
Ohm–meters	Abohm–cm	1 x 10¹¹
	Statohm–cm	1.113 x 10⁻¹⁰
Omers (Old Testament)	Ephah (Old Testament)	0.1
	Liters	2.2
Orguia (Ancient Greece)	Amma	0.1
	Digits	100
	Feet	6
Ounces (apoth or troy)	Dekagrams	3.11035
	Drams (apoth or troy)	8
	Drams (avdp)	17.554
	Grains	480
	Grams	31.1035
	Milligrams	31103.5
	Ounces (avdp)	1.0971
	Pennyweights	20
	Pounds (apoth or troy)	0.0833
	Pounds (avdp)	0.06857
	Scruples (apoth)	24
	Tons (short)	3.429 x 10⁻⁵
Ounces (avdp)	Drams (apoth or troy)	7.2917
	Drams (avdp)	16
	Grains	437.5
	Grams	28.3495
	Hundredweights (long)	0.000558
	Hundredweights (shrt)	0.000625
	Ounces (apoth or troy)	0.91146
	Pennyweights	18.229
	Pounds (apoth or troy)	0.07596
	Pounds (avdp)	0.0625
	Scruples (apoth)	21.875
	Tons (long)	2.79 x 10⁻⁵
	Tons (metric)	2.835 x 10⁻⁵
	Tons (short)	3.125 x 10⁻⁵
Ounces (Brit,flu)	Cu cm	28.413
	Cu inches	1.7339
	Drachms (Brit,flu)	8
	Drams (US,flu)	7.6861
	Gallons (Brit)	0.00625
	Milliliters	28.413
	Minims (Brit)	480
	Ounces (US,flu)	0.96076
Ounces (US,flu)	Cu cm	29.5735
	Cu inches	1.80469
	Cups	0.125
	Cu meters	2.9574 x 10⁻⁵
	Drops	360
	Drams (US,flu)	8
	Fifths	0.039
Ounces (US,flu)	Gallons (US,dry)	0.006714
	Gallons (US,liq)	0.00781

Convert From	Into	Multiply By
	Gills (US)	0.25
	Jiggers	0.66667
	Liters	0.02957
	Minims (US)	480
	Ounces (Brit,flu)	1.0408
	Pints (US,liq)	0.0625
	Ponys	1.0
	Quarts (US,liq)	0.0312
	Shots	1.0
	Teaspoons	6.0
	Tablespoons	2.0
Ounce–force	Newtons	0.2780
Ounce–force/sq inch	Dynes/sq cm	4309.2
	Gram–force/sq cm	4.39418
	In of H_2O @ 39.2°F	1.730097
	In of H_2O @ 60°F	1.73166
	Newton/sq meter	430.922
	Pascals	430.922
	Pound–force/sq foot	9
	Pound–force/sq inch	0.0625
Ounces (avdp)/ton (L)	Milligrams/kg	27.9018
Ounces (avdp)/ton (S)	Milligrams/kg	31.25
Ounces (troy)/ton (L)	Ounces (troy)/ton (Met)	0.984
	Ounces (troy)/ton (S)	0.8929
	Parts per million	30.612
Ounces (troy)/ton (S)	Ounces (troy)/ton (L)	1.120
	Ounces (troy)/ton (Met)	1.1023
	Parts per million	34.286
Ounces (troy)/ton (met)	Ounces (troy)/ton (L)	1.016
	Ounces (troy)/ton (S)	0.9072
	Parts per million	31.103
Paces (US Survey)	Centimeters	76.200152
	Chains (Gunter's)	0.03788
	Chains (Ramden's)	0.02500005
	Feet (US Survey)	2.5
	Hands	7.500015
	Inches (US Survey)	30
	Meters	0.762
	Ropes (Brit)	0.12500025
Palmi (Ancient Rome)	Inches	2.9
	Digiti	4
	Pes	0.25
Palms	Centimeters	7.62
	Chains (Ramden's)	0.0025
	Cubits	0.16667
	Feet	0.25
	Hands	0.75
	Inches	3
Parsecs	Kilometers	3.08568×10^{13}
	Meters	3.08568×10^{16}
	Miles (statute)	1.9174×10^{13}
Parts/billion	Milligrams/metric ton	0.90909
Parts/million	Grains/gal (Brit)	0.070155
Parts/million	Grains/gal (US)	0.05842
	Grams/liter	0.001
	Grams/ton (Met)	1
	Milligrams/liter	1

Convert From	Into	Multiply By
	Ounces (troy)/ton (S)	0.0292
	Percent	0.0001
	Pounds/million gal	8.345
Pascal	Atmospheres	9.869233×10^{-6}
	Atmospheres (technical)	1.01972×10^{-5}
	Bars	1.0×10^{-5}
	Baryes	10
	Dynes/sq cm	10
	Foot of Water (0°C)	3.34552×10^{-4}
	Inch of Hg (0°C)	2.953×10^{-4}
	Inch of Water (0°C)	4.01463×10^{-4}
	Kg-force/sq cm	1.01972×10^{-5}
	Kg-force/sq meter	1.01972×10^{-1}
	Lbf/sq inch (psi)	0.00014504
	Millibars	0.01
	Newton/square meter	1
	Poundals/sq foot	0.671969
	Pound-force/sq ft	0.0208854
	Torr	7.50062×10^{-3}
Pascal-sec	Centipoises	1.0×10^{3}
	Kg-force sec/sq meter	0.102
	Newton sec/sq meter	1.0
	Poises	10
Passus (Ancient Rome)	Feet	4.86
	Pes	5
	Stadium	0.008
Pecks (Brit)	Bushels (Brit)	0.25
	Coombs (Brit)	0.0625
	Cu cm	9092.18
	Cu inches	554.84
	Gallons (Brit)	2
	Gills (Brit)	64
	Hogsheads	0.038095
	Kilderkins (Brit)	0.1111
	Liters	0.90922
	Pints (Brit)	16
	Quarterns (Brit,dry)	4
	Quarters (Brit,dry)	0.03125
	Quarts (Brit)	8
	Quarts (US,dry)	8.25645
Pecks (US)	Barrels (US,dry)	0.07619
	Bushels (US)	0.25
	Cu cm	8809.77
	Cu feet	0.31111
	Cu inches	537.6
	Gallons,(US,dry)	2
	Gallons (US,liq)	2.3273
	Liters	8.8098
	Pints (US,dry)	16
	Quarts (US,dry)	8
Pennyweights	Drams (apoth or troy)	0.4
	Drams (avdp)	0.87771
Pennyweights	Grains	24
	Grams	1.55517
	Ounces (apoth or troy)	0.05
	Ounces (avdp)	0.05486
	Pounds (apoth or troy)	0.00417

Convert From	Into	Multiply By
	Pounds (avdp)	0.003429
Perch (Masonry)	Cu feet	24.75
	Stone 18 in x 12 in x 16.5 feet long	
Pes (Ancient Rome)	Inches	11.7
	Palmi	4
	Passus	0.2
Petrograd standard	Cu feet	165
Phots	Foot–candles	929.03
	Lumens/sq cm	1
	Lumens/sq meter	10000
	Lux	10000
Picas (printing)	Centimeters	0.4233
	Inches	0.16667
	Points	12
Picofarads	Farads	1×10^{-12}
	Microfarads	1×10^{-6}
Picul (Malaysia)	Katis	100
	Kilogram	60.48
	Pound	133.33
Pie (Rome)	Inches	11.73
Pinch	Teaspoon	1/3 to 1/4
Pints (Brit)	Cu cm	568.261
	Gallons (Brit)	0.125
	Gills (Brit)	4
	Gills (US)	4.8038
	Liters	0.56826
	Minims (Brit)	9600
	Ounces (Brit,flu)	20
	Pints (US,dry)	1.03206
	Pints (US,liq)	1.20095
	Quarts (Brit)	0.5
	Scruples (Brit,flu)	480
Pints (US,dry)	Bushels (US)	0.0156
	Cu cm	550.61
	Cu inches	33.6003
	Gallons, (US,dry)	0.125
	Gallons (US,liq)	0.14546
	Liters	0.5506
	Pecks (US)	0.625
	Pints (US,liq)	1.16368
	Quarts (US,dry)	0.5
Pints (US,liq)	Cu cm	473.1765
	Cu feet	0.01671
	Cu inches	28.875
	Cu meters	4.731765×10^{-4}
	Cu yards	0.000619
	Cups	2
	Drams (US,flu)	128
	Fifths	0.625
Pints (US,liq)	Gallons (US,liq)	0.125
	Gills (US)	4
	Jiggers	10.6667
	Liters	0.473176
	Milliliters	473.176
	Minims (US)	7680
	Ounces (US,flu)	16.0
	Pints (Brit)	0.8327
	Pints (US,dry)	0.85934

Convert From	Into	Multiply By
	Ponys	16.0
	Quarts (US,liq)	0.5
	Shots	16
	Teaspoons	96
	Tablespoons	32
Pipe (English, wine)	Gallons	126
	Liters	572.796
Planck's constant	Erg–seconds	6.6255×10^{-27}
	Joule–seconds	6.6255×10^{-34}
	Joule–sec/Avogad.	3.99×10^{-10}
Points (printing)	Centimeters	0.0351
	Inches	0.013837
	Picas	0.0833
Poises	Dynes sec/sq cm	1
	Grams/(cm x sec)	1
	Newtons sec/sq meter	0.1
	Pounds/foot hour	241.91
Poise–cu cm/gram	Sq cm/sec	1
Poise–cu ft/lb	Sq cm/sec	62.428
Poise–cu in/gram	Sq cm/sec	16.3871
Ponys	Fifths	0.02933
	Jiggers	0.5
	Ounces, (US,fluid)	0.75
	Pints	0.020833
	Shots	0.75
Pottles (Brit)	Gallons (Brit)	0.5
	Liters	2.273
Poud (Russia)	Pounds	36.113
Pounce (France)	Millimeters	27.07
Poundals	Dynes	13825.5
	Gram–force	14.098
	Joules/cm	1.383×10^{-3}
	Joules/meter	0.1383
	Kilogram–force	0.0141
	Newtons	0.1383
	Pound–force	0.03108
Pounds (apoth or troy)	Drams (apoth or troy)	96
	Drams (avdp)	210.65
	Grains	5760
	Grams	373.24
	Kilograms	0.37324
	Ounces (apoth or troy)	12
	Ounces (avdp)	13.166
	Pennyweights	240
	Pounds (avdp)	0.82286
Pounds (apoth or troy)	Scruples (apoth)	288
	Tons (long)	0.000367
	Tons (metric)	0.000373
	Tons (short)	0.0004114
Pounds (avdp)	Drams (apoth or troy)	116.667
	Drams (avdp)	256
	Grains	7000
	Grams	453.59
	Hundredweights (long)	0.008929
	Hundredweights (shrt)	0.01
	Kilograms	0.4536
	Ounces (apoth or troy)	14.583
	Ounces (avdp)	16

Convert From	Into	Multiply By
	Pennyweights	291.667
	Pounds (apoth or troy)	1.21528
	Scruples (apoth)	350
	Slugs	0.03108
	Tons (long)	0.0004464
	Tons (metric)	0.0004536
	Tons (short)	0.0005
Pound–force	Dynes	444822.166
	Joules/cm	0.04448
	Joules/meter	4.44822
	Kilogram–force	0.453592
	Newtons	4.44822
	Poundals	32.17405
Pounds/cu foot	Grams/cu cm.	0.016018
	Kg/cu meter	16.018
	Lbs/cu inch	5.787×10^{-4}
	Lbs/cu yard	27
	Lbs/mil–foot	5.45415×10^{-9}
Pounds/cu inch	Grams/cu cm	27.6799
	Grams/liter	27.6807
	Kg/cu meter	27679.9
	Lbs/cu foot	1728
	Lbs/mil–foot	9.425×10^{-6}
Pounds/cu yard	Lbs/cu foot	0.037
Pounds/foot	Kilograms/meter	1.488
Pounds/gal (Brit)	Pounds/cu ft	6.2288
Pounds/gal (US,liq)	Grams/cu cm	0.11983
	Pounds/cu ft	7.48052
Pounds/inch	Grams/cm	178.5797
	Grams/ft	5443.11
	Grams/inch	453.59237
	Ounces/cm	6.2992
	Ounces/inch	16
	Pounds/meter	39.37008
Pounds/mil–foot	Grams/cu cm	2.93693×10^{6}
Pounds/minute	Kilograms/hr	27.2155
	Kilograms/min	0.45359
Pound–force/sq ft	Atmospheres	0.00047
	Bars	0.000479
	Cm of Hg @ 0°C	0.03591
	Dynes/sq cm	478.803
Pound–force/sq ft	Feet of Water (32°F)	0.01602
	Gram–force/sq cm	0.48824
	In of Hg @ 32°F	0.014139
	In of H_2O @ 39.2°F	0.19223
	Kg–force/sq meter	4.88243
	Mm of Hg @ 0°C	0.35913
	Newtons/sq meter	47.8803
	Pascals	47.8803
	Pound–force/sq inch	0.00694
Pound–force/sq in	Atmospheres	0.06805
	Bars	0.06895
	Cm of Hg @ 0°C	5.17149
	Cm of H_2O @ 4°C	70.3087
	Dynes/sq cm	68947.6
	Feet of water (32°F)	2.3067
	Gram–force/sq cm	70.307
	In of Hg @ 32°F	2.036

Convert From	Into	Multiply By
	In of H$_2$O @ 39.2°F	27.6778
	Kg–force/sq cm	0.07031
	Kilopascals	6.89476
	Mm of Hg @ 0°C	51.715
	Newtons/sq meter	6.89476 x 10^3
	Pascals	6.89476 x 10^3
	Pound–force/sq foot	144
Pounds of water (0°C)	Cu feet	0.01602
	Cu inches	27.68
	Gallons (US)	0.1198
Pounds of water/min	Cu ft/sec	2.67 x 10^{-4}
Pound–force feet	Cm–dynes	1.356 x 10^7
	Cm gram–force	13825
	Joules	1.35582
	Meter kg–force	0.1383
	Newton meter	1.35582
PPM	See parts/million	
Prospecting dish	Gallons	2
	Cu Yards	0.008929
Pu (China)	Inches	70.5
Puncheons (Brit)	Cu meters	0.31797
	Gallons (Brit)	70
	Gallons (US)	84
Quadrants	Degrees	90
	Minutes	5400
	Radians	1.5708
Quarterns (Brit,dry)	Buckets (Brit)	0.125
	Bushels (Brit)	0.0625
	Cu cm	2273.045
	Gallons (Brit)	0.5
	Liters	2.27305
	Pecks (Brit)	0.25
Quarterns (Brit,liq)	Cu cm	142.065
	Gallons (Brit)	0.03125
	Liters	0.142065
Quarters (US,long)	Kilograms	254.0117
	Pounds (avdp)	560
Quarters (US,short)	Kilograms	226.796
	Pounds (avdp)	500
Quarts (Brit)	Cu cm	1136.52
	Cu inches	69.355
	Gallons (Brit)	0.25
	Gallons (US,liq)	0.30024
	Liters	1.1365
	Quarts (US,dry)	1.0321
	Quarts (US,liq)	1.2009
Quarts (US,dry)	Bushels (US)	0.03125
	Cu cm	1101.2
	Cu feet	0.03889
	Cu inches	67.2006
	Gallons (US,dry)	0.25
	Gallons (US,liq)	0.29091
	Liters	1.10112
	Pecks (US)	0.125
	Pints (US,dry)	2
Quarts (US,liq)	Cu cm	946.353
	Cu feet	0.0334
	Cu inches	57.75

Conversion Tables

Convert From	Into	Multiply By
	Cu meters	9.464 x 10⁻⁴
	Cu yards	1.238 x 10⁻³
	Drams (US,flu)	256
	Fifth	1.25
	Gallons (US,dry)	0.2148
	Gallons (US,liq)	0.25
	Gills (US)	8
	Liters	0.94635
	Magnums	0.625
	Ounces (US,flu)	32
	Pints (US,liq)	2
	Quarts (Brit)	0.83267
	Quarts (US,dry)	0.859367
	Shots	32
Quintals (metric)	Grams	100000
	Hundredweights (long)	1.9684
	Kilograms	100
	Pounds (avdp)	220.462
Quintal (USA, old)	Kilograms	45.36
	Pounds	100
Quires	Ream	0.05
	Sheets	24 or 25
Radians	Circumferences	0.15915
	Degrees	57.29578
	Minutes	3437.747
	Quadrants	0.63662
	Revolutions	0.15915
	Seconds	206265
Radians/cm	Degrees/cm	57.29578
	Degrees/ft	1746.37
	Degrees/in	145.531
	Minutes/cm	3437.75
Radians/sec	Degrees/sec	57.29578
Radians/sec	Revolutions/min	9.5493
	Revolutions/sec	0.15915
Radians/(sec x sec)	Revolutions/(min x min)	572.96
	Revolutions/(min x sec)	9.549297
	Revolutions/(sec x sec)	0.15915
Rattel (Arabia)	Pounds (avdp)	1.02
Ream	Quires	20
Ream	Sheets	480 or 500
Register tons	Cu feet	100
	Cu meters	2.8317
Rems	Sieverts	0.01
Revolutions	Degrees	360
	Grades	400
	Quadrants	4
	Radians	6.2832
Revolutions/min	Degrees/sec	6
	Radians/sec	0.1047
	Revolutions/sec	0.01667
Revolutions/(min x min)	Radians/(sec x sec)	1.745 x 10⁻³
	Revolutions/(min x sec)	0.01667
	Revolutions/(sec x sec)	2.778 x 10⁻⁴
Revolutions/sec	Degrees/sec	360
	Radians/sec	6.283
	Revolutions/min	60
Revolutions/(sec x sec)	Radians/(sec x sec)	6.283

Convert From	Into	Multiply By
	Revolutions/(min x min)	3600
	Revolutions/(min x sec)	60
Reyns	Centipoises	6.8948 x 10⁶
Rhes	Poises⁻¹	1
	(Pascal sec)⁻¹	10
Ri (Japan)	Miles	2.440
Rods (US Survey)	Centimeters	502.92
	Chains (Gunter's)	0.25
	Chains (Ramden's)	0.16500033
	Feet	16.500033
	Feet (US Survey)	16.5
	Furlongs (US Survey)	0.025
	Inches (US Survey)	198
	Links (Gunter's)	25
	Links (Ramden's)	16.500032
	Meters	5.0292
	Miles (statute)	0.003125
	Perches (US Survey)	1
	Yards (US Survey)	5.5
Rontgens	Coulombs/kg	2.58 x 10⁻⁴
Ropes (Brit)	Feet	20
	Meters	6.096
	Yards	6.66667
Sabbath's Day Journey	Cubits	2000
	Yards	1000
Schoppen (Germany)	Liters	0.5
Score	Units	20
Scruples (apoth)	Drams (apoth or troy)	0.3333
	Drams (avdp)	0.73143
Scruples (apoth)	Grains	20
	Grams	1.29598
	Ounces (apoth or troy)	0.041667
	Ounces (avdp)	0.045714
	Pennyweights	0.8333
	Pounds (apoth or troy)	0.00347
	Pounds (avdp)	0.002857
Scruples (Brit,flu)	Minims (Brit)	20
Se (Japan)	Square Yards	118.615
Sea Mile	Degree of latitude	1/60th
Seahs (Old Testament)	Liters	7.3
Seams (Brit)	Bushels (Brit)	8
	Cu feet	10.275
	Liters	290.95
Seconds (angle)	Degrees	0.000278
	Minutes	0.016667
	Quadrants	3.086 x 10⁻⁶
	Radians	4.8481 x 10⁻⁶
Seconds (mean solar)	Days (mean solar)	1.1574 x 10⁻⁵
	Days (sideral)	1.1606 x 10⁻⁵
	Hours (mean solar)	0.0002778
	Hours (sideral)	0.0002785
	Minutes (mean solar)	0.0166667
	Minutes (sideral)	0.016712
	Seconds (sideral)	1.002738
Seconds (sideral)	Days (mean solar)	1.1542 x 10⁻⁵
	Days (sideral)	1.1574 x 10⁻⁵
	Hours (mean solar)	0.000277
	Hours (sideral)	0.0002778

Convert From	Into	Multiply By
	Minutes (mean solar)	0.016621
	Minutes (sideral)	0.0166667
	Seconds (mean solar)	0.99726967
Seer (India)	Pounds (avdp)	2.057
Shaku (Cloth, Japan)	Meters	0.37878
Shaku (Building, Japan	Meters	0.30303
Shekels (Old Palestine)	Grains (troy)	320
	Grams	16.33
	Pounds (avdp)	0.035999
	Talents	0.00033
Shekels (Old Testament)	Bekahs (Old Testament)	2
	Grams	11.3
	Minas (Old Testament)	0.02
	Talents (Old Testament)	0.00033
Sheng (China)	Liters	1.035
Shih (China)	Pounds	157.89
Sho (Japan)	Liters	1.804
Shots	Fifths	0.039
	Jiggers	0.6667
	Ounces, (US, fluid)	1
	Pints	0.0625
	Ponys	1.333
	Quarts	0.03125
Shot of Chain (Nautical)	Feet of chain	90.0
Siemens	Abmhos	1×10^{-9}
	Mhos or (Ohms)$^{-1}$	1.0
	Statmhos	8.988×10^{11}
Sieverts	Curies/kg	21.6
	Joules/kg	1.0
	Newton meter/kg	1.0
	Rems	100
	Rontgens	8.4 (approx)
Skeins	Feet	360
	Meters	109.728
Slugs	Geepounds	1
	Kilograms	14.594
	Pounds (avdp)	32.174
Slugs/cu ft	Grams/cu cm	0.51538
Spans	Centimeters	22.86
	Fathoms	0.125
	Feet	0.75
	Inches	9
	Quarters (Brit)	1
Span (Old English)	Inches	6
Sphere	Steradians	12.57
Sq centimeters	Ares	1×10^{-6}
	Circ mm	127.324
	Circ mils	197352.5
	Sq chains (Gunter's)	2.471×10^{-7}
	Sq chains (Ramden's)	1.0764×10^{-7}
	Sq decimeters	0.01
	Sq feet	0.001076391
	Sq feet (US Survey)	0.001076387
	Sq inches	0.155
	Sq meters	0.0001
	Sq mm	100
	Sq miles	3.861×10^{-11}
	Sq mils	155000

Convert From	Into	Multiply By
	Sq rods	3.9537 x 10⁻⁶
	Sq yards	0.0001196
Sq chains (Gunter's)	Acres	0.1
	Sq feet	4356
	Sq feet (US Survey)	4355.98
	Sq inches	627264
	Sq links (Gunter's)	10000
	Sq meters	404.69
	Sq miles	0.000156
	Sq rods	16
	Sq yards	484
Sq chains (Ramden's)	Acres	0.22957
	Sq feet	10000
	Sq feet (US Survey)	9999.96
	Sq inches	1.44 x 10⁶
	Sq links (Ramden's)	10000
	Sq meters	929.03
	Sq miles	0.000359
	Sq rods	36.7309
	Sq yards	1111.11
Sq decimeters	Sq cm	100
Sq decimeters	Sq inches	15.50003
Sq degrees	Steradians	0.000305
Sq dekameters	Acres	0.02471
	Ares	1
	Sq meters	100
	Sq yards	119.599
Sq feet	Acres	2.2957 x 10⁻⁵
	Ares	0.000929
	Circular mils	1.833 x 10⁶
	Sq cm	929.03
	Sq chains (Gunter's)	0.0002296
	Sq feet (US Survey)	0.999996
	Sq inches	144
	Sq links (Gunter's)	2.2957
	Sq meters	0.0929
	Sq miles	3.58701 x 10⁻⁸
	Sq millimeters	9.290 x 10⁴
	Sq rods	0.003673
	Sq yards	0.1111
Sq feet (US Survey)	Acres	2.2957 x 10⁻⁵
	Sq centimeters	929.034
	Sq chains (Ramden's)	0.0001
	Sq feet	1.0000040
Sq hectometers	Sq meters	10000
Sq inches	Circular mils	1273239
	Sq cm	6.4516
	Sq chains (Gunter's)	1.5942 x 10⁻⁶
	Sq decimeters	0.064516
	Sq feet	0.00694
	Sq ft (US Survey)	0.00694
	Sq links (Gunter's)	0.01594
	Sq meters	0.000645
	Sq miles	2.491 x 10⁻¹⁰
	Sq mm	645.16
	Sq mils	1 x 10⁶
Sq inches/sec	Centistokes	645.2
	Sq cm/hour	23226

Convert From	Into	Multiply By
	Sq cm/sec	6.4516
	Sq meter/sec	6.452×10^{-4}
	Sq ft/min	0.41667
	Stokes	6.452
Sq kilometers	Acres	247.1054
	Sq centimeters	10^{10}
	Sq feet	1.07639×10^{7}
	Sq feet (US Survey)	1.07639×10^{7}
	Sq inches	1.550003×10^{9}
	Sq meters	1×10^{6}
	Sq miles	0.3861
	Sq yards	1.196×10^{6}
Sq links (Gunter's)	Acres	1×10^{-5}
	Sq cm	404.686
	Sq chains (Gunter's)	0.0001
	Sq feet	0.4356
	Sq feet (US Survey)	0.4356
	Sq inches	62.726
Sq links (Ramden's)	Acres	2.2957×10^{-5}
	Sq feet	1
Sq meters	Acres	0.000247
	Ares	0.01
	Hectares	0.0001
	Sq cm	10000
	Sq feet	10.7639
	Sq inches	1550.003
	Sq kilometers	1×10^{-6}
	Sq links (Gunter's)	24.71054
	Sq links (Ramden's)	10.764
	Sq miles	3.861×10^{-7}
	Sq mm	1×10^{6}
	Sq rods	0.03954
	Sq yards	1.19599
Sq meter/sec	Centistokes	1×10^{6}
	Sq feet/hr	3.875×10^{4}
	Sq in/sec	1550
	Stokes	1×10^{4}
Sq miles	Acres	640
	Hectares	258.999
	Sq chains (Gunter's)	6400
	Sq feet	2.78784×10^{7}
	Sq feet (US Survey)	2.7829×10^{7}
	Sq kilometers	2.58999
	Sq meters	2589988
	Sq rods	102400
	Sq yards	3.098×10^{6}
Sq millimeters	Circular mm	1.2732
	Circular mils	1973.5
	Sq cm	0.01
	Sq feet	1.076×10^{-5}
	Sq inches	0.00155
	Sq meters	1×10^{-6}
Sq mils	Circular mils	1.273
	Sq cm	6.452×10^{-6}
	Sq inches	1×10^{-6}
	Sq mm	0.000645
Sq rods	Acres	0.00625
	Ares	0.25293

Convert From	Into	Multiply By
	Hectares	0.00253
	Sq cm	252928.5
	Sq feet	272.25
	Sq feet (US Survey)	272.249
	Sq inches	39204
	Sq links (Gunter's)	625
	Sq links (Ramden's)	272.25
	Sq meters	25.293
	Sq miles	9.7656×10^{-6}
	Sq yards	30.25
Sq yards	Acres	0.000207
	Ares	0.00836
	Hectares	8.3613×10^{-5}
Sq yards	Sq cm	8361.27
	Sq chains (Gunter's)	0.002066
	Sq chains (Ramden's)	0.0009
	Sq feet	9
	Sq feet (US Survey)	8.99996
	Sq inches	1296
	Sq links (Gunter's)	20.661
	Sq links (Ramden's)	9
	Sq meters	0.8361
	Sq miles	3.228×10^{-7}
	Sq millimeters	8.361×10^{5}
	Sq rods	0.03306
Stadia (Ancient Rome)	Miles	0.114
	Milliare	0.125
Stadion (Ancient Greece)	Ammas	10
	Yards	200
Stadium (Ancient Rome)	Passus	125
	Yards	202.3
Statamperes	Abamperes	3.3356×10^{-11}
	Amperes	3.3356×10^{-10}
Statcoulombs	Ampere–hours	9.2656×10^{-14}
	Coulombs	3.3356×10^{-10}
	Electronic charges	2.082×10^{9}
Statfarads	Farads	1.11265×10^{-12}
	Microfarads	1.11265×10^{-6}
Stathenries	Abhenries	8.9876×10^{20}
	Henries	8.9876×10^{11}
	Millihenries	8.9876×10^{14}
Statohms	Abohms	8.9876×10^{20}
	Ohms	8.9876×10^{11}
Statvolts	Abvolts	2.9979×10^{10}
	Volts	299.79
Statvolts/cm	Volts/cm	299.79
	Volts/inch	761.47
Statvolts/inch	Volts/cm	118.028
Steradians	Hemispheres	0.15915
	Solid angles	0.079577
	Spheres	0.079577
	Spher. right angles	0.63662
	Square degrees	3282.81
Steres	Cubic meters	1
	Decisteres	10
	Dekasteres	0.1
	Liters	1000
Stilbs	Candles/sq cm	1

Convert From	Into	Multiply By
	Candles/sq inch	6.4516
	Lamberts	3.14159
Stokes	Sq cm/sec	1
	Sq inches/sec	0.1550003
	Sq meter/sec	1 x 10⁻⁴
Stones (Brit,legal)	Centals (Brit)	0.14
	Pounds	14
Talents (Old Palestine)	Kilograms	20 to 60
	Pounds	60 to 140
Talents (Old Testament)	Minas (Old Testament)	60
	Shekels (Old Testament)	3000
Tablespoons	Cups	0.0625
	Drops	180
	Gills	0.125
	Ounces (US, fluid)	0.5
	Quarts	0.015625
	Teaspoons	3
Teaspoons	Cups	0.0208333
	Drops	60
	Gills	0.04167
	Ounces (US, fluid)	0.16667
	Pinch	3 to 4
	Pints	0.01042
	Quarts	0.00521
	Tablespoons	0.3333
Teslas	Gausses	1 x 10⁴
	Lines/sq inch	6.452 x 10⁴
	Webers/sq cm	1 x 10⁻⁴
	Webers/sq inch	6.452 x 10⁻⁴
	Webers/sq meter	1.0
Therm	Btu	100000
Tierce	Gallons (wine)	42
To (Japan)	Liters	18.039
Toise (France)	Meters	1.949
Tonnes	Kilograms	1000
Tonos (Greece)	Pounds (avdp)	3315
Tons (long)	Hundredweights (long)	20
	Hundredweights (short)	22.4
	Kilograms	1016.05
	Ounces (avdp)	35840
	Pounds (apoth or troy)	2722.2
	Pounds (avdp)	2240
	Tons (metric)	1.01605
	Tons (short)	1.12
Ton–force (long)	Dynes	9.964 x 10⁸
	Newtons	9964.02
Tons (metric)	Grams	1 x 10⁶
	Hundredweights (short)	22.0462
	Kilograms	1000
	Ounces (avdp)	35273.96
	Pounds (apoth or troy)	2679.23
	Pounds (avdp)	2204.62
	Tonne	1.0
	Tons (long)	0.98421
	Tons (short)	1.1023
Ton–force (metric)	Dynes	9.80665 x 10⁸
	Newtons	9806.65
Tons (short)	Hundredweights (short)	20

Convert From	Into	Multiply By
	Kilograms	907.185
	Ounces (avdp)	32000
	Pounds (apoth or troy)	2430.55
	Pounds (avdp)	2000
Tons (short)	Tons (long)	0.89286
	Tons (metric)	0.90718
Ton–force (short)	Dynes	8.8964×10^8
	Newtons	8896.44
Tons–force (long)/sq ft	Atmospheres	1.0585
	Dynes/sq cm	1.0725×10^6
	Gram–force/sq cm	1093.66
	Newton/sq meter	1.0725×10^5
	Pascals	1.0725×10^5
	Pound–force/sq ft	2240
Ton–force (short)/sq ft	Atmospheres	0.9451
	Dynes/sq cm	957605
	Gram–force/sq cm	976.49
	Newtons/sq meter	9.5761×10^4
	Pascals	9.5761×10^4
	Pound–force/sq inch	13.889
Ton–force (long)/sq in	Atmospheres	152.423
	Dynes/sq cm	1.544×10^8
	Gram–force/sq cm	157488
	Newtons/sq meter	1.5443×10^7
	Pascals	1.5443×10^7
Tons-force (short)/sq in	Dynes/sq cm	1.37895×10^8
	Kg–force/sq mm	1.40614
	Newtons/sq meter	1.379×10^7
	Pascals	1.379×10^7
	Pound–force/sq inch	2000
Tons-refrigeration	Btu/hr	12000
Tons of water/24 hrs	Pounds of water/hr	83.333
	Gallons/min	0.16643
	Cu ft/hr	1.3349
Torr (0°C)	Mm of Hg @ 0°C	1
	Pascals	133.322
Townships	Acres	23040
	Sections	36
	Sq kilometers	93.2396
	Sq miles	36
Tu (China)	Miles	100.142
Tuns	Gallons (US)	252
	Hogsheads	4
	Pipes	2
	Puncheons	3
Vara (Old Spanish)	Feet	2.6816
	Meters	0.8359
Vara (S. America)	Meters	0.8 to 1.1
Vedro (Russia)	Liters	12.3
Verst (Russia)	Feet	3500
	Meters	1067.07
Volts	Abvolts	1×10^8
	Statvolts	0.003336
	Volts (Int)	0.99967
Volts (Int)	Volts	1.00033
Volt–coulombs	Joules (Int)	0.9998
Volt–seconds	Maxwells	1×10^8
	Webers	1.0

Convert From	Into	Multiply By
Volts/meter	Abvolts/cm	1×10^6
Volts/meter	Kilovolts/cm	1×10^{-5}
	Newtons/coulomb	1.0
	Statvolts	3.33565×10^{-5}
Volts/in	Volts/cm	0.393701
	Volts/meter	39.3701
	Volts/mil	1000
Watts	Btu/hr	3.41214
	Btu (mean)/hr	3.4095
	Btu (mean)/min	0.056825
	Btu/sec	0.000948
	Btu (mean)/sec	0.000947
	Cal,g/hr	860.42
	Cal,g (mean)/hr	859.18
	Cal,g (@20°C)/hr	860.85
	Cal,g/min	14.34
	Cal,g (IST)/min	14.331
	Cal,g (mean)/min	14.3197
	Cal,kg/min	0.01434
	Cal,kg (IST)/min	0.01433
	Cal,kg (mean)/min	0.01432
	Ergs/sec	1×10^7
	Foot pound–force/min	44.2537
	Foot pound–force/sec	0.737562
	Horsepower	0.00134
	Horsepower (boiler)	0.0001
	Horsepower (electric)	0.00134
	Horsepower (metric)	0.0013596
	Joules/sec	1
	Kilogram–calories/min	0.01433
	Kilowatts	0.001
	Liter–atmosphere/hr	35.529
	Watts (Int)	0.99984
Watts (Int)	Btu/hr	3.41499
	Btu (mean)/hr	3.41008
	Btu/min	0.569165
	Btu (mean)/min	0.0568
	Cal,g/hr	860.56
	Cal,g (mean)/hr	859.326
	Cal,kg/min	0.0143
	Cal,kg (IST)/min	0.01433
	Cal,kg (mean)/min	0.01432
	Ergs/sec	1.000165×10^7
	Joules (Int)/sec	1
	Watts	1.000165
Watts/sq cm	Btu/(hr x sq ft)	3172.1
	Cal,g/(hr x sq cm)	860.421
	Foot lbf/(min x sq ft)	41113
Watts/sq in	Btu/(hr x sq ft)	491.68
	Cal,g/(hr x sq cm)	133.365
	Foot lbf/(min x sq ft)	6372.5
Watt/sq meter	Foot lbf/hr sq meter	2655.2
	Horsepower/sq meter	0.00134
	Joules/hr sq meter	3600
	Joules/sec sq meter	1.0
Watt/sq meter	Kilowatts/sq meter	0.001
Watt/meter K	Btu/hr foot °F	0.5778
	Kilocalories/hr foot °C	0.26208

Convert From	Into	Multiply By
Watt–hours	Btu	3.4144
	Btu (mean)	3.4095
	Cal,g	860.42
	Cal,kg (mean)	0.85918
	Cal,g (mean)	859.18
	Ergs	3.60×10^{10}
	Foot pound–force	2655.22
	Hp–hours	0.00134
	Joules	3600
	Joules (Int)	3599.41
	Kg-calories	0.8604
	Kg–force meter	367.098
	Kw–hours	0.001
	Watt–hours (Int)	0.9998
Watt–sec	Foot pound–force	0.73756
	Gram–force cm	10197.2
	Joules	1
	Liter–atmospheres	0.00987
	Volt–coulombs	1
Webers	Kilolines	1×10^{5}
	Lines	1×10^{8}
	Maxwells	1×10^{8}
	Volt–seconds	1
Webers/sq cm	Gausses	1×10^{8}
	Lines/sq cm	1×10^{8}
	Lines/sq in	6.4516×10^{8}
	Teslas	1×10^{4}
Webers/sq in	Gausses	1.550003×10^{7}
	Lines/sq inch	10^{8}
	Webers/sq cm	0.1550
	Webers/sq meter	1550
	Teslas	1.550003×10^{3}
Webers/sq meter	Gausses	10^{4}
	Lines/sq inch	6.452×10^{4}
	Teslas	1.0
	Webers/sq cm	10^{-4}
	Webers/sq inch	6.452×10^{-4}
Weeks (mean calendar)	Days (mean solar)	7
	Days (sidereal)	7.01916
	Hours (mean solar)	168
	Hours (sidereal)	168.46
	Minutes (mean solar)	10080
	Minutes (sidereal)	10107.6
	Months (lunar)	0.237042
	Months (mean calendar)	0.230137
	Years (calendar)	0.019178
	Years (sidereal)	0.0191646
	Years (tropical)	0.019165
Weys (Brit)	Pounds (avdp)	256
Yards	Centimeters	91.44
	Chains (Gunter's)	0.454546
	Chains (Ramden's)	0.03
	Cubits	2
	Fathoms (US Survey)	0.499999
	Feet	3
	Feet (US Survey)	2.999994
	Furlongs (US Survey)	0.004545
	Inches	36

Convert From	Into	Multiply By
	Kilometers	9.144 x 10⁻⁴
	Meters	0.9144
	Miles (naut)	4.937 x 10⁻⁴
	Miles (statute)	5.682 x 10⁻⁴
	Millimeters	914.4
	Poles (Brit)	0.181818
	Quarters (Brit)	4
	Rods (US Survey)	0.181818
	Spans	4
Years (calendar)	Days (mean solar)	365
	Hours (mean solar)	8760
	Minutes (mean solar)	525600
	Months (lunar)	12.360065
	Months (mean calendar)	12
	Seconds (mean solar)	3.1536 x 10⁷
	Weeks (mean calendar)	52.14286
	Years (sidereal)	0.999298
	Years (tropical)	0.999337
Years (leap)	Days (mean solar)	366
Years (sidereal)	Days (mean solar)	365.2564
	Days (sidereal)	366.2564
	Years (calendar)	1.000702
	Years (tropical)	1.000039
Years (tropical)	Days (mean solar)	365.242
	Days (sidereal)	366.242
	Hours (mean solar)	8765.81
	Hours (sidereal)	8789.81
	Months (mean calendar)	12.00796
	Seconds (mean solar)	3.15569 x 10⁷
	Seconds (sidereal)	3.16433 x 10⁷
	Weeks (mean calendar)	52.17746
	Years (calendar)	1.0006635
	Years (sidereal)	0.99996
Zoll (Switzerland)	Centimeters	3
Zolotnik (Russia)	Grains	65.8306

Calendar

Perpetual Calendar

Calendars on the following 14 pages apply to years other than those listed on each calendar. A look up table for additional years is provided on page 752. Simply locate the year you want and the **C#** to the right of that year is the number of the calendar you want.

Although a detailed list of national and state holidays is listed on page 230, the following special dates are listed on each of the 14 calendars in this section.

Abbrev.	Holiday and Date
N	New Years Day - January 1 (check for observed day)
K	Martin Luther King Day - 3rd Monday in January
P	Presidents Day - 3rd Monday in February
-	Easter - 1st Sunday after the 1st full moon after the Spring equinox. 2002=3-31; 2003=4-20; 2004=4-11 2005=3-27; 2006=4-16; 2007=4-8; 2008=3-23; 2009=4-12 2010=4-4; 2011=4-24; 2012=4-8; 2013=3-31; 2014=4-20 2015=4-5; 2016=3-27; 2017=4-16; 2018=4-1
S	Secretaries Day - Wednesday of the last FULL week in April
M	Memorial Day - Last Monday in May
I	Independence Day - July 4 (check for observed)
L	Labor Day - 1st Monday in September
C	Columbus Day - 2nd Monday in October
V	Veterans Day - November 11 (check for observed day)
T	Thanksgiving - 4th Thursday in November
Z	Christmas - December 25 (check for observed day)

"Observed day" indicates that if the holiday occurs on a Saturday, then the work day taken off is Friday and if it occurs on a Sunday, then the work day taken off is Monday.

Calendar 1 2005

January

S	M	T	W	T	F	S
					N	1
2	3	4	5	6	7	8
9	10	11	12	13	14	15
16	*K*	18	19	20	21	22
23	24	25	26	27	28	29
30	31					

February

S	M	T	W	T	F	S
		1	2	3	4	5
6	7	8	9	10	11	12
13	14	15	16	17	18	19
20	*P*	22	23	24	25	26
27	28					

March

S	M	T	W	T	F	S
		1	2	3	4	5
6	7	8	9	10	11	12
13	14	15	16	17	18	19
20	21	22	23	24	25	26
27	28	29	30	31		

April

S	M	T	W	T	F	S
					1	2
3	4	5	6	7	8	9
10	11	12	13	14	15	16
17	18	19	20	21	22	23
24	25	26	*S*	28	29	30

May

S	M	T	W	T	F	S
1	2	3	4	5	6	7
8	9	10	11	12	13	14
15	16	17	18	19	20	21
22	23	24	25	26	27	28
29	*M*	31				

June

S	M	T	W	T	F	S
			1	2	3	4
5	6	7	8	9	10	11
12	13	14	15	16	17	18
19	20	21	22	23	24	25
26	27	28	29	30		

July

S	M	T	W	T	F	S
					1	2
3	*I*	5	6	7	8	9
10	11	12	13	14	15	16
17	18	19	20	21	22	23
24	25	26	27	28	29	30
31						

August

S	M	T	W	T	F	S
	1	2	3	4	5	6
7	8	9	10	11	12	13
14	15	16	17	18	19	20
21	22	23	24	25	26	27
28	29	30	31			

September

S	M	T	W	T	F	S
				1	2	3
4	*L*	6	7	8	9	10
11	12	13	14	15	16	17
18	19	20	21	22	23	24
25	26	27	28	29	30	

October

S	M	T	W	T	F	S
						1
2	3	4	5	6	7	8
9	*C*	11	12	13	14	15
16	17	18	19	20	21	22
23	24	25	26	27	28	29
30	31					

November

S	M	T	W	T	F	S
		1	2	3	4	5
6	7	8	9	10	*V*	12
13	14	15	16	17	18	19
20	21	22	23	*T*	25	26
27	28	29	30			

December

S	M	T	W	T	F	S
			1	2	3	
4	5	6	7	8	9	10
11	12	13	14	15	16	17
18	19	20	21	22	23	24
25	*Z*	27	28	29	30	31

Holiday calendar on page 230; Calendar year selector on page 752.

January

S	M	T	W	T	F	S
1	*N*	3	4	5	6	7
8	9	10	11	12	13	14
15	*K*	17	18	19	20	21
22	23	24	25	26	27	28
29	30	31				

July

S	M	T	W	T	F	S
						1
2	3	*I*	5	6	7	8
9	10	11	12	13	14	15
16	17	18	19	20	21	22
23	24	25	26	27	28	29
30	31					

February

S	M	T	W	T	F	S
			1	2	3	4
5	6	7	8	9	10	11
12	13	14	15	16	17	18
19	*P*	21	22	23	24	25
26	27	28				

August

S	M	T	W	T	F	S
		1	2	3	4	5
6	7	8	9	10	11	12
13	14	15	16	17	18	19
20	21	22	23	24	25	26
27	28	29	30	31		

March

S	M	T	W	T	F	S
			1	2	3	4
5	6	7	8	9	10	11
12	13	14	15	16	17	18
19	20	21	22	23	24	25
26	27	28	29	30	31	

September

S	M	T	W	T	F	S
					1	2
3	*L*	5	6	7	8	9
10	11	12	13	14	15	16
17	18	19	20	21	22	23
24	25	26	27	28	29	30

April

S	M	T	W	T	F	S
						1
2	3	4	5	6	7	8
9	10	11	12	13	14	15
16	17	18	19	20	21	22
23	24	25	26	*S*	28	29
30						

October

S	M	T	W	T	F	S
1	2	3	4	5	6	7
8	*C*	10	11	12	13	14
15	16	17	18	19	20	21
22	23	24	25	26	27	28
29	30	31				

May

S	M	T	W	T	F	S
	1	2	3	4	5	6
7	8	9	10	11	12	13
14	15	16	17	18	19	20
21	22	23	24	25	26	27
28	*M*	30	31			

November

S	M	T	W	T	F	S
			1	2	3	4
5	6	7	8	9	*V*	11
12	13	14	15	16	17	18
19	20	21	22	*T*	24	25
26	27	28	29	30		

June

S	M	T	W	T	F	S
				1	2	3
4	5	6	7	8	9	10
11	12	13	14	15	16	17
18	19	20	21	22	23	24
25	26	27	28	29	30	

December

S	M	T	W	T	F	S
					1	2
3	4	5	6	7	8	9
10	11	12	13	14	15	16
17	18	19	20	21	22	23
24	*Z*	26	27	28	29	30
31						

Holiday calendar on page 230; Calendar year selector on page 752.

January

S	M	T	W	T	F	S
	N	2	3	4	5	6
7	8	9	10	11	12	13
14	*K*	16	17	18	19	20
21	22	23	24	25	26	27
28	29	30	31			

July

S	M	T	W	T	F	S
	1	2	3	*I*	5	6
7	8	9	10	11	12	13
14	15	16	17	18	19	20
21	22	23	24	25	26	27
28	29	30	31			

February

S	M	T	W	T	F	S
				1	2	3
4	5	6	7	8	9	10
11	12	13	14	15	16	17
18	*P*	20	21	22	23	24
25	26	27	28	29		

August

S	M	T	W	T	F	S
				1	2	3
4	5	6	7	8	9	10
11	12	13	14	15	16	17
18	19	20	21	22	23	24
25	26	27	28	29	30	31

March

S	M	T	W	T	F	S
					1	2
3	4	5	6	7	8	9
10	11	12	13	14	15	16
17	18	19	20	21	22	23
24	25	26	27	28	29	30
31						

September

S	M	T	W	T	F	S
1	*L*	3	4	5	6	7
8	9	10	11	12	13	14
15	16	17	18	19	20	21
22	23	24	25	26	27	28
29	30					

April

S	M	T	W	T	F	S
	1	2	3	4	5	6
7	8	9	10	11	12	13
14	15	16	17	18	19	20
21	22	23	*S*	25	26	27
28	29	30				

October

S	M	T	W	T	F	S
		1	2	3	4	5
6	7	8	9	10	11	12
13	*C*	15	16	17	18	19
20	21	22	23	24	25	26
27	28	29	30	31		

May

S	M	T	W	T	F	S
			1	2	3	4
5	6	7	8	9	10	11
12	13	14	15	16	17	18
19	20	21	22	23	24	25
26	*M*	28	29	30	31	

November

S	M	T	W	T	F	S
					1	2
3	4	5	6	7	8	9
10	*V*	12	13	14	15	16
17	18	19	20	21	22	23
24	25	26	27	*T*	29	30

June

S	M	T	W	T	F	S
						1
2	3	4	5	6	7	8
9	10	11	12	13	14	15
16	17	18	19	20	21	22
23	24	25	26	27	28	29
30						

December

S	M	T	W	T	F	S
1	2	3	4	5	6	7
8	9	10	11	12	13	14
15	16	17	18	19	20	21
22	23	24	*Z*	26	27	28
29	30	31				

Holiday calendar on page 230; Calendar year selector on page 752.

January

S	M	T	W	T	F	S
			N	2	3	4
5	6	7	8	9	10	11
12	13	14	15	16	17	18
19	*K*	21	22	23	24	25
26	27	28	29	30	31	

July

S	M	T	W	T	F	S
		1	2	3	*I*	5
6	7	8	9	10	11	12
13	14	15	16	17	18	19
20	21	22	23	24	25	26
27	28	29	30	31		

February

S	M	T	W	T	F	S
						1
2	3	4	5	6	7	8
9	10	11	12	13	14	15
16	*P*	18	19	20	21	22
23	24	25	26	27	28	

August

S	M	T	W	T	F	S
					1	2
3	4	5	6	7	8	9
10	11	12	13	14	15	16
17	18	19	20	21	22	23
24	25	26	27	28	29	30
31						

March

S	M	T	W	T	F	S
						1
2	3	4	5	6	7	8
9	10	11	12	13	14	15
16	17	18	19	20	21	22
23	24	25	26	27	28	29
30	31					

September

S	M	T	W	T	F	S
	L	*2*	*3*	*4*	*5*	*6*
7	*8*	*9*	*10*	*11*	*12*	*13*
14	*15*	*16*	*17*	*18*	*19*	*20*
21	*22*	*23*	*24*	*25*	*26*	*27*
28	*29*	*30*				

April

S	M	T	W	T	F	S
		1	2	3	4	5
6	7	8	9	10	11	12
13	14	15	16	17	18	19
20	21	22	*S*	24	25	26
27	28	29	30			

October

S	M	T	W	T	F	S
			1	2	3	4
5	6	7	8	9	10	11
12	*C*	14	15	16	17	18
19	20	21	22	23	24	25
26	27	28	29	30	31	

May

S	M	T	W	T	F	S
				1	2	3
4	5	6	7	8	9	10
11	12	13	14	15	16	17
18	19	20	21	22	23	24
25	*M*	27	28	29	30	31

November

S	M	T	W	T	F	S
						1
2	3	4	5	6	7	8
9	10	*V*	12	13	14	15
16	17	18	19	20	21	22
23	24	25	26	*T*	28	29
30						

June

S	M	T	W	T	F	S
1	2	3	4	5	6	7
8	9	10	11	12	13	14
15	16	17	18	19	20	21
22	23	24	25	26	27	28
29	30					

December

S	M	T	W	T	F	S
	1	2	3	4	5	6
7	8	9	10	11	12	13
14	15	16	17	18	19	20
21	22	23	24	*Z*	26	27
28	29	30	31			

Holiday calendar on page 230; Calendar year selector on page 752.

Calendar 5   2009

January

S	M	T	W	T	F	S
				N	2	3
4	5	6	7	8	9	10
11	12	13	14	15	16	17
18	K	20	21	22	23	24
25	26	27	28	29	30	31

February

S	M	T	W	T	F	S
1	2	3	4	5	6	7
8	9	10	11	12	13	14
15	P	17	18	19	20	21
22	23	24	25	26	27	28

March

S	M	T	W	T	F	S
1	2	3	4	5	6	7
8	9	10	11	12	13	14
15	16	17	18	19	20	21
22	23	24	25	26	27	28
29	30	31				

April

S	M	T	W	T	F	S
			1	2	3	4
5	6	7	8	9	10	11
12	13	14	15	16	17	18
19	20	21	S	23	24	25
26	27	28	29	30		

May

S	M	T	W	T	F	S
					1	2
3	4	5	6	7	8	9
10	11	12	13	14	15	16
17	18	19	20	21	22	23
24	M	26	27	28	29	30
31						

June

S	M	T	W	T	F	S
	1	2	3	4	5	6
7	8	9	10	11	12	13
14	15	16	17	18	19	20
21	22	23	24	25	26	27
28	29	30				

July

S	M	T	W	T	F	S
			1	2	I	4
5	6	7	8	9	10	11
12	13	14	15	16	17	18
19	20	21	22	23	24	25
26	27	28	29	30	31	

August

S	M	T	W	T	F	S
						1
2	3	4	5	6	7	8
9	10	11	12	13	14	15
16	17	18	19	20	21	22
23	24	25	26	27	28	29
30	31					

September

S	M	T	W	T	F	S
		1	2	3	4	5
6	L	8	9	10	11	12
13	14	15	16	17	18	19
20	21	22	23	24	25	26
27	28	29	30			

October

S	M	T	W	T	F	S
				1	2	3
4	5	6	7	8	9	10
11	C	13	14	15	16	17
18	19	20	21	22	23	24
25	26	27	28	29	30	31

November

S	M	T	W	T	F	S
1	2	3	4	5	6	7
8	9	10	V	12	13	14
15	16	17	18	19	20	21
22	23	24	25	T	27	28
29	30					

December

S	M	T	W	T	F	S
		1	2	3	4	5
6	7	8	9	10	11	12
13	14	15	16	17	18	19
20	21	22	23	24	Z	26
27	28	29	30	31		

Holiday calendar on page 230; Calendar year selector on page 752.

January

S	M	T	W	T	F	S
					N	2
3	4	5	6	7	8	9
10	11	12	13	14	15	16
17	*K*	19	20	21	22	23
24	25	26	27	28	29	30
31						

February

S	M	T	W	T	F	S
	1	2	3	4	5	6
7	8	9	10	11	12	13
14	*P*	16	17	18	19	20
21	22	23	24	25	26	27
28						

March

S	M	T	W	T	F	S
	1	2	3	4	5	6
7	8	9	10	11	12	13
14	15	16	17	18	19	20
21	22	23	24	25	26	27
28	29	30	31			

April

S	M	T	W	T	F	S
				1	2	3
4	5	6	7	8	9	10
11	12	13	14	15	16	17
18	19	20	*S*	22	23	24
25	26	27	28	29	30	

May

S	M	T	W	T	F	S
						1
2	3	4	5	6	7	8
9	10	11	12	13	14	15
16	17	18	19	20	21	22
23	24	25	26	27	28	29
30	*M*					

June

S	M	T	W	T	F	S
		1	2	3	4	5
6	7	8	9	10	11	12
13	14	15	16	17	18	19
20	21	22	23	24	25	26
27	28	29	30			

July

S	M	T	W	T	F	S
				1	2	3
4	*I*	6	7	8	9	10
11	12	13	14	15	16	17
18	19	20	21	22	23	24
25	26	27	28	29	30	31

August

S	M	T	W	T	F	S
1	2	3	4	5	6	7
8	9	10	11	12	13	14
15	16	17	18	19	20	21
22	23	24	25	26	27	28
29	30	31				

September

S	M	T	W	T	F	S
			1	2	3	4
5	*L*	7	8	9	10	11
12	13	14	15	16	17	18
19	20	21	22	23	24	25
26	27	28	29	30		

October

S	M	T	W	T	F	S
					1	2
3	4	5	6	7	8	9
10	*C*	12	13	14	15	16
17	18	19	20	21	22	23
24	25	26	27	28	29	30
31						

November

S	M	T	W	T	F	S
	1	2	3	4	5	6
7	8	9	10	*V*	12	13
14	15	16	17	18	19	20
21	22	23	24	*T*	26	27
28	29	30				

December

S	M	T	W	T	F	S
		1	2	3	4	5
6	7	8	9	10	11	12
13	14	15	16	17	18	19
19	20	21	22	23	*Z*	25
26	27	28	29	30	*N*	

Holiday calendar on page 230; Calendar year selector on page 752.

January

S	M	T	W	T	F	S
					N	1
2	3	4	5	6	7	8
9	10	11	12	13	14	15
16	*K*	18	19	20	21	22
23	24	25	26	27	28	29
30	31					

July

S	M	T	W	T	F	S
						1
2	3	*I*	5	6	7	8
9	10	11	12	13	14	15
16	17	18	19	20	21	22
23	24	25	26	27	28	29
30	31					

February

		1	2	3	4	5
6	7	8	9	10	11	12
13	14	15	16	17	18	19
20	*P*	22	23	24	25	26
27	28	29	←see below*			

August

		1	2	3	4	5
6	7	8	9	10	11	12
13	14	15	16	17	18	19
20	21	22	23	24	25	26
27	28	29	30	31		

March

		1	2	3	4	
5	6	7	8	9	10	11
12	13	14	15	16	17	18
19	20	21	22	23	24	25
26	27	28	29	30	31	

September

					1	2
3	*L*	5	6	7	8	9
10	11	12	13	14	15	16
17	18	19	20	21	22	23
24	25	26	27	28	29	30

April

						1
2	3	4	5	6	7	8
9	10	11	12	13	14	15
16	17	18	19	20	21	22
23	24	25	*S*	27	28	29
30						

October

1	2	3	4	5	6	7
8	*C*	10	11	12	13	14
15	16	17	18	19	20	21
22	23	24	25	26	27	28
29	30	31				

May

	1	2	3	4	5	6
7	8	9	10	11	12	13
14	15	16	17	18	19	20
21	22	23	24	25	26	27
28	*M*	30	31			

November

		1	2	3	4	
5	6	7	8	9	*V*	11
12	13	14	15	16	17	18
19	20	21	22	*T*	24	25
26	27	28	29	30		

June

			1	2	3	
4	5	6	7	8	9	10
11	12	13	14	15	16	17
18	19	20	21	22	23	24
25	26	27	28	29	30	

December

					1	2
3	4	5	6	7	8	9
10	11	12	13	14	15	16
17	18	19	20	21	22	23
24	*Z*	26	27	28	29	30
31						

Holiday calendar on page 230; Calendar year selector on page 752.

*Pope Gregory XIII, creator of today's calendar, rescheduled leap year to fall every 4th yr. <u>except</u> century years not divisible by 400. **2000 <u>will be</u> a leap year** but 1700, 1800 and 1900 were not.

Calendar 8 — 2007

January

S	M	T	W	T	F	S
	N	2	3	4	5	6
7	8	9	10	11	12	13
14	*K*	16	17	18	19	20
21	22	23	24	25	26	27
28	29	30	31			

February

S	M	T	W	T	F	S
				1	2	3
4	5	6	7	8	9	10
11	12	13	14	15	16	17
18	*P*	20	21	22	23	24
25	26	27	28			

March

S	M	T	W	T	F	S
				1	2	3
4	5	6	7	8	9	10
11	12	13	14	15	16	17
18	19	20	21	22	23	24
25	26	27	28	29	30	31

April

S	M	T	W	T	F	S
1	2	3	4	5	6	7
8	9	10	11	12	13	14
15	16	17	18	19	20	21
22	23	24	*S*	26	27	28
29	30					

May

S	M	T	W	T	F	S
		1	2	3	4	5
6	7	8	9	10	11	12
13	14	15	16	17	18	19
20	21	22	23	24	25	26
27	*M*	29	30	31		

June

S	M	T	W	T	F	S
					1	2
3	4	5	6	7	8	9
10	11	12	13	14	15	16
17	18	19	20	21	22	23
24	25	26	27	28	29	30

July

S	M	T	W	T	F	S
1	2	3	4	*I*	6	7
8	9	10	11	12	13	14
15	16	17	18	19	20	21
22	23	24	25	26	27	28
29	30	31				

August

S	M	T	W	T	F	S
			1	2	3	4
5	6	7	8	9	10	11
12	13	14	15	16	17	18
19	20	21	22	23	24	25
26	27	28	29	30	31	

September

S	M	T	W	T	F	S
						1
2	*L*	4	5	6	7	8
9	10	11	12	13	14	15
16	17	18	19	20	21	22
23	24	25	26	27	28	29
30						

October

S	M	T	W	T	F	S
	1	2	3	4	5	6
7	*C*	9	10	11	12	13
14	15	16	17	18	19	20
21	22	23	24	25	26	27
28	29	30	31			

November

S	M	T	W	T	F	S
				1	2	3
4	5	6	7	8	9	10
11	*V*	13	14	15	16	17
18	19	20	21	*T*	23	24
25	26	27	28	29	30	

December

S	M	T	W	T	F	S
						1
2	3	4	5	6	7	8
9	10	11	12	13	14	15
16	17	18	19	20	21	22
23	24	*Z*	26	27	28	29
30	31					

Holiday calendar on page 230; Calendar year selector on page 752.

Calendar 9   2002

January

S	M	T	W	T	F	S
		N	2	3	4	5
6	7	8	9	10	11	12
13	14	15	16	17	18	19
20	K	22	23	24	25	26
27	28	29	30	31		

July

S	M	T	W	T	F	S
	1	2	3	I	5	6
7	8	9	10	11	12	13
14	15	16	17	18	19	20
21	22	23	24	25	26	27
28	29	30	31			

February

S	M	T	W	T	F	S
					1	2
3	4	5	6	7	8	9
10	11	12	13	14	15	16
17	P	19	20	21	22	23
24	25	26	27	28		

August

S	M	T	W	T	F	S
				1	2	3
4	5	6	7	8	9	10
11	12	13	14	15	16	17
18	19	20	21	22	23	24
25	26	27	28	29	30	31

March

S	M	T	W	T	F	S
					1	2
3	4	5	6	7	8	9
10	11	12	13	14	15	16
17	18	19	20	21	22	23
24	25	26	27	28	29	30
31						

September

S	M	T	W	T	F	S
1	L	3	4	5	6	7
8	9	10	11	12	13	14
15	16	17	18	19	20	21
22	23	24	25	26	27	28
29	30					

April

S	M	T	W	T	F	S
	1	2	3	4	5	6
7	8	9	10	11	12	13
14	15	16	17	18	19	20
21	22	23	S	25	26	27
28	29	30				

October

S	M	T	W	T	F	S
		1	2	3	4	5
6	7	8	9	10	11	12
13	C	15	16	17	18	19
20	21	22	23	24	25	26
27	28	29	30	31		

May

S	M	T	W	T	F	S
			1	2	3	4
5	6	7	8	9	10	11
12	13	14	15	16	17	18
19	20	21	22	23	24	25
26	M	28	29	30	31	

November

S	M	T	W	T	F	S
					1	2
3	4	5	6	7	8	9
10	V	12	13	14	15	16
17	18	19	20	21	22	23
24	25	26	27	T	29	30

June

S	M	T	W	T	F	S
						1
2	3	4	5	6	7	8
9	10	11	12	13	14	15
16	17	18	19	20	21	22
23	24	25	26	27	28	29
30						

December

S	M	T	W	T	F	S
1	2	3	4	5	6	7
8	9	10	11	12	13	14
15	16	17	18	19	20	21
22	23	24	Z	26	27	28
29	30	31				

Holiday calendar on page 230; Calendar year selector on page 752.

Calendar 10 — 2004

January

S	M	T	W	T	F	S
				N	2	3
4	5	6	7	8	9	10
11	12	13	14	15	16	17
18	*K*	20	21	22	23	24
25	26	27	28	29	30	31

February

S	M	T	W	T	F	S
1	2	3	4	5	6	7
8	9	10	11	12	13	14
15	*P*	17	18	19	20	21
22	23	24	25	26	27	28
29						

March

S	M	T	W	T	F	S
	1	2	3	4	5	6
7	8	9	10	11	12	13
14	15	16	17	18	19	20
21	22	23	24	25	26	27
28	29	30	31			

April

S	M	T	W	T	F	S
				1	2	3
4	5	6	7	8	9	10
11	12	13	14	15	16	17
18	19	20	*S*	22	23	24
25	26	27	28	29	30	

May

S	M	T	W	T	F	S
						1
2	3	4	5	6	7	8
9	10	11	12	13	14	15
16	17	18	19	20	21	22
23	24	25	26	27	28	29
30	*M*					

June

S	M	T	W	T	F	S
		1	2	3	4	5
6	7	8	9	10	11	12
13	14	15	16	17	18	19
20	21	22	23	24	25	26
27	28	29	30			

July

S	M	T	W	T	F	S
				1	2	3
4	*I*	6	7	8	9	10
11	12	13	14	15	16	17
18	19	20	21	22	23	24
25	26	27	28	29	30	31

August

S	M	T	W	T	F	S
1	2	3	4	5	6	7
8	9	10	11	12	13	14
15	16	17	18	19	20	21
22	23	24	25	26	27	28
29	30	31				

September

S	M	T	W	T	F	S
			1	2	3	4
5	*L*	7	8	9	10	11
12	13	14	15	16	17	18
19	20	21	22	23	24	25
26	27	28	29	30		

October

S	M	T	W	T	F	S
					1	2
3	4	5	6	7	8	9
10	*C*	12	13	14	15	16
17	18	19	20	21	22	23
24	25	26	27	28	29	30
31						

November

S	M	T	W	T	F	S
	1	2	3	4	5	6
7	8	9	10	*V*	12	13
14	15	16	17	18	19	20
21	22	23	24	*T*	26	27
28	29	30				

December

S	M	T	W	T	F	S
			1	2	3	4
5	6	7	8	9	10	11
12	13	14	15	16	17	18
19	20	21	22	23	*Z*	25
26	27	28	29	30	*N*	

Holiday calendar on page 230; Calendar year selector on page 752.

January

S	M	T	W	T	F	S
		N	2	3	4	5
6	7	8	9	10	11	12
13	14	15	16	17	18	19
20	*K*	22	23	24	25	26
27	28	29	30	31		

July

S	M	T	W	T	F	S
		1	2	3	*I*	5
6	7	8	9	10	11	12
13	14	15	16	17	18	19
20	21	22	23	24	25	26
27	28	29	30	31		

February

S	M	T	W	T	F	S
					1	2
3	4	5	6	7	8	9
10	11	12	13	14	15	16
17	*P*	19	20	21	22	23
24	25	26	27	28	29	

August

S	M	T	W	T	F	S
					1	2
3	4	5	6	7	8	9
10	11	12	13	14	15	16
17	18	19	20	21	22	23
24	25	26	27	28	29	30
31						

March

S	M	T	W	T	F	S
						1
2	3	4	5	6	7	8
9	10	11	12	13	14	15
16	17	18	19	20	21	22
23	24	25	26	27	28	29
30	31					

September

S	M	T	W	T	F	S
	L	2	3	4	5	6
7	8	9	10	11	12	13
14	15	16	17	18	19	20
21	22	23	24	25	26	27
28	29	30				

April

S	M	T	W	T	F	S
		1	2	3	4	5
6	7	8	9	10	11	12
13	14	15	16	17	18	19
20	21	22	*S*	24	25	26
27	28	29	30			

October

S	M	T	W	T	F	S
			1	2	3	4
5	6	7	8	9	10	11
12	*C*	14	15	16	17	18
19	20	21	22	23	24	25
26	27	28	29	30	31	

May

S	M	T	W	T	F	S
				1	2	3
4	5	6	7	8	9	10
11	12	13	14	15	16	17
18	19	20	21	22	23	24
25	*M*	27	28	29	30	31

November

S	M	T	W	T	F	S
						1
2	3	4	5	6	7	8
9	10	*V*	12	13	14	15
16	17	18	19	20	21	22
23	24	25	26	*T*	28	29
30						

June

S	M	T	W	T	F	S
1	2	3	4	5	6	7
8	9	10	11	12	13	14
15	16	17	18	19	20	21
22	23	24	25	26	27	28
29	30					

December

S	M	T	W	T	F	S
	1	2	3	4	5	6
7	8	9	10	11	12	13
14	15	16	17	18	19	20
21	22	23	24	*Z*	26	27
28	29	30	31			

Holiday calendar on page 230; Calendar year selector on page 752.

January

S	M	T	W	T	F	S
1	*N*	3	4	5	6	7
8	9	10	11	12	13	14
15	*K*	17	18	19	20	21
22	23	24	25	26	27	28
29	30	31				

February

S	M	T	W	T	F	S
			1	2	3	4
5	6	7	8	9	10	11
12	13	14	15	16	17	18
19	*P*	21	22	23	24	25
26	27	28	29			

March

S	M	T	W	T	F	S
				1	2	3
4	5	6	7	8	9	10
11	12	13	14	15	16	17
18	19	20	21	22	23	24
25	26	27	28	29	30	31

April

S	M	T	W	T	F	S
1	2	3	4	5	6	7
8	9	10	11	12	13	14
15	16	17	18	19	20	21
22	23	24	*S*	26	27	28
29	30					

May

S	M	T	W	T	F	S
		1	2	3	4	5
6	7	8	9	10	11	12
13	14	15	16	17	18	19
20	21	22	23	24	25	26
27	*M*	29	30	31		

June

S	M	T	W	T	F	S
					1	2
3	4	5	6	7	8	9
10	11	12	13	14	15	16
17	18	19	20	21	22	23
24	25	26	27	28	29	30

July

S	M	T	W	T	F	S
1	2	3	*I*	5	6	7
8	9	10	11	12	13	14
15	16	17	18	19	20	21
22	23	24	25	26	27	28
29	30	31				

August

S	M	T	W	T	F	S
			1	2	3	4
5	6	7	8	9	10	11
12	13	14	15	16	17	18
19	20	21	22	23	24	25
26	27	28	29	30	31	

September

S	M	T	W	T	F	S
						1
2	*L*	4	5	6	7	8
9	10	11	12	13	14	15
16	17	18	19	20	21	22
23	24	25	26	27	28	29
30						

October

S	M	T	W	T	F	S
	1	2	3	4	5	6
7	*C*	9	10	11	12	13
14	15	16	17	18	19	20
21	22	23	24	25	26	27
28	29	30	31			

November

S	M	T	W	T	F	S
				1	2	3
4	5	6	7	8	9	10
11	*V*	13	14	15	16	17
18	19	20	21	*T*	23	24
25	26	27	28	29	30	

December

S	M	T	W	T	F	S
						1
2	3	4	5	6	7	8
9	10	11	12	13	14	15
16	17	18	19	20	21	22
23	24	*Z*	26	27	28	29
30	31					

Holiday calendar on page 230; Calendar year selector on page 752.

January

S	M	T	W	T	F	S
					N	2
3	4	5	6	7	8	9
10	11	12	13	14	15	16
17	*K*	19	20	21	22	23
24	25	26	27	28	29	30
31						

July

S	M	T	W	T	F	S
					1	2
3	*I*	5	6	7	8	9
10	11	12	13	14	15	16
17	18	19	20	21	22	23
24	25	26	27	28	29	30
31						

February

S	M	T	W	T	F	S
	1	2	3	4	5	6
7	8	9	10	11	12	13
14	*P*	16	17	18	19	20
21	22	23	24	25	26	27
28	29					

August

S	M	T	W	T	F	S
	1	2	3	4	5	6
7	8	9	10	11	12	13
14	15	16	17	18	19	20
21	22	23	24	25	26	27
28	29	30	31			

March

S	M	T	W	T	F	S
		1	2	3	4	5
6	7	8	9	10	11	12
13	14	15	16	17	18	19
20	21	22	23	24	25	26
27	28	29	30	31		

September

S	M	T	W	T	F	S
				1	2	3
4	*L*	6	7	8	9	10
11	12	13	14	15	16	17
18	19	20	21	22	23	24
25	26	27	28	29	30	

April

S	M	T	W	T	F	S
					1	2
3	4	5	6	7	8	9
10	11	12	13	14	15	16
17	18	19	20	21	22	23
24	25	26	*S*	28	29	30

October

S	M	T	W	T	F	S
						1
2	3	4	5	6	7	8
9	*C*	11	12	13	14	15
16	17	18	19	20	21	22
23	24	25	26	27	28	29
30	31					

May

S	M	T	W	T	F	S
1	2	3	4	5	6	7
8	9	10	11	12	13	14
15	16	17	18	19	20	21
22	23	24	25	26	27	28
29	*M*	31				

November

S	M	T	W	T	F	S
		1	2	3	4	5
6	7	8	9	10	*V*	12
13	14	15	16	17	18	19
20	21	22	*T*	24	25	26
27	28	29	30			

June

S	M	T	W	T	F	S
			1	2	3	4
5	6	7	8	9	10	11
12	13	14	15	16	17	18
19	20	21	22	23	24	25
26	27	28	29	30		

December

S	M	T	W	T	F	S
				1	2	3
4	5	6	7	8	9	10
11	12	13	14	15	16	17
18	19	20	21	22	23	24
25	*Z*	27	28	29	30	31

Holiday calendar on page 230; Calendar year selector on page 752.

January

S	M	T	W	T	F	S
			N	2	3	4
5	6	7	8	9	10	11
12	13	14	15	16	17	18
19	K	21	22	23	24	25
26	27	28	29	30	31	

July

S	M	T	W	T	F	S
			1	2	I	4
5	6	7	8	9	10	11
12	13	14	15	16	17	18
19	20	21	22	23	24	25
26	27	28	29	30	31	

February

S	M	T	W	T	F	S
						1
2	3	4	5	6	7	8
9	10	11	12	13	14	15
16	P	18	19	20	21	22
23	24	25	26	27	28	29

August

S	M	T	W	T	F	S
						1
2	3	4	5	6	7	8
9	10	11	12	13	14	15
16	17	18	19	20	21	22
23	24	25	26	27	28	29
30	31					

March

S	M	T	W	T	F	S
1	2	3	4	5	6	7
8	9	10	11	12	13	14
15	16	17	18	19	20	21
22	23	24	25	26	27	28
29	30	31				

September

S	M	T	W	T	F	S
		1	2	3	4	5
6	L	8	9	10	11	12
13	14	15	16	17	18	19
20	21	22	23	24	25	26
27	28	29	30			

April

S	M	T	W	T	F	S
			1	2	3	4
5	6	7	8	9	10	11
12	13	14	15	16	17	18
19	20	21	S	23	24	25
26	27	28	29	30		

October

S	M	T	W	T	F	S
				1	2	3
4	5	6	7	8	9	10
11	C	13	14	15	16	17
18	19	20	21	22	23	24
25	26	27	28	29	30	31

May

S	M	T	W	T	F	S
					1	2
3	4	5	6	7	8	9
10	11	12	13	14	15	16
17	18	19	20	21	22	23
24	M	26	27	28	29	30
31						

November

S	M	T	W	T	F	S
1	2	3	4	5	6	7
8	9	10	V	12	13	14
15	16	17	18	19	20	21
22	23	24	25	T	27	28
29	30					

June

S	M	T	W	T	F	S
	1	2	3	4	5	6
7	8	9	10	11	12	13
14	15	16	17	18	19	20
21	22	23	24	25	26	27
28	29	30				

December

S	M	T	W	T	F	S
	1	2	3	4	5	5
6	7	8	9	10	11	12
13	14	15	16	17	18	19
20	21	22	23	24	Z	26
27	28	29	30	31		

Holiday calendar on page 230; Calendar year selector on page 752.

Calendar Year vs. Calendar Number

Calendars on the preceding pages apply to other years as listed in the table below. Simply locate the year you want and the **c#** to the right of that year is the number of the calendar for that year.

Year	C#	Year	C#	Year	C#	Year	C#
1858	6	1900	8	1942	5	1984	12
1859	1	1901	9	1943	6	1985	9
1860	12	1902	4	1944	7	1986	4
1861	9	1903	5	1945	8	1987	5
1862	4	1904	13	1946	9	1988	13
1863	5	1905	2	1947	4	1989	2
1864	13	1906	8	1948	10	1990	8
1865	2	1907	9	1949	1	1991	9
1866	8	1908	14	1950	2	1992	14
1867	9	1909	6	1951	8	1993	6
1868	14	1910	1	1952	11	1994	1
1869	6	1911	2	1953	5	1995	2
1870	1	1912	3	1954	6	1996	3
1871	2	1913	4	1955	1	1997	4
1872	3	1914	5	1956	12	1998	5
1873	4	1915	6	1957	9	1999	6
1874	5	1916	7	1958	4	2000	7
1875	6	1917	8	1959	5	2001	8
1876	7	1918	9	1960	13	2002	9
1877	8	1919	4	1961	2	2003	4
1878	9	1920	10	1962	8	2004	10
1879	4	1921	1	1963	9	2005	1
1880	10	1922	2	1964	14	2006	2
1881	1	1923	8	1965	6	2007	8
1882	2	1924	11	1966	1	2008	11
1883	8	1925	5	1967	2	2009	5
1884	11	1926	6	1968	3	2010	6
1885	5	1927	1	1969	4	2011	1
1886	6	1928	12	1970	5	2012	12
1887	1	1929	9	1971	6	2013	9
1888	12	1930	4	1972	7	2014	4
1889	9	1931	5	1973	8	2015	5
1890	4	1932	13	1974	9	2016	13
1891	5	1933	2	1975	4	2017	2
1892	13	1934	8	1976	10	2018	8
1893	2	1935	9	1977	1	2019	9
1894	8	1936	14	1978	2	2020	14
1895	9	1937	6	1979	8	2021	6
1896	14	1938	1	1980	11	2022	1
1897	6	1939	2	1981	5	2023	2
1898	1	1940	3	1982	6	2024	3
1899	2	1941	4	1983	1	2025	4

Index

Index

Index 763

Pocket Ref

Metric - Millimeters